MASTERPLOTS II

WOMEN'S
LITERATURE
SERIES

MASTERPLOTS II

WOMEN'S LITERATURE SERIES

6

Spr-Z

Indexes

Edited by

FRANK N. MAGILL

SALEM PRESS

Pasadena, California   Englewood Cliffs, New Jersey

Library of Congress Cataloging-in-Publication Data
Masterplots II. Women's literature series / edited by
Frank N. Magill.
    p.   cm.
Includes bibliographical references (p.) and index.
    1. Literature—Women authors—History and criti-
cism. 2. Literature—Stories, plots, etc. 3. Women in
literature. I. Magill, Frank Northen, 1907-   . II. Ti-
tle: Masterplots 2. III. Title: Masterplots two.
PN471.M37   1995
809′.89287—dc20   94-25180
ISBN 0-89356-898-8 (set)   CIP
ISBN 0-89356-904-6 (volume 6)

LIST OF TITLES IN VOLUME 6

LIST OF TITLES IN VOLUME 6

MASTERPLOTS II

WOMEN'S
LITERATURE
SERIES

SPRING MOON
A Novel of China

Author: Bette Bao Lord (1938-   )
Type of work: Novel
Type of plot: Historical realism
Time of plot: 1892-1972
Locale: China
First published: 1981

Principal characters:

SPRING MOON, the wife of Glad Promise and the niece and
    mistress of Bold Talent
LUSTROUS JADE, the daughter of Spring Moon and Glad Promise
BOLD TALENT, the patriarch of the Chang family
AUGUST WINDS, an orphaned relative of the Chang family
    adopted by Bold Talent, a typical capitalist
ENDURING PROMISE, the illegitimate son of Spring Moon and
    Bold Talent
NOBLE TALENT, a professional soldier and Spring Moon's
    unmarried uncle
RESOLUTE SPIRIT, Lustrous Jade's husband, the son of a peasant
    farmer

Form and Content

Bette Bao Lord's *Spring Moon: A Novel of China*—chronicles the tribulations of a
family—the Changs—and in particular one woman—Spring Moon—between 1892
and 1972. In addition to a prologue and an epilogue, the novel contains thirty-eight
chapters arranged in six sections. The first section, "West Wind," focuses on Spring
Moon's adolescence in Soochow, and the second section, "Spring Fire," celebrates
Spring Moon's marriage to Glad Promise and her sojourn in Beijing (Peking). In the
third section, "Golden Ashes," the widowed Spring Moon returns to Soochow with
her daughter, Lustrous Jade. The fourth section, "Summer Wine," is unified by Spring
Moon's affair with Bold Talent in Shanghai. Lustrous Jade's revolutionary activities
dominate the fifth and longest section, "Jade Phoenix." In the sixth section, "Sowing
Dawn," political unrest forces the Changs to flee Soochow for Hong Kong, and
eventually the family disintegrates, only to be reunited in Soochow years later. Forty-
five years pass between the last chapter in section 6 and the novel's epilogue.

The events in the prologue prefigure much of the novel's action. Told that she must
marry an aged friend of the Chang family, Spring Moon's servant girl, Plum Blossom,
kills herself. Her death is the first in a series of deaths and antitraditional acts that
organize the work. Within weeks after Plum Blossom's suicide, the patriarch dies, and
the House of Chang begins to crumble. It is a gradual decline, occurring over a period

of eighty years, from 1892 to 1972, but it is also steady and irreversible. As the new patriarch Bold Talent squanders the clan's assets to promote his reforms. Spring Moon and her two uncles become fugitives after they conspire against a corrupt official. Lustrous Jade crops her hair and participates in demonstrations and finally revolution. Throughout the novel, friends and loved ones die at intervals: Glad Promise; Fierce Rectitude; the Matriarch; Fatso, a loyal servant; Lotus Delight; and eventually Bold Talent, who is killed by a stray bullet during a political uprising in Shanghai. Lustrous Jade's and Resolute Spirit's suicides occur in the narrative gap between 1927 and 1972 and are reported to Enduring Promise by Spring Moon.

Each chapter begins with an epigraph from Chinese history, folklore, or literature. These epigraphs serve to illuminate the plot, through either contrast or parallel, and to broaden the scope of the novel by associating the specific with the general and the concrete with the universal. Lord occasionally experiments with form. For example, one chapter consists of a series of letters between Spring Moon and Bold Talent. This epistolary format allows the author to cover several years very quickly and lends variety to the narration. Another chapter relates Bold Talent's death in stream of consciousness, a stylistic device that imitates the natural, often disjointed "stream" of a person's thinking.

Lord's 1973 trip to China was the inspiration for *Spring Moon*. Although born in China, she moved with her family to the United States in 1946 and stayed permanently after the Communists had taken control of China. She attended Tufts University and Fletcher School of Law and Diplomacy. In 1963, she married Winston Lord, who later became a member of President Richard Nixon's diplomatic corps, joining Secretary of State Henry Kissinger's delegation to China. When the Lords traveled to China in 1973, Bette was able to visit her relatives. Upon her return, she decided to write a nonfiction work about her family, but political considerations and the safety of her relatives in China prompted her to write a novel instead. *Spring Moon* took more than six years to complete and was intended to help Americans understand China.

Analysis

The necessity of yielding is an important theme in *Spring Moon*. On his deathbed, the Old Venerable (the first patriarch) tells nine-year-old Spring Moon, "We are mere mortals who must learn not to contend with life but to yield to it." This message becomes the guiding principle of her life. To console her daughter at their parting, Spring Moon says that, "both of us, you and I, must yield," but Lustrous Jade unlearns this lesson at school and becomes an unyielding adult. Recalled by her mother-in-law, Spring Moon ends her affair with Bold Talent, saying, "We shall eventually think that our separation is a natural state. Yielding more, we shall desire less." Bold Talent challenges her resolution, but she remains constant to the precept, paradoxically contradicting herself. Before leaving for Hong Kong, as she pays homage to her relatives and ancestors at their graves, Spring Moon says, "In yielding we are like the water, by nature placid, conforming to the hollow of the smallest hand; in time, shaping even the mountains to its will." The characters who yield usually survive, while the characters who resist often die needlessly. At the end of the novel, only August Winds and ninety-year-old Spring Moon remain to greet Enduring Promise. By yielding and surviving, Spring Moon is able to fulfill her destiny of reuniting five generations of Changs at the graves of their ancestors.

Juxtaposition is the author's primary method of conveying theme. In chapter 31, the characters play a game called "antithetical couplets," in which one person composes the first line of a poetic couplet and a second person matches it with a contrast and a parallel. Thus, "green trees" becomes "red flowers" because green is the opposite of red and trees belong to the same family as flowers. This game mirrors the author's extensive use of contrasts and parallels in the plot. Plum Blossom's suicide parallels Lustrous Jade's suicide; neither woman is willing to yield to fate. Spring Moon's bridal trip to Peking contrasts with her return to Soochow after the death of her father-in-law. Though in opposite directions, both trips are the result of Spring Moon's willingness to yield to circumstance. Noble Talent's exploits with Resolute Spirit in chapter 18 parallel Lustrous Jade's exploits with Resolute Spirit in chapter 37. In the epilogue, Enduring Promise shows Spring Moon a photograph of his daughter delivering a graduation speech. This picture parallels Spring Moon's memory of Lustrous Jade's graduation speech. By juxtaposing opposites and parallels, the author encourages the reader to engage in meaningful comparison.

The differences between Spring Moon and Lustrous Jade reflect the metamorphosis of China between 1900 and 1930. In contrast to Spring Moon's "golden lilies," Lustrous Jade's feet are unbound and "big." Whereas Bold Talent and the Matriarch arrange Spring Moon's marriage, Lustrous Jade chooses her own husband and even proposes to him. Ever the dutiful mother, Spring Moon stays at home with her children and cares for them (though she leaves Lustrous Jade at a boarding school for several years). Lustrous Jade, on the other hand, leaves her son, New Destiny, with Spring Moon and returns to the Hunan Province to catechize peasant women. Whereas Spring Moon represents the thesis of tradition, Lustrous Jade represents its antithesis. The promise of synthesis is offered by Jade Spring, Lustrous Jade's great-granddaughter, who takes Spring Moon's hand at the end of the novel and prepares to listen to a clan story.

Context

Spring Moon is one of the few books in American literature to portray the traditional life of an upper-class Chinese woman at the beginning of the twentieth century. Nominated for an American Book Award in 1982, Lord's novel addresses such issues as arranged marriages, foot binding, and cloistering—all from a woman's point of view. The American reader is shown the impersonal business of betrothal, which always entailed submission and servitude for a woman, though not always to an agreeable mother-in-law or a kind husband. Spring Moon's husband is both agreeable and kind, and his love makes it possible for Spring Moon to tolerate her mother-in-law's sour disposition. The American reader is also introduced to the cruel practice of foot binding, the binding of a woman's feet to produce small "golden lilies." It is a painful practice that Spring Moon bewails and later rejects for her own daughter. Finally, the American reader is afforded a sense of the isolation that upper-class Chinese women must have felt in seclusion. Cloistered since birth, these women seldom knew a world beyond the confines of their Edenic courtyards. Spring Moon yearns for a glimpse of the outside world, but even after her marriage she is forbidden to leave the Woo estate. When she finally ventures out into the world, her elation is overwhelming to her and pathetic to the reader.

Lord's novel can be viewed as a literary precursor of Amy Tan's successful novel *The Joy Luck Club* (1989), which tells the stories of four Chinese women and their American daughters. The two novels have many similarities. In "A Pair of Tickets," the last chapter of Tan's novel, the protagonist, June Woo, travels to China to meet her long-lost sisters. Similarly, in the epilogue to *Spring Moon*, Enduring Promise returns to China to find his mother, whom he still believes to be his sister (a lie that Spring Moon had to tell him to conceal his illegitimacy). The ordeal of June Woo's mother as she fled from the Japanese forces in the late 1940's parallels the tribulations of the Chang clan as they flee from the Kuomintang in the late 1920's. Just as June Woo's mother played mah jongg with her friends during air raids in Kweilin, so does Spring Moon play mah jongg with her family during air raids in Hong Kong.

The parallels even extend to the lives of the authors. Lord was inspired by her 1973 trip to China to write *Spring Moon*. Likewise, Tan was enabled by her 1987 trip to China to complete *The Joy Luck Club*. Lord's third book, *In the Year of the Boar and Jackie Robinson* (1984), and Tan's third book, *The Moon Lady* (1992), are both children's novels. Tan's mother's sisters were left behind in China when their family immigrated to the United States. Likewise, Lord's sister was left behind in China when her family immigrated to America. In her first book, entitled *The Eighth Moon: The True Story of a Young Girl's Life in Communist China* (1964), Lord tells about her sister's childhood in exile from her family.

Sources for Further Study

Bonner, Joey. Review of *Spring Moon*. *The New Republic* 185 (October 21, 1981): 38-39. This review discusses the novel in the context of China's political and cultural history. It identifies the plot as "a family saga," describes Spring Moon as "curiously apolitical," and credits the novel's success to domestic delineation rather than political exegesis.

Lehmann-Haupt, Christopher. "Books of the Times." *The New York Times*, December 2, 1981, p. 29. This review criticizes the novel for its heavy-handed use of history but compliments its "narrative velleity." Includes especially interesting comments about the prologue.

Lord, Bette Bao. "China Doll." *New York* 19 (May 12, 1986): 50-51. In this article, Lord discusses her childhood in America, her children's book, and her life as the wife of the U.S. ambassador to China. The article illuminates the personality of the author.

McMurran, Kristin. "Winston Lord May Be an Old China Hand but Wife Bette Wrote the Book on Mandarins." *People Weekly* 220 (November 23, 1981): 90, 93-94. This article provides biographical information about Lord and her husband and useful information about the genesis of *Spring Moon*.

Madden, Kathleen. "Bette Bao Lord: A Wife, Mother Writes Her Own Text." *Vogue* 172 (February, 1982): 182. Discusses Lord's career as an author from a feminist perspective. Lord's comments on Chinese women illuminate the characters in *Spring Moon*. For example, Lord states that the role of women in Chinese society has been "revolutionized," but not "necessarily liberated."

Nevans, Ronald. Review of *Spring Moon. Saturday Review* 8 (October, 1981): 75-76. This review touts *Spring Moon* as "one of the most remarkable novels ever to explain the East to the West." Briefly discusses Chinese society's mistreatment of women and Lord's "low-key style," which captures "the understatement of tradition."

Paterson, Katherine. "From the Manchu to Mao: One Woman's Journey." *The Washington Post Book World* 11, no. 41 (October 11, 1981): 1-2. This substantive review comments on Lord's use of epigraphs to "clarify and enrich" the plot. It also discusses the difficulty of translating Chinese idioms and names into English.

Edward A. Malone

A SPY IN THE HOUSE OF LOVE

Author: Anaïs Nin (1903-1977)
Type of work: Novel
Type of plot: Psychological realism
Time of plot: The 1940's, during World War II
Locale: New York City
First published: 1954

> *Principal characters:*
> SABINA, a passionate woman who has sexual relationships with a
>   variety of men
> THE LIE DETECTOR, a surreal father figure who represents
>   Sabina's guilty conscience
> ALAN, Sabina's husband, who seems oblivious to her affairs
> PHILIP, one of Sabina's lovers, a handsome opera star
> MAMBO, a drummer at a small jazz club and another of Sabina's
>   lovers
> JOHN, a grounded aviator and another of Sabina's lovers
> DONALD, Sabina's final lover before she breaks down
> JAY, an artist and Sabina's former lover
> DJUNA, Sabina's friend and confidante

Form and Content

The best known of Anaïs Nin's novels, *A Spy in the House of Love* is a surreal journey through one woman's mind as she attempts to satisfy her sexual desire and to understand love. Like all Nin's fiction, the narrative form of the text is experimental. Poetic impressions reflecting the complicated nature of Sabina's personality are linked by semichronological events; supporting characters are minimally described, and only in reference to Sabina. Dialogue is restricted to the most relevant exchanges; setting and action are included only when their symbolic weight provides insight to Sabina's frame of mind. The result is a novel that explores the various layers of a single personality, undermining the notion that a woman's identity can be categorized or limited to a single facet.

A telephone awakens the lie detector at the beginning of the novel. Sabina has placed a call at random, seeking comfort from a strange voice in the middle of the night. The lie detector tells her that she needs to confess or she would not have called a stranger, since "Guilt is the one burden human beings can't bear alone." He has the call traced and finds Sabina in a bar, where he observes and analyzes her voyeuristically. At dawn, he follows her.

The point of view shifts to Sabina, where it remains for most of the rest of the work. She awakens anxiously, then hides her chaotic expression with makeup. She dresses in a black cape for its protectiveness, its masculinity, as though dressed for battle.

Outside on the streets of New York City, however, she is panicked by enormous trucks that block the sun with their rolling wheels; she feels insignificant and threatened. At such moments of insecurity, Sabina visualizes her husband, Alan. She returns to the hotel, checks out, then walks two blocks home where she finds Alan and the fleeting happiness of safety.

As after all of her affairs, Sabina is worried about hurting her husband—or worse, losing him and the stability that he provides. So she lies to him, describing her week-long acting role as Madame Bovary. Later, beside him in bed, she silently recalls her affair with Philip, a handsome opera star who discovered her lying naked on the beach. Philip is used to noncommittal sexual relationships and is easily satisfied by their lovemaking. Sabina, however, does not climax and feels angry, defeated, and jealous of Philip's casual ability to possess a stranger.

Attempting to mimic Philip's sexual freedom, she enters an affair with Mambo, a drum player at a local jazz club. This time it is Mambo who is disappointed, because he realizes that Sabina desires him sexually but is unwilling to form a commitment. Though Sabina achieves her goal of physical fulfillment with relational freedom, she is increasingly afraid of seeing Alan while with Mambo. Her inability to experience both love and passion in a single relationship makes her feel that she is a spy in the house of love.

Her next affair is with John, a grounded aviator who completely satisfies Sabina physically but refuses to see her more than once. He cannot love the kind of woman who would have sex so easily, and he leaves her filled with guilt. Seeking atonement for his curse, she seeks a relationship with someone resembling John and finds Donald, the least adequate of her lovers. Donald worships Sabina as a mother and is therefore afraid of having sex with her. She mothers him until she finds her own passion fading.

Fragmented from playing so many roles, she seeks advice from her friend Djuna. The lie detector reappears; he and Djuna help Sabina realize that negative self-judgment and unrealistic expectations of others have prevented her from experiencing love.

Analysis

A Spy in the House of Love is the fourth in a series of five works that Nin wrote as a continuous novel called *Cities of the Interior*. The novels can be read in any order, with the overall meaning preserved. The theme of the entire collection is female psychology: Each book examines a different aspect of female identity, and though a number of women are depicted in the series, the characters can ultimately be read as overlapping aspects of one persona. The series is a thorough reworking and expanding of the female ideal depicted in traditional literature, and it is most remembered for expressing previously unfashionable or forbidden subjects in a lyrical, accurate, and analytical manner.

Sabina is a recurring figure throughout Nin's fiction, always appearing as a sensual, sexually assertive woman. Like all Nin's female characters, Sabina is torn between her sense of responsibility and her desire to experience pleasure. Developed most fully in *A Spy in the House of Love*, Sabina enjoys sex but finds herself emotionally fragmented by attempting to satisfy and be satisfied by so many lovers. Sabina's quest is to emulate Philip's, or any man's ability to enjoy sex with a stranger. She assumes that she will find emotional gratification this way, but she learns otherwise in her relationships with Philip, Mambo, and John. When she does make commitments, she limits her identity in order to please her partners. She tries to be the child she thinks Alan wants and the mother Donald needs, and in both cases she is physically unsatisfied.

Nin makes it clear that Sabina is at fault not for having affairs but for failing to confront her own subconscious, with its simmering confusion of passion and guilt. This is particularly true of Sabina's affair with John, whose seed is described as poison. His own shame for surviving the war is taken out on Sabina: "He had mingled poison with every drop of pleasure, . . . every thrust of sensual pleasure the thrust of a knife killing what he desired, killing with guilt." Sabina unconsciously soaks up John's attitude: Because he thinks she is bad, she thinks so too. She attempts to cleanse her spirit by nurturing Donald, but her plan fails. After Sabina becomes the mother Donald desires, she compares herself to a caged bird with faded plumage.

In yielding to her lovers' needs, Sabina is depleted, her spirit broken and dismembered. Jay's portraits of her, which she had not understood years before while they were lovers, finally make sense when she sees them hanging at the jazz club:

> His figures exploded and constellated into fragments, like spilled puzzles, each piece having flown far enough away to seem irretrievable and yet not far enough to be disassociated. . . . By one effort of contraction at the core they might still amalgamate to form the body of a woman.

What Sabina sought in her affairs was solace, a synthesis of emotional and physical pleasure. Instead, she has been pulled apart by separating her roles as seductress, lover, mother, and child. The aspects of her identity are still connected, however, suggesting their validity. If she can locate the core, she might realize stability by accepting her own multifaceted nature.

Alone, tired, and emotionally lost, Sabina finally understands Marcel Duchamp's famous painting *Nude Descending a Staircase*, which outlines the same woman in numerous positions, "like many multiple exposures of a woman's personality, neatly divided into many layers, walking down the stairs in unison." An actress, a wearer of many disguises, Sabina no longer senses a single inner identity. Afraid that she can no longer portray an isolated aspect of her personality, that of the innocent child, she fears going home to Alan for the first time and seeks forgiveness and atonement from a confessor. The lie detector, her own guilty conscience, must be confronted.

It is Djuna who points out that Alan's paternal attitude is nurtured by Sabina's refusal to display her maturing selves. Because Sabina acts like a child with Alan, he acts like a parent. This is a revelation for Sabina, who has looked to others for personal fulfillment. Literature is filled with stories about women finding complete satisfaction

THE STONE ANGEL

Author: Margaret Laurence (1926-1987)
Type of work: Novel
Type of plot: Bildungsroman
Time of plot: The 1870's to the 1960's
Locale: The fictional town of Manawaka and Vancouver, British Columbia
First published: 1964

Principal characters:
>HAGAR CURRIE SHIPLEY, a ninety-year-old woman who reveals her past
>JASON CURRIE, Hagar's father
>MATT and DAN CURRIE, Hagar's brothers
>BRAMPTON SHIPLEY, Hagar's husband
>LOTTIE DREISER SIMMONS, a classmate of Hagar
>MARVIN SHIPLEY, Hagar's oldest son
>DORIS SHIPLEY, Marvin's wife
>JOHN SHIPLEY, Hagar's younger son
>MURRAY LEES, a man whose kindness to Hagar shows her the possibility of hope

Form and Content

Margaret Laurence's *The Stone Angel* is told through Hagar's ninety-year-old eyes, with small events triggering flashbacks that reveal her history. The novel's title is explained in the opening pages: The stone angel was a monument erected by Hagar's father for his wife, who died giving birth to Hagar. Intended to impress, the angel is doubly blind: Made of unfeeling stone, she is also eyeless, and harkens people to heaven without knowing them. As Hagar's narrative reveals, she has similar faults: Her pride and her unswerving sense of superiority often "blind" her to other people. Hagar is not apologetic about her past, but she does desire understanding.

Hagar's thoughts of the angel spark memories. As youngest child and only daughter of the town's storekeeper, Hagar is sure of her high place in the world. Her father is strict and undemonstrative, and he teaches Hagar these qualities. Inordinately proud of his position in the town, he will not jeopardize it. Laurence shows Manawaka's social hierarchy: "No-Name" Lottie Dreiser is barred from the Curries' house, and the "half-breeds" on the fringes of society are unacknowledged—although the Currie children secretly socialize with both.

Hagar's fear of weakness is shown with her brother Dan's death. Matt realizes that their dying and delirious brother wants to see their mother. He asks Hagar to wear her old shawl and to comfort Dan. Hagar refuses, remembering what she has heard about her mother's meekness and frailty—qualities she detests. At age eight, Hagar has chosen her father's steeliness and determination.

At eighteen, Hagar is sent to finishing school, where she learns social niceties such as embroidery, menu planning, and managing servants. Her father is pleased with her polish. Refusing Hagar's wish to teach, he asks her to stay in Manawaka to act as his hostess. Bitterly, Hagar does his bidding for three years. To her father's horrified disapproval, she then recklessly marries Bram Shipley and begins life on his farm. She hates Bram's shiftlessness and vulgarity. Though he is unaware of it, Bram appeals to her sexually; Hagar will not admit her feelings for him because she sees the expression of love as a weakness.

Her life of grinding hard work and humiliation from Manawaka's townspeople becomes increasingly difficult. One day Hagar, unkempt and overweight, realizes that she resembles Bram's cowlike first wife. She has become what she most loathes. After selling her few heirlooms, she deserts Bram. She and her son John settle in Vancouver, where ironically Hagar becomes a housekeeper for a man much like her father. Though Hagar is glad to be independent, she is lonely and often wonders about Bram. She is jealous, however, when John returns to live with his father, saying that he might fit in better back on the farm. Two years later, she hears that Bram is ill and returns to Manawaka.

Like her father, Hagar abhors the thought of her child marrying beneath him. After Bram's death, John wants to marry Arlene Simmons, Lottie Dreiser's daughter, over Hagar's strenuous objections. Hagar claims that the Great Depression has made them too poor to marry and that they are too young (though John is nearly thirty). Hagar knows that Lottie shares her feelings, and the two mothers scheme to have Arlene leave for a year. John, who has stopped drinking and carousing, despairs at the thought of being alone again. That night, he and Arlene are killed in a drunken accident.

Hagar says little about the intervening years; her employer dies the next year and leaves her enough money to buy her own home. Her son Marvin and his wife, Doris, both in their sixties, eventually move in with her. Hagar details her efforts to maintain her dignity and privacy through the humiliations of endless discussions of her physical, spiritual, and mental health. When Marvin and Doris discuss placing Hagar in a nursing home, she escapes again to Shadow Point. She tells much of her story to Murray Lees—not realizing that she has revealed more of herself to this stranger than to anyone in her family. Her tears before him show her renunciation of her previous steely calm and her regret for her "lost men"—her brothers, her son, and her husband.

At Shadow Point, Hagar is able to sort out her feelings, but Marvin "rescues" her and takes her to a hospital. As she lies in bed trying to think of some free and unconstrained action in her life, only two things come to mind: One is to tell Marvin that he is a better son than John. She admits to herself that this is a lie, but a well-meant one. Her new openness becomes painfully evident when she tells Marvin that she is frightened of what will happen to her. When a minister comes to see her, Hagar realizes that she has wanted all her life simply to rejoice. Her joy in life has been stymied, though, by worries about "proper" appearances. The novel ends with Hagar's insistence on fighting to the very end, as befits the epigraph "Do Not Go Gentle into That Good Night."

Analysis

The Stone Angel examines the patterns that damage successive generations. Hagar's hatred of emotionality, instilled by her father, blunts her enjoyment of life and ensures her harsh and overly critical attitude toward other people. Hagar comments on the stone angel's blindness, but she does not see that she herself also unseeingly tries to force people into her own model of proper behavior. Later the angel is desecrated: After Hagar has married and left Bram, she briefly returns to Manawaka to find that, to her horror, the angel has toppled. When John grudgingly raises her, Hagar sees that the angel's mouth has been garishly lipsticked. She tries to scrub away the red, but a stain remains. After that day, the angel crookedly marks the Currie-Shipley resting place. Hagar's experiences have similarly knocked her from her pedestal, and she is also "crooked" in the way in which she sees the world. Only at the age of ninety does she realize that she wanted to speak her heart's truth, unrestrained by pride and propriety. Like her father, she was shackled by a pride born of fear.

Laurence juxtaposes Hagar's parallel stories. Hagar's present, as an unwillingly frail and often tyrannical old woman, is carried throughout, but Hagar's memories and explanations of the past are equally important. There are nineteen major changes between past and present time, often triggered by Hagar's present sensations: For example, a painting, children playing on the beach, or a flowered dress can spark her painful and often comic memories. The first four chapters detail Hagar's thoughts before she runs away from Marvin; the next four focus on her actions and thoughts while at Shadow Point; and the last two center on the hospital and her last days before death. In the last chapters, past and present become blurred: Hagar's remembering becomes so intense that she essentially relives the pain and happiness that she experienced. Toward the end of the novel, Hagar begins to think about events from others' points of view—insights that have been all too rare.

Laurence unflinchingly reveals Hagar's many faults—intolerance, pride, discontent—but she also shows Hagar's determination, her struggle for independence, and her reluctant love of her family. Hagar's voice is pugnacious, ironic, and bitter. She has an odd ability to freeze a memory and to examine her past self, an ability that brings about some of the novel's tragicomic moments and poignance. The "re-seeing" of her past leads to her enlightenment at novel's end.

Hagar rails at the frailties of her aged body, likening herself to a firmly rooted stump or an old hawk caught in a net. Images of the natural world run throughout: Like many women, Hagar felt torn between "natural" impulses and social restraints. Hagar twice escapes to nature from the "civilized" world of town and hypocrisy. The first is when she marries and lives with all the brutality and beauty of the farm, but because of her sense of superiority she will not allow Bram to know how she feels. The second time is her escape to Shadow Point, where she relies on nature to shield her. Her desperate escape allows her to "confess" to Murray Lees.

Thirst is another important metaphor: Bram and John both drink for recreation, and Bram's wedding gift to Hagar is a cut-glass decanter. Hagar thirsts for self-knowledge, and the novel focuses on this quest. At Shadow Point, she remembers to bring food but not water; Murray Lees gives her wine and the sparrows point her to rainwater. When she awakens after her night in the abandoned fish cannery, she can only think of water: Her grief of the previous night has parched her. As Hagar lies dying, she cries out that she is thirsty, but she insists that no one can give her the water. She must drink it herself, or spill it, just as she chooses.

Hagar's physical escapes are futile; she is still chained by pride and her uncompromising nature. Each escape demands sacrifice: Her marriage causes her to renounce her refinement and sensitivity and to isolate herself from her family. When she leaves Bram, she gives up her sexuality; when she flees Marvin, she endangers her health and also hurts Marvin deeply. At Shadow Point, Hagar digs deep into her self and her past and tries to reconcile them. Murray Lees's guilt in the death of his baby son prompts a storm of memories about John's last months with Hagar and forces her to remember her role in his death. Befuddled by wine and exhaustion, she mistakes Murray Lees for John and apologizes for her bad temper, saying that she needs no one but him, that he can have Arlene to the house whenever he wants. As Hagar refused to do for her brother all those years ago, Murray Lees plays the role of someone long dead and reassures Hagar that everything is all right. In this last and desperate physical escape, Hagar has found some measure of spiritual redemption.

Context

The Stone Angel is applauded as a Canadian classic and Laurence's best work. Beloved in Canadian literature and widely studied, it is one of the few authentic and unsentimental views of old age and dying; Hagar's voice is truthful and uncompromising. Laurence, who was only thirty-eight when the novel was published, made Hagar's complexity believable; she once proudly wrote that the novel had been studied in hospital geriatrics courses. *The Stone Angel*, along with Scottish writer Muriel Spark's *Memento Mori* (1959), is one of the few novels to focus on the disintegration of the body, the role of memory in aging, the pride in independence, and the struggle for identity among older people.

Laurence, a feminist and activist, often wrote about the damage done to the individual by internalizing standards of "proper" behavior. This novel is part of her "Manawaka cycle," books that focus on a small community. Manawaka's hypocrisy and condemnation of those who breach acceptable standards leads Hagar to rebellion and, later, despair. The town's (and her father's) attitude to the illegitimate Lottie and the half-Indian children reinforced rigid intolerance. The pride of Hagar's father in his social standing made him reject his children when they needed him. Pride's painful results culminate when Hagar objects to her son's marriage because she believes that John's background is superior, and this attitude leads to John's and Arlene's deaths. After this tragedy, Hagar says that she has turned to stone. Until the end of the novel, when she confesses her pain, she is unable to weep or show great joy.

Hagar is admirable for her courage, her willingness to strike out on her own, and her strength; as Marvin says, she is a "holy terror." As in several of Laurence's other works, the main character's motherlessness is important: Lacking strong female role models, Hagar becomes as inflexible and distant, and as blind, as her father. Her father repeatedly tells her of men's "terrible thoughts"; Hagar consequently denies her sexuality and sees love as a weakness. Hagar is hurt by the double standard that denies women's enjoyment of sex and need for independence. Laurence described herself as a religious writer, and Hagar's enlightenment at novel's end, though not specifically religious, shows hope for even the most "unregenerate sinner."

Sources for Further Study

Cameron, Donald. *Conversations with Canadian Novelists*. Toronto: Macmillan of Canada, 1973. In one chapter, a close friend of Laurence talks with her about family, religious influences, travels, and sources for her novels. Laurence discusses the influence of her grandfather and the women in her family on *The Stone Angel*.

Gunnars, Kristjana, ed. *Crossing the River: Essays in Honour of Margaret Laurence*. Winnipeg, Manitoba: Turnstone Press, 1988. A variety of essays examine various themes in Laurence's work. Two essays focus on *The Stone Angel*: one on Hagar as storyteller and the other on the work as a novel of "completion." The bibliographies and footnotes are useful in stimulating research.

Laurence, Margaret. *Dance on the Earth*. Toronto: McClelland and Stewart, 1989. Laurence's memoirs, which praise the women who influenced her development. Biographical connections to her novels are discussed. An invaluable source for in-depth knowledge of her inspirations.

Morley, Patricia. *Margaret Laurence: The Long Journey Home*. Montreal: Queens-McGill University Press, 1991. Offers a clear and helpful analysis of Laurence's life and work. The chapter on the "Manawaka cycle" examines *The Stone Angel* in detail, especially Laurence's use of religious imagery and tragicomedy.

Thomas, Clara. *The Manawaka World of Margaret Laurence*. Toronto: McClelland and Stewart, 1976. A critical assessment of Laurence's Manawaka novels. Examines *The Stone Angel* and Laurence's storytelling techniques and methods of characterization.

Michelle L. Jones

THE STORIES OF ELIZABETH SPENCER

Author: Elizabeth Spencer (1921-   )
Type of work: Short stories
First published: 1981

Form and Content

The Stories of Elizabeth Spencer is a collection of short stories by one of the most-admired writers in that genre. As a native Mississippian, Elizabeth Spencer is well aware of the restrictions that a traditional society places on all of its members and especially on its women. Many of the characters in her stories are torn between their desire for freedom from family and community pressures and their equally intense need for the sense of stability and permanence that they derive from their heritage.

The collection is introduced by two brief but significant essays. In her preface, the author asserts that even though many of her stories were written while she was living in Italy or in Montreal, she can see that at least in memory the South was always with her. While she was always conscious of place, however, it was not until she had been writing for three decades that a unifying theme appeared in her fiction: the affirmation that girls and women can find ways to make what is for them a very difficult world "possible, livable."

The foreword by Eudora Welty points to one source of support for such women. As Welty describes their friendship of long standing, which began when Spencer was still in college, it is evident that this relationship, based on respect for each other as individuals and as writers, meant much to both women. Spencer's fellow Mississippian sees qualities in her friend's fiction that reflect the tradition of Southern storytellers: the sense of place, the understanding of people, and the delight in absurdity. Spencer's "detachment" and "scope," Welty believes, are not so typical of Southern writers.

Since Spencer has arranged these stories in the order in which they were written, it is easy to see how her vision has broadened as she has moved on to new places and new experiences. In the first part of this volume, covering the years from 1944 to 1960, four of the six stories are set in Mississippi. The final story in the first section, however, is set in Italy, as are half of the six stories in the second part, which is dated 1961-1964. By the time that she wrote these stories, Spencer had time to reflect on her life in Italy, where she had gone as a Guggenheim Fellow in 1953, eventually to marry and remain there for several years.

Spencer notes, however, that although she was physically absent from the South, it remained a strong presence in her memory and her imagination. More than half of the thirteen stories in the third and longest segment of the book, consisting of works written between 1965 and 1971, are placed in the South, most of them specifically in Mississippi. Interestingly, though Spencer and her husband had moved to Montreal in 1958, the first of her stories set in Canada does not appear until the final section of this volume, which is dated 1972-1977.

It is not surprising that a writer whose fiction is so much admired for its structure should have displayed her customary precision in the organization of her collection. The work covers thirty-three years, and it contains thirty-three stories—each of which, it should be noted, is unique. When one realizes that in addition to so many stories of uniformly high quality during this period Spencer also published five novels and two novellas, it is evident that she deserves her high standing among contemporary fiction writers.

Analysis

In her article "Storytelling, Old and New," Spencer describes how her stories are conceived. Each of them begins, she says, with a specific event which somehow sparks her imagination. By writing, she tries to penetrate the surface of what she has observed, in order to find out not only why the event occurred but also what it signifies.

Written as they are out of a kind of creative curiosity, Spencer's stories quite naturally move toward a final revelation, when her narrators or protagonists come to a new understanding of the self, of human nature, or of the substance of life. Such revelations may be merely the reestablishment of domestic tranquillity after some momentary tension, as in "A Bad Cold" and "The Adult Holiday." They can involve a momentous change, however, as when in "The Girl Who Loved Horses" the protagonist recognizes herself in a man she has learned to fear or when in "The Bufords" the teacher realizes that the boisterous family whose offspring she cannot control forgive her for her intolerance and absorb her into their clan and their way of life.

Typically, in the course of a story, Spencer will pose a problem by setting up thematic oppositions. For example, in "Moon Rocket" a young boy must choose between illusion and reality; if he does not abandon his fantasy of life in space and beam down to earth, at least temporarily, he will lose his new girlfriend. Similarly, it is an overactive imagination that causes difficulties for the protagonist of "The Eclipse." After young Weston realizes that his plan to run away to Chicago with his music teacher is nothing but a hopeless dream, he finds another way to exercise his imagination and exert his will. By pulling the emergency cord and bringing the train to a stop, he becomes a local hero and shows his father that he is a real boy, after all.

Sometimes the issue is what to do with the past. In "A Southern Landscape," Marilee Summerall sees the need for decayed plantations and decayed aristocrats; they are, she feels, "a permanent landscape of the heart." In "First Dark," however, the past represents a threat. When a couple must choose between staying in the house that would trap them and leaving it forever, they flee, fearful even of looking back.

Often one must decide between dreams and duty, between the desire to be free, on one hand, and the sense of responsibility, often to one's family, on the other. For Cousin Félice in "A Kiss at the Door," there was no real choice; while she could hardly help resenting the waste of her life, she still believes that she could not do anything but her duty. In contrast, when the protagonist of "Indian Summer" has been ignored and outvoted by his wife and his grown son one time too many, he walks out. Though he does return eventually, it is on his own terms. In "Knights and Dragons," Martha Ingram is also determined to escape. In fleeing from the husband she has divorced, however, she withdraws further and further from everyone else. When at last she thinks herself free, she has to recognize the fact that she has lost her humanity in the process. Like many of Spencer's women, she has paid a high price for her independence.

Context

As Spencer has indicated in various essays and interviews, in her fiction she explores complex situations and relationships, then looks for some way in which her protagonists' lives can be bettered, if not perfected. As she wrote in the preface to this volume, she seems increasingly to be applying this pattern to what she calls "seeking girls and women."

From the beginning of her career, Spencer has tended to choose a female point of view for her narratives. In her works of the 1980's and 1990's, however, one can see a new emphasis on women's issues. This is as evident in her novels as in her short stories. In *The Night Travellers* (1991), although the young draft protester is a sympathetic character and his eventual fate a tragic one, Spencer focuses on the predicament of his young wife—abandoned in a foreign country, left with a child to support but without funds, friends, or family to help her. So often, Spencer sees, it is women who are expected to pick up the pieces.

As a tough-minded realist, however, Spencer does not spend her time bemoaning the problems that women face but instead, especially in the final stories in this collection, tries to see what her characters can do with the hands that they are dealt. Sometimes fortune favors her women. The young girl in "A Christian Education" has a self-sufficient grandfather to imitate; his gift to her is indeed the gift of freedom. Similarly, when her own family scoffs at her ambitions, the protagonist in "Mr. McMillan" finds an academic environment to nurture her. Yet Spencer points out that no matter how hard they try, few women can escape from the past. Thus in "The Search," although in a symbolic gesture the mother casts off her grief for her missing daughter, her anguish remains with her.

Although some feminist writers see only the positive side of women's new independence, Spencer admits that the "seeking" women with whom she obviously identifies do pay a price for their unconventionality. There is no question that the narrator of "I, Maureen" had to escape from a stifling family situation; however, her one significant artistic triumph is a photograph of pain. In addition to the fact that she is superb in her craft, Spencer's sympathy toward her women characters, her sensitivity about their inner conflicts, and most of all, her uncompromising honesty about women's issues make her works among the most important in contemporary fiction.

Sources for Further Study

Cole, Hunter McKelva. "Windsor in Spencer and Welty: A Real and an Imaginary Landscape." *Notes on Mississippi Writers* 7 (Spring, 1974): 2-11. Compares the use made by Eudora Welty and Elizabeth Spencer of the same picturesque ruin. Though the protagonist of Spencer's story "A Southern Landscape," Marilee Summerall, knows that both Windsor and the aristocratic Foster Hamilton are doomed, she sees them as symbols of something unchanging.

Evoy, Karen. "*Marilee:* 'A Permanent Landscape of the Heart.'" *Mississippi Quarterly* 36 (Fall, 1983): 569-578. A review of *Marilee* (1981), which consisted of the three stories told in the voice of Marilee Summerall. Like Spencer herself, Marilee sees how stultifying a traditional society can be, while at the same time finding that only in her recognition of family ties and of the presence of the past can she attain the sense of stability that she desperately needs.

Neely, Jessica. "Personal Allegiances." *Belles Lettres: A Review of Books by Women* 7 (Winter, 1991-1992): 11-12. Argues that the theme of "personal allegiances—to community, family, friends" dominates Spencer's later collection, *Jack of Diamonds and Other Stories* (1988). Stories set in places as different from each other as Canada and the Deep South show how relationships between individuals are affected by group pressures. The reviewer calls Spencer "one of our most accomplished writers."

Park, Clara Claiborne. "A Personal Road." *Hudson Review* 34 (Winter, 1981-1982): 601-605. The South seen through the eyes of Elizabeth Spencer is markedly different from that shown in the fiction of Flannery O'Connor or Eudora Welty. The "dirty little secret" of Spencer's world is not its infatuation with history, not even its remnants of racism, but the existence of a rigid class structure which tells individuals who they are and keeps them where they belong. This is the reason that so many of Spencer's characters leave the South, or at least attempt to do so.

Prenshaw, Peggy Whitman. *Elizabeth Spencer*. Boston: Twayne, 1985. A valuable study, written by an outstanding scholar and checked for accuracy by Spencer herself. Although the bulk of the volume is devoted to the novels, one chapter is devoted to Spencer's short stories. In another chapter, Prenshaw looks at the novella *Knights and Dragons* (1965), which she sees as closely related to the short story "Ship Island." Essential reading.

Spencer, Elizabeth. *Conversations with Elizabeth Spencer*. Edited by Peggy Whitman Prenshaw. Jackson: University Press of Mississippi, 1991. A collection of interviews in which the author speaks candidly about her life and her works. In view of the fact that she had left her native South and was living elsewhere during some extremely productive years, the comments that Spencer makes regarding the relationship between memory, place, and fiction are particularly interesting.

——————— . "Storytelling, Old and New." *The Writer* 85 (January, 1972): 9-10, 30. Explains how a work of fiction begins with a question, to which the story provides an answer. Spencer voices her disgust with writers' seeming obsession with sexual fulfillment, suggesting that they devote their energies to exploring how people can learn to live together in harmony.

Rosemary M. Canfield Reisman

THE STORIES OF KATHERINE MANSFIELD

Author: Katherine Mansfield (1888-1923)
Type of work: Short stories
First published: 1984

Form and Content

The Stories of Katherine Mansfield, edited by Antony Alpers, is the most authoritative and probably the most complete of the collections of Mansfield's short stories made since her death in 1923. Mansfield is regarded as one of the greatest female authors of the first quarter of the twentieth century. Not only can she be said, along with James Joyce, to have created the modern short story, but almost all of her stories have women as central characters and focus on women's lives and concerns.

Of the approximately 120 stories that Mansfield left complete or unfinished when she died, this edition prints 85. This number includes the 42 stories that Mansfield published in book form and a representative selection of her other stories. They are divided into thirteen sections, arranged chronologically according to the time they were written. At the end of the volume, Alpers supplies a "Commentary" on each story, telling when it was written and published, as well as supplying essential background information. The "Commentary" also notes stories not printed in this selection.

The thirteen sections of *The Stories of Katherine Mansfield* show the great range of Mansfield's stories and allow the reader to follow her development closely. The first two sections contain stories that she wrote as a girl in New Zealand and as a young woman attending Queen's College in London. A number of these youthful stories contain hints of the themes and settings of her later work. The next section contains bitter stories set in Germany, based on her life during a short stay in that country in 1910 and influenced by the stories of Anton Chekhov. The next five sections show the products of her apprenticeship in London and Paris between 1911 and 1917. During these years, she experimented with many styles and forms, such as parodies, satires, and dialogues.

The last five sections in this collection contain Mansfield's mature work, the stories that she wrote in London and on the Continent between 1917 and her death in 1923. These are the stories for which she is remembered and by which her place in literary history is judged. Some stories are set in London and some in the French and Swiss towns and cities where Mansfield sought relief from tuberculosis; a great many (and probably the best) are based on childhood memories of New Zealand life. The ways in which Mansfield tells these stories are also varied. Some, such as "The Fly," are short and pointed. Some, such as "The Garden Party," are longer, richly evocative, and conventional in form. Two, "Prelude" and "At the Bay," are brilliant experiments in telling a complex story by a series of vignettes.

Analysis

Mansfield said that two things caused her to write. One was the "joy" and "peace" that she felt when "something delicate and lovely seems to open my eyes, like a flower without thought of a frost." She often communicates joy in her stories by describing such things as flowers, waves, and beams of light. Her second motive for writing was quite different: "an *extremely* deep sense of hopelessness, of everything doomed to disaster" which made her cry out against "corruption." She pillories injustice and depravity. For example, in "The Fly" she presents a businessman who treats an old employee badly and sadistically tortures an insect.

Corruption is only one source of hopelessness in Mansfield's world. Men and women in love always misunderstand each other and talk at cross-purposes. The timid and tongue-tied fail to declare their passion; ambitious lovers have more important people to conquer; some are confused by sex. In "Psychology," two artists are so painfully conscious of the complexities of their relationship that their passion fades. In this world, there are many failures, often lonely women in lonely rooms thinking or trying not to think about their loneliness. For failures and nonfailures alike, time is the enemy.

Katherine Mansfield's style is economical; each word counts. Yet although she is precise, her stories are seldom easy to understand. Her tone is elusive, for she mixes witty satire with romantic evocation. Because she mainly writes dialogue, indirect speech, and descriptions, readers do not hear her own voice giving directions. Mansfield often employs symbols that suggest much but tell the reader nothing definite. The way in which she tells stories causes problems as well, for their actions do not surge forward to climaxes that reveal their "meanings." Mansfield's quick shifts of time and surprise turns of plot are designed to lead her readers (and some characters as well) to epiphanies, unexpected moments of illumination that are difficult to summarize.

Four of her most famous stories show the nature of her achievement. "Miss Brill" is a lonely woman; the reader lives through her story without the author making any direct comments. She is an English teacher in a French resort city. On Sunday afternoon, she dresses up with her fox fur to sit in the public gardens, where she enjoys listening to the band and to the conversations of other people. She is pleased by talk that most readers find banal and imagines what others are saying. Her joy intensifies when she reflects that all of them—including herself—are in a great play; she turns the drama of public life into a consolation for her lonely state. Then, just when the reader is happiest for Miss Brill, two lovers ridicule her to her face. The reader imagines her pain. Silently she returns to her room, and as she packs her fox fur away, she thinks she hears it cry. Mansfield's is a poignant story of a woman's pathetic joys and solitude.

"Bliss" tells of Bertha Young, a youthful wife happy about her beautiful day, her wonderful baby, her wealthy husband, and her fascinating friends. The lovely pear tree blooming in her garden symbolizes her happiness. The story moves forward slowly; at a party readers meet Harry, her down-to-earth husband, some silly guests, and the cool Miss Fulton, dressed in silver. Then something happens. Bertha touches Miss Fulton's arm and feels a "fire of bliss." Later, when the two women regard the pear tree, Bertha thinks that they achieve a wordless understanding. The story has more surprises. Suddenly, "For the first time in her life Bertha Young desired her husband." Her homoerotic feelings have changed to heterosexual ones, but her bliss is soon shattered when she glimpses Miss Fulton and Harry making an assignation. Bertha is alone, wondering what will happen to her. The reader has been led through a maze of sexual shifts, of momentary exhilaration and despair.

"At the Bay" is one of Mansfield's longer narrative experiments. In its thirteen short episodes, she introduces the extended Burnell family and a few others. The children are growing up; boys and girls jockey for status. Among the adults are two men, the ineffectual Uncle Jonathan and the bluff businessman father, Stanley. Stanley's wife, Linda, still loves the boy behind his bluster, but she is worn out by her pregnancies and dislikes her children. The story's most striking drama involves Linda's unmarried sister, Beryl, and the handsome and menacing Harry Kember. When Beryl's fantasies threaten to become real, she backs away from sexual intimacy with horror. The story interweaves its characters' yearnings and frames their day with pictures of the timeless and destructive sea. Mansfield displays these dreams and sets them in a cosmic context.

In "The Garden Party," Mansfield evokes the joy that the young Laura feels about having a perfect day for the perfect garden party and depicts corruption and destruction as well. Even though its plot is more conventional than "At the Bay," this story leads both Laura and the reader to an epiphany. The corruption in "The Garden Party" centers on Laura's mother. When Laura wants to postpone the event because a poor man nearby has been killed, her mother refuses and bribes Laura into happiness by giving her an extravagant hat to wear at the party. Yet Laura cannot forget the dead man. When the party is over, she gathers some leftover sandwiches, rushes down the hill, and enters a strange world of darkness, tears, poverty, and death. When she enters the room where the corpse is laid out, she is not horrified; she sees death as something calm and even beautiful, something far different from her silly party. "Forgive my hat," she asks the dead man. She has had an illumination. What she says is woefully inadequate, but the reader sees her moment of understanding and growth. Mansfield has led the reader to an epiphany, though it is not the same as Laura's. When Laura tries to tell her brother what has happened, it is not clear that he understands. As usual, Mansfield does not explain everything.

Context

Biographies of Katherine Mansfield show that she was one of the courageous women who, during the opening decades of the twentieth century, attempted to live a free and unconventional life. She left her home in New Zealand as soon as she could. She was probably bisexual. She lived unconventionally and dedicated her life to art. She paid a heavy price, however, both emotionally and physically. Her emotional life was stormy, and a sexually transmitted disease so weakened her that she developed the tuberculosis that caused her early death.

Yet she may be regarded as one of the greatest writers of her day. Not only was she a leader in creating the modern short story (and thereby one of the most important modernist writers), but many of her stories are regarded as among the finest examples of that genre as well. Mansfield's achievements as an artist were recognized in her own lifetime and had a great impact on many later women writers, in particular Elizabeth Bowen and Katherine Anne Porter. Moreover, she was one of the most important artists of her day to write about women's concerns from a woman's point of view. Although the stories treat men with understanding, they focus on an impressive range of female characters. They show young girls and adolescents beginning to experience life's joys and injustices; women yearning for, yet fearing, love; wives estranged from or coming to love their husbands; mothers loving their children, or feeling indifferent to them; and elderly women patiently looking on and waiting for death.

Sources for Further Study
Alpers, Antony. *The Life of Katherine Mansfield*. Rev. ed. New York: Viking Press. A standard biography by the editor of *The Stories of Katherine Mansfield*. Alpers' sensible, balanced, and detailed revised work draws on years of research and on interviews with people who knew Mansfield and who commented on his earlier biography. Includes notes, illustrations, an index, a detailed chronology, and a good bibliography.

Boddy, Gillian. *Katherine Mansfield: The Woman and the Writer*. Ringwood, Australia: Penguin Books, 1988. An introduction to Mansfield's life and work. This volume is noteworthy for its many photographs and reproductions of documents. Includes the texts of some stories.

Hankin, C. A. *Katherine Mansfield and Her Confessional Stories*. New York: St. Martin's Press, 1983. Hankin calls Mansfield's fiction "confessional" and connects many stories to biographical sources. Her analyses of characters and symbols in the major stories are subtle and detailed.

Kaplan, Sydney Janet. *Katherine Mansfield and the Origins of Modernist Fiction*. Ithaca, N.Y.: Cornell University Press, 1991. A feminist perspective. Although Kaplan examines Mansfield as a major modernist writer, she argues persuasively throughout that hers is a recognizably feminist brand of modernism and that Mansfield should be regarded as important a feminist as Virginia Woolf.

Kirkpatrick, B. J. *A Bibliography of Katherine Mansfield*. Oxford, England: Clarendon Press, 1989. The complete bibliography of Mansfield's published writings, their various editions in foreign languages, reports of her speech, music, and manuscripts. The volume also lists works about Mansfield, from television productions to ballets.

Nathan, Rhoda B., ed. *Critical Essays on Katherine Mansfield*. New York: G. K. Hall, 1993. Good essays, including the editor on Mansfield's methods and three treatments of "Bliss." David Daiches sets Mansfield's poetic way of "telling truth" in the English tradition.

Tomalin, Claire. *Katherine Mansfield: A Secret Life*. New York: Alfred A. Knopf,

1987. A very readable biography. Though it lacks critical comments, this book describes the medical consequences of Mansfield's sexual freedom.

George Soule

THE STORIES OF MURIEL SPARK

Author: Muriel Spark (1918-   )
Type of work: Short stories
First published: 1985

Form and Content

The Stories of Muriel Spark contains twenty-seven short stories written over a thirty-year period. Six original stories are included in this volume, while the remainder had appeared in earlier collections. The settings are modern times, usually post-World War II, in various locations, such as England, Scotland, and Africa. Although Muriel Spark's use of point of view is varied, nineteen of the stories are first-person narratives. Her focus is the observation of human behavior, particularly of female characters. The themes of the stories can be divided into four subject groups: supernatural stories, stories about corruption and evil, stories exposing foolishness and hypocrisy, and stories featuring "lost souls."

The tales containing supernatural elements often feature women protagonists who encounter strange phenomena, as does the title character in "Miss Pinkerton's Apocalypse" when a flying Spode china saucer sweeps through her antique shop. In "The Exccutor," Susan Kyle is troubled by the spirit of her late uncle until she discloses the missing pages of his manuscript and gives up her notion of writing the last chapter of his unfinished novel to publish as her own instead. Spark is at her best in "The Portobello Road," which is narrated by a ghost named Needle, who has been murdered by her friend George and comes back to pay him a visit.

Spark's stories of corruption and evil often feature controlling women who seek power. "The Pawnbroker's Wife" and "The Curtain Blown by the Breeze" are set in Africa and portray two female characters whose manipulative desires bring disastrous results. In "Bang-Bang You're Dead" and "The Ormolu Clock," two ambitious women use their intelligence and determination to acquire success at the expense of others. Spark uses a complex narrative in "Bang-Bang You're Dead" that juxtaposes the past and present to reveal the unfeeling nature of the main character, Sybil. In "The Ormolu Clock," Frau Lublonitsch works tirelessly to make her Austrian Inn a commercial success. While she appears "undefined and dumpy" in her boots and brown apron, the narrator discovers that Frau Lublonitsch is ruthless and ambitious in eliminating her competitors.

In "Daisy Overend," "You Should Have Seen the Mess," "The Black Madonna," and "A Member of the Family," female protagonists are portrayed as hypocritical or foolish. Spark satirizes the women, because they never learn from their mistakes or see themselves as they really are. The narrator in "Daisy Overend" takes delight in conspiring with the audience to expose Daisy, a stunted social climber, trying to succeed as a 1940's socialite with a flapper mentality left over from the 1920's. Daisy's "tawdry" garters left in the drawing room during her soiree prove to be her undoing. In "You Should Have Seen the Mess" and "A Member of the Family," both protagonists, Lorna and Gwen, lack common sense. They live by superficial values, judging others by appearances and expecting to be judged themselves by the same shallow standard. In "The Black Madonna," Lou Parker prays to a Madonna carved from black wood; she asks for a child of her own. Yet when the child is born, Lou rejects her baby daughter because she has black skin. While priding herself on being tolerant of people of all races during the course of the story, Lou rejects her own child based on skin color; thus, Spark exposes Lou's hypocrisy and misplaced values.

The fourth group of stories centers on individuals who are somehow "lost" or isolated from the society. In " 'A Sad Tale's Best for Winter' " a middle-aged man dies contemplating corruption. In "Come Along Marjorie," an assembly of recovering neurotics watch Marjorie's decline from reality to madness. In "The Go-Away Bird," Daphne, the female protagonist, is murdered on her return to Africa during her search to find herself and her home.

Analysis

Spark satirizes the foibles of human nature in her short stories. Her Catholic belief in humankind's fall from grace and Original Sin are crucial to her worldview. Often she is the detached observer who describes her characters in a reserved tone, never passing judgment directly but exposing the characters for what they really are—good or evil, sincere or corrupt. Spark enlists the reader as her comrade even when her characters narrate a tale in the first person. Yet Spark's frequent use of a first-person narrator does not necessarily bring the reader closer to the story's action. Often she maintains a detached tone that effectively removes the reader from the emotion of the plot's situation. For example, in "The Portobello Road" Needle's ghost voice calmly relates the details of her murder. Her matter-of-fact tone in describing her death reinforces a sense of detachment and irony. Spark's wry humor is evident when Needle explains that her "*good* friend" George strangled her with hay in a deserted pasture, and the resulting news headline read, "Needle Found in Haystack."

Spark often employs supernatural elements in her stories to expose the frailties of her characters. In her first story, "The Seraph and the Zambesi," which won a 1951 writing contest sponsored by the *Observer*, arrogant playwright Samuel Cramer feels only jealousy and contempt when a genuine heavenly angel makes an appearance in his Christmas masque. Similarly, Susan Kyle in "The Executor" is haunted by her late uncle's spirit when she tries to claim his unpublished novel as her own. Spark often uses supernatural forces to expose the selfish motives of her characters.

Adults are not the only ones to fall under Spark's scrutiny. *The Stories of Muriel Spark* contains several stories about young girls who embrace or confront evil. She contrasts the innocence of children with the cruelty of adults or reverses the irony and explores the "devilish" nature of children, who are shielded by a guise of adult politeness. For example, in "The Twins" two seemingly normal children exercise some invisible yet insidious control over their parents and other adults who enter their household. In "Alice Long's Dachshunds," eight-year-old Mamie's innocent neglect of the five dachshunds left in her charge is contrasted with the conscious cruelty of the gamekeeper who intentionally kills the dogs. Thus, Spark suggests that even childhood does not ensure innocence; all people possess the knowledge of good and evil.

Spark is at her best when she exposes women characters who use their femininity or identity to gain power or control. "The Pawnbroker's Wife" portrays a woman corrupted by power. Mrs. Jan Cloote, known only by her husband's name, carries on as the pawnbroker in her husband's absence. Hence, in her name and speech she employs distance to separate her actions from her image as innocent wife. Such distancing allows Mrs. Cloote freedom to deny responsibility for her conduct, no matter how cruel or petty.

In "The Ormolu Clock," Spark uses symbolism to amplify the ambitious nature of Frau Lublonitsch. An innkeeper, she seems to live plainly, working hard and behaving kindly; nevertheless, her private living quarters reflect her ambition. Richly adorned in scarlet quilts and gilt-edge furniture, her bedroom and the ormolu clock epitomize her fierce drive to succeed. The clock becomes a symbol that she will soon defeat her competitor Heir Stroh by overtaking his business and destroying his livelihood. The narrator neither condemns nor praises Frau Lublonitsch's ambition; she only comments that everyone likes to be on a winning side. It seems that Spark's disapproval stems from Frau's duplicity and cold-heartedness, not her ambition.

"The Go-Away Bird," Spark's longest story, describes one woman's quest for identity. Daphne, the central figure, is caught between two cultures, that of the Dutch Afrikaaners and the English colonists in Africa. As one of Spark's "lost souls," Daphne seeks to find herself. Spark links Daphne's struggles with the African Go-Away Bird, illustrating an individual's difficulty in trying to find love and identity within diverse cultural and social structures. Daphne is bound by fate and by the men around her: She is murdered by the man who resents her and goes unmourned by the man she loved.

Context

Spark presents an array of female characters in *The Stories of Muriel Spark*. She is concerned with twentieth century morals and manners without being a heavy-handed moralist. Spark's stylized satire exposes the eccentricities and hypocrisies of her age. Though Spark is best known for her novel *The Prime of Miss Jean Brodie* (1961), her short stories also reflect her interest in exploring human behavior in a world in which one must choose between good and evil.

Spark invites her readers to identify with her characters and also to evaluate them. In some cases, the distance that Spark creates as part of her narrative structure makes it impossible for the reader to be anything but an evaluator of the deeds of her protagonists. She portrays women involved in a search for identity; some willingly embrace malevolence while others search for self-respect. Spark's feminists do not seek special rights for women, nor do they view themselves as victims oppressed by society. Yet her characters, such as Needle in "The Portobello Road," do seek to find themselves.

When her women characters become victims, it is usually because they are overcome by outside forces of evil, as is Daphne in "The Go-Away Bird." Other characters meet with disaster through their own willingness to engage in evil, as does Sonia Van der Merwe in "The Curtain Blown by the Breeze." Spark's grasping females, such as Frau Lublonitsch and Mrs. Jan Cloote, are intent on imposing their will on others, regardless of the consequences. Even less sympathy is afforded to hypocritical women, such as Lou Parker in "The Black Madonna" and Gwen in "A Member of the Family," because Spark implies that a woman unable to face the truth is a traitor to herself.

Spark's tone is ironic or satiric. Supernatural elements are often used in her plots to bring judgment regarding a character's vice or sin. She is adept at illustrating the slightly macabre, evil, or hypocritical nature of human beings. While her characters might never be thoroughly explained psychologically, they are believable. She reveals a thorough understanding of the feminine mind—the struggles that women face in a search for identity—and the supernatural forces that shape the unseen elements of contemporary society.

Sources for Further Study

Bold, Alan. *Muriel Spark*. London: Methuen, 1986. Bold is concerned with the relationship between Spark's personal background and the development of her characters, particularly links between Spark's religious experience and the religious elements of her fiction. He includes biographical information and then discusses Spark's works in chronological order, specifically the novels. An extensive bibliography is included, listing criticism, articles, essays, interviews, and books related to Spark and her work.

Hynes, Joseph. *Critical Essays on Muriel Spark*. New York: G. K. Hall, 1992. Hynes's extensive collection contains three sections. The first focuses on Spark's life and art. The second group contains general criticism of Spark's themes, both positive and negative. The remaining eighteen essays discuss Spark's individual works, her novels in particular.

Sproxton, Judy. *The Women of Muriel Spark*. New York: St. Martin's Press, 1992. Spark's female characters are discussed in four chapters under the topics of mature women, women of power, women as victims, and narrative and faith. "Narrative and Faith" is a chapter summation of Spark's vision of Christianity and her worldview. Each chapter is devoted to a discussion of specific women characters in Spark's novels. While the work does not contain a bibliography, a biography of Spark is included.

Walker, Dorothea. *Muriel Spark*. Boston: Twayne, 1988. Walker is interested in the vision underlying Spark's plots and characters, particularly in her novels. The seven chapters are organized by themes. An important feature in Walker's volume is an extensive annotated bibliography of primary and secondary sources.

Whittaker, Ruth. *The Faith and Fiction of Muriel Spark*. New York: St. Martin's Press, 1982. Whittaker's work elaborates on the diversity of Spark's themes, meanings, and purpose. The chapter divisions are organized according to topics: religion, style, structure, and form. Limited primarily to a discussion of Spark's novels. Includes a biographical section, as well as an extensive bibliography.

Paula M. Miller

THE STORY OF GÖSTA BERLING

Author: Selma Lagerlöf (1858-1940)
Type of work: Novel
Type of plot: Historical realism
Time of plot: The end of the 1820's
Locale: Värmland, Sweden
First published: Gösta Berlings saga, 1891 (English translation, 1898)

Principal characters:

GÖSTA BERLING, a drunken but brilliant minister who leads a
  rebellion of cavaliers
MARGARETA CELSING, a beautiful young woman married to
  Major Samzelius
ANNA STJÄRNHÖK, one of the several local women whose hearts
  are broken by Gösta Berling
MARIANNE SINCLAIRE, a great beauty given to self-observation
ELISABETH DOHNA, the beautiful wife of Henrik Dohna
HENRIK DOHNA, a foolish nobleman
SINTRAM, a local landowner who represents evil

Form and Content

The Story of Gösta Berling consists of thirty-six chapters, each of which can be
regarded as one complete episode. Taken together, however, the various tales constitute a unified plot. This plot is centered on one year in the life of Gösta Berling,
although information about his life prior to that year is also presented. Gösta's life is
portrayed as dynamic and even dramatic, with a large number of important events,
and extends from the moment when he loses his position as a minister in the Swedish
church to some time after his marriage to Elizabeth Dohna.

While a number of dramatic events in the life of Gösta Berling provide the
backbone of the novel's plot, it is, however, the life history of its female protagonist,
Margareta Celsing, which provides the most engaging part of the story. She, and such
other female characters as Anna Stjärnhök, Marianne Sinclaire, and Elisabeth Dohna,
stand at the center of the author's interest and the novel's meaning. Lagerlöf's concern
is primarily ethical and philosophical, and it is the actions of Margareta Celsing, who
is also known as the Major's Wife, which are placed in the reader's focus. Through
her portrayal of Margareta and the other women in the novel, Lagerlöf created one of
the earliest examples of high-quality women's fiction in Swedish literature.

The role of love in human life is the novel's most important motif, and it connects
with the book's central theme, which is the question of how to defeat evil and establish
justice. The power of evil is represented by the character of Sintram, who is in league
with the Devil or perhaps is even the Devil himself. He enters into a pact with the
twelve cavaliers, who, at the invitation of the Major's Wife, are living at Ekeby Manor.
The cavaliers promise to refrain from any kind of useful labor for a period of one year,

and in return they will be given control of Ekeby during that year. They reveal to Margareta's husband, Major Samzelius, that Altringer, who willed Ekeby to the major, was the long-time lover of his wife. Consequently, Margareta is cast out of her home by her husband, after which he moves to another one of his farms, thus leaving the cavaliers in control of Ekeby. Yet Lagerlöf also shows that this unfair treatment of a woman by her husband becomes a blessing in disguise, as it gives Margareta an opportunity to expiate her sins, leave behind the undesirable personality traits that she had acquired in the course of many years, and return to her youthful state of innocence and gentleness.

Equally important to the development of the novel's theme is the story of Gösta Berling's love affairs. A handsome man much admired for his social graces but troubled by alcoholism, Gösta attracts the attention of several women, the most important of whom are Anna Stjärnhök, Marianne Sinclaire, and Elisabeth Dohna. All but one of these attractions are met with disappointment, but thereby the women learn the value of renunciation, as does Gösta himself. When he finally marries Elisabeth Dohna, the rejected wife of a local nobleman, he does so out of a sense of duty and not for love. The end of the book comes when the cavaliers' year of reign at Ekeby is over and they return to useful labor. Work, the author seems to say, is a major component of virtue and a chief defense against evil.

Analysis

The Story of Gösta Berling is, above all, an ethical novel, as it takes as its theme how justice and goodness can be established in the face of evil. This theme is made manifest both on the level of individuals, particularly in the lives of Gösta Berling and Margareta Celsing, and on the level of society as a whole.

The male protagonist, Gösta Berling, is a minister who becomes defrocked because of drunkenness. Alcohol is the chief evil in his life, and it destroys not only his personal happiness but also his ability to provide leadership for the people whom he has been called to serve. The chief moral question in Gösta's life is how he can regain his sense of responsibility for service to other human beings.

While Gösta has sinned against his parishioners, against the community as a whole, Margareta Celsing has transgressed primarily against her husband and her mother. Originally a sweet and innocent girl, Margareta has become the coarse wife of Major Samzelius, in which role she does the work of men and is known as the most powerful woman in Värmland. Her negative feelings toward her husband, coupled with her love for the rich man Altringer, have led to an adulterous relationship of long standing. Margareta profited financially from this relationship: Prior to his death, Altringer willed his substantial holdings to her and her husband, as Swedish law at the time prohibited women from controlling property on their own. Margareta's sin against her mother consisted in not listening to her advice. According to the doctrine of the Swedish church, children were to obey their parents, and they never outgrew this obligation.

At the point in time when *The Story of Gösta Berling* begins, Margareta is at the height of her power. Her estate, Ekeby, is highly profitable, as are several other farms and iron works that she controls. She has assembled on her estate a group of twelve cavaliers, who are basically idle yet talented men, and their various activities provide her with entertainment. One of these men is Gösta Berling.

The plot of the novel is set in motion when the cavaliers resolve to rebel against Margareta's rule. This decision is presented in two different ways by Lagerlöf. On the level of myth, the cavaliers believe that the Major's Wife, as she is commonly called, has entered into a pact with the Devil, according to which one of the cavaliers is to be given to him each year of Margareta's continued control of Ekeby. From the perspective of psychology, on the other hand, it appears that the Major's Wife is becoming increasingly troubled by what kind of person she has become and wishes to regain her former identity.

The rebellion breaks out at Christmastime, which is a period when, in Scandinavian folk belief and legend, the forces of evil are particularly active. The cavaliers are offered a deal by the evil Sintram, who may be the Devil incarnate, and are promised control of Ekeby on the condition that they abstain from any useful activity for one year. Sintram, who on the book's realistic level is presented as rapidly losing his sanity, wishes to destroy the material basis for people's lives in the area. On the level of myth, the cavaliers are entering into an agreement with the Evil One and thus sinning grievously. When they tell Major Samzelius about Margareta's adultery, he expels his wife from the estate, moves to one of his other farms, and leaves Ekeby in the hands of the cavaliers.

The consequences of their rule of Ekeby are indeed disastrous. No useful work is performed, and there is thus little opportunity for the people of the district to earn the necessities of life. The economic decline also leads to a general worsening of the moral and ethical conditions in the area. As the year of the cavaliers' rule over Ekeby is coming to its end, the district is faced with a condition that is tantamount to mob rule, as the assembled inhabitants march on Ekeby. It is this crisis that finally brings Gösta Berling to assume a true leadership role. Prodded by his wife, Elisabeth, he brings the mob back to its senses and leads the cavaliers in what can only be termed an act of group reformation, as they work to bring both the economic and the moral conditions in the area back to their former, and happier, state.

Context

The Story of Gösta Berling is regarded as one of the most important novels in Swedish literature; indeed, some critics consider it the most significant one. Serving as a bridge between the naturalistic and the symbolist movements in Scandinavia, it contains elements of both. One of its important characteristics is the faithful depiction of social and historical reality that was common in the literature of the 1880's, while its emphasis on folk belief and legend ties it to the aesthetic concerns of the 1890's.

Upon its publication, the book was not immediately hailed as a masterwork even though it had been eagerly anticipated, as five chapters from it had received an award the previous year. It was judged on narrow realistic criteria, and the critics did not understand the significance of the author's use of myth. A review by the respected Danish critic George Brandes (1842-1927) two years later, however, launched Lagerlöf on her career as one of Sweden's most important writers. The recognition that she received encouraged Lagerlöf greatly, and the financial rewards from her writing enabled her to quit her job as a teacher and to travel widely. Later she was able to purchase her childhood home, which became an anchor for both her life and her activity as an artist.

Lagerlöf went on to receive several important honors, chief among which is the 1909 Nobel Prize in Literature. She also received an honorary doctorate from the University of Uppsala and became a member of the Swedish Academy in 1914. Because of her position in the world of letters, Lagerlöf was able to serve as an effective role model for other Scandinavian woman writers.

A strong feminist thread runs through Lagerlöf's work. This may be seen in some of the portraits of women in *The Story of Gösta Berling*, particularly in that of Margareta Celsing, who is thrown out of her home because she is legally prohibited from controlling property on her own. Lagerlöf also involved herself deeply in the struggle for women's suffrage and made statements which anticipated some of the arguments during the women's movement of the 1970's.

Lagerlöf's work has also meant much to feminist academic criticism. Because of her books, as well as those of other women writers in the Nordic countries, it has been possible to argue convincingly for the view that the Scandinavian novel is truly the creation of women: Lagerlöf stands as one of the mothers of the novel in Scandinavia.

Sources for Further Study

Berendsohn, Walter A. *Selma Lagerlöf: Her Life and Work*. Translated by George F. Timpson. Port Washington, N.Y.: Kennikat Press, 1968. First published in German in 1927, the volume by Berendsohn discusses the relationship between Lagerlöf's life and her books. Emphasizes her connection with Värmland, where *The Story of Gösta Berling* takes place.

Edström, Vivi. *Selma Lagerlöf*. Translated by Barbara Lide. Boston: Twayne, 1984. A highly accessible volume written by a world renowned authority on Lagerlöf, this book contains an overview of her biography and separate chapters on her most important works, including *The Story of Gösta Berling*. Edström discusses the form of the book, the roles played by both historical reality and mythical and folkloric motifs, and its place in Swedish literary history. Also offers extensive analysis of plot, theme, characters, and setting. Contains notes, a bibliography, and an index.

Gustafson, Alrik. *A History of Swedish Literature*. Minneapolis: University of Minnesota Press, 1961. An overview of the literature of Sweden from the beginning to the postwar era, this volume places Lagerlöf's works in the context of Swedish literary history.

_____ . *Six Scandinavian Novelists*. Princeton, N.J.: Princeton University Press, 1971. In the context of five other major Scandinavian novelists, Gustafson offers a comprehensive overview of Lagerlöf's authorship.

Olson-Buckner, Elsa. *The Epic Tradition in Gösta Berling's Saga*. New York: Theo. Gans, 1979. In an extended analysis of the book, Olson-Buckner points out the many points of contact between *The Story of Gösta Berling* and the conventional epic. Examines the novel's structural similarities to the traditional heroic saga.

Wivel, Henrik. *Selma Lagerlöf: Her Works of Life*. Minneapolis: Center for Nordic Studies, University of Minnesota, 1991. This pamphlet contains a brief discussion of the idea of love as it is presented throughout Lagerlöf's works. The section dealing with *The Story of Gösta Berling* presents a helpful analysis of the way in which the characters interact with one another. Includes a good bibliography of both primary and secondary material.

Jan Sjåvik

THE STORY OF MY LIFE

Author: Helen Keller (1880-1968)
Type of work: Autobiography
Time of work: 1880-1903
Locale: Alabama, Massachusetts, and New York
First published: 1903, rev. ed. 1966

> *Principal personages:*
> HELEN KELLER, the author, a blind and deaf young woman
> ANNE SULLIVAN, Keller's first teacher, who helped her
> communicate with the outside world

Form and Content

The Story of My Life is an account of the early years of a woman who overcame incredible problems to become an accomplished, literate adult. The book does not give a complete account of the author's life, as it was written when she was still a college student. It is, however, a unique account of one young woman's passage from almost total despair to success in a world mostly populated by hearing and seeing people. This book is relatively short, but the modern editions also include letters written by and to Helen Keller and an analysis of her education from a later standpoint.

The Story of My Life begins with Keller's vague memories of early childhood. She was born in 1880 in Alabama, an apparently normal child. According to her recollections, she began to speak before she was a year old. The early chapters recount the little girl's love of the natural world, a theme that is repeated many times throughout the work, and her generally happy home life, with loving and nurturing parents.

At the age of nineteen months, however, Keller was stricken with an unexplained disease—certainly unexplained in the nineteenth century, with no suggestion in the book of any later diagnosis—which left her both blind and deaf. She became a domineering child, with behavior that was totally unacceptable. Keller mainly lays the blame for this behavior upon her frustration at the futility of trying to communicate her thoughts and feelings without any ability to speak, read, or write.

The breakthrough came when the Kellers visited noted inventor Alexander Graham Bell in Washington, D.C., who referred them to the Perkins Institution, a school for blind children in Boston. The school sent a woman named Anne Sullivan to teach young Helen to behave properly and, if possible, to teach her to be a "normal" child. Most of the book deals with Sullivan's training of Keller, showing her how to behave decently, to use the manual alphabet to communicate her thoughts, and to read books in raised letters and later in braille. In the last chapters, there is much emphasis on Keller's higher education.

According to her own recollections, young Helen Keller's greatest love, apart from the natural world, was language. She learned to read not only English but also French, German, Latin, and Greek. She began writing in her early teens. There is also

considerable discussion of her examinations and preparation for admission into
Radcliffe College, the sister college to Harvard, and her eventual acceptance.

Keller writes about her attempts to use speech as a means of communication, but
she largely considers these attempts to be failures: She never really learned to speak
well. Keller demonstrates that the process of learning to speak is difficult for any
person who is either blind or deaf and virtually impossible for someone who lacks
both senses. Instead, Keller became a great lover of books, which became her only
real way of relating to the world outside. The book ends on this note, with a list of
favorite authors and a wish to be counted among them.

Analysis

The Story of My Life is the story of one young woman's emergence from the most
extreme isolation possible. It is not a story of an "emerging woman" in the usual sense
of the term; there is no discussion of sexuality, of women's place in society, or of
societal attitudes. Rather, young Helen was an emerging human being. This is a story
of a young woman learning to reach out to the world.

Apart from a few short opening chapters relating to Keller's vague memories of her
early childhood, the tone of this book is largely one of joy. Every new word, every
new concept, is a major revelation. A long passage describes her discovery that all
objects are associated with words, and a special emphasis is placed on water, the first
concept that the young Helen learned to refer to with both speech and sign.

Above all, there is a focus on the essential importance of language. Keller clearly
believes that abstract thought is impossible without language, that language is the
single most important factor that sets human beings apart from other animals. More
than anything else, the author recounts her efforts to use human languages and her
emergence as a "real person" as a result of this newfound ability.

There is more than one way to interpret this emphasis. Most people take language
for granted. Children who have normal senses of sight and hearing and adequate
intelligence do not have to be taught to speak. They learn by listening and watching,
by imitation. This path was closed to the little girl trapped in a dark and silent world.
It is natural that she should focus on her process of learning to communicate with the
outside world.

Keller learned to read and write several foreign languages. At the end of the book,
there are references to her emerging love of the works of William Shakespeare, the
Greek classics, and other great works of literature. There is a long discussion about
her early attempts at becoming a writer herself, at the age of twelve. In later life, Keller
would indeed become a successful writer, among other things. At the time that *The
Story of My Life* was written, however, she was still in the process of learning to
communicate, and there is very little said about what she would later wish to
communicate to the outside world. Language, in itself, is the essential theme of the
book.

In this regard, it is necessary to consider *The Story of My Life* in context. When she
wrote this book, Keller was a student in one of the greatest centers of learning in the

world. Being graduated from Radcliffe College with honors is far from an easy task, even for someone with a normal sensory system. There is a sense of Keller's fierce determination, but it is always tempered with love and understanding and with great praise for the various people who helped her, especially Anne Sullivan, her teacher in childhood and her helper in later life.

Keller uses language in two quite different ways in *The Story of My Life*. She makes the reader very much aware of how the world appears to someone who passes through life deaf and blind. On the other hand, she also makes use of visual and auditory images that she could not have experienced, doing so quite convincingly. These two uses of language underscore the reality of the author's roles as a person who experienced the world in a unique way and as a successful author who could relate to the way in which other people experience life.

Context

When *The Story of My Life* was written in 1902, many female authors were still using male pseudonyms in an attempt to give their work some credence in a literary world dominated by men. It would be almost twenty years before women were given the right to vote and a much longer period before they made any real impact on the political and literary scenes.

Decades later, Helen Keller would be considered one of the great social leaders of the time, and her earlier works would be considered inspirational to women and to society in general. Keller's social work was primarily aimed at helping people with assorted disabilities, but not necessarily physical ones. She took upon herself the task of improving society in general, regardless of sex, race, nationality, or social standing. *The Story of My Life* cannot be considered "feminist" in any real sense, as the author at that time of her life had problems considerably more difficult to overcome than merely being a woman in a male-dominated society. In a broader context, however, this book has been inspirational to people faced with difficulties that must be overcome—physical, emotional, or societal.

Sources for Further Study

Boylan, Esther, ed. *Women and Disability*. Atlantic Highlands, N.J.: Zed Books, 1991. A series of articles on the situation of disabled women in the world. This book places emphasis on the concept that women have a "double handicap" by being female as well as disabled.

Brooks, Van Wyck. *Helen Keller: Sketch for a Portrait*. New York: E. P. Dutton, 1956. A biography of Keller covering her early years, her later development as an adult author and activist, and her continuing relationship with Anne Sullivan Macy, her teacher from early childhood.

Hillyer, Barbara. *Feminism and Disability*. Norman: University of Oklahoma Press, 1993. The story of a woman bringing up a disabled little girl. The stress in this book is on the feminist movement and the movement for the rights of disabled people of both sexes, and on how the two issues may come into conflict.

Keller, Helen. *Midstream: My Later Life*. Westport, Conn.: Greenwood Press, 1968. A reprint of an autobiography of Keller originally published in 1929. This book continues where *The Story of My Life* left off. It offers insights into the author's later development, after she was graduated from college and entered the mainstream of American society.

_____ . *Teacher: Anne Sullivan Macy*. Garden City, N.Y.: Doubleday, 1955. A biography of Helen Keller's early teacher and longtime companion and helper. Explores Keller's training from a later point of view, as well as providing insight into the life of Anne Sullivan and the long-standing relationship between the two women.

Lash, Joseph P. *Helen and Teacher: The Story of Helen Keller and Anne Sullivan Macy*. New York: Delacorte Press, 1980. The story of Keller's training and the relationship between Keller and her teacher. Traces the development of both women from Sullivan's childhood in the 1860's through Keller's death in 1968.

McInnes, J. M., and J. A. Treffry. *Deaf-Blind Infants and Children: A Developmental Guide*. Toronto: University of Toronto Press, 1982. A modern guide to the teaching of children with Helen Keller's problems. This book provides a discussion of modern methods used in treating such children, which have changed greatly since the days of Keller's childhood.

Marc Goldstein

STORYTELLER

Author: Leslie Marmon Silko (1948-   )
Type of work: Folklore, memoir, poetry, and short stories
First published: 1981

Form and Content

Although it includes materials from many different literary genres—poetry, short story, myth, memoir, and biography—*Storyteller* viewed in its entirety is essentially an autobiography, a portrait, as its title makes explicit, of the artist as a young storyteller. In addition to the literary materials, interspersed throughout are photographs of Leslie Marmon Silko and her family and of various scenes in and around her childhood home, Laguna Pueblo in New Mexico. What unifies these diverse materials is the pervasive focus on Silko's development as an artist, on the familial and cultural factors that shaped her conception of herself as a writer—or, as she prefers to think of herself, a storyteller—working in the tradition of oral storytelling as it was practiced from the earliest times among the Laguna people and concentrating, though not exclusively, on female experience in both the autobiographical and the fictional parts of the book.

The biographical sections, mostly concerning relatives who told Silko stories when she was a child, and the autobiographical sections, mostly concerning experiences related to the stories, are scattered throughout the book and function as introductions to and links between the stories, poems, and Laguna myths that make up the bulk of the book. Some critics have been troubled by what they have seen as a lack of originality in *Storyteller* since much of this latter material had already been published elsewhere: many of the poems in *Laguna Woman* (1974), many of the short stories in a collection edited by Kenneth Rosen entitled *The Man to Send Rain Clouds* (1974), and many of the Laguna myths in Silko's novel *Ceremony* (1977). Silko's defenders have pointed out, however, that this "retelling" is perfectly consistent with and indeed necessary to Silko's concept of storytelling. In the oral tradition, which Silko is attempting to adapt to the circumstances of a literate culture, storytellers have a repertoire of tales that they tell over and over again. Indeed, Silko believes that one of the beauties of the oral tradition is that every time a story is retold, even if repeated word for word by the same teller sitting in the same chair, it becomes a new and unique story. Silko's intention is to help readers get a sense of how a story would sound if they were hearing it.

In keeping with this desire to approximate the oral tradition, *Storyteller* begins by explaining the importance of storytelling in Laguna culture and in Silko's own life through a brief biography of her father's Aunt Susie, a member of the last generation of Laguna people who maintained the oral tradition whereby the entire culture and the people's sense of identity were passed on from one generation to the next. From her, Silko heard several of the traditional stories that are included in *Storyteller*, among them two which appear early in the book and which Silko has said derive from the matriarchal nature of Laguna culture in which the mother is the real authority figure. The first is about a little girl, Waithea, who wants corn mush to eat and drowns herself when her mother refuses to give her any, and the second is about a little girl and her baby sister who are left behind by their mother when the people flee to a mesa to escape a flood. Other stories taken from the Laguna oral tradition include the story of the evil magician who persuaded the Lagunas to abandon the care of the Mother Corn altar and to rely on his magic instead; the story of the quarrel between Reed Woman and Corn Woman; the story of Kaup'a'ta, the Gambler, who shut up the storm clouds until they were rescued by the Sun; and the story of how Arrowboy, a hero figure prominent in Laguna myth, escaped from the power of his witch-wife. If Aunt Susie is the last of the traditional Laguna storytellers, Silko is the first of the new generation of storytellers, and she accepts the responsibility although hers is a literate rather than an oral tradition.

Just what accepting this responsibility entails is the subject of the first of the original short stories in the book. It is also entitled "Storyteller," and its plot deals with two Inuit storytellers, an old man and the young girl who lives with him. The old man, who represents the traditional storyteller, is compelled to tell in endless detail over a long period of time a story about a hunter and a giant white bear which will ultimately kill him at the same time that the old storyteller dies. The young girl represents the storyteller in the modern world. She is compelled to tell the story of her revenge on the white man who sold her parents the contaminated alcohol that killed them. It is a story of the dishonesty, prejudice, and sexual depravity of the white men, and of their exploitation of the Inuits, the Inuit land, and especially the Inuit women. In *Storyteller*, Silko assumes the functions both of the traditional storyteller, who must preserve the legacy of the past, and of the new generation storyteller, who must tell the truth about the present. The materials in the rest of the book fit into one or the other of these categories, or else deal with the cultural, biographical, and autobiographical information needed to understand them.

Analysis

In addition to generating Silko's sense of identity, the theme of the storyteller and storytelling gives unity to the diverse materials collected in *Storyteller*. Growing up as a person of mixed blood, Silko was not fully accepted in Laguna culture or in white culture. As a storyteller who both preserves the oral tradition and functions in the tradition of literate authorship, however, she can establish a bridge between the two cultures and find an identity worthy of respect in both. Moreover, one of the major themes in this book, as it is in her novel *Ceremony*, is that the traditional stories are not merely relics of the past but are relevant to the very different world of today. As Silko says in the selection entitled "Storytelling," it is important for people to understand, through stories, how things were in the past, not only to have an accurate knowledge of history but also because history repeats itself and "it is the same/ even now." This theme is developed further in the short story "Yellow Woman," which is often anthologized and is perhaps Silko's best-known work. Yellow Woman, known to the Lagunas as Kochininako, is the subject of many stories in the oral tradition. In Silko's story, a young Laguna wife has a sexual encounter with a stranger. She remembers and identifies with the story of Yellow Woman's encounter with a spirit from the north with whom she went away and lived. The story emphasizes Silko's cyclical view of history and her belief in the importance of stories in providing a sense of identity.

The exploitation of American Indians by whites is another major theme in *Storyteller*, not only in the short story "Storyteller" but also in three other stories. In "Lullaby," the white rancher for whom the Navajo Chato has worked loyally for many years heartlessly evicts him and his old wife from their shack when Chato gets too old to work. In "Tony's Story," a sadistic state policeman harasses two young pueblo men. In "A Geronimo Story," Laguna scouts who are forced to help the white men track down Apaches are not allowed to sleep in the house with the white soldiers and must sleep outside with the horses. In addition, many of the biographical and autobiographical sections deal with the bigotry that Silko and her family encountered in their dealings with whites.

The natural world, the environment, and animals also constitute important interests in *Storyteller*, as they do in all of Silko's works. Silko's love of the mountains and the desert surrounding Laguna is apparent. Hiking and hunting are activities that she enjoyed as she was growing up, and the stories and poems are filled with careful observations of nature and of animal behavior. Deer, bears, goats, roosters, horses, coyotes, badgers, and sheep all figure prominently in them.

The most striking and pervasive theme to emerge from *Storyteller*, however, is the theme of the importance of family. Silko speaks of her family—her great-aunts and great-uncles, great-grandparents, grandparents, aunts and uncles, father, and sisters—with unfailing love and respect. They are important parts of her story and important influences on her as a storyteller. (References to her mother, however, are notably absent.) Through the biographical and autobiographical segments and the photographs, readers are introduced to the members of the Stagner and Marmon families who played such an important role in Silko's development as an author and who continue to play an important role in her affections.

Context

Silko is one of the best-known and most highly acclaimed American Indian writers. She has received many awards for her work, including the so-called genius prize, a MacArthur Foundation Fellowship, in 1981. One of her greatest strengths as a writer is her ability to portray not only female but also male experience realistically and convincingly. She believes that at the deepest levels of human consciousness, men and women are the same, and she has attributed her success in portraying male experience to the fact that in the Laguna culture boys and girls are not segregated as they are in white American society. Consequently, when growing up she was able to observe both male and female experience equally.

As Silko has also pointed out, however, traditional Laguna society is matriarchal, and she grew up in the midst of a group of strong-minded, intelligent, and hard-working women—such as her Aunt Susie, her Grandma A'mooh (Marie Anaya Marmon), and her Grandma Lillie (Francesca Stagner)—and in a community in which the homes are considered the property of the women and in which the women do much of what white American society would consider man's work. The matriarchal nature of Laguna culture is reflected in its concept of the deities, the most important of which are female. Corn Woman and Spider Woman figure prominently in the traditional stories that are incorporated in *Storyteller*. Thus, Silko is important in the history of women's literature not only because she is the first American Indian woman to achieve considerable recognition as a writer but also because her work embodies the matriarchal consciousness of Laguna culture and presents with great accuracy, realism, and psychological insight the experiences of both genders within that culture.

Sources for Further Study

Graulich, Melody, ed. *"Yellow Woman": Leslie Marmon Silko*. New Brunswick, N.J.: Rutgers University Press, 1993. Includes an excellent introduction by Graulich setting *Storyteller* in its cultural, biographical, and critical contexts. Also includes essays dealing with *Storyteller* by Linda Danielson, Patricia Jones, Bernard A. Hirsch, and Arnold Krupat.

Seyersted, Per. *Leslie Marmon Silko*. Boise, Idaho: Boise State University, 1980. A good introduction to Laguna culture and to Silko's early work up to and including *Storyteller*, which was in press and available to Seyersted when he published his analysis.

Silko, Leslie Marmon, and James Wright. *The Delicacy and Strength of Lace: Letters Between Leslie Marmon Silko and James Wright*. Edited by Anne Wright. St. Paul, Minn.: Graywolf Press, 1986. Correspondence between Silko and poet James Wright from 1978 to 1980, in which Silko discusses *Storyteller*: its genesis and structure, the decision to include photographs, and several of the people, stories, and poems that appear. The best source for biographical information on Silko up to 1980.

Studies in American Indian Literatures 5, no. 1 (Spring, 1993). A special edition devoted to *Storyteller*. Linda Danielson summarizes its critical reception to 1993. Toby C. S. Langen discusses it as a treatise on literature at the same time that it is a work of literature. Robert M. Nelson compares Silko's tellings of traditional Laguna stories to the tellings of John Gunn, which were published in 1917. Helen Jaskoski discusses five writing assignments related to *Storyteller* that provide insight into American Indian literatures and to literature in general. Also included are several photographs taken by Silko's father that are relevant to *Storyteller*.

Wiget, Andrew. *Native American Literature*. Boston: Twayne, 1985. Discusses Silko's achievement in terms of her realization of the possibilities of American Indian myths and storytelling as a principle for plot construction and characterization.

Dennis Hoilman

THE STREET

Author: Ann Petry (1911-   )
Type of work: Novel
Type of plot: Naturalism
Time of plot: 1944
Locale: Harlem, in New York City
First published: 1946

> *Principal characters:*
> LUTIE MAE JOHNSON, a hardworking, African American single
>   mother with middle-class aspirations
> BOOTS, a musician and pimp
> MRS. HEDGES, a tenant in Lutie's building who runs a house of
>   prostitution for Junto
> JUNTO, the Jewish owner of the nightclub where Boots works
>   and the brothel that Mrs. Hedges operates
> THE "SUPE," the demented superintendent of the apartment
>   building
> MIN, the superintendent's common-law wife

Form and Content

Ann Lane Petry was the first African American woman writer to record book sales of more than one million copies. She reworked her experiences as a reporter for two Harlem newspapers, *The Amsterdam News* and *The People's News*, into her novel *The Street*. Organized into eighteen chapters and set in 1944, *The Street* introduces Lutie Mae Johnson, who has moved to 116th Street in Harlem following the dissolution of her marriage. Lutie was forced into an early marriage because of the security that it would provide, but the marriage failed primarily because of the inability of her husband, Jim, to find work. His continual unemployment caused Lutie to accept work as a live-in domestic for a wealthy white family in Connecticut. While working for the Chandlers, Lutie became imbued with white American cultural values, which emphasize the belief that success (seemingly equated with money) is possible if one works hard enough.

Lutie adopted this work ethic, choosing Benjamin Franklin as her hero. She accepted the American myth that Franklin had arrived in Philadelphia with only two loaves of bread and prospered. Although she learned from the Chandlers' experiences that the mere possession of money does not bring happiness, she now uncritically pursues the American Dream.

Lutie has been exposed to the American Dream not only through her work for the "filthy rich" Chandlers but also through her education and her friendship with the Prizzinis, an Italian immigrant couple who operate the local grocery store. Following these models, Lutie continually strives to achieve her dream of upward mobility.

During the day, she works in a laundry, and at night, she studies to pass a civil service exam. No matter how much Lutie tries, however, she cannot progress economically. She is unable to accumulate the extra money that she needs for her and her son to move from their dingy apartment. She believes that she will obtain success somehow if only she works hard enough.

The door opens a crack when she meets Boots, a musician who tells her that she can become a singer in his band. To prepare for this career change, Lutie decides to take singing lessons. Mr. Cross, the teacher, offers her lessons in exchange for her body. Lutie refuses to use her sexuality to advance her career, although it seems to be the only way that she can attain the financial security she seeks.

Boots must renege on the job offer when Junto, the Jewish owner of the Casino nightclub, tells Boots that he wants Lutie for himself. Lutie refuses both Boots and Junto, recalling bits of conversation that she overheard while working for the Chandlers about the immorality of African American women. Lutie understood perfectly this type of thinking that automatically evoked cultural stereotypes of African American women. She knew that her race and her gender made her immediately suspect and available. Lutie's grandmother had frequently cautioned her about the indecent intentions of white men.

Her grandmother forgot to warn Lutie, however, about African American men. The urban North produced little contact between white men and African American women, and the white man was not always the enemy, as Lutie discovers. In desperate need of money to obtain the release of her eight-year-old son, who has been arrested, Lutie goes to Boots. Boots tells her that she can have the money but that she must submit sexually to both him and Junto. Boots's slap after she spurns his sexual advances triggers the release of a lifetime of suppressed anger and frustration. Her subsequent killing of Boots is the culmination of years of disappointment.

Analysis

Petry's stated purpose in writing *The Street* was "to show how simply and easily the environment can change the course of a person's life." The wind symbolically represents the environment in the opening paragraph. It portends the life that awaits Lutie Johnson and her son, Bub. Like the wind that scatters litter and people alike, Lutie's life will be buffeted by social, economic, and cultural forces that will assault her sense of self and dignity, never allowing her to meet her goals. She is ultimately defeated because she yearns for more than the choices allowed African American women within a tripartite system of oppression: racism, sexism, and classism.

Unlike Richard Wright's Bigger Thomas, in *Native Son* (1940), Lutie neither fears nor hates whites. She is naïve, however, in her opinion of their system: She does not understand that as an African American woman in the 1940's she is excluded from the American Dream. Lutie believes that she has as much chance for success as a white person or an immigrant because she has accepted the myths of American culture. From her education to her observation of the Chandlers to the machinations of Madison Avenue, she has unthinkingly accepted these myths. She knows from personal observation that money does not equate contentment, but she disregards the unhappiness that permeates the Chandler family. When a suicide committed on Christmas Day in the Chandlers' home is treated as an accident in order to avoid social difficulty, Lutie only notes the power of money to change perceptions.

She not only accepts the myth of Benjamin Franklin but also embraces the idea of a "woman's place." Lutie assumes that her place is in the home and consequently feels guilt because she must work. She does not understand that the system is not designed for her aspirations. Although she indiscriminately accepts white social values, she uncritically rejects the surrounding African American community. She considers herself and her son superior to the other blacks on "the street" by virtue of her education and exposure to the white elite. By isolating herself from the community, she lacks the support that would have sustained her and challenged her ideas for realizing the American Dream. By attempting to achieve autonomy without the support of the African American community and by being too judgmental of other African American women, she sabotages herself.

Yet Petry does not naïvely blame the African American men in *The Street* for the problems in the black community. Boots, Jim, and the "Supe" are as much victims as Lutie. The source of the problems plaguing the African American community are people like Junto and the Chandlers. These white representatives of an oppressive system gain their privilege and power through the racial and economic exploitation of African Americans.

Lutie seemingly is unaware of how white patriarchal power functions and of her inability to change the system or to work within it. She—like many other women— blames herself for the failures in her life. Even so, Lutie never loses her dignity as a woman. The stereotypical images of African American women held by the dominant society were never the images that she had of herself.

Context

The Street was the first work by an African American woman in which a woman faced the challenges of a hostile environment in the same manner as a man. As a result of the inequities inherent in the American social system, Lutie's outward behavior resembles that of Bigger Thomas or of Bob Jones in Chester Himes's *If He Hollers Let Him Go* (1945). She murders out of frustration that comes from her inability to achieve material success in accordance with the precepts of the American Dream.

The Street conforms to the naturalistic mode of writing that was prevalent in African American literature of the 1940's. Naturalism stresses the power of external forces, the environment or the social system, to block human freedom. It may also emphasize the power of internal forces, irrational beliefs or the subconscious, to limit human rationality and responsibility. A standard characteristic of naturalism is that life for the protagonist is a downhill struggle ending in acceptance of the oppressive forces or in death. Lutie's naturalistic flaw seems to be her inability to understand or intellectually accept that black life and the American Dream of material success are diametrically opposed.

As she was writing in the naturalistic mode at the same time as Richard Wright and Chester Himes, Petry's novel was dismissed as an ineffectual imitation of her contemporaries, probably because of her focus on a woman. Although the novel has received much critical attention, until quite recently it had received little literary acclaim. The limited reception of the novel by literary critics did not prevent it from becoming a best-seller. Although the first few chapters won the Houghton Mifflin Literary Fellowship of $2,400 in 1943, many critics missed a crucial difference between Petry's novel and those of her contemporaries: gender.

Although African American men and African American women share a common history, the women have faced and continue to face triple oppression: race, class, and gender. Lutie is female, and her reality is distinct from that of Bigger Thomas or Bob Jones. In *The Street*, Petry chronicles the consequences of racial, sexual, and economic oppression on the psyche of an African American woman. Because of the societal conventions to which Lutie is subjected, particularly sexual exploitation, an extra dimension is added to her experiences that would be missing in a man's. The stereotyping of Lutie as an immoral African American woman denies her certain privileges within society. In addition, she is battered not only spiritually and economically by society but also physically and mentally by African American men.

The Street, published in 1946, was a forerunner of the women's movement of the 1960's and 1970's. By illustrating the abusive and controlling nature of some African American men as well as of white men, Petry allowed African American women to question the assumption that race was their only obstacle to full participation in American society.

Sources for Further Study

Bell, Bernard W. "Ann Petry's Demythologizing of American Culture and Afro-American Character." In *Conjuring: Black Women, Fiction, and Literary Tradition*, edited by Marjorie Pryse and Hortense J. Spillers. Bloomington: Indiana University Press, 1985. Through an examination of Petry's three major novels—*The Street*, *Country Place* (1947), and *The Narrows* (1953)—Bell concludes that Petry's characters have been shaped differently by their environment than those of her contemporaries, Wright and Himes. Petry's more complex delineation of black personality allows for women characters who are more varied and complex.

Clark, Keith. "A Distaff Dream Deferred? Ann Petry and the Art of Subversion." *African-American Review* 26, no. 3 (Fall, 1992): 495-505. Clark suggests that Petry offers alternative methods of achieving the American Dream of success through two minor female characters, Mrs. Hedges and Min.

Dempsey, David. "Uncle Tom's Ghost and the Literary Abolitionists." *Antioch Review* 6 (September, 1946): 442-448. Petry is one of several literary "abolitionists" writing during the 1940's who do not include a lynching.

Gayle, Addison. *The Way of the New World*. Garden City, N.Y.: Doubleday, 1975. Claims that Petry is more concerned with the effects of the environment on her characters than with the characters themselves.

Ivey, James. "Ann Petry Talks About Her First Novel." In *Sturdy Black Bridges: Visions of Black Women in Literature*, edited by Roseann P. Bell, Bettye J. Parker, and Beverly Guy-Sheftall. Garden City, N.Y.: Anchor Press, 1979. The source of Petry's often-quoted statement that her purpose "is to show how simply and easily the environment can change the course of a person's life."

Pryse, Marjorie. " 'Patterns Against the Sky': Deism and Motherhood in Ann Petry's *The Street*." In *Conjuring: Black Women, Fiction, and Literary Tradition*, edited by Pryse and Hortense J. Spillers. Bloomington: Indiana University Press, 1985. Besides exploring and expanding references to Benjamin Franklin in the text, Pryse analyzes two other female characters, Mrs. Hedges and Min.

Shinn, Thelma J. "Women in the Novels of Ann Petry." *Critique: Studies in Modern Fiction* 16, no. 1 (1974): 110-120. Shinn argues that women, both African American and white, must conform to society's notions of feminine behavior or be ostracized.

Yarborough, Richard. "The Quest for the American Dream in Three Afro-American Novels: *If He Hollers Let Him Go, The Street, Invisible Man*." *MELUS* 8 (1981): 33-59. Yarborough argues that according to these three novels, the American Dream is not possible for African Americans.

Mary Young

SULA

Author: Toni Morrison (Chloe Anthony Wofford, 1931-   )
Type of work: Novel
Type of plot: Bildungsroman
Time of plot: 1919-1965
Locale: "The Bottom," a community in Medallion, Ohio
First published: 1973

> *Principal characters:*
> SULA PEACE, a resident of "the Bottom," an African American
>   community, who rebels against tradition
> NEL WRIGHT, Sula's best friend and foil
> HANNAH PEACE, Sula's mother
> EVA PEACE, Sula's grandmother
> HELENE WRIGHT, Nel's mother
> SHADRACK, a shell-shocked soldier who starts his own holiday
>   called National Suicide Day
> ALBERT JACKS (AJAX), Sula's lover

Form and Content

In *Sula*, Toni Morrison explores a community's role in the individual's search for wholeness. The story begins at the end, after the African American community known as "the Bottom" has been destroyed and replaced with a golf course. The narrator reveals the history of "the Bottom" forty years before it was destroyed, in chapters titled simply by the year of focus, beginning with 1919 and ending with 1965.

The community gained its name from a joke played on a slave by a white farmer. After promising his slave freedom and land upon the completion of some difficult chores, the farmer did not want to part with his choice land. So he told the slave that the hilly land—difficult to plant and plagued by high winds and sliding soil—was the bottom of heaven, the "best land there is." Consequently, the slave accepted the land, and "the Bottom" is where Sula Peace and Nel Wright are born.

Nel, her mother Helene, and her father live in a home Nel considers to be oppressively neat. Carefully groomed by her mother, who is admired in the community for her beauty and grace, Nel prefers the disorder that she finds in Sula's home, where "something was always cooking on the stove, . . . the mother, Hannah, never scolded or gave directions" and "all sorts of people dropped in." During her only trip outside Medallion, ten-year-old Nel meets Helene's estranged mother and sees her own mother's usual grace disturbed by Southern remnants of racist oppression. Nel and Helene must sit in the "colored only" car of the train, and because there were no "colored only" restrooms past Birmingham, they urinate in the woods when the train stops. Helene is pleased to return home. After Nel insists, Helene welcomes the young Sula into her home, in spite of Hannah Peace's reputation for being "sooty."

Sula and Nel's development into adults follows some predictable and some unpredictable patterns. Nel becomes a carbon copy of her mother. She marries, has children, and bases her entire identity on the roles of mother and wife, an identity disrupted by her best friend. After attending college and traveling to some major American cities, Sula returns to Medallion, where she continues her mother's legacy of promiscuity and has her mean-spirited grandmother placed, against her will, in a home for the elderly.

To Nel's dismay, Sula has sex with Nel's husband, Jude. Feeling betrayed by her husband and her best friend, Nel says that her life and her "thighs . . . [are] truly empty and dead." After nearly three years of not speaking to each other, Nel visits Sula after hearing that she is sick. Nel leaves unsatisfied with Sula's shallow reason for having sex with Jude. Sula dies of an unnamed illness at the age of thirty.

On January 3, 1941, the National Suicide Day after Sula's death, Shadrack continues his tradition, although with less passion since he misses Sula. This year, many town members participate in his parade. They march gayly to "the white part of town," distinguished by the tunnel excavation and beginnings of remodeling for the city. Angered by not being permitted to work on the renovations, many citizens of "the Bottom" crowd into the tunnel as an action of self-assertion and protest. Unfortunately, the tunnel collapses, killing an unspecified number of them (approximately twelve to fifteen).

By 1965, the hills of "the Bottom" are largely populated by whites, and the narrator laments the lack of cohesion among the African Americans who have moved to the valley. As the narrator notes, there were not as many spontaneous visits and everyone had his or her own television and telephone. After Nel visits Eva in the home for the elderly, Nel remembers calling the hospital, mortuary, and police after Sula's body was found—eyes open and mouth open—in Eva's bed. Only after Nel leaves the cemetery does she discover that all the pain and loneliness that she had been feeling was from missing having Sula in her life, not Jude.

Analysis

In *Sula*, the concept of class and its relation to sex and race occupies much of Morrison's attention as she chronicles the development of Sula and Nel. A few fundamental concepts shape Morrison's vision of the human condition—particularly, as critic Dorothy Lee points out, her preoccupation with how a community affects the individual's achievement and retention of an acceptable self.

The African American citizens of "the Bottom" were victims of a cruel joke begun by the white farmer who gave the hilly land its ironic name by refusing to surrender to the slave the land that he deserved. Although African Americans work hard and serve their country in war, their rewards are few. Morrison's presentation provides a bleak look at a community suffering from oppression and the denial of rewards or even acknowledgment. The men are limited to menial jobs that do not even give them the pleasure of muscle-fatiguing labor; they cannot work on the tunnel. The women are placed in the positions of mothers, wives, or whores; there is no in-between.

Though victims, they all victimize one another, maintaining a status quo that they themselves did not set.

Sula Peace is a significant part of this community's history. As her name suggests, she seeks inner peace, a personal wholeness that the restrictions of life deny her. These restrictions are largely a result of limited traditional roles designated for women and racial prejudice aimed at African Americans. Determined to face life truthfully, Sula rebels against nearly all tradition and endures the wrath and scorn of her community. She embodies much of the frustration and pain of her community members.

Nel and Sula represent conformity and rebellion, respectively, to their community's expectations. Nel marries a man from "the Bottom" and performs her duties, including sex, as a mother and wife. After her husband's infidelity with Sula, Nel describes her thighs—a metaphor for her sexuality and her self—as "empty and dead." Jude leaves Nel, and without the role as wife condoned by society, Nel becomes unsure of her identity.

Sula chooses to stand outside society, to define herself as a revolt against it. Unlike Nel, she ignores traditional roles and society's expectations: "She went to bed with men as frequently as possible." Consequently, Sula functions as pariah for her community: "She was pariah, then, and knew it. Knew that they despised her and believed that they framed their hatred as disgust for the easy way she lay with men." Sula's promiscuous behavior makes her the chaos and evil against which the community must define and protect itself.

Helene Wright attempts to transcend the boundaries set by race by denying her New Orleans roots, cleaning incessantly, and wearing nice clothes. Shadrack tries to cope with his pain by dedicating a special day to it. Eva copes with her pain by inflicting pain on herself and others.

The lack of a happy ending, the deaths of many community members near the end of the work, and the lack of cohesion in the 1965 community as emphasized by the narrator in the final chapter all indicate the power that Morrison perceives in communal energy. She seems to imply that without the strength and support that a healthy community provides—that is, a community made up of strong, supportive, loving individuals who are not oppressed and subjugated by society—the development of people into productive, content, spiritually whole individuals is stifled or, at worst, impossible.

Context

Morrison's exploration of friendship between African American women makes *Sula* a major link between Zora Neale Hurston's *Their Eyes Were Watching God* (1937) and Alice Walker's *The Color Purple* (1982). Furthermore, the friendship between Sula and Nel does not depend on or revolve around men. Morrison explores this friendship, its maturity and its eventual dissolution.

Nel and Sula's relationship blossoms out of mutual admiration, for Sula appreciates the quiet orderliness of Nel's home. In stark contrast, and in addition to Hannah's sexual liaisons, the Peace home is characterized by Eva's unpredictability. Sula's grandmother has one leg, and the town rumor is that she either placed the other on a railroad track or sold it to a hospital. In either case, Eva provides food and shelter for her family. Yet Eva is not simply a provider; she is also a sacrificer. When her son, Plum, returns from the war in a questionable mental and physical condition, she burns him to death as he sleeps in his room.

Helene, Nel, Sula, Eva, and Hannah continually challenge stereotypes as the narrator reveals these women's thoughts, fears, and concerns. Morrison's depictions stress the fact that women cannot be limited to select roles; they are too wonderfully diverse. Not unlike Hurston, Walker, and a host of other female writers, Morrison gives voices to the many women who remained silent when required to choose between severely limited life options.

Although the possibilities for women in American society have expanded since the publication of *Sula* in 1973, the novel reminds its readers of a time that should be remembered. In the late 1960's, the women's liberation movement was in full force to combat sexual discrimination and gain legal, economic, vocational, educational, and social rights and opportunities for women that were equal to those of men. It is important to women, and clearly important to Morrison, that the history of this struggle and the stories of these women not be forgotten.

Sources for Further Study

Carby, Hazel V., ed. *Reconstructing Womanhood*. New York: Oxford University Press, 1987. This collection of essays includes a thorough study of the female characters found in African American literature. The authors explore the works of African American women writers from Harriet Jacobs, the author of *Incidents in the Life of a Slave Girl* (1861), to Toni Morrison.

Christian, Barbara, ed. *Black Feminist Criticism: Perspectives on Black Women Writers*. New York: Pergamon Press, 1985. This compilation of criticism and commentary on literature by African American women addresses literature by Toni Morrison, Alice Walker, Gloria Naylor, and Gwendolyn Brooks. The book is composed of essays that include extensive analyses of individual works, as well as examinations of common traits found in literature by African American women. Each essay contains many explanatory notes and lists of sources.

Gates, Henry L., Jr., ed. *Reading Black, Reading Feminist: A Critical Anthology*. New York: Meridian/New American Library, 1990. This collection of critical essays explores the effects that African American female writers have had on literature. Includes the work of May Helen Washington, Barbara Christian, Hazel V. Carby, Mae Gwendolyn Henderson, and many other leaders in the field of African American literary studies. Their critical analyses go far beyond the surface as they examine the characters (mostly female) from the novels of Morrison and other African American female authors.

Lee, Robert A. *Black Fiction: New Studies in the Afro-American Novel Since 1945*. London: Vision Press, 1980. These insightful essays explore the African American novel in order to identify recurring themes and techniques. One particular essay, by

Faith Pullin, addresses *Sula* and Morrison's creation of women in this text who do not fit common stereotypes.

Morrison, Toni. "Toni Morrison's Black Magic." Interview by Jean Strouse. *Newsweek* 97 (March 30, 1981): 52-56. Morrison appeared on the cover of this issue of *Newsweek*, and she was the first African American woman to do so. It is one of the most revealing interviews she has given. Provides valuable biographical information, starting from her childhood, and she discusses her writing as a reflection of her perception of life.

Jeryl J. Prescott

SURFACING

Author: Margaret Atwood (1939-   )
Type of work: Novel
Type of plot: Social criticism
Time of plot: About 1970
Locale: An island in northern Quebec
First published: 1972

Principal characters:

THE NARRATOR, an unnamed woman in her late twenties who
     works as a commercial artist
JOE, the narrator's boyfriend, an artist who makes pots
ANNA, the narrator's closest female friend
DAVID, Anna's husband of nine years
THE NARRATOR'S FATHER, a retired botanist who is missing
THE NARRATOR'S MOTHER, who died of cancer
THE NARRATOR'S BROTHER, a prospector in Australia

Form and Content

The story of *Surfacing* covers nine days that the four younger people—the narrator, Joe, Anna, and David—spend on the island that had been the narrator's childhood home and several more days when she is there alone. Though the unnamed narrator is attempting to find explanations for her father's mysterious disappearance, the others treat it more as a vacation, filming quaint Quebec oddities during the trip and their own outdoorsy exploits on the island. They expect the narrator to entertain them by taking them fishing and blueberry picking.

The detective-novel feel of the early part of the novel is emphasized as the group hunts for traces of the narrator's father on the island and as the narrator searches the cabin for something that might indicate his whereabouts. The past gradually comes into sharper focus for the narrator as she finds things in the cabin that trigger memories of her childhood and her young adult years. Memories of her wedding and her child are juxtaposed with memories of her school years and images from drawings she produced as a child that her mother kept in scrapbooks.

After finding childlike drawings of strange animals and figures among her father's papers, the narrator concludes that he must have gone crazy as he spent another winter alone in the isolated cabin. She fears that he is alive on the island and a danger to her friends. The forced intimacy on the island is also proving dangerous, as David and Anna bicker and insult each other while Joe broods silently.

Digging further into her father's papers, while the others try to amuse themselves with reading old paperbacks from the cabin or working on a film called "Random Samples," the narrator comes across letters from an archaeologist to her father. Apparently, the odd drawings were not indications of her father's madness but sketches of ancient Indian rock paintings from around the area. She does not share her theories with the others but feels compelled to prove to herself that her father is not crazy, but dead. Realizing that the water level would have risen and covered the rock paintings when the timber company dammed the lake decades ago, the narrator plans a solitary trip to a nearby site, where she will be able to dive underwater and search for the paintings.

Diving in search of not only the paintings but some sort of answer about her father's fate as well, the narrator is also forced to confront her own past and repressed memories. She does not see any paintings, but as her breath is running out, she sights a body below her in the murky lake. Bursting out of the water, she has surfaced to the knowledge that her father is indeed dead and that she can no longer lie to herself about her past. The former husband and abandoned child assume their real forms as an art professor with whom she had an affair and their child, which was aborted. Her father's death is confirmed the next day as some men stop by the island to tell her that his body was hooked by a fisherman.

Her cleared vision causes the narrator to realize that she needs to stop fighting nature with her modern Americanized life and redeem her past by producing a child. The night before they are to leave the island, she knows that she is fertile and leads Joe outside to have sex on the ground. The narrator continues her revolt against civilization as she destroys the men's film and refuses to leave with the others when the boat comes to pick them up. Hiding in the woods, she knows that she must find answers about her parents, her past, and who she is.

Over the next few days, she becomes increasingly like an animal, as she somehow knows that it is taboo for her to enter the cabin, wear clothes, or eat prepared food. She believes that she must destroy man-made things and breaks, ruins, or burns much of the cabin's contents. She knows that there is a child growing inside her, and she does not want it tainted by modern life. The narrator is physically weakened by several days with little food, but she becomes more powerful spiritually. She finds her answers as visions of her parents appear to her—her mother feeding the birds with outstretched arms and her father as a half-human, half-animal figure resembling the cliff drawings. This mystical experience transforms her, and she is again able to enter the cabin, eat, wear clothes, and perhaps return to civilization. The novel ends ambiguously as Joe returns to the island and calls for her.

Analysis

Atwood's unstable and less-than-trustworthy narrator undermines the security of the plot but causes readers to focus instead on her mental state and interpretations. The events that she reports are not as important as how she sees them. Because of her scrambled and deliberately evasive memories, the narrator provides an example of a mind unable to accept modern civilization and a psychological study of a woman attempting to cope.

Atwood's didacticism and moral message are especially evident in the conflict between civilization and nature. She questions whether the so-called progress of culture is only an illusion. Canadian nationalism also figures in the story, as David and the narrator rail against Americans or people with Americanized attitudes who kill animals for fun and pollute the environment. The narrator becomes increasingly alienated from civilization, yet David and Anna are securely anchored in modern technological society. Joe remains on the border—his silence shows that he has not been completely coopted by modern existence. At the end of the story, he is described as an ambassador or mediator between civilization and wilderness.

After she has surfaced to the knowledge about her delusions and past lies, the narrator needs to reject the trappings of modern life. Her destruction of the film is one aspect of this, as is her abandonment of her clothing in the lake—a baptism or ritual cleansing. She is attempting to become part of nature because her years of trying to become civilized were unsuccessful. When searchers return to the island for her, she is afraid that the natural woman she is becoming will be treated like an animal—brutally killed or put on display.

The question "What is natural?" is also raised in the love relationships in *Surfacing*. The narrator feels incapable of love and feels trapped when Joe, instead of asking the expected "Do you love me?" asks her to marry him. She is unable to commit, fearfully remembering past relationships, while Joe wants a yes-or-no answer. For him, there is no middle ground. By contrast, Anna claims that she and David have remained married because they have an emotional bond. After observing their warped interaction, the narrator begins to wonder if that emotion is hate rather than love.

Parent-child relationships are also questioned. While the others have cast off their parents, the narrator is equivocal toward her family and her past. She distanced herself from them because of her own failure to become a parent: She felt too guilty to face them after her abortion. Achieving harmony with her parents' spirits is the climax of her period of heightened sensory awareness. She realizes that she can learn from her parents, even after their deaths. The narrator's vision of what her father has become functions as a warning about trying to get too close to ancient gods and meanings without proper reverence. Her vision of her mother feeding the birds somehow satisfies her need to explain this mysterious woman's significance. Her confrontation with their spirits is prefigured by the token that she believes her mother has left for her in one of the scrapbooks: a drawing that the narrator had made as a child showing a pregnant woman confronting a horned god, while her baby watches from inside her stomach.

The novel's title indicates the complex theme and image pattern involving birth and abortion. The narrator's constructed memories about her child have double meanings when reread with the knowledge that she actually had an abortion. Images of body and blood fit both situations. Linked to this is her "memory" (though the event happened before she was born) of her brother's near drowning and images of the frogs and other animals that he kept in jars in his secret laboratory. She remembers his anger when she released the animals that had not already died, while she is haunted with her own created memories of dead babies in jars like laboratory specimens.

The death images are contrasted with those of rebirth: the narrator's surfacing to life and knowledge after she sees her father's body in the water and her symbolic baptism as she is cleansed by the lake after the others have left. Her sunny childhood drawings of rabbits and eggs suggest fertility and reinforce her powerful pregnant condition at the novel's close. The themes of drowning and surfacing also resonate with the narrator's descent into her unconscious, nonrational mind to seek explanations for questions about her parents and her life.

Context

Atwood's novel raises many issues about women and about modern society. The narrator's need to control her destiny at the end of the novel arises out of the drifting young adult years when she let others—such as the married professor with whom she had the affair—make choices for her. Atwood explores how women react when they cannot live as they desire. The narrator responded to her abortion by building more socially acceptable fantasies to hide her behavior from herself and others. Anna responds by playing the victim role: She loves David and defines herself as his wife, so she endures his cruel jokes and his infidelity.

Likewise, the narrator's namelessness can be seen to signify the role of women in a society where they are not valued as individuals. Her lack of a title emphasizes her lack of secure role or position. Her namelessness also suggests that the search that she undertakes is something all women must do—she is Everywoman. Many critics see the novel as exemplifying a female quest. The characters and events can be viewed as archetypal patterns that resonate with mythology and folklore about heroic women.

Because of the recognition gained by Atwood's poetry and her first novel, *The Edible Woman* (1969), *Surfacing* was not released in obscurity. Critics recognized in it Atwood's previously established patterns of feminism, Canadian nationalism, and ecological issues. *Surfacing*, however, is the novel after which Atwood began to be considered as a public voice for women. Some critics made the link between the victimization of female characters and a postcolonial Canadian attitude of victimization.

Sources for Further Study

Davey, Frank. *Margaret Atwood: A Feminist Poetics*. Vancouver: Talonbooks, 1984. Provides a useful biography of Atwood which is interspersed with quotes from interviews. Also examines her poetry, novels, short fiction, and criticism.

Davidson, Arnold E., and Cathy N. Davidson, eds. *The Art of Margaret Atwood*. Toronto: Anansi, 1981. Thirteen essays dealing with Atwood as a poet, novelist, and critic. Two fairly contrasting views of *Surfacing* are presented, one a feminist archetypal view and the other a psychological comparison with Atwood's first and third novels.

Grace, Sherrill E., and Lorraine Weir, eds. *Margaret Atwood: Language, Text, and System*. Vancouver: University of British Columbia Press, 1983. A varied collection of essays by Canadian scholars. Those addressing *Surfacing* deal with shamanism and syntax.

Rigney, Barbara Hill. *Margaret Atwood*. Totowa, N.J.: Barnes & Noble Books, 1987. A chronological exploration of Atwood's work with a feminist interpretation. The examination of *Surfacing* deals especially with thematic patterns and symbols and connections with Atwood's poetry.

Van Spanckeren, Kathryn, and Jan Garden Castro, eds. *Margaret Atwood: Vision and Forms*. Carbondale: Southern Illinois University Press, 1988. Presents fifteen essays on Atwood's poetry and prose, with two specifically on *Surfacing*. An interview with Atwood and a foreword written by the author provide insight into her writings.

Woodcock, George. *Introducing Margaret Atwood's "Surfacing."* Ontario: ECW Press, 1990. Woodcock provides background information on Atwood, discusses the reception of *Surfacing* in Canada and the United States, and explores at length its style, structure, and themes.

Rebecca L. Wheeler

SWEET TALK

Author: Stephanie Vaughn (1943-   )
Type of work: Short stories
First published: 1990

Form and Content

The stories in Stephanie Vaughn's *Sweet Talk* all have young women at their centers and are presented in the realistic mode. In the stories that have Gemma as their central character, the narrative is in the first person, as it is also in "Other Women," whose central character is named Angelina. Third-person narration is used in "The Architecture of California" and "Snow Angel," which are centered on characters named Megan and Marguerite. The stories are straightforward narratives, although some of Gemma's are clearly written from a later perspective. Devices such as flashbacks, fantasies, dreams, or time shifts are not used. The overall impression given by most of the stories is of emotional moments seen from a distance; the emotions are real and affecting, but with an important exception, they are not immediate.

The first and last stories in the volume, "Able, Baker, Charlie, Dog" and "Dog Heaven," are reminiscences of youth told from the perspective of adulthood; both concern a time when Gemma was twelve years old and the family lived on an Army post near Niagara Falls, New York. The other Gemma stories—"My Mother Breathing Light," "Kid MacArthur," and "The Battle of Fallen Timbers"—are primarily concerned with her relationships with other members of her family. The stories "Sweet Talk" and "We're on TV in the Universe" have as narrators unnamed young women who might be Gemma. These relationships are drawn with a subtlety which is the most impressive aspect of Vaughn's writing. Especially in "Able, Baker, Charlie, Dog" and "Kid MacArthur," Gemma's resentment of her father's obsession with discipline and order is set against a child's love, which aches for her father's frustrations and failures even as it struggles to break free of the rigid constraints that the parent imposes. The scene in which the twelve-year-old Gemma, knowing her father's career has fallen apart, watches his progress across ice floes in the Niagara River and wishes that she could call out to him, but is unable to do so, is a starkly memorable one.

Of the other characters, the most clearly drawn is Gemma's brother, MacArthur. He hates his name, which reflects his father's admiration for a military hero, and he resents the standards of appearance and conduct that his father imposes on him. Yet until he joins the Army himself, he tries to live up to his father's expectations. His experiences in Vietnam, however, leave him with hatred of the violence that military life entails. The souvenir ears that some soldiers brought back as trophies from Vietnam play a major role in "Kid MacArthur" as a means of permitting Gemma to understand her brother's anguish.

The mother and grandmother are less distinctive characters. The mother is pitiable in her attempts to live independently after the father's death and in her denial of the cancer that is killing her, but although she provides warmth for her young children, she is too weak to stand up to her husband. The grandmother is almost a comic figure in her resentment of her son-in-law's domination of the household and in her role as the target of his occasional jokes, but she is not a substantial character.

The women who appear in the other stories all demonstrate the difficulties of relationships. The nameless narrator of "Sweet Talk," who may be Gemma, is involved in a disintegrating marriage. When her husband has an affair, she pretends to have a lover of her own, but the stratagem fails. The reconciliation at the end of this story is terribly fragile. Angelina, in "Other Women," is having an affair with a married man who gives her crabs, which he has gotten from Susu, his estranged wife. In "The Architecture of California," Megan finds out that her best friend, Vera, is pregnant and that the father is Megan's husband, George. Marguerite, in "Snow Angel," makes a figure by lying down in the snow in a desperate effort to escape domesticity and motherhood.

Analysis

The tone of the stories in *Sweet Talk* is uniformly subdued. There is evocative description of countryside in some of the stories, but in all the stories characters are effectively sketched through action and speech rather than through detailed physical description. Gemma is the narrator of the stories dealing with her family, but her voice is far from strident—fittingly, since she is not an assertive character. She depicts herself as a normal teenager, more interested in being a cheerleader than in anything serious, and even when she later rebels against her father's way of life she does so in secret. She tries to help her sick mother but does not seem to have much effect. In "We're on TV in the Universe," the central character, perhaps Gemma, is passive, allowing things to happen to her, not taking the initiative. The actions taken by Gemma and the other female figures tend not to be drastic or dramatic.

The stories about Gemma deal with the problems of a girl and young woman growing up in a restrictive environment. She struggles to find ways to assert her own personality and to find a warmth which her father seems unable to provide. Especially in "Dog Heaven," her friendship with a schoolmate and the loyalty of a favorite dog combine to give Gemma a memory which she obviously treasures for the rest of her life. The tenor of most of the stories, however, is subtly tragic. The father's attempt to rule his family and provide his children with rules for living is no more successful than his military career. There is something pathetic in his decision to name his son after a soldier far more successful than he is.

Gemma eventually throws off her father's direct influence; in "Kid MacArthur," her father warns her against participating in marches protesting the Vietnam War, but she is already doing so. In that story, however, it is clear that her brother has a more difficult time dealing with the heavy hand of their father. As a boy, MacArthur had become an expert marksman at his father's urging, despite his own distaste for firearms. When the family moved to a new base, MacArthur got in trouble for trying to be one of the boys by stealing cigarette lighters and was humiliated by his father's punishment; Gemma's efforts to help him were fruitless. At the end of the story, when MacArthur is living in isolation where Gemma visits him, the mood is bleak. Gemma's love for her brother cannot help him deal with the effects of their father's influence or with the aftereffects of MacArthur's experience in Vietnam.

There is a sense throughout the book that the characters have little success in finding happiness, that moments of joy are to be treasured because they are rare and fleeting. Marguerite's moment of ecstasy in making a snow angel is heightened by the very impermanence of what she does. The most sentimental of the stories, and the only one in which Gemma's voice is openly emotional, is "Dog Heaven," in which the adolescent Gemma finds a friend and is made briefly joyous by a dog named Duke. The family is leaving Niagara Falls to go to another Army base, and the dog is being temporarily left behind in the care of a mess sergeant. The dog escapes, however, and returns to the family home before they have left. Gemma, MacArthur, Gemma's friend, and the dog have a few minutes of pure joy as the children are skating on an ice rink. The pathos of the situation intrudes in the repetition that closes the story: "We skated across the darkening ice into the sunset, skated faster and faster, until we seemed to rise together into the cold, bright air. It was a good day. It was a good day. It was a good day." As Gemma tells the story, however, she has already revealed that on the same day she learned of her friend's accidental death and Duke was killed by poisoned hamburger distributed by a dog hater.

Context

The stories in *Sweet Talk* are not feminist in any doctrinaire sense. They do, however, provide a consistent sense of the struggle that a young woman faces in a world dominated by masculine values, and the relationship between Gemma and her father may be regarded as a paradigm of the complexities of that situation. The love she has for her father, most obvious in her memory of watching him on the day that his career fell apart, is very real, but it does not offset the fact that at every stage she is intent on subverting the code that he is trying to impose on her. Her mother's subservience is a reminder of what a woman's life may become if she fails to resist, but resistance may not always be possible.

It is true that MacArthur probably suffers more than does Gemma from the long-term effects of their father's impositions, but the stories that are not part of the chronicle of Gemma's family help demonstrate that a persistent subject of *Sweet Talk* is women's subordinate position. The wife in the title story shares her husband's poverty, but it is she who must try to retaliate for the man's infidelity and who makes the effort to try to define their situation and try for a reconciliation. Similarly, Angelina in "Other Women" is the victim of her lover's failure to be faithful either to her or to his estranged wife; in "The Architecture of California," both Megan and her friend Vera are in a sense the victims of the husband. The women in these stories are, with few exceptions, spirited in their resistance, but that resistance is not always successful.

Sources for Further Study

Henken, Joshua. "The Facets of Gemma." *Mother Jones* 15 (February/March, 1990): 42. Of the many flattering reviews of *Sweet Talk*, this is among the most perceptive and least pretentious.

Palmer, Paulina. *Contemporary Women's Fiction: Narrative Practice and Feminist Theory*. New York: Harvester Wheatsheaf, 1989. This study of practice and theory in the works of a number of women writers insists on the significance of contemporaries and provides an instructive background for reading Vaughn's stories.

Vaughn, Stephanie. Interview by Hillel Italieo. *Associated Press Interviews*, March 23-25, 1990. The only published interview with Vaughn, this article contains her comments on the process of writing and some information about how stories take shape in her mind. She finds that many stories create their own endings.

Yaeger, Patricia, and Beth Kowalski-Wallace. *Refiguring the Father: New Feminist Readings of Patriarchy*. Carbondale: Southern Illinois University Press, 1989. This study of fictional interactions between fathers and daughters provides considerable information on one of the central themes of Vaughn's stories, examining how the theme has been used in the fiction of other contemporary women.

John M. Muste

THE TALE OF GENJI

Author: Murasaki Shikibu (978?-1014?)
Type of work: Novel
Type of plot: Romance
Time of plot: The eleventh century
Locale: Japan
First published: Genji monogatari, 1001-1015 (English translation, 1925-1933)

> *Principal characters:*
> PRINCE HAIKARU GENJI, the offspring of the Emperor and his
>   concubine, called the Shining Prince
> KIRITSUBO, the Emperor's concubine and Genji's mother
> THE EMPEROR, Genji's father, who has great affection for him
> LADY KOKIDEN, the Emperor's consort, who is unhappy that her
>   son's future as heir apparent is challenged
> PRINCESS AOI, Genji's first wife, whom he ignores
> YUGAO, one of Genji's paramours
> MURASAKI, an orphaned girl whom Genji secretly rears and who
>   later becomes his second wife
> UKIFUNE, the lover of Genji's son and grandson
> KAORU, the illegitimate but official son of Genji
> PRINCE NIOU, the grandson of Genji

Form and Content

The Tale of Genji opens with a reference to a beloved "lady not of the first rank" loved by the sovereign and reflects the Chinese Po Chu'i's "Song of Everlasting Sorrow," which provides the prototype for Japan's "Paulownia Court" and initially gives the work political overtones. Murasaki Shikibu was learned and uses this evocative poem to preface her *monogatari,* or prose narrative, about royal succession as determined by blood ties and political power struggles.

In part 1 of the novel, Prince Genji's nature is an aristocratic ideal: His political acumen is marvelous; his public behavior manifests wise judgments and correct actions; and his private life offers a parallel, being colorful and elegantly woman-centered. Yet, from part 2 onward, *The Tale of Genji* becomes uniquely Murasaki's creation. Her transcendent structure builds in a regard for the element of time, producing a remarkably "modern" narrative style based on karma, or the cause and effect of previous existences. Murasaki implies that the lives and actions of her characters originate in acts committed in previous lives.

Part 2 of the novel depicts suffering, sometimes caused by acts committed before the characters were born. Genji's affair with Fujitsubo, the concubine of his father, the Emperor, probably results from his awareness of his inferior lineage but may also be influenced by karma. This pattern of karmic suffering continues in part 3, in which his descendants, Niou and Kaoru, both love women of inferior lineage, especially Ukifune. The novel's three themes gradually develop. Reality and clear insight predominate in the opening section, the second section adds the themes of karma and predetermined suffering, and the third section complements these with the addition of piety and spiritual blindness.

In order to express these themes, Murasaki's narrative techniques include the incorporation of *waka*, traditional five-line poems, and classical techniques of poetic lyricism. Through this blending of narrative and poetic, she acknowledges the *monogatari* as of equal worth with the older *waka*, Japan's premier art form. The author's poetic echoes in her narrative text also reinforce the novel's prestigious historical framework.

Additionally, Murasaki develops *soshiji*, narrational intrusion, as the author makes her presence known and offers explanations or opinions from a first-person perspective. For example, there is her comment about Genji's leaving for exile in Suma: "I have no doubt that there were many fine passages in the letters with which he saddened the lives of his many ladies, but, grief-stricken myself, I did not listen as carefully as I might have."

Murasaki also experimentally controls the psychological distance between the audience and the circumstances and characters in her work by developing a multilayered narrative technique, such as building in accounts from secondary narrators. She masters the technique of effectively distancing psychological portrayals by linking the reader's consciousness to the primary narrator's viewpoint, while transmitting the character's emotions at the same time. In part 2, a full psychological portrayal evolves as the reader is led to follow clues that lead to discovery, which encourages repeated, careful reading.

Part 3 relies upon symbolism to present disappointing human experiences; it is a dark world, in Buddhist terms the symbol of spiritual blindness, leaving Genji's "shining" world behind. In fact, his son's and grandson's names signify, not light, but perfume and scent. Here four images reoccur: mountains for piety, rivers for spiritual blindness, boats for human drifting, and growing darkness.

Today called the first psychological novel in the world, the fifty-four chapters of *The Tale of Genji* spread the action over three-quarters of a century and involve four generations. As an artistic entity, its three units are frequently divided: books 1 through 12 concern Prince Genji's youth and glory; books 13 through 41 present his conflicts, maturity, and death; and books 42 through 54 reveal the story of his transcendence of death and of his descendants.

Unifying the novel are psychological relationships between men and women that sustain an awareness of time's passage, including seasonal changes, social vicissitudes, and human emotions. The incremental repetitions of situations, settings, and characters' relations structure the novel so that occurrences reveal their resemblance to earlier episodes, thus showing how the past overlaps on the present. These echoes demonstrate the flow of time, for example showing how a man loves a woman who reminds him of another.

Murasaki's interest in Fujiwara power, as opposed to natural impermanence, on the surface focuses *The Tale of Genji* on the career and amorous adventures of its idealized hero, the Shining Prince, Genji. His adulterous loves are individually treated, as are episodic sections about his ascents and descents at court. Genji is an aesthetic and emotional ideal in terms of good looks, talent in the arts, and captivating power as a charmer of ten women. The concluding thirteen chapters follow Genji's death and trace the darkening triangle relationship between his wife and his best friend's illegitimate son, his grandson, and a beautiful, disinterested girl.

Analysis

Murasaki's original handwritten manuscript is lost, but fragments of the text exist from the twelfth century, by which time it had become the subject of scholarly interest. *The Tale of Genji* has been praised for its brilliant realism of setting and depiction of the everyday life of Heian aristocrats. Through the influence of this novel, the era's refined emotions and sensibilities have affected Japanese writers for hundreds of years, whether in fiction, poetry, or theater. Murasaki's views on the art of the novel are presented in *The Tale of Genji*'s "Fireflies" chapter, which rebuts the prevailing Chinese attitude that "frivolous" literature was dangerous. The passage begins by praising romances that teach about how people once lived. Murasaki's Genji himself explains that the art of the novel goes beyond a romantic story of someone's adventures; it happens, he says, because of the storyteller's passionate desire to save and share experiences, both autobiographical events and things that have been indirectly encountered. Genji adds that the storyteller must go beyond the theme of virtue and also illustrate vice and folly. Anything may become the subject of a novel, he declares, provided that it is part of mundane life.

Shinto rituals are important in Genji's world and reflect the prerogatives of imperial succession. Buddhism plays an even larger role, helping to explain the novel's premise—that life is suffering as a consequence of thwarted human desire. In order to interrupt the cycle of birth, death, and rebirth, Buddhism teaches that one may negate desire, which creates enlightenment. This is the challenge before Prince Genji. The novel traces a series of desires that lead men and women astray: For example, the Emperor's love for Kiritsubo causes him to protect their boy from his wife's wrath by removing Genji from imperial succession. Nevertheless, Genji is drawn to court and, like his father, loves one of the concubines, Fujitsubo, who is a sort of mother figure. Though the boy is married off to a Fujiwara princess, he continues to seek happiness, first by courting her niece and then by seducing Fujitsubo. Genji then becomes involved with a series of women, including Kokiden's sister, Lady Oborozukiyo.

Behind these willful liaisons lie the further dangers of court politics—the Emperor's death leaves power in the hands of Kokiden's father, the Minister of the Right who resents Genji's inept romancing of Fujitsubo and Oborozukiyo and causes the Prince's exile in Suma. The novel's style thus shows how actions are repeated; just as seasons succeed each other, people repeat essential patterns. In this Buddhist world, human desires are thwarted by transgressions that are often immoral both in personal and in political terms. Genji's sins require expiation because his sexual adventures unwisely lead him into the enemy camp. Since Japanese Buddhists see love as a dangerous and demeaning loss of self-control, Genji's passionate character is flawed, as he particularly reveals in his obsessive passion for the young orphan Murasaki.

Evil passion in the novel is perhaps even more clearly illustrated by Lady Rokujo, a lover of Genji whose malign spirit apparently kills both Princess Aoi and Yugao and pursues little Murasaki. Lady Rokujo is a widow frustrated by the withdrawal of Genji's undivided attentions; her loss of control over her own spirit leads it to invade and destroy others, a sin which even her travels to Ise cannot cleanse.

Originally seen as a diversion, then attacked as immoral, *The Tale of Genji* was used to justify the city's merchant class and pleasure quarters. Murasaki's Genji was called a modern rake in the name of cultural authority to condone pleasure. Later, Motoori Norinaga (1730-1801), a famous Japanese literary critic, explained that the novel is about life; his phrase *mono no aware*, the "pathos of things," provides the novel's ongoing aesthetic justification.

Many Western readers were introduced to *The Tale of Genji* by Arthur Waley's 1935 translation. Readers have since called it the greatest of novels, produced centuries before the form emerged in Europe.

Context

Murasaki Shikibu's central intention was to provide a woman's response to events at Heian court, including a refreshing view of courtiers, romance, and political power. This revolutionary intention is confirmed in her diary for the years between 1007 and 1010, which rounds out the picture given in the novel of Japanese court life. She was a member of the Fujiwara clan, a widow who became part of Princess Shoshi's entourage in 1005 or 1006. Her interest in people created a contemporary audience of women, a remarkable feat in an era when men wrote formally in Chinese. Murasaki's world in the novel ignores Confucianism, synonymous with men's Chinese scholarship, except for the precept of filial piety.

She represents the Emperor as an important spiritual and psychological center of Japanese court life, but he is politically impotent, a pawn in the game of aristocratic family leadership who fears his wife and is not free to promote his favorite son. Her depiction of the Fujiwara clan reveals a network of marriage ties to the imperial family that emphasize the usually overlooked importance of women's role in securing family leadership. In her novel, women become both men's political and sexual pawns, providing links in chains of family connections, and people who wield power in their own right through the ability to provide and withhold love.

Yet women's lives are also revealed to be sedentary, passive, and restricted; they are named by patriarchal affiliation, place, rank, office, or family relation. Even the author of *The Tale of Genji* is known only by a name given her as a tribute to a female character in her novel.

In the novel, women appear serially. In the Hahakigi section, Murasaki presents a description of different kinds of women; Genji's involvements present contrasting examples of noble women, among the most memorable Aoi, his unbending wife; the gentle Yuago; the proud Rokujo; the resisting Utsusemi; and Fujitsubo, the Emperor's beloved concubine. Only in the Uji section of the novel, away from the capital, are female characters found happily together, but they are mother and daughter. Here a few tenuous affirmative connections are shown. In the novel, women's frequent unhappiness in personal relationships leads to the significance of religion for them. Of Genji's ten loves, five become nuns, one wishes to do so, and two meet untimely deaths. Only two do not become nuns but may have entered a temple, one of the customs of female aristocracy.

The author reveals men's language as a tool of cultural and sexual domination. Murasaki and the women diarists of her day virtually invented a written Japanese language that created a medium for their attempts to define themselves in textual terms. Among the brilliant diaries of court life in this era are *The Gossamer Years, The Pillow Book of Sei Shonagon, The Sarashina Diary,* and *The Murasaki Shikibu Diary.* These women, led by Murasaki, became Heian historians describing the parameters of a world where men were placed in the center of a polygamous society of wives and concubines, which created endless rivalry and jealousy. Her example of Prince Genji's political marriage illustrated how aristocrats caused such women as Princess Aoi to be defined by pining, waiting, and responding, but never by initiating passion. Murasaki's world is one in which women are hidden; viewing was identified as violation. Language became women authors' sole way of ratifying themselves, an attempt to break out of the subjective limitations of aristocratic Heian culture by building a new social context for themselves that included the broader world of politics and history.

Sources for Further Study

Bowring, Richard J. *Murasaki Shikibu: Her Diary and Poetic Memoirs.* Princeton, N.J.: Princeton University Press, 1982. A useful study of Heian politics and Murasaki's life.

Field, Norma. *The Splendor of Longing in "The Tale of Genji."* Princeton, N.J.: Princeton University Press, 1987. Concentrates on the relationships between the hero and his women in the novel.

Keene, Donald. *Japanese Literature.* New York: Grove Press, 1955. The definitive commentator on Japanese literature, Keene discusses the Japanese novel's indebtedness to *The Tale of Genji* and its sad obsession with mutability.

McCullough, Wilt. "Japanese Marriage Institutions in the Heian Period." *Harvard Journal of Asiatic Studies* 27 (1967): 103-167. A closely annotated translation of *Eiga monogatari,* a fictionalized history of the Fujiwara clan. Borrows techniques of *The Tale of Genji*; its introduction, notes, and appendices are a gold mine of information on Heian customs.

Morris, Ivan. *The World of the Shining Prince.* Oxford, England: Oxford University Press, 1964. An entertaining discussion of the Heian court's cultural milieu, with much information taken from literary sources. Includes helpful appendices, charts of relationships, genealogical information, a glossary, a bibliography, and an index.

Takehiko, Noguchi. "The Substratum Constituting Monogatari: Prose Structure and Narrative in the *Genji monogatari.*" In *Principles of Classical Japanese Literature*, edited by Earl Miner. Princeton, N.J.: Princeton University Press, 1985. Describes how Murasaki's novel is structured by pairing, foreshadowing, cause and effect, generational correspondences, contrasts, and ellipses. These categories create depths in the *monogatari*'s narrative structure, with the deepest substratum consisting of the narrator's voice.

Sandra Parker

TAR BABY

Author: Toni Morrison (1931-   )
Type of work: Novel
Type of plot: Social criticism
Time of plot: The 1970's
Locale: Isle de Chavaliers in the Caribbean, New York City, Florida
First published: 1981

> *Principal characters:*
> VALERIAN STREET, a rich Philadelphia candy manufacturer
> MARGARET STREET, Valerian's wife
> SYDNEY CHILDS, the Streets' butler
> ONDINE CHILDS, the Streets' cook
> JADINE "JADE" CHILDS, a well-educated black model who is the
>   niece of Sydney and Ondine
> WILLIAM "SON" GREEN, an uneducated American black

Form and Content

Jade Childs is the tar baby that Toni Morrison refers to in her title. Jade is a black woman, intelligent, orphaned, and educated in Paris, who at twenty-five stands poised between two worlds. Her natural world is that of her aunt and uncle, Sydney and Ondine, servants to the affluent Streets who, impressed by Jade's unique abilities, have sent her to study art history at the Sorbonne. Jade can function in both of her worlds.

Tar Baby is a polemical novel. Morrison examines two worlds by putting into sharp contrast the marriages of the Childses and their employers, the Streets. Although legitimately a member of both worlds, Jade wishes that race were not a part of her social context. She wants to be accepted for the person she is inside, but in her native setting, the United States, this is not possible.

Much of *Tar Baby* concerns Jade's attempts to establish her identity. This emphasis is reinforced by Margaret Street's desperate struggle to retain the identity she gained when she married Valerian. In order to marry him, she sacrificed the personal identity she had gained as a beauty queen. For more than half of her life, she has been Valerian Street's wife—nothing more, nothing less. Now, having retired to the land of heart's desire, she is totally alone, afraid of losing Valerian's love.

Morrison places the durable marriage of Sydney and Ondine Childs in dramatic juxtaposition to the Streets' deteriorating marriage. These two, hobbled by racism, lack of education, and relative, if genteel, poverty, have everything the Streets lack. Sydney and Ondine are unabashedly in love, caring deeply about each other, as is shown in the touching scene in which Sydney lovingly massages his wife's aching feet at the end of a hard day.

Into this mix, Morrison introduces the spoiler, William "Son" Green, a street-savvy black who is fleeing a murder rap in the United States. Son is the first major character that Morrison introduces. In *Tar Baby*'s epilogue, Son is a sailor on a ship not far from Isle des Chevaliers. It is Christmastime.

Son, homesick and disheartened, jumps ship and is borne by the currents to the island where the Streets live. He enters their kitchen surreptitiously and is caught stealing food. Valerian Street, ever the idealist, invites Son to dine at his table, much to the chagrin of Margaret and of Jade, who is visiting Sydney and Ondine for the holidays.

Jade, who is struggling with her own identity, is frightened and appalled by the intruder Valerian has befriended, but underlying her antipathy is a fascination with Son's deep blackness and raw primitiveness—what Morrison elsewhere calls the "true and ancient properties" of her race. Jade is drawn to Son as irresistibly as a leaf caught in a whirlpool. Jade is to Son the fulfillment of his dreams, the tar baby that attracts him hypnotically but that can trap and destroy him utterly.

Morrison's setting reinforces Jade's situation. Isle des Chevaliers is a primitive island of overgrown jungle. It was settled by Africans who, struck blind at their first sight of the island, lost their value as slaves and were left there to survive as best they could. Their progeny still inhabits the island's remote areas. L'Arbe de la Croix, the Streets' luxurious estate, is surrounded by jungle that, if not controlled constantly, will reclaim its manicured acres and, with its encroaching tendrils, bring its buildings down.

Jade, like L'Arbe de la Croix, is an artificial creation on a primitive tableau. She can elude her roots in Paris, but in this setting, they reclaim her. She goes off with Son for a time. When they return, Son goes to the remote end of the island to live among its primitive settlers.

Analysis

In *Tar Baby*, Toni Morrison explores a theme that fascinated playwright Eugene O'Neill, who, in *The Emperor Jones* (1920) and *The Hairy Ape* (1922) focused on the primitive versus the civilized. In the former play, the Emperor Jones, a black Pullman porter, finds himself elevated to a position close to sainthood in a jungle not unlike that of the Isle des Chevaliers. In the latter play, Yank, a stoker on a freighter, finds himself in the Easter Parade on New York's highly civilized Fifth Avenue, which becomes his undoing.

Morrison combines in a single novel the elements that O'Neill treated separately in his two plays. On the one hand, she creates a highly civilized setting in the Streets' retirement paradise, L'Arbe de la Croix, to which they have retreated after Valerian's lifetime of hard work in Philadelphia as a successful manufacturer of candy.

L'Arbe de la Croix has sweeping lawns and well-tended gardens, but they are at any given time only weeks—perhaps days—away from being reclaimed if the rain forest surrounding them is not continually chopped back. The encroaching jungle constantly mocks the civilized, affluent image that l'Arbe de la Croix projects. The jungle has been tamed, but only temporarily and only with the greatest of difficulty. If the Streets' servants turn their backs on it for a day, the jungle will advance on the artificial world the Streets have created for themselves and reclaim it.

L'Arbe de la Croix has all the outward appearances of a well-ordered estate of happy, affluent people. Appearances, however, deceive. Within the walls of the house live a man and a woman who have ceased to mean much to each other. The woman has spent her life being a wife, giving that role priority over her role as a mother. Her deepest secret has to do with her abuse of their son, who now has little to do with his parents.

Isolated in the retirement world that Valerian has created, Margaret has no female friends in whom she can confide. She had turned to her cook, Ondine, sharing her deepest secrets and greatest fears with this wise and trustworthy servant, but the two are now distant with each other. In her portrayal of Margaret, Morrison makes a strong feminist statement about what happens to a woman whose identity is totally dependent on her role as a wife, as Margaret's has been since she was twenty.

Like l'Arbe de la Croix, Jade Childs is a creation of Valerian Street. Orphaned in infancy, Jade has been reared by her aunt and uncle, the Streets' lifelong servants. The Streets look upon Jade as a surrogate daughter and have enabled her to escape the racist environment that would limit her possibilities substantially by sending her to Paris to study art history at the Sorbonne. Jade has grown into a cultivated woman of twenty-five who, in Paris, has been accepted as a person rather than as a black person.

Having moved beyond the limiting racism that faces American blacks, Jade comes to the idyllic Caribbean to spend the holidays at l'Arbe de la Croix. She arrives a self-assured young woman, able to interact easily with her aunt and uncle but equally graceful in her social dealings with the Streets. Jade appears to be on an even keel, secure in her accomplishments and optimistic about her future.

When Morrison brings Son into the Streets' world, it is as though the jungle is invading Jade's manicured existence. Jade's early resistance to Son is transparent: It is based upon her terror at being fascinated by a primitive black man, the very sort of person whose company she would have avoided in her own, artificially created, European world.

Because Son is Valerian Street's guest, Jade cannot escape him. The inevitable happens. Jade leaves the island with Son, going first to New York with him and then to Son's native Florida, where Jade realizes how impossible their relationship is. Jade leaves Son, returning to Isle des Chevaliers, but Son follows her and is brought to the island's primitive side to live with the descendants of the original blind Africans who settled the island.

Jade can attempt to reclaim her hard-won security and racial equality by returning to Paris, but will she ever again know the equanimity she experienced before Son came into her life? Son is likely ever to cast his threatening shadow of primitiveness over Jade's existence because in his blood pulsates the jungle drumbeat that also is a part of Jade's bloodline, no matter how vigorously she has tried to deny it.

Context

Tar Baby focuses on many social issues, particularly race, class, and gender.

Although the book makes significant feminist statements, it is much more than a feminist tract. Its social statements are encompassing, its range of vision broad.

In Jade Childs, readers find Morrison presenting all three of the social issues identified above. Issues of race and class receive greater emphasis than do gender issues; the discussion of race and class, however, brings significant gender issues to the fore. Jade Childs has almost shaken the bonds of racism. Her education has been sound. Her social, intellectual, and racial identity seem to be well established.

Son, however, delivers a devastating jolt to Jade's carefully built structure. In his black "primitiveness," Jade finds a dominance that something in her seems to need. In their relationship, Jade is not the decision maker or the equal partner; she is the female, subordinated to the prototypical black male that Morrison seems to be projecting—a prototype, incidentally, modeled on Morrison's own father. Morrison in no way implies that this relationship is right. She presents it as it is, making no value judgment. Indeed, Morrison herself would likely deplore such a relationship, but as the observant writer she is, she cannot deny that a pattern exists to justify her depiction.

In many ways, Morrison makes a more strident feminist statement in her depiction of the Valerian-Margaret relationship than she does in depicting the Son-Jade relationship. Margaret had her Warholian moments of glory as the toast of the beauty contest. Valerian Street was deemed a fortunate man to have won her hand. At that moment, Margaret was her own person, but then something happened: She became a wife.

As a typical stay-at-home rather than a working wife, Margaret began to play the role of promoting her husband's interests over her own. The result was that she had few female friends, and even those few disappeared when she was drawn into her husband's retirement exile on a remote Caribbean island. Morrison gives hints of Margaret's frustration during the Philadelphia days. She abused her son, which surely does not suggest a happy motherhood.

Margaret Street is presented as a nonentity. Morrison offers little to suggest either that she could or could not have been a contributing member of society. Her life has been a comfortable little island, but a strangely isolated one. Only Ondine Childs emerges from *Tar Baby* as a fully realized, well-adjusted woman. She is an equal member in a partnership of her own choosing and making. She is at peace with herself.

Sources for Further Study

Awkward, Michael. *Inspiring Influences: Tradition, Revision, and Afro-American Women's Novels.* New York: Columbia University Press, 1991. Awkward deals with Morrison's place among African American women writers. He compares her to Zora Neale Hurston, Alice Walker, Gloria Naylor, and others.

Bloom, Harold, ed. *Toni Morrison.* New York: Chelsea House, 1990. This 247-page book has an introduction by its editor and extensive contributions from more than a dozen scholars of Morrison's work. The essays that deal directly with *Tar Baby* are thoughtful and sometimes profound.

Harris, Trudier. *Fiction and Folklore: The Novels of Toni Morrison.* Knoxville:

University of Tennessee Press, 1991. The overall coverage of Morrison's fiction is solid. Harris traces the folkloristic roots of Morrison's fiction to West African origins.

McKay, Nellie Y., ed. *Critical Essays on Toni Morrison.* Boston: G. K. Hall, 1988. All the essays in this collection will be useful to readers who are interested in Morrison. Of particular note is Craig H. Werner's "The Briar Patch as Modernist Myth: Morrison, Barthes, and *Tar Baby* As-Is."

Mobley, Marilyn Sanders. *Folk Roots and Mythic Wings in Sarah Orne Jewett and Toni Morrison: The Cultural Function of Narrative.* Baton Rouge: Louisiana State University Press, 1991. This book complements Harris' study. Mobley shows how a Maine writer of the nineteenth century and Morrison, a black writer of the late twentieth century, used similar folk motifs.

Pacquet, Sandra Pouchet. "The Ancestor as Foundation in *Their Eyes Are Watching God* and *Tar Baby.*" *Callaloo* 13 (Summer, 1990): 499-515. This article appears in a special section of *Callaloo* that focuses on Morrison. Pacquet shows consistent patterns of character and plot development in two of the author's novels.

R. Baird Shuman

A TASTE OF HONEY

Author: Shelagh Delaney (1939-)
Type of work: Drama
Type of plot: Psychological realism
Time of plot: The 1950's
Locale: Manchester, England
First produced: May 28, 1958, at the Theatre Royal, Stratford, London, England
First published: 1959

Principal characters:
> Jo, a clear-eyed, quick-witted girl of about seventeen
> HELEN, Jo's mother, who enters into relationships with men for financial reasons
> PETER, the latest of a series of men in Helen's life
> GEOFFREY, Jo's homosexual friend, an art student

Form and Content

Through a series of loosely related episodes, *A Taste of Honey* follows its teenage, working-class protagonist through the process of her entry into womanhood. As the play begins, Jo and her mother, Helen, have just moved into their latest dwelling, a dingy hole in a lower-class neighborhood that leaves Jo suitably unimpressed. Moving from place to place is an old story for these two, but it seems to Jo that they are moving down in the world and from a position that was hardly exalted. Helen refuses to be discouraged; the place will do, if only because it has to do. The arrival of Peter terminates the tentative stability of Jo and Helen's arrangement. An old friend of Helen, he wants to renew their relationship. When he proposes marriage, Helen shows an interest that catches her daughter's sometimes-caustic attention.

Responding both to her desires as a young woman and to her mother's apparent indifference, Jo becomes involved with a young black seaman. She fantasizes that he is an African prince; in fact, he is from Cardiff, Wales. Wherever he is from, Jo finds him impossible to resist, even though she probably at least half realizes that the ring he gives her does not commit him to any permanent relationship. He must return to his ship, and Helen's impending marriage to Peter means that Jo will be alone. Before leaving, Helen tells Jo, whether truthfully or not, that Jo's father was a retarded man with whom Helen had an affair shortly after her marriage to her puritanical first husband.

At the beginning of the second act, Jo is visibly pregnant. Her young man is nowhere in evidence, and Jo, although she still alludes to the fantasy that he is an African prince, wastes little time in regretting his departure. She has been befriended by Geoffrey, a gay art student. Fortuitously, he is looking for a place to stay. In offering him the use of the couch, Jo assures herself of a nurturing companion in what could otherwise have been a bitterly lonely time. Noticing some sketches Jo has done, Geof acknowledges her undeveloped talent. The talent is likely to remain undeveloped, since setting a goal and working toward it are not congenial to Jo's temperament. She is no planner, whether the issue is art or motherhood.

Geof's concern for Jo leads him to go surreptitiously in search of Helen. Jo does not want her mother to play any role in this part of her life, and she is a bit angry with Geof for his interference. She dismisses Helen's suggestion that Jo might come and live with her and Peter, and it turns out that Peter is unwilling to have Jo and her baby anyway. Impatiently, he tells Helen to come along with him. Jo is not surprised that Helen does what Peter says.

Yet Helen has not gone for good. When she turns up again, it is because Peter has moved on to another woman. Helen now asserts her prerogatives as mother. She, not Geof, will look after Jo; in fact, Geof had better move out entirely. Neither Jo nor Geof can resist Helen's force. Now alone with Helen, Jo tells her mother that the baby will be black. Helen's first reaction is to say that in that case she will drown it, but as she leaves for the drink she decides she needs, she offers another idea. Perhaps they can put the child on the stage and call it Blackbird. Alone at the final curtain, Jo sings a song that Geof has taught her.

Analysis

The early critics of *A Taste of Honey*, most of whom greeted the play with enthusiasm, commented especially on three features of the play: its looseness of structure, the authentic flavor of its dialogue, and its overall vitality.

The play's structural looseness may reflect the limits of its young and inexperienced playwright's skill at plotting. Shelagh Delaney was only seventeen years old when she began writing *A Taste of Honey*, and she was for the most part unfamiliar with the classics of dramatic literature. What spurred her to write was her belief that she could come up with something better than the play by Terence Rattigan, a successful commercial playwright, that she had been watching while working as an usher at a local theater.

Thus, there was a pleasing air of amateurism about Delaney's emergence as an important new playwright of the British theater in the late 1950's. Yet the structural openness of Delaney's play may not be merely a consequence of amateurism. Whatever his limitations as an artist, Rattigan was a polished craftsman; the structure of his plays was normally impeccable. It was probably in part against this very quality, the neatness with which everything is made to fit together, that Delaney was reacting. The absence of a conventionally constructed plot, in favor of a structure closer to the random nature of life as it is lived, may then reflect a conscious decision on the part of the young playwright. At any rate, audiences have accepted the play's structure as appropriate to the dramatic material. Unlike the conventional dramatic hero, Jo is not defined by her pursuit of goals. She lives in the moment, accepting what life gives her. She could hardly have been realized in a more tightly constructed play.

If Delaney's sense of plot was uncertain, her ear for dialogue was remarkable. The speech in this play often has the air of discontinuity that one hears in everyday speech, in which one is accustomed to speakers jumping from topic to topic with minimal respect for the rules of coherent composition. Yet because of its unfailing truth to character, the dialogue contributes positively to the coherence of the play as the plotting does not. It also captures the diversity of the characters, each of whom has an individual style of speech; but it is dramatically right that in Jo's style there are clear echoes of Helen's.

It is ultimately the characters who give the play its remarkable vitality, although Jo's lover is more a function than a character and Peter seems rather a thin creation (nevertheless, a good actor can bring him to life on the stage). In Geoffrey, Delaney has created a character who explodes two stereotypes, that of homosexuality and that of masculinity. What may be more impressive, however, is that Geoffrey assumes an individual identity as well. In giving him a conventional streak and in finding his emotional vulnerabilities, Delaney moves beyond commenting on stereotypes to the much more difficult accomplishment of creating a living character.

Jo and Helen remain Delaney's greatest achievements, both as individual characters and in their relationship to each other. The relationship of mother and daughter has rarely been explored on the stage with such unsentimental, but not uncompassionate, clarity. Their differences create vital dramatic tensions, yet one never forgets that Jo is Helen's daughter—that Jo's amused resignation in the face of an indifferent world, her resilience in response to adversity, and her focus on the here and now are variations on qualities that are present in Helen. The interplay of similarity and difference gives a vital edge to the relationship between these two characters, and that relationship is a significant source of the vitality of the play.

Context

At the time of the first production of *A Taste of Honey*, the talk of the English theater was of the work of the "Angry Young Men," who were rejecting the genteel conventions of the English stage in favor of a new directness of emotion and of social and political protest. In this context, it was Shelagh Delaney's considerable accomplishment to shift the focus of attention to women. Delaney not only situates the mother-daughter bond at the center of the play but also examines that bond with an honesty and an absence of moralism that remain impressive. Moreover, she allows the women to control the action. Although not goal-oriented in the manner of the conventional male hero, they are the active forces in the play.

The playwright was not the only creative artist involved in the evolution of *A Taste of Honey* as a theater work. The play's original director, Joan Littlewood, as founder of the Theatre Workshop, was a major figure in the advanced British theater at the time. She made a number of significant contributions, including the characters' direct addresses to the audience (sometimes called "breaking the fourth wall"), that complicate the play's realism without violating it. Littlewood's importance in the theater may be equal to that of any British playwright of her generation, and *A Taste of Honey* takes on added importance as a collaboration of women in the theater.

The success of her first play created for its remarkably young playwright great expectations that were not fulfilled in the years that followed. *A Taste of Honey* remained its author's one theatrical success. Yet in defining new possibilities for women in theater, *A Taste of Honey* constitutes at least a significant forerunner to a woman's theater. Jo and Helen must be numbered among the great roles for women in the English theater of the twentieth century.

Sources for Further Study

Brockett, Oscar G., and Robert R. Findley. "Absurdity and Anger." In *A Century of Innovation: A History of American Theatre and Drama Since 1870*. Englewood Cliffs, N.J.: Prentice Hall, 1973. A clear and concise analysis of the work of Joan Littlewood and the Theatre Workshop provides an often-illuminating context for a consideration of *A Taste of Honey*.

De Jongh, Nicholas. "Out of Bondage Towards Being." In *Not in Front of the Audience: Homosexuality on Stage*. London: Routledge, 1992. Examining *A Taste of Honey* in the light of gay and lesbian studies, de Jongh finds in Geof a recognition of the full humanity of the homosexual character unusual for its time. However tentatively, the play marks the beginnings of a revolt against conventional relationships and in favor of personal liberation.

Jellicoe, Ann. "Motherhood and Masculinity." In *Look Back in Gender: Sexuality and the Family in Post-War British Drama*, edited by Michelene Wandor. London: Methuen, 1987. Examining *A Taste of Honey* from a feminist perspective that would not have been available to Delaney in 1958, Jellicoe finds that while the play violates a number of taboos, the old values still rule. Nevertheless, especially in its treatment of relationships between women, the play marks a significant departure from the established conventions of the British theater as it existed at the time.

Keyssar, Helene. "Foothills: Precursors of Feminist Drama." In *Feminist Theatre: An Introduction to Plays of Contemporary British and American Women*. New York: Grove Press, 1985. While praising Delaney's unsentimental portrayal of the mother-daughter bond, Keyssar finds the male characters, other than Geoffrey, poorly drawn. She is also troubled by the device of breaking the fourth wall, but she finds it effective as means of awakening the audience to its responsibilities.

Taylor, John Russell. "Shelagh Delaney." In *Anger and After: A Guide to the New British Drama*. Baltimore: Penguin Books, 1963. Argues that although Joan Littlewood, the play's first director, added a number of distinctive touches, the essence of the play was realized in Delaney's original script. The collaboration of Delaney and Littlewood produced a work of magnified realism. Taylor's discussion is also available in his book *The Angry Theater* (1963).

Tynan, Kenneth. "Joan Littlewood." In *Tynan Right and Left: Plays, Films, People, Places, and Events*. New York: Atheneum, 1968. A portrait sketch of the director of the original production of the play by a critic who was closely in touch with what was most exciting in British theater at the time.

_____. Review of *A Taste of Honey*. In *Curtains: Selections from the Drama Criticism and Selected Writings*. New York: Atheneum, 1961. One of the important reviews of the first British production, by the most influential British drama critic of the period. While Tynan finds crudities in the play, he also detects the smell of life.

Wellwarth, George E. "Shelagh Delaney: The Drama of Alienated Youth." In *The Theater of Protest and Paradox: Developments in the Avant-Garde Drama*. Rev. ed. New York: New York University Press, 1971. Like many of the important plays of its period, *A Taste of Honey* presents loneliness as the human condition. Wellwarth praises Delaney's dialogue but finds her plotting weak.

W. P. Kenney

TELL ME A RIDDLE

Author: Tillie Olsen (1913-   )
Type of work: Novella and short stories
First published: 1961

Form and Content

The title story of this collection, "Tell Me a Riddle," is a novella in which Tillie Olsen depicts the inevitably destructive dynamic in a dysfunctional marriage that has endured for almost half a century when both elderly members are forced to confront their regrets. Divided into four parts, it portrays the current anguish and past tribulations of a dying woman, Eva, whose terminal illness, like so much that she deserved and desired to know, has been kept from her. Part 1 opens with the first of many riddles that haunt the novella. The adult children of the couple married forty-seven years are puzzled that their parents cannot get along. Eva and Dave literally and figuratively tune each other out during part 1: he, by turning up the television volume; she, by turning off her hearing aid. The major conflict that their relentless banter surrounds is David's desire to move to the Haven, a comfortable and "carefree" retirement community for the aged, and Eva's refusal to sell the house and do so, since she has finally realized a "reconciled peace" in her own space.

Determined to preserve her hard-won ability "at last to live within and not move to the rhythms of others," she ignores her husband's various derogatory and dismissive names for her (Mrs. Live Alone and Like It), though she cannot ignore her physical pain. She agrees to see doctor and son-in-law Phil after her first doctor could not determine the cause of her discomfort. Part 1 ends with son Paul's silencing of his wife Nancy's cruel allegation that it was merely psychosomatic, for Phil has reported that the gall bladder operation revealed cancer everywhere.

Part 2 includes subsequent visits to her children (Hannah and Vivi) which exacerbate Eva's frustration in wishing to be alone and to forget; she cannot do so when daughter Vivi's guilt, gratitude, and sorrow pour forth in a deluge of memories. Part 2 brings them to Los Angeles, where granddaughter Jeannie, a nurse, takes care of them both. When they meet Mrs. Mayes, an old friend whose life has gone from eight children to aloneness in a coffin-like room, Eva realizes the extent of her own suffocation. At the end of part 3, upon seeing for the first time David's concern for her, Eva solves the riddle of the incessant travel: She understands now that she is dying. Part 3, then, involves Eva and David's gradual acceptance not only of her swiftly consuming death but also of the truth of their lives. Eva struggles to remember and articulate the trauma of her Siberian imprisonment during the revolution and the tragic forfeiture of her and David's ideals as their lives became determined by familial needs.

In his own last efforts to reconstruct the past as worthwhile and happy, David resents Eva's stream-of-consciousness focus on the hardships that permeated her existence, children's quarrels and endless demands, her humiliation in poverty, and so forth. Yet the revolutionary songs she utters exact his own confrontation with reality. Jeannie assuages this blow and becomes very close to both of them. Indeed, her art of healing captures the love that is still inherent in their embrace; she is at once able to help David redeem his grief at Eva's loss and ease his remorse. Tillie Olsen has rendered in this moving work of fiction the reality of her own mother's difficult life as a struggling social activist, wife, and caretaker who, in parallel fashion, lost a battle with cancer.

Analysis

Olsen's novella within this collection breathlessly illustrates the mental, emotional, spiritual, and physical agony that results from the disintegration of love and idealism. David and Eva are no longer able to grant each other true peace, so they must settle for the ironic and fraudulent quiet of willfully not listening to each other. Eva holds her lifetime investment in futile housewifely duties against David, because these continual obligations make her family the enemy of her own aching wants and needs: to be a social activist, to read, to listen to music, to discuss philosophy. One important riddle, in fact, is that now that she has the time and space to pursue these passions (the children are grown), her degenerating health cruelly limits her. Her eyesight and hearing are failing.

Eva's all-consuming love for her children had suffocated all of her other desires. These maternal capacities all used up, she cannot bear to be near Vivi's newborn baby, who reminds her of her personal history of deprivation. The literal and figurative drain of maternity had drowned her beyond the ability to risk reopening wounds by touching any other baby. In a sense, she is recovering from the "lovely drunkenness" that has usurped her passion; she would not dare to endanger her "reconciled peace" by submitting to the temptation of another drink. Thus do grudges and manipulation now preoccupy Eva and David's interaction; for example, David's constant badgering about the Haven forces Eva to relive old grievances in spite of their children's meager efforts to make them compromise on the basis of their years invested, as son Lenny— who, saddened by what in his mother and himself never lived and who learned at an early age to mother himself—argues they should.

For Eva, her investment has exacted an extraordinary intensity and anxiety, and thus she welcomes the poetic justice inherent in David's finally having to worry about how they are going to make do. This justified revenge stems from Eva's disdain for the way David has always opted to run from life rather than face it. As she tells her granddaughter, she can no longer tell riddles, perhaps because she has endured too many riddles in her life, which has been replete with contradictions and unresolvable dilemmas: She cannot bear her husband, yet they still love each other.

Eva's life as wife and mother has become a riddle. Clara, her oldest daughter, regrets that she and her mother have lost each other in harshness, silence, and withdrawal. She wants Eva to repay the affection she lost because she had so many younger siblings and laments that she and Eva never knew each other. Further, Eva's obligation to attend to Vivi's children's interests (Richard's rock collections, Ann's autumn leaves) tires Eva, for the weight of the trust is too burdensome, the agonizing self-effacing past it calls up, too oppressive. The screaming of the children, for example, reminds her of Lisa, her beloved friend and cellmate in a Siberian prison, whose rage and anguish at their betrayal by their traitorous friend compelled Lisa to murder the traitor in heinous fashion, by attacking her and biting her jugular vein—a savage act that Eva witnessed fifty years ago and cannot forget.

Again one senses the disparity between Eva and David, for he runs from the pain and the past. He recalls not the suffering but rather their ideals and dreams, and Eva's elegance in expressing those hopes during the revolution. Amazed by the profundity of Eva's convictions, David nevertheless regrets how much he has lost, finally confronting the bereavement he had repressed through the century. Eva's reminiscence—in their final days, she focuses on the negative only—David takes as her betrayal of them both. He wonders if their beliefs were false, for his self-pity and egocentric perception distort the realities of the past. He can no longer accept Eva's brutal honesty about the multiple imprisonments—including wifehood and motherhood—which have constituted her life.

One such incarceration from which she has liberated herself is religion, which she deems a farce that has perpetuated and sanctioned, even glorified, women's subordination. By exempting herself from the tidy and conventional classifications society imposes to confine, define, and divide people—race and religion—Eva defies conventional categories that have made sacrosanct the dual persecution she has endured as a Jewish woman. She declares that her "race" is "human," her "religion," "none."

Stream-of-consciousness technique—noted in the graphics of the text as italics—literally and figuratively casts a particular slant on these major themes. Reinforced by the power of words to wound, verbal and nonverbal sounds evoke inescapable images and memories, unifying the intense novel through associative prose and prominent motifs, including noise and other pollution, singing as a catalyst for memory, paper dolls, riddles rooted in oxymoron (Eva's "swollen thinness"), the importance of women's own self-cultivated, maintained, and desired space, and human regression to infant or animal-like status (Eva's clasping hands become clawlike as she reverts inward to a fetal position).

Stream of consciousness also prevails in other stories in this collection. For example, in "Hey Sailor, What Ship?"—the second story—Whitey is a drunken sailor who tries to buy the affection and reluctant acceptance of his former shipmate Lennie's family. After their rebellious teenager, Jeannie, rejects his misguided generosity, he turns more solidly to his bottle, his only constant and solace. A biting commentary on the likely destructiveness of life in the service, this classic is painfully realistic.

Context

Olsen's novella has had an inexhaustible impact upon and relevance to women's literature. Even in one of the mother-daughter conflicts surrounding Eva's disgust with institutionalized religion, the reader witnesses the intergenerational gap between social activist Eva and religious conformist daughter Hannah, who lost her childhood in the premature responsibilities of helping to rear younger siblings and now duplicates her mother's selfless exhaustion. When Hannah was growing up, Eva had neither the luxury of excess time nor the desire to pass on what she deemed to be "superstition" (the lighting of Sabbath candles). Indeed, she resented others' blind obeisance to such traditions in times of severe poverty: using potatoes as candle holders when there was nothing to eat, buying candles when there was no money for soap. She sees Hannah invoking these submissive gestures to appease her husband and his family and to fill in the emptiness and darkness that Hannah has yet to admit also fills her traditional life. Eva is angry that Hannah would opt to teach her offspring these practices rather than the pragmatic and realistic ways in which social activism could improve the world.

Nevertheless, the cyclic repetition of women's lives pains Eva. She sees that Hannah, too, is run ragged by her children's and her husband's needs and has no time left for herself. Similarly, Vivi's wornness worries Eva. Vivi's own empathy with her mother's past self-sacrifice gushes forth in her gratitude over the catalog of humiliations and grief that Eva suffered for their sake: sewing all their clothes; taking them to the train station when they had no heat; begging for bones, allegedly for their dog in the winter. No wonder, then, that the paper dolls Ann makes for Eva assume disproportionate significance. Like Eva's and Vivi's, their eyes are fatigue-ringed, their one-dimensional bodies flattened, aproned, and flowery in their ancient pliability.

Eva wishes that the new generation would break this merciless repetition of women's lives: She wishes that granddaughter Dody, like her brother Richard, would climb trees and hang freely from them. With her oldest granddaughter and ultimate caretaker, Jeannie, as well, Eva bears witness to the hope that this second generation of women has the potential to offer and cultivate. Eva tells Jeannie that by the time she was her age, both her own mother and her grandmother had already buried children, as Eva had buried Davy; significantly, Jeannie is tied to neither husband nor children. Eva fantasizes that, by extension, Jeannie will not have to sacrifice her youthful vigor and generous capacity to give, and that she will not have to beg a self-absorbed man to honor her dying request to return to her home and hard-won "reconciled peace." Perhaps Jeannie will not fall prey to doctors who, assuming that women's ailments are psychological, contribute to the abbreviation of their lives by not diagnosing soon enough a problem as grave as cancer.

Olsen, as the second of seven children of Jewish immigrant parents who fled Russia after the 1905 rebellion, knew at firsthand the poverty and political activism she portrayed. A member of the Young Communist League, she wrote a proletarian novel, *Yonnondio*, after serving a jail term for union organizing. Because she supported four daughters through a series of blue-collar jobs, she was not able to finish it until forty years later. She began work on *Tell Me a Riddle* in 1955, when a Stanford University fellowship gave her the economic freedom to focus on her writing. Typical of many struggling working-class women writers, Olsen was not able to complete the novella until a Ford Foundation grant in 1959 again offered her the wherewithal to do so.

The novella's universal themes of race, class, and gender obstacles and implications won for it an enthusiastic reception as well as the O. Henry Award for the best short story of 1961, the same year in which she published "I Stand Here Ironing," the second most well-known of the stories in this collection. This confessional narrative is a remorseful retrospective of Olsen's oldest daughter Emily's problematic childhood with a single working mother whose husband left them and of her troubled adolescence as a helping "mother, housekeeper, and shopper" of four smaller children by Olsen's second marriage.

Like those of Clara, Hannah, and Vivi, Emily's youth was short-lived because of the expectations of the need for assistance with childrearing. Like Eva, the autobiographical "I" in "I Stand Here Ironing" is still haunted by her daughter's unmet needs and the consequent rivalry between them. This story exemplifies the difficult, distracting lives of working-class mothers and explains in part why recognition by Radclyffe Institute and National Endowment of the Arts fellowships, a MacDowell Colony grant, and teaching at three universities made it possible for Olsen to complete *Yonnondio* forty years after she had begun it (1974).

Olsen again addresses the interstices of race, class, and—to a lesser degree—gender in the third story of this collection, "O Yes." Here, she dramatizes the differences in religious expression across race lines when twelve-year-old, white Carol attends the baptismal service of her black friend Parialee. The revivalistic hype of this service overwhelms the unprepared Carol, who—as a result of the trauma—comes to realize the emotional cost of caring. Her mother simultaneously recognizes the blessing that these "negroes" have in their loving, supportive, and understanding acceptance of and strength in one another's woe.

Olsen's interest in women's writing was rekindled by the 1960's, and she has been instrumental in retrieving such works as Rebecca Harding Davis' *Life in the Iron Mills*, which the Feminist Press published in 1972 and for which Olsen wrote an afterword that was longer than the poignant novel itself. *Silences* (1978), Olsen's third book, describes how circumstances of the disenfranchised (poor Jewish women) preclude the resources and space necessary to create, since wives and mothers place others' needs before their own—a theme that resurfaces in each of the other works of this collection as well, including "Hey Sailor, What Ship?" and "O Yes." The recipient of several honorary degrees, Olsen continues to encourage women to develop the potential of their own creative powers and transformative imaginations and to offer a voice to the inarticulate and silent.

Sources for Further Study

Culver, Sara. "Extending the Boundaries of the Ego: Eva in 'Tell Me a Riddle.' " *Midwestern Miscellany* 10 (1982): 38-49. Culver suggests the waste that results from using women as servants and breeders. Suppressing their intellect, artistic ability, courage, and idealism causes women bitterness and is a blight on their children as well, in part because those children learn to assume a mother's self-sacrifice as their due. Eva is thus betrayed by the cultural confinement of motherhood.

Jacobs, Naomi. "Earth, Air, Fire, and Water in *Tell Me a Riddle*." *Studies in Short Fiction* 23, no. 4 (1986): 401-406. Jacobs contends that earth, air, fire, and water are metaphors for Eva's various spiritual states on the continuum between isolation and union, quarrel and embrace, silence and song, life and death.

Kamel, Rose. "Literary Foremothers and Writers' Silences: Tillie Olsen's Autobiographical Fiction." *MELUS* 12, no. 3 (Fall, 1985): 55-72. Kamel discusses each of Olsen's works, including her postscript to Rebecca Harding Davis' *Life in the Iron Mills*, which blend critical analysis and self-scrutiny. Davis and Olsen both experienced working-class hardship, observed human misery, and suffered sexism's demands on women, which Kamel discovers in such stylistic features as inverted syntax, run-on sentences, fragments, repetitions, alliterative parallels, and incantatory rhythms that reflect the chaos and drudgery of working women's lives.

Nilsen, Helge Normann. "Tillie Olsen's *Tell Me a Riddle*: The Political Theme." *Etudes Anglaises* 37, no. 2 (April-June, 1984): 163-169. Nilsen suggests the essentially political identity that Eva needs to cultivate once her children are grown, in order to offset the stunted development of her talents and faculties incurred by stifling motherhood. With a radicalism that Nilsen argues is rooted in American transcendentalism, Eva sees that love transcends personal, familial boundaries to include a commitment to better the world.

Olsen, Tillie. *Silences*. New York: Delta Press, 1978. The self-referential voice of the extended wail in *Tell Me a Riddle* offers an apologia or lamentation for Olsen's own sparse literary output and for the waste of creative potential in working-class women's lives. Olsen cites the ongoing tension between artists who crave a voice and an audience, and societally imposed, psychically internalized silence.

Trensky, Anne. "The Unnatural Silences of Tillie Olsen." *Studies in Short Fiction* 27, no. 4 (Fall, 1990): 509-516. Trensky studies silence as a theory and metaphor that give form and definition to women's lives in *Tell Me a Riddle*.

Roseanne L. Hoefel

TENDENCIES

Author: Eve Kosofsky Sedgwick (1950-   )
Type of work: Literary criticism
First published: 1993

Form and Content

Tendencies is a collection of essays dealing with the general theme of homosexuality and literature. The essays vary considerably in form; Sedgwick lists some of the genres she intends to include—"the autobiographical narrative, the performance piece, the atrocity story, the polemic, the prose essay that quotes poetry, the obituary"—and the collection includes these and other genres. Many essays combine several genres, as does "White Glasses," which is part creative writing, part autobiography, and part obituary.

The book is subdivided into three sections: "Queer Tutelage," "Crossing of Discourses," and "Across Genders, Across Sexualities." Because the book consists of essays conceived and written independently, it lacks a single thesis, but it nevertheless displays methodological and thematic unity. Sedgwick's goal throughout is to explore at a theoretical level the connections between human sexual desire and identity.

Sedgwick accomplishes this goal primarily through literary criticism. In *Tendencies*, the examples of literature range from eighteenth century French literature (Denis Diderot's *The Nun*), through British literature (represented by Jane Austen and Oscar Wilde) and American modernists such as Willa Cather and Henry James, to contemporary popular culture, and especially the cult films of John Waters. Sedgwick thus draws on mainstream and canonical authors but also undercuts the distinction between high and low culture, canonical versus cult, through her juxtaposition of traditional literary figures with popular and contemporary culture.

Sedgwick focuses relentlessly on sexuality as the key to philosophical questions of identity, but her definition of "sexuality" is unusually broad. For Sedgwick, sexuality is not an essence that remains fixed across all space and time; instead, it is socially constructed, and different forms of sexual expression have specific histories. For Sedgwick, identity is inextricably bound up with sexuality, as she explains in the "Christmas effects" section of the opening essay "Queer and Now." Thus, she traces the forms of desire as they are channeled through sexual taxonomies and behavior as a way to address the construction of identity itself.

In "Jane Austen and the Masturbating Girl," for example, Sedgwick focuses on the work of a canonical author to discuss the historical changes in society's view of masturbation. Sedgwick shows that the behavior of one of Jane Austen's heroines (Marianne in *Sense and Sensibility*) is described in terms that would be used throughout the nineteenth century to characterize the "masturbation addict" or "onanist." Sedgwick charts the history of this "addiction" and uses this Victorian case history to show how, in the course of the century, a wide variety of sexual identities has "boiled down" into one basic dichotomy (homo/hetero). It is generally assumed that this is an adequate taxonomy that efficiently describes everyone. Sedgwick wishes to expose and explode this assumption, to show that there is more at stake than a simple binary system and that various interests are at work to obscure this fact. Not surprisingly, essays such as "Jane Austen and the Masturbating Girl," with its (typically) provocative title, have attracted much negative criticism from hostile readers.

Sedgwick extends her discussion of sexual taxonomies throughout *Tendencies*. In "Tales of the Avunculate," Sedgwick focuses on Wilde's play *The Importance of Being Ernest* but shifts the focus away from the end of the play, which has traditionally occupied critics' attention, to focus instead on the role of aunts and uncles in the rest of the play. Sedgwick's exploration of these often-overlooked family members leads her to conclude that their role as figures of identification may have been overlooked by the Freudian oedipal model. This analysis once again opens onto larger political questions as Sedgwick relates her treatment of Wilde's play to the emphasis on "family" in contemporary politics.

Sedgwick also focuses on specific sexual categories when she discusses the lack of writings about female anal pleasure (in "A Poem Is Being Written") and why the trope of irony is associated with lesbian sexuality (in "Is the Rectum Straight?"). Elsewhere, she describes trends in the way behavior is categorized when she explores the addiction paradigm (in "Epidemics of the Will"), and she questions what it means to "have" a gender (in "Nationalisms and Sexualities"). In "How to Bring Your Kids Up Gay," she responds to the hidden homophobic assumptions in some recent psychiatric books. Although each essay is organized around a specific theme, the essays in *Tendencies* nevertheless form a coherent collection.

Analysis

To label the focus of these essays as simply "homosexuality and literature" is to oversimplify; Sedgwick is generally credited as one of the founders of the growing field of "queer theory." This hybrid field derives from the cross-fertilization of gay and lesbian studies as they have developed in the United States over the last two decades, on the one hand, and recent continental philosophy, history, and psychoanalysis as exemplified in the work of figures such as Jacques Derrida, Michel Foucault, Luce Irigaray, Julia Kristeva, and Jacques Lacan, on the other. Queer theory often uses literary texts as both object of analysis and illustration, but with its emphasis on theory and its interdisciplinarity, it also invariably questions the social order. Sedgwick also uses mainstream European American philosophy, particularly the discourse of "speech acts" developed by the philosopher J. L. Austin and his followers. In this context, language not only represents reality but also affects reality. The very fact of using certain kinds of language in certain contexts is sufficient to bring into being certain states (an example often cited is when someone says, "I promise").

Sedgwick also draws on a rich tradition of feminist and gay/lesbian writing. This includes the work of already notorious authors such as Oscar Wilde as well as authors whose sexual identity may be ambiguous, such as Henry James, and the growing body of "queer" criticism.

Queer theory does not treat only marginal issues; it attempts to theorize not homosexual experience alone but all human experience. It asks broad questions about the role of sexuality in society, the mechanisms of its construction and maintenance, and its role in shaping thought and human endeavor in every field. Sedgwick cites Foucault's contention that in modern society, the production and articulation of identity takes place through the construction of a sexual identity. Sexuality is thus not an add-on to a preexisting human subject, but part of what produces that subject; not a peripheral or secondary concern, but central to an understanding of what and how it means to be human.

Although the focus of Sedgwick's work is literature, her approach is experimental and personal. She writes in a sometimes brutally honest first-person voice and makes frequent reference to the circumstances in which she is writing and the personal events that have shaped her thought. She draws on her experiences with breast cancer, for example, which she describes as "an adventure in applied deconstruction," shares with her reader poems she wrote as a child, and does not shrink from admitting a rather narcissistic, comical, and ultimately poignant admiration for a friend's pair of white glasses. She writes about her experience as a "fat" woman and meditates on taboo subjects such as female anal pleasure.

Sedgwick pays great attention to style and is not afraid to be difficult. She mocks the anti-intellectualism that claims that anything worth saying should be said clearly, preferring instead to treat writing, including literary critical writing, as an art form. As a result, Sedgwick risks being viewed as inaccessible and elitist, but there is an important distinction to be made between obscurity for its own sake and complexity of thought that requires some effort on the reader's part. For Sedgwick, resisting a false sense of transparency and facility also has political ramifications. An illusion of comprehension often masks underlying contradictions, textual knots, and paradoxes. It is precisely the implications of these points of conflict and contradiction that interest Sedgwick, because they may represent issues that remain unresolved, unrecognized, and repressed in society.

Sedgwick offers a more specific critique of the politics of ignorance in "Privilege of Unknowing: Diderot's *The Nun*," in which she analyzes the relationship between power and ignorance. Although it is frequently assumed that knowledge is power, Sedgwick shows that ignorance can also be powerful, using the example of Suzanne in Diderot's eighteenth century novel *The Nun* to make her point. Although Sedgwick's discussion focuses on literature, she points out some of the political and social consequences of this recognition; for example in the contemporary justice system and in fascism.

Context

Sedgwick's most important contribution to the field of women's literature has been her work in the field of "queer theory." Two major works—*Between Men: English Literature and Male Homosocial Desire* (1985), and *The Epistemology of the Closet*

(1990)—have established her reputation as one of the founders and foremost theorists and practitioners in this area, and *Tendencies* continues this direction.

In addition, Sedgwick has enriched the field of women's literature by demanding that it address complex theoretical questions, ones that do not pertain only to women. As a woman who is forging close personal and political links with gay men, Sedgwick has created new coalitions within feminist criticism. She has been criticized for her inattention to lesbian issues in her work, since she focuses on—and repeatedly identifies with—gay male experience, but she has also suggested and theorized connections between men and women that negate gender separatism. In this way, she has brought about a significant reconfiguration of the field.

Sources for Further Study

Abelove, Henry, Michele Aina Barale, and David M. Halperin, eds. *The Lesbian and Gay Studies Reader*. New York: Routledge, 1993. This multidisciplinary anthology of articles on lesbian and gay studies contains articles referred to by Sedgwick and samples of the work of authors who have influenced and have been influenced by Sedgwick. It gives the reader a sense of the variety of the emergent field of queer studies.

Austin, J. L. *How to Do Things with Words*. 2d ed. Cambridge, Mass.: Harvard University Press, 1975. Austin presents and illustrates his philosophy that speaking can be a form of action in this founding text of speech act philosophy.

Butler, Judith. *Gender Trouble: Feminism and the Subversion of Identity*. New York: Routledge, 1990. Butler's founding work in the field of queer theory analyzes the work of several European thinkers and argues that sex and gender are performative (in the philosophical sense).

Castle, Terry. *The Apparitional Lesbian: Female Homosexuality and Modern Culture*. New York: Columbia University Press, 1993. Castle faults Sedgwick for ignoring lesbians in *Between Men* and remedies this oversight by offering her own readings of the way lesbianism haunts modern culture.

Felman, Shoshana. *The Literary Speech Act: Don Juan with J. L. Austin, or Seduction in Two Languages*. Ithaca, N.Y.: Cornell University Press, 1983. An application of philosophical speech act theory to literature, through the figure of Molière's Don Juan.

Foucault, Michel. *The History of Sexuality: An Introduction*. New York: Pantheon Books, 1978. Foucault is considered one of the most important historians and theorists of sexuality. His history of sexuality argues that the cultural definition of sexuality has varied over time, thus challenging the essentialist view.

Fuss, Diana, ed. *Inside/Out: Lesbian Theories, Gay Theories*. New York: Routledge, 1991. A collection of essays illustrating the range of voices and issues explored by means of queer theory.

Grosz, Elizabeth. *Sexual Subversions: Three French Feminists*. Sydney: Allen & Unwin, 1989. Grosz's book presents an overview and critique of three French feminists: Julia Kristeva, Luce Irigaray, and Michèle Le Doeuff. The first two have been particularly influential in North America.

Van Leer, David. "The Beast of the Closet: Homosociality and the Pathology of Manhood." *Critical Inquiry* 15 (Spring, 1989): 587-605. Van Leer criticizes Sedgwick, arguing that she reproduces certain homophobic assumptions (that gay men are passive, for example) and that her appropriation of gay male culture constitutes a form of imperialism.

Melanie C. Hawthorne

TENDER MERCIES

Author: Rosellen Brown (1939-   )
Type of work: Novel
Type of plot: Domestic realism
Time of plot: The present
Locale: A small town in New Hampshire, with flashbacks to New York City and
    Boston
First published: 1978

> *Principal characters:*
> DAN COURSER, a high-school shop teacher whose carelessness
>   has caused an accident that has left his wife a quadriplegic
> LAURA SHURROCK COURSER, Dan's quadriplegic wife
> JONATHAN COURSER, the son of Dan and Laura
> HALLIE COURSER, the daughter of Dan and Laura
> MR. and MRS. SHURROCK, Laura's parents
> CAROL SHURROCK, Laura's sister
> JOHN COURSER, Dan's older brother

Form and Content

Tender Mercies focuses on the aftermath of a terrible accident and its effects on the
family involved. The quotations from Virginia Woolf and May Swenson cited at the
novel's beginning pose a question: What happens when, freed of her body, a woman
is reduced to the core of herself? The novel explores this question, primarily through
the poetic monologues of the victim, Laura, whose body has been reduced to an
unfeeling object by the carelessness of her husband of twelve years. Yet *Tender
Mercies* turns an intense and unsentimental light on social relationships beyond the
internal one between victim and self. It examines the relationships between husband
and wife, among family members, and between a family and the community in which
it lives. Stripped of tradition by the accident, these relationships require redefining,
and regarding this redefinition the novel poses basic questions related to gender
issues. What motivates men and women to marry the people they marry? What is
expected from the relationship? What function does a wife or husband serve? In
narrative flashbacks throughout the novel, Dan describes his family background, his
meeting and courtship of Laura, the accident, and the period of recuperation in New
York City. As narrator, he continues to describe the painful struggle to adjust, with
Laura's internal monologues providing the inner landscape from which she faces her
dilemma.

The novel begins a year after the accident in which Dan turned the moving propeller
of a boat into the body of his wife, paralyzing her from the neck down. The family has
spent that year in New York City where Dan drove a taxi while his wife recuperated
in a hospital. After their daughter Hallie disappears for a night, Dan literally kidnaps

Laura from the rehabilitation facility against the doctors' advice and brings his family home.

During the weeks that follow, Dan assumes total care of Laura and the family. Tensions build as Dan and Laura attempt to communicate and as the children try to adjust to a disabled mother. The community members come to pay their respects, which is not a painless experience, since they, too, need to adjust to Laura's situation. Dan decides to throw an impromptu party and seems somewhat encouraged by Laura's reaction, believing that their relationship is beginning to move, although he is not sure in what direction.

Shortly after the party, Laura's family arrives with aid and accusations. Dan is forced to face the fact that they must move from the house he loves because it is not wheelchair accessible. Unable to cope, Dan leaves Laura and the children to the Shurrocks' care.

One month later, he returns to find only his sister-in-law Carol remaining to care for Laura. When he learns that Laura had been hospitalized for a time, he goes to his brother John for details. After a fight in which he allows himself to be beaten by John, Dan returns to Laura and makes love to her. After weeks of painful silences, cruel ironies, and hopeless guilt, for the moment at least, this family remains intact.

Analysis

Brown forces her characters to confront the core of an individual life and of a marriage by stripping them of all ordinary roles through a tragic accident. What is left for a woman with no feeling or movement in her body? What is left of the marriage? What is left for the guilty husband? Reading this novel is a remarkably painful experience that is heightened by Brown's honesty, by her choice of narrator, by the tensions that she creates, and by her language, which is rich with metaphor, imagery, and allusion.

Without sensationalism, Brown confronts the reader with all the ugly physical and psychological detail involved in surviving as and caring for a quadriplegic, including catheters and wet dreams. Although Laura accuses her husband of sounding like a script for *The Dick Van Dyke Show*, the Coursers are not a 1960's television sitcom family. Laura is silent and uncommunicative. Dan appears selfish and uncaring at times, clowning in an attempt to cope with the experience, escaping to another woman for a brief fling. His sense of guilt is crushing. The children are embarrassed and uncertain. Someone in the community sends Dan ads for professional "escorts" and a diaper service. Brown does not flinch from the truth.

The author's choice of narrator is brilliant. Laura has lost her ability to speak for a time and had has to relearn these skills. Her monologues, which are scattered throughout the book, are often surreal and at times disconnected, but effective. It is Dan's point of view, however, that controls the story. With remarkable insight into a man's life, Brown describes Dan's past, his feelings of inadequacy, his indiscretions, his hopes and fears, and his terrible guilt. At one point, when he has allowed Laura to fall from her chair:

He stands still and looks at what he's done. That slow irrevocable tinkling down of something valuable breaking—his mother, his brother uncovering the mess of shards, his teacher finding the missing object stuffed in his desk, destroyed. Car in the ditch, dog smashed on the center line. Shreds of Laura's bathing suit bobbing in the bloodied water, small patches of green and orange and blue. Long reddish hair in thick clusters streaming on the water's surface. What has he learned since that day?

Constant exposure to Dan's pain prevents the reader from judging him too harshly.

This empathy, juxtaposed with the knowledge of Dan's actions, is the basis for the tension that Brown creates; there is no black or white. The pages crackle with tension from the very beginning. He has stolen her from the hospital, from a secure place where she was learning ways of surviving. He wants to help her, but she is silent and uncommunicative. The children want to help, but they are awkward and embarrassed. There is a tension between their pasts: Her refrigerator contained white wine, mayonnaise, and guava shells, while his held dry milk and bologna. According to Dan, Laura maintains a perfect and tensive balance between the two poles of strength and weakness. Tension exists between what Laura communicates (or at least what Dan perceives) and what she is feeling, as revealed in her monologues. She wants to be touched but gives Dan the impression that it would be boorish of him to do so. He waits for her to melt, to communicate with him. He believes that if the first sexual encounter is "yielding," the next one will be a "salvation," an "absolution." The sexual tension is unrelieved until the very last pages, when Dan, absolved by the physical beating, is able to assert himself and make love to Laura.

Therefore, the family and the reader survive the pain, at least for the time being. Although Brown provides no pat answers to the questions she raises, she ends on an upbeat note. Dan remembers that the Tin Soldier did have an indestructible heart. It is interesting that, while Brown adds depth to her painful portrayal through her use of imagery, metaphor, and literary allusion, the primary source of her allusions is the fairy tale. This use of allusion helps to trace Dan's progress from an ignorance of childhood fantasy to an understanding of the basic truths such fantasy provides. "Fairy tales! he thinks. Holy Jesus, times have changed since he used to sail beer cans and condoms effortlessly out into this river, and all the nights of his life flowed downstream with them."

Context

Rosellen Brown specializes in the portrayal of families in the midst of traumatic and often tragic events. In these circumstances, the ordinary, the stereotype, the ritual fall away and the characters must confront the roots of their existence and their relationships. Brown believes that being a mother has shaped her fiction. She writes about all the terrible possibilities about which mothers dream. In her first novel, *The Autobiography of My Mother* (1976), a daughter returns home to her mother with a small baby; the mother and daughter are basically incompatible and must learn to live together. In *Civil Wars* (1984), a couple who are active in the civil rights movement are awarded custody of two children orphaned by an accident. The children are adamant racists. In *Before and After* (1992), an adolescent son murders his girlfriend, and the parents must define their roles in the light of the crime. In *Tender Mercies*, Brown portrays a couple who are forced by a terrible accident to redefine their relationship; she does so with all the tender and brutal honesty of Tillie Olsen's "Tell Me a Riddle."

With a profound understanding of the traditional male attitude toward women, Brown creates a character who is forced to move beyond this traditional philosophy. Dan Courser views women as they have been portrayed in literature for centuries. On the one hand, woman is the temptress to be conquered, even broken, which makes the man strong and just a little bad. Laura, however, is the other extreme: the woman on the pedestal, Snow White, the mermaid. She is the goddess to be worshipped, to aspire toward; she is the perfect proportion of strength and weakness. Even in her post-accident state, Laura is his monument to idolize. Ironically, in her paralyzed state, she literally becomes the statue on a pedestal. Now, however, he wants her to melt. Making love with her again would be his salvation, would absolve him of his guilt.

Fortunately, Laura brings Dan into the era of feminist enlightenment with her patience, her strength, and her desire to rise above the conformity of her past. Ironically, she minimizes his "badness" and sees herself as bad. She defines marriage as a "concentration" rather than a series of promises, an unbroken thing unseen, but understood, between two people. Dan believes that he can accept that definition because it puts Laura in the middle yet gives him room to negotiate. Brown's characters are noble in their struggle, and hope prevails because they are willing to change.

Sources for Further Study

Craig, Patricia. "Cripples." *New Statesman* 98 (July 13, 1979): 62-63. This article presents a not entirely complimentary review of *Tender Mercies*. Craig believes that the author has gone a little too far and that the novel contains errors in form and taste. She sees the novel as contributing style, however, and she identifies rehabilitation as the major theme.

Epstein, Joseph. "Is Fiction Necessary?" *The Hudson Review* 29 (1976-1977): 593-594. This article contains a review of Brown's *The Autobiography of My Mother*. Although Epstein thinks that the novel lacks the direction of a real story, he admits that the characters are remarkable, that the book is intelligent, and that Brown is a novelist worth reading.

Hulbert, Ann. "In Struggle." *The New Republic* 190 (May 7, 1984): 37-40. Hulbert's article contains an insightful and extensive review of *Civil Wars* and several cursory remarks about the first three Brown novels. Hulbert speaks of Brown's "Keatsian" inclination and, interesting in relationship to *Tender Mercies*, defines the word "concentration," a word that Brown uses often.

Rosenbert, Judith. "Rosellen Brown." *Publishers Weekly* 239 (August 31, 1992): 54-55. This article contains a review of Brown's fourth novel, *Before and After*, brief mention of all of her publications, and a brief biographical sketch. It also focuses on the relationship between Brown as a parent and her fiction. In the article, Brown discusses the economic relationship between female writers and their spouses.

Thurman, Judith. "Rosellen Brown." *Ms.* 13 (January, 1985): 82. In 1985, *Ms.* honored Brown for her willingness to confront major issues in her fiction. This article contains Brown's comments about her fiction, about reader expectations, and about her home life, as well as a review of *Civil Wars*.

Karen Ann Pinter

THE TENTH MUSE LATELY SPRUNG UP IN AMERICA

Author: Anne Bradstreet (1612-1672)
Type of work: Poetry
First published: 1650

Form and Content

The Tenth Muse Lately Sprung Up in America is a collection of poems by Anne Bradstreet (née Dudley) which was published in London by an admiring brother-in-law. The volume begins with a number of short poems honoring Bradstreet by various New England worthies, followed by a respectful poem dedicated to her father Thomas Dudley, after which appear longer scholarly poems ("quaternions") on the four elements (fire, earth, water, and air); the four humors (or bodily fluids); the four ages of life; the four seasons; and the four "monarchies" (a truncated world history up to the Romans). Following these come shorter verses such as "A Dialogue Between Old and New England: An elegy Upon Sir Philip Sidney" (the courtier and poet the Dudleys claimed as kinsman); a poem in praise of the French poet Guillaume Du Bartas (1544-1590), whom the Puritans held in high esteem; and poems, many of them dedicatory, on a variety of other subjects. Before her death, Bradstreet made emendations and added still more poems for a projected revised edition; some of these added poems are regarded as her finest. This new book, known as *Several Poems*, was published in Boston, Massachusetts, in 1678.

The Tenth Muse (the full title runs more than two dozen lines) is certainly not a title that Anne Bradstreet chose herself, for while she was realistically aware of her talent, she would have considered it pretentious to call herself "the tenth muse," a latter-day addition to the nine immortal sisters whom the ancient Greeks saw as inspiring artists of every sort. Yet *The Tenth Muse* and *Several Poems* constitute one of the two most remarkable poetic achievements in English of the colonial period—the other being the work of Edward Taylor (1644-1729). Although her keen and scholarly mind roamed in many directions, even to "the most important political and ecclesiastical problems of her day," it is often when she writes of *Kinder*, *Küche*, and *Kirche* (children, the kitchen [domestic activity], and the church [the devout life]) that she most delights the reader. Wife, mother of eight, and formidable intellect, she was loved as well as admired.

Anne Bradstreet left Boston, England, as a teenage wife in June of 1630 with her husband Simon, her parents, and her brother and sisters. She sailed aboard the *Arbella*, flagship of a fleet of eleven ships and seven hundred colonists under the leadership of John Winthrop (1588-1649). The Great Migration, though not so widely remembered as the journey of the Pilgrims, who landed at Plymouth, Massachusetts, some ten years earlier, was a much better organized and financed project guided by essentially the same purpose: to establish a religious freedom that seemed impossible in the mother country.

Although Bradstreet's family was of considerable ability and means—both her father and her husband became governors—life in the new land proved to be difficult and fraught with dangers. The *Arbella* took sixty days to cross an Atlantic rife with early spring storms and another three to make its way down the northeast coast to the tiny settlement of Salem, Massachusetts, which was only two years old and had fewer than twenty houses.

There the settlers unloaded their ships and built makeshift shelters, some modeled after the huts of the Indians or partially dug into hillsides. The Dudleys and Bradstreets, however, did not stay long. In another month, they left Salem for Charlestown, about twenty-five rugged miles south across the Charles River from Shawmut (Boston), then moved to Cambridge, later to Ipswich, and finally north to Andover.

Analysis

The bulk of Bradstreet's work is perhaps of most interest to the scholar. John Berryman's long biographical ode "Homage to Mistress Bradstreet" (1956), however, served to reawaken a general interest in her poetry, an interest that has been sustained by the poetry's own merits. Sometimes unjustly called "imitative," Bradstreet works within carefully established traditions in which modern notions of originality have less meaning.

In her elegy "In Honor of Du Bartas," an early poem in praise of the "pearl of France," written in the rhymed iambic couplets she found in Joshua Sylvester's translation, "the tenth muse" calls her own muse only a "child" but reverently brings her "daisy" to the religious poet's hearse, using the same conventions that the English poet John Milton (1608-1674) did in "Lycidas" (1637). Although her funeral offering is humble, she hopes someday to do more; in other words, she intends to establish herself as a poet, a goal she would pursue with total dedication.

While Bradstreet is generally subservient to men ("Men do best, and women know it well"), recent feminist scholars have begun to show in her an independence that "subverts biblical patriarchy." In her poem "In Honor of Queen Elizabeth," to mention only one place, she takes issue bluntly with men in general, stating wittily: "Let such as say our sex is void of reason,/ Know 'tis slander now but once was treason."

Her long poems written in Ipswich about 1642 on the four elements and the four humors reflect the poet's wide reading. Bradstreet had before her the example of her respected father Thomas Dudley, who had composed a poem—no longer extant—on the four parts of the world, each represented by a sister. His approbation may have encouraged his daughter further; she composed two more quaternions, one on the ages of man and a second on the four seasons. All these poems are loosely linked to show "how divers natures, make one unity." "The Four Monarchies," the last of the quaternions, is unrelated to the others and is indebted to Sir Walter Raleigh's *History of the World*.

It is a second group of poems, however, found mostly in *Several Poems*, about her life, her family, and her husband that attracts modern readers to Bradstreet. In "Before the Birth of One of Her Children," she refers to herself charmingly as her husband's "friend" and worries that soon she might die and her children might fall into the hands of a "stepdame" (stepmother). The thought of parting from her husband plays a role in several of her "marriage poems." "To My Dear and Loving Husband" expresses the notion that the couple should live such lives that they both will achieve eternal life: "Then while we live, in love let's so persevere/ That when we live no more, we may live ever." This concluding couplet ("persevere" rhymed with "ever" in the seventeenth century) provides the familiar paradox that only in dying does the Christian attain life everlasting. "A Letter to Her Husband Absent Upon Public Employment" states her desire that Simon should quickly return to her as the sun returns to the earth in summer. "Another (Letter to Her Husband)" again identifies her husband with the sun (Phoebus) and makes use of what the English metaphysical poet John Donne (1572-1631) calls "tear-floods" and "sigh-tempests." This poem is entirely secular, however, a rarity for her, as is the following one in *Several Poems*, which is also called "Another (Letter to Her Husband)." It, too, relies on contemporary conventions, especially on puns, as when the poet calls herself "hartless," meaning both that her heart left when her husband had to go away and that she is a "hind" (or doe) whose "hart" (or buck) has gone.

"In Reference to Her Children" identifies each child with a bird, her four boys ("four cocks") and four girls ("four hens"). Children are the subjects of many of Bradstreet's poems, such as one called "In Memory of My Dear Grandchild Elizabeth," in which the poet points out that fruits and vegetables in time mature and die, but that a baby not yet two years old should die can only be evidence of a special Providence. The same theme of unquestioning faith appears in "Upon the Burning of Our House," in which she identifies her house as "His." It is, however, her realistic depiction of fire in the night, the destruction of her library and papers, and the wistful lingering over lost possessions that move the reader most.

Context

Undoubtedly, too much has been made of Nathaniel Ward's (1578-1652) dismissal of Bradstreet as a "girl" in his introductory poem in *The Tenth Muse*. Forgotten are the facts that this eccentric curmudgeon is not speaking in his own voice here, that he was decades older than Anne Bradstreet, and that he personally did as much as he could to further her career.

It seems likely that, while Bradstreet had to contend with prejudice against her sex, she enjoyed loyal support from her family and a wide circle of friends. It is also possible that Puritan society was less repressive toward women—or at least some women—than has been thought. Although she enjoyed praise and assistance from some men, however, she bristles in her "Prologue" at those who will denigrate her accomplishments, believing that "a needle better fits a woman's hand."

It must be remembered that *The Tenth Muse Lately Sprung Up in America* was extremely popular, going through five reprintings in its first year. Indeed, a British bookman later mentions it in a list of best-sellers. *The Tenth Muse* was the only poetry collection in Edward Taylor's personal library, and the famous Boston minister Cotton Mather (1663-1728) enthusiastically includes Anne Bradstreet—admittedly, his great-aunt—in the list of famous women poets of the world.

Anne Bradstreet wrote poetry because she wanted to, for no one writes as much and as skillfully for any other reason. If she wrote chiefly for family members, they could never have been the only audience she envisioned; indeed, before her death, she saw that she had an international one. It has been asserted often that she composed poetry to escape the harsh life of early New England, but the long hours she needed at her desk must certainly have represented a sacrifice rather than escape. In the midst of sickness, births, and myriad household duties in a harsh new land, she found the time to compose both the poems that her contemporaries admired and those that the modern age has found appealing.

Sources for Further Study

Bradstreet, Anne. *The Complete Works of Anne Bradstreet*. Edited by Joseph R. McElrath and Allan P. Robb. Boston: Twayne, 1981. This volume makes accessible to beginning and advanced students all the discovered poetry and writings of Bradstreet. Moreover, it offers a very brief summary of the various views taken toward the poet that have emerged over the years, finally taking its own balanced, moderately feminist position. A publishing history of the poetry and an account of all Bradstreet's work is provided along with discussion of textual variations.

Piercy, Josephine K. *Anne Bradstreet*. New York: Twayne, 1965. Two prominent aspects of this older but widely available book are open to some questions: that Anne Bradstreet underwent a struggle of faith with orthodoxy and that she serves as a sort of pre-Romantic English poet. Neither of these readings detracts from the value of the study, which is sensitive and helpful to the general reader.

Rosenmeier, Rosamond. *Anne Bradstreet Revisited*. Boston: Twayne, 1991. This revisionist and feminist study offers an Anne Bradstreet for the modern time, an intellectual and theologian committed to an impelling and progressive *Weltanschauung*. Rosenmeier makes the too-often-ignored point that Puritanism was a house of many mansions.

Stanford, Ann. "Anne Bradstreet." In *Major Writers of Early American Literature*, edited by Everett Emerson. Madison: University of Wisconsin Press, 1972. Although much work has been done on Bradstreet since this essay appeared, this work remains a valuable introduction. Stanford provides an overview of the author's life, era, and poetry, emphasizing the meditational systems of devotion long popular in Europe among Catholics and Protestants alike that inform Bradstreet's thought.

White, Elizabeth Wade. *Anne Bradstreet: "The Tenth Muse."* New York: Oxford University Press, 1971. Solid scholarship in the fine tradition of historical criticism. White has deep knowledge of both the Old and New World in which Anne Bradstreet lived. An indispensable work with a splendid bibliography and a fine index.

James E. Devlin

TESTAMENT OF EXPERIENCE
An Autobiographical Story of the Years 1925-1950

Author: Vera Brittain (1893-1970)
Type of work: Autobiography
Time of work: 1925-1950
Locale: England and New York
First published: 1957

> *Principal personages:*
> VERA BRITTAIN, an English novelist, essayist, and political
>   activist
> G. (GEORGE EDWARD GORDON CATLIN), her husband, an English
>   political scientist and politician
> WINIFRED HOLTBY, an English novelist, her close friend

Form and Content

   Testament of Experience, the second volume of Vera Brittain's autobiography, follows her *Testament of Youth* (1933) in attempting to trace the history of the generation that came of age in Britain at the time of World War I, through an account of her personal experiences and her responses to public events. The perspective is that of a widely traveled university-educated woman from an upper-middle-class background whose career as a literary journalist married to a political scientist active in the Labour Party enabled her to become acquainted with some of the most prominent public figures of her time, from Sir Oswald Mosley of the British Union of Fascists and Dick Sheppard of the Peace Pledge Union to President and Mrs. Franklin D. Roosevelt and Jawaharlal Nehru. At the same time, living in London and elsewhere in the south of England during and after World War II, Brittain was exposed to the dangers and deprivations then undergone by Londoners of all socioeconomic classes.

   Testament of Experience is a predominantly chronological account of Brittain's life from the time of her marriage in 1925 to that of her return from a speaking tour of India in 1950, shortly before her silver wedding anniversary. Part 1 focuses on the period between the wars, emphasizing the rise of Nazism and Fascism on the public level and Brittain's initial literary success on the personal; part 2 deals with World War II and Brittain's much-maligned efforts in the peace movement; part 3 chronicles the early years of recovery and Brittain's work for famine relief and Indian independence.

   Brittain's personal experiences, as she presents them, are always intertwined with the public events and larger movements of her time. Characteristically, she and her husband George Catlin, to whom she refers as "G.," honeymooned in Vienna, the capital of a recently defeated and dismembered empire, and Budapest, where Brittain observed the full force of the aftermath of war. The initial year of Brittain's marriage set the pattern for the quarter-century of their married life that is chronicled in the book. Stifled personally and professionally by the isolation of Ithaca, New York, where her husband accepted a professorship at Cornell University, Brittain returned alone after a year to London, where she shared a flat with her friend Winifred Holtby and began at once to have success in placing articles and reviews. The couple drifted toward a legal separation until they settled into a pattern in which they spent long periods of work-related travel apart but enjoyed a relationship that Brittain always characterizes as warm, loving, and supportive, and that produced two children and lasted until her death in 1970.

Testament of Experience chronicles Brittain's literary successes, her lecture tours and other travels, her work for the Peace Pledge Union and later for the Bombing Restriction Committee and the Food Relief Campaign, the trials of the Blitz, the pain caused by the death of Winifred Holtby, and the difficulties of extended periods of separation from her husband as a result of their careers and from her children because of the war. It is a story of a woman whose strong antiwar beliefs brought her public opprobrium and personal satisfaction, and who looks back on a career of sometimes prominent and sometimes more obscure literary and political work with gratification.

Analysis

In a sense, *Testament of Experience* is a self-contained memoir of a quarter-century's private and public events, but the book is best read in connection with its predecessor, *Testament of Youth*, and Brittain's biography of Winifred Holtby, *Testament of Friendship* (1940), because it contains many references to the people and events discussed in them. The premise of *Testament of Experience*, like that of *Testament of Youth*, is that one may profitably interpret recent history in terms of one's personal life, using "the technique of presentation hitherto reserved for fiction." In fact, there is little recognizable fictional technique in *Testament of Experience*, except that autobiography perhaps inevitably relies on the use of an unreliable first-person narrator. Brittain's style is not novelistic but direct and relatively unadorned, except in a few reflective passages relating to the deaths of friends or the conclusions of momentous public events. She largely adheres to linear chronology in recounting her experiences, but a reader must be vigilant to follow the time-frames of the various chapters and sections. In an attempt to communicate her sense of the close connection between public and private events, she often shifts abruptly between them—a technique that is often but not always effective.

A number of significant themes emerge from Brittain's account of her life and career. The first of these concerns the problems facing a well-educated and ambitious woman who sought, in the middle decades of the twentieth century, to live in a manner that was both personally and professionally rewarding. Unable to form and maintain fruitful literary connections from the obscurity of upstate New York, Brittain reluctantly left her husband of one year to pursue a relatively independent life. Although G. eventually negotiated an arrangement that kept him at Cornell only in alternate semesters, between his work on behalf of various journals, government departments, international agencies, and the Labour Party and Brittain's political work, lecture tours, and need for solitude in order to pursue large writing projects, the two were seldom together. Similarly, the middle-class English tradition of the boarding school education, compounded by the dangers of World War II in London, caused Brittain to be separated from her son and daughter for extended periods of time—as long as three years when they lived with family friends in Minnesota at the height of the war. Concern, doubt, and self-questioning about this manner of conducting family life recur throughout *Testament of Experience*.

The second most prominent theme concerns Brittain's dedication to the cause of peace. *Testament of Youth*, a poignant narrative that centered on Brittain's loss of both her brother and her fiancé in World War I, was enthusiastically received, for it apparently expressed feelings that were quite common among the British public at the time of its appearance, and Brittain gained considerable prominence on both sides of the Atlantic. Fame turned to notoriety, however, when she began to speak and write against the legacy of the Treaty of Versailles and for policies that she believed would avoid a new war. Her highly visible membership in the Peace Pledge Union and her writing and publication of a personal *Peace Letter* with nearly five hundred subscribers led to her being held in suspicion by various government agencies and, during the war, to a suspension of her passport and a restriction on her movements within Britain. Her peace activities, together with her husband's rather distant association with Sir Oswald Mosely before the latter left the Labour Party, even brought veiled accusations of treason, but she was vindicated when it came to light that both she and G. had been on the infamous Gestapo list of British subjects considered particularly dangerous by the Third Reich. After the war, with the election of a Labour government and the end of bureaucratic nervousness about security, Brittain began again to act as an official representative of her country to various international organizations, and she was at last able to undertake long-delayed visits to the United States, various European countries, and India. *Testament of Experience* is on this level a testament to and demonstration of the value of holding to one's personal political convictions, however unpopular and self-damaging they might become. Brittain saw her work as writer, lecturer, and political activist as being always based on a desire to "enlarge the consciousness of humanity" in order to try to promote peaceful change toward humanistic goals: a self-image that is reflected in the seriousness of this autobiography.

Context

Vera Brittain's story as recounted in *Testament of Experience* is significant in terms of women's issues largely for the example she set as a woman who, in a social environment that was still largely hostile to independent women active in politics, let alone unorthodox politics, sought, as she put it, the right to combine "normal human relationships with mental and spiritual fulfillment." Seeing herself early in her marriage sacrificing her literary career, which she viewed as a devotional crusade for humane values, to her husband's academic and political pursuits, she boldly asserted her independence, and the two worked out a free but apparently successful relationship that enabled both equally to do the work that was important to them. Her personal experiences as a woman influenced the social and literary topics she promoted and developed; for example, her difficult first pregnancy impressed her with the inadequacy of maternity health care in Britain. By the time of publication in 1928 of her book *Women's Work in Modern England*, Brittain had come to be thought of as an important writer on women's issues, with her essays appearing in several major newspapers and journals. She was called as an "expert witness" in the case of the suppression of Radclyffe Hall's *The Well of Loneliness*.

In addition to its account of the struggle to balance literary work and the demands of motherhood, *Testament of Experience* also portrays the ubiquitousness of gender discrimination even in the supposedly progressive works of left-of-center journalism; when *The Nation* merged with *The New Statesman*, Brittain's column was one of very few regular features that were discontinued, another being the contributions of her friend Winifred Holtby. Yet Brittain became a truly prominent voice for the women's movement with the publication of *Testament of Youth*, the great success of which on both sides of the Atlantic she considered an affirmation of the wisdom of her attempt to pursue the dual careers of mother and writer. The book's best-seller status confirmed for her the sense that she had managed to express the gist of the experience of her generation of British women.

In *Testament of Experience*, Brittain depicts herself as a type of transitional figure in the modern movement for women's rights, connecting her mother-in-law's activism in the suffrage movement with the success of her daughter Shirley in national politics. If it is difficult to identify Brittain's influences among later writers, it can be confidently asserted that along with *Testament of Youth*, this book offers an important example of a successful woman writer who, during some of the most troubled decades of the twentieth century, found ways to conduct a prominent literary and political career on her own terms.

Sources for Further Study

Bailey, Hilary. *Vera Brittain*. Harmondsworth, England: Penguin Books, 1987. Part of Penguin's Lives of Modern Women series, this is the first biography of Brittain, and it ends in the middle of World War II. A popular rather than a scholarly biography, it draws heavily on Brittain's works and is useful mainly for supplying the chronology of events that *Testament of Experience* itself sometimes obscures.

Brittain, Vera. *Testament of Friendship: The Story of Winifred Holtby*. London: Gollancz, 1940. Brittain's biography of her friend Winifred Holtby presents a different perspective on many of the events described in *Testament of Experience*, from 1925 until Holtby's death in 1935.

——————. *Testament of Youth*. London: Gollancz, 1933. The first volume of Brittain's autobiography presents her life and its sociopolitical contexts from her birth until 1925. The greatest emphasis is placed on World War I and its personal effect on Brittain and her generation.

Higonnet, Margaret Randolph, et al., eds. *Behind the Lines: Gender and the Two World Wars*. New Haven, Conn.: Yale University Press, 1987. In the company of a group of essays on the roles and perceptions of women in the two world wars, Lynne Layton's essay "Vera Brittain's Testament(s)" explores Brittain's development from patriot to pacifist and feminist as a result of her wartime experiences. The essay offers a brief but insightful overview of Brittain's views on war, gender, and sexuality.

Kennard, Jean E. *Vera Brittain and Winifred Holtby: A Working Partnership*. Hanover, N.H.: University Press of New England, 1989. Kennard discusses Brittain's friendship with Holtby and assesses its impact on their writing and their political activities.

Vicki K. Janik

TESTAMENT OF FRIENDSHIP
The Story of Winifred Holtby

Author: Vera Brittain (1893-1970)
Type of work: Memoir
Time of work: From the late nineteenth century to 1935
Locale: England and France
First published: 1940

Principal personages:
> WINIFRED HOLTBY, an English novelist, journalist, and political activist
> VERA BRITTAIN, an English novelist, essayist, and political activist who is Holtby's close friend
> BILL, a soldier nursed by Holtby
> MARGARET, LADY RHONDDA, founder of the weekly periodical *Time and Tide*
> G. (GEORGE EDWARD GORDON CATLIN), Vera Brittain's husband, an English political scientist and politician

Form and Content

Shortly before her death, Winifred Holtby was asked to write her autobiography; ill health and the press of creative and political work prevented her from undertaking the project. Several years later, Vera Brittain wrote the biographical memoir *Testament of Friendship* from the unique perspective of an intimate friend of sixteen years with whom Holtby had shared apartments, houses, and holidays, both before and during Brittain's marriage to G., whose academic and political activities frequently kept him away from the lodgings the three—and later Brittain's children—shared in London.

The biography begins traditionally, with an account of Holtby's Yorkshire ancestors and her early life at Rudston House in the East Riding, where her father was a farmer and loyal Councillor; her school years and her fifteen months as a Women's Army Auxiliary Corps nurse; and her experiences as a student at Somerville College, Oxford. It was at Somerville that she met Vera Brittain, with whom she formed the extraordinarily close friendship and literary association that provides the principal focus for this biography. The two met because they had the same history tutor, but they soon discovered more significant common ground: Brittain's loss of her brother and fiancé in the war and Holtby's heartfelt but forever unrealized attachment to Bill, a young soldier whose prospects for a normal life were undermined by the war's psychological aftermath; the ambition of both women to become novelists; and the growing conviction of both that the pursuit of peace and social justice is an overriding political and therefore personal value. At the end of the term during which they met, Holtby and Brittain spent a fortnight's holiday together in Cornwall, marking the beginning of a "shared working existence" that was to last continuously for five years, and with intervals for the rest of Holtby's life. *Testament of Friendship* chronicles that relationship and its continuity in spite of Brittain's marriage to the university lecturer and Labour Party stalwart and political candidate she invariably calls "G." It also discusses Holtby's work as a novelist as well as her years as a director of *Time and Tide*, the periodical created by Lady Rhondda and several other women whose social consciousness was raised by their wartime work in the Women's Army Auxiliary Corps (WAAC), and her tireless efforts for the causes of peace and world unity through the League of Nations Union, for equality of the sexes, and against imperialism and racial oppression, primarily as a supporter of progressive forces in South Africa, where she spent six months on a lecture tour in 1926.

The final third of the book unavoidably centers on Holtby's valiant and medically remarkable fight against Bright's disease, which put her in nursing homes for extended periods for nearly four years but which seldom incapacitated her completely until just before her death in 1935. She was able, in spite of chronic fatigue, excruciating headaches, and nausea, to pursue a successful career as a journalist and public speaker, to complete six novels—crowned by the posthumously published international best-seller *South Riding* (1936)—and several important nonfiction books, and to develop a legendary reputation among her friends and acquaintances as a selfless listener, nursemaid, companion, and helper.

Analysis

Although it remains the only full-length biography of Winifred Holtby, *Testament of Friendship* is far from a typical literary biography. Brittain's intimate personal relationship with her subject bars her from even the pretense of objectivity; the book is a labor of love that verges, at times, on hagiography. Indeed, Brittain often refers to Holtby as a kind of secular saint, and some of the anecdotes suggest that the characterization may be deserved. Much of the book is devoted to stories that display Holtby's kindness, decency, generosity, and self-sacrifice. For example, in July of 1935, shortly after a serious bout with the symptoms of Bright's disease and less than three months before her death, Holtby traveled alone from London to Wimereuz, France, where Brittain was on holiday with her children, in order to spare her friend the shock of receiving news of her father's death by telegram. Worn out by her journey, Holtby had a relapse, but she nevertheless accompanied Brittain back to London and shortly thereafter returned to France to look after Brittain's children for a period that extended to several weeks because G. had meanwhile fallen ill with septicemia. Although extreme, the incident was far from unique; throughout her life, by Brittain's account, Holtby gave her time and energy so naturally and cheerfully that the recipients of her kindness often failed to recognize the full extent of her selflessness.

Brittain also emphasizes Holtby's less personal humanitarianism. Like Brittain, Holtby recognized a struggle within herself between the desire for artistic expression and the desire for social reform, and as often as not the claims of her sense of a moral imperative won out over her desire for solitude and time to work on her novels, stories, poems, and plays. Brittain praises Holtby's literary accomplishments, particularly the novels *The Land of Green Ginger* (1927), *Mandoa! Mandoa!* (1933), and *South Riding*, and she demonstrates that her friend's devotion to the cause of reform in South Africa, her lecture tours on behalf of the League of Nations Union, and her journalistic writing on feminist and other social issues constituted distractions, however worthy, from her vocation as a writer of fiction.

The most striking and pervasive theme of *Testament of Friendship*, however, is neither Holtby's personal generosity, her dedication to progressive causes, nor her development as an artist, but the nature of the personal relationship between the book's subject and its author. From 1922 to 1925, when Brittain married, the two women shared not only flats, first near the British Museum and then in Maida Vale, but also lives, in a manner that can only be described as a kind of ideal marriage in everything but (apparently) the sexual aspect. Brittain records how her falling in love with G. was attended almost immediately by her regrets concerning the inevitable effect on her relationship with Holtby, and how when her wedding was postponed for lack of money she and Holtby immediately, almost with relief, undertook three months of travel in Eastern Europe, speaking on behalf of the League of Nations and also enjoying what can only be described as a romantic adventure in Prague, Vienna, and Budapest. Even when Brittain and G. did marry and leave for the United States, where he taught at Cornell University, the plan was for the couple to return to London and share a home with Holtby—a plan that was realized, although over the years G. apparently spent more time away from his wife and her friend than with them.

These unconventional domestic arrangements inevitably drew curiosity and comment among acquaintances, and Brittain returns often to characterizations of her friendship with Holtby that amusedly deny that the two had a sexual relationship. Yet these protestations are called in question by some of Brittain's accounts of both women's feelings and avowals. Whether Holtby and Brittain were lovers in a physical sense is less important to contemporary readers than it apparently was to their acquaintances. Jean Kennard, in her study of the two writers' partnership, comes to the conclusion that it is impossible to determine the nature of their physical relationship, but that if one defines a "lesbian" relationship as one in which two women are the emotional centers of each other's lives, the word is appropriate to that between Holtby and Brittain. What is more significant than questions of sexual orientation is the extent to which their friendship contributed to their personal happiness, gave sustenance to their efforts for social reform, nurtured their development as literary artists, and even contributed to the strength of Brittain's marriage and gave Holtby the benefits of an adult family life. In those senses the book is, as well as a literary biography, an unashamed celebration of genuine friendship between women.

Context

Testament of Friendship has been important to the study of women's literature in three ways. First, Brittain's biography was published long enough after Holtby's masterpiece *South Riding* that it revived interest in a writer who had had her time on the best-seller list but whose works might have fallen into obscurity without the reminder that Brittain's book provided. Brittain is thus at least partially responsible for Holtby's place in the history of British women writers of the twentieth century, along with Virginia Woolf, Elizabeth Bowen, Iris Murdoch, Muriel Spark, A. S. Byatt, and Brittain herself.

Second, along with Brittain's *Testament of Youth* and *Testament of Friendship*, this biography gives an important account of how a talented young woman was able, in the first half of the twentieth century, to succeed in areas such as political journalism that had long been largely male preserves, yet to do so on her own terms, without compromising her identity and integrity as a woman.

Perhaps most significant, Brittain's book is an unabashed and apparently relatively candid picture of a lifelong professional friendship between two women who interacted not only personally but also as writers, encouraging and nurturing each other's talent and helping each other in their careers. In her introduction to the 1981 reprint, Carolyn Heilbrun observed that for them "friendship meant, as it long had for men, the enabling bond which not only supported risk and danger, but comprehended also the details of a public life." *Testament of Friendship* was an early attempt to discuss the potentials and realities of friendship between women in a modern context, and it was, on that level, a precursor of a number of academic studies written from a feminist viewpoint.

Sources for Further Study

Bailey, Hilary. *Vera Brittain*. Harmondsworth, England: Penguin Books, 1987. Part of Penguin's Lives of Modern Women series, this is the first biography of Brittain. This popular biography draws heavily on Brittain's works and is useful mainly for supplying the chronology of events that is sometimes obscured in *Testament of Friendship*. It ends in the middle of World War II.

Brittain, Vera. *Testament of Experience: An Autobiographical Story of the Years 1925-1950*. London: Gollancz, 1957. The second volume of Brittain's autobiography overlaps and provides a different perspective on many of the events described in *Testament of Friendship*, from 1925 until Holtby's death in 1935.

_____. *Testament of Youth*. London: Gollancz, 1933. The first volume of Brittain's autobiography presents her life and its sociopolitical contexts to 1925, emphasizing World War I and its effect on the generation in which Brittain came of age.

Higonnet, Margaret Randolph, et al., eds. *Behind the Lines: Gender and the Two World Wars*. New Haven, Conn.: Yale University Press, 1987. Amid other essays on the lives of women during the two world wars, Lynne Layton's essay "Vera Brittain's Testament(s)" explores Brittain's development of her wartime experiences. Provides an overview of Brittain's views on various subjects.

Kennard, Jean E. *Vera Brittain and Winifred Holtby: A Working Partnership*. Hanover,

N.H.: University Press of New England, 1989. Kennard examines Brittain's friendship with Holtby, focusing on its effects on their writing and their political activities.

Vicki K. Janik

TESTAMENT OF YOUTH
An Autobiographical Study of the Years 1900-1925

Author: Vera Brittain (1893-1970)
Type of work: Autobiography
Time of work: 1900-1925
Locale: England
First published: 1933

Principal personages:
ROLAND A. LEIGHTON, Brittain's fiancé, who was killed in action
EDWARD H. BRITTAIN, the author's younger brother
WINIFRED HOLTBY, the author's friend
VISCOUNTESS RHONDDA, founder in 1921 of the feminist Six
    Point Group
GEORGE GORDON CATLIN, Brittain's husband

Form and Content

Testament of Youth is the story of the loss of an entire generation's youth and innocence to the shattering tragedy of World War I (1914-1918). Though often remembered as one of a very few World War I memoirs written by women, *Testament of Youth* contains only one section devoted to Vera Brittain's wartime experiences as an Army nurse and two equally long sections dealing with her childhood and her experiences as a writer, lecturer, and activist in the postwar years. Woven into the narrative of wartime tragedy and peacetime frustration are consistent threads of puzzlement and irony over the political, social, and sexual double standards that relegated women to ancillary roles in all areas of life. Born into a middle-class British family near the end of Queen Victoria's reign (1837-1901), Vera Brittain, like many women of her generation, chafed against the restrictions imposed on women by the strict morality of the late Victorian and early Edwardian eras. In Brittain's day, any girl might be—as Brittain herself was at the age of eleven by her mother and aunt—severely chastised merely for chatting with boys her own age, and the education of women consisted chiefly of preparation for marriage. Throughout her narrative, Brittain attacks the various legal and social constraints that kept women from becoming equal partners with men in politics, social life, and even in such personal institutions as marriage and parenthood.

Part 1 of *Testament of Youth* chronicles Brittain's sheltered childhood and her growing awareness of feminism, an awareness that was powerfully influenced by her study of two books by the South African feminist Olive Schreiner (1855-1920), *The Story of an African Farm* (1883) and *Woman and Labor* (1911), as well as by the writings of Mary Wollstonecraft (1759-1797), the English author of *A Vindication of the Rights of Woman* (1792), the first great feminist manifesto. Brittain won a scholarship to Oxford University's Somerville College, where in 1914 she began her study of English, then considered the "woman's subject" at Oxford. While at Oxford, Brittain continued her developing romance with Roland A. Leighton, a brilliant and sensitive young man she had met through her brother, Edward. Soon after the war began in August of 1914, Edward and Roland both joined the army, and Brittain followed in 1915, lying about her age in order to be accepted for training as a nurse. This section closes with Brittain's posting to the First London General Hospital, which in 1915 was beginning to receive casualties from the front in France, and with the death of Roland.

Part 2 details Brittain's experiences as a VAD (member of a Voluntary Aid Detachment) stationed in London, Malta, and France. In all three locations, she endured deplorable living conditions, worked long hours, and struggled to harden herself against the suffering of the wounded. Like many people in England, France, and Germany, Brittain suffered the loss of those closest to her, and with them the loss of her sense of purpose.

In part 3, Brittain recalls her postwar efforts to advance the causes of world peace and equal rights for women while beginning to establish a career as a writer. Brittain worked for the establishment of the League of Nations, an organization conceived by President Woodrow Wilson in 1918 to promote international cooperation. Brittain also joined the Viscountess Rhondda's Six Point Group, a women's organization that sought to improve the lot of women by establishing widows' pensions, equal parenting rights, improved legal protection for rape victims and unmarried mothers, equal compensation for women teachers, and equal opportunity for women in civil service positions.

Analysis

Testament of Youth is a touching autobiography. As a wartime memoir, it illuminates the extraordinary courage of Vera Brittain and her contemporaries: the heroic young men who lost their innocence in the mud and the gas of the trenches, and the heroic young women who lost theirs in the blood and the antiseptic of the military hospitals. As a feminist document, it exposes the inconsistency and unfairness Vera Brittain saw in the laws and customs of her society.

The wartime memoir reveals aspects of World War I which are often neglected in less personal histories. Like most Britons in June of 1914, Brittain thought little of the assassination in far-off Sarajevo, Bosnia (later Yugoslavia), of Austria-Hungary's Archduke Francis Ferdinand, the event that triggered World War I. She perceived the outbreak of the war as an interruption to her personal plans for an education and a career as a writer. It proved instead to be a tragedy both personal and global. The war claimed her fiancé, two close friends, numerous casual acquaintances, and her brother, Edward. It also claimed eight million dead in battle and twenty-one million wounded. Vera Brittain's response to the tragedy was human, not nationalistic. She nursed both English and German casualties during the war, and afterward she grieved not only for the English dead but also for the hungry, shivering children of a defeated Germany. The intelligence and compassion of Brittain's narrative lead the reader to a deeper understanding of the human tragedies on both sides in any war, and to an awareness of the need for international cooperation.

As a feminist document, *Testament of Youth* attacks institutionalized sexism, which Brittain saw as riddled with inconsistencies. For example, although women in England had been granted the right to vote in 1918, that right was extended only to women over thirty. Prevailing wisdom in postwar England was that, with the male population decimated by the war, suffrage for all adult women would give women a political majority. Brittain herself, although she had a university degree and four years of national service, could not vote until five years later. Although Oxford University admitted women before the war and subjected them to the same rigorous curricula and examinations as men, it did not grant degrees to women until October of 1920. Brittain's puzzlement over such paradoxes at first seems to be genuine. As more paradoxes come to light, that puzzlement changes to irony.

Brittain's struggles to advance women's rights after the war show how sexism affects even those in the highest seats of power. As a member of the Six Point Group, Brittain worked for the fair enforcement of the Sex Disqualification (Removal) Act of 1919. The Act was intended to remove legal distinctions between men and women, but women were still routinely dismissed from jobs when they married, a state of affairs that forced the best and the brightest to choose between marriage and career. Brittain worked also for the passage of such landmark legislation as the Criminal Law Amendment Bill of 1922, which raised the age of consent in sexual assault cases from thirteen to sixteen and disallowed the previously admissible defense that the attacker believed the victim to be of legal age. Brittain's ironic bafflement over the opposition's argument—that better protection for teenage girls somehow constituted a curtailment of British freedom—swiftly unmasks the sexism behind that argument. The same ironic bafflement lays bare the inanity behind objections to other major pieces of legislation enacted in postwar England. Brittain complains that a bill to give mothers equal rights of guardianship was regarded as an insult to fathers and, inexplicably, to God. A bill to give women equal rights to divorce and to extend the grounds for divorce to insanity, drunkenness, and incompatibility instead of limiting those grounds to adultery (chiefly the wife's adultery) was opposed because male members of Parliament considered adultery, which perhaps threatened a man's "ownership" of his wife, far worse than wife battering or other types of abuse. Again, Brittain's ironic puzzlement lays bare the foolishness she perceives behind such sexist thinking.

Missing from Brittain's narrative is venom. Although she is occasionally sarcastic and frequently ironic, she disinfects each and every discriminatory law and attitude with the aplomb of the veteran nurse. In 1921, prevailing wisdom insisted that the shortage of marriageable men created by the war had rendered large numbers of women "superfluous" and that these "superfluous women," for their own domestic happiness and for the good of the nation, should emigrate in search of husbands and so ease the strain on England's disabled economy. In a letter to Winifred Holtby, Brittain sadly complains that people simply do not understand that not all women want or need husbands, and she points out several times that women should not be forced to choose between marriage and careers. Keeping married women out of the professions, she argues, very nearly amounts to race suicide because it wastes both the professional talents of women who choose marriage and the maternal talents of women who choose careers. The same intelligence and compassion that guided her through the tragedies of the war also guide her through the tragedies—and the tragicomedies—of peace.

Context

A best-seller by the standards of the 1930's, *Testament of Youth* sold 120,000 copies in its first six years and generated 1,300 letters to its author, who suddenly found herself famous. As part of a rising tide of popular feminist literature, Brittain's story helped her generation to establish a new definition of women and their roles, a definition that included not only marriage and motherhood but also careers and, above all, self-determination.

Vera Brittain wrote twenty-nine books and countless essays and poems during a writing career that spanned half a century. Other autobiographical works include *Testament of Friendship* (1940), the story of her close relationship with Winifred Holtby, and *Testament of Experience* (1957), a memoir of the years between 1925 and 1950, including her uncomfortable experiences as an avowed pacifist during World War II. She wrote several collections of poetry, including *Verses of a V. A. D.* (1918), and her novels include *Dark Tide* (1923) and *Account Rendered* (1945). A notable work of history is *Lady into Woman: A History of Women from Victoria to Elizabeth II* (1953).

Sources for Further Study

Higonnet, Margaret Randolph, et al., eds. *Behind the Lines: Gender and the Two World Wars*. New Haven, Conn.: Yale University Press, 1987. These essays reassess women's wartime roles in the light of the twentieth century's development of total war. Lynne Layton's essay "Vera Brittain's Testament(s)" suggests that before the war, Brittain subscribed to an essentially masculine pro-war view, but that because women define themselves in part through relationships, her personal losses during the conflict caused her to move toward an essentially feminine identification.

Kennard, Jean E. *Vera Brittain and Winifred Holtby: A Working Partnership*. Hanover, N.H.: University Press of New England, 1989. While arguing for the literary value of the writings of Brittain and Holtby, this insightful book examines women's relationships as part of the process of self-definition. Kennard suggests that during a fifteen-year friendship, Brittain and Holtby served as second selves, each helping to define and to empower the other.

Leonardi, Susan J. *Dangerous by Degrees: Women at Oxford and the Somerville College Novelists*. New Brunswick, N.J.: Rutgers University Press, 1989. A study of six women writers, this work discusses the novels of Vera Brittain as variations of the traditional romance, although many of Brittain's heroines are examples of the university-educated or "Oxbridge" woman. Ultimately, Leonardi insists, Brittain's feminist themes are overshadowed by the genre of the romance.

Mitchell, Dale. *Women on the Warpath: The Story of the Women of the First World War*. London: Jonathan Cape, 1966. This book argues that the patriotic achievements of women not only played a vital role in winning the war but also spearheaded the drive for equality in England.

Spender, Dale, ed. *Feminist Theorists: Three Generations of Women's Intellectual Traditions*. London: Women's Press, 1983. Spender offers this collection of essays as a refutation of men's right to "ownership" of the realm of theory. Muriel Mellown's essay "Vera Brittain: Feminist in a New Age" argues for Brittain's position as a feminist and an independent thinker who refused to be pigeonholed or swayed from her beliefs by either conservatives or radicals.

Strachey, Ray. *The Cause: A Short History of the Women's Movement in Great Britain*. 1928. Reprint. Port Washington, N.Y.: Kennikat Press, 1969. First published in 1928, this dated but sympathetic work provides important background reading for understanding Vera Brittain's feminism in the context of the struggle for women's rights in Britain.

Craig A. Milliman

THAT NIGHT

Author: Alice McDermott (1953-   )
Type of work: Novel
Type of plot: Social realism
Time of plot: The 1960's to the 1980's
Locale: Long Island, New York
First published: 1987

Principal characters:
>THE NARRATOR, unnamed, who is ten years old
>SHERYL, Rick's teenage heartthrob
>RICK, a seventeen-year-old "hood"
>MRS. SAYLES, Sheryl's mother

Form and Content

The phrase that titles Alice McDermott's second novel, *That Night*, names also the novel's central scene, around which in backward and forward sequence the whole story is told. Vivid in its presentation, the scene revolves in the memory of the unnamed narrator in much the same way that the cars belonging to Rick and his teenage buddies move slowly around and around the several blocks of the suburban neighborhood that provides the major setting of the novel. Slowly, the cars move in intricate patterns in and around the block, passing silently by the Sayleses' house, sometimes pausing and then in slow motion taking up again the intricate patterns. The monotonous movement of the cars around and around becomes ominous, suggesting a funeral, the circlings of mourners around a coffin as they pay last respects. Indeed, in a way, this procession does mark a death—the end of a dream of love strong enough to conquer death. Rick's cry rising above the engines of the idling cars and the window fans of the deserted houses is a kind of death wail, a poignant keen, for his lost love.

When Rick agrees with his leather-jacketed buddies that a proper form of behavior for those warring with a dominant society is to invade the enemy's territory and carry off the enemy's treasure, he must already know the inevitable conclusion, for men of warring tribes do not surrender their women to invaders. Neither do the T-shirted suburbanites. Rick's demand to Mrs. Sayles that she send for Sheryl is already frustrated by Mrs. Sayles' previous action. Sheryl is no longer there. She has been spirited off by the women, who play their roles as if they have been well rehearsed. Rick makes the mistake of reaching for Mrs. Sayles, however, and at that moment the men of the neighborhood, all more than a decade away from their soldiering in World War II, take up hoes, bats, sticks, and the tops of garbage cans to attack the boys, who have come equipped with chains. Many bruises later, Rick is in jail and the men have become comrades in arms, bonded at last in their suburban "paradise," and ready to take up arms again and again, if necessary, to protect the virtue of their daughters and their wives.

Like the circumnavigation of the cars, the narrative follows a circular movement in time. After "that night," the narrator recounts the previous several hours, then returns to the fight, pausing there before taking the reader forward several days and then back even farther to the previous summer, only to bring the reader forward again to the several ensuing days after the fight. All the while, the narrator's comments wind circuitously around previous and forthcoming decades until it is clear that the circumstances of "that night" simply adumbrate what is to come for all the daughters and all the sons: the knowledge that love alone, even first love, which is relatively uncomplicated and fierce, is not enough; that love eventually comes to nothing; that children become adults and lose their children in one of myriad ways; that there is no way to halt the passing of time and beauty, even though one may try as hard as one might and in seemingly ridiculous ways.

Witness Mrs. Carpenter, whose taste for beauty and longing for permanence overwhelm her good sense to the point that she relegates family living to the basement because she believes that living in the house will disturb the pristine beauty of the furnishings. Twenty years later, the neighborhood will be all but abandoned by the people who settled there, looking for the completion of the American Dream promised after World War II, a dream that seemed to guarantee to every American "war hero" a family, a home, and an automobile to transport him to and from his daily work.

Sheryl, delivered into the hands of other women in the family, takes the course expected of all Catholic girls: a waiting period followed by secretion; a birth, followed by an adoption; and a return to a point left off or one reasonably similar to it. Sheryl stays with a cousin who cares for her conscientiously and delivers her promptly back to her immediate relatives, who have moved to another suburb in another state. Sheryl knows what is expected of her. She takes up again where she left off, looking for a boyfriend to help assuage her grief for her father's passing and for Rick, her lost loves. She will eventually marry and have children, as will Rick and the narrator, who, at the end of the novel, has lost a child, left a husband, and is in the act of selling the suburban home in which she grew up.

Analysis

The unnamed narrator, who is ten years old at the time of Sheryl's trouble, is in love with the idea of love; and in Sheryl, the little girl finds a real model, not a play model like her Barbie doll. Sheryl might not have fallen so quickly into the deadly trap of love if her father had lived and had returned his own car to his own garage on the day of his death. Catapulted into Rick's car by her father's early death, Sheryl is still too young to play the game of love with Rick at a time when she still expresses her fascination with the Barbie doll and its wardrobe of clothes, which are cleverly seductive and are clearly designed to attract what would years later become the Ken doll. Not for Barbie and her outfits the real world of living, of loving, losing, compromising, and bearing children only to lose them to houses for unwed mothers, to bitter divorces, or to death by war or by natural causes, even to worn down youth, early marriage, early pregnancy, low wages. Witness Rick with a wife and three children, listlessly looking through the narrator's house after it is put on the market.

The ten-year-old narrator, however, is struck by the beauty of the youthful romance and sees Sheryl as a Barbie doll come alive. One evening, with a playmate, Diane, the narrator witnesses Sheryl and Rick saying goodnight. In the light cast by Sheryl's open front door, the children witness Rick's face pressed into Sheryl's chest and her arms around his head. For a moment the children seem to see lovers as silhouettes. Then Sheryl, like a dancer, gracefully lifts her body and with her face straight up to the sky pauses a moment before dipping back into the shadows, where she kisses Rick's face and throat as though she were blessing him.

In counterpoint to the unwanted pregnancy so easily achieved by Sheryl and Rick are the older women who desire children. Leela pursued pregnancy beyond her optimum age, and learning-disabled Jake is the result. The narrator's mother, the same age as Leela, goes through a series of eccentric acts such as soaking in a solution of Epsom salts and standing on her head to help sperm connect to egg; when a connection is made, she goes through several heartbreaking miscarriages, only to try again to conceive.

Domestic heartbreak is seldom the stuff of tragedy. What Alice McDermott manages to do in this short novel, however, is to raise the thematic material to tragic levels, to make aspirations lost and dreams forgotten the stuff of an American tragedy, and Sheryl and Rick, ordinary suburban teenagers, the emblems of that tragedy. The point of view of an adult looking back at childhood and commenting on points in between provides McDermott with the means to revivify the old myths. Making the narrator the spokesperson for the neighborhood allows both individuation and community in characterization. Perhaps more important, the point of view, allowing for constant revisitation and rumination, provides the vehicle for a prose style whose intricacies of sentence structure match the complexities of theme and whose lyricism provides the elegiac tone.

Context

A relative newcomer to the novelists' calling, Alice McDermott grew up during the decades when women's issues came to the forefront of the concerns of people in the English-speaking world. Standard feminist texts were being published as McDermott made her way through school; she could not have helped but be influenced by so dominant a movement. *That Night* is not a feminist text through proclamation; it is a feminist text in its rendering of the social order both within and without families in Suburbia, U.S.A., during a short period in American history when shared values were stable, when a sense of community was strong, and when men and women knew their "place" in family life.

Men were the breadwinners; women were the caretakers of the home. Men did "manly" things—going to and from work in elaborate machines, using less elaborate machines to cut grass and keep the yards tidy, and using shoulder muscles to lift heavy objects such as garbage cans brought to curbs. These men had just returned from soldiering in another world war—the last, they thought—to save home and family and shared American values. They did not anticipate another war that would call their sons to "duty" and possible death.

Consequently, the men in *That Night* rally to save home and hearth from a group of teenagers—black-jacketed "hoods" in hot rods who represent a threat to a way of life that the dominant culture holds sacred. The male bonding that results confirms their identities as they withstand the threat while women and children stand on the sidelines watching the battle.

After World War II, women gave up the jobs they had taken to replace men who had been called to the service of their country. They took up housewifely duties in little box houses where they cooked and cleaned and bore children—the emblem of their fulfillment as women, as well as insurance against a future when children might be called upon to care for mothers and grandmothers who had been widowed or otherwise left alone.

Consequently, the women in *That Night* take care to protect their daughters from scandal, moving in concert as though they have already rehearsed their actions. Therefore, Mrs. Sayles is bitter and angry when her husband dies prematurely, thus breaking his marital vows; the narrator's mother is furious when she learns that Leela's husband left her to marry a woman who could bear children more easily; and the narrator's mother tries frantically to have another baby even though she already has two. How does one measure a woman's worth? The men and women in this novel would say, "In the light of her ability to mother her husband's child, to care for her husband's house, and to put a meal on her husband's table." It is no wonder that the narrator's father wonders what his wife has to talk about with their friends.

All the shared values, however, and all the unquestioned acceptance of roles in the family and social structures assure no one of happiness or freedom from pain. The events in the novel make this fact clear. It also does not seem to matter what the prevailing social mores are. By the end of the novel, the narrator, a grown women, laments the breakup of her marriage and the postponement of children, for at the end of the novel twenty years have passed and in real time the flower children have come and gone, the Civil Rights movement and the women's movement have brought about many changes, the family, as Americans once knew it, is on its way out, and shared values are only an illusion of a past time.

Sources for Further Study

Balliett, Whitney "Books: Families." *The New Yorker* 63 (August 17, 1987): 71. A discussion of the richness of *That Night* as compared with minimalist fiction that also deals with middle-class values but in spare and bleak ways. Balliett also mentions McDermott's prose style and her use of amplifying and overlapping clauses in sentences. He agrees that the book is about life in the suburbs but insists that *That Night* is more than that. It is about the adolescent passion of a first love that can never be repeated.

Leavitt, David. "Fathers, Daughters, and Hoodlums." *The New York Times Book Review*, April 19, 1987, 1, 29-30. Leavitt also points to the differences between

McDermott's work and that of minimalists whose settings and characters are similar but whose tones, moods, and themes are different. Whereas minimalist work is ironic and bleak, McDermott's is accepting and elegiac. The difference is primarily in the baroque richness of the language, and the complexity of the moral vision McDermott presents, Leavitt says, invests her novel with historical authenticity.

Towers, Robert. "All American Novels." *New York Review of Books* 34 (January 21, 1988): 26-27. Towers calls *That Night* a pleasant piece of bittersweet Americana, faithful to historical time and place. He suggests that too much praise has gone to the novel. Nothing in the book is in any way remarkable, Towers concludes—not characters, not descriptions, not use of language. The novel is, however, Towers says, a small, decent work that is successful within the limits the author sets.

Mary Rohrberger

THEIR EYES WERE WATCHING GOD

Author: Zora Neale Hurston (1891-1960)
Type of work: Novel
Type of plot: Social criticism
Time of plot: The 1930's
Locale: Eatonville, Florida
First published: 1937

> *Principal characters:*
> JANIE CRAWFORD KILLICKS STARKS WOODS, the protagonist and
>   initial narrator
> NANNY, Janie's grandmother
> JOE STARKS, Janie's second husband
> VERIGIBLE "TEACAKE" WOODS, Janie's third husband
> PHEOBY, Janie's best friend

Form and Content

Zora Neale Hurston wrote most of *Their Eyes Were Watching God* in 1937 during a seven-week period she spent in Haiti. Hurston, the recipient of a Guggenheim fellowship, spent her days gathering anthropological data about life in Haiti, but she spent her evenings working on what was to become her greatest novel. The impetus for such an outpouring of words was a love affair with Albert Price III, a young graduate student of West Indian descent whom she had left in New York. Hurston undoubtedly realized that her relationship with Price was doomed, and thus she invested much of her own emotional life in the creation of her protagonist, Janie Crawford Killicks Starks Woods. The reader witnesses the internal maturation of Janie as she embarks on a journey for self-knowledge.

Janie tells the story of her life to Pheoby, her best friend, a woman who sympathizes with her and who is eager to hear Janie's story. Although Janie's brief narration is introduced by and then taken over by a third-person, or "public," narrator, the narrative voices that speak throughout the text always move toward convergence with Janie's voice. Janie's conscious life begins in her grandmother's backyard, where she first experiences sexual ecstasy. When Nanny sees Janie kissing Johnny Taylor, she insists that Janie marry Logan Killicks. Nanny tells Janie that the white man gives his workload to the black man, and the black man gives his workload to the black woman; therefore, the "nigger" woman is the mule of the world. After her marriage to Killicks, Janie quickly discovers that marriage does not equal love, and when the opportunity presents itself, Janie simply walks away and never looks back.

Janie's opportunity to leave Killicks presents itself in the form of Joe Starks. Starks is on his way to a town in Florida that has been established by and for African Americans. He is a man of the world and plans to be a "big voice" in the town of Eatonville. Janie marries Joe and moves with him to Eatonville. She is soon disappointed in her marriage, however, because Joe Starks places Janie on a pedestal, far above the common riffraff of the town, and thus effectively silences her. Janie ceases to love Joe, and their marriage moves from the bedroom into the parlor. During the years of her marriage to Joe, Janie's self-awareness grows. She discovers that she has a "jewel" inside her. Janie discovers that she understands Joe's motives, that she can see a man's head "naked of its skull." Finally, after twenty years of marriage, Joe dies. Janie, rejoicing in her newfound freedom, rejects the community's efforts to marry her to another man.

Janie is unwilling to allow the community of Eatonville to find her another husband; however, she finds a new mate when Teacake Woods enters her store. Although he is much younger than Janie, Teacake teaches her to laugh and to play again, and together they leave Eatonville to work in the Everglades as farm laborers. In the Everglades, or the Muck, their relationship is challenged by the community of laborers, a community whose attitudes and activities present a microcosm of African American society. Janie and Teacake are also challenged by god, or nature, in the form of a hurricane. During their struggle to survive the hurricane, Teacake is bitten by a rabid dog and becomes rabid himself; Janie is forced to shoot him. Janie is brought to trial and acquitted by a white jury. The circularity of the novel is completed as Janie returns to Eatonville. The narrative ends as Janie pulls her life in about her and drapes it over her shoulders like a great fishnet.

Analysis

Although *Their Eyes Were Watching God* is a work of fiction, it is autobiographical as well. Hurston reveals her personality through the narrative events and through the interplay of the author's, narrator's, and protagonist's voices. This novel not only tells the reader about Hurston's emotional life but also "signifies" upon (revises) feminine images in nineteenth century narratives written by African American women. Therefore, it provides an important link between those earlier narratives and novels written by African American women in the last quarter of twentieth century. Unlike literary foremothers such as Jessie Fauset, Frances E. W. Harper, and Pauline Hopkins, Hurston refused either to stereotype her protagonist or to conform to earlier plot lines established by white predecessors. Hurston moved Janie far beyond the boundaries that restrained the "true woman" of the nineteenth century, and in doing so, she provided the model of a heroic African American woman that was to profoundly influence twentieth century writers such as Alice Walker.

Their Eyes Were Watching God is the fist self-conscious effort by an American ethnic writer both to subvert patriarchal discourse and to give voice to women of color. Hurston's protagonist moves from object to subject, from a passive woman with no voice who is dominated by her husband to a woman who can think and act for herself. Janie's change in status begins when she realizes that she is as important and knowledgeable as her husband. Soon after this realization Janie begins to find her voice. The casual conversation of the men on the porch of Joe Starks's store reveals the extent of their sexism. The favorite topics of these men are the stupidity or meanness of mules and women, and the heroics of folk heroes such as Big John de Conquer. On the day that Janie "thrust" herself into the conversation, the men are all in agreement that if the nagging Mrs. Tony were married to any of them, they would kill her. Janie suddenly realizes that female obedience and chatteldom are in themselves a metaphorical death, that they place woman in the position of "the mule." Janie informs the men that they do not know half as much about women as they think they do, that God speaks to women as well as to men, and that men have no idea how much women know about them.

Hurston's use of language is an important and somewhat revolutionary aspect of her narrative. Her characters use African American dialect, a form of speech that is also often adopted by the narrator. The use of dialect with free indirect discourse (dialogue without quotes or direct indication of speaker) serves to move the narrative voice toward convergence with a given character's speech. Hurston uses free indirect discourse most often and most empathetically when Janie speaks.

The use of language is presented in terms of power throughout the narrative. Joe Starks uses his "big voice" to silence Janie. Janie, in turn, uses her voice to rob Joe Starks of his illusion of irresistible maleness and to some extent destroys the authority that Joe has established in the town of Eatonville. The use of language in Janie's discourse with Teacake Woods is quite different. Janie tells her friend Pheoby that Teacake taught her a new language, with new thoughts and new words. Hurston's sentence structure demonstrates the equality that exists in the early phase of Janie and Teacake's' relationship. Hurston uses compound subjects with single active verbs to describe the two lovers at play, two lovers who together are thinking new thoughts and creating a new language that could possibly bridge the communicative chasm that separates male from female.

Unfortunately, Janie and Teacake are unable to complete the creation of their new language. Janie's relationship with Teacake does not survive the challenges posed by society and nature. Hurston was undoubtedly describing her emotional relationship with Albert Price as she wrote about Jane and Teacake. Although Janie returns to Eatonville alone, she returns as a strong, self-actualized woman; in a sense, she is a new woman. Hurston's narrative advocates both freedom from sexist and racist oppression, and the rejection of community and cultural values that enforce such oppression. Hurston also presents an imaginative consciousness that speaks of wandering and independence in a time when women were somewhat restricted. Ultimately, Janie, like Hurston and many African American women of the twentieth century, becomes a woman who can think and act for herself, who can make her own world.

Context

Their Eyes Were Watching God is a groundbreaking narrative. Hurston's protagonist, Janie Woods, is a new kind of African American woman. Hurston revised the images of women presented in earlier African American narratives in which African American women were modeled upon white protagonists or were dedicated to the notion of "uplifting" the entire race. Through Janie, Hurston calls attention to the silencing of women and to their exclusion as storytellers within the African American community. She also demonstrates how the men of Eatonville, the "porch talkers," set the boundaries of discourse for the entire community. The language of the men, unlike the language used by Janie, is a game, a competition; it reveals no internal development. Although Hurston is somewhat ambivalent toward Janie and allows her husband, Teacake, to beat her, she nevertheless depicts her as a questing hero, as a woman who moves from object to subject. *Their Eyes Were Watching God* is a feminist novel, and it may be considered the first such novel in the African American tradition.

Hurston's life and work provided a model for later African American writers. Alice Walker has stated that *Their Eyes Were Watching God* had a profound effect upon her writing and that if she were marooned on a desert island with only ten books, Hurston's masterpiece would be among those she would choose to take with her. Literary critics believe that one of Walker's protagonists, Shug, of *The Color Purple*, is a re-creation of Hurston herself. Hurston has become a literary "foremother" not only for Walker but also for other African American women writers, including Gayl Jones, Gloria Naylor, Toni Cade Bambara, and Toni Morrison. Although Hurston failed to define new parameters for discourse between men and women, she gave her protagonist a voice that allowed her to speak for herself. *Their Eyes Were Watching God* offers a point of departure for a new generation of African American women writers who are attempting to bridge the communicative chasm that exists between men and women.

Sources for Further Study

Awkward, Michael. *Inspiriting Influences: Tradition, Revision, and Afro-American Women's Novels.* New York: Harper Perennial, 1990. Awkward's chapter on Hurston focuses on the importance of community and communal voice in Hurston's novel. He argues that Janie's voice becomes one with the African American community and reflects the emphasis on oral tradition within that community.

Dixon, Melvin. *Ride Out the Wilderness: Geography and Identity in Afro-American Literature.* Chicago: University of Chicago Press, 1987. Dixon's chapter on Hurston's novel includes an analysis of Janie's search for identity as she moves from one geographical location to another, from the porch to the Muck, and back to Eatonville at the end of the narrative.

Gates, Henry Louis, Jr. *The Signifying Monkey: A Theory of African-American Literary Criticism.* New York: Oxford University Press, 1988. This analysis of the African American literary canon includes a chapter on the structure and content of *Their Eyes Were Watching God.* Gates argues that Hurston's combination of African American dialect with free indirect discourse revises, or "signifies" upon, earlier African American texts.

Hemenway, Robert E. *Zora Neale Hurston: A Literary Biography.* Chicago: University of Chicago Press, 1977. In this historical analysis of Hurston's life and writing, the chapter on *Their Eyes Were Watching God* describes how Hurston came to write her most famous novel. Hemenway underestimates the autobiographical content of the novel.

Hurston, Zora Neale. *Dust Tracks on a Road*. 1942. Reprint. New York: Harper Perennial, 1991. Hurston's "official" autobiography, this volume contains both the story of her life and her account of the circumstances surrounding the creation of *Their Eyes Were Watching God*. This book provides insights into the real and fictional worlds created by Hurston.

_____ . *Mules and Men*. 1935. Reprint. New York: Harper & Row, 1990. This account of Hurston's anthropological research offers insight into the folktales contained in *Their Eyes Were Watching God*. The text contains many of the same metaphors that appear in Hurston's other autobiographical books.

Yvonne Johnson

THIS SEX WHICH IS NOT ONE

Author: Luce Irigaray (1930-   )
Type of work: Essays
First published: Ce Sexe qui n'en est pas un, 1979 (English translation, 1985)

Form and Content

Based on Luce Irigaray's work as a psychoanalyst, linguist, and philosopher, the eleven essays collected in *This Sex Which Is Not One* critically analyze Western culture's descriptions of female identity and the many ways in which these representations influence women's psychic, social, and economic development. Irigaray explores a number of related issues, including the restrictive nature of masculinist language systems and the subsequent limitations in male-defined images of female sexuality, women's absence in Western philosophical tradition, and the importance of developing exclusively feminine modes of communication. The nonlinear, poetic writing styles she employs in many of these essays make it difficult to arrive at definitive statements concerning her theories of the feminine, yet this elusiveness is an important part of her undertaking. By unsettling readers' expectations, she challenges them to rethink conventional definitions of masculinity and femininity.

Although many of the essays in *This Sex Which Is Not One* were previously published in various journals and can be read separately, the arguments presented in each chapter are interconnected and mutually dependent. The title essay offers a useful entry into Irigaray's work, for it provides readers with an overview of her theory of the feminine. In addition to arguing that women's pleasure and female sexuality cannot be adequately described in Western culture's patriarchal language systems, Irigaray contrasts women's autoeroticism with men's and offers an alternative perspective on the feminine, which she describes as plural, nonunitary, and fluid.

Irigaray expands her analysis of Western culture's restrictive notions of female sexuality in other chapters and includes more explicit analyses of how psychoanalytic theory's unacknowledged masculine bias prevents the development of autonomous definitions of the feminine. In "Psychoanalytic Theory: Another Look," she begins by summarizing Sigmund Freud's theory of femininity and briefly examines how later psychoanalysts, including Karen Horney, Melanie Klein, Ernest Jones, Helene Deutsch, and Marie Bonaparte, reject, revise, or support Freudian views. "The Power of Discourse and the Subordination of the Feminine" and "Questions" are transcripts of interviews containing Irigaray's comments on her groundbreaking 1974 text *Speculum de l'autre femme* (*Speculum of the Other Woman*, 1985) and her replies to commonly asked questions about her theories and methods. These chapters provide readers with accessible discussions of Irigaray's views on conventional psychoanalytic theory, women's liberation movements, mother/daughter relationships, "sexual indifference," the existence of a feminine unconscious, women's lack of agency, and the economic exploitation of women. In "Cosí Fan Tutte," a witty, sophisticated essay critiquing Jacques Lacan, Freud's major twentieth century proponent and Irigaray's former teacher, Irigaray used Lacan's own words to illustrate the hidden biases in his theory of femininity. In the following essay, "The 'Mechanics' of Fluids," she again indirectly challenges Lacanian descriptions of the feminine and exposes the inadequacies in masculinist language systems. In later chapters, such as "Women on the Market," "Commodities Among Themselves," and " 'Frenchwomen,' Stop Trying," Irigaray explores how Western culture's limited definitions of women and femininity reinforce hierarchical male/female social and economic relations.

Irigaray's writing style is highly original. Although she draws on her own extensive knowledge of classic Western philosophy, she does so primarily to demonstrate that traditional knowledge systems have erased women's presence. She rejects the linear reasoning and the conventional forms of argument found in canonical texts and employs a number of subversive strategies, including puns, paradoxical statements, rhetorical questions, parenthetical comments, and quotation marks around problematic terms. The volume's title illustrates one form that Irigaray's playful technique assumes, for the phrase "This Sex Which Is Not One" refers both to the absence of a specifically female sexuality and to the feminine's plural, nonunitary nature. This ambiguous, subversive style—which Irigaray describes as "jamming the theoretical machinery"—serves two interrelated purposes. First, it enables her to critique patriarchal language systems; and second, it allows her to begin inventing an alternative discourse capable of representing and expressing the feminine. The opening and closing essays, "The Looking Glass, from the Other Side" and "When Our Lips Speak Together," provide the most extensive demonstrations of Irigaray's unique style.

Analysis

Throughout the essays collected in *This Sex Which Is Not One*, Irigaray engages in a twofold movement: She simultaneously critiques the hidden male bias in Western philosophical systems and attempts to develop new forms of writing and speaking that reflect women's specificity. Central to this undertaking is her call for a theory of sexual difference in which femininity and masculinity would indicate autonomous, qualitatively different models of subjectivity, or consciousness. Drawing primarily on psychoanalytic insights developed by Freud and Lacan, Irigaray maintains that Western linguistic and philosophical traditions are based on what she calls "sexual indifference," or an unacknowledged conflation of two independent sexes into a single, pseudo-universal model of personhood that subordinates the feminine. In this representational system, which she and other theorists describe as "phallocentric," woman or the feminine is defined as being quantitatively, rather than qualitatively, different from the masculine. Thus, for example, Freud describes the girl's clitoris as a little penis, not as a specifically female organ.

Irigaray argues that by denying women an independent, sexually specific identity, this phallocentric model reduces the feminine to "the inverse, indeed the underside, of the masculine." Woman, for example, is defined only as man's "other." In "The Power of Discourse" and "Questions," she attributes Freud's restrictive account of femininity to this hierarchical binary system. She explains that because sexuality assumes a single, masculine form in Freudian theory, women's sexual pleasure and women's unconscious have meaning only in relation to the masculine: "The feminine is defined as the necessary complement to the operation of male sexuality, and, more often, as a negative image that provides male sexuality with an unfailingly phallic self-representation."

According to Irigaray, this absence of sexually specific representations of the feminine has significant implications for women in Western cultures. Without a language capable of reflecting their specific needs, they lack an autonomous identity and remain silenced, unable to express, or even to recognize, their desires. In "Women on the Market" and "Commodities Among Themselves," she associates this lack of sexually specific representations of the feminine with what she describes as the "ho(m)mo-sexual monopoly," or the homosocial bonding between men that provides the foundation for patriarchal social orders and the heterosexual contract. Basing her arguments on Claude Lévi-Strauss's anthropological study of kinship structures, in which the exchange of women is used to establish social relations among men from different groups, she explains that phallocentric systems prevent women from actively participating in the creation of culture. Because the feminine has value solely in relation to the masculine, women function only as commodities whose circulation between men maintains the existing social order. In other words, women are products whose use-value is derived solely from their mediational role: Men from nonrelated social groups solidify their relationships with one another by exchanging women in marriage. Irigaray further argues that women's restrictive social roles establish a system of rivalry that prevents them from establishing mutually supportive relationships with one another.

Irigaray combines her critique of phallocentric linguistic and social systems with suggestions for the development of an exclusively feminine discourse, or new ways of speaking and writing that are capable of reflecting women's sexually specific needs. Significantly, she does not simply attempt to overturn existing conditions by elevating the feminine over the masculine; as she explains in "Questions," strategies of reversal remain locked in hierarchical binary systems. Instead, she calls for the creation of a specifically feminine language that would exist in addition to, rather than in replacement of, the masculine. The final essay, "When Our Lips Speak Together," illustrates one form that this exclusively feminine writing might take. Irigaray uses poetic language and the figure of lips both to subvert unitary, phallic models of sexuality and to provide alternative representations of female identity which emphasize autonomy and self-sufficiency, while also acknowledging women's interrelatedness. This description of female sexuality provides a significant alternative to the currently existing social system in which women function only as objects of exchange.

Context

Like traditional psychoanalysts, Irigaray explores the ways in which language constructs gendered identities; however, by using her psychoanalytic training to analyze psychoanalysis itself, she exposes its unacknowledged masculine bias. As in *Speculum of the Other Woman* and her later writings, she attempts in *This Sex Which Is Not One* to develop a theory and practice of sexual difference that demonstrates the secularized nature of all Western philosophical and representational systems. This undertaking has important political implications, for Irigaray maintains that the pseudo-neutrality of rational thought and objective knowledge has led to the development of patriarchal social systems that oppress women economically, socially, and psychically. She suggests that the creation of specifically feminine ways of writing and speaking offers the possibility of developing alternate epistemologies and new forms of society.

Irigaray's theory of sexual difference makes a significant contribution to feminist analyses of twentieth century knowledge systems. With the rise in gender studies in the 1980's, increasing attention has been paid to her analysis of the sexualized nature of all linguistic systems and social structures. By exposing the phallocentric foundations of Western culture's reliance on logical rational thought and the subsequent bias in all supposedly neutral accounts of objective knowledge, Irigaray provides theorists with important tools in their attempts to develop alternatives to analytical forms of thinking.

Yet Irigaray's elusive, ambiguous style; her many references to an extensive body of male-authored texts; her descriptions of the feminine as fluid, nonunitary, and plural; and her poetic allusions to women's anatomical parts have led to many debates concerning her work, especially among European American feminists. A number of theorists argue that Irigaray's attempt to develop sexually specific forms of writing and speaking inadvertently supports stereotypical views of the feminine. They maintain that her Lacanian-influenced belief in an all-encompassing phallocentric representational system denies women's agency, thus reinforcing their subordinate status in Western knowledge systems. Others, however, argue that Irigaray's emphasis on an irreducible difference between the masculine and the feminine and her attempts to establish openly sexualized bodies of knowledge indicate radical breaks from the relational masculine/feminine binary oppositions structuring Western thought systems. The confusion concerning Irigaray's theories is made even more problematic by the inaccurate assumptions that Julia Kristeva, Hélène Cixous, and Irigaray represent a single school of "French feminist" thought. There are, however, significant theoretical, stylistic, and political differences between them. Moreover, all three theorists distance themselves in various degrees from twentieth century feminist movements.

Sources for Further Study

Burke, Carolyn. "Irigaray Through the Looking Glass." *Feminist Studies* 7 (Summer, 1981): 288-306. This essay provides a useful overview of Irigaray's career, including her break with Lacan, the role that Jacques Derrida's deconstructive philosophy plays in her theory of feminine writing, and her impact on feminist studies. It offers a highly sympathetic reading of Irigaray's elusive style and insightful summaries of several essays in *This Sex Which Is Not One*, including "The Looking Glass, from the Other Side" and "When Our Lips Speak Together."

Fuss Diana. *Essentially Speaking: Feminism, Nature, and Difference*. New York: Routledge, 1989. Chapter 4, "Luce Irigaray's Language of Essence," summarizes European American debates concerning Irigaray's use of female anatomy to describe feminine writing. In addition to exploring how literal readings of Irigaray's references to lips lead to misinterpretations, this chapter briefly discusses her theory of sexual difference.

Grosz, Elizabeth. *Sexual Subversions: Three French Feminists*. Sydney: Allen & Unwin, 1989. This examination of recent theories of sexual difference situates Irigaray's work in the context of Kristeva's and Michele Montreley's theories of the feminine. In addition to exploring Irigaray's use of Lacanian psychoanalysis and Derridean deconstruction, the two chapters on Irigaray summarize key concepts, including her analysis of phallocentric language systems, her attempt to develop autonomous representations of the feminine, and her call for alternative descriptions of mother/daughter relationships.

Moi, Toril. *Sexual/Textual Politics: Feminist Literary Theory*. New York: Routledge, 1983. A comparative analysis of European American feminism and French theories of the feminine developed by Cixous, Irigaray, and Kristeva. The chapter on Irigaray discusses *Speculum of the Other Woman*, *This Sex Which Is Not One*, and Irigaray's reception in the United States.

Whitford, Margaret. *Luce Irigaray: Philosophy in the Feminine*. New York: Routledge, 1991. This book provides an extremely comprehensive account of Irigaray's theories and an analysis of her contributions to twentieth century psychoanalytic and philosophic traditions. It includes extensive primary and secondary bibliographies of French and English texts.

AnnLouise Keating

A THOUSAND ACRES

Author: Jane Smiley (1949-   )
Type of work: Novel
Type of plot: Domestic realism
Time of plot: 1979 and 1982
Locale: Northwest Iowa
First published: 1991

Principal characters:

VIRGINIA (GINNY) COOK SMITH, the narrator and the eldest of
    Larry Cook's three daughters, the mainstay of the Cook
    homestead
LAURENCE (LARRY) COOK, a proud Iowa farmer
JESSIE (JESS) CLARK, Harold Clark's prodigal son
ROSE COOK LEWIS, the second daughter of Larry Cook
CAROLINE COOK RASMUSSEN, Larry Cook's youngest daughter,
    the only one not interested in maintaining the farm
HAROLD CLARK, Jess's father
TYLER (TY) SMITH, Ginny's husband, a hard-working farmer
PETE LEWIS, Rose's husband
LOREN CLARK, Jess's brother
PAMMY and LINDA LEWIS, daughters of Rose and Pete

Form and Content

    A Thousand Acres reconceives *King Lear* for an American landscape. Shake-speare's tragedy of a sovereign who prematurely relinquishes power to his daughters becomes a story of the disintegration of a Midwest farming dynasty. Set in 1979, in Zebulon County of northwestern Iowa, the novel is narrated by Ginny, the eldest of Laurence Cook's three rival daughters. She recounts the disastrous consequences of the patriarch's decision to retire from the management of their vast, successful spread and to divide it among his grownup heirs: Ginny, thirty-six; Rose, thirty-four; and Caroline, twenty-eight. Caroline, a lawyer who has moved to Des Moines, wants no part of the arrangement, and Larry regrets ceding control of the largest farm in the region, one that he has expanded to a thousand acres. Ginny and Rose, the new proprietors, have had a reason to resent their father's abusive rule. Cast also in this rural drama are the neighboring Clarks, whose sons Loren and Jess are to their doddering father Harold as Edgar and Edmund are to Shakespeare's sightless Gloucester. When Harold is blinded in a farming accident for which Rose's husband Pete bears responsibility, the event roughly parallels the moment when Gloucester's eyes are plucked out by Lear's son-in-law. *A Thousand Acres* is not so schematic, however, that it merely transposes every plot twist and character trait in *King Lear* to the contemporary American heartland.

A Thousand Acres follows the arc of a woman's enlightenment, her transformation from submission to rebellion against a lethal order imposed by oppressive men. The Ginny whom the reader first encounters is a devoted wife and daughter who rises before 5:00 A.M. each day to prepare breakfast for three households that inhabit the spacious family farm: her widowed father Larry; her sister Rose, who is recovering from a mastectomy, and Rose's husband Pete; and Ginny's own husband, Ty, and herself. Because of five miscarriages, Ginny, who longs to be a mother, is childless, but she adores her two young nieces, Pammy and Linda, whom Rose has sent to boarding school. When their own mother died shortly after Caroline's birth, Ginny and Rose reared their youngest sister, and both are hurt by Caroline's aloofness and her decision to live in Des Moines.

So is Larry, the patriarch who uses the occasion of a pig roast hosted by Harold Clark in honor of his newly returned son Jess to announce startling news; though still vigorous, Larry intends to retire and consign his farm to his three daughters. When Caroline, a lawyer with no interest in raising hogs, balks at the proposal, he disinherits her. Though Larry continues to live on it, the farm that he has spent his life amassing and cultivating now belongs to Ginny and Rose. Conflict soon arises, however, between the cantankerous father and his two eldest daughters. Larry regrets that he ever surrendered control, and, in a clear parallel to act III, scene 2 of *King Lear*, the old man wanders off alone into the night during a raging thunderstorm after calling Rose and Ginny "whores." Coming from Larry, who refuses to acknowledge his sexual exploitation of his own daughters, the term is not an idle insult.

Smiley has added an element to the relationship between the patriarch and his daughters which was undreamt of in Shakespeare's play; as children, Rose and Ginny were victims of their father's sexual abuse. Rose is tormented by memories of coerced incest, and she harbors resentment toward Larry for it. At first, Ginny denies such unseemly occurrences in her own past and suggests that Rose's recollections might be fantasy more than memory. Under the force of exceptional circumstances, however, Ginny recalls how her beloved father came to her bedroom and violated her. That new awareness of the sordid family secret shapes Ginny's subsequent behavior and colors how she narrates the events that lead to the collapse of the Cooks' agrarian kingdom. Even after Ginny and Rose defeat an attempt by Larry and Caroline to recover the farm by court order, Ginny loses enthusiasm for the enterprise. She abandons Ty, whose attitudes toward agriculture and marriage she now recognizes as indistinguishable from Larry's brutal husbandry. Abandoning the thousand acres, she drives off to Minnesota. Ginny returns three years later to assume guardianship of Pammy and Linda after Rose's death from cancer. They live, modestly, in town, after the failure of the Cook dominion. A conglomerate named The Heartland Corporation now lays claim to a thousand acres of once-fertile Iowa soil.

Analysis

It is not necessary to be familiar with *King Lear* in order to read Smiley's novel as an absorbing study in family tensions on a Midwestern farm during a time—a decade before the book's publication—of economic crisis in American agriculture. For those who know Shakespeare, the most striking departure in Smiley's book is her decision to present the events through the eyes of one of the sisters. Ginny becomes an Iowa Goneril, but because she is telling the story and because of the way in which she tells it, she emerges as more sympathetic than Shakespeare's cruel, ungrateful daughter. *A Thousand Acres* is a woman's book—written by a woman, narrated by a woman, and presenting a woman's perspective on a powerful story known as the tragedy of men. The collapse of an agricultural empire and of an Iowa family are recounted by a woman who rejects the abusive values represented by both.

In remarks that she delivered after receiving the National Book Critics Circle Award for *A Thousand Acres*, Jane Smiley described her novel as "a complex argument against a certain kind of farming and land use, that is leading us towards an environmental disaster, the destruction of the lives of people and of the moral life of our country." *A Thousand Acres* is set in the recent past, during a severe slump, particularly in the Midwest in which Smiley—a native of Los Angeles who grew up in St. Louis, studied at the University of Iowa, and taught at Iowa State University— was living.

A Thousand Acres is not merely a mirror of harsh conditions in contemporary Iowa or an exercise in nostalgia for the family farms that were being displaced. It is a critique of patriarchal arrogance, the way that one stubborn man dominates and abuses his female children, and, more fundamentally, the way that human beings, like rapacious males, assert control over nature, as though the environment were theirs to subdue. Violation of the land is a sexual metaphor by which Smiley understands what goes wrong with the Cooks and on the thousand acres that they presume to possess. There is an obvious parallel between Larry Cook's exploitation of his daughters and his appropriation of Iowa soil. As if to avenge human offenses against the environment, Ginny's miscarriages and the cancer that kills Rose are linked to chemicals in the water that are a by-product of large-scale farming. Ginny's final glimpse of the thousand acres that no Cook will ever till again is of a landscape poisoned, like the family itself, by man's abuse.

A pacifist vegetarian, Jess Clark, who is more attractive than their own husbands to Ginny and Rose, offers an alternative to the ethic of violent domination represented by other men in Zebulon County. Rejecting the wanton application of toxic chemicals on the Cooks' property, which is devoted largely to raising hogs for slaughter, Jess plans to introduce organic methods of cultivating healthful grains and vegetables. Jess is defeated, however, by local inertia and his own inability to commit. Even after Larry's death, the spirit of the imperious father prevails. Renouncing triumphalist visions of family achievement and national expansion, Ginny, in her final words to Ty, offers a feminist critique of patriarchal presumption:

> You see this grand history, but I see blows. I see taking what you want because you want it, then making something up that justifies what you did. I see getting others to pay the price, then covering up and forgetting what the price was. Do I think Daddy came up

with beating and fucking us on his own? . . . No, I think he had lessons, and those lessons were part of the package, along with the land and the lust to run things exactly the way he wanted no matter what, poisoning the water and destroying the topsoil and buying bigger and bigger machinery, and then feeling certain that all of it was "right," as you say.

Smiley writes convincingly about quotidian activities on a large Midwestern farm, about the details of planting tomatoes, canning sausages, and building slurries. It is usually, as Ginny notes, "a life where many things go unsaid." By giving those things utterance, this novel and its defiant woman narrator exorcise the horror and begin to restore a proper balance to the world.

Context

Although Smiley's seven previous books had received respectful attention, the appearance of *A Thousand Acres* catapulted her into prominence and wealth. Extensively and enthusiastically reviewed, it received two of the most prestigious annual awards—the Pulitzer Prize and the National Book Critics Circle Award. The hardcover and paperback editions were both best-sellers. The category of "women's literature" was widely studied and admired, and the forty-three-year-old author could now count on a large and eager readership for her subsequent books.

A Thousand Acres appeared at a time when incest and paternal sexual abuse were increasingly being discussed in the United States. Scholars were documenting their frequency, prosecutors were bringing lurid cases to public trial, and tabloids, talk shows, and television dramas gravitated toward the topic. Oprah Winfrey's announcement that she had been abused as a child, and, though dismissed in court, accusations that Woody Allen had molested the children he shared with Mia Farrow drew widespread attention to a problem thought to be epidemic. In a manner that is not itself exploitive, Smiley employs the resources of fiction to explore the enduring damage of incest and sexual violation.

Much of Smiley's earlier fiction exposed the hollowness of overbearing males. Her men are often not very sympathetic, and, if her texts are not merely exercises in male-bashing, they are critiques of the oppressive attitudes and practices that she associates with androcracy. Both novellas collected in *Ordinary Love and Good Will* (1989), the book that Smiley published immediately prior to *A Thousand Acres*, are stories of women and children victimized by charismatic men. In particular, *Free Will* exposes Bob Miller, who runs a fifty-five-acre subsistence family farm that, to an outsider, seems like paradise, as a destructive egomaniac. He is an earlier avatar of Larry Cook in *A Thousand Acres*, the novel that drew national attention to Smiley's feminist revision of traditional farm fiction.

Sources for Further Study

Carlson, Ron. "King Lear in Zebulon County." *The New York Times Book Review*, November 13, 1991, 12. Reluctant to invoke *King Lear* as a paradigm, Carlson analyzes *A Thousand Acres* as a novel about American farming, the loss of family farms, an d the power of the family. He praises the vividness and immediacy of Smiley's rural Iowa. He contends that one of the novel's strengths is its selection of Ginny, who is reluctantly drawn into the events and made to acknowledge stark realities, as storyteller. Carlson reads the novel as an examination of the burdens of daughterhood.

Fuller, Edmund. "Kind and Unkind Daughters." *The Sewanee Review* 101, no. 2 (Spring, 1993): 50-52. Comparing *A Thousand Acres* with another variation of *King Lear, The Quondam Wives* (1993), by English author Mairi MacInnes, Fuller prefers Smiley's version. He finds both novels woman-oriented and contends that Shakespeare's universal vision eludes both. He regrets the lack of redemptive self-knowledge at the conclusion of *A Thousand Acres* and judges Larry's monstrousness to be the novel's greatest weakness.

Purkiss, Diane. "Uncovering Iowa." *The Times Literary Supplement*, October 30, 1992, 20. Purkiss analyzes *A Thousand Acres* as a feminist version of *King Lear*, one that transforms the play's silences into a metaphor for the unspeakableness of incest and rape. Insisting that Smiley, who is intent on uncovering unpalatable truths about women's lives rather than juggling narratives, is not postmodern, Purkiss locates her within the tradition of women revisionists of Shakespeare such as Mary Cowden Clarke and Mary Lamb rather than Virginia Woolf and H. D. She reads *A Thousand Acres* as a realistic novel that offers the pleasures of detailed evocation, of an Iowa that is Eden lost.

Steven G. Kellman

THREE LIVES

Author: Gertrude Stein (1874-1946)
Type of work: Novel
Type of plot: Psychological realism
Time of plot: The early twentieth century
Locale: The fictional town of Bridgepoint
First published: 1909

> *Principal characters:*
> ANNA FEDERNER, a forty-year-old German American domestic
>   servant
> MISS MATHILDA, Anna's employer
> MRS. LEHNTMAN, a widow, Anna's closest friend
> MELANCTHA HERBERT, an eighteen-year-old mulatta
> ROSE JOHNSON, Melanctha's married friend
> JANE HARDEN, Melanctha's footloose friend with a yearning for
>   men
> DR. JEFF CAMPBELL, physician to Melanctha's mother
> JEM RICHARDS, a gambler
> LENA MAINZ, a young German American girl
> MRS. HAYDON, Lena's overbearing aunt
> HERMAN KREDER, a German American tailor
> MRS. KREDER, Herman's mother

Form and Content

Three Lives consists of three episodes, the novella-length "Melanctha" and two short pieces, "The Good Anna" and "The Gentle Lena." The work is generally called a novel because of its thematic unity, although it is not a novel in the conventional sense of the word. Stein set out to portray "the bottom nature," as she called it, of three lower-middle-class women employed as domestic servants. In all three episodes, Stein pushes language to its extremes, using her rhetoric to reflect salient elements in the three women about whom she writes.

Each of the women—Anna Federner, Melanctha Herbert, and Lena Mainz—represents a generalized type of character, although Melanctha rises above the stereotypical and becomes the best realized character of the three. "Melanctha" is among the first works by a white writer to depict a black character in depth.

The episodes, told in the present with ramblings into the past, are not overtly connected to one another, nor do characters from one episode recur in either of the other two. A major connecting thread from one episode to another is love: Stein uses each episode to speculate on a different kind of love.

Stein, shortly before she wrote *Three Lives*, was herself working through a triangular love affair with May Bookstaver and Mabel Haynes and had, for some time, been

Bookstaver's lover. Much of this book is Stein's attempt to work out her own feelings and organize her own thoughts about love.

The good Anna idolizes her employer, Miss Mary Wadsmith, as she had her previous employers, Dr. Shonjen and Miss Mathilda. Generous to a fault, Anna can always be depended upon—and this is precisely what she wants in her relationships with people. She is fulfilled when others depend upon her. Anna loves her dogs, Peter and Rags, almost as much as she loves her employers, but in her love of both dogs and people, Anna must have control.

Melanctha Herbert's love is quite different from Anna's. Melanctha is a sensuous kind of woman who loves erotically more than spiritually. Her friend Jane Harden has helped to make Melanctha streetwise. She has felt no real emotional attachment to any man, but when Jeff Campbell, a physician, comes to treat her mother, she finds him attractive, and they fall into a relationship in which neither has very deep emotional involvement. Melanctha throws Jeff over for Jem Richards, whose life as a gambler offers little hope of stability. He tells Melanctha that he does not love her at about the same time that her friend Rose Johnson tells Melanctha that she never wants to see her again. Melanctha contracts tuberculosis and, as this segment of *Three Lives* ends, she is alone and confined to a home for "consumptives." She dies there.

Lena Mainz represents antilove more than she does any positive form of love. She lacks the emotional depth to feel any profound emotions, and her husband, Herman Kreder, is as emotionally bankrupt as Lena. Herman, who is twenty-eight years old, lives with his parents, who dominate him completely. When it is arranged that Herman and Lena will marry, Herman runs away, delaying the nuptials for a week, but his father brings him back and the wedding takes place.

The main implication in this bleak story seems to be that human beings are meant to reproduce, to continue the species. Herman does this. Lena, having borne four children, is expendable. Her death is not mourned by those who knew her or, indeed, by many who read about her in *Three Lives*.

Analysis

Three Lives, an extensive literary experiment in language and psychology, is generally called a novel, as noted above, because of the unifying thematic threads that run through it. The book is more than three disparate episodes gathered together in a single volume. Much influenced by Gustave Flaubert's *Trois Contes* (1877; *Three Tales*, 1903), *Three Lives* is as realistic in its recording of the speech patterns of commonplace people as Stein can make it. Stein's medical research took her into lower-middle-class neighborhoods in Baltimore, where she became fascinated by the way people spoke. The characters in her books speak in the same repetitive, stream-of-consciousness constructions that Stein heard from the working-class people of Baltimore with whom she came into contact.

Stein is unfailingly interested in the psychological underpinnings of the characters of the three servant women she has chosen to portray. She reveals each in her relationships with other people, and in so doing, she develops with considerable insight and sensitivity three distinctly different personalities, each with a unique view of love and life.

Lena (whose name suggests that she is a "leaner") is best summed up in her response when her aunt, Mrs. Haydon, presses her to marry Herman Kreder, whom she has no desire to marry. Lena merely tells her aunt that she will do whatever she (Mrs. Haydon) tells her is right to do. She agrees to marry Herman because Mrs. Haydon wants her to.

Juxtaposed with Lena in this episode is Herman, who is as weak and spineless as his bride-to-be. When his parents decide that he will marry Lena, they tell Mrs. Haydon not to discuss the matter with their son. Mrs. Kreder tells Herman that Lena is thrifty, a good worker, and never wants her own way. Herman's response is a grunt that is taken for assent.

Unlike Lena, both Anna and Melanctha have considerable backbone. Anna is more resolute than Melanctha, but she is also more than twice Melanctha's age and appears to have gained self-confidence over the years. Anna's pattern in life has been to seek out bungling, dependent people who need her, then to run their lives for them.

Anna is unswerving in her notions of decency, as a result of which she occasionally suffers grave disappointments, as she did when she discovered that Mrs. Lehntman, whom Stein describes as the "romance in Anna's life," has been involved in something shady with the doctor with whom she is working. Having once made a judgment of this sort, Anna is intractable.

Melanctha's development depends on Stein's showing her in relation to her two close female friends, Rose Johnson and Jane Harden, as well as in relation to the three men who are important in her life: her father, Jeff Campbell, and Jem Richards. As it turns out, Melanctha loses everyone she cares about, but she has never really cared deeply about anyone. Her death is sad but falls far short of being tragic because of Stein's portrayal of Melanctha as insensitive. Stein exposes her readers neither to Melanctha's eventual physical decline nor to her death throes. Instead, she reports Melanctha's death almost incidentally at the end of this longest section of *Three Lives*.

As Stein portrays them, both Anna and Lena, despite the great differences in their personalities, are mundane characters whose intellectual and emotional compasses are limited. Stein captures their banality well, particularly in her faithful depiction of their speech patterns. The endless repetition in their dialogue reinforces the lack of drama and the constant recurrences in their lives.

Melanctha, however, is a far more romantic character than is either Anna or Lena. As a mulatta, she has a foot in the black world and one in the white, even though the milieu in which Stein presents her is black. Jeff Campbell, a professional who represents the rising black upper middle class, displays many of the characteristics and values of whites.

Melanctha, however, rejects Jeff in favor of Jem, a man who fits Stein's conceptions of the black men of her day, only to be discarded by him. Melanctha is the most fully realized character in *Three Lives*, although each of Stein's three major characters is memorable.

The components of *Three Lives* reflect the personal problems with which Stein was dealing when she wrote the book: moral uncertainty, fear of rejection, mixed emotions about her relationship with May Bookstaver, and sexual desire without a stable object toward which she might direct it. Alice B. Toklas was not yet in Stein's life when *Three Lives* was being conceived, although the two were living together by the time it was published. This book, in a sense, is a cry by a highly intelligent woman who had not yet found what she was seeking for herself.

Context

For Gertrude Stein, *Three Lives* was a quite personal book. In writing it, Stein did not consciously aim to write a feminist tract, and the book did not turn into one. It is a penetrating psychological study of three distinctly different women and of the three faces of love that they represent. As women's issues have become a prominent concern in assessing and analyzing literature, however, *Three Lives* has emerged as an important book in that regard.

The world of *Three Lives* is one of male dominance. The three women whom Stein portrays are locked by their social class into a setting that definitely limits their possibilities in life. Anna Federner, who shows definite signs of having lesbian tendencies, lived a life of willing self-sacrifice, inviting—indeed, needing—people to take advantage of her good will and generosity. Perhaps this is Anna's means of expiation for essentially having desires of which she, as staunchly moral as she is and living in the age in which she lived, can hardly approve and possibly cannot admit even to herself. If she has lesbian tendencies, as seems quite probable, it is unthinkable that she has ever acted on them or has even considered doing so.

Lena has the sexuality of a slug. She seems to be living life just to get it over with. She has no enthusiasms, no *joie de vivre*. She is in a class with Frank Norris's McTeague (*McTeague*, 1899), a fictional character with whom Stein may have been familiar. McTeague has a bit more gumption than does Lena, who seems totally lacking in that characteristic.

The news that Lena has died leaves some readers thinking, "Thank heaven. What a terrible mother she would have made!" Then, however, one remembers that her children will be left with Herman Kreder, and the scenario darkens. Naturally, someone—his parents or Mrs. Haydon—will probably tell Herman to remarry, and he will accommodate that wish.

Lena might be viewed as a woman who has been beaten down by a male-dominated society, but more accurately, she is a person so lacking in personality and potential that, brought up in nearly any other environment, she probably would have been no different. Indeed, viewing Lena in medical terms, one might wonder whether she suffered from a deficiency in her body chemistry. So lacking is she in emotion and personality that she cannot even be viewed as depressive.

Only Melanctha emerges from *Three Lives* as someone who finds a degree of normal joy in life—or, at least, has the potential to do so. Melanctha, however, is young and undeveloped. Emotionally, she is still sending out trial balloons. Her selfhood is tied to the personalities of the men in her life, and they treat her only as an object. The women in her life—Rose Johnson and Jane Harden—certainly provide her with no role models.

Sources for Further Study

Bloom, Harold, ed. *Gertrude Stein*. New York: Chelsea House, 1986. Part of the Modern Critical Views Series, this work includes fifteen essays on Stein, a chronology, and a bibliography. Donald Sutherland's essay on *Three Lives* and Richard Bridgman's on *Things as They Are* and *Three Lives* are instructive.

Hobhouse, Janet. *Everyone Who Was Anybody: A Biography of Gertrude Stein*. New York: G. P. Putnam's Sons, 1989. This book gives a good run-down of the significant people who frequented 27 rue de Fleurus. Well illustrated.

Mellow, James R. *Charmed Circle: Gertrude Stein and Company*. New York: Praeger, 1974. The well-illustrated book captures the vibrant spirit of the circle of painters, sculptors, writers, and fascinating passersby that came within the Stein-Toklas social orbit.

Souhami, Diana. *Gertrude and Alice*. New York: HarperCollins, 1991. The most thorough account of Gertrude Stein's long lesbian relationship with Alice B. Toklas, this book shows how strong Toklas was and how she dominated many aspects of her forty-year association with Stein.

_____ . Introduction to *Three Lives*. New York: Bantam Books, 1992. In her thirteen-page introduction, Souhami provides a strong feminist reading of *Three Lives*.

Sprigge, Elizabeth. *Gertrude Stein: Her Life and Work*. New York: Harper Brothers, 1957. Like Mellow's book, this well-written biography is replete with excellent illustrations. Tells much about the genesis of *Three Lives*.

R. Baird Shuman

THROUGH THE IVORY GATE

Author: Rita Dove (1952-   )
Type of work: Novel
Type of plot: Psychological realism
Time of plot: Between the early 1960's and the mid-1970's
Locale: Phoenix, Arizona; and Akron and Oberlin, Ohio
First published: 1992

> *Principal characters:*
> VIRGINIA EVANS, the protagonist
> CLAYTON, a tall, deeply sensitive gay musician with whom
>   Virginia falls in love and has an affair while in college
> GRANDMA EVANS, Virginia's maternal grandmother
> AUNT CARRIE, Virginia's father's sister
> BELLE, Virginia's mother
> TERRY, a handsome black architect

Form and Content

Rita Dove's *Through the Ivory Gate* uses a series of flashbacks that weave a tapestry of narratives that span three generations of African American women. At the center of the narratives is Virginia, a musician, artist, and puppeteer whose memories generate the flashbacks that serve as counterpoints to a present narrative about Virginia, who works with children in a public school, teaching them how to use their imaginations through puppetry. She returns to Akron, Ohio, her childhood home, to make contact with her memories and with at least two important people in her life—her Aunt Carrie and her Grandma Evans. Virginia, a well-educated and cultured woman, passionately and unpretentiously immerses herself in the study and appreciation of classical music, cello playing, puppetry, theater, and literature. Throughout the narrative, she grows increasingly aware of her blackness in the world of the early 1970's. This awareness is generated by her recollection of past memories about being black as a child in Akron, Ohio, a teenager in Arizona, and a college student in Wisconsin. Her memories contextualize her present experience and allow her to come to grips with her emotions and thoughts on issues of race, gender relationships, and adulthood.

While working as an artist-in-residence in the elementary school, Virginia discovers details about her family history that date back to the turn of the century. One of the central discoveries in the work is that of her father's affair with his sister, Aunt Carrie, when he was a teenager. Aunt Carrie calmly and candidly narrates this scandalous story to Virginia, explaining in the process why she has been ostracized from Virginia's family for so many years. This revelation also provides insight into Belle's (Virginia's mother's) dominating personality. Belle, according to Aunt Carrie's narrative, demands that the family move to Arizona to get away from the painful memories of Akron. Virginia seeks out her relatives with a combination of trepidation and curiosity; however, she develops a sense of her own identity through the historical grounding that they provide. Virginia does not want to be like them, but she learns from them.

Virginia's life, as presented in the nonlinear back-and-forth of flashbacks and memories, is characterized by progressive emotional, intellectual, and psychological growth. Dove uses the puppet/doll metaphor to provide insights into Virginia's development. The novel opens with an explosive but revealing dilemma in which Virginia as a child is given a Sambo doll to play with along with her white Penelope doll. Virginia rejects the Sambo doll. The act haunts her for life, and in later passages, she has dreams in which she tries to explain the symbolic significance of the Sambo doll in her life. Her dreams are prompted by her sense of regret and guilt for having betrayed her core self—her black self. Later, as a puppeteer, she creates a doll called Gina who becomes her alter ego. Gina, black, afro-haired and dressed in Afrocentric garb, represents a self-conscious attempt by Virginia to assert her blackness. The puppet becomes a way for her to declare her racial identity.

Virginia's romantic attachments reveal more about her character. Her selfish and driven side emerges during her affair with Terry, a young black architect whom she eventually abandons in the interest of her professional aspirations. After her affair with Clayton while in college, she develops an emotional toughness when he rejects her after he realizes that he cannot change his preference for men. Her evolving selfishness appears again when she develops an unbalanced relationship with a child, Renee, which she fails to sustain because of her inability to recognize the child's intense and jealous attachment to her.

At the end of the novel, Virginia leaves Akron to pursue a career as an actress. She leaves with a greater understanding of herself in the context of her race and her family history. The women of her family—her grandmother and her Aunt Carrie, and through flashbacks and recollections, her mother, Belle—provide this knowledge. The women also supply her with a knowledge of the tradition of strength and independence which she claims as a part of her makeup and identity.

Analysis

Dove's focus on the experience of a female protagonist makes this work fit subject matter for a feminist reading. Such a reading reveals that Dove tries to shape female characters who have a strong sense of themselves and who assume the right to explore their creativity in self-involved ways. In this sense, Virginia represents an important portrayal of the woman who has evolved out of the feminist movement of the 1960's and 1970's. Virginia's crucial decisions are founded on a conscious challenge of the stereotypical roles of the female—that of wife and homemaker. She likes children but is clearly not "a natural" with them, and she does not betray any "maternal instincts." Virginia is decidedly "unmotherly." Her quest for self-understanding constitutes the feminine equivalent of the archetypal journey into the "heart of darkness." In her journey into her psychic interior, she is guided by both male and female characters whose relationships with her allow her to come to grips with her relationship with herself.

This distinctly feminine journey becomes complicated by the parallel journey that characterizes Virginia's life. Her memories and the manner in which they emerge in her mind indicate that racial questions are crucial to her understanding of herself. She has experienced direct racism, yet she has had the peculiar experience of living an ostensibly white existence in terms of her artistic and social interests and activities. Dove expands the concept of the woman as intellectual and the black woman as free of any limitations that have been imposed by society through her positive portrayal of Virginia. Part of this articulation rests on the sophisticated narrative style in which the central character demonstrates her profound and wide-ranging intelligence through her contemplation of classical music, anthropology, race theory, classical puppetry, and the sociopolitical state of African Americans in American theater. These subjects are effectively woven into the narrative in a manner that makes them appear to be elemental features of Virginia's character. Such natural assumptions about intellectualism and race and gender equity as expressed in the work demonstrate Dove's own political inclinations, which suggest that the African American female has the capacity to challenge the limitations that society places on her.

Dove's shaping of character is deftly rendered. Her often flawed characters have peculiar qualities that make them engaging. In many ways, however, Dove has a tendency to understate or downplay conflict and tension in her writing. She constantly removes the characters from potentially explosive situations as soon as they appear to be moving toward an emotional complexity that could challenge the narrative control of the author. As a result, the work at times appears somewhat contrived and self-consciously constructed. Nevertheless, Dove displays her ability to sketch quickly characters who leave an indelible mark on the reader's psyche. Characters such as Parker, the puppeteer; Clayton, the gay musician; Aunt Carrie, the woman with a tainted and mysterious past; Ernie, Virginia's father, whose peculiar idiosyncrasies make him at once mysterious and unique; and Belle, whom the reader rarely meets but constantly hears about through the emotionally complex filter of Virginia's mind, are all distinct, engaging, and compelling characters.

The structure of the novel allows the chronological sequence of events to be presented through a complex system of echoes and connections. Dove uses dreams, literary and musical criticism, proverbs, anecdotes, essays, dramatic dialogue, and simple oral narrative techniques to render her story through the eclectic mixture of styles that one normally associates with poetry. Thematically, also, the novel shares much of what fascinates and engages Dove in her poetry. The art of making the mundane details of the simple histories of ordinary people resonate with sublime poetry is central to what Dove seeks to do in collections such as *Museum* (1992) and the Pulitzer Prize-winning *Thomas and Beulah* (1986). As do those two collections of poetry, *Through the Ivory Gate* gives attention to the histories of African American peasant folk and the impact of such histories on those African Americans who have come from that stock. In her work, Rita Dove celebrates the power and beauty of these lives.

Context

Dove's distinction with this work lies in her desire to explore an element of the black woman's experience that is not often explored in much of American literature. Dove's protagonist is, like Dove, an intelligent and profoundly educated woman whose commitment to the study and performance of art defies stereotypical perceptions of the African American woman as nonintellectual and wholly "passionate." Dove, unlike a number of black women novelists, locates her work in the American heartland, the Midwest, and situates her characters as the typical figures described as the backbone of America—middle-class college-educated people. In so doing, she succeeds in broadening the reader's perception of what constitutes the African American experience.

This novel celebrates Virginia's ability to assert her right to make her own decisions about her life and its direction. The characters of three other women in the work reflect this quality of independence and strength: Aunt Carrie, the isolated and victimized woman who has an affair with her brother; Grandmother Evans, a strong black woman who determines whom she is going to marry and further determines how her husband must behave in relation to her through force of arms; and Belle, Virginia's mother, who guides the family away from Akron and the negative histories associated with it to a new life in Arizona. Indeed, these women are all pivotal to the work, and they literally shape the lives of all the men in the work.

As a novel about art and artists, *Through the Ivory Gate* is a timely work that chronicles a period in American history when the role of women was assuming a distinctive identity that would affect society in the late 1970's and early 1980's. Dove shows this movement to be grounded on the efforts of women from decades before the 1970's.

Sources for Further Study

McDowell, Robert. "The Awakening Vision of Rita Dove." *Callaloo* 9, no. 1 (Winter, 1986): 61-70. In this article, which focuses on Dove's poetry, McDowell celebrates the writer's instincts as a storyteller and her distinct style of "assembling" seemingly eclectic narrative modes into a cohesive vision.

Ryman, Geoff. "Nothing Succeeds Like Virginia." *The New York Times Book Review*, October 11, 1992, 11-12. Ryman's review is a positive appraisal of the work that identifies as its central theme the black woman artist coming of age in a racist world. He comments on the poetic influence on her narrative style.

Stitt, Peter. "Coherence through Place in Contemporary American Poetry." *The Georgia Review* 40, no. 4 (Winter, 1986): 1021-1033. Stitt looks briefly at Dove's narrative style of the understated and the unsaid as evidence of her maturity as a poet with a strong narrative inclination. The article discusses primarily *Thomas and Beulah*.

Vendler, Helen. "In the Zoo of the New." *The New York Review of Books* 33, no. 16
(October 23, 1986): 47-52. Vendler, reviewing *Thomas and Beulah*, points to a key
factor of Dove's writing that bears uncanny relevance to her fiction. Vendler argues
that Dove eschews editorializing and leading the reader.

Kwame S. N. Dawes

TIRRA LIRRA BY THE RIVER

Author: Jessica Anderson
Type of work: Novel
Type of plot: Social criticism
Time of plot: The late 1940's to the late 1970's
Locale: Brisbane and Sydney, Australia, and London, England
First published: 1978

> *Principal characters:*
> NORA ROCHE, a restless, frustrated romantic
> GRACE ROCHE, Nora's sister, who lives out most of her life in the family home
> COLIN PORTEOUS, Nora's husband, an aggressive bully
> DOROTHY IREY, the Roche family's neighbor, who murders her husband and all of her children but one
> OLIVE PARTRIDGE, Nora's friend from her youth who experiences success and happiness

Form and Content

In *Tirra Lirra by the River*, expatriate Australian Nora Roche Porteous comes back to suburban Brisbane to live out her days in her family home after forty-five years away. She arrives with pneumonia, and alternating between the present and the past, she ends up reconstructing and restoring her sense of self. Spinning her "globe of memory" so that even its dark side is no longer hidden, Nora reviews her lifelong quest for self-acceptance, self-knowledge, and freedom, a journey often foiled by the oppressive requirements of the traditional female role.

Now in her seventies, Nora remembers herself as an imaginative girl, whose embroideries earned high praise though she did not think much of them at the time. Restless and unhappy, an outsider in her provincial hometown, she escapes through relentless walking and through her imagination. An avid reader, she recites Alfred Lord Tennyson's poem "Lady of Shallot," from which the book's title is taken. Through the distortion of a cheap piece of window glass, she envisions her own Camelot in her backyard, complete with a dim, grief-filled memory of Lancelot. After her friend Olive Partridge inherits enough money to leave Brisbane, Nora's vision of other, better worlds nudges her into marriage with Colin Porteous. Thinking that she is leaving behind stodgy, rule-bound tradition, she moves with him to Sydney. Like the Lady of Shallot, however, Nora dies many times over in the world of reality.

In her marriage, Nora is at first as submissive as Porteous is domineering. Initially sexually unresponsive, when Nora begins to respond in bed, her husband is horrified at her unfeminine behavior and chastises her to "just lie still." Also to her husband's distaste, Nora finds friends—a single woman dressmaker, who teaches her to sew, and a possibly gay man. During the Great Depression of the 1930's, Porteous demands that they move in with his mother, a move that Nora does not want but that she does not fight. Under the additional thumb of her mother-in-law, without money or friends, Nora becomes a virtual prisoner in the house. Porteous eventually asks for a divorce, for he has found someone else. He justifies his unfaithfulness with his conviction that Nora was an unfit wife.

In her newfound freedom, Nora takes a boat to England, but London too fails to live up to her expectations of Camelot. After a shipboard affair during which she becomes pregnant, Nora has a humiliating, illegal abortion which nearly kills her. She then gets a job as a theatrical costumer and spends the damp winters chronically ill with bronchitis. After a facelift that leaves her face stiff and unnatural, she attempts suicide. Nora recovers and moves in with two women to form a comfortable, if emotionally unattached, home at Number Six. When the household breaks up, Nora returns to Australia.

Having faced her most painful memories, Nora begins to recover from her pneumonia. Enjoying the sun in the backyard, she discovers that her traditional sister Grace has created a green Eden despite years of drought by composting, a mulching method not then accepted as a gardening technique. Gradually, she settles once again into life in Brisbane, but without the desperate walking of her youth. In the final paragraph, Nora remembers that her true Lancelot, her father, died when she was six years old. The pain of that trauma, she realizes, stunted her ability to access her deeper emotions and kept her looking for something external—a Lancelot, a place—to make her happy. Now, with her new sense of completeness, Nora knows that she can take care of herself; she is finally "home."

Analysis

The theme of *Tirra Lirra by the River*, the woman artist's search for self within the constraints of the traditional female role, is connected to Jessica Anderson's use of imagery from Tennyson's poem "The Lady of Shallot." Tennyson's main character is a weaver, as Nora is an embroiderer. Nora is as much an outsider in her hometown on the Brisbane river as the Lady in her island tower. Nora, too, sees the world through the reflection in a mirror, the mirror of books, and yearns for Camelot, some larger life away from the constraints of post-World War I suburbia. Her incomplete childhood memory of "the nod of a plume" also conjures up the image of a Lancelot. Nora, however, does not heed the poem's warning: that following Lancelot's song would mean her death and that even the mythical Camelot offered no equitable place for women.

Nora's physical and mental journeys echo the quests undertaken by medieval knights. As she travels from Brisbane to Sydney, then to London, and back to Brisbane, she takes many wrong turns and faces many dangerous trials. Her difficulties stem from the fact that her life choices are limited by the traditional female role, a role to which she generally submits passively. Also, her decisions are often made without any understanding of herself or the world, just as the Lady, unaware of the consequences of the curse, rushes to the window at the sound of Lancelot's song. That look at the world results in her death.

Nora's journey toward spiritual death begins with her marriage. She first looks at her husband as her knight in shining armor, but she soon learns the repressiveness of the female role in patriarchal marriage, with its traditions of legal, sexual, and economic subjection. Despite her attempt to free herself with the move to London, there, once again, she experiences the indignities particular to her female role. Searching for love and sexual fulfillment, she has a shipboard affair with a married man and then, alone, undergoes a nearly fatal abortion. Her search for physical beauty results in a mummifying facelift and causes her to attempt suicide.

Her search for herself is also constrained. Her identity as an expatriate in London and her emotional distance from the residents of Number Six also keep intact her outsider status. She maintains the mask that hides her inner self and fails to find roots in her new country. Her job as a theatrical costumer provides some economic independence, but it does not fulfill her as an artist. Like the results of the facelift, Nora's work is symbolic of her masking her true nature.

Yet while Nora suffers many "deaths" and difficulties in her life, she does not finally physically die, like the Lady of Shallot, without having overcome her sense of isolation and inferiority. Through an uncensored reweaving of the tapestry of her life and by facing buried emotional realities, she comes to self-awareness and self-acceptance. Unlike the Lady, she survives and is strengthened by her look at the real world. Nora's final vision of her father's funeral, the loss of her true Lancelot, provides the insight into her early emotional death that frees her to live in relative peace.

Nora's personal search ending in self-acceptance and awareness parallels another, political, theme in the novel. Her struggles and expatriate status symbolize Australia's historic status with England. Since its eighteenth century appropriation as a British penal colony, many Anglo-Australians believed that their country was morally and culturally inferior to Great Britain, a perception shared by the English. This sense of insignificance led many Australians to imitate British habits or to leave home for England and other places with "real" culture and a longer, more respected history. That attitude changed during the nationalism movement in the 1970's. Australians stopped looking overseas for their identity and began to examine themselves. This movement created an increasing regard for things Australian, particularly in the arts, and a growing interest the country's native, aboriginal culture. While Anderson does not assert that Australia is paradise, Nora's discovery of Grace's Eden in her own backyard underscores the author's love for her home country.

Context

The most highly regarded of Anderson's novels, *Tirra Lirra by the River* won the Miles Franklin Award and the Australian Natives Association Literature Award. Feminists praised the book as a paradigm of the oppressiveness of the lives of women born early in the twentieth century. Women had to face the tyrannies of place, patriarchal marriage and family, illegal abortion, and ideals of youthful feminine beauty. Like those women, Nora has no role models to follow should her search for herself fall outside the traditional boundaries of women's sphere. Her marriage, shipboard affair, job, and life at Number Six are Nora's attempts to find her way within those narrow boundaries. The consequences of her choices are sometimes disastrous—the abortion nearly kills her, the facelift makes her face an unnatural mask. When she does connect with some deeper part of herself, as when she awakens sexually, she is slapped down by those enforcing her traditional role.

Alongside Nora, four other female characters depict various options for women's lives early in the century. Dorothy Irey marries a doctor and lives in "the best home in the street," but the public facade conceals Dorothy's rage against her stultifying domestic role, which explodes when she kills her husband, her children, and herself. Dorothy needed the freedom that a larger life would provide, which Nora was seeking in her travels. Olive Partridge—who leaves Brisbane, becomes a successful novelist, and later marries and remains happily childless—is Anderson's model for a freedom that eluded both Dorothy and Nora. Unlike Nora, Olive accepted her identity as an artist and found both personal happiness and professional success. Like Olive, the character Ida Mayo is a single, successful woman. Her professional success, however, is in the traditional women's field of dressmaking. Another successful woman character is Grace, Nora's older sister and her early nemesis. While traditioanl and limited in many ways, Grace is also strengthened by her deep sense of loyalty toward her country. Her creativity goes into making her home a better place, overcoming the difficulties of life in what was once the Australian bush—something the restless Nora could not do. Grace's initiative and vision cause her to try a new gardening method that turns her drought-stricken home into a green Eden.

Nora's status as an expatriate also symbolizes the outsider status of all women, especially women artists, from the mainstream, male-defined culture. Because of her outsider status in her society, Nora never conceived of herself as an artist, sharing instead society's traditional failure to consider women's crafts—such as her embroidery, dressmaking, and costuming—as art. Only after she is shown her early embroideries, and through her reflection on her life, does she recognize their worth and her own stunted potential as an artist.

Sources for Further Study

Baker, Candida. *Yacker 2: Australian Writers Talk About Their Work.* Sydney: Pan Books, 1987. A collection of interviews with contemporary Australian authors, including Anderson. The interview touches on Anderson's life, her writing technique, Australian nationalism, and expatriation.

Barry, Elaine. "The Expatriate Vision of Jessica Anderson." *Meridian* 3, no. 1 (1984): 3-11. Explores Anderson's use of the theme of expatriation in five of her novels as a vehicle for social satire and as a metaphor for the plight of society's outsider, especially for the life of the artist.

Ellison, Jennifer, ed. *Rooms of Their Own.* Victoria, Australia: Penguin Books, 1986. A collection of interviews with Australian women writers, including Anderson. The author reveals biographical information and discusses her literary influences, as well as the character of Nora in *Tirra Lirra by the River*.

Gallagher, Donat. "Tirra Lirra by the Brisbane River." *Literature in North Queensland*. 10 (1981): 101-110. A generally favorable review of Anderson's novel, exploring themes of memory and imagination and the author's use of various symbols to layer the meaning of the narrative.

Haynes, Roslynn D. "Art as Reflection in Jessica Anderson's *Tirra Lirra by the River*." *Australian Literary Studies* 12 (May, 1986): 316-323. Focuses on the theme in *Tirra Lirra by the River* connected with the poem "The Lady of Shallot" as a reflection of Anderson's belief that art represents intense emotions and that experiences can be created only after the artist has achieved emotional distance.

Sykes, Alrene. "Jessica Anderson: Arrivals and Places." *Southerly* 46 (March, 1986): 57-71. Examines arrivals as representative of characters' inner journeys and the comparisons between Australia and Europe in five of Anderson's novels, including *Tirra Lirra by the River*.

Willbanks, Ray. *Australian Writers and Their Work*. Austin: University of Texas Press, 1991. A collection of interviews with sixteen contemporary authors. Willbanks' introduction outlines his ideas on current trends in Australian fiction. The interview with Anderson offers both biographical information and a discussion of her writing.

——————. "The Strength to Be Me: The Protagonist in the Fiction of Jessica Anderson." *SPAN: Journal of the South Pacific Association for Commonwealth Literature and Language Studies* 27 (October, 1988): 58-63. Compares several female characters in three of Anderson's works, including *Tirra Lirra by the River*. Willbanks suggests that each is an outsider figure—strong but alienated from male-dominated societies.

Kristen Montgomery

TO KILL A MOCKINGBIRD

Author: Harper Lee (1926-　　)
Type of work: Novel
Type of plot: Social criticism
Time of plot: The 1930's
Locale: Maycomb, Alabama
First published: 1960

Principal characters:
　　SCOUT FINCH, a six-year-old girl living in a small Southern town
　　JEM FINCH, Scout's older brother
　　ATTICUS FINCH, the father of Scout and Jem, an honorable lawyer
　　TOM ROBINSON, a young black man wrongly accused of raping
　　　　Mayella Ewell
　　BOB EWELL, the shiftless father of Mayella Ewell
　　BOO RADLEY, the recluse of the town

Form and Content

To Kill a Mockingbird is narrated by Jean Louise Finch, nicknamed Scout, who recalls her childhood spent in the sleepy Southern town of Maycomb, Alabama. Set in the Great Depression of the 1930's, part 1 of the novel mainly consists of Scout's everyday trials and tribulations with her father, Atticus; her older brother, Jem; their black housekeeper, Calpurnia; and their neighbors. Scout and Jem are becoming more aware of the adult world around them. Atticus Finch desires his children to be more tolerant in a town that has certain deep-rooted prejudices. Scout and Jem begin this struggle for understanding when Dill, a precocious nephew of their neighbor Stephanie Crawford, visits one summer. Dill proposes that they try to make Boo Radley come out of his house. Fascinated by the town's rumors that Boo is insane, the children make several attempts to lure the mysterious recluse out into the open.

When Dill leaves in the fall, the children's ideas concerning Boo fade. Scout encounters the school system for the first time. On the first day of school, she gets in trouble with her new teacher because Atticus has been teaching Scout to read; the teacher insists that Scout learn to read "properly"—that is, in school. From this encounter, Atticus teaches Scout about compromise—they will continue to read together every night, but Scout must learn her teacher's reading methods as well—and about the value of seeing things from another person's perspective.

Later in the school year, Jem discovers gifts left in the knot hole of a tree on the Radley place. The children realize that Boo Radley may have left these gifts for them. The children's pondering over Boo Radley's existence is overtaken, however, by Atticus' involvement with the trial of Tom Robinson, a black man wrongfully accused of raping a white woman. Atticus tries his best to prepared his children for the months ahead. At Christmas, Atticus gives the children their first air rifles but cautions that it is a sin to kill a mockingbird because mockingbirds only bring pleasure. Later, Scout connects this comment about the innocent mockingbird to Boo Radley.

Part 2 is the more serious section of the novel, moving from the happy memories of Scout's childhood to Tom Robinson's trial and its long-reaching effects on Atticus and the children. On the night before the hearing, a lynch party is narrowly diverted when Scout, having followed Atticus to the jail along with Jem and Dill, recognizes a classmate's father. Her innocent remarks to the man cause him to disband the lynch mob.

The trial brings the whole county of Maycomb to hear the testimony of Mayella Ewell, a white girl who lives in extreme poverty with her shiftless father, Bob Ewell. During cross-examination, Atticus proves that the Ewells are lying about Tom, but unfortunately, as Jem and Scout learn, the jury upholds Ewell's word, and Tom is convicted of rape. The children and their father barely get over the pain of this conviction before word comes that Tom has been killed while trying to escape from prison.

By the fall of Scout's eighth year, the controversy has died down, but Bob Ewell continues to threaten members of the court who he feels discredited him. He publicly spits on Atticus. Later, Ewell attacks Jem and Scout on their way home from the town's Halloween pageant. Scout survives the attack unscathed, but Jem is badly hurt. Reunited with a frightened Atticus, she learns that it was their reclusive neighbor, Boo Radley, who killed Ewell and saved the children's lives. Atticus and the town sheriff decide not to tell the town of Boo's deed, and Scout agrees, reminding Atticus that it would be "like shootin' a mockingbird." After walking Boo home, Scout stands on his front porch and finally understands her father's words about seeing things from another's point of view.

Analysis

Most critics agree that the strength of *To Kill a Mockingbird* lies in Harper Lee's use of the point of view of Scout. This point of view works in two ways: It is the voice of a perceptive, independent six-year-old girl and at the same time it is the mature voice of a woman telling about her childhood in retrospect. Lee skillfully blends these voices so that the reader recognizes that both are working at the same time but that neither detracts from the story. Through the voice of the child and the mature reflection of the adult, Lee is able to relate freshly the two powerful events in the novel: Atticus Finch's doomed defense of Tom Robinson and the appearance of the town recluse, Boo Radley. The child's voice gives a fresh approach to looking at the racism issue in the novel. Both Scout and Jem struggle with confusion over why some people are acceptable in the social strata of their community and others are not. As Scout wisely answers Jem, "There's just folks." The mature adult voice serves to give the reader reflections on the events that a child could not yet see.

Regarding the plights of Tom Robinson and Boo Radley, Lee draws on the symbol of the mockingbird. Both Tom and Boo are victims of the prejudices of their community. Tom, who is an innocent black man accused of rape, is convicted by a white jury even though Atticus Finch proves that the evidence against Tom is false. Boo is another victim—first, of his father's harsh religious views, and second, of the town's ignorance and gossip. Both men are closely related to the symbol of the mockingbird. Atticus and Miss Maudie, their wise neighbor, tell the children it is a sin to kill a mockingbird because the bird brings only pleasure to humans. When Tom is killed trying to escape, the editor of Maycomb's newspaper likens Tom's death to the senseless killing of songbirds by hunters and children. Later, after Atticus and the sheriff decide not to tell anyone that Boo Radley killed Ewell in defense of the Finch children, Scout agrees and equates exposing Boo Radley to the curious town to killing a mockingbird.

Two major themes dominate the novel: that of growing from ignorance to knowledge and that of determining what is cowardice and what is heroism. The "ignorance-to-knowledge" theme is developed through the characterization of the maturing children. Scout and Jem both develop understanding and an awareness of the adult world as they grow through their experiences. Lee represents children as having a fairer sense of justice than adults. Thus, when Robinson is convicted, the children are the ones who cannot accept it. Atticus' insistence that his children learn to be tolerant and not judge people only on appearances becomes one of the moral lessons of the book.

The other theme regards the children's growing awareness of what is cowardice and what is true heroism. The central figure and model for them here is their father, Atticus. In part 1, the children do not consider their father much of a hero because he will not play football with the Baptists. Only when Atticus shoots a rabid dog do the children learn that their humble father is "the deadest shot in Maycomb county." Atticus tries to redefine heroism for the children when he has Jem and Scout read to the hated Mrs. Dubose. He tells them after her death that she was a morphine addict trying to free herself of her addiction before dying. Atticus comments that true heroism is "when you're licked before you begin but you begin anyway." In part 2 of the novel, Atticus lives up to this definition of heroism by his courageous defense of Tom Robinson.

Context

Published in 1960, *To Kill a Mockingbird* has become an American literary classic. It won the Pulitzer Prize in 1961 and was made into an Academy Award-winning film in 1962, with Gregory Peck playing Atticus Finch. The novel also won the Brotherhood Award of the National Conference of Christians and Jews in 1961 and was *Best Sellers* magazine "Paperback of the Year" in 1961.

Although Harper Lee has not published a major work since *To Kill a Mockingbird*, the book retains its place in American literature for its telling of a regional story with a universal message. Also, although it is not a main issue, the novel features a feminist struggle. Even though the main focus of the novel remains Scout's growing recognition of the prejudices of her surroundings, Scout struggles for an understanding of womanhood. Through the strong, lyrical voice of this independent tomboy, the reader sees a young girl unsure of her place in Southern femininity. Scout struggles with how to fit into the world of "ladies," as exemplified by her Aunt Alexandria, and how to retain the independence that she has had as a child. Men still hold the main arena, and their world seems much more interesting to Scout than the world of caretaking that her aunt enjoys. Only Miss Maudie, Scout's outspoken neighbor, offers a good model for Scout. Maudis is independent and speaks her mind, yet she enjoys her baking and tending her garden.

Lee has been linked to other Southern writers who emerged in American literature after World War II, such as Truman Capote (who was the model for Dill in the novel), Carson McCullers, William Styron, and Eudora Welty. Along with these writers, Lee celebrates the Southern tradition of looking back on the past as did her predecessor William Faulkner. The new Southern writers, however, wrote about a "new South," a region that looked not only to its past but also to its future. Critics praised Lee for her portrayal of the new Southern liberal in the character of Atticus Finch. They also praise her technical use of point of view and her strong evocation of place as the strengths of *To Kill a Mockingbird*.

Sources for Further Study

Dave, R. A. "*To Kill a Mockingbird*: Harper Lee's Tragic Vision." In *Indian Studies in American Literature*, edited by M. K. Naik et al. Dharwar, India: Karnatak University, 1974. Dave provides an interesting discussion of the history of the mockingbird as a symbol of innocence and joy in American literature. He draws parallels between *To Kill a Mockingbird* and Walt Whitman's poem "Out of the Cradle Endlessly Rocking." Dave also explores how Lee, like Jane Austen, evokes a regional place yet makes it a macrocosm describing a range of human behavior.

Erisman, Fred. "The Romantic Regionalism of Harper Lee." *Alabama Review* 26 (April, 1973): 123-136. Erisman's article discusses in depth Lee's evocation of the "new South," one that looks back on its past but is beginning to look forward and not dwell on pre-Civil War glories. Also contains a good discussion of Atticus Finch as Lee's strong portrayal of the new Southern liberal trying to come to terms with the old traditions and prejudices of the South.

Going, William T. "Store and Mockingbird: Two Pulitzer Novels About Alabama." In *Essays on Alabama Literature*. University: University of Alabama Press, 1975. Contains a good discussion on Lee's use of point of view to relate the story's themes in a fresh manner. Going also discusses Lee's ties to the other new Southern writers who emerged in the late 1950's and early 1960's.

Johnson, Claudia. "Secret Courts of Men's Hearts: Code and Law in Harper Lee's *To Kill a Mockingbird*." *Studies in Fiction* 19, no. 2 (1991): 129-139. Johnson gives an excellent overview of the history of racial conflicts in Alabama during the 1930's, when the novel is set, and conflicts in the late 1950's, when the novel was being written, that Harper Lee drew upon for the trial of Tom Robinson.

Rubin, Louis D., Jr., ed. *The History of Southern Literature*. Baton Rouge: Louisiana State University Press, 1985. A brief history of Harper Lee's place among the new

Southern writers such as Capote, Welty, Styron, and McCullers. Rubin discusses how the new writers reflect on the past yet look toward the future, explore the plight of the black man in the South, and focus on portrayals of the new type of Southerner—the liberal who is in conflict with his or her environment because of an awareness of racism.

Shelley Burkhalter

TO THE LIGHTHOUSE

Author: Virginia Woolf (1882-1941)
Type of work: Novel
Type of plot: Psychological realism
Time of plot: 1910-1920
Locale: The Isle of Skye in the Hebrides
First published: 1927

Principal characters:
> MRS. RAMSAY, the matriarch of the Ramsays, a Victorian wife, mother, and hostess
> MR. RAMSAY, the patriarch, an aging philosopher
> LILY BRISCOE, an artist who disdains social conventions
> JAMES, the Ramsays' youngest son
> CAM, the Ramsays' youngest daughter
> PRUE, the prettiest of the Ramsay daughters
> ANDREW, the Ramsay son who is killed in World War I
> JASPER, the young Ramsay son who shoots birds
> NANCY, ROGER, and ROSE, the other Ramsay children
> WILLIAM BANKES, a botanist and an old friend of Mr. Ramsay
> CHARLES TANSLEY, a protégé of Mr. Ramsay
> MINTA DOYLE and PAUL RAYLEY, a young couple who become engaged through the machinations of Mrs. Ramsay
> AUGUSTUS CARMICHAEL, a minor poet
> MRS. MCNAB, the Ramsays' elderly housekeeper

Form and Content

Departing from the nineteenth century formalities of literary realism, Virginia Woolf pioneered, along with James Joyce and William Faulkner, the stream-of-consciousness technique employed in *To the Lighthouse*. Composed of three discrete but intimately related sections, the novel provides a poetic examination of English Victorian domesticity and social roles.

Woolf stealthily weaves through her characters' psyches to reveal realities that are not necessarily apparent in either their actions or their speech. Section 1, aptly entitled "The Window," invites the reader's observation of the Ramsays' summer household. Mrs. Ramsay sits by the window with James. She has promised him that they will sail to the lighthouse tomorrow to take provisions to the lighthouse keeper and his son. When Mr. Ramsay, backed by Charles Tansley, insists that the weather will prevent their journey, an angry Mrs. Ramsay offers a more optimistic forecast. It is Mr. Ramsay's pursuit of Truth without any regard for people's feelings that so upsets her. Although Mr. Ramsay repeatedly offends Mrs. Ramsay, she remains the dutiful Victorian wife, accepting his word over hers, accompanying him on silent strolls, and making him feel needed although she is the one who truly rules the house.

Standing at her easel a distance from the window, Lily Briscoe works to capture Mrs. Ramsay and James on canvas. William Bankes lounges nearby. Mrs. Ramsay invites Charles Tansley to join her for a walk into town, where she makes social calls and visits the sick. Mrs. Ramsay also spends time knitting, and Mr. Tansley discusses philosophy with Mr. Ramsay. In the meantime, the children play outside.

Andrew and Nancy have embarked upon a daring walk along the cliffs with Minta and Paul. Stealing a moment alone, Minta and Paul embrace, causing temporary discomfort to Nancy and Andrew, who spy the couple from afar. Having lost her grandmother's brooch among the rocks, Minta provides Paul with the opportunity to conduct a heroic search. Unable to find the brooch before the tide rolls in, he devises a chivalric plan to present her with a new one. Their search for the brooch causes their late return to the house, leading Mrs. Ramsay first to worry and then to agitation, since they will disrupt her perfectly planned dinner.

The dinner, nevertheless, is a victory for Mrs. Ramsay, affording positive moments of cohesion for most present, though not without its bobbles. After dinner, Mrs. Ramsay picks up the nursemaid's slack: She successfully puts James and Cam to bed by solving the dilemma of a decorative, but frightening, boar's skull that keeps the children awake. She then joins her husband in the library while some of the guests go out to watch the waves.

Section 2, "Time Passes," is short in length but covers ten years in time. Detailing the house's deterioration, this section also brings news of World War I and the deaths of Mrs. Ramsay, Prue, and Andrew, which are announced in parenthetical asides.

The third and final section, "The Lighthouse," introduces the return of Mr. Ramsay, Cam, James, Lily, and Mr. Carmichael to the Ramsay home on the Isle of Skye. With their enthusiasm for the trip to the lighthouse completely disintegrated, James and Cam nevertheless concede to their father's insistence. Forgoing the trip herself, Lily remains on shore and completes the painting of Mrs. Ramsay and James that she had begun ten years earlier.

Analysis

The Ramsay family portrait is one that was intimately familiar to Virginia Woolf's Victorian sensibilities. She presents an outwardly functional social structure. Beneath the surface of her characters' actions and spoken words, however, rest contempt, frustration, and dissatisfaction with an outmoded code of behavior that nevertheless continues to be enforced.

To the Lighthouse is a novel propelled almost entirely by internal thoughts. The physical activities undertaken by the characters serve merely as jumping-off points for Woolf to comment upon and interpret the underlying realities. The voices of Lily Briscoe and Mrs. Ramsay most clearly delineate the problems that Woolf chooses to address. Both display reservations and confusion regarding their chosen codes of behavior. Lily proudly rejects Victorian conventions. Opting to remain single, she can paint and develop platonic relations with men primarily because she refuses to compromise herself by either aiding insecure men, such as Mr. Ramsay, or indulging the egos of overweening men, such as Charles Tansley. Unfortunately, however, Lily suffers insecurities about her bold differentness. Mrs. Ramsay, on the other hand, recognizes that society is sexually polarized, and she sees it as her duty to uphold the system. Consequently, she suppresses her individuality to serve the dominant male society.

Mrs. Ramsay's sacrifices are not without remorse; she frequently registers disdain for her role. At dinner, for example, she regrets that her lack of a formal education prevents her participation in conversations about square roots, literature, and politics. After dinner, when some of the guests announce that they are going out to watch the waves, "Instantly, for no reason at all, Mrs. Ramsay became like a girl of twenty, full of gaiety. A mood of revelry suddenly took possession of her." Nevertheless, Mrs. Ramsay suppresses her longings; she knows that she must stay in the house to attend to her husband.

Woolf portrays Mr. and Mrs. Ramsay, the man and the woman, as vastly different creatures. Whereas Mrs. Ramsay's thoughts are more imaginative and jump back and forth in time relating to specific events, people, and emotions, Mr. Ramsay's thoughts progress rationally along a linear plane. He moves, as he says, step by step from A to Z and laments that he may not possess the intellectual acumen to move beyond Q. In the process, he "wears Mrs. Ramsay to death." She restlessly works to counteract, or eradicate, his personal self-doubts and feelings of inadequacy.

Literary critics have readily compared the character of Lily with her creator, Virginia Woolf: They are both revolutionary artists who find themselves out of place in a sexually polarized society. In *To the Lighthouse*, Mr. Ramsay represents the purely masculine and Mrs. Ramsay the purely feminine; neither functions successfully. Woolf offers Lily as an androgynous figure who unifies the two extremes. It is Lily who becomes the central figure in the final section of the novel. Her ideas about Mrs. Ramsay and her visions of Mr. Ramsay and the children landing at the lighthouse enable her to complete her painting. She unites the rational and the imaginative into the androgynous whole that the painting represents.

Context

The small revolutions fought by Lily for choosing against marriage, by Minta for wearing a torn stocking, and by Cam for refusing to give Mr. Bankes a flower are representative of the literary and social revolutions inspired by the publication of *To the Lighthouse*. By the time that the novel was published, Woolf had already achieved critical acclaim and was an outspoken member of the Bloomsbury group. She was constantly engaging the dominant voices of her society, and her ideas about gender and domestic life were seriously addressed as a consequence.

To the Lighthouse does not provide solutions to the problems of sexual polarization. In fact, Lily's androgynous convergence is far from ideal. By raising the issues of gender so honestly and openly in her novel, however, Woolf laid the foundations for a feminist discourse that has not lost its momentum.

Sources for Further Study

Beja, Morris. *Critical Essays on Virginia Woolf.* Boston: G. K. Hall, 1985. This text attempts to reconcile disparate schools of Woolf criticism. Includes a review of *To the Lighthouse*, written by Conrad Aiken, that appeared in 1927 upon the novel's publication.

Kelley, Alice van Buren. *The Novels of Virginia Woolf: Fact and Vision.* Chicago: University of Chicago Press, 1973. A study of the significance of creative tension between objective reality and inconfirmable poetic insight in Woolf's novels. Includes a chapter on *To the Lighthouse* that explores the influences of fact and vision upon the novel's plot, characterization, and imagery.

Leaska, Mitchell A. *Virginia Woolf's Lighthouse: A Study in Critical Method.* New York: Columbia University Press, 1970. An exhaustive study of the narrative methods Woolf employs in *To the Lighthouse*. Includes an extensive bibliography and concordance-like appendices.

Love, Jean O. *Virginia Woolf: Sources of Madness and Art.* Berkeley: University of California Press, 1977. A biography investigating the paradoxical connection between Woolf's life and art. Provides a psychological interpretation of the author based on primary documents.

Marcus, Jane, ed. *New Feminist Essays on Virginia Woolf.* Lincoln: University of Nebraska Press, 1981. An insightful collection of essays that approach the author from an unabashedly feminist perspective. Includes a chapter by Jane Lilienfeld discussing the Ramsays' marriage.

Zwerdling, Alex. *Virginia Woolf and the Real World.* Berkeley: University of California Press, 1986. A study of Woolf's social vision and her response to the historical events and sociopolitical currents of her age. Included an enlightening chapter on the domestic politics of *To the Lighthouse*.

Debra L. Picker

TOP GIRLS

Author: Caryl Churchill (1938-   )
Type of work: Drama
Type of plot: Psychological realism
Time of plot: The early 1980's
Locale: England
First produced: 1982, at Royal Court Theatre, London, England
First published: 1982

> *Principal characters:*
> MARLENE, the managing director of the Top Girls employment
> agency
> JOYCE, Marlene's sister, a housewife separated from her husband
> ANGIE, Joyce's sixteen-year-old daughter
> WIN and NELL, employment counselors at Top Girls
> JEANINE, a Top Girls applicant, a secretary wanting a better job
> LOUISE, a Top Girls applicant whose career has stagnated in
> middle management
> SHONA, a Top Girls applicant, a gifted charlatan with no actual
> business experience

Form and Content

Top Girls is the story of one woman's rise to success and of the other women in her life (as well as those in history) whose experiences call hers into question. Its all-female cast speaks from a wide variety of cultural and political positions in dialogue that is orchestrated on the page almost like musical lines and themes, with numerous interruptions, dual conversations, and simultaneous speeches which undercut or highlight one another. The cast must also be prepared to perform multiple roles, particularly in the long opening scene, which may be Marlene's dream or a fantasia outside the plot serving as a prologue.

The play opens in a stylish restaurant as Marlene prepares for the celebration of her promotion at Top Girls. As the guests arrive, the dinner party takes on the nature of a celebration of "top girls" from history and legend who fought and achieved: Isabella Bird, a nineteenth century Scottish woman who became a noted world traveler after the age of forty; Lady Nijo, a medieval courtesan forsaken by her lover, the Japanese emperor, to wander as a Buddhist nun; Dull Gret, a figure in a Hans Brueghel painting who leads a band of peasant women into hell to fight the devils; Pope Joan, who is fabled to have ruled as pope in the ninth century, disguised as a man; and Patient Griselda, an exemplary, long-suffering wife in Geoffrey Chaucer's *Canterbury Tales*. The women's lively conversation veers into anguish as each woman reveals the high toll that her success exacted: exhaustion, neglect, abuse, loneliness, even murder. Much of this came at the hands of men or from the societal expectations against which these women struggled. The dinner party dissolves into a cacophony of broken dishes, tears, and outbursts of rage.

The rest of act 1 begins in the offices of the Top Girls agency the first day of Marlene's new position, then moves to Joyce's house the day before; likewise, the two scenes of act 2 begin by continuing the day at Top Girls, then shifting a year earlier, to Joyce's house. In the first scene at the agency, Marlene interviews Jeanine; Marlene's energy and drive are shown in counterpoint to Jeanine's uncertainty. Following this, Angie is seen playing with Kit, a younger playmate; Angie seems not to relate to children her own age. Kit, who is good in school, both admires the older girl and finds her strange and threatening. Joyce and Angie argue, while Joyce worries about Angie's chances in life. The tension escalates between them, and Angie confides to Kit that she wants to kill Joyce.

In act 2, between job interviews Win and Nell discuss their own prospects in love and careers, none of which seem promising. Angie turns up at the office, surprising Marlene, who is fond of Angie but does not know what to do with her, particularly as Angie hints that she wants to stay and become a success as well. Angie watches as Marlene is confronted by the wife of the runner-up for Marlene's new position, who accuses Marlene of taking away jobs meant for men, even of betraying other women who support their husbands' careers. Marlene angrily defends her success and her life. Later, Win relates a similar but less happy story to Angie, involving burnout from having to outwork and prove herself to men. The scene closes with Marlene, Nell, and Win discussing Angie, who has fallen asleep; Marlene concedes ultimately that Angie is "not going to make it."

The final scene is a flashback to Marlene's visit to Joyce and Angie the previous year after many years away. The center of the scene is an angry discussion between the sisters over their lives, their agreement that Joyce would rear Angie (who is actually Marlene's child), and the political philosophies that divide them. The argument goes unresolved, as does the sisters' attempt to relate as family despite their differences. Finally, a shaken, tipsy Marlene tries to comfort herself and Angie, who cannot sleep. Marlene tries to persuade Angie that things will be fine, but Angie only repeats one word: "Frightening."

Analysis

Caryl Churchill has commented that *Top Girls* grew from two particular initial ideas: that of women from the past appearing to and speaking with present-day women, and the idea of the variety of jobs that women fill, both in the economy and in culture. Though her work is strongly influenced by Churchill's feminism—she wrote *Vinegar Tom* (1976) in collaboration with a feminist theater group—the scenarios she presents here open up the question of what feminism is for different women, how they define the concept not only in theory but also through their actions and choices.

The solidarity of women becomes both a theme and a problem. The historical figures of the dinner party in act 1 can be seen as a context for Marlene's success, a tradition of women who took risks and made their presences felt. Yet each is also presented as isolated in her historical moment, unsupported by a larger society of women and actively discouraged or attacked by men or institutions created by men. Similarly, in the ensuing modern scenes, Marlene and the other Top Girls are shown to have paid high prices in the attempt to succeed in a "man's world" not established with their ascent or their needs in mind.

Perhaps gender equity has improved if a woman such as Marlene can rise into management or Margaret Thatcher can be named prime minister; these advances form the basis for Marlene's claim that women do not need a movement or feminist politics to move forward. This seeming rise is potentially damaging to women; Joyce and Angie's scenes show that, in Churchill's view, most women face disadvantages and lack of opportunity and that the career track of Marlene is a rare exception, not a prototype that all women can follow. For every Lady Nijo or Isabella Bird, there have been uncounted women restricted in their options, left to obscurity and poverty.

For every Marlene, there are many women like the three job applicants: underqualified, unconfident, and lacking the rare combination of intelligence, beauty, drive, and style that have propelled Marlene. Marlene offers to help them, and companies pay her well to do so, but the women must play by her rules—for example, keeping quiet about plans to marry someday. Remaking women in her own image is the key to Marlene's success, and supposedly to theirs. Aggressive confidence and the power to persuade employers and sales clients are methods recognized by the men with whom such women must work and against whom they must compete. Yet even the women who manage to "beat" the patriarchal system are merely outwitting it, not reforming it to make the field more fair to all women.

The connection between economics and feminism is continually at issue in *Top Girls*. Women have traditionally been relegated to the private sphere of homemaking and parenting, and a woman such as Marlene, who dares not only to enter but also to insist on advancement in the public sphere of economic activity, necessarily embodies a larger, inherent cultural tension. Giving up her daughter, beating out other women, and living without a partner are Marlene's particular instances of the larger disjunctions between women's rights and the rules of capitalist society, as Churchill sees it.

The problem is not simple: The issue is not whether successful businesswomen are paragons of feminist victory or bloodthirsty man-haters (though characters in the play express both these notions) but whether these women, like all beneficiaries of capitalism, have lost much in the quality of their lives, even as they appear to reject economic subservience to men. Such women, like their male counterparts, have acquiesced to a system of domination and profit refined over centuries by men in power, and even if they benefit from it as individuals, they ultimately are complicit in the oppression of their own gender. Marlene works at eradicating the signs of inequality between women and men in public life, but she does not pay attention to the larger patterns of dominance. This can take the form of Marlene's competing subtly with her friends Win and Nell, her apparent neglect of her sister and daughter, or even the spiritual emptiness and despair behind her bright demeanor, glimpses of which Churchill allows at moments throughout the play.

Context

Perhaps the most immediate impact of *Top Girls* is visual as well as structural: Its audience sees a play where every actor on stage is a woman. Churchill's casting strategy is striking seen against a dramatic tradition in which the great majority of characters are male, with perhaps a handful of female characters at most, usually in stock roles such as romantic interest, villain, or servant. The historical figures in the dinner scene serve as a reminder that, regardless of whether they were acknowledged by dramatists, women have played a number of "dramatic" roles in lived experience, as full of adventure and conflict as the male-centered stories of most traditional dramas. The action of the contemporary story points out that many of the lives and experiences of women have not been encompassed by traditional dramatic narrative.

Churchill has often relied on writing practices that also go against traditional notions of authorship. Several of her plays, including *Owners* (1972), *Cloud Nine* (1979), and *A Mouthful of Birds* (1986), were developed in a group process. Playwright, actors, and staff discuss ideas in an open workshop and do collective research; then Churchill works with the collected material in a writing period, after which the group moves into rehearsals. Though this process was not in effect for *Top Girls*, other elements of the play show Churchill's interest in changing traditional forms. Her interlaced conversational lines and transformations of the linear narrative time frame combine with her casting and thematic choices to show that there are stories not yet heard that women can tell, both on stage and as authors, and that there may be new ways to communicate them dramatically.

Churchill's impact is felt widely in the theater, as she has become one of the most widely produced women playwrights in English, writing for British radio and television as well as the stage. *Serious Money* (1987) was a success in London's West End, as well as at the influential producer Joseph Papp's Public Theater in New York; her other works have been performed in many regional and university theaters in the United States and the United Kingdom.

Sources for Further Study

Cousin, Geraldine. *Churchill the Playwright*. London: Methuen Drama, 1989. This study views Churchill's plays in the context of her experimentations with collaborative productions, in which the author, actors, and director research, write, and develop a play together through a prerehearsal workshop period. Cousin examines *Top Girls* for the way in which it manipulates traditional time schemes and questions notions of achievement, success, and what Churchill considers "joy."

Fitzsimmons, Linda, comp. *File on Churchill*. London: Methuen Drama, 1989. A useful compilation of materials on Churchill's plays, their contexts and critical reactions. The volume includes a chronology of her career, brief synopses of the plays, comments from reviews and interviews, a select bibliography, and statements from the writer on her work.

Kritzer, Amelia Howe. *The Plays of Caryl Churchill: Theatre of Empowerment*. New York: St. Martin's Press, 1991. A wide-ranging study of Churchill's plays for radio, television, and the stage, as they move from traditional to more alternative forms of writing and staging. Kritzer focuses on Churchill's use of theater to give voice to formerly silenced groups, and she argues that *Top Girls* rejects ideas of feminist progress without their connection to socialist politics.

Randall, Phyllis, ed. *Caryl Churchill: A Casebook*. New York: Garland, 1989. The first book-length collection of essays on Churchill. The essay on *Top Girls* discusses it in the light of the "second wave" of feminism, which moves from individual struggles for rights to envisioning a transformation of society as a whole. Includes primary and secondary bibliographies.

Keith Todd

TOWARD A NEW PSYCHOLOGY OF WOMEN

Author: Jean Baker Miller (1927-   )
Type of work: Social criticism
First published: 1976

Form and Content

Created by one of a group of women who were struggling to formulate a theory and practice of feminist therapy in the early 1970's, Jean Baker Miller's *Toward a New Psychology of Women* affirms a distinctly female psychology. Because men dominate in society, Miller contends that a woman's way of being has been forced underground and, if it is seen at all, has been highly suspect. She claims that psychoanalysis, in its attempt to probe the depths of the human mind, has unearthed this domain of suppressed qualities that are, essentially, the feminine psyche.

Toward a New Psychology of Women is composed of three sections. In part 1, Miller argues that the male-female relationship is predicated on inequality. This fundamental inequality between men and women is not unlike the sociological imbalances of power found between races, religions, nationalities, and classes. The dynamic of domination-subordination demands that the subordinate group's identity be constructed around the dominant group's perceptions and needs. The male-dominated culture has deemed certain human potentials more valuable than others and has shunted the "less desirable" qualities onto women.

Part 2 develops the theme that these very characteristics relegated to women which seem to be weaknesses are, in fact, strengths that hold the potential for an advanced way of living. Qualities such as vulnerability, weakness, caretaking, dependency, and cooperation fuel the drive to be connected in relationships. The problem for women is that these propensities become subsumed into the male-centered system and that the female identity, apart from who a woman is in relation to others, is eclipsed.

Part 3 addresses the direction in which women are headed. Miller contends that the future holds a more authentic female identity for women who, grounded in the understanding that the organizing principle for women's selfhood is affiliation, embrace cooperation, their own creativity and personal power, and constructive conflict.

Throughout the book, Miller illustrates her ideas with vignettes of women who struggle with these issues. One example is Anne, an artist with two children and a husband who feels free to paint only when she has done everything possible to meet her family's needs. When her husband dies at a young age, she is overwhelmed by a sense of purposelessness. Her children and the need to support them keep her going, however, and she is able to embrace her art with deep concentration because it is now essential to her family's livelihood. In doing so, Anne comes to feel a greater sense of herself than she ever had when her life centered solely on her husband's and children's needs. When she remarries and her work is not essential financially, she struggles once again with her commitment to her work. "She felt that she did not have the right to devote herself to something 'just for me.'" Anne's dilemma typifies that of many of the women Miller portrays. A woman's tendency, Miller believes, is to derive meaning and satisfaction from her work "when it takes place in the context of relationships to other human beings—and even more so when it leads to the enhancement of others."

Analysis

Toward a New Psychology of Women emerged out of Miller's therapeutic work with women. Through observing the problems that women confront in their lives, Miller became convinced that there is a distinction between male and female psychological development. Miller believes that traditional psychoanalytic theory's organizing principle for personality development, autonomous selfhood, is descriptive of male experience. The goal of autonomy is separateness and self-direction. Women's selfhood, is predicated on the opposite principle of affiliation, or the need to be in relationships.

Miller contends that the culture sets up a double bind for women. On the one hand, the male-dominated society relegates the very qualities it fears to women. Women are conditioned to develop passivity, dependency, cooperation, emotion, and nurturing of others. On the other hand, women are seen as psychologically immature for making relationships central to their lives and are thus punished for having the very qualities that have been assigned to them by the culture. Miller concedes that there are women who have chosen to follow self-directed paths of growth but holds that the woman who does so violates "a dominant system of values that says she is not worthy . . . that there must be something wrong with her for even wanting alternatives."

In the context of a dominant-subordinate culture, truly mutual affiliation is impossible. In this relationship of unequals, women relinquish their own personal power. Conditioned from an early age to attend to the needs of others, women experience difficulty establishing an identity apart from what others expect of them. Miller has found this often to be the root of women's psychological problems.

The answer to the dilemma lies in abandoning the model of domination-subordination without abandoning the drive toward affiliation and reclaiming one's personal power. A woman must attend to herself, focusing on her own needs and desires, even if it means displeasing others. This is no small task. A woman is so conditioned to think of others' needs before her own that she often has difficulty ascertaining what she wants. Moreover, the perceived risk of abandonment or condemnation for self-care can be terrifying and can seem to be utterly contrary to the need for affiliation. Miller maintains, however, that it is a necessary risk.

Miller views the dominant male culture as a "low-level, primitive organization built on an exceedingly restricted conception of the total human potential. It holds up narrow and ultimately destructive goals for the dominant group and attempts to deny vast areas of life." Psychoanalysis has revealed that those denied areas, embodied in the female psyche, have to do with the desire for relationship. Miller believes that as women attend to themselves in the context of their affiliations, they will challenge their partners into adopting new ways of living more creatively and cooperatively. Conflict, which was either denied or played out destructively under the old model, will be embraced as good and as a pathway to growth.

Context

Miller's small volume has become a classic in circles concerned with women's issues. In the years since *Toward a New Psychology of Women*'s publication, the frequency of its citation in journal articles has only increased. In 1979, there were twelve references to this work in professional articles; in 1992, there were sixty-three. Miller's book has broad implications, since it is cited in fields as diverse as women's issues, health and medicine, psychology, sociology, education, and the law.

Toward a New Psychology of Women was seminal in suggesting that female psychological development is distinctive, thus challenging a cultural icon, the psychoanalytic tradition. Refuting the notion that a woman must either defer to expected roles or feel guilty for not doing so, Miller maintained that a woman's impulse toward personal growth is good. She links one of the most common psychological problems women face, depression, directly to the suppression of the impulse toward personal growth.

Sources for Further Study

Chernin, Kim. *Reinventing Eve: Modern Woman in Search of Herself.* New York: Harper & Row, 1987. Chernin offers her own journey of self-discovery and an interpretation of modern culture's limitations on women's lives. She uses religion, myth, literature, and psychoanalysis to suggest transformative images for women.

Chodorow, Nancy. *The Reproduction of Mothering: Psychoanalysis and the Sociology of Gender.* Berkeley: University of California Press, 1978. Chodorow provides extensive psychoanalytic grounding for her argument that parenting should be shared equally by both men and women.

Gilligan, Carol. *In a Different Voice: Psychological Theory and Women's Development.* Cambridge, Mass.: Harvard University Press, 1982. Gilligan argues that developmental theories in psychology have been built on the observations of men. Grounded in research, her study illuminates the distinctiveness of female identity and moral development as rooted primarily in connectedness with others.

Gilligan, Carol, Annie G. Rogers, and Deborah L. Tolman, eds. *Women, Girls, and Psychotherapy: Reframing Resistance.* New York: Haworth Press, 1991. This collection of essays focuses on the psychological development of adolescent girls. Highlighting the unique problems they face, how they cope through the teenage years, and how teenage experiences affect their adult lives, the essays also reveal the social pressures placed on girls to submit and "be nice," and illuminate their resistance to accepting the limits of socially defined femininity.

Schaef, Anne Wilson. *Women's Reality: An Emerging System in White Male Society.* 3d ed. San Francisco: Harper San Francisco, 1992. Schaef elucidates the psychosexual differences between men and women. Based on her experiences as a psychotherapist, she writes an accessible analysis of women's experience and reality vis-à-vis those of men.

Kim Dickson Rogers

TOWARD A RECOGNITION OF ANDROGYNY

Author: Carolyn G. Heilbrun (1926-   )
Type of work: Literary criticism
First published: 1973

Form and Content

Written during the height of the women's movement, at a time when women were questioning society's rigid definitions of what it meant to be a woman or man, *Toward a Recognition of Androgyny* suggests that the salvation of the human race depends upon the ability to transcend gender stereotyping and allow individuals a full range of human behaviors. This ideal state of understanding is "androgyny," a term derived from the Greek *andro* ("male") and *gyn* ("female"), meaning "a condition under which the characteristics of the sexes, and the human impulses expressed by men and women, are not rigidly assigned." Turning to literature for examples of this androgynous vision, Carolyn G. Heilbrun, then professor of English literature at Columbia University, finds them in writers as diverse as Sophocles, William Shakespeare, Emily Brontë, and Virginia Woolf in this ambitious reexamination of some of the major texts of Western literature.

The book is divided into three separate but interrelated sections. The first traces "The Hidden River of Androgyny" embodied in Greek mythology and literature and continuing through the Renaissance, finding its fullest expression in Shakespeare's complex heroines. Proceeding chronologically and shifting, for the most part, to fiction, "The Woman as Hero" section is the longest. This section examines mostly female characters from some of the most important novels written in English from the eighteenth through the twentieth centuries who embody both "female" and "male" characteristics. In novels by writers including Samuel Richardson, Emily Brontë, William Makepeace Thackeray, Nathaniel Hawthorne, Henry James, and E. M. Forster, it identifies vibrant, atypical heroines who rebel, in their various ways, against their societies' gender constraints. The last section, "The Bloomsbury Group," moves from fiction to fact by examining Virginia Woolf, Lytton Strachey, Clive Bell, and their circle, the group of writers and artists who met in Bloomsbury Square in London from 1904 to the 1930's, as the first example of the androgynous life in practice.

Heilbrun's work includes references to philosophers and literary critics, to Greek mythology, the Bible, and writers as disparate as Sophocles and George Bernard Shaw. A literary critic, Heilbrun is primarily concerned with reading the various texts, often in startling new ways, and understanding them in their historical context. Although the reader who has read the works to which she alludes will benefit most from this ambitious study, Heilbrun provides enough examples so that most readers can understand her main point: that in great literature, particularly novels, there has been, consistently, a recognition, whether conscious or not, of the limitations placed on the individual by gender expectations. As a result, such literature has imagined other, sometimes freer but always more complex, possibilities for women and men.

Toward a Recognition of Androgyny is both scholarly and accessible. Heilbrun includes the mandatory notes and index, but both are kept to a minimum. Moreover, the writing style is direct and clear, without the inflated rhetoric that is typical of much academic prose.

Analysis

Claiming in her introduction that "androgyny seeks to liberate the individual from the confines of the appropriate," Heilbrun sets out to find examples of this liberating impulse in Western thought and literature. Moving freely between cultures and through time, she hones in on specific examples that prove her point, often contrasting them with works expressing an opposing (and she would say more limited) vision.

In Greek literature, Heilbrun finds a "hidden" tradition of androgyny embodied in such plays as *Antigone* (c. 441 B.C.) by Sophocles and *Medea* (431 B.C.) by Euripides. She argues that in the former, for example, by reversing the expected gender roles played by Antigone and Haemon, Sophocles makes his female protagonist play the "male" part: a woman acts to avenge her brother's death. Haemon, Antigone's lover, sacrifices himself for his beloved in proper "female" fashion. To further underscore the theme, Heilbrun adds that Sophocles provides Ismene, Antigone's sister, as an ineffectual woman following a prescribed gender role, and the blind prophet Teiresias, who is both male and female, as the true visionary.

Although the Judeo-Christian tradition and that of Islam emphasized patriarchy almost exclusively, feminine, civilizing principles reenter in the medieval period, according to Heilbrun, with the rise of romance and the growth of popular adoration of the Virgin Mary. By the Renaissance, and particularly in Shakespeare's women, Heilbrun argues that the androgynous impulse emerged in full flower. Citing several examples—Hamlet's sacrificing of Ophelia as an example of his killing his "feminine" self in *Hamlet* (1603); the recognition of the daughter as her father's true inheritor in *King Lear* (1608) and the late romances; the vitality and moral force of the comic heroines disguised as men, such as Rosalind in *As You Like It* (1623)—she argues convincingly for Shakespeare's androgynous vision.

In part 2 of the work, "The Woman as Hero," Heilbrun turns to fiction to trace the continuation of the androgynous impulse in literature written in English from the eighteenth century through the early twentieth century. Beginning with Samuel Richardson's *Clarissa* (1747-1748), which she calls the first androgynous novel, Heilbrun goes on to discuss others, including William Makepeace Thackeray's *Vanity Fair* (1847-1848), Emily Brontë's *Wuthering Heights* (1847), and Nathaniel Hawthorne's *The Scarlet Letter* (1850). Each contains an example of the androgynous female hero, who is, according to Heilbrun, a dominant figure that is unlike the traditional, more passive heroine. By juxtaposing these novels, Heilbrun uncovers startling similarities: For example, in their sense of themselves, their wasted talents, and their qualities of martyrdom and sainthood, Richardson's Clarissa and Hawthorne's Hester Prynne achieve a similar kind of mythic grandeur and moral authority in their respective novels.

Examining the work of the great women writers of the nineteenth century—Jane Austen, Charlotte and Emily Brontë, and George Eliot (Mary Ann Evans)—Heilbrun demonstrates the ways in which all but one demonstrate the androgynous vision in their fiction. Although she is "no more a feminist than Dickens," Jane Austen is also not the "feminine" writer whom critics for years have been patronizing, according to Heilbrun. Austen's genius, instead, is her ability to imagine a society in which women and men are equally responsible for their actions and equally able to imagine their own selfhood. Therein lies her claim to androgyny.

To Heilbrun, Emily Brontë's *Wuthering Heights* reveals the androgynous ideal in the love between Catherine and Heathcliff, which represents an unattainable merging of male and female principles. Abandoning Heathcliff, her "masculine" self, Catherine succumbs to the limited "female" role that society has prescribed for her: the protection and "respect" of marriage. Unlike Jane Austen, George Eliot was not able to envision androgynous characters, Heilbrun explains. She also did not suggest a way in which a talented woman could discover a destiny equal to her talents. Yet Eliot's androgynous vision emerges in her suggestion in the novel *Middlemarch* (1871-1872), for example, that "the separation of the sexes is somehow fundamentally connected with the impotence of society to hasten human progress." It is Charlotte Brontë whose vision is not androgynous, according to Heilbrun, perhaps because she was so passionately aware of the disabilities under which gifted women struggle.

Heilbrun claims that it was not until the late nineteenth century that "the woman as hero" appeared. Unlike earlier women in fiction, the woman hero, Heilbrun explains, "is sustained by some sense of her own autonomy as she contemplates and searches for a destiny; she does not wait to be swept up by life as a girl is swept up in a waltz." This character is thus more like the traditional male hero in her awareness of her own individuality and selfhood. Perhaps ironically, she was also exclusively the creation of male writers. As Heilbrun explains, she was invented by Norwegian playwright Henrik Ibsen and American-born novelist Henry James. Nora Helmer in *A Doll's House* (1879) and Isabel Archer in *The Portrait of a Lady* (1881) are her earliest manifestations.

In characters such as Margaret Schlegel in E. M. Forster's *Howard's End* (1910) and Ursula Brangwen in D. H. Lawrence's *The Rainbow* (1915), Heilbrun finds independent women who are literary ancestors of these earlier heroes. Demonstrating that androgyny is not limited to female characters, she examines James Joyce's "womanly" hero, Leopold Bloom, from *Ulysses* (1922). In the post-World War II worlds created by American writers such as Philip Roth, Bernard Malamud, Norman Mailer, and Saul Bellow, Heilbrun finds the death of the woman as hero as their male characters exploit, demean, or escape women.

Finally, in "The Bloomsbury Group," Heilbrun discusses the writers who met in Bloomsbury Square in London from 1904 to the 1930's as the first example of the androgynous way of life in practice. Contending that in their lives and works masculinity and femininity were mixed, reason and passion holding equal sway, Heilbrun examines at some length the works of Clive Bell and Lytton Strachey. In the novels of Virginia Woolf, she finds the fullest expression of a synthesis between female and male vision, rereading *To the Lighthouse* (1927) as a search for balance between the individually limited ideas of Mr. and Mrs. Ramsay, not as a celebration of femininity, as it has been read more commonly.

In her afterword, Heilbrun calls for writers to create, once again, androgynous works in which characters are conceived in all their human complexity. Convinced that women writers should not only write about their victimization, she hopes that they will eventually discover a literary form in which to represent their autonomy.

Context

Toward a Recognition of Androgyny elicited strong responses from its supporters and detractors. The former, many of them women, found it liberating: For the first time, someone had articulated what (among other things) made some writers great and others not so great. The giants, women and men, possessed a certain vision that enabled them to see beyond rigid gender boundaries. The book's detractors, many of them men, wanted a more precise definition of androgyny and failed to recognize the difference between the androgynous writer and the feminist, a distinction that Heilbrun makes a few times in the text. Some critics questioned individual interpretations.

The book's position in the history of literary criticism, and feminist literary criticism in particular, is secure. Only three years after the publication of Kate Millett's *Sexual Politics* (1970), in which Millett exposed the misogyny in authors such as Norman Mailer and Henry Miller, Heilbrun's book contributed a different perspective. By examining the idea of androgyny, a notion that had been introduced into literary criticism by Samuel Taylor Coleridge and had been discussed by Virginia Woolf, Heilbrun not only reread the literature of the past but also offered a blueprint for writers of the future.

In later works, including *Reinventing Womanhood* (1978), *Writing a Woman's Life* (1988), and *Hamlet's Mother and Other Women* (1990), Carolyn Heilbrun has continued to examine women's lives, in fiction and in fact, in order to make sense of them.

Sources for Further Study

Diamond, Arlyn, and Lee Edwards, eds. *The Authority of Experience: Essays in Feminist Criticism.* Amherst: University of Massachusetts Press, 1977. An early collection of excellent feminist essays on writers including Shakespeare, Richardson, Charlotte Brontë, and Virginia Woolf.

Edwards, Lee R. *Psyche as Hero: Female Heroism and Fictional Form.* Middletown, Conn.: Wesleyan University Press, 1984. A study of the fulfillment or frustration of heroic possibilities in a variety of English and American novels from the mid-eighteenth century to the present. Edwards examines many of the same novels that Heilbrun does.

Gilbert, Sandra M., and Susan Gubar. *The Madwoman in the Attic: The Woman Writer and the Nineteenth-Century Literary Imagination.* New Haven, Conn.: Yale University Press, 1979. A bold interpretation of the major women writers of the nineteenth century that traces in their works a distinctly female literary tradition.

Heilbrun, Carolyn G., and Margaret R. Higonnet, eds. *The Representation of Women in Fiction*. Series: Selected Papers from the English Institute, 1981. Baltimore: The Johns Hopkins University Press, 1983. Six important essays from the English Institute's first session on feminist criticism. Relevant are Jane Marcus on Virginia Woolf and Mary Poovey on Jane Austen. Heilbrun contributes a brief introduction.

Springer, Marlene, ed. *What Manner of Woman: Essays on English and American Life and Literature*. New York: New York University Press, 1977. A superb collection of essays on women in literature from the medieval period to the present which deals with many of the authors in Heilbrun's study. Includes an essay by Heilbrun on marriage in English literature from 1873 to 1941.

Donna Perry

TRACKS

Author: Louise Erdrich (1954-   )
Type of work: Novel
Type of plot: Domestic realism
Time of plot: 1912-1924
Locale: North Dakota
First published: 1988

> *Principal characters:*
> NANAPUSH, one of two first-person narrators, an old and
>   authoritative Chippewa
> PAULINE PUYAT, a young mixed-blood woman whose unreliable
>   narration moves from prevarication to madness during the
>   course of the book
> FLEUR PILLAGER, a woman who is rescued by Nanapush
> ELI KASHPAW, the son of Margaret (Rushes Bear) and the lover
>   of Fleur
> MARGARET KASHPAW, the fourth wife of Nanapush
> NECTOR KASHPAW, Margaret's practical son
> LULU PILLAGER, Fleur's daughter

Form and Content

Tracks shares with the other novels of Louise Erdrich's Chippewa tetralogy—*Love Medicine* (1984, rev. 1993), *The Beet Queen* (1986), and *The Bingo Palace* (1994)— its form, a series of short interconnected tales reminiscent of oral Indian narrative cycles; its use of contrasting voices, often recounting the same episodes from different points of view; and many of the same characters. Erdrich's continuing concern with American Indian family formation and with the development of character over many years here focuses on the crucial time of 1912 to 1924, when widespread disease; the consequences of the Allotment Acts of 1887 and 1904, when reservation land was divided and sold off (usually to whites); and the bitter division between full-bloods and mixed-bloods (in current slang, "skins" and "breeds") over policy all tore apart the fabric of Chippewa society. This breaking of the "sacred hoop" is Erdrich's main subject here, and she examines her subject through various memorable portraits of strong Indian women.

Strong is not always, however, good. Pauline Puyat—along with Nanapush, one of the two first-person narrators of the novel—is an unreliable and steadily deteriorating character. She does not have, like Nanapush, a direct narratee for her story. Nanapush reminds the reader throughout that his primary audience is Lulu, whom he has helped to rear, has saved from the government school she loathed, and now attempts to dissuade from an unwise marriage to a Morrissey) one of the "breed" families of villains, profiteers reminiscent of Faulkner's Snopeses). Pauline, however, seems to be addressing herself, which is appropriate, considering the self-absorption that she constantly exhibits in the novel. Since no omniscient narrator spans both worlds, as is the case in *Love Medicine* and *The Beet Queen*, readers must choose between Nanapush's and Pauline's often conflicting reports. Because Nanapush's is a seasoned, comic, and often touching voice, one tends to rate his account as being more accurate than Pauline's, especially as she moves from the comparatively normal tone of her first narration through increasing psychosis and utter madness.

For both of them, the focal character is Fleur, "the last Pillager," who comes from a clan that is legendary for its magic and shamanistic power. Three times she almost drowns in Lake Matchimanito, and three times she is saved. During her brief summer in Argus—the only time she lives away from the bush—she is raped (or so Pauline says), revenges herself on the three men responsible, and conceives Lulu, to whom her story is being told. Her passionate mating with Eli results in another pregnancy, Pauline's jealousy, and Pauline's deliberate causing of the death of her child. Eli's familial connection with Margaret and Nector, who cheat Nanapush and Fleur of their land, causes the couple's permanent rupture and, eventually, Fleur's sending Lulu away to government school. In a stunning climax, Fleur's magic and woods knowledge defeat, at least temporarily, a logging company's attempt to rape her land. Nanapush's late-blooming love for Margaret Kashpaw and Pauline's murderous movement from marginal status to sisterhood in a convent and proclamation of her own pure white blood, as well as her bearing and discarding of Marie, are interwoven with Fleur's fascinating but ultimately tragic destiny.

Analysis

As in the other books of the Chippewa tetralogy, Erdich's themes are enduring and interlinked: the necessity for belonging to a family, whether natal or adoptive, and often not conventionally formed; the lure of home, in its difference from alien places and its necessary welcome; and the awe-inspiring power of love, whether erotic or familial. Because this is the earliest in time of all the novels, the contrast between a still mostly virginal reservation and even a small town (as Argus is then, early in this century) is a drastic one for the mostly Indian cast of characters. Besides the residents of Argus, only the priest and the nuns of the convent are white, although there is a sharp division between the "skins" such as Nanapush, Fleur, and Eli, all of them wise in the ways of the woods, and the "breeds," such as the Morrisseys and Lazarres, who tend to take the white man's road. Although Erdrich's decision to forgo the omniscient narrator who might have directly reflected her own sympathies makes the reader dependent for information on the two contrasting first-person voices of Nanapush and Pauline, one easily infers that it is the former and not the latter with whom she empathizes, and, as a corollary, the woods-loving rather than the town group that she favors. Visiting Nanapush at his cabin, Fleur sums it up: " 'I shouldn't have left this place.' "

Tracks has a structure that, for the sections Nanapush narrates, is necessarily circular. At some indeterminate time after 1924 (when she would have been only ten), he is trying to explain her mother to a Lulu who is nubile enough to have engaged herself to a Morrissey. He begins with his rescue of the girl Fleur during the terrible winter of 1912; her stubbornness emerges at once in her refusal of his nurturing any longer than is absolutely necessary and her return to Lake Matchimanito to live alone: "A young girl had never done such a thing before." A mature woman at the end of the book, she again refuses Nanapush's offer of a home and, her cabin forfeit and surrounded by the dozens of oaks she has felled in a final magic gesture, sets off alone hitched to a greenwood cart. Fleur's stubbornness is parallel to her daughter Lulu's, as Nanapush knows, and his role in the story is not only to explain to Lulu that it was her mother's love that sent her away but also to urge her, implicitly, toward a similar independence that he sees she will forfeit if she marries an unworthy man. Pauline's chapters, as they alternate with this circular story, are necessary to let the reader know what Nanapush does not—the Argus episode, for example. They are informed by malice, however, and are correlative in their lying and warped view of events to the threat that assimilation represents to the Chippewa way of life.

Symbolism, too, has much to do with contrasts between the assimilated and the traditional way of life. The umbrella that Fritzie Kozka gives Fleur in Argus she later uses to shade her dead baby's traditional Chippewa grave—a box set high in a tree. The white woman's white fan that Nanapush has kept in his third wife's French trunk he lends Eli to aid in his initial wooing of Fleur. A pair of patent leather shoes, so inappropriate for the woods, a gift to Lulu from Eli, are charred when Margaret, angry that they have injured her little girl's feet, throws them into the fire. All these icons are piled in Fleur's cart with her family's gravemarkers as she leaves Nanapush's sight at the end of the novel.

A complex narrative device revolves around the trope of playing cards. Fleur's skill at cards earns for her not only the money with which to pay the annual fee on all the Pillager lots she has inherited but also the animosity of her male opponents and Lulu. Her gift from her earnings to Nanapush is a new deck of cards to replace his years-old pack. Finally, drawing on actual Chippewa myth involving the presence in heaven of gambling (along with all other pleasures), Pauline sees Fleur involved in a ghostly card game with her three dead former opponents: This time the stakes are her and Eli's child's life, and this time she loses. Of such combinations of myth and reality is the whole novel made.

Context

All of Erdrich's fiction offers believable portraits of strong, capable, and interesting women. This is probably as reflective of the pronounced matriarchal tradition in Chippewa tribal life as it is of the role models that Erdrich has credited among her relatives and friends. Of all of her female portraits, Fleur, Pauline, and Margaret Kashpaw (Rushes Bear, a name she earns from a confrontation in this novel) are among the most memorable. In *Tracks*, there is no female bonding such as that seen in *The Beet Queen*: Each of these women is bound into her own psyche and her own world. Their coming together in the novel results from need rather than from any genuine liking. None of them, however, is reducible to the kind of stereotype—love object, goddess, mother figure—so prevalent in (mostly male-authored) earlier portraits of women.

Margaret, who is in the process of assimilation, is a churchgoing Catholic whose family name ("cash-paw") implies a turning away from the woods and toward the white man's road. Her sons are divided: Eli prefers the woods and the old ways, as is seen in both *Love Medicine* and *The Beet Queen*; Nector represents the future of the tribe, as is especially apparent in *Love Medicine* but also here in his selfish use of Nanapush and Fleur's allotment money to pay the fine on Kashpaw land. Fleur's late-blooming love affair with Nanapush is damaged (although not permanently) by her acquiescence in this act, and she—along with Nanapush—redeems Lulu from the government school and rears her. She is a strong representative of matriarchy in the book.

Pauline represents the most evil presence in the series, here in her role as *provacateuse* and prevaricator, and in *The Beet Queen* and *Love Medicine* as the disturbed (and disturbing) hater disguised in a nun's robe. She seems to be an objective correlative of the baneful influence of the Catholic church on the Chippewa, and, as a half-breed, she is vulnerable to the lure of whiteness (her own is revealed to her in a vision). Yet even here Erdrich tends to resist stereotype: Pauline's consciousness of her own unattractiveness is a strong impetus to her bizarre actions and ultimate madness, and a reminder of the premium that was placed on beauty in earlier literature and the price that women must pay for it in social terms.

Fleur's portrait is Erdrich's masterpiece. In her gallery of remarkable females, no other is so enigmatically attractive. Fleur's passion, independence, and endurance win the reader's heart. Her brief appearances in both *The Beet Queen* and *The Bingo Palace* indicate the extent of her influence in the whole series. In all Western literature there are very few women like Fleur: To use the term "Earth Mother" of her is to suggest one of her dimensions but not to encompass her totality. Fleur indicates Erdrich's ability to penetrate through previous female characterizations and to find for modern women a role model that is significant not only for Native Americans but also for all women who read to discover themselves in the imaginations of gifted writers.

Sources for Further Study
Flavin, James. "The Novel as Performance: Communication in Louise Erdrich's *Tracks*." *Studies in American Indian Literature* 3, no. 4 (Winter, 1991): 1-12. Noting that the novel form, unlike the indigenous oral song or tale, is questionable as a vehicle for expressing American Indian subjects, Flavin discusses Erdrich's use of assumed orality to overcome this difficulty. Particularly with the narrator Nanapush, addressing a listener and constant reference to the Chippewa language are noticeable devices.
Larson, Sidner. "The Fragmentation of a Tribal People in Louise Erdrich's *Tracks*." *American Indian Culture and Research Journal* 17, no. 2 (1993): 1-13. *Tracks* is partially an autopsy for the phenomenon, begun by the General Allotment Acts of

1887 and 1904, by which Indian land became European American property. The exploitation of mixed-bloods resulting from intermarriage and Catholicism provides a primary tension in the novel.

Schumacher, Michael. "A Marriage of Minds." *Writer's Digest*, June, 1991, 28-59. Erdrich and her husband, Michael Dorris, discuss the collaboration they claim for all their work, whether jointly published or bearing only the name of one (as in *Tracks*). They note the importance of orality in this process, both as they talk out their ideas to each other and as they attempt to reproduce Indian oral tradition.

Sergi, Jennifer. "Storytelling: Tradition and Preservation in Louise Erdrich's *Tracks*." *World Literature Today* 66, no. 2 (1992): 279-283. The storyteller relies on memory and a chain of tradition. In *Tracks*, Nanapush uses repetition, parallelism, rhythms suggestive of speech to a named audience (Lulu), and actual Chippewa myths to give poetic and historic voice to the story.

Walker, Victoria. "A Note on Narrative Perspective in *Tracks*." *Studies in American Indian Literature* 3, no. 4 (Winter, 1991): 37-40. Of the two participatory narrators in *Tracks*, one (Pauline) is a liar and the other (Nanapush) speaks not to the reader but to his "adoptive" granddaughter Lulu. Erdrich's refusal to use an omniscient narrator means that one must judge for oneself between a mean-spirited, lying woman and a warm, humorous, appealingly talkative old man.

Maureen Fries

TRIBUTE TO FREUD

Author: H. D. (Hilda Doolittle, 1886-1961)
Type of work: Memoir
Time of work: 1933-1934
Locale: Vienna, Austria
First published: 1974

> *Principal personages:*
> SIGMUND FREUD, the founder of psychoanalysis and H. D.'s analyst
> HILDA DOOLITTLE, an American expatriate poet who signed herself H. D.
> WINIFRED ELLERMAN, known as Bryher, H. D.'s lifelong companion
> D. H. LAWRENCE, H. D.'s friend, a novelist and poet

Form and Content

H. D.'s *Tribute to Freud* is her memoir of her psychoanalysis over a period of five or six months in 1933-1934 at Berggasse 19 in Vienna with Sigmund Freud. Since Freud's intention was to turn H. D. back upon herself, the book is in some ways more about H. D., her life and her poetry, than about Freud himself. The work is in two parts: "Writing on the Wall" and "Advent," which is "the continuation of 'Writing on the Wall,' or its prelude."

"Writing on the Wall" consists of eighty-five numbered sections or meditations written in London in 1944 from memory—without reference to the notes that H. D. had taken, against Freud's suggestion, during the course of her analysis. It was also the first part to be published, first in *Life and Letters Today* in 1945-1946 and then as a book under the title "Tribute to Freud" in 1956. It is dedicated "to Sigmund Freud, blameless physician." "Advent" is both a gloss on "Writing on the Wall" and in a sense its raw material. It was written when H. D. returned to Lausanne, Switzerland, after World War II and recovered her original notes of her analysis: It is thus both closer to the source of her experience than "Writing on the Wall" and able to comment upon it. Nine of Freud's letters to H. D. form an appendix. *Tribute to Freud* also contains a foreword by Norman Holmes Pearson and an introduction by Kenneth Fields.

H. D. begins "Writing on the Wall" with an account of the approach to Freud's house. She had hour-long sessions with Freud five days a week; he was seventy-seven, H. D. forty-seven. H. D. and Freud talk of many things: the gardenias in Rome; H. D.'s jealousy of Princess Marie Bonaparte; Freud's grandchildren; H. D.'s father, mother, and brother; her visions and dreams; Judaism; Greece; and Egypt. At one point, "uncanonically," H. D. sits "stark upright" on the couch with her feet on the floor. Equally uncanonically, Freud himself is beating "the old-fashioned horsehair sofa that has heard more secrets than the confession box." Freud picks up one or another statue from his collection to show her and offers to lend her books. He gossips with her, listens to her, and then suggests interpretations that H. D. sometimes finds "too illuminating," making her "bat-like thought-wings" beat painfully in their searchlight. At times, H. D. prefers her intuition to Freud's considered judgment.

Central to the work is H. D.'s description of a series of visions that she had while in Corfu in 1920, visions which she saw as if projected on the wall of her hotel and which she terms "pictures" or "writing"—the "writings on the wall" of her title. Sections forty-three through forty-five record H. D.'s growing awareness of Nazism: She sees showers of golden paper swastikas ("the gold clear as Danae's legendary shower"), then swastikas in chalk on the Berggasse ("It is not so easy to scrub death-head chalk-marks from a pavement"), and then rifles stacked neatly at the street corners. H. D. is afraid for Freud: Clearly, she loves him. "Writing on the Wall" closes with an analysis of Johann Wolfgang von Goethe's lyric *Kennst du das Land*.

"Advent" is based on H. D.'s 1933 notebooks and was "assembled" in Lausanne in 1948. The entries are dated and contain more mundane details of H. D.'s life than "Writing on the Wall"—and at the same time, some deeper insights into Freud and psychoanalysis. Yet through the whole work runs H. D.'s constant awareness, as poet and as woman, that she "cannot classify the living context" of their talks. It was, she writes, an atmosphere.

Analysis

Memory is at the heart of any psychoanalysis, and hence memory and the problems that it brings with it—the problems of the past in the present, the influence of the past on the future—are major themes in H. D.'s account of her own analysis. "The years went forward, then backward," she writes. "The shuttle of the years ran a thread that wove my pattern into the Professor's."

Specific memories provided the occasions for H. D. and Freud to explore together the peculiarly defensive, allusive, and finally creative character of memory itself, and so of a life's story—H. D.'s own—constantly rewritten. The visions in "Writing on the Wall" constitute one such memory, leading back into others from H. D.'s own life and also into that great reserve of memory that is world culture. Another was the memory of a strange visionary shipboard romance in 1920 with one Peter Van Eck (Rodeck) who was or was not physically present, was or was not somehow her father, was or was not somehow D. H. Lawrence, too—this last discovery being made only after her analysis had ended, her book written. It is the allusiveness of her tone that captures this shuttling of years backward and forward, of memory into analysis and so back into life and forward into the written word.

Yet H. D. is not only an analysand but also woman and poet. Therefore specifically feminine concerns are also thematic in the work, though largely subsumed in her search for an authentic voice and vision. "I do *not* like to be the mother in transference," Freud tells H. D. He sees her bisexuality and constant recourse to ancient mythologies as resulting from her desire to return to the mother: more specifically to the mother of her early years, before gender complicated her life with its identification of her as a girl, while she could still be the boy-god of one of her analytic dreams. While attempting to provide a more positive alternative to her cold fish of a father, Freud is careful never to criticize H. D.'s lesbian aspect. He maintained simultaneously a warm friendship with H. D.'s companion, Bryher, who was herself a major supporter of the psychoanalytic venture.

Freud was in some sense the completion of H. D.'s experience of family. "I am on the fringes or in the penumbra of the light of my father's science and my mother's art—the psychology or philosophy of Sigmund Freud," she writes. This leads immediately to creation: "I must find new words as the Professor found or coined new words to explain certain as yet unrecorded states of mind or being." With new words come new forms: H. D., ever the classicist, was also a constant innovator and experimentalist, in prose and poetry alike. It is not surprising that *Tribute to Freud* can be read as an experiment in autobiography—a capturing of the allusiveness of the psychoanalytic method of free association—or as a set of extended prose meditations, akin to Thomas Traherne's *Centuries of Meditations* (1908) in modern idiom.

Finally, Freud himself is the theme central to this work—that is, H. D.'s Freud. She writes that theirs was "the most luscious sort of vers libre relationship"—and Lisa Appignanesi and John Forrester, in their monumental exploration, *Freud's Women* (1992), suggest that for Freud too the relationship had a special, even amorous quality. As they write, "Only perhaps with Lou Andreas-Salomé, his other literary patient-pupil, did Freud display a similar tone—a loving care, compounded with respect and imaginative interest." He is virtually deified in *Tribute to Freud*, which is dedicated to him as "blameless physician"—a phrase classically used to describe Asclepios, Apollo's son—and views him in turn as a Moses, a guardian of sacred treasures, a magician, and Faust.

Yet H. D. is rewriting Freud as she goes: "He has to stick to his scientific guns, but I have to stick to mine too." What he sees as a dangerous symptom, she sees as mystical vision. Characteristically, immediately after her phrases about finding new words, H. D. turns to alchemy: "We retreat from the so-called sciences and go backward or forward into alchemy." Alchemy is hardly popular among psychoanalysts of the Freudian school, although Herbert Silberer's *Probleme der mystik und ihrer symbolik* (1914; *Problems of Mysticism and Its Symbolism*, 1917) deals sensitively with it. As a territory, it has largely been ceded to Carl Jung and his followers, the analytical psychologists. Yet here is H. D. speaking of her work with Freud as alchemical. "He is Faust, surely," she writes.

Context

The redoubtable Ernest Jones, Freud's biographer, called this work "surely the most delightful and precious appreciation of Freud's personality that is ever likely to be written. . . . It will live as the most enchanting ornament of all the Freudian literature." Many psychoanalysts have indeed turned to "Writing on the Wall," hoping to learn something about Freud's methodology from it. Norman Holland writes: "I know of no account by an analysand that tells more about Freud, his techniques, or the analytic experience as it seems from within."

Clearly, *Tribute to Freud* is first and foremost the account of an analysis with Freud, and its primary impact is therefore in the realm of psychoanalytic studies. Yet H. D.'s life and work have, as Appignanesi and Forrester note, "served as something of an exemplum in feminist literary history." Her struggle to find a voice true to her erotic and creative life as a woman—whether that struggle involved wrestling with Erza Pound, D. H. Lawrence, Freud, or (as always) with herself—lies at the heart of that life. It is that which has made her life paradigmatic for so many later readers.

Paradoxically, because that true voice comes from the mothers—that is, from the realm of intuition, dream, and myth—H. D. is perhaps more likely to find a sensitive reading among the goddess-feminists, who are Jungian in sympathy, than among their Freudian counterparts. It is this more sympathetic reading of H. D. herself in *Tribute to Freud* that finally permits her to emerge from the shadow of Erza Pound and to be seen by writers such as Margaret Dickie as so much more than an early Imagist. She was an important figure in the transition to modernism and, more than that, a major poet of feminine erotic and mystical sensibility.

Sources for Further Study

Appignanesi, Lisa, and John Forrester. *Freud's Women*. New York: Basic Books, 1992. A major work dealing with Freud's opinions on and relationships with women, ranging from Dora to Anna Freud and from Sabina Spielrein to Lou Andreas-Salomé. The section devoted to H. D. portrays their relationship as among the warmest and most sympathetic of his life. With notes and an index.

Chisholm, Dianne. *H. D.'s Freudian Poetics: Psychoanalysis in Translation*. Ithaca, N.Y.: Cornell University Press, 1992. An extended study of H. D.'s later poetry in the light of her reading of and analysis with Freud. Some knowledge of standard Freudian terminology (such as "screen memory") helps. Offers extensive notes, a bibliography, and an index.

Dickie, Margaret. "Women Poets and the Emergence of Modernism." In *The Columbia History of American Poetry*, edited by Jay Parini. New York: Columbia University Press, 1993. A sensitive essay offering an extended treatment of H. D., Marianne Moore, and Gertrude Stein. Dickie views them as figures who were rendered marginal by the assumptions of their male colleagues in literary modernism. They had to wait almost a century for the recognition that they deserved and the readers who would cherish them, because they were "at least that far ahead of their times."

Gay, Peter. *Freud: A Life for Our Time*. New York: W. W. Norton, 1988. The definitive biography of Freud, in which for the first time his theories and writings are fully integrated into his life story. H. D. is given only slight mention, but this work is the simplest and most complete introduction to both the life and the work of Freud and thus provides an invaluable tool in understanding H. D.'s very personal and idiosyncratic sense of the man. Notes, a bibliographical essay, and an index are included.

Guest, Barbara. *Herself Defined: The Poet H. D. and Her World*. London: Collins, 1985. An excellent biography of H. D., tracing the many strands that, woven together, constitute the complex life of a woman whose work was always autobiographical, always rooted in the concrete event as it flowered in symbolic and mythic thought. With a bibliography and an index.

Robinson, Janice. *H. D.: The Life and Work of an American Poet*. Boston: Houghton Mifflin, 1982. A biography of H. D. which puts slightly greater emphasis on the psychoanalytic aspect of her life than Barbara Guest's work (above). Contains notes, a bibliography, and an index.

Charles Cameron

TRILOGY

Author: H. D. (Hilda Doolittle, 1886-1961)
Type of work: Poetry
First published: 1973

Form and Content

Trilogy brings together in one poetic sequence three volumes of poems, *The Walls Do Not Fall* (1944), *Tribute to the Angels* (1945), and *The Flowering of the Rod* (1946). Each of the three volumes in turn consists of forty-three numbered poems.

The poems of *The Walls Do Not Fall* were written during World War II while the bombs fell on London: "but when the shingles hissed// in the rain of incendiary,/ other values were revealed to us,// other standards hallowed us." They are war poems, but the war in question is not only World War II but also the war of the biblical book Revelation—apocalyptic war when that which has been hidden is revealed: "over us, Apocryphal fire,/ under us, the earth sway, dip of a floor." *The Walls Do Not Fall* is also about Egypt, and specifically Karnak, which H. D. had visited with her companion Winifred Ellerman, known by the pen name Bryher. The tombs of the Egyptian dead opened to the air by archaeology resemble the rooms sliced open in London by German bombs: "we pass on// to another cellar, to another sliced wall/ where poor utensils show/ like rare objects in a museum." Still the walls do not fall. Visionary experiences, a kind of ecstasy in the heart of wartime London, and the uncovering and assimilation of memories thread through the poems of this sequence until, at the last, some hope of reaching safe "haven, heaven" can be found.

H. D. called *Tribute to the Angels* a "premature peace poem." Osbert Sitwell had recommended *The Walls Do Not Fall* to the Oxford University Press and suggested in a review that more was needed in the same vein, and *Tribute to the Angels* was H. D.'s response. The sequence opens with Hermes Trismegistus, patron of alchemists and founder of Hermetism; passes to St. John of Patmos, the author of Revelation (the key text here); and then in the central poems invokes a succession of seven angels (as in Revelation), beginning with Azrael, angel of death. In the alchemical crucible that London was for her, H. D. could not escape "the spear/ that pierces the heart," but she can "admit the transubstantiation." She can sense the rood, the tree of the Crucifixion which is also a half-dead London tree, beginning to put forth new blossoms. The sequence ends with a vision of the Virgin Mary, carrying a book that is yet to be written, containing a wisdom that is yet to be revealed. While that wisdom has not yet been written, it can no longer be prevented from coming into existence, because Mary is also "Psyche, the butterfly,/ out of the cocoon."

The Flowering of the Rod was written in the two weeks surrounding Christmas, 1944. Its title refers back to the twenty-third poem in *Tribute to the Angels*, and this sequence picks up the image of Mary from the last poems in that volume: Only here, Mary is at first the Magdalen, the whore, the pagan. The wise men from the East— Kaspar, Melchior, Balthasar, the Magi with their gifts—figure largely in the body of the text, in much the same way that the angels figured in *Tribute to the Angels*. The whole sequence describes the shift by which Kaspar comes to perceive a pure and heavenly Mary in Mary Magdalen; by giving the Magdalen an alabaster jar, he offers her the means to anoint the feet of Christ.

Taken together, the three books in *Trilogy* move from the desolating actuality of London in the Blitz, via passion, death, and resurrection (mediated by the angels) toward the revelation of a new wisdom, to be born like a Christ Child of the female psyche.

Analysis

In *The Walls Do Not Fall*, the walls are those of Karnak and London, physically, and the walls of that view of life which was under attack by Adolf Hitler. Yet they are also H. D.'s own walls—the walls of what she calls "our own house of life," in which "outer violence" touches "the deepest hidden subconscious terrors." If Karnak is London, then the Egyptian scribes and their gods are also present in London: H. D. herself is scribe, visionary, and poet, and the gods are her protectors, the protectors of poetry and vision. As H. D. suggests in a letter to her friend Norman Holmes Pearson, "Protection for the scribe seems to be the leit-motif. And the feeling of assurance back of it, of the presence of the God of the Scribe."

The angels in *Tribute to the Angels*, as a hint in the twenty-fourth poem suggests ("Every hour, every moment/ has its specific attendant Spirit"), can be read as the different Angels of the Hours venerated during H. D.'s Moravian childhood. They are also the angels she helped her friend Gustav Davidson research for *Dictionary of Angels*. Again, they are the angels of Revelation, of John Milton's *Paradise Lost* (1667, 1674) and the literary tradition of which she is a part. Finally, they are the men she termed "initiators" in her life, from Ezra Pound ("Azrael") on. Likewise the Mary of her vision is herself. This is implicit in the reference to Mary as Santa Sophia, Holy Wisdom (that is, poetic inspiration) in the thirty-sixth poem and explicit in the statement that she is Psyche (that is, the soul) in the thirty-eighth poem. So "her book is our book," the book of a feminine wisdom yet to be written.

The theme of *The Flowering of the Rod* is introduced in *Tribute to the Angels* as "a tale of a Fisherman,/ a tale of a jar or jars." The tale of the fisherman is that of Christ, which also contains the tale of an "alabaster jar" that Mary Magdalen found, although "it is not on record/ exactly where and how" she found it. Jars, indeed, are a central image. These are the "unguent jars" of an Arab—one at least filled with myrrh for a "double ceremony, a funeral and a throning," while the other, at poem's end, an offering of Kaspar of the Magi at the Christ Child's feet. These and the Arab's other jars have "sigils and painted figures" on them, but "though the jars were sealed,/ the fragrance got out somehow." No doubt the jars themselves recall such jars on the shelves of Sigmund Freud, with whom H. D. experimented with psychoanalysis. More than that, they figure for symbols within dreams, sealed yet fragrant, unreadable yet filled with ancient meaning. The Arab—who might be a Chaldean, Balthasar, Melchior, "that other" wise man Kaspar, an angel, an old lover, or God (but who, "of course" was Kaspar)—brings (or does not bring, or brings in endless ritual repetition) the jar to Mary, who is herself myrrh (Mary-myrrh) and who pours it with kisses on Christ's feet. There is also a door "ajar" between two rooms, two worlds. In all this—the doorway between rooms, the sigils on the side of the jars, the sealed jars and their fragrance that escapes—there are hints of hidden things that shall be revealed and that shall pertain to funeral and crowning, death and glory.

Such layering of meaning, in *The Flowering of the Rod* and in the rest of *Trilogy*, is achieved by an allusive style of writing which in itself constitutes both an archaeology of the unconscious (uncovering layers of buried memory) and a palimpsest (concealing and revealing layers of meaning). Frequent shimmering transformations occur between kindred figures from different iconographic traditions and from her own life. Word associations ("jar" and "ajar"), of a kind certainly encouraged by H. D.'s time in analysis with Freud, play their part. Yet H. D. can be seen as reversing Freud's own reductionist tendency. For while it is Freud's trope to draw a moral out of myth—to reduce the Oedipus myth to a complex, and thus to equate Sophocles' *Oedipus Rex* with a proposition about childhood trauma—H. D.'s trope is, literally, the "re-verse": to derive myth from her psychoanalytic insights and thus to reinstate their inherent poetry.

Context

H. D.'s style, from the beginning, sat well with Pound's call for a modern poetry that would avoid unnecessary words and stick to "the thing"—so well, indeed, that at times she seemed almost invisible: the perfect Poundian, rather than herself. Yet her voice is a woman's voice, her vision a woman's vision. As *Trilogy* appeared, first volume by slim volume during the war years in England, it must have given succor to many women whose male counterparts were finding it in T. S. Eliot's *Four Quartets* (1943). With the reemergence of feminism in the 1960's and 1970's, her voice was an exemplary woman's voice, heard alongside those of her contemporaries, Gertrude Stein and Marianne Moore.

Yet H. D. was more than a woman poet: She was a seer, a visionary. Louis Martz, in his introduction to *H. D.: Collected Poems 1912-1944*, calls *The Flowering of the Rod* "a new myth of redemption." She was, herself, the carrier of "a book" that "is not/ the tome of the ancient wisdom," whose pages "are the blank pages/ of the unwritten volume of the new." It is a specifically feminine myth that H. D. is not only writing herself in *Trilogy* but also proposing as her poetic solution to the troubles of a world. In Dianne Chisholm's terms, she "resets the stage . . . for the uncanny return of the mother of prehistory, the mother from whom Freud withdrew in horror and despair, the mother who brings with her a song even more 'originary' than that of the prehistoric father."

Thus she is the precursor of that specific tradition in feminism which draws more on her disliked Carl Jung than on her beloved Freud, a feminism which sees in a return to the goddess its root and flower. Hers was neither the loudest nor the first voice of postwar feminism, but she was far ahead of her times.

Sources for Further Study

Chisholm, Dianne. *H. D.'s Freudian Poetics: Psychoanalysis in Translation*. Ithaca, N.Y.: Cornell University Press, 1992. Examines H. D.'s later poetry, of which *Trilogy* is the centerpiece, in the light of her relationship with Freud. Requires some knowledge of standard Freudian terminology. Extensive notes, a bibliography, and an index are provided.

Dickie, Margaret. "Women Poets and the Emergence of Modernism." In *The Columbia History of American Poetry*, edited by Jay Parini. New York: Columbia University Press, 1993. A sensitive essay that covers H. D., Marianne Moore, and Gertrude Stein. Dickie argues that all three women were almost a century ahead of their overshadowing male contemporaries—and thus required that much time to find their audience.

Guest, Barbara. *Herself Defined: The Poet H. D. and Her World*. London: Collins, 1985. A biography of H. D. which analyzes the complex life of a woman whose work was always autobiographical but which contained symbolic and mythic themes. A bibliography and an index are included.

H. D. *Tribute to Freud*. Boston: D. R. Godine, 1974. H. D.'s own account of her psychoanalysis with Sigmund Freud, which provides an entrance into the understanding of her life and mode of work. Crucial to understanding of *Trilogy* and the works that were to follow. Widely recommended as the first of H. D.'s books to read. With an appendix of letters from Freud to H. D.

Robinson, Janice. *H. D.: The Life and Work of an American Poet*. Boston: Houghton Mifflin, 1982. An excellent, introspective biography of H. D. Notes, a bibliography, and an index are provided.

Charles Cameron

THE TRIUMPH OF ACHILLES

Author: Louise Glück (1943-   )
Type of work: Poetry
First published: 1985

Form and Content

The poems in *The Triumph of Achilles* explore sexuality and power, the relation of Eros and Art, the conditions of endurance, and the differences between the aesthetics of men and women. Louise Glück employs a stark, declarative poetry that often grounds its arguments in classical Greek mythology or biblical allusions. Throughout these poems, Glück anatomizes desire and reveals the deep structures that still define the female body.

The twenty-six poems in *The Triumph of Achilles* are arranged in three parts. Of these poems, eight are long poems divided into sections, some of which are titled. Most illustrative of her long poems is "Marathon." Placed at the heart of this collection, "Marathon" consists of nine titled sections that trace, through juxtaposition rather than any sequential ordering, the course of a romantic relationship. This emphasis on the long poem, like that on fusing myth with contemporary life, first appears in Glück's previous collection, *Descending Figure* (1980). Through her use of the long poem, Glück not only recasts the idea of lyric but also redefines the nature of confessional poetry.

Whereas "Marathon" draws together many of Glück's thematic and stylistic concerns, the collection's opening poem, "Mock Orange," establishes the stringent tone that runs throughout the collection. In this poem, Glück rejects the romantic, sensual qualities of the fragrance of mock orange; in its cloying scent, it is as paralyzing as a man's body, "the man's mouth/ sealing my mouth." The oppressive division between the genders is explicit. The aesthetic choices allowed women are controlled—or usurped—by the male: He seals—either approving or silencing—the poet's voice.

"Mock Orange" is typical of Glück's poetry in that it relies on few particularizing details. There is a refusal of any rapture with language, the world, or the body. Indeed, each of these elements has been distilled into an abstraction. Ironically, only the poet's voice conveys a sense of its own history and narrative—that it is a particular voice, one that has been, however, forced into desolation and obsession.

Glück creates drama through the urgency of an implicit and revelatory dialogue with the reader. "Mock Orange" conveys this in the aside that completes the first line: "It is not the moon, I tell you." The asides, however, function as rhetorical questions; at the conclusion of the poem, for example, the poet asks, "How can I rest?" The response is yet another question: "How can I be content/ when there is still/ that odor in the world?" The collection responds to these questions of the dominion of the body and its inescapable desires.

The arrangement of the poems in *The Triumph of Achilles* emphasizes the juxtaposition between the varied tones of the poems. For example, "Mock Orange" is followed by "Metamorphosis," which is a meditation on Glück's father's death and which insists on survival and life. "Metamorphosis" expands on the confessionalism implicit in the asides in "Mock Orange." Signaled by the allusion to the Latin poet Ovid's *Metamorphoses*, "Metamorphosis" turns the anger and desolation of "Mock Orange" into self-affirmation. In the penultimate sentence of "For My Father," the third and final section of "Metamorphosis," Glück states, "I feel/ no coldness that can't be explained." Against this assumption of complete knowledge—an assertion of power and control—Glück concludes, "Against your cheek, my hand is warm/ and full of tenderness."

The first part of the collection concludes with "Liberation," which reverses the conditions of power that were established in "Mock Orange." The poet realizes that power—that which can kill—negates the possibility of reflection and questioning. "Only victims have a destiny," states Glück, whereas it is the hunter who "is paralyzed." This reversal of the conditions of domination is further explored in the second part of the collection, especially in "Marathon," the concluding section of the poem of the same title. Here, the patriarchal power of objectification and control, particularly of sexuality, is assumed by the woman poet, even while her position is that of the victim. In the third part of the collection, Glück further explores this reversal of power as well as the duplicity of Eros in such poems as "The Reproach," "Elms," and "Horse." With Eros comes power and inescapable desire that paradoxically overwhelms life, as Glück states in "Horse," the concluding poem of the collection: "Look at me. You think I don't understand?/ What is the animal/ if not the passage out of this life?"

Analysis

Glück's poetry challenges definitions of desire, and her work also redefines lyric and confessional poetry. Revelations of the personal are counterbalanced by the need of the woman poet to mask herself. By grounding her poems in myth, Glück distances herself from the personal, though she may be addressing issues of desire, relationships, or sexuality that among her contemporaries, such as the poet Sharon Olds, would be given explicit expression. Eschewing outright narratives and favoring allusive but disjunctive dramas, Glück risks a nihilistic vision in which the contemporary world is always constructed in mythic archetypes. Glück finds in classical myth and biblical allusions, however, a way of preempting narrative structures (since the stories are already known) and favoring the lyric aria or collapse that follows; for Glück, that is where the possibility of reflection is the greatest.

In "Mythic Fragment," death and freedom are bound together in sexuality. Adapting the myth of Daphne, Glück sees in her transformation not rescue from Apollo but stasis and the loss of freedom. The myth is not recast; instead, Glück emphasizes the depth of desolation that is implicit in such myths of transformation and desire. Daphne says, "Reader,/ pity Apollo," for in his arms she was able to stiffen into a laurel tree, thereby thwarting his desires—yet her power was granted only by her father, a river god, who otherwise abandons her: "of his encompassing love/ my father made/ no other sign from the water." Within the compass of myth, argues Glück, female sexuality can either be denied or be the object of ravishment.

In "Marathon," Glück utilizes elements of confessional poetry while also muting the reader's expectations. Stylistically, "Marathon" departs from much of Glück's poetry in its use of longer lines that are often end-stopped. Nevertheless, this emphasis on the pause or silence at the line's end corresponds to her use of shorter lines that usually end at what would have been a caesura or at the point at which the breath breaks on an accented word or syllable. This use of end-stops is one form of control that Glück exerts over the embedded drama of her poems. Such control over the line is also found in the use of syllabically short phrases, which further underscores the necessity to pause or restrain the movement of the poem. Thus, Glück transforms the seemingly excessive emotionalism of confessional poetry into formal restraint. This corresponds to the thematic tension between desire and order, body and reason, excess and freedom. As Glück writes in "The Beginning," the sixth section of "Marathon," "what began as love for you/ became a hunger for structure."

"Marathon" anchors its drama in the classical allusion of its title: It refers not only to the endurance race, in which the runner's body tests its own limits, and to the celebrated battle in which the Athenians repelled the Persians in 490 B.C. but also to the monumental site of the tumulus that was raised over the bodies of the Athenians killed in that battle. The poem encompasses these aspects in that it is thematically concerned with conflict and endurance, as suggested in the fifth section, "Night Song":

> You're tired; I can see that.
> We're both tired, we have acted a great drama.
> Even our hands are cold, that were like kindling.
> Our clothes are scattered on the sand; strangely enough,
> they never turned to ashes.

The poem is also a monument, like the tumulus at Marathon: "you must have known, then, how I wanted you./ We will always know that, you and I./ The proof will be my body." The woman's body is the object of desire and the site where that desire is made manifest.

Desire negates identity. In sexual consummation, people lose their particularity and become, in Glück's words in "Song of Invisible Boundaries," the eighth section of "Marathon," "interchangeable/ with anyone, in joy/ changed to a mute couple." To lie "in the bright light without distinction," Glück argues, "is what we craved." Juxtaposed to this craving is Glück's self-definition, "we who would leave behind/ exact records." These lines, which conclude this section, are set off by a dash, as though to indicate their provisionality and to emphasize that, ultimately, the ethical action of witnessing is overwhelmed by desire. If the loss of self defines desire's fulfillment, then it also negates the freedom to question and to take account of oneself. The final lines of "Marathon" emphasize this moral collapse: "the bond with any one soul/ is meaningless; you throw it away."

The Triumph of Achilles puts forward a critique of desire. In these poems, desire is antithetical to freedom and is in fact the expression of domination and objectification of women. Transcendence through passion is impossible, as Glück relates in the title poem: Achilles, who was part god, was also "a man already dead, a victim/ of the part that loved,/ the part that was mortal." How people construct their inner lives and their social relationships is expressed through past myths; indeed, myths are the informing deep structures of language and actions. Thus, as Glück reads relationships or myths, she sees the implicit violence of hierarchy and domination: "Always in these friend-ships/ one serves the other, one is less than the other."

Context

Glück's poetry marks a turn away from strict confessionalism. Her reliance on a classicist poetics—spare, distanced, allusive—suppresses any outright identification with aesthetics of a woman-centered poetry that emphasizes a direct experiential poetry that bears witness. The recipient of the National Book Critics Circle Award, the Boston Globe Literary Press Award, and the Poetry Society of America's Melville Cane Award, *The Triumph of Achilles* raises the issue of complicity in one's own oppression. Although Glück's tone is critical of the myths she invokes, those myths are presented as inescapable dramas.

In these poems, passion leads to oblivion rather than transcendence, art risks being overcome by Eros, the body too easily overwhelms knowing, and sexual consumma-tion erases freedom. If there is to be some solace, then it is that poems are written in the face of such conditions, that against this structured violence one has the choice to write or make art. Nevertheless, the implicit distrust of the body is a disturbing element of Glück's poetry. The extreme passivity exposed in these poems—exemplified in the detached narrative of the "I" or the controlling elements of myth—is clearly what Glück seeks to criticize, yet such passivity seems also to come to define her poetics.

Sources for Further Study

Dodd, Elizabeth. *The Veiled Mirror and the Woman Poet: H. D., Louise Bogan, Elizabeth Bishop, and Louise Glück.* Columbia: University of Missouri Press, 1992. Contains a most useful and extended discussion of Glück's poetry, with particular emphasis on Glück's postconfessional classicism.

Keller, Lynn. "'Free/ of Blossom and Subterfuge': Louise Glück and the Language of Renunciation." In *World, Self, Poem: Essays on Contemporary Poetry from the "Jubilation of Poets,"* edited by Leonard M. Trawick. Kent, Ohio: Kent State University Press, 1990. An overview of Glück's poetry arguing that it "raises crucial, disturbing issues about women's complicity in their own oppression."

McMahon, Lynne. "The Sexual Swamp: Female Erotics and the Masculine Art." *Southern Review* 28, no. 2 (Spring, 1992): 333-352. Concentrates on the long poem "Marathon," and reads Glück's poetry in relation to the work of the poets Marianne Moore and Elizabeth Bishop.

Raffel, Burton. "The Poetry of Louise Glück." *The Literary Review* 31, no. 3 (Spring, 1988): 261-273. This overview of Glück's work is largely critical of *The Triumph of Achilles*, seeing the collection as overdramatized, artificial, and often trite.

Vendler, Helen. *The Music of What Happens: Poems, Poets, Critics*. Cambridge, Mass.: Harvard University Press, 1988. A brief chapter on Glück emphasizes the demands of writing poems employing myth.

James McCorkle

TROPISMS

Author: Nathalie Sarraute (1900-   )
Type of work: Novel
Type of plot: Psychological realism
Time of plot: The 1930's
Locale: Paris, London, and unspecified locations
First published: Tropismes, 1939; rev. ed. 1957 (English translation, 1963)

Form and Content

Tropisms is a collection of brief, nonnarrative prose pieces. Very little, on the surface, links these two- or three-page fragments together. Upon close reading, however, certain patterns emerge: the almost constant use of the third person, the tension between childhood and adulthood, a deep suspicion and even fear of the spoken word. There are twenty-four such texts, each preceded by a roman numeral like a chapter in a more conventional novel. Each of these texts proposes a distilled version of a phenomenon of human existence: crowds of housewives gathered in front of a store window (number I), an old man taking his grandson for a walk (number VIII), the moment before teatime in a small cottage in the suburbs of London (number XVIII).

The word "tropism" originally refers to the tendency of plants to respond to certain outside stimuli, such as light, but growing (and thereby "moving") in a particular direction. Nathalie Sarraute applies the word to the human sphere; therefore, she suggests that there is a level of consciousness which is almost plantlike in its simplicity—one might say its primitiveness—yet which underlies all human actions and emotions in the world. The purpose of *Tropisms* is to encircle, in writing, the almost imperceptible movement that occurs at the point of origin of human consciousness. By so doing, Sarraute tries to reinvest writing with the ability to convey the truth: If language can serve to represent a state of consciousness that precedes a human being's sense of self in the world, then it will also be purged of the corrupting influence that life in society has upon the written and spoken word.

The theory behind *Tropisms* is difficult to explain without reference to the work itself and to the means by which it suggests the existence of a latent reality. One of Sarraute's strategies, for example, is to portray scenes of people who are clearly out of touch with the world that surrounds them. In number III, she describes the lives of the inhabitants of a small neighborhood in Paris, people who are unaware of others except as occasional, phantomlike presences and who do not even know their own past. In very stark terms, she shows how life has radically separated these individuals from the real world, so that they exist in a state of perpetual blindness or illusion.

Some of the pieces in *Tropisms* bring into play the role of literature and art in human society. Number XI, for example, speaks of a woman who has learned the secret of appreciating culture. She reads about art and literature, convinced that they contain the key to real value in life. Her appreciation is simply a mode of snobbery, however, and she and others like her use great art to claim membership in an elite group of initiates. By suggesting that most people respond to art in the same way, Sarraute indicates that there is a parallel between one's way of reading and viewing great works of art and one's way of perceiving reality: Although people think that they are in touch with what is genuine and real, they are in reality deluding themselves. The actual meaning of the world and human existence becomes manifest only when one has succeeded in stripping away these layers of false consciousness and arriving at the primitive source of the human relationship to the world, the tropism itself. The next-to-last fragment in the book, number XXIII, reaffirms the false attitude of people toward art, as a small assembly discusses the film that they have just seen: They appear to the protagonist of the scene (a woman referred to only as "she") not as real people, but as characters from realist fiction by Honoré de Balzac, Gustave Flaubert, Guy de Maupassant, and others. The stereotyped world of conventional narrative has infiltrated, and even replaced, everyday life.

Finally, it is important to point out the role of children in some of the fragments that make up *Tropisms*. Sarraute apparently takes the position that life in the world involves a loss of innocence, a descent into deceit and corruption. It is only logical, therefore, that children should be somewhat more immune to the deluding qualities of language than adults. An example of this is number XV, in which a young girl (probably adolescent) has a conversation with an elderly man who comes to visit. The girl looks forward to the conversation, impressed as she is by the man's age and the history that he represents (he even kissed the hand of the Empress Eugénie, the wife of Napoleon III). The encounter becomes increasingly unpleasant, however, as the old man seizes the girl and carries on a nonsensical conversation about her trip to England, in which names and fragments of names of English writers and cities tumble out of his mouth. Only when her parents enter the room is she finally able to escape his grasp. The moment is fraught with a kind of terror of the old man, whose behavior is attributable partly to senility but is also symptomatic of the world at large that the young girl trusts so much, but that will sooner or later hold her in its grip as well. The notion of something sinister and grotesque lurking beneath the benign aspect of everyday reality is also strongly characteristic of the work as a whole, making this a representative fragment on a number of levels. The final tropism, number XXIV, seems to be written from the point of view of an infant, a final indictment of the adult world from the only person who can effectively judge it.

Analysis

The difficulty of placing *Tropisms* in any preexisting category suggests that Sarraute may have invented a whole new literary genre. It is not a novel in any recognized sense of the term, since it shares none of the structural elements—plot, dialogue, characterization—that even the most experimental works tend to display to some degree. *Tropisms* cannot be called prose poetry either, because the various fragments nevertheless cohere into some sort of a narrative whole by virtue of being variations on the idea contained in the title: Human consciousness is constituted by tropisms, tiny movements "of which we are hardly cognizant, [and which] slip through us on the frontiers of consciousness in the form of undefinable, extremely rapid sensations." The preceding quote is from Sarraute's introduction to the 1963 English edition, translated by Maria Jolas, and must count as an important key to the interpretation of the novel itself.

In fact, Sarraute's work is of great importance to the development of twentieth century literature precisely because it occupies a position on the border separating philosophy from the novel. She begins with an epistemological problem: What element of human consciousness, if any, precedes language? Is there a state of innocence in which humans already exist as conscious entities, but have not yet been contaminated by the meaninglessness and deception inherent in human speech? The quest for such an idealized state dominates this and much of the rest of Sarraute's work, and it goes far toward explaining why children often seem to be her protagonists.

By asking these questions, Sarraute had a far greater impact on the history of the novel than anyone could have anticipated at the time. When *Tropisms* first appeared in 1939, it hardly left a trace in the literary world. The first work by Sarraute that more clearly fit the designation of a "novel" was *Martereau* (1953), and it achieved much greater recognition. It was not until the 1950's, after her work had attracted the attention of philosopher Jean-Paul Sartre and the growing movement of the French New Novel, that her influence began in earnest.

Her philosophical concerns made her concentrate on certain elements in her prose that had previously fallen outside the purview of the novel: the emphasis, for example, on tiny, quotidian gestures, as ends in themselves, rather than as the means toward a more encompassing narrative; the perception of human activity, even of thought and emotions, as a conglomerate of tiny movements, of yearnings and frustrations, analogous to life in its most basic form; and the constant suspicion of language in all its permutations, and of the society in which it functions.

Many of these elements found their way into the theory of the New Novel, which revolutionized narrative literature in France after World War II. The proponents of the New Novel, such as Michel Butor, Alain Robbe-Grillet, and Claude Simon, were very conscious of Sarraute's achievements, and *Tropisms* was an important early influence on their work. Sarraute has resisted being grouped together with the members of the movement, yet in spite of her artistic independence, her work helped the New Novelists explore the implications of the theory of an "antinovel," which seemed at the time to open up entirely new fields of narrative investigation. Because it was in many ways a forerunner of the New Novel, it is important to consider *Tropisms* a novel as well: Even its resistance to such a categorization, because of its lack of resemblance to any novel written up to that time, became part of the radical new way of conceiving the genre that was popular in the 1950's and early 1960's.

Context

Just as Nathalie Sarraute explicitly resisted being grouped together with other authors and literary trends of any sort, she denied that her work can be associated with a particular political stance, feminist or otherwise. Furthermore, many readers have criticized her way of portraying female characters: Tropism number X, for example, shows women on an outing together, whose behavior and birdlike chatter makes them paradigms of the superficiality of human existence and stereotypical, idle, upper-class women. Similar characterizations abound throughout her work. Under these conditions, one can ask whether it is possible to speak of Sarraute in connection to women's issues without distorting her work beyond recognition.

As Lucille Frackman Becker proves, however, there are many important interpretations of Sarraute that claim her relevance to the question of women's writing. By rejecting linear narration and causality, Becker argues, Sarraute successfully developed an alternative to masculine modes of writing. The question that one must address in connection to a novelist as avant-garde and experimental as Sarraute is whether the alternative that she proposes can actually be termed feminine, as distinct from other types of nonconventional (and even anticonventional) prose that do not aspire to the term "women's writing." To phrase the question differently, what is specifically feminine, or feminist, about Sarraute's search for a style which reflects the deeper reality behind the masks and appearances of the social world? Her own literary criticism, such as the essays gathered in the collection *The Age of Suspicion* (1956), does not address this problem directly.

The answer to such a question lies not so much in the actual text of *Tropisms* and Sarraute's other novels as in the impact that they have had on the development of a sophisticated and influential theory of "women's writing" in France. Monique Wittig, for example, is one French feminist theorist whose work shows strong ties to Sarraute. By giving a voice to that which is inarticulate or silent (like the many children or childlike characters who inhabit the novel) and trying to capture a level of consciousness which precedes or altogether avoids the act of rational self-reflection, Sarraute made a substantial case for the possibility of a privileged female perspective. At any rate, such is the argument of those who would advocate the idea of a gendered writing. One has to remember that many writers, both male and female, resist the idea that writing can manifest such a gendered nature, and that Sarraute herself must be counted among them.

Sarraute's influence on the relatively new concept of women's writing has been compared to that of Marguerite Duras, another novelist who opens up the possibility of a mode of writing that lies outside the boundaries of patriarchal speech. The greatest difference between the two on the level of their relationship to women's writing is that Duras does not resist the label of "woman writer," at least not as explicitly as Sarraute. By the 1980's, both women had earned the reputation as France's foremost living novelists, the first time in French history that women were so prominent in this area.

Sources for Further Study
Becker, Lucille Frackman. *Twentieth-Century French Women Novelists*. Boston: Twayne, 1989. This overview of contemporary French women's writing places

Sarraute in the broader literary context of her time. By constantly emphasizing a feminist theoretical viewpoint, Becker brings the question of women's writing in connection to Sarraute into clear focus.

Besser, Gretchen Rous. *Nathalie Sarraute*. Boston: Twayne, 1979. Part of a series on world literature, Besser's book is a very good introduction to Sarraute's life and work. She particularly emphasizes Sarraute's role in the origin and development of the New Novel in France, while at the same time demonstrating her independence and individuality in comparison with other contemporary writers. Contains a useful chronology and a bibliography.

Cohn, R. "Nathalie Sarraute's Sub-Conversations." *Modern Language Notes* 78 (1963): 261-270. The notion of "sub-conversation," or the true dialogue that takes place implicitly within actual exchanges of words, is an important concept for the understanding of *Tropisms*. Cohn's article is one of the better analyses of this phenomenon, along with Sarraute's own piece on the subject contained in *The Age of Suspicion*.

Fleming, John A. "The Imagery of Tropism in the Novels of Nathalie Sarraute." In *Image and Theme: Studies in Modern French Fiction*, edited by W. M. Frohock. Cambridge, Mass.: Harvard University Press, 1969. Starting from the premise that *Tropisms* contains the key to the understanding of Sarraute's work as a whole, this article explores the tropism as a narrative and stylistic device. In addition to *Tropisms*, Fleming analyzes several other of her novels from the same point of view. He also addresses another key concept in the novel, "sub-conversation."

Minogue, Valerie. *Nathalie Sarraute and the War of the Words*. Edinburgh, Scotland: Edinburgh University Press, 1981. Minogue analyzes each of Sarraute's major novels, including *Tropisms*, in an attempt to show how Sarraute searches for a purer reality than what language usually conveys. The fact that Sarraute uses language itself as a tool for her search is the paradox that underlies this useful and accessible study.

Oppenheim, Lois, ed. *Three Decades of the French New Novel*. Urbana: University of Illinois Press, 1986. The proceedings of a colloquium on the New Novel held at New York University in 1982, this anthology provides a useful and accessible overview of some more recent interpretations of the movement. Contains a contribution by Sarraute herself, which sheds light on her rich and ambivalent relationship to the movement. A bibliography is included.

Temple, Ruth Z. *Nathalie Sarraute*. New York: Columbia University Press, 1968. Though only forty-eight pages long, this introduction to Sarraute's work is still one of the clearest presentations of some of the major issues in her fiction. Contains a dated but useful bibliography which lists several interviews and articles that have appeared in the nonacademic English and American press.

M. Martin Guiney

TROUBLE IN MIND

Author: Alice Childress (1920-1994)
Type of work: Drama
Type of plot: Protest drama
Time of plot: Monday and Tuesday mornings in fall, 1957
Locale: A Broadway theater in New York City
First produced: 1955, at Greenwich Mews Theatre, New York City, New York
First published: 1971

> *Principal characters:*
> WILETTA MAYER, an attractive middle-aged African American
>   actress
> AL MANNERS, a white racist director
> EDDIE FENTON, an eager young white assistant director
> JOHN NEVINS, a young African American actor
> JUDY SEARS, a young white actress
> MILLIE DAVIS, Wiletta's foil, an attractive middle-aged African
>   American actress
> SHELDON FORRESTER, a veteran black actor
> HENRY, a seventy-eight-year-old Irish theater doorman
> BILL O'WRAY, an old white character actor

Form and Content

Trouble in Mind presents a play within a play, pointing out ironic parallels between the frame story of the actors rehearsing and "Chaos in Belleville," the play being rehearsed, a naturalistic portrayal of Southern lynching. In reality, "Chaos" acts out the racist stereotypes it seems to be protesting. It presents civil rights struggles in the late 1950's in which a young black man named Job, played by John, wants to register to vote, although his mother, Petunia, played by Wiletta, tries to restrain him for fear of racist reprisals. Meanwhile, Carrie, the plantation owner's Southern belle daughter, played by Judy, urges her father to let the "darkies" have a "stomp" to celebrate her maid Ruby's birthday (played by Millie). The scene does nothing to advance the plot but plays up the playwright's assumptions about black/white relations in the South. When Job faces racist reprisals, Carrie begs her father to protect him by carting him off to jail and away from a lynch mob. Predictably, the mob lynches Job, while his mother, Petunia, croons sentimental spirituals. Throughout the crisis, Job's father (played by Sheldon) sits on the porch whittling a stick and uttering nonsense in theatrically garbled black dialect.

In the opening scene, the actors express delight at landing roles in a Broadway play. Before the other actors arrive, Wiletta tells John that she thinks the play is worthless both from an artistic and a political perspective. She plans to praise Manners for choosing it, however, to laugh when expected to, and to do exactly what he asks. John calls her survival strategy "Tommish."

When Al Manners and Eddie Fenton arrive, Wiletta finds it difficult to act out the hypocrisy she has been promoting. In order to illustrate the value of "method" acting, a psychological technique by which the actor gets inside the character, Manners demands that Wiletta pick up a scrap of paper that he tosses on the stage. Her spontaneous fury and grudging compliance draws applause from the director, who congratulates her for her display of genuine unmediated emotion. Although shaken by the director's manipulative power play, the cast begins rehearsing the scene in which Carrie petitions her father. The scene reveals the playwright's subtle racism through his depiction of African American servants fawning like children on their white masters. Millie's character utters fawning, self-deprecating lines straight out of the movie *Gone with the Wind*. When Wiletta sings a dirge at the end of the first act, which Manners and the whole cast find moving, he tries to get Wiletta to verbalize her motivation. Whereas he expects her to describe her "natural" feelings of a mother worrying about her son, Wiletta's acting comes from craft. When Manners forces her through a word association game to get at her "true" feelings, he and the others see that Wiletta is truly angry at Manners and the whole white racist world. She can, however, act a convincing version of the "Mammy" stereotype the white world expects. When Manners has Wiletta sing the spiritual after he gets her to "loosen up" through word association, she sings in a voice powerful enough to lead people to march against their oppressors with pride. Shocked, Manners dismisses the cast for the day.

In the second act, Wiletta tries to get Manners to listen to her critique of the play and her character. She argues that the third act is not the logical outcome of the first, that her character would never send her son out to a lynch mob, and that the play is designed to make Job's parents look ignorant and irresponsible and to make the white man the hero. In other words, she demonstrates that the script lacks psychological realism. The more intelligent her analysis, the more condescending Manners becomes: "Make me a solemn promise, don't start thinking." Continuing his attempt to draw "natural" acting from the cast, Manners has them imagine a lynching. Sheldon, whom Wiletta and Millie consider a "Tom," announces that he witnessed a lynching. He describes a scene of horror from his boyhood more vivid and credible than anything in the script they are rehearsing.

In the final climactic scene when Manners refuses to hear Wiletta, she calls him "a prejudiced racist." "Would you send your son out to be murdered?" she asks. His "natural" and unrehearsed reply, "Don't compare yourself to me!" proves her point to the shocked cast. Manners walks out. At the final curtain, Wiletta stands alone in the lights on stage reciting a psalm about brotherhood while Henry turns on the applause machine.

Analysis

Like the blues song from which it takes its title, *Trouble in Mind* portrays the no-win plight of African Americans struggling to survive in a white racist society. Wiletta can survive as an artist only by lying. Her opening scene advice to John foreshadows her final heroic catastrophe. Her honest assertion of pride and intelligence after a lifetime of capitulation echoes the historic heroism of Rosa Parks, who chose to sit down on a segregated bus and who thus began the end of segregation. Childress forces the audience or reader to acknowledge that Wiletta's courage is the toll that racism demands every day from African Americans who can be honest or survive but not both. As a bourgeois tragedy protest play, *Trouble in Mind* calls U.S. citizens to action.

Never simplistic in her presentation of racism, Childress never presents all black characters as good and all white characters as evil. On the contrary, she shows how racism negatively affects everyone. As in her other plays, she makes her political statements through a meticulous creation of realistic characters who experience a classical recognition and reversal that forces them to change and grow in the two-day span of a drama that comes close to observing Aristotelian unities of time, place, and action. With compassion, she creates complex characters who exhibit painful contra-dictions.

Being cast in "Chaos" forces each of the five white characters to respond to daily racism in ways that exhibit their true mettle. Al Manners, who initially presents himself to the cast as a liberal fighting against racism, is unmasked, even to himself, as racist. At the outset, he wields directorial power and unexamined white privilege. Manipulative and condescending, he bolsters his ego at the expense of the racial pride and artistic integrity of his African American actors. His sidekick Eddie survives by being a yes man and reinforcing Manners' racism and his own impotence. Judy is shown to be capable of learning the realities of racism and ways of supporting the struggle against racism. She grows from the naïveté of one who believes the myths of her sugar-coated suburban upbringing to become a true ally of African Americans. Bill O'Wray recognizes but evades the horror of racist injustice and prejudice because it gives him indigestion. He is guilty of culpable ignorance and responsible for his own suffering. Henry, the doorman, is the only white character who does not see color. Possibly because of his own heritage of Irish oppression, he chooses to notice only artistic talent and personal integrity.

Each of the four African American characters responds to racism in a different way. Sheldon Forrester, who has perfected the "Uncle Tom" pose, has previously, although indirectly, supported racism by his complicity and by permitting racists such as Manners to continue to feel superior. The playwright, however, allows his character to grow from his first appearance, laughing at everything Manners says, to his rawly honest monologue describing a lynching in the second act. Wiletta's display of courage and artistic integrity affects him. John Nevins seems to have made moral choices in the opposite direction. He chooses to play the role that the white director expects rather than assert his honest pride. It is ironic that after he initially resists Wiletta's advice to act what he calls "Tommish," he does, in fact, play the hypocrite in order to win Manners' approval. By the second act, he, like Manners, is calling Wiletta his "sweetheart." John and Sheldon exchange the "Tom" role in the end. Millie compensates for the humiliation of racist treatment by strutting around in expensive clothes, as if pride of race and class were found in costumes. Wiletta's honesty cracks her façade; she admits that she too needs acting jobs to survive. Even Wiletta's heroism is not unmixed. Like Rosa Parks, she seems to have reached an inevitable boiling point at which hypocrisy is more killing to her soul than is losing a job. She must recognize, however, that her moral choice has consequences for others. Her resistance to the white director may close the play and put everybody out of work. Nevertheless, she chooses racial and artistic integrity above the economic survival of the whole cast. Like the classic tragic hero, she isolates herself from society by her act of hubris and heroism.

Context

Trouble in Mind is the first full-length play produced on the professional New York stage with a middle-aged black woman as protagonist. Childress began her career in theater as an actress. Like Wiletta, she was discouraged by the lack of substantial roles for actresses such as herself and by having only sexist and racist stereotypes to choose. Her first play, the one-act *Florence* (1949), set in a Jim Crow train station in the deep South, features a middle-aged black woman. Her two most famous feminist plays, *Wedding Band* (1966) and *Wine in the Wilderness* (1969), which have been frequently anthologized in collections of women's drama, along with *Trouble in Mind*, present intelligent, courageous, self-educated, working-class black women as heroes. In all three full-length plays, the protagonists stand up to racists and sexists who see the women only through their own prejudice.

Childress often compares her diversely oppressed, solitary, middle-aged black female heroes with other black female characters who have similar problems but who make different choices. In *Trouble in Mind*, Childress presents both Wiletta and Millie as working artists. As Wiletta's foil, Millie mentions her husband, who works as a dining car porter; but Wiletta has no outside life or family. Both Millie and Wiletta work to support themselves as other working women do. Throughout the history of Western drama, female characters rarely appear except as mother of, daughter of, or wife of a more significant male character. To create isolated heroic female characters (regardless of race, class, or age) is an act of feminist courage. When Wiletta argues with the dishonest creation of the character she plays, she speaks out against mother-blaming with no reference to her own maternal status. By contrast, Judy regards her first Broadway role as a means of escape from the stultifying suburbs. Whereas Judy's situation is less severe than that of the black women, Childress invites spectators to applaud Judy's flight from bourgeois boredom. She also shows Judy learning about racism and developing a social conscience that conflicts with the ready-made answers of racist white America.

Sources for Further Study

Abramson, Doris E. *The Negro Playwright in the American Theatre 1925-1959*. New York: Columbia University Press, 1967. A survey of significant dramas that have been professionally produced. Includes a lengthy discussion of the first production of Childress' *Trouble in Mind.*

Brown-Guillory, Elizabeth. *Their Place on the Stage: Black Women Playwrights in America.* Westport, Conn.: Greenwood Press, 1988. A chapter on Childress, Lorraine Hansberry, and Ntozake Shange describes production difficulties experienced by three award-winning playwrights who rejected stereotypes and broke new artistic and literary ground.

Miller, Jeanne-Marie A. "Black Women in Plays by Black Playwrights." In *Women in American Theatre*, edited by Helen Crich Chinoy and Linda Walsh Jenkins. New York: Theatre Communications Group, 1987. Professor Miller discusses Childress' characters in the context of American racial stereotypes.

Mitchell, Loften. *Black Drama: The Story of the American Negro in the Theatre.* New York: Hawthorne, 1966. Narratives describing the history of acting and directing as well as playwrighting are presented in chapters devoted to each decade of the twentieth century up to the 1960's. Childress is discussed as an important contributor to black drama in several chapters. Several pages are devoted to describing the first production of *Trouble in Mind.*

Rosemary Keefe Curb

TURTLE MOON

Author: Alice Hoffman (1952-   )
Type of work: Novel
Type of plot: Mystery
Time of plot: The 1980's
Locale: Verity, Florida, and Great Neck, New York
First published: 1992

> *Principal characters:*
> LUCY ROSEN, a divorced woman in her late thirties
> JULIAN CASH, a police detective who trains and owns tracking
>   dogs
> KEITH ROSEN, Lucy's son, "the meanest boy in Verity"
> BETHANY LEE, Lucy's neighbor, who is known to the people of
>   Verity as Karen Wright
> THE ANGEL, the ghost of Julian's cousin Bobby

Form and Content

The central plot of *Turtle Moon* follows Lucy Rosen's and Julian Cash's efforts to solve the murder of Bethany Lee as well as the development of their own relationship. The novel also emphasizes the problems that women face after divorce, especially child custody and single parenting. The story is set in motion when Bethany flees Great Neck with her baby in an effort to protect herself and the child from her former husband. When Bethany is murdered and her baby disappears, Julian is called in to track the baby. Lucy soon learns that her son, Keith, has also disappeared, and Julian starts tracking him, also. Along with tracing the mystery surrounding Bethany's murder, the novel explores the mystery of human relationships. In the relationships between Bethany and Randy, Lucy and Julian, and Keith and Arrow, Hoffman shows the difficulties of understanding oneself and others.

Hoffman establishes a mysterious, almost supernatural mood in the first chapter, which explains that strange things always happen in Verity in the month of May, including the events covered in the novel. Hoffman also establishes several points of tension in the early chapters, including Bethany's escape into hiding, Lucy's worries about Keith, and Julian's feeling of being haunted by his own past. When Lucy learns that her neighbor, whom she knows as Karen Wright, has been murdered and that both the neighbor's baby and her own son have disappeared, she fears that Keith will be charged with the murder. She learns that "Karen Wright" was a pseudonym, and she believes that if she can find her neighbor's true identity, she may locate the real killer and protect her son from suspicion. She knows that "Karen" had her hair done at the same salon she used to go to, so she uses her high school reunion as an excuse to return to Great Neck and try to track down "Karen's" real identity.

As she and Julian begin working together, each is strongly attracted to the other. As their relationship grows, the narrator reveals more of Julian's past to explain how Julian's history of losing those he loves or being left by them has convinced him not to look for bonds with other people. His attraction to Lucy, however, draws him further into the case. He finds the children, leaves them with Miss Giles, and follows Lucy to Great Neck. When Lucy is attacked by Randy Lee, Julian rushes in to protect her. They learn that the man Randy hired to kill Bethany is now tracking the only witness to the murder. They hurry back to Verity, believing that the killer is now after Keith.

When Julian follows Lucy to Great Neck, he leaves Keith in charge of feeding Arrow, and the boy and the dog discover an instant rapport. The boy ignores Julian's instructions and lets Arrow out of his pen, but with Keith the dog behaves well. Their relationship saves Keith's life. When the killer tracks Keith into the woods, Arrow attacks him. Julian arrives and sees that the dog has lost control. He shoots Arrow. Although Keith is heartbroken over the loss of his dog, he is also now ready to get on with his life.

Julian, too, has come to terms with himself. He feels a connection with Keith, who reminds him of himself, and he begins to understand his own childhood better. Although he does not expect the relationship to continue, his love affair with Lucy has also helped him face some of his own fears. He finally returns to the Burger King parking lot, where he confronts his past: As a teenager, Julian crashed his car into the gumbo-limbo tree in the parking lot, killing his cousin Bobby. He is finally able to release both his own spirit and that of the Angel, who is Bobby's ghost.

Over the course of the novel, Lucy comes to understand her son better, in part through her relationship with Julian. She also learns that she can do some things she had not thought she could do, such as confront a murderer. She decides to let Keith return to Great Neck to live with his father, and although she knows she will miss him, she also determines to make the most of her own life, including her relationship with Julian.

The novel includes several subplots that complicate the story line but also help develop the theme of the mystery of human relationships. For example, in several chapters focusing on the Angel, the narrator describes how he falls in love with a teenage girl who comes to sit under the gumbo-limbo tree and sort out her life. His love for her reflects both his own longing for life and his nostalgia for his past, which had included a romance with the girl's mother. The girl seems to sense this feeling, and she takes on the Angel's longing for escape as she decides to leave Verity and go to college.

Analysis

The central theme of this novel is the mystery of human relationships. People never really know or understand others, much less themselves, the story suggests, and all human connections must be based on a leap of faith. Neither people nor human emotions can really be understood. Sometimes, trusting such mysterious connections leads to strong, mutually fulfilling relationships, but sometimes this trust is misplaced and relationships lead to separation, hurt, and even death. The problem of determining when to trust and when to protect oneself faces both women and men, this novel suggests, but men have more difficulty taking the leap into relationships.

Hoffman raises this theme of the uncertainty of relationships and human behavior in her short history of Bethany's marriage to Randy early in the novel. Bethany thought that Randy was a caring, romantic man, but soon after their marriage, and in the course of just a few sentences of narrative, he is revealed as a distant, even violent husband. The idea that people cannot trust relationships to last or people to behave consistently is also presented when Hoffman describes Verity as "home to more divorced women from New York than any other town in the state of Florida." The very setting of the novel, then, underscores the problem of establishing lasting relationships.

Even good relationships between men and women are uncertain, Hoffman suggests, because the people involved do not always understand their own feelings. She describes the attraction between Lucy and Julian as something that neither comprehends but that neither can avoid. The narration suggests that some instinct draws the two characters together. When they first make love, both are described as feeling out of control, and as their relationship continues, both act on emotions they neither understand nor believe will last. Their relationship does not make sense, but it is powerful nevertheless.

The difficulty of understanding relationships arises in other connections within the novel, too. Keith's relationships with the baby and with Arrow develop this theme clearly. When Keith first picks up the baby, he is acting on instinct. He does not know why he believes that he must protect her, but he does, and he soon finds that the child clings to him and depends upon him to provide food and water. He becomes quite protective of her and he cannot bring himself to leave her, even after she is safe at Miss Giles's house. Keith also feels an almost mystical connection with Arrow, and the dog seems to reciprocate. Arrow will not even let Julian pet him, but he curls up protectively next to Keith as soon as he sees him. Keith learns that despite his feeling of being isolated from others, he can become involved. He begins to think more of others than of himself, and these connections help him retreat from his growing delinquency.

Although both women and men within the novel find relationships confusing, male characters seem to find trusting others and their own feelings particularly difficult. Julian reminds himself constantly not to trust that his relationship with Lucy will last, and he seems to believe that getting involved is dangerous. His personal history of lost relationships explains this; Lucy, however, has similar experiences but does not feel so strong a fear of relationships. She is more willing to become involved without worrying about the outcome. Keith's resistance to his mother's concern also suggests a male desire for independence, especially when seen in contrast to the feelings of another teenager, Shannon Bass. Shannon is struggling to break the strong bond she has with her mother so that she can begin a more independent life away from home. The characters in this novel thus exemplify the differences between masculine and feminine psychology described by Nancy Chodorow, who argues that boys learn to think of themselves in terms of independence, while girls learn to think in terms of relationships.

Hoffman uses several stylistic features to support the theme of uncertainty and the pattern of gender difference in this novel. First, she uses two distinct storytelling patterns: short summaries, such as the history of Bethany and Randy's marriage; and slowly unfolding histories, such as the story of Julian's relationship with his cousin. Most of the short summaries are told about the female characters in the novel, while the male characters' stories, especially Julian's, emerge more slowly. This pattern suggests that women's intentions and even their experiences in relationships are clearer than men's. Despite histories that include difficult relationships, the women enter more willingly into relationships and leave with fewer regrets.

Another stylistic feature that relates to the novel's central themes is a shifting perspective. Within each chapter, the story is told by following different characters. This creates a fragmented but understandable narrative. In several places, the identities of characters change slightly. For example, the reader is introduced to both Bethany Lee and Karen Wright in different sections of chapter 1 and must make the connection between the two. The reader also observes Bethany/Karen from two perspectives: her own and Lucy's. Such shifting perspectives suggest how difficult it is to understand others.

Finally, the supernatural elements in this novel, especially the presence of the Angel, add to the sense that some things go beyond ordinary human understanding. The novel both opens and closes with passages that emphasize such experiences. The strange power that Verity residents assign to the month of May, for example, suggests that people's behavior might be affected by a force that they do not even comprehend. Similarly, the final scene of the novel shows Julian's reconciliation with the Angel as the two meet under the gumbo-limbo tree. Julian first feels and then actually sees Bobby's presence, and the final image of the novel is a bright light surrounding the tree as both men, apparently, find release from their pasts. Such elements not only advance the plot of the novel but also establish and support the theme of uncertainty.

Context

With *Turtle Moon*, Hoffman joins the growing ranks of American women mystery writers, a field that includes authors such as Sara Paretsky and Sue Grafton. Like the works of these novelists, *Turtle Moon* features a female character who is acting independently to solve a mystery, even though Lucy is not a detective and is, at times, aided by Julian. Although Julian provides protection, it is Lucy who locates the murderer.

Although two of the three central characters in this novel are male, the plot emphasizes three key issues for contemporary women: the problems associated with divorce, violence against women, and the concept that men and women may approach relationships differently.

Although it does not ignore the economic problems associated with divorce that have dominated feminist discussion of the issue, the novel emphasizes the emotional difficulty of single parenting. The novel features several divorced women who are rearing their children alone, and the relationship between Lucy and Keith places this problem at the heart of the novel.

In addition, the novel highlights the problem of violence against women by focusing on Bethany's murder. Randy Lee uses violence against his wife first in an attempt to claim custody of their child and later as a means of revenge. Later, he also threatens Lucy with violence. Although he is not represented as a "typical" male, his behavior does suggest that men too often use physical force against the women in their lives.

Hoffman also develops the idea that women and men approach relationships differently, a concept that has been examined in the psychological research of Nancy Chodorow, in Deborah Tannen's writing about how men and women use language, and in a large number of popular psychology books.

Sources for Further Study

"Alice Hoffman." *Current Biography* 53 (September, 1992): 14-18. This biography identifies the major developments and influences in Hoffman's career. It emphasizes her ability to write convincingly and compassionately about Americans of nearly all ages and social strata and to make ordinary life seem magical.

Hunnewell, Susannah. "Florida Is a Character." *The New York Times Book Review*, April 26, 1992, 1. This brief profile of Hoffman includes comments on how the landscape of Florida inspired her. She explains that she considers it a character in *Turtle Moon.*

Telgen, Diane. "Alice Hoffman." *Contemporary Authors.* New Revision Series. Vol. 34. Detroit: Gale Research, 1991. A useful summary of Hoffman's career, this reference entry lists her other books and reviews of her work. It also provides a brief biography and a discussion of the central themes of her fiction.

Sherry Lee Linkon

TWENTY YEARS AT HULL-HOUSE

Author: Jane Addams (1860-1935)
Type of work: Autobiography
Time of work: 1860-1910
Locale: The United States and Europe
First published: 1910

Principal personages:

JOHN H. ADDAMS, Jane's father and the primary influence on her

LOUISE DE KOVEN BOWEN, president of the Juvenile Protective Association

DR. ALICE HAMILTON, a specialist in industrial medicine

FLORENCE KELLEY, a socialist resident who transformed Addams from a philanthropist to a reformer

JULIA C. LATHROP, the organizer of the Cook County Juvenile Court and the first head of the Children's Bureau

JOHNNY POWERS, a corrupt alderman

MARY ROZET SMITH, a trustee of Hull-House

ELLEN GATES STARR, a cofounder of Hull-House

ALZINA STEVENS, a textile worker active in unions and the first probation officer in Cook County

LEO TOLSTOY, a Russian novelist who sought peace by undertaking to do his daily share of the physical labor of the world

Form and Content

Jane Addams wrote *Twenty Years at Hull-House* for two main reasons: to present a record of the founding and first years of the Hull-House settlement in Chicago, and to stop the publication of two biographies of herself. The first four chapters trace Addams' life from her childhood through college and tours of Europe to her decision to begin Hull-House. The primary influence in these years was Addams' wealthy abolitionist father, who stressed morality and sensitivity to the poor. The second important influence was Abraham Lincoln. John H. Addams was both a supporter and a personal friend of Lincoln, and although Jane Addams was only a small child when Lincoln was assassinated, she had heard many stories of him from her father. Addams saw Lincoln as the best role model for the new immigrants, since Lincoln too had emerged from humble surroundings without ever forgetting his past and the lessons that he had learned from his experiences. These two men helped to form Jane Addams' character and influenced the direction that her life took.

It is in these early chapters that Addams makes clear the problem that the first generation of college-educated women faced: what to do with their lives. As happened to other women of this generation, Addams suffered psychological conflict that resulted in physical distress. One result of her ailment was a physician's recommendation to visit Europe for two years. Had she been male, a tour of Europe would have been part of her maturing experiences. Addams and Ellen Gates Starr, her college friend, visited not only museums and art galleries but also the wretched poor in the East End of London. Although Addams had spent a year in medical school before illness resulted in her tour, she now realized that there might be other ways to help the poor besides practicing medicine.

Addams' experiences in Europe brought into focus the problem that she and other women faced. As she described it herself, they were smothered with advantages and had lost the ability to react to human suffering. The assumption of society was that an educated "girl" could have nothing to do with the poverty that was particularly acute in the large cities. Addams' trip did not cure her physical ailments, but a second trip with Starr, when she attended a meeting of the striking London match girls, began the crystallization of her plans for renting a house in Chicago where she might live and work among those mired in poverty.

The other fourteen chapters deal with Addams' life work at Hull-House, which involved a wide variety of activities and an amazing array of exceptionally talented women who were nurtured, trained, and readied there to do social battle on larger fronts than that of the neighborhood of Halsted Street. The activities at Hull-House involved almost every important person of the late nineteenth and early twentieth centuries, from John Dewey and Henry George to Prince Peter Kropotkin.

Although these later chapters begin with a chronological chapter telling of the first days at Hull-House, Addams soon switches to a topical approach, discussing poverty, economics, labor problems, immigrants, ideas from European settlements and experiments, local political campaigns, social clubs, and the arts at Hull-House and ending with the story of revolutionaries from Russia. These chapters are filled with engaging stories that illustrate what Hull-House was attempting on these various fronts.

Analysis

The central issue in Hull-House is that the various socioeconomic classes have a reciprocal dependency and can therefore learn from one another. As Addams saw it, a settlement house would provide a place where "young women who had been given over too exclusively to study, might restore a balance of activity along traditional lines and learn of life from life itself." Here was the crux of the matter: maintaining traditional lines while at the same time doing things that were very nontraditional. A few examples of Hull-House residents will demonstrate this mode of operation. Julia Lathrop, a lawyer, moved to Hull-House in 1890 and soon became a member of the State Board of Charities and organized the first juvenile court. Florence Kelley was the first factory inspector for the State of Illinois, and one of her deputies, Alzina Stevens, became the first president of the Working Woman's Union and later the first probation officer of the Cook County Juvenile Court. Alice Hamilton identified flies as the carriers of disease and later wrote *Hamilton and Hardy's Industrial Toxicology*, which was printed in its fourth edition in 1983. At one point, Addams herself was named garbage inspector for her ward, which shocked her neighbors, because that was "unwomanly work." Addams replied that if it was a womanly task to nurse the sick, then it certainly was a womanly task to prevent those conditions that caused the illness. As one biography opined: "She revolted against the stereotype of woman as submissive, gentle and intuitive but did not publicly challenge the stereotype."

Addams had considerable skill as a writer, and in *Twenty Years at Hull-House*, she captured the reader's attention with engaging anecdotes that proved her points. These range from a cooking class that enabled a young woman to keep the husband who had threatened to leave her if he did not get a decent meal to the tale of a young Italian boy who died at seventeen because of his use of legally available cocaine. Because of her writing skill, Addams became one of the best known and most revered settlement leaders of the early twentieth century.

In her autobiography, Addams followed the typical format of a heroine's life story: a weak and handicapped ugly child who had a childhood dream of helping the poor and being sensitive to their needs. This is illustrated by the story of Addams' father advising her not to wear her new and beautiful coat because those who did not have one might feel badly at seeing hers. The second part of the format is a conversion experience, or epiphany, in which the heroine changes her life's path. According to Addams, this took place at a bullfight in Madrid in 1888. Here Addams realized that she had been deluding herself with travel and study as a preparation for some promise of future action. Putting aside further procrastination, Addams began speaking about her plans to move into the city and live with the poor. The next January she and Starr sought a place in Chicago. That place was Hull-House. At last, the heroine had found her life's task.

Addams' biography defined and consolidated her position as a social reformer and identified and presented her as a symbol of Americanism. Addams, taking her cue from Lincoln, wanted to ensure that democracy would endure, and the only way that could happen with the influx of immigrants from southern and eastern Europe was for the settlements to socialize democracy by means of educational, philanthropic, civil, and social undertakings. It was in this way that the finer and freer aspects of living would be incorporated into the common life of the country, providing mobility for all.

Context

Addams' effect on women's issues was a result of her activities rather than of any specific writings. Addams supported the suffrage movement and worked to secure the vote in municipal elections, but her feminism saw women as morally superior. To such feminists, suffrage was not only a right but also something that would result in a moral uplifting of the political world. It was not Addams' role in suffrage, however, that had the most long-lasting effect; it was her life, which served as a role model. In addition to working at Hull-House, she was an academic who taught college extension courses, published in professional journals, and at times referred to herself as a sociologist.

Addams' effect as a role model is best seen in the life of Hilda Polacheck, who wrote of her experiences in *I Came a Stranger: The Story of a Hull-House Girl* (1989).

After her marriage, she moved to Milwaukee, where she supported Addams' feminist activities and invited her to inaugurate Milwaukee's chapter of the Women's International League for Peace and Freedom. When she later worked on the Work Projects Administration's Writer's Project, she wrote on Hull-House. She gave full credit to Jane Addams for the effect she had had on her life.

Among Addams' other writings are *Hull0House Maps and Papers* (1895), *Democracy and Social Ethics* (1902), *Newer Ideals of Peace* (1906), *Spirit of Youth and the City Streets* (1909), *A New Conscience and an Ancient Evil* (1912), *Women at the Hague* (1915), *The Long Road of Woman's Memory* (1916), *Peace and Bread in Time of War* (1922), *Second Twenty Years at Hull-House* (1930), and *My Friend Julia Lathrop* (1935).

Sources for Further Study

Brieland, Donald. "The Hull-House Tradition and the Contemporary Social Worker: Was Jane Addams Really a Social Worker?" *Social Work* 35 (March, 1990): 134-138. Based on six objectives from the mission and purpose statement of social workers, Brieland concludes that the answer to the question posed in the article's title is yes.

Carson, Mina. *Settlement Folk: Social Thought and the American Settlement Movement, 1885-1930.* Chicago: University of Chicago Press, 1990. Emphasizes how well Jane Addams exemplified the Victorian cult of personality. Sees her as a master at publicizing her causes. Describes settlement houses as agents of social control and claims that their promotion of industrial education was to keep the immigrants in the working class.

Davis, Allen F. *American Heroine: The Life and Legend of Jane Addams.* New York: Oxford University Press, 1973. A critical yet sympathetic treatment of Addams which explores her self-created legend, relates it to the facts of her life, and shows how the two became intertwined. Includes a good bibliography.

Davis, Allen F., and Mary Lynn McCree. *Eighty Years at Hull-House.* Chicago: Quadrangle Books, 1969. Contains reprinted articles by Starr, Mary Kenney (O'Sullivan), Kelley, Hamilton, Bowen, Dr. Dorothea Moore, and Edith Abbott as well as by men who lived in or visited Hull-House in its first twenty years. Shows Hull-House through the eyes of its residents and those most closely involved in its work.

Farrell, John C. *Beloved Lady: A History of Jane Addams' Ideas on Reform and Peace.* Baltimore: The Johns Hopkins University Press, 1967. Contains a superior annotated bibliography and a complete listing of Addams' writings. Places Addams in the context of the Progressive Era and examines her views on education and urban recreation as well as peace.

Levine, Daniel. *Jane Addams and the Liberal Tradition.* Madison: State Historical Society of Wisconsin, 1971. Places Jane Addams and her work in the liberal tradition of alleviating suffering by reforming society. Part 1 ("Jane Addams and Hull-House") and part 2 ("Rousing the New Conscience") most closely parallel her work from 1889 to 1909.

Linn, James Weber. *Jane Addams: A Biography*. New York: D. Appleton-Century, 1935. The author, Jane Addams' nephew, provides insights into Addams' personality. "Six Women" is a good discussion of Starr, Lathrop, Kelley, Bowen, Hamilton, and Smith.

Lissak, Rivka Shpak. *Pluralism and Progressives: Hull House and the New Immigrants, 1890-1919*. Chicago: University of Chicago Press, 1989. Like Carson, Lissak sees Hull-House as an instrument of social control, pushing assimilation to keep the immigrants in their place for the benefit of the middle class. The work's focus is on eastern European Jewish immigrants, but some attention is devoted to Italian and Greek immigrants in the Hull-House neighborhood.

Polacheck, Hilda Satt. *I Came a Stranger: The Story of a Hull-House Girl*. Edited by Dena J. Polacheck Epstein. Chicago: University of Illinois Press, 1989. A view of Hull-House from the neighborhood. Part 3, "Growing Up with Hull-House," is particularly valuable. A good counterbalance to Carson and Lissak.

Anne Kearney

TYPICAL AMERICAN

Author: Gish Jen (1955-   )
Type of work: Novel
Type of plot: Social realism
Time of plot: 1947-1970
Locale: China and the United States
First published: 1991

Principal characters:
RALPH CHANG, a professor of mechanical engineering
THERESA CHANG, Ralph's sister
HELEN, Ralph's wife
GROVER DING, a Chinese American businessman who was born
    in the United States
HENRY CHAO, Ralph's colleague and department chair

Form and Content

Typical American appeared contemporaneously with *The Kitchen God's Wife*, by Amy Tan; *China Boy*, by Gus Lee; *Donald Duk*, by Frank Chin; and *Pangs of Love*, by David Wong Louie. Yet Gish Jen does not believe that her novel and the other Asian American authors' works are "comparable in intention or level of writing"; her work is not only about the immigrant experience but also very much about the United States. The phrase "Typical American" is meant to be doubly ironic: It refers to how the mockery, which starts out as a farfetched stereotype, gradually turns into a self-fulfilling prophecy for the characters who have invented the term. The novel consists of short chapters organized into five parts—a structure reminiscent of the five-act play.

"Sweet Rebellion" (part 1) recounts the life of Ralph as a dimwit graduate student in New York during the late 1940's. As mainland China falls to the communists and his expired visa becomes unrenewable, he is turned into an illegal alien. Gradually, he runs out of money to pay for rent and food. He is rescued by his sister Theresa, who has fled to the United States with Helen, whom Ralph marries. The three live together in a rundown apartment, and a sense of complacency begins to emerge in their family life (part 2, "The House Holds"). For entertainment, the three often poke fun at the incompetence of "typical Pete," their apartment manager, whose shortcomings they generalize to be typical of Americans. In time, thanks to his family, Ralph earns his Ph.D. and becomes a professor of mechanical engineering. A crisis begins to loom, however, when Ralph, inspired by "positive thinking" and the example of self-made millionaire Grover Ding, starts "imagineering" the good life for himself.

"This New Life" (part 3) is the success story of Ralph and his family. Against all odds, he receives tenure. He owns a car and, with the support of Helen and Theresa, purchases a home in suburban Connecticut. Meanwhile, Theresa has also earned a medical degree and has become a doctor. Coincidentally, Henry (Ralph's department chair) becomes her patient and—although he is a married man—her lover. The Chang household undergoes severe "Structural Weakening" (part 4) when Ralph opens a fried chicken restaurant with financial "assistance" from Grover. Blinded by Grover's deceitful advice and his own worship of money, Ralph is unaware of Grover's seduction of his wife. Out of arrogance and contempt, he insults his sister and causes her to move out of the family.

Before long, Ralph's American Dream comes to a rude awakening when his unsafely expanded restaurant has to be demolished. The aftermath of this failure is captured in "A Man to Sit at Supper and Never Eat" (part 5). Reluctantly, Ralph lets Theresa move back and sullenly puts up with Henry's frequent visits to her. Later, discovering his having been cuckolded by Grover, he forces Helen into his car and threatens to kill both Helen and himself. In the process, however, the car knocks down Theresa, putting her into a coma.

Although the novel ends on a note of faith and hints at the remorse of Ralph, it comes close to being a full-fledged tragedy. The distanced and comic-ironic voice permeating the greater portion of the narrative, however, suggests that the book can be more appropriately seen as a social satire. The author's avoidance of psychological analysis and emotional descriptions also hints at the allegorical nature of the work.

Analysis

Rather than dwelling upon the issue of racism and idealizing the notion of ethnic heritage, *Typical American* offers a relentless critique of how the cultural "baggage" that immigrants bring with them to America can undermine their well-being.

Ralph is a perfect example of this baggage. Because of his Confucianist (pseudo-Confucian) upbringing in a functionary's family in precommunist China, Ralph has a sense of self and other that does not fit in with the American environment. The Confucianist veneration for (and fear of) teachers has prevented him, early in the novel, from seeking help from Pinkus, the department chair, in a candid manner. His dissatisfaction with his teaching career can also be attributed to the frustration of his Confucianist precepts. In marriage, Ralph has not taken Helen seriously as a person; instead, he views her as potentially the first of many possible wives, as if he were in China. He even dictates the way she is supposed to breathe. The most deplorable aspect of his character that is a part of his pseudo-Confucian ethic is his attitude toward Theresa; in his eyes, the education of women is superfluous if done at all, and unacceptable if it is better than men's. Sarcastically, Ralph often refers to Theresa as "Know-It-All," and she succumbs to his denigration by pretending that her scholarship has been turned down so that he can feel better. More important, once he learns about Theresa's affair with Henry, out of pseudo-Confucian morality Ralph calls her a "rotten egg" (whore) in front of his daughters. It hardly crosses Ralph's mind that to her he owes not only his career but also his very life.

Theresa is also burdened with her cultural baggage—deference to male members of one's family in particular. Reared to be "married off," she has always subordinated her personal interests to those of her brother, despite her superior talents. She is more than self-effacing; her sense of self is deficient because of her patriarchal morals, as if it is through her brother that she has to define her own being. The marriage she arranges for her brother is in a sense also an arrangement that allows her to define herself; it reduplicates a family structure in which the male is the head of the household and the women are subordinates. Theresa's own need for a male companion does not occur to herself until she has become a doctor, and even then the need is fulfilled in the form of an adulterous affair involving her brother's boss—indeed, Ralph's tenure and promotion would not have been possible without Theresa's influence on Henry.

Helen also has burdens of her own from the old country. Having grown up in an affluent and therefore overprotective environment, she is rather delicate, susceptible to creature comforts, and vulnerable to materialistic as well as romantic temptations. Grover, the self-made millionaire who is "helping" Ralph set up a business, hence finds her seducible. If she could ensure that Grover would keep his promises of providing for her, she might very well leave Ralph for good. As hinted in the novel, the adultery terminates not so much for moral as for pragmatic reasons. On the occasion of the breakup, when Helen grabs Grover by his exposed penis and threatens to do it harm if he does not keep his promise (she actually does so with her flashing fingernails), she is issuing a desperate ultimatum on the firm price that Grover must pay in order for their relationship to continue.

Jen's metaphor of the house being transported intact to America is emblematic of the cultural baggage that immigrants bring with them. Inevitably, however, the lives of immigrants are transformed, willingly or not. Hence, the focal irony of the novel is that as the Changs become Americans they are caught up in the American Dream and begin to acquire what they have previously denigrated as "typical American" qualities. The author thematizes this ironic transformation by dramatizing the fortunes and misfortunes of Ralph's "Chicken Palace." This fast-food joint not only reminds the reader of Ralph's having been a chicken butcher but also serves as yet another metaphor for the destiny of the Chang household.

There is nothing objectionable about the typical American enterprise of having a business of one's own; after all, democracy and capitalism go hand in hand in America. Yet Ralph has become too greedy and too aggressive. A worshipper of money, he is not satisfied with his thriving business and sets out to make illegal profits by falsifying cash register receipts every night (to save tax money). This trick, which he has learned from Grover, is unfortunately also part of Grover's scheme to seduce his wife. Grover's "generous" financial support for Ralph's expansion of his restaurant also turns out to be a sellout, because the restaurant is built on an unstable landfill. Thus, the "structural weakening" and impending demise of the joint are also symbolic of what goes on in Ralph's family. Ralph as a character holds the promise of being an epic hero in quest of the American Dream, but in the process he turns into a monstrosity.

Ralph's downfall illustrates how a person is essentially the sum total of his or her limits, but the American Dream represses such a fact, thus exacting a high price on people who plunge into the Dream with misguided visions and improper expectations. In this sense, *Typical American* also offers a serious critique of the American experience.

Context

Although *Typical American* is primarily the story of Ralph's mock-heroic quest for fortune, it also addresses important gender issues in its subplots about Theresa and Helen, both of whom have quests of their own. The main issue pertaining to such efforts is their pursuit of individuality, an integral part of which is the question of their sexuality.

In spite of Theresa's contribution to the well-being of the Chang family, she has always been the victim of what Jen calls "sibling rivalry," mainly because of her gender. Her brother, since childhood days in China, has learned to call her "Know-It-All," and he continues to do so even in America. The derisive nickname stems from her superior talents, which are discouraged according to the patriarchal precepts of Confucianism. In America, although Theresa does not openly rebel against such precepts, she has nevertheless fulfilled her potentials and become a doctor through careful negotiations. Thanks to her professional status, she has achieved a certain level of financial security and —if necessary—independence, without which she would not have been able to survive Ralph's insults about her being a "rotten egg." To a lesser degree, although she is not a career woman, Helen also has the potential of achieving individuality if given the opportunity, as is evident from the way she takes charge of matters related to the business loan, home improvements, and family finances. Her quest as a woman, however, is seriously marred by her role as a susceptible consumer and discontented housewife.

In either case, the shadow of Ralph looms too large over Theresa and Helen for them to achieve self-liberation on their own terms. Seen from this perspective, both women's adulteries are acts of transgression with ambiguous outcomes. Theresa, who sees herself as a stereotypical "spinster" until her affair with Henry, starts out as a sexual object (when making love, Henry orders her not to look) but progresses toward being a human subject (when Henry respects her enough to be divorced). For Helen, although her affair with Grover is a pathetic case of romantic fantasy and sexual exploitation, on its conclusion she has nevertheless "gained" a fuller sense of her being. If Gish Jen had given her a tragic touch, Helen could easily rank among heroines found in such novels as Gustave Flaubert's *Madame Bovary* and Kate Chopin's *The Awakening*.

Sources for Further Study

Gornick, Vivian. "Innocents Abroad." *The Women's Review of Books* 8, nos. 10-11 (July, 1991): 14. Discussing *Typical American* in the historical context of the immigrant novel, the reviewer points out the inadequacies and the conservatism of the novel.

Jen, Gish. "Gish Jen Talks with Scarlet Cheng." Interview by Scarlet Cheng. *Belles Lettres: A Review of Books by Women* 7, no. 2 (Winter, 1991): 20-21. Distinguishing her novel from other Asian American books about immigrants, Jen argues that ethnic identity should not be used as the basis for the judgment of an author's work. Humor, dislocation, and assimilation are also discussed. Contains a brief biographical sketch. The interview is followed by Scarlet Cheng's "The Typical American Comes to Town—*Typical American* by Gish Jen," which praises the work but points out problems in characterization.

_____ . "The Intimate Outsider." Interview by Marilyn Berlin Snell. *New Perspectives Quarterly* 8, no. 3 (Summer, 1991): 56-60. An interview in which Jen discusses the odyssey of the immigrant in the New World: how any ethnic group coming to the United States attempts to re-establish the Old World in America, but is ultimately changed by the new environment. Related issues covered include visions of America through immigrant eyes and Asian Americans as a "model minority."

_____ . "Writing About the Things That Are Dangerous: A Conversation with Gish Jen." Interview by Martha Satz. *Southwest Review* 78, no. 1 (Winter, 1993): 132-141. An interview in which Jen discusses the writing of her novel, the generation gap, cultural conflicts, Asian American identity, and Ralph as a metaphor for the passage of America's adolescence.

Mojtabai, A. G. "The Complete Other Side of the World." *The New York Times Book Review*, March 31, 1991, 9. A review of *Typical American* focusing on the challenge of materialism and consumerism for immigrants; the lack of contending forces in the downfall of the Chang family is also questioned.

Balance Chow

UNCLE TOM'S CABIN
Or, Life Among the Lowly

Author: Harriet Beecher Stowe (1811-1896)
Type of work: Novel
Type of plot: Social criticism
Time of plot: 1850
Locale: Kentucky and the swamps of Louisiana
First published: 1851-1852 (serial), 1852 (book)

Principal characters:
> TOM, a loyal, virtuous Christian slave
> ELIZA HARRIS, a beautiful slave woman
> GEORGE HARRIS, Eliza's husband and Harry's father
> MR. AUGUSTINE ST. CLARE, the second kind owner of Tom
> EVANGELINE, or LITTLE EVA, the angelic daughter of the
> St. Clare family
> TOPSY, the wayward St. Clare family slave girl
> MISS OPHELIA, the old-fashioned Calvinist aunt of the St. Clare
> family
> SIMON LEGREE, Tom's jealous and vicious owner

Form and Content

Uncle Tom's Cabin: Or, Life Among the Lowly is the most powerful and enduring work of art ever written about American slavery. It was the greatest fiction success of the nineteenth century. Uncle Tom, Simon Legree, and Little Eva became symbols known to most people. Although the book was out of print in the middle of the twentieth century, in the 1960's, with the renewed struggle over civil rights in the South, the book became available again and there was a new interest in the book.

The purpose of *Uncle Tom's Cabin* is to provide powerful propaganda against slavery. The theme of the novel is the idea that slavery and Christianity cannot exist together. Stowe believed that the owning, buying, and selling of slaves was inhumane and un-Christian. The widest opposition to slavery, Stowe believed and demonstrated, stemmed from an individual's—usually a woman's—outraged feeling. She gave constant examples, presented emotionally, from the world she knew, the world of home and family, of incidents she had seen herself or of stories she had heard that dealt with atrocities to individuals or to family units. She felt that to describe the process of so harshly tearing child from mother, husband from wife, was to expose the heartlessness and cruelty of slavery. The audience to which she appealed consisted largely of women such as herself who could comprehend the horror of families being separated, churchgoing women whom she made to see the inhumane and un-Christian aspects of slavery. She showed her readers how slavery violated the home and went against the religion of her readers. She wrote the book out of religious inspiration.

The passage of the Fugitive Slave Act of 1850, which not only gave slave owners the right to pursue their escaped slaves even into free states but also forced the people of these free states to assist the slave owners in retrieving their "property" led to Stowe's decision to write *Uncle Tom's Cabin*. She wrote the book in serial format, to be published in the *National Era*, an abolitionist paper in Washington, D.C. The first chapter was published on June 5, 1851, the last on April 1, 1852.

One learns much about how *Uncle Tom's Cabin* was written through anecdotes in the biographies of Harriet Beecher Stowe written by Annie Fields, a fellow author and close friend, and compiled by the son of Harriet, the Reverend Charles Edward Stowe.

According to an account of the creation of *Uncle Tom's Cabin*, certain scenes flashed before the eyes of Stowe and she included them in the book. One account said that the dramatic scene of the death of Uncle Tom came to her in church. She finally suggested that she had not written *Uncle Tom's Cabin* herself but had taken it in dictation from God.

Analysis

During her life, Harriet Beecher Stowe had been personally disturbed by slavery but socially and publicly uncommitted to action until the passage of the Fugitive Slave Act. The passage of this cruel, inhumane, un-Christian act caused her to write *Uncle Tom's Cabin*. Stowe brought a moral passion to her indictment of slavery which was impossible for Americans to forget. Harriet Beecher Stowe had great dramatic instincts as a novelist. She saw everything in terms of polarities: slavery as sin versus Christian love; men active in the cruel social process of buying and selling slaves versus women as redeemers, by virtue of their feelings for family values. She depicts the glory of family life in Uncle Tom's cabin—glory that is contrasted with Tom's separation from his family and his unhappy end at the Legree plantation.

Undoubtedly, many events in the novel were taken from Stowe's life. While her husband Calvin Stowe, a biblical scholar, was a teacher at Lane Theological Seminary, she had lived in Cincinnati, Ohio, where slavery was a prominent issue because Cincinnati was a location where many slaves tried to escape North. She understood slavery as an economic system and had also heard many details and anecdotes about slavery from family members. Her brother Charles had worked in Louisiana, and her brother Edward had lived through riots over slavery in Illinois. Harriet Beecher Stowe knew Josiah Henson, an escaped slave, who was the model for Uncle Tom. Eliza Harris was drawn from life. She may have been a fugitive who was helped by Calvin Stowe and Henry Ward Beecher. The original of Eva was the dead daughter of Stowe herself. The original of Topsy was a slave named Celeste, who was known to the Stowe family in Cincinnati. The character Simon Legree, although sketched by Charles Stowe, owes much to writers of melodrama and gothic novelists as well as the imagination of Harriet Beecher Stowe herself.

The novel is divided into three sections. The first section takes place on the Shelby estate. It is an accurate description of the scene, since Stowe had been as far South as Kentucky. The second section, which introduces Topsy, Evangeline, and St. Clare, enriches the novel with wit and humor. This section, containing descriptions of the efforts of Miss Ophelia to discipline Topsy, points to the true moral of the tale—that love is above the law. After the efforts of Miss Ophelia are unsuccessful, it is the superhuman love of Little Eva that starts Topsy on the path toward decency and honesty. The third section, containing Simon Legree, introduces terror into the novel. In the wild flight of Eliza at the beginning of the novel, one sees a similar terror, which is a dramatic foreboding of the powerful conclusion of the novel. The secluded wilderness plantation of Legree, with its grotesque and cruel inhabitants, its pitiable victims, and the intervention of supernatural powers, could be material for a gothic novelist such as Ann Radcliffe.

The last few chapters of the novel, which are reflections on slavery, are anticlimactic. The true end of the story comes with the end of Tom in chapter 40, when "Legree, foaming with rage, smote his victim to the ground." Tom nobly suffered martyrdom, lingering long enough to bid farewell to his young master from Kentucky, who had reached him too late to buy his freedom. George Harris was a new man once he regarded himself as "free," but Uncle Tom had an outlook that was different from that of George Harris and his creator, Harriet Beecher Stowe. Tom was a true Christian among the heathen, and for him, slavery was only one added indignity. His reading of the New Testament, an "unfashionable old book," separated him more completely from his fellows than did either his race or his status as a slave. Tom wanted his freedom as ardently as Stowe wanted it for him, but he preferred slavery and martyrdom to dishonorable flight. He was a black Christ who was shaming a Yankee Satan. The conviction of Stowe against slavery was so strong that she had "religious" visions, such as that of the killing of Uncle Tom—visions that she included as scenes in the novel.

Context

Harriet Beecher Stowe visited the White House in 1863 to urge President Abraham Lincoln to do something positive about the thousands of slaves who had fled to Washington, D.C. The often-quoted statement by Abraham Lincoln on that occasion, that Mrs. Stowe was "the little woman who wrote the book that made this great war," points to the role of *Uncle Tom's Cabin* in the history of women's literature, not only because of its impact on the history of women's literature but also because of its impact on American literature and American history in general. Because of her religious background, Stowe strongly opposed slavery because it was un-Christian. The buying and selling of slaves violated Christian regard for human rights, for the rights of other human beings.

The strongest objection to slavery expressed by Stowe as a woman was that slavery broke up slave families. In Mark Twain's *The Adventures of Huckleberry Finn*, the strongest, most emotional feelings expressed by the slave Jim were that he missed his family. Stowe stressed the dangers of capitalism to family values. She saw the slave trade as a masculine, unfeeling occupation and appealed to her female readers to end slavery because it destroyed the family. She never viewed women as abolitionists; that was a masculine pursuit. She believed that by writing her novels and appealing to her female reading audience, she could effect a change and abolish slavery. She reflected on the suffering that she herself felt when she lost a child and compared it to what a slave mother must feel when her child is sold away from her.

The enactment of the Fugitive Slave Act led Stowe to write *Uncle Tom's Cabin.* From the beginning, Stowe had unequivocally advocated absolute legal freedom for all slaves. She shows in the novel the difference that being free makes on the former slaves. George Harris, once he regarded himself as "free," held his head up higher and spoke and moved like a different man, even though he was unsure of his safety. Slavery, in its criminal disregard for human souls, in its treatment of human beings as property, was different from and worse than any other atrocity in life.

Sources for Further Study

Adams, John R. *Harriet Beecher Stowe*. Rev. ed. Boston: G. K. Hall, 1989. This work expands Adam's earlier study, the first and only comprehensive analysis of the life and works of Stowe. Adams discusses recently disclosed biographical information about the Beecher family and numerous critical examinations of Stowe written in the twenty-five years since the early study was published. The author connects *Uncle Tom's Cabin* to the religious ideas and personal experiences of Stowe. The volume includes an up-to-date bibliography and chronology.

Beach, Seth Curtis. *Daughters of the Puritans: A Group of Brief Biographies*. 1905. Reprint. Freeport, N.Y.: Books for Libraries Press, 1967. This book contains a forty-page introductory biography of Harriet Beecher Stowe, a background against which to study *Uncle Tom's Cabin*. The object of the study is to show the influences that molded Stowe, to present the salient features of her career and her characteristic qualities. The selection is interesting and informative and provides background material for all readers. It can be read by high school students as well as college undergraduates.

Fields, Annie. *Life and Letters of Harriet Beecher Stowe*. Boston: Houghton Mifflin, 1898. The second definitive biography of Harriet Beecher Stowe after the book by her son Charles, this sympathetic portrait was written by her personal friend and professional associate who was also a celebrity in her own right. This readable biography contains many now-famous anecdotes about Harriet Beecher Stowe.

Gossett, Thomas F. *Uncle Tom's Cabin and American Culture*. Dallas: Southern Methodist University Press, 1985. This excellent, detailed book shows why *Uncle Tom's Cabin* was the most widely read American novel of its time. The first section, about eighty pages long, describes the conditions that led to the creation of the book. The second section, another eighty pages, is an analysis of the book as fiction and social criticism. The remaining two hundred and fifty pages recount the reception of the book in the North, the South, and Europe; the replies; the dramatic versions; and adverse criticism. Contains extensive notes and a comprehensive bibliography.

Stowe, Charles Edward. *The Life of Harriet Beecher Stowe*. Boston: Houghton

Mifflin, 1889. This excellent biography of Harriet Beecher Stowe was compiled by her son, the Reverend Charles Edward Stowe, from her letters and journals. The authorized family biography, it contains the first printing of indispensable letters and other documents and is the foundation of all later biographies. It tells the story of the life of Harriet Beecher Stowe as she had wished and had hoped to tell it herself in her autobiography. Two later books by members of the Stowe family add additional material: Charles Edward Stowe and Lyman Beecher Stowe's *Harriet Beecher Stowe: The Story of Her Life* (1941) and Lyman Beecher Stowe's *Saints, Sinners, and Beechers* (1934).

Wangenknecht, Edward. *Harriet Beecher Stowe: The Known and the Unknown.* New York: Oxford University Press, 1965. A combination of biography and literary criticism, this book contains an accurate description of the literary and personal character of Harriet Beecher Stowe. The details are arranged topically, with chapters on Stowe as writer, reader, and reformer as well as daughter, wife, and mother.

Linda Silverstein Gordon

AN UNFINISHED WOMAN

Author: Lillian Hellman (1905-1984)
Type of work: Memoir
Time of work: 1905-1969
Locale: The United States, Spain, and the Soviet Union
First published: 1969

Principal personages:
MAX HELLMAN, Hellman's father
JULIA HELLMAN, Hellman's mother
SOPHRONIA, Hellman's African American nurse
ARTHUR KOBER, Hellman's first and only husband
DASHIELL HAMMETT, a writer of classic detective stories and
    Hellman's mentor and lover
DOROTHY PARKER, a fellow writer and Hellman's close friend
HELEN, Hellman's African American maid

Form and Content

An Unfinished Woman is a memoir, not an autobiography. In Hellman's case, the distinction is important because she is not claiming to present an orderly, elaborated, and chronological account of her life. Instead, she is remembering those events that shaped her character; sometimes they are presented in chronological fashion, but just as often she is apt to skip ahead in time or shift backward to a number of different incidents in her past. She does include a number of the elements of a traditional autobiography—including a description of her family background and history—but she refuses to be consistent. Parts of An Unfinished Woman are interrupted by extracts from diaries she kept many years before she began to compose her memoir, so that the book is not even a consistent narrative; on the contrary, it insists on the disjointed aspects of Hellman's life.

Although the title of Hellman's work mentions her sex, her memoir is not an overtly feminist work. She does not dwell on her character as a woman per se, although she certainly gives evidence of what it is like to be a woman in professions (playwriting and screenwriting) dominated by male producers and corporation executives. In her relationship with Dashiell Hammett, she dramatizes (without much comment) the problematic nature of loving a man who encourages her work but who also is unfaithful to her and is unwilling, at times, to treat her as an equal.

The title emphasizes incompleteness and fragmentation and makes a virtue of it. To Hellman, it seems more honest to have gaps—to leap, for example, from Russia in 1944 to Russia in 1966. That is how memory works. The grain, the feel of experience recalled is her aim. As she remarks, she does not intend to be the bookkeeper of her life, minutely recording in mechanical sequence each event as it occurred. Certain experiences are more important than others, and thus her memoir is highly selective in what she chooses to tell about her life.

She begins, conventionally enough, with the story of her parents and her childhood in New Orleans and New York City. She is a precocious only child with a vivid imagination and a lively tongue. It seems natural to her that at a very early age she should have decided to become a writer. She is not good in school, and she is a restless adolescent. She skims over these parts of her life rapidly, showing how she got to know Arthur Kober when she worked at the publishing firm of Horace Liveright. A writer of short stories and plays, Kober married Hellman and took her with him to Hollywood, where she got a job reading books that might be transformed into scripts for movies. There she met Dashiell Hammett, then at the peak of his fame as a detective story writer. He serves as a constant touchstone in the memoir; even when she is not directly writing about him, she will refer to comments he made or use his values as a way of defining her own or of assessing her own experience.

Hellman devotes separate chapters to her visits to Spain during the Spanish Civil War and to Russia during World War II and then again in the 1960's. Her writing in these chapters tends to be elliptical, partly because she relies on passages from her diaries that give the immediate feel of her journeys but do not allow room for a retrospective, analytical account of what Hellman later thought of her radical politics and sympathy for the Soviet Union. She does befriend Soviet dissidents in the 1960's, but it is not clear how she came to adopt this position in the light of her earlier support of Stalin. She seems to have changed her position, but she is not forthcoming on how her political views developed.

Hellman's last two chapters are devoted to portraits of Dashiell Hammett and Dorothy Parker, close friends who had an enormous influence on her personality and politics. Her ability to evoke their distinctive characteristics makes these chapters the highlight of *An Unfinished Woman*, and they presage her brilliant gallery of portraits in her next memoir, *Pentimento* (1972).

Analysis

Hellman's choice to write a memoir rather than an autobiography affects not only the way she presents her politics but also the way she views her writing career. Several reviewers of *An Unfinished Woman* noted that she said relatively little about her career as a distinguished playwright. What had it meant to write both screenplays and dramas? What were the influences on her writing? These questions are addressed obliquely. She meets Ernest Hemingway in Spain and writes about his hard-boiled personality, but it is not clear whether she recognizes that his style has influenced hers. Similarly, she tells amusing anecdotes about her period in Hollywood and vividly re-creates the flavor of her stay there, but it is not clear what it meant to her to be a screenwriter or how she viewed the extraordinary privilege Samuel Goldwyn gave her of working alone at a time when almost no writer was given the sole responsibility of developing a screenplay. In other areas of her life, Hellman is equally reticent. She mentions her psychiatrist, Gregory Zilboorg, for example, but the reader learns very little about him, why she turned to him, or what place psychoanalysis held in her life.

Hellman is candid and penetrating, however, on the subject of her own irritability. She presents herself as a willful, spoiled only child and realizes that her upbringing gave her tremendous strength but also blinded her, in certain respects, so that she acted before she had thought out her reasons for doing so. She also tends to be dismissive of people she does not like or positions she does not hold. One of her favorite expressions is "to hell with that." It is no wonder, then, that her literary and political likes and dislikes are the stuff of melodrama but rarely the material for a probing intellectual and emotional self-examination.

An Unfinished Woman concludes very strongly because it deals with Dorothy Parker, Helen, and Dashiell Hammett—the people Hellman loved. The form of the reminiscence—short and tightly controlled—is her forte. Hellman emphasizes that she and Parker were of a different generation, had different kinds of wit, did not like each other on first meeting, and struck up an improbable friendship that lasted to the day of Parker's death. They tended to avoid certain subjects—such as their writing— and did not like each other's male companions. Yet they never had a fight, and Hellman treasured Parker as much for her faults as for her virtues. They wanted to amuse each other and evidently did not feel that they were in competition. As they grew older, the friendship became tenuous. Parker continued to drink heavily, and Hellman felt estranged from her friend at such times.

One of the most fascinating aspects of Helen presented in *An Unfinished Woman* is her ability to handle certain situations better than her employer could. An incident in Hellman's home with a peculiarly excited young black man proves to Hellman that she does not even glimpse what is immediately apparent to Helen—that the boy is on drugs. Rather than enlisting Hellman's help, Helen banishes her from the room and deals swiftly and authoritatively with what otherwise might have been an ugly incident. It is one of those moments when Hellman, without saying so, realizes she is out of her depth. In relationships with people she loves, she is able to see her limitations clearly.

The portrait of Hammett that pervades *An Unfinished Woman* is of Hellman's male counterpart. He is fierce and uncompromising, loyal to the Communist Party, for all of its faults, because it represents the future to him—a political ideal that will survive the imperfections of its instrument. Although he was a celebrated writer and had many friends, he is presented as a loner, a quintessential American individualist.

Context

Hellman's first two volumes of memoirs, *An Unfinished Woman* and *Pentimento*, were an enormous success, garnering for her the best reviews of her life. She became a cult figure lionized by young people, especially women, who saw in her a role model who had held her own in a man's world while remaining feminine. There was criticism of her long-term relationship with Hammett—some women viewed Hellman as the subordinate partner—but on the whole she was praised for confronting the temper of her times with magnificent courage and candor.

Hellman's life and work represent a challenge and an inspiration to women's studies. On the one hand, she was a product of her time—especially of the 1930's—when her works reflected the need of many writers to take part in some form of political engagement. She chose to pursue the hard-boiled creed of her mentor, Dashiell Hammett, never excusing or rationalizing her actions. On the other hand, her memoirs and plays provide ample criticism not merely of male chauvinism but also of her characters and of herself. She knew that she was "unfinished" and that many of her actions were contradictory. The very terms she used—such as "pentimento"—suggest that she recognized that human identity entailed constant revision and remaking—like the artist's repenting, or changing and painting over, of his or her work. This dynamic process of self-creation is what accounted for the tremendous success of Hellman's memoirs, and it is what is likely to repay study in considering Hellman's place as a woman writer.

Regardless of the criticism that Hellman's politics may receive, the style of her memoirs ensures continued interest in her work. She has made a distinctive contribution to autobiography because she has questioned the form itself, noting the fallibility of memory and the way in which the personality of the autobiographer or memorist inevitably shapes what he or she remembers. Several scholars have suggested that women are particularly sensitive to these issues, of the way in which the personality shapes the content of biography and autobiography. Because women were largely excluded from the genre of biography and autobiography until the twentieth century, many women writers have sought new, innovative ways of telling their life stories. Hellman has been recognized as a precursor of these experimental efforts because she is not content to retell her life in traditional narrative form. Instead, she uses the technique of the diary form, for example, to interrupt the narrative, and the conventions of the short story to suggest the art that must be employed in shaping any life story. This consciousness of the mode of storytelling puts her in the forefront of studies of women's literature and especially of women's autobiographies and memoirs.

Sources for Further Study

Gellhorn, Martha. "On Apocryphism." *Paris Review* 23 (Spring, 1981): 280-301. An influential, highly critical view of *An Unfinished Woman* that contests the book's veracity.

Lederer, Katherine. *Lillian Hellman*. Boston: Twayne, 1979. A sound introductory study that includes a chapter on Hellman's biography, discussions of her major plays and memoirs, notes, a chronology, a bibliography, and an index.

Spacks, Patricia Meyer. *The Female Imagination*. New York: Alfred A. Knopf, 1975. Contains a searching and highly critical discussion of Hellman's memoirs.

Wright, William. *Lillian Hellman: The Image, the Woman*. New York: Simon & Schuster, 1986. A full-length biography concentrating on Hellman's life. Wright is less concerned with her plays and memoirs than with her politics, which he treats in a fairly objective manner. Includes notes, and an index.

Carl Rollyson

UNION STREET

Author: Pat Barker (1943-   )
Type of work: Novel
Type of plot: Social realism
Time of plot: The 1970's
Locale: A working-class neighborhood in a city in northern England
First published: 1982

Principal characters:
> KELLY BROWN, a twelve-year-old girl whose prospects at home
> are bleak
> JOANNE WILSON, a woman who has a menial job in a cake factory
> LISA GODDARD, a woman who is married to an abusive husband
> MURIEL SCAIFE, the wife of a hardworking man who has a
> history of health problems
> IRIS KING, a middle-aged woman who works for a home health
> service
> BLONDE DINAH, an aging prostitute
> ALICE BELL, a widow in her seventies

Form and Content

Each of the seven chapters in the novel re-creates the experiences of a different woman who lives on Union Street. Each chapter portrays the experiences of a woman older than the primary character in the previous chapter, so that the novel provides a view of the intergenerational "stages of life" of all the women on Union Street. Although each chapter stands alone in the context of the overall work, the novel is best read as a series of interlocking stories that provide insights into different dimensions of women's experience. The women in this novel are trapped by poverty, poor educational backgrounds, cycles of family violence, narrowly defined sex roles, physical limitations, and children who have lost a sense of filial piety.

The opening and closing chapters provide a framework for the other five stories. In both chapters, the youngest and the oldest characters encounter each other at the climactic moment in each woman's story. In the first chapter, Kelly Brown's childhood comes to an abrupt end when a stranger she befriends rapes her in an alley. From that moment, Kelly begins an emotional and psychological journey that will be made by all the women in the novel: She faces her grief work alone until she encounters someone who helps her find a way to complete a transition from her former self to a new self—in Kelly's case, from a child to an adult. When Kelly meets Alice Bell, an old woman, in the park at the end of her story, she realizes the ways in which her life has meaning because it is connected to the old woman's experience.

Their encounter is portrayed from Alice Bell's point of view in the last chapter. After she suffers a stroke, Alice refuses to move into a nursing home. She commits herself to a defiant act; she ends her life on a park bench on a cold winter night. Before she dies, however, she experiences a vision that unifies her experiences with all the experiences of the other women in the novel. She also has a brief yet intimate conversation with Kelly.

The stories of Joanne Wilson and Lisa Goddard are natural extensions of Kelly's experiences. Joanne is unmarried but pregnant; Lisa is expecting her third child. All three women have been "violated" by men. Kelly's rape robbed her of her childhood; Joanne realizes that her boyfriend does not really love her; and Lisa realizes that she is trapped in an abusive relationship. Like Kelly, Joanne and Lisa face their dilemmas squarely and maintain hope for a better life someday.

The stories of Muriel Scaife and Iris King shift the perspective from childhood and young adulthood to that of middle age. Muriel and Iris have children of their own, and both have achieved a sense of security and inner peace in their lives. Muriel is part of a family system that works. Iris rose from extreme poverty on Wharfe Street, and her move to Union Street has meant stability, respect, and a clearly defined role for her in the neighborhood. Yet the happiness of both women's lives is undermined by changing family circumstances. Muriel's husband, long suffering from a chronic lung disease, dies suddenly; and Iris learns that her sixteen-year-old daughter, Brenda, is pregnant. The two middle-aged women face difficult choices in order to recover a sense of security in their lives.

Analysis

Union Street explores the implications of the statement that one of the characters makes in an early chapter: "Every older woman becomes an image of the future, a reason for hope or fear." Each woman in the novel occupies a different stage in human development; thus, the crisis for each woman concerns the pain and anxiety associated with moving from one stage of human development to another. Every woman in the novel shares with all of the other women characteristics that, when examined together, become part of a continuum of experiences which bonds each woman to another across the generations. In some respects, the lives of all the women represent the experience of every woman. Each woman shares with all the other women the task of finding, for her own sake, a balance between the opposing forces that dominate her life: love and hate, courage and fear, hope and despair. On the one hand, women experience each stage of their lives alone; on the other hand, each woman's overall experience is part of the shared experience of all women. Barker's internal organization within chapters repeats the tension between opposites: Something is born in each chapter, and something dies in each chapter. Each woman faces the decision of either turning toward a new challenge or yielding to the pain and despair of her lot and thus turning away from further challenges. Each woman's self-esteem and personal development is hampered by impersonal and abusive relationships, yet each woman has the capacity to affirm herself and others by fostering intimacy and bonding in relationships.

In other words, the individual experiences of each of the seven women are interchangeable, complementary, and communal. All the women speak with the same voice about the experiences that they share. Barker takes this metaphor one step further by allowing the oldest character, Alice Bell, whose experiences are documented in chapter 7, access to the memories of the other women. Moments before she dies, she becomes a kind of medium through which the voices of the other women are reaffirmed and united. Thus, her voice reflects the communal voice of women as it is represented in the crises that women face in the different stages of their lives. Through these memories, Alice interacts, in one way or another, with every other woman in the novel. In each case, Alice is with these women in her memories. In some sense, she *is* each woman: the child Kelly Brown being raped, Joanne Wilson trying to fend off her boyfriend's unwanted sexual advances, Muriel Scaife running out of the house in grief and horror when her husband dies, Iris King suffering the ordeal of being with her daughter when the latter aborts her child, and Blonde Dinah, the aging prostitute, magnificently seducing a newly retired man. Alice feels confused momentarily, but then she resolves her confusion by integrating those memories: "These fragments. Were they the debris of her own or other lives? She had been so many women in her time." Her words, as well as her voice, represent the voices of all the other women in the novel, the collective identities of all women across the generations.

The characters in this novel perceive the chaos of this life as a force to be reckoned with. Their lives have been governed by poverty, illiteracy, abuse, abandonment, alcoholism, unemployment, and other realities of a harsh existence. Happiness exists only as a brief respite from that chaos. Kelly's sharing of the park bench with Alice Bell, Joanne's cozy interlude with a friend, Lisa's bonding with her daughter in the hospital, Muriel's intimate conversation with her son after her husband's funeral, Iris King's embrace of her oldest daughter's baby, and Blond Dinah's sexual intimacy with a retired man are examples of intimate, hopeful, and restorative moments in these women's lives. Somehow the women in this novel find a measure of self-renewal and fulfillment through these quiet, reflective moments. Barker suggests that although women face a variety of ordeals, with their attendant fears, they have the capacity to reaffirm their bonds with others, sometimes within families, sometimes across generations, by opening themselves to the gifts of hope and life.

Context

In Barker's first three novels, *Union Street* (1982), *Blow Your House Down* (1984), and *The Century's Daughter* (1986), the experiences of working-class women are central to the themes of the works. In that respect, Barker's work deserves recognition for its contribution to the tradition of British working-class novels. Novelists such as D. H. Lawrence, Alan Sillitoe, and John Braine told stories of working-class men. Their characterizations of women were often negative; women were portrayed as limited characters who held men back and kept them from realizing their dreams. Barker extended, and to some extent revised, this working-class tradition by writing about women who were oppressed by abusive, controlling, and insensitive men. The women overcome that oppression through their fortitude, their capacity for intimacy and sharing in relationships, and their commitment to children and the family structure. The women in *Union Street*, the prostitutes in *Blow Your House Down*, and the old woman in *The Century's Daughter* exemplify these strengths of character. Barker emphasizes her characters' ability to survive adversity in her stories of working-class women.

To some extent, *Union Street* can be compared, in terms of structure and theme, to the works of three American writers. Structurally, Barker's novel is reminiscent of Gloria Naylor's *The Women of Brewster Place* (1982) because it tells the interlocking stories of several women. Thematically, however, Barker's novel is closer to the works of Tillie Olsen and Alice Walker. Olsen's famous novella *Tell Me a Riddle* (1961) and her unfinished novel *Yonnondio: From the Thirties* (1974) focus on the lives of working-class women whose strengths of character enable them to survive despite overwhelming odds. The character Eva in the former work possesses strengths of character similar to those of Muriel Scaife, Iris King, and Alice Bell in *Union Street*. Alice Walker's classic novel *The Color Purple* (1982) addresses similar themes of oppression, intimacy and bonding, and women's realization of new roles and hopeful prospects for the future.

Readers of *Union Street* will recognize, however, that Barker should not be labeled as a novelist of the working-class, as a regional writer, or as a feminist writer. Barker incorporates plots that reveal insights into men's experiences in her novels: *The Man Who Wasn't There* (1990), *Regeneration* (1992), and *The Eye in the Door* (1993). Her work transcends labels because of its insights into character, its compassion for the problems that men and women face in a postindustrial age, and its complexity of themes.

Sources for Further Study

Barker, Pat. "Going Home Again: An Interview with Pat Barker." Interview by Donna Perry. *Literary Review* 34 (Winter, 1991): 235-244. The occasion for the interview was the publication of Barker's novel *The Man Who Wasn't There*. Other subjects include Barker's political themes, her process of writing, and her attitudes toward feminist writing.

Fairweather, Eileen. "The Voices of Women." *New Statesman* 103 (May 14, 1982): 21-23. The author provides insights into the genesis of *Union Street* and suggests ways in which Barker's work is a major revision of the tradition of British working-class novels. She notes relevant details of Barker's childhood environment, family life, and early attempts at writing fiction.

Gorra, Michael. "Laughter and Bloodshed." *Hudson Review* 37 (Spring, 1984): 151-159. The article includes reviews of six new works of fiction. Two pages are devoted to a response to *Union Street*. Gorra believes that the achievement of the novel is greater than its label as a working-class masterpiece would lead one to believe. He comments on the ways in which sex and violence form the basis of the characters' experiences.

Pykett, Lyn. "The Century's Daughters: Recent Women's Fiction and History."

Critical Quarterly 29 (Autumn, 1987): 71-77. Pykett evaluates Barker's third novel, *The Century's Daughter* (1986), as a significant example of women's perspective on history and compares the novel to a similar contemporary work. She considers some of the themes in Barker's work, including social realism, feminism, and class conflicts.

Stone, Les, and Jean W. Ross. "Pat Barker." In *Contemporary Authors*, edited by H. May and S. M. Trosky. Detroit: Gale Research, 1988. A bibliographical essay that surveys critical response to Barker's early novels. In an interview, Barker explains how her writing style evolved and notes the concept of a "communal voice," which is used in two of her novels. She also discusses her reputation as a "regional writer." A listing of reviews of Barker's work is appended.

Robert E. Yahnke

THE UNLIT LAMP

Author: Radclyffe Hall (1880-1943)
Type of work: Novel
Type of plot: Bildungsroman
Time of plot: The beginning of the twentieth century
Locale: Seabourne, a fictional town on the south English coast
First published: 1924

> *Principal characters:*
> JOAN OGDEN, the eldest daughter of a retired British colonel and
> his pretentious wife
> MARY OGDEN, Joan's mother and her antagonist
> ELIZABETH RODNEY, Joan's governess and friend
> RICHARD BENSON, the "sensitive" son of a prominent local family
> MILLY OGDEN, Joan's sister, a pretty, self-centered, musically
> gifted child
> JAMES OGDEN, Joan's cruel father

Form and Content

The Unlit Lamp, Radclyffe Hall's first novel, was her second to be published, enjoying good sales. In the *Bildungsroman* tradition, it chronologically recounts the life of protagonist Joan Ogden, detailing her childhood, adolescence, and young adulthood, while compressing later years. Hall styles her characteristically conventional, naturalistic prose to good effect in *The Unlit Lamp*, only sometimes lapsing into floridity.

The novel's working title, *Octopi*, suggests Hall's interpretation of the plot and the antagonist, Joan's mother. Joan detested her dictatorial father but was dedicated to maintaining family harmony. In her caretaking role, she shielded her sister from paternal hostility, and she gave her mother the affection that her father did not provide. Taking advantage of Joan's extreme sensitivity, Mary gained excessive control over her eldest daughter; this control resembles the crushing grip of an octopus. Although she is monstrously selfish regarding Joan's love, Mary Ogden is ultimately depicted as a pitiable woman whose incompetence makes her utterly dependent on Joan.

The Ogdens' life in provincial Seabourne poignantly portrays fading English manners during the fin-de-siècle, when women began earnest agitation for suffrage, employment, and education. Joan's character is designed to reflect the ambiguous dynamics of social change. As a child, she is naturally disinclined to the more patriarchal, arbitrary aspects of her femininity. When Elizabeth enters the Ogden household to tutor Joan and Milly, she personifies the educated, independent "modern" woman; she amplifies those "unfeminine," "antisocial" traits Joan already possesses. Because she encourages Joan personally and intellectually, Elizabeth soon has Joan's respect and love, becoming her most trusted friend.

Not unexpectedly, Mrs. Ogden hates Elizabeth's increasing significance. Fiercely jealous, she attempts to remove the governess; she plays on Joan's love and duty in a thousand petty, insistent ways, to bind Joan to her and to defeat her perceived rival, Elizabeth, a "mere" employee. In this hostile atmosphere, young Joan is trapped amid opposing forces of self and society. She seeks higher education to fulfill her personal potential, though she seems unconvinced of her right to it. She thrives in the company of Elizabeth, slaving over her books to please the governess, ever eager to meet Elizabeth's expectations. She seizes the chance to serve Elizabeth more intimately when Elizabeth's hand is accidentally burned during an act of heroism. Joan loves Elizabeth.

Yet Joan seems to be unable to defy her family's hold on her, no matter how hard she tries to "individuate." Never inclined to marry, she rejects even Richard's advances. Her father's and sister's deaths position her as sole emotional and domestic support for her mother, who clings ever more pathetically to Joan. When Joan makes plans to take exams, to go off to university, to cohabit with Elizabeth, to build an independent life, her mother tightens the noose of duty. The tenacity of Mary's hold on Joan places Elizabeth in the unenviable position of seeming to alienate the daughter from her mother—which she eventually seeks to do, for Joan's own good.

A peculiar love triangle emerges in *The Unlit Lamp*. Mrs. Ogden's "love" for Joan is a suffocating, self-gratifying thing, unlike Elizabeth's strong, generous love. Joan's consuming love for her mother is conditioned by social mores, painful but irresistible. Joan loves Elizabeth deeply, but no authorizing force affirms her pure emotion. Thus, Joan repeatedly spurns Elizabeth, denying herself for her mother's satisfaction. Elizabeth at last sorrowfully concedes Mrs. Ogden's overmastery of Joan and disengages from the conflict, refusing further contact with Joan.

By late middle age, the once-vibrant Joan transforms into a grey, dulled spinster, the handmaid of her mother's dotage, lifeless beyond her patriarchal servility. The suffragists have surpassed her; her disused intellect has faded; her dreams have crumbled. When Richard sees her once again, an aging prisoner of misbegotten choices, he is appalled and briefly hopes to rescue her. He cannot. Obdurate in her resignation, Joan wishes only for news of Elizabeth, long-since married and moved to South Africa, resigned to an agreeable, conformative existence.

Joan's romantic friendship with Elizabeth succumbed to the deterministic power of Victorian standards for domestic femininity. The mother is all-powerful, the family superior to the individual. By novel's end, with her mother dead, Joan is forced to obtain employment as a nursemaid-cum-governess for a middle-aged, mentally deficient man. Her self-appointed sterile, repressed existence grinds on without any possibility of redemption.

Analysis

The initial drafts of *The Unlit Lamp* (then titled *After Many Days*) were rejected by several publishers as overlong and unexceptional. When Cassell brought out the still-lengthy novel in 1924, following Hall's successful "lighter" novel, *The Forge*, the book sold well despite its overwhelmingly depressing nature and what reviewer Alec Waugh described as its only "adequate" treatment of an interesting subject. Like many first novels, *The Unlit Lamp* is based on its author's life. It offers a forbidding projection of what the future might have held for young Marguerite Radclyffe Hall had she not rejected her mother's domination and formulated a highly independent existence as "John," the "invert" lesbian companion first of Lady Mabel Batten and then of Lady Una Troubridge.

Joan Ogden presents a distasteful feminized version of her author, "John": The nominal similarity is indicative. Like Radclyffe Hall herself, Joan dislikes and resents her mother yet obliges every parental whim. Hall avoided her own unlikable mother after receiving an emancipatory inheritance from her idolized absentee father, yet she shouldered financial filial responsibilities until her mother's death. Hall's first serious lesbian relationship, with a sophisticated and cultured singer twenty years her elder, parallels the relationship between Joan and her mother to some degree: *The Unlit Lamp* was even dedicated "To Mabel Veronica Batten in deep affection, gratitude and respect." After "Lady's" untimely death, Hall and the romantic usurper Una Troubridge engaged in a strangely cultish deification of Hall's late motherly lesbian mentor.

Joan's connection with Mary Ogden, her biological mother, is constructed as a sort of abnormal Oedipal relationship far more perverse than the quasi-lesbian relationship between Joan and Elizabeth which simmers just beneath the novel's surface. A reader cannot fail to notice the disconcertingly intimate, pathologically physical ways in which Joan expresses her love for her mother—kissing her, caressing her, embracing a distraught Mary upon her lap. After James and Milly Ogden die, hypochondriacal Mary insists that her daughter share her bed; she snuggles up to Joan's warmth at night in a way that disgusts Joan, who nevertheless tolerates the nocturnal arrangements. Joan permits her mother's passive-aggressive domination out of inordinate sympathy for what she sees as her mother's sad, helpless, disappointed life. She believes that it is her duty to ease her mother's melodramatic sufferings.

Yet Mary's expressions of near-sexual intimacy with Joan constitute an emotional incest that Elizabeth strives unsuccessfully to shatter. Although Elizabeth's authoritative position enables Joan to idealize her tutor, to emulate her intellectual idol, and, for a time, to seek an exclusive and romantically charged relationship with Elizabeth, Joan has a morbid fear of her mother's rejection. She wounds Elizabeth and herself through the bizarre, self-abnegating love of her parent that blots out all other desires. If Joan had managed to escape her mother's hold and to set up house with Elizabeth, it is implied that the stimulating relationship of intellectual equals would have included a sensual component.

That Elizabeth herself occupies a mother-like position as Joan's teacher, as an older woman, cannot be denied; their close association would now be considered unethical, though directed toward Joan's benefit. Yet the pathological intimacy of Joan's relations with Mary could have been supplanted by an emotionally and sexually satisfying, relatively "normal" lesbian relation with Elizabeth. The parochial, repressive morality of the times prevented such a satisfactory resolution to Joan's dilemma. Elizabeth cannot overcome Mary's irrational bondage of Joan; therefore, to preserve her own integrity, she finally abandons not only her loving relationship with Joan but also her independent life. The triangle is shattered, and not one of the three characters can lead a really happy life thereafter.

In a Victorian shadow world where mothers such as Mary can consume their daughters, there is no place for the sort of woman that Elizabeth represents throughout most of the *The Unlit Lamp*. Female economic dependence—Joan's and Mary's—is a primary obstacle. Joan and Elizabeth cannot create their own lesbian world, as Radclyffe Hall and her lovers could, with independent financial means. Whereas Hall presents each female character sympathetically, rendering the plot more complex, Joan is finally cast as a pathetic victim of her own emotional inadequacies and of social conventions. She cannot live up to her exceptional potential; her talent is wasted; her life is a ruin. The novel concludes with a leaden sense of women's inevitable misery, for Joan, the "lamp," remains forever "unlit."

Context

Radclyffe Hall evidently did not consider *The Unlit Lamp* to be "a lesbian novel"; instead, she construed it as a cautionary tale about the dangers that domineering Victorian mothers presented to overcompliant daughters. In this light, the work's quick success with "progressive," post-Edwardian readers makes perfect sense. The modern reader's hindsight, however, cannot overlook the crucial interplays between this first novel and Hall's classic lesbian saga *The Well of Loneliness* (1928). If Joan struggled in a personal darkness, her successor Stephen Gordon strove knowingly against a social gloom no less destructive in its effects.

Clearly, *The Unlit Lamp* made a vital step in Hall's developing career as a novelist, although it has not achieved lasting popularity. In retrospect, it forges a significant link between the limiting domestic purview of late nineteenth century women—the milieu of Hall's youth—and the relatively liberated realm of women in the early twentieth century. The modernizing influence of World War I had a tremendous impact on English society, and women in the postwar era emerged from the restricted family environment Joan suffered to demand their rights to education, political participation, and a public life. Elizabeth previews the "New Woman" of the 1920's, a type personified by minor female characters sporting short hair and mannish dress near the novel's conclusion. Joan reacts to them with a repelled wistfulness.

Like much of Hall's work, *The Unlit Lamp* displays an essentially negative, melancholy worldview. Its female characters are crushed by sexist social forms and by their own excessive sensitivity to others' needs; its male figures alternate between being boorish and sentimental, often sad and ineffectual, but no less authoritarian for that. The feminist reader can only find the historical scenario oppressive, the unrelentingly grim life of the heroine simply depressing. *The Unlit Lamp* ends with only the slightest hint of a better future for "spinsters" or any other women.

Radclyffe Hall herself avoided the unpleasant (if realistic) fates she meted out to her female characters, although her literary vision remained focused on the unsavory aspects of human relationships. Her descriptions of Joan's, Mary's, and Elizabeth's mutual obsessions outlines a dismal, conflict-centered triangle of homosocial affections that only pervasive societal change could mitigate. Finally, despite its literary conventionality, *The Unlit Lamp* can aid in a reader's understanding of the early modern context from which both contemporary feminism and modern lesbianism have sprung.

Sources for Further Study

Baker, Michael. *Our Three Selves: The Life of Radclyffe Hall.* New York: William Morrow, 1985. This highly readable biography focuses on Hall's life without minimizing or sensationalizing her lesbianism. It provides useful insights into her writings, including *The Unlit Lamp.*

Benstock, Shari. *Women of the Left Bank: Paris, 1900-1940.* Austin: University of Texas Press, 1986. Benstock's voluminous work addresses Radclyffe Hall and her work only incidentally but details Hall's modernist milieu and literary acquaintances.

Faderman, Lillian. *Surpassing the Love of Men: Romantic Friendship and Love Between Women from the Renaissance to the Present.* New York: William Morrow, 1981. The preeminent lesbian historian, Faderman discusses the historical context that marks *The Unlit Lamp* as a novel of proto-lesbian friendship and explains Hall's role in early lesbian social psychology.

Gilbert, Sandra M., and Susan Gubar. *Sexchanges.* Vol. 2 in *No Man's Land: The Place of the Woman Writer in the Twentieth Century.* New Haven, Conn.: Yale University Press, 1989. These distinguished feminist critics undertake the monumental task of articulating modern women's literature as a textual and sociohistorical phenomenon, referring to Hall and her work as significant examples of "sexchanges."

Hall, Radclyffe. *The Well of Loneliness.* New York: Anchor Books, 1990. First published in 1928 and banned in England, Hall's fifth and best-known novel fulfills the lesbian implications of *The Unlit Lamp*; the protagonist, the sexual invert Stephen Gordon, accomplishes what the earlier Joan Ogden could not dare.

Rule, Jane. *Lesbian Images.* Garden City, N.Y.: Doubleday, 1975. In this classic literary history, Hall stands at the forefront. The discussion focuses on her lesbian groundbreaker *The Well of Loneliness.*

Penelope J. Engelbrecht

AN UNSUITABLE JOB FOR A WOMAN

Author: P. D. James (1920-   )
Type of work: Novel
Type of plot: Mystery
Time of plot: The 1970's
Locale: London and Cambridge, England
First published: 1972

> *Principal characters:*
>> CORDELIA GRAY, a twenty-two-year-old detective on her first
>> case
>> SIR RONALD CALLENDER, a noted scientist who hires Cordelia to
>> investigate the suicide of his son Mark
>> ELIZABETH LEAMING, Sir Ronald's beautiful secretary and
>> housekeeper
>> LUNN, Sir Ronald's sinister young laboratory assistant
>> SOPHIA TILLING, Mark Callender's former lover
>> ISABELLE DE LINGERIE, an exchange student from France who
>> visited Mark on the night of his death
>> MISS MARKLAND, a woman who employed Mark as gardener
>> MARK CALLENDER, the subject of Cordelia's investigation

Form and Content

An Unsuitable Job for a Woman traces P. D. James's detective Cordelia Gray in her first solo case. While investigating the death of Mark Callender, Cordelia also learns about herself and about the suitability of detective work as a job for a woman. In the tradition of detective fiction, the reader accompanies Cordelia through the major stages of her investigation as she gradually uncovers the truth.

At the novel's opening, Cordelia learns that her partner has cut his wrists after learning that he has terminal cancer. Bernie Pryde had once served in the CID (Criminal Investigation Department) for the London Metropolitan Police, where he had studied under Superintendent Adam Dalgliesh (the central detective in many of James's other novels). Dalgliesh had later fired Pryde, but Pryde continued to regard him as the final authority in how detection should be done, and Cordelia adopts a similar attitude toward Pryde and indirectly toward Dalgliesh as well. Throughout the novel, she reminds herself of the precepts that Pryde supposedly learned from Dalgliesh.

During her first interview with Sir Ronald Callender, Cordelia is struck by his odd detachment from his dead son, but she takes him at his word, that he accepts the police's conclusion and merely wishes to understand why Mark committed suicide. At Mark's cottage, however, Cordelia quickly begins to suspect that Mark was actually murdered. Nothing else could account for the peculiarities of the uneaten dinner and the coffee jug. Cordelia soon begins to identify with the dead young man. When she talks to the Cambridge police, Cordelia discovers that they too considered the suicide odd, mostly because of the way in which the strap that made the noose had been tied to the hook.

As she interviews Mark's university friends, Cordelia likes them, Sophia especially, but realizes that they are hiding some essential information from her. The friends agree that Mark had no reason to kill himself and that he had shown no signs of stress before his sudden departure from school. Gradually, Cordelia learns some bits of information concerning Sir Ronald's attendance at a university dinner the night of Mark's death and a visit which Mark made to a rural doctor a few weeks before he died.

During a visit to Mark's elderly nurse, Nanny Pilbeam, Cordelia learns that Mark's mother, who had died a few months after his birth, had left him a prayerbook in which she had written a cryptic clue regarding their two blood types. Another breakthrough comes when, under duress, exchange student Isabelle de Lingerie confesses that she had visited Mark on the night of his death and had found him already dead, hanging by the neck wearing only a woman's bra and panties, his mouth painted with garish purple lipstick. When Isabelle returned to the cottage with Sophia's brother Hugo, they found Mark still hanging, but wearing jeans, his face clean.

Shortly after this revelation, someone makes an effort to kill Cordelia by throwing her down an abandoned well. Ironically, the strap with which Mark was strangled saves her life. The bits of information send Cordelia back to accuse Sir Ronald of murdering Mark: He realized that Mark had discovered that the blood types made it seem impossible for Sir Ronald to be his true father. Cordelia tells him that he disguised the murder to look like death during some sort of sexual experiment. During their confrontation, Miss Leaming shoots Sir Ronald; she confesses later that she was Mark's mother, which explains the incongruent blood types.

To protect Mark's memory, Cordelia helps Miss Leaming destroy the evidence, and they succeed in deceiving the police, even though Cordelia suspects that Inspector Dalgliesh knows what really happened. At the end of her interview with the inspector, Cordelia accuses him of lacking sensitivity by ignoring Bernie Pryde after he fired him.

Analysis

As the novel's title indicates, an important theme in *An Unsuitable Job for a Woman* examines whether in fact a woman is suitable as a detective. Throughout the novel, many characters tell Cordelia that she is unsuitable, but the three exceptions are important. In an imaginary conversation, Cordelia's mother (who died at her birth) assures her that the job is perfectly suitable. Mark's history teacher suggests that women's patience, curiosity, and desire to manage others should make them fine detectives. Most important, Dalgliesh is finally confounded by the very precepts about lying that Cordelia learned from Pryde, and he seems to acknowledge as well that Cordelia is right in condemning him for his insensitivity.

Sensitivity and emotional involvement are primary issues in this novel, and they seem to account for Cordelia's success. Almost from her first moments in Mark's cottage, Cordelia is doing what theory might say the detective should never do—she is becoming involved with the victim. Indeed, as she interviews Mark's friends, she becomes involved with them as well. She feels comfortable in Mark's cottage and admires his tidy gardening. She even wears his clothes, including the strap with which he was hanged (and which saves her life in the well). Mark was attending the university that she had hoped to attend, and in the end, she acts to protect Mark's memory even though it means that she must violate some basic precepts of detection (such as preserving the evidence).

Throughout the novel, Cordelia responds to events emotionally as well as intellectually. Thus she spreads a blanket over Isabelle's drunken and unconscious chaperone at a party, and she even wishes to offer help to the unpleasant wife of the senile doctor from whom she seeks information. Her effort to help Miss Leaming escape the consequences of her crime seem to rise partly from her sympathy for Miss Leaming as thwarted mother who loves the child she has been forced to give to another woman.

Most significant, the heart of the accusation that Cordelia makes against Sir Ronald is that, as a scientist, he is making a world in which love can have no place. The truth of that accusation sends him into a diatribe which ends in his death. Readers may be surprised that Cordelia, whose own life has been nearly loveless, should place a high value on emotion, but James gives credit to Cordelia's formative years in a convent school, surrounded by peace and order and informed by the loving but still scholarly example of Sister Perpetua, who had hoped to send her to the University of Cambridge. Those years were enough to give her the human heart that, as the novel suggests, detection requires.

Although in many of his appearances in James's fiction Inspector Adam Dalgliesh is indeed a man of sensitivity, in *An Unsuitable Job for a Woman* he falls a bit short, and the reader thinks that Cordelia is right to condemn him for paying too little heed to what happened to Bernie Pryde. In fact, Dalgliesh confesses that he had forgotten Pryde. Still, Dalgliesh has enough heart to suspect that Cordelia has made the right choices in helping Miss Leaming cover up her crime. Although he interrogates Cordelia minutely, in the end (aided in part by Pryde's teachings) she is allowed the victory, having demonstrated that the job is perfectly suitable for her.

The novel also addresses other themes; notably, the great variety of fathers and children, real and spiritual. Thus Cordelia's real father, the Marxist poet, is portrayed as never having been more than a destructive force in her life. It is from her spiritual father, the seedy Bernie Pryde, who nevertheless took enough pride in his work to teach Cordelia the "rules" of detection, that Cordelia has learned her craft. Pryde's relationship with Dalgliesh makes the inspector a spiritual father to Cordelia as well. Sir Ronald is the father who functions as foil to Pryde and Dalgliesh. Sir Ronald denied his son so thoroughly that at last, just as Mark was about to break off the relationship, Sir Ronald broke it himself by murdering him. Yet even Sir Ronald has a spiritual heir in this book; it is the sinister Lunn, whom he first rescued from an orphanage and then imprisoned by training him only as a laboratory assistant instead of as the scientist that the young man's intellect deserved.

Detective fiction is always concerned with uncovering the hidden, and literature has always implied that the greatest mystery is that of identity. *An Unsuitable Job for a Woman* addresses this idea in a way classic to mysteries, by making identity part of the puzzle itself, but in this case the knowledge of self becomes the issue not only for Mark Callender but also for Cordelia Gray, his defender.

Context

Many traditions in detective fiction emphasize the detective as the embodiment of traditionally masculine qualities, particularly regarding powers of reasoning and physical courage. In the British tradition, detectives such as Arthur Conan Doyle's Sherlock Holmes, Dorothy L. Sayers's Lord Peter Wimsey, and Agatha Christie's Hercule Poirot exemplify the rational abilities of the detective while anyone investigating murder (the commonest of all crimes in detective fiction) must be brave.

In *An Unsuitable Job for a Woman*, P. D. James seems to turn the traditions inside out by creating a detective who exemplifies some traditionally feminine qualities as well. Cordelia Gray is no intellectual slouch, but she seems to have particular powers of empathy that are traditionally associated with women. Although she makes no claim for great physical courage, when she is tested her bravery leaves nothing lacking. Beyond simply asserting that being female is no hindrance to Cordelia as a detective, James seems to imply that it gives her special advantages for success.

James has noted that Sayers had a particular influence on her, and Sayers's most explicitly "feminist" detective novel was *Gaudy Night* (1935). In that work, she used a university setting to examine the roles of men and women in the intellectual world as well as in work and marriage. Indeed, in *Gaudy Night*, the very crime involves a series of written attacks on academic women who, the attacker says, are taking jobs away from men. In that novel, Sayers betroths her male detective Lord Peter Wimsey, to her female detective, the crime writer Harriet Vane. In *An Unsuitable Job for a Woman*, James uses the *Gaudy Night* model to look at similar themes. Like Sayers, James uses a university setting; like Sayers, she gives her characters some discussion of the roles of men and women in the world. Unlike Sayers, she does not intend those themes to dominate the novel, but Cordelia Gray, like Harriet Vane before her, is a portrait of female independence in a male-dominated world. Like her predecessor, Gray has neither an intention of rejecting the world of men nor a need to define herself in purely masculine terms.

Sources for Further Study

Campbell, SueEllen. "The Detective Heroine and the Death of Her Hero: Dorothy Sayers to P. D. James." *Modern Fiction Studies* 29 (Autumn, 1983): 497-510. Campbell compares Cordelia Gray to Sayers's Harriet Vane in terms of their age, their independence, and the fates of their heroes. In *An Unsuitable Job for a Woman*, the detective's "lover" (Mark Callender) is dead throughout the novel.

Gidez, Richard B. *P. D. James*. Boston: Twayne, 1986. This useful guide contains a bibliography and chapters on all James's fiction, including *An Unsuitable Job for a Woman*. After some analysis of the novel, Gidez relates the work to that of Dorothy L. Sayers and Ross MacDonald, an American crime writer.

James, P. D. Interview by Patricia Craig. *The Times Literary Supplement*, June 5, 1981, 641-642. James discusses her youth, her adult life, and the early influences on her writing. She also examines her character Cordelia Gray as an involved detective.

Klein, Kathleen Gregory. *The Woman Detective: Gender and Genre*. Urbana: University of Illinois Press, 1988. Klein's discussion of James gives five pages to *An Unsuitable Job for a Woman*, placing it in the Sayers tradition and noting the intrusiveness of Cordelia's interview with Dalgliesh at the end. Includes a bibliography of women writers of detective fiction.

Maxfield, James F. "The Unfinished Detective: The Work of P. D. James." *Critique: Studies in Contemporary Fiction* 28 (Summer, 1987): 211-223. In a detailed psychological reading of *An Unsuitable Job for a Woman*, Maxfield argues that Cordelia Gray's emotional involvement in her case prevents her from being considered an exemplary feminist heroine. He points out similarities between James and Gray.

Ann D. Garbett

VEIN OF IRON

Author: Ellen Glasgow (1873-1945)
Type of work: Novel
Type of plot: Naturalism
Time of plot: December, 1901, to April, 1933
Locale: Ironside and Queenborough, a fictional village and town in Virginia
First published: 1935

> *Principal characters:*
> ADA FINCASTLE MCBRIDE, the daughter of John Fincastle and
>   Mary Evelyn Fincastle
> JOHN FINCASTLE, a Presbyterian minister who was ousted from
>   the pulpit
> GRANDMOTHER FINCASTLE, John's mother
> JANET ROWAN, Ada's pretty, ambitious, pretentious village rival
> RALPH MCBRIDE, Ada's first and permanent love

Form and Content

Ellen Glasgow's *Vein of Iron* is a novel of many messages, the principal one of which is encapsulated in a brief dialogue on its last page. The protagonist, Ada, and her husband, Ralph, in middle age have returned to Ironside, their native village in Virginia's Shenandoah Valley. Misunderstandings, failures, poverty, sicknesses, deception, and deaths lie behind them. Ralph gently chides Ada for being a dreamer but adds that it is queer that a dreamer nevertheless should be a rock upon which to lean. Understanding in her heart that Ralph is confessing his softness and his dependence upon her, Ada exclaims, "And you . . . Oh, Ralph we have been happy together!" Less open and communicative than Ada, Ralph at last replies, "Yes, we've had a poor life, but we've been happy together." Through fortitude, Ada had kept her heart and femininity alive to appreciate the gifts of life. Love had made everything worthwhile for her even if Ralph, the recipient of it, was weaker than she. Not least, Ada understands that happiness is a blessing, not a right.

Casting herself as the third-person narrator, Glasgow divided *Vein of Iron* into five parts of unequal length. Part 3, for example, "Life's Interlude," is composed of two brief chapters, while part 5, "The Dying Age," the novel's lengthiest section, has eighteen chapters. The story unfolds chronologically, opening in part 1, "Towards Life," when Ada is ten, a portion of the novel that provides the cultural setting and introduces Ada, John Fincastle and his wife, Mary Evelyn, Grandmother, Ralph McBride, and Janet Rowan and her family. Subsequent parts advance the characters toward middle age.

Some of the novel's reviewers and critics have focused on John Fincastle, the admirable, almost mystical philosopher who is portrayed as an anachronism in an age enamored of science and devoted to riches, as the central figure. The book's major events do transpire within his ken and are shaped in important ways by his intellectual and moral integrity. Glasgow provided no clues, however, as to the substance of John's intellections and gave no indications about what precisely his four volumes of philosophy contained. In so doing, she made it abundantly clear that *Vein of Iron* is Ada's story.

Reared in a Southern Presbyterian stronghold, the village of Ironside in Shut-In Valley, Ada is the child of strong people who endure hard times and who live somewhat on the defensive. Her father, John Fincastle, chose foremost to live by his principles and make whatever sacrifices that decision imposed upon him and those dear to him. Intelligent, caring, an idealist and a dreamer, Ada is exposed in early life to conventional village mores, to the blessings and cruelties of a tightly knit community. The family, friends, and acquaintances that are important to her or affect her life are those who were around her during childhood.

Ada, in Glasgow's depiction, is a "single heart." She has but one love; she clings to it, pursues it, and nourishes it as the key to meaningful existence. Attracted as a child to Ralph McBride, Ada by twenty has committed her heart to him. Ralph lacks Ada's constancy, although he has promise. John Fincastle sees a future for him in the law, for Ralph is bright, hard working, and intelligent. With help, he even begins studying law. Nevertheless, he is easily influenced by others and shows a feckless streak. Even as he confesses his love to Ada, he simultaneously allows himself to fall into a compromising situation with Janet Rowan, the pretty, well-to-do, conniving village bitch. Janet claims that Ralph impregnated her and, availing herself of village conventions, she forces him into marriage. His prospects in ruins, Ralph and Janet move from the Valley. Janet has lied about her pregnancy. Years later, however, Ralph, on his way overseas, leaves Ada with child, one she must rear, amid the shame of the village and her family, alone.

Ada bravely confronts her fate: rearing her child; caring for a dying mother and a withdrawn, often ill, father. Still, she dreams of Ralph's return. He does return, as a soldier whom Janet is divorcing. Ralph appears on leave before going to France, and he and Ada run secretly into the mountains, sharing an idyllic interlude that is marred only by Ralph's vain moods and anxieties.

Glasgow has firmly established her characters by part 4. Thus, Ada's and Ralph's responses to city life; to coping with low incomes; to Ralph's funks, his flirtations, and his disabling auto accident; to the Great Depression, and to the deaths of family members are predictable. The struggles brought on by events as well as by Ada's trials with Ralph and her father simply reveal Ada's somewhat stoical dedication to her love and to the preservation of her hopes. When in middle age she and Ralph, accompanied by their blossoming daughter and the dying John Fincastle, return to their roots in Ironside, they do so as survivors who have gleaned a measure of happiness, but little joy, from dreary, wearying lives.

Analysis

Vein of Iron was written when Ellen Glasgow was in her early sixties. She was plagued by deafness and lifelong frailties, and despite many friends, she remained unmarried, introspective, and alone. Over forty years of writing, she had produced twenty novels touching upon an immense range of Virginia's and the New South's characters, behavior, and culture. In this, her nineteenth novel, which she considered one of her best, she shifted away from the ironic comedies of manners that had gained her popularity and the highest critical praise to address more solemn themes.

In *Vein of Iron*, Glasgow juxtaposes the mores and values of one Ironside family with what she perceived as the inchoate, distasteful, and confused mores and values of Queenborough—of urbanized America amid the materialism of the 1920's and its failures of the early 1930's. The Fincastles and the rest of Ironside's inhabitants reflected what remained of rural Virginia's pioneer character and conventions, particularly the puritanism of its heavily Scots-Irish Presbyterian population who lived in the mountains framing the Shenandoah Valley. Having focused many of her novels on the outworn elements of Southern culture, she sought in *Vein of Iron* to concentrate on the culture's durable aspects. She did so in the context of the Great Depression, which profoundly challenged the nation's faith in business, prosperity, and progress.

Glasgow records that when she began to write this novel, she intended to produce a family chronicle. No one understood better than she that the South's traditional design for living and its central institution has been and continues to be family. Her effort, she noted, involved more than studying a character or group of characters. Through the Fincastles, she illuminated the "vital principle of survival" that had enabled individuals and races to withstand the destructive forces of nature and civilization. For source material, she drew upon the experiences of the families from whom her father was descended who had been inhabitants of their own Shut-In Valley in the Virginia wilderness between the Blue Ridge and the Allegheny mountains.

What she emphasized, therefore, was the strength that Ada, John, and other Fincastles drew from their spirit and their theology. Their heritage of Scottish Presbyterianism taught them that the world was a hard place where victories for individuals, if they came at all, came from continuous sacrifice and persistent struggle. Sacrifice and struggle were not meaningless and were not directed toward achieving security behind barricades of wealth or material comforts. Instead, they gave these people freedom to examine their consciences, freedom of belief, and an intellectual freedom that were of transcendent value to them. Whatever their personal shortcomings or the limitations of their Calvinism, they knew themselves and remained morally responsible souls.

Context

Glasgow was a self-defined feminist who informed readers of *Good Housekeeping* in 1914 that feminism represented a "revolt from pretense of being" and "a struggle for the liberation of personality." Half a century after her death, a number of prominent feminists continued to regard her as an illustrious predecessor.

From personal experience, Glasgow distilled her beliefs that feminism expressed women's desire to be themselves and to have their achievements measured without reference to their sex. To her, the evolution of this total perception of women was more important than gaining economic opportunities and political recognition.

Ellen Glasgow's personal conduct throughout her life, although she was unmarried, childless, and alone, remained conventional. Unlike other noted feminists, she did not abandon family, religion, home, or husband to live with men to whom she was not married and thereby defy the male-dominated world around her. She did distinguish herself by early rebellion against her father and his religion. Because she revealed in her memoirs, *The Woman Within*, published posthumously in 1954, that she never really felt "liberated," however, scholars and critics have sought a fuller understanding of her feminism, of her unsettled emotions, illusions, and dreams in her novels.

In these, her protagonists invariably are strong women. Besides John Fincastle and one or two other exceptions, Glasgow's representative males, regardless of the advantages vouchsafed to them by customs, are weak or flawed creatures who, like Ralph McBride, must be sustained by their Adas. Profoundly influenced by Darwinism, Glasgow made it clear that women, not men, were best fitted for survival. After having been sexually harassed by a publisher while she was still young, moreover, Glasgow's reactions to male sexual aggressiveness, to sex, and to the offspring that frequently resulted from such behavior, was a disdainful one, and her fantasies tended to be lived out by her heroines. Otherwise outwardly a model of grace and charm in society as well as a self-assured, self-supporting, tough, and efficient businesswoman, she set lofty standards for the women novelists who were to follow her.

Sources for Further Study

Glasgow, Ellen. *The Woman Within*. New York: Harcourt, Brace, 1954. The author's review of herself. A warm straightforward, introspective, and informative account that must be read by those who are seriously interested in Glasgow's work. Includes an appendix that traces Glasgow's family history and a useful index.

Holman, C. Hugh. *Three Modes of Southern Fiction*. Athens: University of Georgia Press, 1966. An excellent treatment of Glasgow in company with William Faulkner (whom Glasgow detested) and Thomas Wolfe in the various contexts of Southern writing. Contains a bibliography and a useful index.

Inge, M. Thomas, ed. *Ellen Glasgow*. Charlottesville: University Press of Virginia, 1976. Ten splendid centennial essays on Glasgow by literary scholars, covering the woman, her novels, her ideas, and her place among Southern authors. Contains a superb biographical essay and Monique Frazee's essay on Glasgow as a feminist. Includes photographs and an index. Essential reading.

Raper, Julius Rowan. *From the Sunken Garden: The Fiction of Ellen Glasgow, 1916-1945*. Baton Rouge: Louisiana State University Press, 1980. An outstanding, well-written analysis of Glasgow's fiction from 1916 to 1945 by a Glasgow specialist. Probes the emotional core of her writing and the influences of modern social psychology on the creation of her characters. Chapter 9 deals in detail with *Vein of Iron*. Contains a good bibliography and an index.

Rubin, Louis D., Jr. *No Place on Earth*. Austin: University of Texas Press, 1959. This excellent commentary on Glasgow and her fellow novelist and friend James Branch Cabell is intended to indicate their places in cultural and literary history. Includes footnotes.

Clifton K. Yearley

VICTORY OVER JAPAN
A Book of Stories

Author: Ellen Gilchrist (1935-   )
Type of work: Short stories
First published: 1984

Form and Content

The stories in *Victory over Japan* explore the conflicts facing women in post-World War II America, particularly in the South. In this, Ellen Gilchrist's second collection of short stories, the author revives two of the characters introduced in her first collection, *In the Land of Dreamy Dreams* (1981): Rhoda Manning, the only major character in that collection to appear in more than one story but whose personality was repeated in several of the other stories' protagonists; and Nora Jane Whittington.

In the Rhoda section, the first section of this second collection, Gilchrist provides three more independent stories of her prototypical character: The first, a story from her childhood, takes place during World War II while her father is serving overseas; the second, from her adolescence, focuses on her conflicts with her father; and the third, from her adulthood, situates her in the process of getting a divorce. The stories are connected by the development of Rhoda's sexual knowledge in each and by the oppression of Rhoda by her father or husband.

The second section of the book, "Crazy, Crazy, Now Showing Everywhere," includes stories of Rhoda-type characters, with one exception, a story with a male protagonist, a rarity in Gilchrist's canon. The section title reflects the connection between the stories of this section: Each one deals with characters who are experiencing some kind of mental breakdown.

The Nora Jane section of the book follows and, unlike the Rhoda stories, picks up right where the earlier Nora Jane story in *In the Land of Dreamy Dreams* had ended and then proceeds chronologically. Nora Jane may be a generation younger than Rhoda, but she is as dependent as Rhoda is upon a man's approval for her happiness, in spite of her own personal strengths and talents. After arriving in California and finding her boyfriend Sandy no longer living at the address from which he'd last written her, she becomes involved with another man. Ultimately, she takes up with Sandy again, too, so that, on finding herself pregnant, she does not know which man is the father.

In the last section of the collection, Gilchrist introduces a new character who will reappear in several later books. Rhoda's cousin, Crystal Manning Weiss, is another manifestation of the prototype in personality, although she has an incredible outward beauty that leads to her own set of conflicts with men. With Crystal, Gilchrist introduces another recurring character, Crystal's maid Traceleen, who also adds a new perspective for her employer/friend's stories, all but one of which are told from Traceleen's point of view. Traceleen reports on the violence within the Weiss household as well as on the relationships between Crystal and her son from a previous marriage and between Crystal and her brother, which reveals that, like Rhoda, Crystal's problems with men began during her childhood and continue in her later relationships with men.

Analysis

Repeatedly in these stories, the women come up against patriarchal oppression in one form or another, from Rhoda's father's attempts to mold her into his own expectations of a daughter to Crystal's husband's attempts to mold her into his expectations of a wife. In between the stories of these two women is a story of two women who are obsessively dieting in order to mold themselves into the patriarchy's ideal of women. The women in this collection who step outside their "proper" roles as reflections of the men in their lives or as incarnations of men's desires—Rhoda, who at the end of "Music," it is reported, has become a writer; Lady Margaret, who at the time of her story is a book reviewer but who, it is revealed, aspires to be a writer herself; Fanny, who rebels against the family she has married into, a family much like the Weiss family Crystal finds herself up against; and Crystal, who stages a grand showdown with her brother—are ultimately tried and convicted in their stories for their "crimes" against the social order. Their punishment is a lifetime of dissatisfaction with themselves, their families, and their lovers. Rhoda cannot find satisfaction with her writing, because she continues to need her father's approval and he condemns her work. Lady Margaret is apparently not a very talented writer. Fanny is viewed as and treated like a mental patient in her husband's home. Crystal's triumphant moment against her brother is undermined by her final realization that one success cannot make up for the years of his unloving behavior toward her. Only Gilchrist's second-generation heroine, Nora Jane, seems to escape unpunished for—even to benefit from—her ultimate rebellion against the two men in her life. After running out on the boyfriend who had once deserted her, discovering that she is pregnant, and even then rejecting the marriage proposal from her other lover while choosing to go through with the illegitimate pregnancy, Nora Jane recovers her talent for singing and uses her voice to comfort herself and some children caught on a bridge during an earthquake.

Gilchrist's development of a prototype and creation of various manifestations of this prototype in the tradition of Ernest Hemingway's Nick Adams and the other manifestations of Nick in Hemingway's *In Our Time* (1925) is a means of revealing that the conflicts facing her female characters are experienced by many different women, particularly since World War II. Like Rhoda, many women got a taste of life without patriarchal oppression while their fathers, brothers, and lovers were overseas fighting in World War II and during this time discovered their own talents and desires. Upon their return from the war, however, the men wanted the social order to go back to the way it had always been, which meant that the women had to return to their subservient positions. With irony and humor, Gilchrist portrays women using their newfound strengths to fight against such regression, usually to the bafflement of the men, who often suspect that these women have, to some extent, gone mad.

Just as *Victory over Japan* continues to develop the characters and themes found in

Gilchrist's earlier collection of short stories, as well as in her 1983 novel *The Annunciation*, the stories and themes of this collection continue to appear in Gilchrist's later books. In particular, Rhoda, Nora Jane, Crystal, Traceleen, and Anna Hand (a minor character in one of the stories from the "Crazy, Crazy, Now Showing Everywhere" section) reappear in her other books, where they continue to come into conflict within their partriarchally dominated communities. The author's vision, however, darkens. Whereas in *Victory over Japan* even an incident such as Crystal's being pushed downstairs by her husband can be handled with some humor and Nora Jane's pregnancy out of wedlock can be optimistically viewed, the author appears to find it difficult to treat lightly Rhoda's abortion in the novel *Net of Jewels* (1992) or Crystal's immature son's impregnation of an equally immature young girl in the collection of novellas *I Cannot Get You Close Enough* (1990).

Context

In these stories, Gilchrist, like her precursor Katherine Anne Porter, continues to concern herself with upper-middle-class women (with some exceptions, including Nora Jane), particularly those of the South. Indeed, Porter's recurring character Miranda may have served as a model for Gilchrist's prototype. Gilchrist begins her later novel *The Anna Papers* (1988) with a suicide by drowning that, although it takes place in the 1980's, calls to mind Kate Chopin's *The Awakening* (1899). In following both of these earlier Southern women writers, Gilchrist picks up where they left off—that is, whereas Porter's novel *Ship of Fools* (1962) ended in anticipation of World War II, Gilchrist's work begins with that war, and, whereas Chopin ended her novel with Edna Pontellier's suicide, Gilchrist begins hers with the similar suicide of her protagonist, Anna Hand. These connections emphasize the dark message behind Gilchrist's quite humorous fiction. Even into the late twentieth century, women are still fighting against the same patriarchal oppression that Chopin's nineteenth century heroine and Porter's early twentieth century heroines faced.

As she does with her other collections of short fiction, Gilchrist expands upon the tradition of short-story cycles of which Sherwood Anderson's *Winesburg, Ohio* (1919) is the exemplary text. Her story cycle is not confined to any one collection. Each of her collections, as well as each of her three novels, is part of a larger story cycle, which is made up of her whole canon and is still evolving. She creates a community of interrelated characters like those of Faulkner's Yoknapatawpha but extending beyond any one region of the South and even beyond the South itself. In *Victory over Japan* alone, she sets the title story outside the South in Indiana, and she sets the whole Nora Jane section in California.

In addition to widespread praise, Gilchrist's *In the Land of Dreamy Dreams*, first published by the University of Arkansas Press, won for its creator a contract with Little, Brown to publish a novel and a second collection of stories, the latter of which was *Victory over Japan*. Although the intervening novel, *The Annunciation*, received mixed reviews, *Victory over Japan* was lauded almost unanimously by the reviewers and then won the 1984 American Book Award for Fiction. The author is praised repeatedly in the reviews of this book for her "nervy talent" in developing her outrageous heroines. Reviewers have been less enthusiastic about her later works. Although Gilchrist is less able to find humor in the patriarchal oppression that she depicts continuing into the late twentieth century, her reviewers seem to still want a comedic approach to the uncovering of male domination.

Sources for Further Study

Bauer, Margaret D. "Water and Women: Ellen Gilchrist Explores Two Life Sources." *Louisiana Literature* 7, no. 2 (1990): 82-90. Traces the water imagery through several of Gilchrist's works, showing how connection to water empowers the female characters and reflects their own life-giving capability.

Larue, Dorie. "Progress and Prescription: Ellen Gilchrist's Southern Belles." *Southern Quarterly* 31, no. 3 (1993): 69-78. Argues that the weaknesses of Gilchrist's work are the author's apparent approval of her heroines' prolonged immaturity and these women's consistent inability to learn from their mistakes.

McDonnell, Jane Taylor. "Controlling the Past and the Future: Two-Headed Anna in Ellen Gilchrist's *The Anna Papers*." In *The Anna Book: Searching for Anna in Literary History*, edited by Mickey Pearlman. New York: Greenwood Press, 1992. Explores the significance of writing and mothering in Gilchrist's second novel.

Matthews, Betty A. "The Southern Belle Revisited: Women in the Fiction of Ellen Gilchrist." *Publications of the Arkansas Philological Association* 16, no. 1 (1990): 63-81. Holds that the source of Gilchrist's female characters' conflicts is their "tend[ency] to define themselves in relation to men." The author also provides an insightful reading of the relationship between the recurring characters Crystal and Traceleen, noting that Traceleen is "the voice of common sense and order" in the Crystal/Traceleen stories and the only Gilchrist woman "undamaged by her relationships with men."

Thompson, Jeanie, and Anita Miller Garner. "The Miracle of Realism: The Bid for Self-Knowledge in the Fiction of Ellen Gilchrist." *Southern Quarterly* 22, no. 1 (1983): 100-114. This first article to be published on Gilchrist's work provides a reading of the Calvinist elements in her first two books, *In the Land of Dreamy Dreams* and *The Annunciation*.

Woodland, J. Randall. " 'New People in the Old Museum of New Orleans': Ellen Gilchrist, Sheila Bosworth, and Nancy Lemann." In *Louisiana Women Writers: New Essays and a Comprehensive Bibliography*, edited by Dorothy H. Brown and Barbara C. Ewell. Baton Rouge: Louisiana State University Press, 1992. Reads several of the Gilchrist stories (from various books) set in New Orleans, including "Looking over Jordan" from *Victory over Japan*.

Margaret D. Bauer

VILLETTE

Author: Charlotte Brontë (1816-1855)
Type of work: Novel
Type of plot: Domestic realism
Time of plot: The early nineteenth century
Locale: England and Belgium
First published: 1853

Principal characters:

LUCY SNOWE, an orphaned young woman who leaves England to earn her own living as a governess and teacher on the European continent

GRAHAM BRETTON (DR. JOHN), a young physician who attends students and staff at the school where Lucy teaches

MME BECK, a headmistress who hires Lucy

MRS. BRETTON, Graham's mother and Lucy's godmother

GINEVRA FANSHAWE, a coquettish student at the school where Lucy teaches

PAULINA DE BASSOMPIERRE (POLLY HOME), a young woman who was befriended as a child by the Brettons

PAUL EMMANUEL, a senior teacher at the school where Lucy works

Form and Content

In *Villette*, Charlotte Brontë effectively uses the format of the traditional romance novel to tell a story of a most unlikely heroine who achieves an unusual fate for ladies who inhabit the pages of such works. Like many of her fictional sisters, Lucy Snowe is an orphan; unlike them, however, she is plain looking and seemingly unaffected by the social interactions that characterize the lives of so many heroines in women's novels of the nineteenth century.

As a teenager, Lucy spends a brief time with her godmother, Mrs. Bretton, and Graham Bretton, a haughty young man given to ignoring Lucy and innocently flirting with ten-year-old Polly Home. That interlude in Lucy's life plays a key role in determining many of her later actions, but it hardly characterizes her early adult years, eight of which are spent in lonely service to an elderly lady whose only gracious act is to die and free the heroine to travel to the Continent in search of employment. Aided by advice from a shipboard acquaintance, Ginevra Fanshawe, and a mysterious stranger who helps her find her way in the foreign city of Villette, Lucy ends up at the Pensionnat, where Mme Beck runs a girls' school. Hired by Mme Beck initially as a governess, Lucy soon becomes a teacher, and much of the novel relates her efforts in dealing with the students at Mme Beck's establishment.

Through Lucy's first-person narration, Brontë introduces readers to Paul Emmanuel, an unlikely hero to match with her unlikely heroine. Emmanuel teaches at Mme Beck's school; he is opinionated, cantankerous, and demanding. He seems to be unusually critical of Lucy's dress and deportment at various social functions; she is decidedly put off by his behavior on more than one occasion. Beneath his gruff exterior, however, he is deeply concerned about Lucy; eventually, he expresses his love for her, and he provides for her when an emergency calls him away from Villette.

For most of the novel, however, Lucy is not interested in Paul Emmanuel. First, she is infatuated with the school's physician, Dr. John—who turns out to be Graham Bretton, grown up and living with his mother in Villette. Lucy is reunited with her godmother in circumstances that lend a Gothic atmosphere to the novel. Left alone at the school during a break in the term, she becomes exceedingly distraught and eventually leaves the Pensionnat to wander aimlessly about the streets of Villette; she even stumbles into a church and makes her way into a Catholic confessional. Collapsed outside the church, she is discovered by the priest and is brought to the home of Dr. John, the school physician; there, she awakes to an even greater shock, finding the house exactly like the one she knew as a child. The similarities are explained when she discovers that Dr. John is really Graham Bretton and that he and his mother are living in Villette. The happy reunion proves, however, to be bittersweet. In love with Graham, Lucy vies silently for his attention with Ginevra Fanshawe, who attends Mme Beck's school. She feels pangs of jealousy, too, when Polly Home reappears in her life and Graham's as the eligible and attractive Mademoiselle de Bassompierre. Only gradually does she come to realize that she and Graham are not meant for each other; readers may sense the problems between them, but since Lucy is controlling the narrative, the realization is delayed.

She is infuriated with Paul Emmanuel, however, when he forces her to perform in a play. She defies him on occasion, expresses frustration at his awkward attempts to express affection, and even seems to fear his attention. When she finally realizes that he cares for her and she for him, it is too late for the traditional happy ending.

The final pages of the novel offer an unusual twist. In most works of this genre, the heroine is united with the man she adores. In *Villette*, however, Lucy ends up separated from Paul Emmanuel. Although he sets her up as a schoolmistress in her own school, he departs for the West Indies and does not return; there is a suggestion that he has died. Lucy goes on with her life, however, and since she reveals at one point that she is now a white-haired lady telling a story of long ago, readers realize that she has been, for years, independent of both male and female benefactors.

Analysis

Beneath the surface story that resembles so many other romance novels of the Victorian period, Charlotte Brontë examines in *Villette* several important and enduring questions about women's roles in society and their obligations to others and to themselves.

Brontë originally intended to name her heroine Lucy Frost; the name and the change are significant. Although both names convey the heroine's cold nature, Frost suggests a frigidity not softened by the paradoxical warmth conveyed by snow. There is significance in the given name as well; Lucy calls to mind images of lumination or lucidity but also suggests the pride exhibited by the first light-bearer, Lucifer. Lucy Snowe is a proud young woman, too proud on occasion to reveal her innermost thoughts not only to other characters but also to readers. As a result, she is an unreliable narrator, and readers are often left wondering how to interpret the actions of those whose stories Lucy relates, or those of the heroine herself.

Brontë's chief concern in *Villette* is to expose and examine the role of women in her society. Having been the jilted lover in a triangle that included an older teacher when she was a governess, Brontë fully understands the plight of her heroine. She realizes the expectations society places on women such as Lucy, who are constricted in their opportunities for both economic and personal advancement. Although she seldom talks candidly to the reader, Lucy Snowe is clearly a woman with a sensitive nature and a strong personal desire to succeed in the world on her own terms and to make choices about her lifestyle. Unfortunately, being a single woman in her century, she finds herself circumscribed by convention and law, forced to accept the supervision and direction of others whose help she requires if she is to survive without benefit of marriage. In one sense, the novel is a *Bildungsroman*, the story of the heroine's growth toward self-awareness and, more important, self-acceptance. The adventures of her youth steel her for the long life she is to lead as an unmarried schoolteacher.

The novel is also a tale of alienation, highlighting the plight of individuals who find themselves alone in a society in which few understand them and few care about them as persons. Brontë accentuates her heroine's isolation in many ways: Lucy is an orphan; she is plain of feature in a society in which female beauty is valued; she is set amid a group of foreigners in Villette who find her odd and aloof; she is a staunch Protestant in a land where Roman Catholicism is the dominant religion; she is unable to communicate her feelings for Graham Bretton, and she must watch as he pays court first to Ginevra Fanshawe and then to Polly de Bassompierre.

The focus of attention on Lucy Snowe may tend to obscure another important theme: Brontë's investigation of the society in which her heroine lives. Although the novel seems to focus on the heroine's exploits—paralleling many popular and senti-mental romances that were consumed with great zeal by Victorian readers—the author is concurrently concerned about the larger social issues that force Lucy to become the reserved, alienated, and sometimes manipulative figure she appears to be. Brontë offers a subtle hint of her aims in the title of the novel: Villette is not the name of the heroine but that of the city in which she passes her life. Brontë wants readers to realize that the story of Lucy Snowe is not simply one of character; it is also an exposé of the world that forces women to behave as Lucy does, and to suffer the disappointments that come from the constraints under which the many Lucy Snowes of the nineteenth century were forced to live. The satiric impact of Brontë's vision is evident in her transformation of the cosmopolitan city of Brussels into the "little village"—Villette. The name stresses the provincialism that characterizes the behavior of individuals—women as well as men—that leads to the social tragedy that is Lucy Snowe's life. In that respect, *Villette* is a forerunner to that greatest of all nineteenth century novels of provincial life, George Eliot's *Middlemarch*

Context

Brontë is frequently celebrated as one of the earliest feminist novelists; her works express discontent, sometimes even anger, with the patriarchal society that limited the possibilities for both economic advancement and personal fulfillment for women. Many critics have viewed Lucy Snowe in *Villette* as a feminist heroine refusing to succumb to the expectations of society, rejecting the traditional route for achieving social acceptance through marriage. Her decision at the end of the novel to reject Paul Emmanuel and remain single is touted as a courageous act of defiance against custom.

Reception to *Villette* by Brontë's contemporaries was decidedly mixed; even some women reviewers criticized her for creating a heroine who did not conform to the expectations of the reading public, which was accustomed to having romances end with a happy marriage. The author's choice of a plain heroine who remains guarded in her relationships—even with readers—was disturbing for some. Nineteenth century critics who praised the novel, and many writing in the first decades of the following century, qualified their enthusiasm by focusing first on the fact that the novel was written by a woman rather than on Brontë's accomplishments in creating complex characters or pursuing an important social and political theme.

Scholars writing later in the twentieth century, especially feminist critics, have judged the novel Brontë's finest work. They applaud her for creating a complex, independent central character who is willing to challenge preconceptions about the role of women and to examine her own social and psychological circumstances honestly and directly. Feminists have embraced all Brontë's works, seeing beneath the conventional surface of her romances a strong, critical voice attacking the social conventions that circumscribed opportunities for women. Although they have not ignored the autobiographical genesis of much of her work, they have noted her special genius as an observer and chronicler of the plight of women in a society that was decidedly male dominated.

Sources for Further Study

Evans, Barbara, and Gareth Lloyd Evans. *The Scribner Companion to the Brontës*. New York: Charles Scribner's Sons, 1982. An excellent handbook outlining the plots and offering brief but insightful analysis of each of the novels written by the three Brontë sisters. Includes sections on the family life, juvenilia, and criticism by nineteenth century contemporaries.

Ewbank, Inga-Stina. *Their Proper Sphere: A Study of the Brontë Sisters as Early-Victorian Female Novelists*. Cambridge, Mass.: Harvard University Press, 1968. An important feminist study of the Brontë sisters, correcting years of patriarchal criticism that had relegated most of their work to secondary status. The chapter on Charlotte attempts to separate her artistic skills from biographical interpretations that dominated previous critical studies.

Keefe, Robert. *Charlotte Brontë's World of Death*. Austin: University of Texas Press, 1979. Offers a reading of the novels based on the premise that all Charlotte Brontë's works are influenced by the death of her mother and siblings. Includes a lengthy chapter on *Villette*, which is judged the finest of her works.

Knapp, Bettina L. *The Brontës: Branwell, Anne, Emily, Charlotte*. New York: Continuum, 1991. A general study of the Brontë family and its contributions to English literature. Contains a chapter on the lives of the siblings, as well as short analyses of their major works. Considers *Villette* a feminine *Bildungsroman*.

Knies, Earl A. *The Art of Charlotte Brontë*. Athens: Ohio University Press, 1969. A comprehensive examination of Brontë's major works which focuses on the novelist's artistry. Includes a lengthy chapter on *Villette* concentrating on the development of Lucy Snowe.

Linder, Cynthia A. *Romantic Imagery in the Novels of Charlotte Brontë*. London: Methuen, 1978. Examines Brontë's reliance on Romantic ideology for the construction of her novels. A chapter on *Villette* analyzes the complex structure of the novel to show how the author effectively dramatizes the effects of Lucy's abortive love affairs.

Moglen, Helene. *Charlotte Brontë: The Self Conceived*. New York: W. W. Norton, 1976. A full-length biography interweaving discussion of Brontë's life with an examination of her works. Pays special attention to the influence of Romantic ideology on her works. Discusses *Villette* as an autobiographically inspired work.

Nestor, Pauline. *Charlotte Brontë*. Savage, Md.: Barnes & Noble Books, 1987. A penetrating assessment of the novelist from a decidedly feminist perspective. A chapter on *Villette* examines Brontë's concern with female powerlessness and repression. Includes a useful summary of Charlotte's reputation among contemporaries and later generations.

Pinion, F. B. *A Brontë Companion*. New York: Harper & Row, 1975. A general reference book about the Brontë sisters and their works. Includes a biographical sketch of Charlotte and critical commentary on her novels. Contains character sketches of principal personages in the works and Charlotte's own comments on her fiction.

Laurence W. Mazzeno

A VINDICATION OF THE RIGHTS OF WOMAN

Author: Mary Wollstonecraft (1759-1797)
Type of work: Social criticism
First published: 1792

Form and Content

First published in London in 1792, in the wake of the American and French revolutions, Mary Wollstonecraft's *A Vindication of the Rights of Woman* was itself a revolutionary book—a powerful argument for the establishment of legal, political, and social equality between men and women. Though by no means the first "feminist" writing in English (that honor should properly go to Mary Astell, who wrote approximately a hundred years before Wollstonecraft), Wollstonecraft spoke with uncommon force and vigor about the institutionalized, culturally sponsored oppression of women. Wollstonecraft's governing premise in *A Vindication of the Rights of Woman* can be traced back through Thomas Jefferson and the American Declaration of Independence to the English philosopher John Locke: She claims that men and women are moral and intellectual (if not physical) equals, and are thus equally entitled to the same "natural rights." Her first steps in presenting her case are to set forth the problem and to establish her authority—the grounds on which she will argue against the oppression of women.

The problem, simply put, is that women have traditionally been relegated to a secondary, subordinate place in society—assigned a role, as a modern feminist put it, as the "second sex." Wollstonecraft recognizes that this is hardly a phenomenon of her time alone. Throughout history, women have been represented as intellectually and morally inferior to men, and this supposed inferiority has been used as the excuse to keep them in a subordinate position, without the power to act—or even to think—freely. Society has further conspired to institutionalize sexual oppression, reinforcing and perpetuating this subordination by denying women access to the same "rational" education as men and by insisting instead that they concern themselves only with finding ways to make themselves more attractive to men. The result, as Wollstonecraft trenchantly puts it, is that women have been kept in a state of "perpetual childhood," a state that inhibits moral and intellectual growth and only increases their dependence on men. Independence, which Wollstonecraft sees as the necessary basis for true equality, can only come about through a "revolution in female manners" built on the recognition that women are as capable of moral and intellectual improvement as men are.

Wollstonecraft's authority in making such claims is fundamentally religious. She argues that men and women alike have been created in the image of the "Supreme Being" and have thus been equally endowed with reason, which she sees as the attribute that defines what it means to be human and thus sets humankind above "brute creation." Reason is not, however, simply a proof of humanity or of humankind's superiority over the rest of creation; it is the divine gift by means of which human beings can attain knowledge, acquire virtue, and ultimately perfect themselves spiritually and morally. That "spiritual" equality guarantees both moral and intellectual equality is the basic principle upon which Wollstonecraft constructs her argument for women's rights. For her, the fact that fully half of humankind has been forced into a position "below the standard of rational creatures" is not merely wrong; it is an affront against God. The only way to remedy this situation, as Wollstonecraft points out time and again, is to abandon the idea of essential sexual difference and to provide women with the educational opportunities that will allow them to think and act as full moral beings.

Wollstonecraft's argument most frequently proceeds by way of analogy. As she moves through her discussion, considering the specific problem of female oppression within the context of society as a whole, she repeatedly discovers similar examples of oppression, some of them involving men as the subjects of the oppression. The behavior of military officers toward their men, of monarchs toward their subjects, of parents toward their children, of bishops toward their curates—all serve to illustrate Wollstonecraft's proposition that the subordination of one group to another through the exercise of arbitrary power will nearly always result in the abuse of that power; in other words, in oppression—and oppression of any kind degrades men and women alike and presents nearly insuperable barriers to social progress.

Analysis

In *A Vindication of the Rights of Woman*, Wollstonecraft sets an enormous task for herself—nothing less than a wide-reaching critique of human society—and she meets the challenge head on. Her aim, she says early on, is to be "useful," and from the first page the reader senses her determination to shun "delicacy" and to pursue the truth wherever it leads her. In order to appreciate the full extent of Wollstonecraft's vision, it is important to note precisely where and how far the truth does lead her. Her critique does not stop at the issue of female oppression but reaches out further to examine the ways in which society functions to oppress and enslave whole classes of people across the social spectrum. What finally makes *A Vindication of the Rights of Woman* so important and "relevant" a document is Wollstonecraft's tacit recognition that the establishment of women's rights can only be accomplished through a radical, sweeping transformation of society as a whole that abolishes all oppression.

Although Wollstonecraft's political and social views were without doubt radical and even revolutionary, she was in other ways—especially in terms of her intellectual heritage—a child of her age. As was the case with many of her contemporaries, two of the chief influences on her thought were the English philosopher John Locke (1632-1704) and the French writer-philosopher Jean-Jacques Rousseau (1712-1778). By the 1790's, Locke's ideas about education and government, in particular, had long been incorporated into mainstream thought, as had his "sensationalist" theory of how people learn. If the mind at birth is, as Locke held, a *tabula rasa* (clean slate), and humans acquire knowledge only through experience, by way of the senses, then both men and women begin life with equal intellectual potential, and the importance of environment and education—so vigorously argued by Wollstonecraft—is supreme. Rousseau's more current ideas influenced an entire generation of thinkers and writers, and were formative in the early stages of what is now called the "Romantic" age of English literature. Wollstonecraft repeatedly refers to Rousseau, both in her text and in extensive footnotes, most often to take issue with him on his view of women as weak and passive creatures born only to please men.

Another important influence on Wollstonecraft was Catharine Macaulay, whose *Letters on Education* (1790) was enthusiastically reviewed by Wollstonecraft in the *Analytical Review*, an important liberal journal. Like Wollstonecraft after her, Macaulay was interested not only in reforming female manners through physical exercise and education but also in challenging the traditional idea that women were intrinsically inferior to men. Equally influential, though in a negative sense, were such writers of female "conduct" literature as James Fordyce and John Gregory, whose popular books advised young women to avoid all physical and intellectual endeavors and to concentrate instead on making themselves more attractive and pleasing to men. Wollstonecraft clearly recognized such texts as lying near the heart of the problem: Men who instructed young women to behave as meek and passive objects of desire, as though such behavior were "natural" to their sex, were in essence preparing them for a life of subordination and oppression. To Wollstonecraft, such instruction was itself a form of enslavement, aimed at fashioning creatures fit only for life in a "seraglio."

In any discussion of *A Vindication of the Rights of Woman*, it is also important to recognize—as her critics often have not—the limits of Wollstonecraft's radicalism. Although the work may rightly be called a "feminist manifesto," and although Wollstonecraft's program for social reform may have required fundamental changes across the sociopolitical spectrum, it most certainly did not call for or entail an essential reconfiguration either of the family or of woman's role in the family. Nothing in *A Vindication of the Rights of Woman* even remotely suggests that women should abandon the idea of motherhood. If anything, Wollstonecraft's theoretical "model" for the enlightened society was the middle-class household seen as an independent social-economic unit managed by the middle-class woman. Wollstonecraft would never have agreed with the idea that a woman's only place is in the home, but she did see the "domestic sphere"—where, in her capacity as wife and mother, a woman functions as primary educator and caregiver—as the place where the progress of civilization can most effectively be advanced.

Context

History did not treat Wollstonecraft kindly—or at all fairly. The initial reception of *A Vindication of the Rights of Woman* was largely positive (although it can be argued that the early reviewers of Wollstonecraft's work, most of whom regarded it as a treatise on "female education," either missed or overlooked its more radical implications). Shortly after her death in 1797 (of complications following the birth of her second child—a daughter, Mary, who was later to marry the poet Percy Shelley and write her own story of power and oppression, *Frankenstein*), however, the press began to vilify Wollstonecraft. As reactionary forces gathered in the wake of the failure of the French Revolution to produce the kind of apocalyptic social change its adherents had thought certain, Wollstonecraft's work came to be ridiculed and her life treated as scandal: In time, she became an object lesson, a cautionary example of the dangers of female education and emancipation. As late as the 1940's, it was still fashionable to ignore the sweeping, humanitarian vision of her work and to focus instead on her life and personality, portraying her as a shrill, man-hating neurotic whose vision was based on a contempt for all traditional values. Following the advent of the women's movement in the 1960's, however, feminist writers turned to Wollstonecraft for direction and inspiration, in the process demanding that she be judged for what she really was: a powerful force in the struggle for human freedom.

Sources for Further Study

Ferguson, Moira, and Janet M. Todd. *Mary Wollstonecraft*. Boston: Twayne, 1984. An excellent introduction to Wollstonecraft and her work. Particularly good on the intellectual background of *A Vindication of the Rights of Woman*.

Flexner, Eleanor. *Mary Wollstonecraft*. New York: Coward-McCann, 1972. A sound biography with a thorough discussion of Wollstonecraft's writings.

George, Margaret. *One Woman's "Situation": A Study of Mary Wollstonecraft*. Urbana: University of Illinois Press, 1970. Though much has been written about Wollstonecraft since 1970, this remains a sensitive discussion of her life and work.

Poovey, Mary. *The Proper Lady and the Woman Writer*. Chicago: University of Chicago Press, 1984. An important study of the emergence of the woman writer. Poovey's psychoanalytic reading of Wollstonecraft's work is fascinating and revealing.

Posten, Carol H., ed. *A Vindication of the Rights of Woman*, by Mary Wollstonecraft. 2d ed. New York: W. W. Norton, 1988. Perhaps the best place to begin a detailed study of Wollstonecraft's work. A fully annotated text, together with a bibliography, selected modern criticism and background material, and a section outlining the "Wollstonecraft debate."

Todd, Janet. *A Wollstonecraft Anthology*. New York: Columbia University Press, 1990. Selections from all Wollstonecraft's works together with a very useful introduction and bibliography.

Michael Stuprich

VIOLET CLAY

Author: Gail Godwin (1937-   )
Type of work: Novel
Type of plot: Psychological realism
Time of plot: The 1970's
Locale: Charleston, South Carolina; New York City; and the Adirondacks
First published: 1978

Principal characters:

VIOLET CLAY, an illustrator of gothic romances
AMBROSE CLAY, Violet's uncle
SAMANTHA DE VERE, a poor unwed mother and Ambrose's
    neighbor in Plommet Falls
GEORGETTE CLAY ("GRANNY"), a woman who gave up a
    promising career as a concert pianist to marry Violet's
    grandfather
VIOLET PARDEE, Georgette's best friend, who is called "the Big
    V." to distinguish her from Violet (her namesake)
LIZA LEE CLAY, Violet's mother
LEWIS LANIER, the Big V.'s nephew and Violet's husband
IVOR SEDGE, an embittered Hungarian refugee and a conceptual
    artist
JAKE, a musician and Violet's lover
MILO HAMILTON, Violet's best friend
SHEILA BENTON, an editor at *Vogue* and Ambrose's lover
CAROL GRUBER, a tycoon who becomes Ambrose's wife
DORIS KOLB, an art director at Harrow House Publishers who
    fires Violet
MINERVA MEANS, Ambrose's landlady in Plommet Falls
CHEYENNE DE VERE, Sam's illegitimate daughter

Form and Content

Violet Clay is a thoughtful, carefully crafted tale of one woman's development as a painter. The novel alternates between accounts of Violet's present experiences—during a two-month period in New York City and the Adirondacks—and flashbacks to the past: her Southern childhood; a summer spent with her grandmother in Charleston after graduating from college; her short-lived marriage; her early struggles as a young divorcée and would-be artist in New York; and her ambivalent relationship with her beloved uncle Ambrose, a writer. By the end of the novel, Violet has exorcised her past failures, confronted her present circumstances, and moved confidently toward a new future as a successful painter.

When the novel begins, Violet is contemplating "the fate of fleeing maidens" (the first chapter's title) while painting one such maiden for the cover of a gothic romance—a job that has paid her rent for nine years but falls far short of the glorious future that she once imagined for herself. A sudden phone call interrupts both her work and her reverie, and initiates the end of her complacent life. This call, from the new art director at Harrow House, is the harbinger of Violet's dismissal later that day. Yet losing her job is not the worst thing that happens on this "Day of Lost Options," as Violet calls it. Later, after she has spent an evening drinking, rehashing her past, and feeling sorry for herself, Violet receives another call: Her uncle Ambrose has shot himself in the Adirondacks, where he had gone to complete his second novel.

Grieving, hung over, and ashamed of her earlier self-pity, Violet packs a bag and flees to the house of her friend Milo. The next morning, she calls Ambrose's former wife, Carol, to tell her of his death, and then she sets off for Plommet Falls. During the trip, Violet remembers her complicated feelings about her uncle at the time of his opportunistic marriage to Carol and his girlfriend Sheila's breakdown. Violet also wonders what became of Ambrose's novel, what drove him to commit suicide, and what role his elusive neighbor, Sam, played in these mysteries. Eventually, Violet decides to stay in Plommet Falls herself, in order to come to terms with Ambrose's death and to confront her own situation.

At first, Violet works hard at her painting there, but she soon grows despondent and disillusioned. Wondering whether this was how Ambrose too had felt, she tries to reenact his suicide—even holding his unloaded gun to her head. Suddenly, Sam, who has avoided Violet's overtures, storms into the cabin, wrests the gun from her grasp, and tells her to take herself and her sickness elsewhere. Sam later gives Violet the unfinished manuscript of Ambrose's novel, which she had hidden from the police. It helps Violet to make sense of his death.

This climactic encounter transforms the lives of both women. Violet encourages Sam to return to school and study architecture; Sam, in turn, models for Violet and inspires her new series of extraordinary paintings. One such painting, "Suspended Woman," brings about Violet's long-awaited success as an artist. More important, it portrays the way in which she and Sam are both reaching toward the future and the fulfillment of their dreams.

Analysis

The novel's primary theme, Violet Clay's artistic and personal development, is emphasized by its design. Violet's first-person narration alternates smoothly and effortlessly between chapters set in the past—during her summer in Charleston, her brief marriage, or her early days in New York—and chapters set in the present, as she confronts the meaning of her uncle's suicide. Even within these specific chapters, Violet constantly refers to stories and memories of her past in order to make sense of her present. As a result of this narrative strategy, Godwin creates in Violet a fictional character of unusual depth and psychological complexity. More important, Godwin emphasizes Violet's ability to learn from her past experiences. Indeed, the novel's ending—which features a shift in narrative time—further illustrates Violet's growth in terms of a movement from past to present. In the last chapter, "Sketches for a New Woman," Violet's narration suddenly changes tenses. She describes the painting of her extraordinary portrait of Sam (which has made her reputation as an artist) as occurring in the past rather than the present: "I like to remember that October morning. I like to go back into it from the 'future,' where I now live, and retrospectively paint into it all the prescient signs of my belated emergence." Such a shift in narrative time provides the perfect ending for a novel whose narration consistently emphasizes its heroine's growth.

Violet's breakthrough painting, "Suspended Woman," becomes itself a symbol for her development as a woman and an artist. At the beginning of the novel, Violet amuses herself by using her own face in an illustration of a gothic heroine fleeing from a shadowy mansion. That self-portrait suggests the many ways in which Violet, at the outset of her story, actually resembles the heroine, trapped in romantic plots of the past; it also foreshadows Violet's own imminent flight. At the end of the novel, after her journey of self-discovery and after she has resolved her complex feelings about Ambrose, Violet paints a very different self-portrait. Now her subject is no imaginary gothic heroine, but Sam, an actual woman. Whereas the gothic heroine's fate is predetermined—she will return to that shadowy mansion and live happily ever after with its brooding master—Sam's fate is unknown. It is clear, however, that Sam will shape her own destiny as much as possible. Instead of the inherited mansion of the romance (or of Violet's own Southern past), Sam lives in a shipshape little cabin that she has fixed up herself, and she eventually plans to design and build her own house. Unlike the gothic heroine, Sam looks resolutely to the future, and she has helped Violet to do the same.

"Suspended Woman" is thus both a portrait of Sam and a self-portrait of Violet, because it reflects the aspirations that they both share. For Violet, the painting embodies the way in which each woman has encouraged the other to reach toward her goals. As Sam modeled for the work of art she inspired, she studied for her high-school equivalency diploma and told Violet what she would like to accomplish with it. Violet remarks, "I like to believe I held the mirror for her. While she modeled for me, so patient and generous with the planes and curves of her body and what she had made of them, I held the mirror for her and helped her put into words what an indomitable spirit, even when victimized, can achieve."

Godwin's implicit analogy, in this passage, between paintings, mirrors, and words, invites her readers to identify "Suspended Woman" with *Violet Clay* itself. The painting, like the novel, is a complex psychological portrait of Violet. Yet both painting and novel are also "sketches for a new woman" (the title of the last chapter)—depictions of any woman who endeavors to realize her dreams on her own. In form and content, Gail Godwin's novel emphasizes a woman's ability to leave the past behind and to design her own future.

Context

Violet Clay is comparable to other pioneering novels of the 1970's, in which feminist writers created new self-reliant heroines and imagined new futures for them. In *Violet Clay*—as in her previous novel, *The Odd Woman* (1974)—Gail Godwin focuses on a single independent working woman. In each of these novels, Godwin seeks a happy ending for her heroine, but one that does not depend on her marriage.

Indeed, *Violet Clay* can be read as a critique of the formulaic marriage-centered plots of women's gothic romances—such as the paperbacks that Violet herself illustrates at the beginning of the novel. This literary tradition is exemplified by such classic works as Ann Radcliffe's *The Mysteries of Udolpho* (1794), Charlotte Brontë's *Jane Eyre* (1847), and Daphne du Maurier's *Rebecca* (1939). *Violet Clay* parodies the narrative conventions of such novels—particularly the happily-ever-after marriage, which in Violet's case occurs before the action begins, does not last long, and is largely irrelevant to the story of her life. In its self-reflexive feminist critique of the female gothic tradition, *Violet Clay* can also be compared to other contemporary novels such as Margaret Atwood's *Lady Oracle* (1976) and Fay Weldon's *The Life and Loves of a She-Devil* (1983).

Godwin's novel, however, is less satirical and less overtly feminist than *Lady Oracle* or *She-Devil*. This is partly because Godwin does not merely subvert the formulaic plot of the gothic romance. Instead, she replaces it with another familiar plot structure, the *Künstlerroman*—a narrative about an artist's development, which is, perhaps, best exemplified by James Joyce's classic *A Portrait of the Artist as a Young Man* (1914). *Violet Clay*, however, portrays the successful development of the artist as a young woman. For this reason, it can be read in counterpoint to *The Story of Avis* (1877), Elizabeth Stuart Phelps's early feminist novel about a woman of genius whose brilliant artistic career ends with her marriage.

As a feminist *Künstlerroman*, *Violet Clay* most resembles (and was perhaps influenced by) Margaret Atwood's *Surfacing* (1972). In both novels, a young female artist must retreat to the wilderness in order to free herself from her own past and from patriarchal structures. Whereas *Surfacing* ends on an ambivalent note, however, *Violet Clay* holds out hope that a woman can find freedom, power, and self-fulfillment through art. Godwin's novel encourages all women to realize their dreams through their own efforts rather than through their relationship to a man.

Sources for Further Study

Allen, John Alexander. "Researching Her Salvation: The Fiction of Gail Godwin." *Hollins Critic* 25, no. 2 (1988): 1-9. Although Allen focuses on Godwin's *A Southern Family* (1987), he provides a useful account of the search for human dignity pursued by characters in all of her novels. The essay is followed by a brief note on her life.

Brownstein, Rachel M. "Gail Godwin: *The Odd Woman* and Literary Feminism." In *American Women Writing Fiction: Memory, Identity, Family, Space*, edited by Mickey Pearlman. Lexington: University of Kentucky Press, 1989. In an insightful essay, Brownstein analyzes Godwin's development and critical reception in the context of her feminism. The essay is followed by two useful bibliographies, complied by Pearlman, of Godwin's complete works and of writings published about them.

Cheney, Anne. "Gail Godwin and Her Novels." In *Southern Women Writers: The New Generation*, edited by Tonette Bond Inge. Tuscaloosa: University of Alabama Press, 1990. This comprehensive essay, prefaced by a sketch of Godwin's life and augmented by original biographical research, traces the autobiographical elements in her novels, up to and including *A Southern Family*. A bibliography of Godwin's major works cites stories and essays as well as novels.

Frye, Joanne S. "Narrating the Self: The Autonomous Heroine in Gail Godwin's *Violet Clay*." *Contemporary Literature* 24, no. 1 (Spring, 1983): 66-85. Frye's exciting essay focuses on the novel's complex narrative technique. It argues that Violet first defines herself in terms of others' stories but gradually learns to create the narrative of her own life.

Godwin, Gail. "Becoming a Writer." In *The Writer on Her Work*, edited by Janet Sternburg. New York: W. W. Norton, 1980. A candid and witty account of Godwin's artistic development.

Westerlund, Kerstin. *Escaping the Castle of Patriarchy: Patterns of Development in the Novels of Gail Godwin*. Uppsala, Sweden: University of Uppsala Press, 1990. This solidly researched book—the first ever published on Godwin's fiction—shows how consistently she focuses on her heroines' gradual journeys toward self-discovery. It also shows that Godwin's novels, read in chronological order, reveal her own development as feminist writer. Westerlund's fourth chapter, "Suspended Woman," compares *The Odd Woman* and *Violet Clay* as novels whose heroines seek fulfillment outside marriage and traditional gender roles but who still perceive men as obstacles to that goal.

Wimsatt, Mary Ann. "Gail Godwin's Evolving Heroine: The Search for Self." *Mississippi Quarterly* 42, no. 1 (1988/1989): 27-45. During the course of Godwin's career, Wimsatt argues, her female characters have steadily grown in confidence, independence, and self-definition.

Susan Elizabeth Sweeney

WAITING TO EXHALE

Author: Terry McMillan (1951-   )
Type of work: Novel
Type of plot: Psychological realism
Time of plot: 1990
Locale: Phoenix, Arizona
First published: 1992

> *Principal characters:*
> SAVANNAH JACKSON, an independent thirty-six-year-old single
>   black woman who is looking for the right man
> BERNADINE HARRIS, Savannah's college roommate and friend
> ROBIN STOKES, a friend of Bernadine and Gloria
> GLORIA MATTHEWS, a friend of Robin, Bernadine, and Savannah
> TARIK, Gloria's fifteen-year-old son

Form and Content

Terry McMillan has created four protagonists whose personalities represent aspects of contemporary middle-class African American women. The narrative structure of *Waiting to Exhale* is rather unusual, with alternating chapters told from different main characters' perspectives. Savannah and Robin tell their own stories, while Gloria's and Bernadine's narratives are related in the third person. Taken together, McMillan's four protagonists mirror the concerns, the joys, and the struggles of contemporary African American women. The problems these fictional women encounter and over-come are problems to which many women can directly relate. The lives of these women—indeed, the women themselves—are the major focus of the novel.

Waiting to Exhale follows the lives and loves of four middle-aged African American women who struggle to change the tenor and direction of their lives. The changes do not seem great, in some cases, but they represent the small, internal shifts that give individuals new perspectives and renewed power in their lives. These women are drawn together by bonds of friendship and sharing, and together or singly they deal with issues such as job changes, divorce, aging and ailing parents, and the desire to establish a relationship with a good man. The desire for and the lack of a fulfilling relationship with someone of the opposite sex dominates much of the discourse of the narrative; however, the search for a man is only the surface content of the narrative. At a deeper level, the narratives explore the lack of connection between men and women, and the quests for self and voice of the four main characters.

All these women are more or less frustrated by the lack of an opposite-sex relationship, because they are no longer young, and all of them have family and career concerns that demand their time and energies. Savannah is involved in establishing a new career in the television industry and in financially and emotionally encouraging her mother. Bernadine's eleven-year marriage is ending in divorce, and she is facing not only the challenges of pulling her own life and career goals together but also the mixed blessing of rearing her two children. Robin is the only one of the women who absolutely needs a man in her life in order to maintain her self-image, yet even she has other concerns—concerns about her career and about her father's struggle with Alzheimer's disease. Only Gloria seems to have accepted life without a lover; however, Gloria has simply put her feelings aside and has devoted herself to her son, career, and community. While these women are "waiting to exhale," waiting for the right man, they are in reality forging bonds with one another and their communities.

Waiting to Exhale covers the lives of these four women through most of 1990. The narrative begins with Savannah's decision to move from Denver to Phoenix and with her New Year's resolution not to spend another year without a man to share her holidays. Bernadine's year begins with an encounter of a very different kind. Her husband returns home early one Sunday morning to tell her that he is divorcing her to marry his accountant—a younger, white woman. Robin's year begins with the breakup of her relationship with her lover, Russell, and Gloria's year begins with a confrontation with her son, Tarik. Throughout the year, all these women face life-changing situations; from these situations, they forge bonds of friendship with one another and, to varying degrees, make the changes that point toward new self-images.

Analysis

McMillan's central intention is to portray African American women who are actively taking control of their lives. They all belong to an organization called Black Women on the Move, an organization whose goals are to change society and give voice to African American women. Although all these women want to establish long-term relationships with men, the men in the novel seem to fear commitment. Because her heroines are gutsy and resilient, McMillan's books have been compared to those of Zora Neale Hurston and Alice Walker. In her award-winning anthology *Breaking Ice* (1990), McMillan states that writing became her way of making sense of what she saw, her way of trying to "fix what was broken." *Waiting to Exhale* is both descriptive and prescriptive, an attempt to diagnose and to cure.

The alternating voices in McMillan's book give substance and reality to her characters. First-person narratives are delivered by the seemingly strongest and, in some ways, the weakest characters in the novel, Savannah and Robin. Both are single women without children who are hoping to meet and marry someone. Yet there are some important differences between them. Savannah's narrative actually sets the tone for the novel. Her narrative is the emotional center of the novel, while the other narrative voices, as individualistic as they are, seem to revolve around this model. Savannah hopes to meet a man but is willing to live alone until she finds someone who makes her feel that she was born "with a tiara" on her head. Her self-image is stronger than Robin's, because Robin must have a man in her life in order to feel good about herself. Robin is attracted to losers who ultimately leave her or to men she cannot have. Ironically, Savannah's first-person narration serves to elicit empathy for her from the reader, whereas Robin's first-person narration tends to distance her from the reader.

Unlike the first-person narrations, the third-person narratives of both Bernadine and Gloria elicit sympathy from the reader. Bernadine and Gloria both have children, are both homeowners and homemakers, and hope to own their own businesses. Actually, Gloria is the owner of a hair salon, whereas Bernadine is still working toward establishing her own catering business. There are obvious differences between the two women. Gloria has never been married, but Bernadine's marriage is ending in a messy divorce. Gloria has raised her son alone, has founded a fairly successful beauty salon, and has seemingly accepted the fact that she does not have a man in her life. Consequently, her anger and her lack of self-esteem are turned inward. They are apparent only in the weight she carries and in the heart attack that results from her weight and her repressed anger. Bernadine, however, has sacrificed her career goals to her husband's, has remained dependent on him, and is now, for the first time, being forced to become an independent being. She is angry and somewhat vengeful. The reader, however, retains sympathy for both these women as they struggle through their anger to change their lives.

McMillan's characters win only small victories in their lives. There are no earth-shattering revelations, and no major changes are evident in the lives of these four women. They do, however, make the emotional moves that could lead to major change. Bernadine moves away from her anger toward acceptance. She is able to move toward the establishment of her own business and to establish a tentative relationship with a man. Gloria has a heart attack that causes her to reassess her relationship with her son and opens the door for a possibly romantic relationship with her new neighbor. Although McMillan's portrayal of most men's ability to relate to women is somewhat bleak and pessimistic, her book allows for the possibility of fulfilling male-female relationships. Her main emphasis, however, is on the cooperative development and empowerment of African American women.

Context

Like McMillan's earlier novels, *Waiting to Exhale* offers a feminist perspective not unlike those of Zora Neale Hurston and Alice Walker. The changing roles of women, their feelings, and their voices are central to this work. Although many of the men in this book are portrayed as immature or ineffectual, McMillan, like Walker and Hurston, offers some amount of hope for male-female communication and cooperation. Unlike the women in Hurston's and Walker's novels, McMillan's independent, career-oriented women form their own community and set the parameters for discourse within that community. McMillan's novel is not a groundbreaking work, but as a reiteration of the search for self and voice found in such works as Hurston's *Their Eyes Were Watching God*, it definitely makes an important contribution to the growing body of African American women's literature.

Although all of her novels contribute to the African American women's literary canon, McMillan seems consciously to model certain aspects of her work upon Hurston's. Like Hurston's, McMillan's characters are not representative of large classes of African American women. Instead, McMillan focuses on the individual difficulties and small victories of women in their day-to-day lives.

Although McMillan focuses on individual lives and small victories, she does not hesitate to use her characters to voice political concerns. She does not, however, focus totally on racial concerns. In her introduction to *Breaking Ice*, McMillan states that many contemporary African American writers are a "new breed" of artists who are free to "comment on ourselves in our work." McMillan considers herself representative of these new artists, writers who come from many different backgrounds, who concentrate not on the entire African American people, but on the lives of the individuals that they create.

Despite the fact that McMillan writes about individual lives, *Waiting to Exhale* is part of the literature of African American women. According to Mary Helen Washington, the single distinguishing feature of literature by African American women is that it centers on women, on the "thoughts, words, feelings, and deeds" of these women. *Waiting to Exhale* belongs to this category. It centers not only on the words, thoughts, and actions of Savannah, Bernadine, Robin, and Gloria but also on the shared intimacies that allow McMillan to represent her women more fully.

Sources for Further Study

Awkward, Michael. "Chronicling Everyday Travails and Triumphs." *Callaloo* 11, no. 3 (Summer, 1988): 649-650. In his review of McMillan's first novel, *Mama*, Awkward discusses the novelist's goals and style of writing. Although he compares her to Zora Neale Hurston, he also points to significant differences between the two writers.

Gates, Henry Louis, Jr. *Reading Black, Reading Feminist*. New York: Penguin Books, 1990. The first nine essays in this anthology discuss the construction of the African American women's literary canon. Mary Helen Washington's essay on the emotional support afforded by female kindred spirits is helpful in understanding the construction of *Waiting to Exhale*.

Hine, Darlene Clark, ed. *Black Women in America*. Brooklyn, N.Y.: Carlson, 1993. This volume of short biographical entries about African American women provides an overview of McMillan's life and work. Kathleen Thompson also discusses the public reaction to McMillan's novels.

McMillan, Terry. *Breaking Ice: An Anthology of Contemporary African-American Fiction*. New York: Penguin Books, 1990. In the introduction to her anthology, McMillan explains how and why she became a writer. In her explanation of the reasons for the creation of this anthology, she includes a discussion of her goals as a creative writer.

—————. *Disappearing Acts*. New York: Washington Square Press, 1989. McMillan's second novel met with both critical acclaim and a landmark legal battle. Modeled on McMillan's life with her former living partner, it describes the trials and tribulations of an educated woman named Zora who lives with a construction worker. McMillan's former lover claimed that the central male character was modeled on his life; fortunately, however, the court dismissed the case.

———————. *Mama.* New York: Washington Square Press, 1987. McMillan's first novel met with critical acclaim and comparisons to Zora Neale Hurston. The story centers on a tough, gritty woman, Mildred, who is determined to raise her family despite the almost overwhelming challenges presented by single motherhood, low cash, dependence on drink and "nerve pills," and many other problems.

Yvonne Johnson

THE WAR BETWEEN THE TATES

Author: Alison Lurie (1926-   )
Type of work: Novel
Type of plot: Social criticism
Time of plot: 1969-1970
Locale: Upstate New York and New York City
First published: 1974

> *Principal characters:*
> BRIAN TATE, a forty-six-year-old political science professor at
>   Corinth University
> ERICA TATE, Brian's wife
> WENDY GAHAGHAN, the graduate student with whom Brian
>   becomes entangled
> DANIELLE ZIMMERN, Erica's best friend and a divorcée who
>   teaches French at Brian's university
> SANFORD FINKELSTEIN ("ZED"), owner of the Krishna Bookshop
> MUFFY and JEFFO, the Tates' teenagers, formally christened
>   Matilda and Jeffrey

Form and Content

The War Between the Tates is told from the omniscient point of view, allowing Alison Lurie to alternate between camps in reporting from the front. Along with their private war, the Tates wage a joint campaign against the generation of the late 1960's. As Erica and Brian face off over the marital disruption introduced by Wendy Gahaghan, they are both adjusting to a world that threatens their established values. Moreover, both have private battles with themselves that cloud their perceptions of their situations. The all-knowing narrator keeps up with all this strife in a series of well-observed and sometimes quite comic scenes that move rapidly toward the Tates' armistice day.

Brian's career at Corinth University has been safe, conventional, and dull. At forty-six, he yearns for more—not only more from the academy but also something more from Erica in terms of conjugal excitement, something raging and Faustian. He is always conscious of being only five feet five, and he has an unhappy sense of a stunted life.

Erica has grown up safe, too. Conservative in her social, sexual, and cultural values, she now finds her traditionalism sorely tested. She has always worshiped the children, whose boorish adolescence has her on the brink of apostasy. A shopping center is about to blot her pastoral landscape, a gut-blow from the industrial-commercial bogeyman that troubles the dreams of all liberals such as the Tates. Brian has not become the mighty scholar she had hoped he would be, leaving her as the woman behind less of a man than she had fantasized.

Wendy Gahaghan, then, can be seen as the Tates' salvation in that she rejuvenates their lives. Wendy has a raffish flower-child sexiness, and when she presents herself to Brian as an offering to his solid goodness, the war is on. The sequence is an old one: adulterous liaisons, wifely rage on discovery, a bristly truce, pregnancy of the mistress, and the husband's removal to an apartment.

Much of Brian's estrangement not only pains him in every way but also bores him. A serious student of George Kennan is hardly suited to camping out with dope-smoking counterculture guerrillas. Yet he fights on.

Erica, meanwhile, consults her friend Danielle Zimmern, who is already divorced from her English-professor husband, Leonard. Encouraged, perhaps, by Danielle's happy affair with a robust, easygoing veterinarian, Bernie Kotelchuk, Erica timidly accepts the futile love of Zed Finkelstein. When Erica knew Zed at Radcliffe and Harvard, he was Sanford, but "Zed" suits the higher purpose evident in one who runs an establishment called the Krishna Bookstore and serves as guru to the socially alienated. Unfortunately, Erica does not have the luck of her worldly friend Danielle, and the spiritual Zed fumbles where the carnal Bernie moves with swift purpose.

During this domestic turmoil, Brian facetiously suggests to Wendy's feminist collaborators that they take hostage the much-despised target of their rage, Don Dibble, a conservative colleague of Brian's whom he much dislikes. To Brian's shock, they do precisely that, and it then falls to Brian to rescue the victim by smuggling a rope into Dibble's office. The furious women get revenge by beating Brian in a ridiculous denouement.

This slapstick virtually concludes Brian's tour of duty with the psychedelic underground, but Wendy, after having had one abortion, announces that she is pregnant again. The *deus ex machina* for Brian is a foreign one—a Pakistani graduate student in engineering who may be the father. The new friend with whom Wendy leaves for a "far-out commune" in Northern California is Ralph, who "really digs kids" and is eager to work out "a total relationship" with Wendy. With Zed's departure from Corinth at the same time, the Tates are left to survey the battle damage and begin postwar reconstruction. Such a finale is an inkblot that everyone with interpret to her or his satisfaction, but the gentleness with which Lurie puts her characters through their paces suggests that life will not be more than usually intolerable for the Tates if they remain under their creator's care.

Analysis

The main characters in *The War Between the Tates* are set in motion by acts of adultery. In their reactions to the marital betrayals of the two husbands, Brian Tate and Leonard Zimmern, the two couples reveal totally different visions of life. They define themselves by means of their sexual behavior.

The Tates are social and political liberals but cultural conservatives. Deep down—and not always so deep—they prize bourgeois family life and see themselves as upholders of a tradition. They are religious people without a church, heirs of rationalism and believers in progress. Thus, their self-images suffer a great shock as they entangle themselves with people whose values and orientations they cannot share. After the erotic regeneration that Brian enjoys with Wendy begins to wear off, he does not really want to endure her trivial chitchat any longer simply to have her young body at his disposal, and he does not want to move on to ever fresher Wendys. What he really wants to do is to go home to Erica and burrow back into the security of the middle-class life for which he has worked. Certainly, that is also what Erica wants.

The Zimmerns are another case. Leonard Zimmern is unique among Lurie's characters in that he appears in four other of her novels. In *Real People* (1969), Leonard Zimmern is a scholar at a writers' colony, a ruthless critic and an intent marauder among vulnerable women. *Only Children* (1979) goes back in time to show the fourteen-year-old Lennie, already disgruntled with life and living with his detested father and stepmother while taking out his malign urges in teasing and cruel jokes. Later on, in the early 1980's, the setting of *Foreign Affairs* (1984), L. D. Zimmern surfaces as the sixtyish critic who attacks Vinnie Miner's scholarship; his daughter, Ruth Zimmern Turner, is married to Fred Turner, Vinnie Miner's coprotagonist. In *The Truth About Lorin Jones* (1988), Leonard Zimmern pops up as the half brother of the title character.

Leonard Zimmern is what Brian Tate could never be: a man apparently driven to seek out sexual alliances without regard for consequences. Moreover, he must be an accomplished seducer of a kind that Brian would not even aspire to be. His former wife, Danielle, although obviously hurt by Leonard's adulteries, is tougher than Erica. After all, Danielle teaches French literature, which is hardly more than a series of studies in the vicissitudes of passion, whereas Erica writes children's books about an ostrich named Sanford. Danielle rebounds quickly, too. It is a fair inference that what drew Leonard and Danielle together in the first place was a mutual excellence in sex, and when Danielle accepts another man it is not a sexual incompetent (such as Erica's Zed) to whom she turns, but a man who is at home with all of life's challenges— Bernie Kotelchuk, a veterinarian who feels no urge to be a Don Juan. Danielle does not need another intellectual; the self-confident Bernie comforts her spirit.

If adultery occupies the foreground of *The War Between the Tates* in a sort of Shakespearean comic do-si-do of shifting partners, then it is the raucous social scene of the late 1960's that fills up the background. Social chaos and change recapitulate domestic chaos and change. The peace march at the end of the novel is a perfect vignette of the 1960's and includes all of what Brian calls "freakish, violent, and socially disruptive elements": guerrilla theater players, Maoist troublemakers, Gay Power advocates, and a delegation from WHEN. The good liberal Brian, however, would probably agree that despite their scruffiness and the many opportunities they presented for satire when caught in ludicrous postures, the various civil rights campaigners evolved better lives for their subjects. Who would not choose as companions the campus protesters over the pharisee Dibble?

Lurie has a sharp eye for social satire, but only self-oriented manipulators such as the ubiquitous Leonard Zimmern seem to be without salvation in her world. Herself an academic—an English professor at Cornell University, an authority on children's literature, and a student of changing habits of dress—she is well positioned to survey the social anthropology of university families and departmental clan structures. She adopts a policy of justice tempered by mercy—and a warning to keep a sharp eye out for the Lennie Zimmerns of the world.

Context

Alison Lurie is a teacher, a scholar, and a writer of fiction about upper-middle-class professors and creative people in the arts, and she usually depicts the struggles and crises of women in this mixed milieu. Many of these struggles—*most* of them—are, by the nature of things, with men, and these contests between the sexes are seen predominantly from the woman's point of view and imply a special sympathy for her ordeal but without caricaturing all men as demons.

Lurie's own career should be a testimony to the possibilities of achievement open to women. While still an undergraduate at Radcliffe, she published poems in *Poetry* and stories in *Commentary* and *Woman's Press*, but after eight years of rejections, she quit writing. During this dry period, she married Jonathan Peale Bishop, son of the poet John Peale Bishop, and moved with him to western Massachusetts, where he taught English at Amherst College. Before their separation in 1975, they had three sons.

Lurie was jolted out of the barrenness in her creative life by two significant events. First was the death in 1956 of a close friend, the poet, playwright, and actress V. R. (Bunny) Lang; the writing *V. R. Lang: A Memoir* (privately printed, 1959) changed Lurie's life irrevocably. In studying the career of a talented woman who overcame many obstacles, Lurie escaped the frustrating round of domestic duties that preoccupied her and further educated herself about the lifestyle she would soon depict in her novels of manners.

The second important change in Lurie's life was moving with her family in 1957 to Los Angeles, where her husband was to teach at the University of California. She soon freed her mind of Amherst by writing her first published novel, *Love and Friendship* (1962), followed by a novel treating the culture shock of a New England girl transplanted to California, *The Nowhere City* (1965). Two other novels came next, *Imaginary Friends* (1967) and *Real People* (1969), before the critical and popular success of *The War Between the Tates* established Lurie as a major figure in American fiction. Official honors came with the Pulitzer Prize for *Foreign Affairs* (1984).

Sources for Further Study

Ackroyd, Peter. "Miss American Pie." *Spectator* 232 (June 29, 1974): 807. Praise for *The War Between the Tates* from a British critic. Ackroyd plays down the significance of the novel's background in the troubled Vietnam years and emphasizes its comic elements in the vein of James Thurber.

Aldridge, John W. "How Good Is Alison Lurie?" *Commentary* 59 (January, 1975): 79-81. Aldridge faults Lurie for what he sees as a trivial approach to academic life. This article is one of the more authoritative negative judgments on Lurie's work.

Costa, Richard Hauer. *Alison Lurie*. New York: Macmillan, 1992. An indispensable source for biographical information. The perceptive commentary includes a whole chapter on *The War Between the Tates*, and the bibliography is excellent.

Cowen, Rachel B. "The Bore Between the Tates." *Ms.* 4 (January, 1975): 41-42. This is a strong feminist reading. Cowen argues that Erica Tate should have aligned herself with the women revolutionaries and used the whole episode of Brian's affair as an occasion to grow as a woman.

Helfand, Michael S. "The Dialectic of Self and Community in Alison Lurie's *The War Between the Tates*." *Perspectives on Contemporary Literature* 3 (November, 1977): 65-70. Helfand's major interest in *The War Between the Tates* is the political commentary that he identifies. Brian Tate's interest in the foreign policy doctrines of George Kennan helps Helfand to understand some of the problems of modern liberalism.

Rogers, Katharine M. "Alison Lurie: The Uses of Adultery." In *American Women Writing Fiction: Memory, Identity, Family, Space*, edited by Mickey Pearlman. Lexington: University Press of Kentucky, 1989. An excellent broad treatment of adultery and its significance in women's lives. All of Lurie's novels through *Foreign Affairs* are analyzed.

Frank Day

THE WELL OF LONELINESS

Author: Radclyffe Hall (1880-1943)
Type of work: Novel
Type of plot: Tragedy
Time of plot: World War I
Locale: England and France
First published: 1928

> *Principal characters:*
> STEPHEN GORDON, the only daughter of English gentry
> SIR PHILIP GORDON, Stephen's father, who waited ten years for a
> son only to have a daughter
> LADY ANNA GORDON, Stephen's mother, the "archetype of the
> very perfect woman"
> MISS PUDDLETON, known as "Puddle," Stephen's schoolmistress
> at Morton and her later companion
> MARTIN HALLAM, Stephen's friend and rival
> ANGELA CROSSBY, the neighbor with whom Stephen falls in love
> MARY LLEWELLYN, a woman with whom Stephen falls in love

Form and Content

The Well of Loneliness examines the lonely life of Stephen Gordon. The only child of English country gentry, she is reared as the son her parents never had. Boyish and awkward, Stephen is close to her father, sharing his interests in riding, hunting, and learning. Yet her mother never finds a way to love this odd and ungraceful child. Stephen's isolation is rather acute: She is educated at home by governesses.

In one of her first attempts at finding love, the young Stephen forms an intense crush on a family maid, becoming enraged upon discovering the woman embracing the footman. After he learns of his daughter's heartache, Sir Philip involves himself even more in Stephen's upbringing, although he never tells Stephen or his wife of his suspicions. Neither does the schoolmistress, Puddle, although the author heavily implies that this woman's own oddness gives her special insight into her young charge.

Once Martin Hallam enters the picture, it appears that Stephen may not be as strange or different as her father has suspected. Yet, after Stephen is insulted and enraged by Martin's proposal, it is clear that she will never marry. Soon after, Stephen's father dies, and Stephen turns to Angela Crossby for emotional consolation. Angela uses Stephen, however, returning the girl's love with betrayal: Although she had spent much time in Stephen's arms, talking of love and accepting expensive gifts, Angela shows her husband one of Stephen's passionate letters. Angela's attempt to end the relationship with Stephen results in her husband's exposing Stephen to her mother. Lady Anna condemns her daughter, banishing her from Morton, the family estate.

Stephen and Puddle move to London, where Stephen becomes a successful novelist. At the urging of a homosexual acquaintance, Jonathan Brockett, they move to Paris, where Stephen has her first glimpse of lesbian culture. With the outbreak of World War I, Stephen becomes an ambulance driver, receiving both a medal and a scar of honor and becoming acquainted with Mary Llewellyn. Although the relationship proceeds rather slowly, Mary's love for Stephen overcomes Stephen's reservations, and they finally set up housekeeping back in Paris.

Yet their relationship is not an easy one. Stephen is forbidden to bring Mary to Morton. The only acquaintances they make in respectable society cancel invitations and refuse to associate with them. Stephen is busy with her writing, and Mary has little to do. With no place else to turn, they venture into the lesbian subculture, finding friends among "their own kind." Yet many of the women they meet lead tragic lives, drowning in alcohol, poverty, and self-loathing.

At this point, Martin Hallam reappears. Although his friendship with Mary begins innocently enough, providing a welcome reentry to mainstream society, he falls in love with her. He and Stephen begin a battle of the heart and will. Mary clings to Stephen devotedly, although she does have feelings for Martin. Determined to save Mary from the pain and isolation of lesbian life, Stephen feigns an affair with another woman, deliberately pushing Mary into Martin's waiting arms.

Analysis

As it depicts "the love that dare not speak its name," *The Well of Loneliness* clearly portrays the isolation, condemnation, and struggle of lesbian life as it was in the recent past and unfortunately remains in some pockets of contemporary society. In so doing, however, it gives a dignity to lesbian relationships, showing the suffering and sacrifices made in the effort to find and give love. Although the writing has the tenor of other late Victorian novels, with its detailed pastoral scenes, attribution of human insights and emotions to animals, and vagueness and delicacy with regard to sex, its controversial subject matter marks it as on the cusp of modernity. The pain and angst of its heroine has an existential quality that resonates with the struggle for meaning and identity that is often thematized in the modern novel.

Not once in the novel does Radclyffe Hall use the word "lesbian," and rarely does she use the medical term often employed by early sexologists: "invert." Instead, through her descriptions of the young Stephen's oddness, boyishness, and disdain for traditionally feminine clothing and pursuits, the writer evokes her heroine's lesbianism. While Stephen's strong sense of honor, her religious faith, and her respect for the land and traditions of Morton establish her as a strong and sympathetic character, the author's reluctance to name Stephen's "condition," to say "what" she is, creates the dramatic tension that enables the reader to identify Stephen. More specifically, both Sir Philip and Puddle refuse to tell Stephen what she is. This refusal replays within the novel the tension between naming and suspicion which marks the reader's relationship to the author. Like Stephen, the reader suspects that a certain difference and abnormality is afoot, but is left to pull the pieces together.

Just as the avoidance of naming signifies Stephen's separateness from the world of accepted societal norms and definitions, so is her isolation rendered explicit by the tension between her own sense of the worthiness and naturalness of her love and the condemnation of the world around her. At one point, as she speaks the language of love to Angela Crossby, describing how they could run away together, Angela asks, "Could you marry me, Stephen?" Knowing all too well the answer to this question, Stephen faces the loneliness of her position: "She could only debase what she longed to exalt, defile what she longed to keep pure."

To be sure, as some critics have pointed out, Hall's own sense of purity and endorsement of social conventions tend to lead her to depict lesbian life ambiguously. On the one hand, the lesbian subculture in Paris provides Stephen and Mary with a circle of accepting friends. Yet, on the other, many of those in this subculture are haunted and tormented, a decadent, miserable army of society's outcasts. Forced either to live a lie or to remain in the darkness of bars and nightclubs, they are bereft of social dignity. Although their situation is ultimately blamed on society's failure to accept difference, such a melancholy portrayal of homosexuality has been said to undermine Hall's general defense of same-sex love.

In one of the book's most memorable scenes, the depth of Stephen's pain and isolation comes out with particular poignancy. Her mother has read the letter describing Stephen's love for Angela Crossby and has found this love shameful, unnatural, and unworthy. Tormented by her mother's rejection and condemnation, Stephen refuses to be ashamed. She attempts to defend her love as the best part of her, comparing it to the bond between her parents. Despite the eloquence of her appeal to this sacred tie, Lady Anna cannot accept her daughter and, indeed, finds the comparison an abomination, thus damning herself and forever cutting her daughter off from the familial tie that is so important to her.

Similarly, Stephen cuts herself off from the relationship that she and Mary have built together for the sake of allowing Mary to live in the type of family that is legitimized by society. The book thus culminates with a tragic lament that nevertheless contains within it the possibility of hope. As she watches Mary leave in Martin's arms, she hears the cries of other men and women who are similarly cut off from love by societal dictates. Their call is both to her and to God to acknowledge their right to existence. As a writer, then, Stephen is uniquely placed to describe and defend homosexual love. Ultimately, her sacrifice of Mary becomes the cost to be paid for fighting this lonely battle and earning the right to happiness.

Context

The significance of *The Well of Loneliness* cannot be overestimated. It was banned in England shortly after its publication as obscene, and the publicity surrounding its trial helped to establish the book as an heroic defense of homosexuality. Additionally, as the press at the time and many critics since have noted, Radclyffe Hall's own public life as a lesbian added to the book's success, although the book is not autobiographical. Since 1928, *The Well of Loneliness* has been translated and reissued numerous times and remains the best-known lesbian novel.

For many women, this novel proved to them that they were neither alone nor unnatural in their love for other women. Heterosexual readers, moreover, often responded to its dignified account of lesbianism. To be sure, because it is one of the few lesbian novels, the impact of the book has been mixed. Its stereotypic equation of lesbianism with masculinity, with the concomitant disavowal of femininity, seemed to confirm restrictive prejudices regarding lesbian identity. This led some women into "butch" styles that were foreign to their own identities and desires. Additionally, its strict adherence to early theories of the "cause" and "symptoms" of lesbianism adds to the view of lesbianism as pathology: Few lesbians want to be men, and fewer still can be said to have "become" lesbians because their fathers wanted sons. Despite these drawbacks, however, *The Well of Loneliness* and the courage of Radclyffe Hall helped to increase the visibility of lesbians and pave the way for further writers.

The Well of Loneliness is Hall's only novel to take up specifically lesbian themes. Her other writings include a collection of poetry, *A Sheaf of Verses* (1908); *The Unlit Lamp* (1924); *Miss Ogilvy Finds Herself* (1934); and *The Sixth Beatitude* (1936).

Sources for Further Study

Baker, Michael. *Our Three Selves: The Life of Radclyffe Hall.* New York: William Morrow, 1985. A comprehensive biography of Radclyffe Hall which examines the publication and reception of *The Well of Loneliness.* Several chapters deal with the trial and publicity surrounding the banning of the book in England. Includes photographs of Radclyffe Hall, her family, and lovers. The discussion connecting *The Well of Loneliness* to Hall's other novels is also helpful.

Faderman, Lillian. *Odd Girls and Twilight Lovers.* New York: Penguin Books, 1991. This history of lesbianism in twentieth century America provides a historical framework for understanding the experiences of women who love women and includes a discussion of the role of *The Well of Loneliness* in providing women with knowledge of lesbianism.

Franks, Claudia Stillman. *Beyond "The Well of Loneliness."* Aldershot, Hampshire, England: Avebury, 1984. One of the most thorough critical treatments of the novel.

Jay, Karla, and Joanne Glasgow, eds. *Lesbian Texts and Contexts: Radical Revisions.* New York: New York University Press, 1990. A collection of critical essays on lesbian fiction and literature, a number of which discuss Radclyffe Hall and her work. A selective bibliography lists numerous fiction, nonfiction, and critical works by and about lesbians.

O'Rourke, Rebecca. *Reflecting on "The Well of Loneliness."* London: Routledge, 1989. A critical examination of *The Well of Loneliness* with a selected bibliography of books and articles by and about Radclyffe Hall. Especially interesting is the author's discussion of the reactions of lesbian and heterosexual readers of the book.

Troubridge, Una Vincenzo, Lady. *The Life and Death of Radclyffe Hall.* London: Hammond & Hammond, 1961. A biography of Hall by her longtime companion.

Jodi Dean

WEST WITH THE NIGHT

Author: Beryl Markham (1902-1986)
Type of work: Autobiography
Time of work: 1906-1936
Locale: Africa, Australia, and Europe
First published: 1942

> *Principal personages:*
> LORD and LADY DELAMERE, Kenyan colonialists who owned the
>   Equator Ranch
> TOM BLACK, a pioneer aviator
> BARON BROR BLIXEN-FINECKE, a Kenyan big game hunter and
>   the husband of Karen Blixen-Finecke (Isak Dinesen)
> DENYS FINCH-HATTON, a Kenyan big-game hunter and pioneer
>   aviator

Form and Content

Beryl Markham wrote her autobiography in four sections she called books, which she subdivided into twenty-four chapters. Of those chapters, twenty take place in East Africa. Yet the title of the book, *West with the Night*, refers to her record solo flight across the Atlantic in September, 1936. She flew from Gravesend, England, to Cape Breton Island, Newfoundland. Other plots had flown solo from West to East, most notably Charles Lindbergh and Amelia Earhart, but Markham was the first pilot, male or female, to fly solo across the Atlantic against the prevailing winds. When the book was originally published in 1942, her international fame and reputation was built on that flight.

The title is also symbolic of Markham's life. Her twenty-one-hour, twenty-five-minute flight in a Vega Gull plane culminated a life spent breaking stereotypes and records. The material she selected for the autobiography illustrates how her life shaped her into a person who flew alone across the Atlantic under adverse circumstances. By extension, her life, and, perhaps, every woman's life is seen as the process of soloing a small plane across the Atlantic in adverse circumstances.

Book 1 is composed of four chapters describing a flight in 1935 to deliver medicine to a dying miner in a remote area of Kenya. Book 1 ends with the flight back to Nairobi; en route, Markham rescues a friend whose plane has crashed.

Book 2 is composed of chapters 5 through 10. These cover Markham's childhood years from the age of four on her father's farm at Njoro, Kenya, to the age of seventeen, when she leaves the farm. Prophetically, in the last chapter, she helps to birth a colt she names Pegasus. On Pegasus, she rides away to a neighboring farm when her father emigrates to South America.

Book 3 relates Markham's successes at a farm in Molo, Kenya. As result of her skill with horses, she wins the prestigious Kenya Derby. She also meets Tom Black in an encounter she describes as destiny. Black, a pioneer aviator and the 1934 winner of the International Air Race from England to Australia, becomes her flight instructor and mentor.

The chapters dealing with the period from the beginning of her flying lessons to the transatlantic crossing are contained in book 4. With Black as her instructor and a DeHavilland Gipsy Moth for a plane, Markham earns her commercial license in eighteen months by virtue of hundreds of hours of study and more than a thousand hours of flying time. She also tells of her experiences with Denys Finch-Hatton. Finch-Hatton was an early aviator, an Eton-educated big-game hunter, and Markham's lover. This last fact is not discussed in the autobiography. Finch-Hatton teaches her to scout elephants from a plane for European safaris, and she states that this was her most lucrative freelance flying job. Markham describes Finch-Hatton's death in a plane crash.

She frequently flies for one of her best friends, Baron Bror Blixen-Finecke, who is better known as the husband of Isak Dinesen, author of *Out of Africa*. Dinesen, too, was a close friend of Markham. With Bror Blixen-Finecke as a passenger, Markham tells how she pilots a plane from Kenya to London in March of 1936. In London, she meets the people who finance her Atlantic solo flight. Chapter 23 is the title chapter, and, in it, she describes her flight.

Analysis

Beryl Markham's autobiography can be analyzed on the basis of details she included and details she excluded. Those that are included illustrate what she believes is required of a person who breaks stereotypes and records. Those that are excluded are details that might detract, because of their controversial nature, from the case she attempts to build about herself. The details that she included present a woman who lived an unorthodox life and loved it. The three passions of her unorthodox life were Africa, horses, and flying.

Markham's love of Africa is clear. Brought to Kenya at the age of four, she chose to live most of her adult life there, and she died there. Her early years provided her with rigorous training. Of particular importance are the descriptions of her childhood, when she lived close to the Nandi and Masai tribes. She writes of being attacked by lion and leopard, of being left alone at night on the plains after a hunt with her Nandi friends, and of being left to fend for herself at the age of seventeen.

Horses provided her opportunities early in life to break stereotypes, and they, like Africa, remained a lifelong love. The triumph of her horse Wise Child at the Kenya Derby gives Markham her first taste of fame and fortune in the predominantly male world of horse racing. Her success in horse racing foreshadows her success in flying. In both cases, she credits her success to prodigious labor and reading. She writes frequently about the hours of work she logged with her horses, even sleeping in their stalls, and she read volumes about horses. Markham left nothing to chance, and this same attitude applied later to flying.

Some particularly revealing lines about how Markham perceived herself are found in one of the chapters dealing with horses. In them, she incorporates one of her numerous literary allusions. She compares Pegasus to a knight's beautiful steed and identifies herself with Don Quixote. Ultimately, Markham died in 1986 as the result of injuries suffered when she fell from a horse. She was eighty-four years old and still riding.

Moving from the male-dominated worlds of rural Kenya and horse racing to the new, dangerous world of flying was natural for the adventurous Markham. By detailing her pilot's lessons, elephant tracking by plane, and white-knuckle-flying rescue missions, Markham shows that she is adequately prepared to fly the Atlantic alone.

An event not related to Africa, horses, or flying reveals Markham's one fear: orthodoxy. The event described is her meeting with a prostitute in Benghazi, Libya, in 1936. It is noteworthy because almost as much space is devoted to this woman as to the transatlantic flight. Markham learns that the woman had been sold into white slavery as a child and describes her as helpless and trapped. For Markham, there is little difference between the prostitute's life and that of the ordinary housewife.

Markham carefully selected for inclusion events in her life which ultimately led to her successful solo flight. Of equal importance are the details of her life which she omitted. They reveal a person who did what was necessary to achieve, and what she did and achieved was highly unconventional for a woman in the early twentieth century.

The exclusion of other women is surely deliberate. There is no mention of Markham's mother, Clara, who returned to London and left Beryl, at age four, in Kenya with her father. No mention is made of her stepmother, Ada. Lady Delamere is given one line. No reference is made to her friend Isak Dinesen. The importance of her relationship with Baron Blixen-Finecke is discussed at length, but not her relationship with his wife.

She also does not mention any of her three husbands: Jock Purves, Mansfield Markham, and Raoul Schumacher. Schumacher is thanked on the dedication page of the book, but the book is dedicated to her father. Her only child, a son, Gervaise Markham, born in 1929, is omitted. In a move reminiscent of her own mother's, she left him in London to be reared by his grandmother, and she returned to Kenya. She rarely saw him again. When he died, she could not afford to fly from Kenya to Europe for the funeral.

She discusses none of her lovers, yet she is reputed to have had many. A mystery surrounds the birth of her son, whom some believe to be the child of one of her most famous paramours, Prince Henry, Duke of Gloucester, who was third in line to the British throne. Her divorce from Mansfield Markham was occasioned by her public affair with Prince Henry. For fear of scandal, the prince was not named in the divorce proceedings, and Beryl left the palace. From 1929, the year of her son's birth, until her death in 1986, an annuity was paid to her from a trust in Prince Henry's name. Neither this affair nor any other is even hinted at in the autobiography.

Another omission is the source of her name. She used her second husband's surname, yet her maiden name was Clutterbuck. Perhaps Beryl Clutterbuck did not have the lyrical ring necessary for a woman who could ride winged horses.

Context

Houghton-Mifflin was the first publisher of *West with the Night*. The book should have been a success, but in 1942, the world's attention was fixed on World War II. Small royalties were generated for about two years, but then the book disappeared and did not emerge again until 1983. Despite its lack of commercial success in 1942, the book was universally acclaimed by critics from *The New York Times*, *Boston Globe*, and *Saturday Review of Books*. The positive reviews mentioned the fascinating content of the story and the lyrical quality of the writing. Critics believed that Markham had contributed to the literature of Africa, flying, and the philosophy of the human spirit.

Some reviewers saw in her lyrical writing the influence of her friend Antoine de Saint-Éxupéry, another writer and aviator. Indeed, isolated passages bear a resemblance to his published works. Nevertheless, the consensus seems to be that he helped her to discover her literary style.

A significant controversy surrounding the original publication was based on rumors that Markham's third husband, Raoul Schumacher, had ghostwritten the book. The history of events surrounding the book's publication, however, seems to belie this theory. In March of 1941, Markham met with representatives of Houghton Mifflin. On the basis of four sets of typewritten manuscripts submitted by June 26, 1941, the company accepted her book, and she signed a contract in mid-July of 1941. Markham was introduced to Schumacher in California in August of 1941. It is true that the last six chapters of the book were written after she began living with Schumacher, but her biographer sees no change in writing style. Schumacher at various times made claims that he had been the writer, but chronology and style are cited as the salient arguments against him. He is credited with some editing.

The autobiography's republication in 1983 continues to bear out the view that Markham added to the literature of the early colonial period of East Africa, to the early history of avionics, and to the literature that speaks about the unyielding spirit of humans to fly, literally and metaphorically. Such bold adventure stories are often the province of men, and this fact may account for the book's disappearance until 1983. Social attitudes regarding what is proper and acceptable for women have changed substantially since 1942. It is likely that this fact accounts for the continuing revival of Markham's story.

Sources for Further Study

Bull, Bartle. *Safari: A Chronicle of Adventure*. New York: Viking Press, 1988. Bull chronicles the history of safaris in Africa from 1836. He provides detailed descriptions and photographs of Markham, her friends, and their lifestyles in the British colony of Kenya.

Lomax, Judy. *Women of the Air*. New York: Dodd, Mead, 1987. Lomax examines women's contributions in the field of aviation. The chapter on Markham contains anecdotes about her entire life and specific details about her transatlantic solo flight.

Lovell, Mary S. *Straight On Till Morning*. New York: St. Martin's Press, 1987. This definitive biography was written after Lovell conducted extensive interviews with Markham. Included is information on her family's English background and the controversial material that Markham kept out of her autobiography. Numerous pictures of Markham, her family, and friends are presented. Lovell uses for her title one of the titles originally considered by Markham for her autobiography.

Judith L. Steininger

THE WHEEL OF LOVE

Author: Joyce Carol Oates (1938-   )
Type of work: Short stories
First published: 1970

Form and Content

The Wheel of Love is a collection of short stories that have to do with the complex nature of love in a degenerate society. Although nearly every story includes at least one relationship between a man and woman, romantic love is not the focus. Violence, adultery, religious vocations, and academia are part of the external setting, contributing to a confusing, empty inner life for individuals. Characters seem almost like sleepwalkers, unable to control their own actions yet acutely aware of the emptiness of their daily routines, their relationships and behaviors dictated by a society that has ceased to hold any meaning for the individual.

A prevalent theme in these stories is that of women being trapped in the terror of love and in a patriarchal system of relationships that seems to have changed little since the previous generation. All efforts by younger women to "break out" of the oppressive system seem to land them right back in the same circumstances of their mothers and the women before them. In "Unmailed, Unwritten Letters," a young woman confesses her confusion and disappointment with life in letters that the reader assumes she will not actually write or send to her husband, lover, lover's child, lover's wife, and editor of the newspaper. "Accomplished Desires" is a disturbing story about how young Dorie moves in with the scholarly Arbers and then smoothly becomes the third Mrs. Mark Arber when the second, Pulitizer Prize-winning poet Barbara Scott, commits suicide. The women in this story suffer painfully in silence because, as the reader is told, Mr. Arber hates disruptions. Sharon, a young widow in "What is the Connection Between Men and Women," searches for her elusive identity by moving to five different apartments after her husband dies, and still, when she makes eye contact with a stranger in the street who reminds her of her husband, she knows immediately that they have formed a mysterious bond and that he now "owns her."

The difficult relationship between fathers and daughters is also explored in this collection. The stories "Demons," "The Assailant," and "The Heavy Sorrow of the Body" all contain a grown daughter who is present at the death of her father. The emotions are complex because each daughter feels strangely connected with a father to whom she was never emotionally close, as if to break the bounds of patriarchy a daughter must identify with men, look at the world "without comment or shame," and become "no longer a woman," as Nina does in "The Heavy Sorrow of the Body." Yet the death of the father, perhaps the ultimate symbol of a patriarchal culture in the life of each daughter, is significant. Like the legendary phoenix, each daughter rises, either successfully or unsuccessfully, out of the ashes of her father's death.

Oates also makes use of a theme that is common in contemporary fiction—that of things not being what they seem. The terror of the familiar suddenly being transformed into something unfamiliar is found in many of these stories, including the well-known "Where Are You Going? Where Have You Been?" in which Arnold Friend, a supposed criminal who pretends to be a teenager, chooses fifteen-year-old Connie as his next victim. At first, his clothes, manner, and slang are all familiar to Connie as the trappings of her teenage crowd. With dawning terror, however, she realizes that he is not a teenager; he is a "fiend" rather than a "friend," as his name implies. In "Convalescing," amnesiac David Scott is in the awkward position of trying to familiarize himself with the life he cannot remember, including his love for his wife and her extramarital affair. "I'm older than you think. . . . I'm not the way you think," is what Pauline, a sculptor in "Bodies" tries to tell Anthony, a disturbed young man who keeps following her because he cannot stop looking at her face. He eventually slashes his throat at her feet, leading to her mental breakdown. "An Interior Monologue" offers the thoughts of a young man who is fascinated by his best friend's wife and the "normal" life that she and his friend lead as a couple.

Another recurrent theme in contemporary fiction is the plight of the individual against society. The society in Oates's stories reflects the turbulent late 1960's, with conflicts between races, classes, and generations. Oates often uses a person with artistic inclinations to represent the vulnerable individual in a cruel world, and some stories seem to suggest that a sensitive soul cannot survive in today's world. The two most common "escapes" for the individual are insanity or death. "In the Region of Ice" gives an example of a young, artistic soul, Allen Weinstein, who cannot be saved by Sister Irene, his college literature instructor, who is torn between her role as a representative of the cold world of academia and as a human being. In "How I Contemplated the World from the Detroit House of Correction and Began My Life Over Again," a young, artistically inclined girl from a wealthy family recounts her foray into the criminal world, culminating in her beating at the House of Correction and her eventual return home. Both "The Wheel of Love" and "Matter and Energy" focus on the sorrow and anger that family members experience when an individual seems to "choose" insanity or suicide as an alternative to real life.

Many of the stories in this collection portray children as the innocent victims of a society in which values are up for grabs. On a symbolic level, children seem to represent the individual, innocent soul born into a world that is indifferent to its needs. The best example of such a portrayal is "Wild Saturday," in which young Buchanan is promised a trip to the zoo by his divorced father but, as usual, spends the day in the apartment of his father's girlfriend, Sonya, lying in the dark bedroom with Sonya's sniffling son, Peter, while the adults party in the other room. After things get out of hand and the police arrive, Buchanan lies to his mother and insists, through his tears, that he went to the zoo. There is violence against children, or at least the suggestion of it, in this story as well as in "Four Summers," "I Was In Love," "Boy and Girl," and "You." As their training for life, the children are offered only neglect, indifference, and empty promises by their parents, and if they survive childhood, they seem to be destined to repeat the same meaningless lives of their parents.

Analysis

Oates has said that the "serious writer, after all, bears witness," and the suffering and frustration of her individual characters seem to be symbolic of American society as a whole, a society with nothing left to worship, full of empty words and slogans, with popular music that drones endlessly in the background. Yet while Oates's realistic portrayal of society in these stories is not uplifting, she has said that "no writer is a pessimist; the very act of writing is an optimistic act. I think of it primarily as a gesture of sympathy."

Indeed, there is something almost loving in Oates's nearly obsessive attention to detail in everyday life. In her hands, the careful description of an ordinary room or a street can sound reverent. Their compressed nature and highly charged emotional content, along with the attention to syntax, make the stories in *The Wheel of Love* seem almost like prose poems. Some stories clearly reach an allegorical level that is most apparent in the "demon lover," Arnold Friend, who arrives unbidden to Connie in "Where Are You Going? Where Have You Been?" Another demon lover seems to materialize in "Demons," romancing Eileen and then killing her father and his dog. In each case, the demon lover is a twisted form of wish fulfillment: He does nothing that Connie and Eileen have not already imagined, however innocently. In "Bodies," a tomb monument of a man receiving his fate from the angel of death serves as a symbol for the two main characters. Pauline explains to Anthony that both the man and the angel are dead, foreshadowing her and Anthony's fate.

Oates experimented with form in other ways. "Unmailed, Unwritten Letters" is written in a series of letters. "Matter and Energy," "An Interior Monologue," and "How I Contemplated the World" are all written as a series of notes, the latter presented as notes on an essay for an English class. "Four Summers" consists of four sketches of different summers as the main character grows from child to young, married woman. All the sketches take place at a certain tavern on the lake. Each of these forms makes the stories more realistic by presenting a narrative in fragments, imitating snatches of human thought and memory.

The stories in *The Wheel of Love* concern themselves with different perceptions of reality within the society of the 1960's. Each story contains a psychological reality that makes everyday occurrences and behaviors seem like a mere distraction, a reality that lies beneath life's surface.

Context

For almost three decades, Oates has continually produced highly acclaimed fiction, poetry, drama, and essays. She has been the recipient of many awards, including a Guggenheim Fellowship and the National Book Award. Nearly every story in *The Wheel of Love* has won an award. Oates received the O. Henry Award for "In the Region of Ice," which went on to win an Academy Award as a short film.

Sensitivity to women's issues has been a hallmark in Oates's writing. Many of her stories lend themselves to feminist readings. In *Understanding Joyce Carol Oates*, Greg Johnson wrote that the story "Where Are You Going? Where Have You Been?"

is a description of "a young and sexually attractive girl's enslavement within a conventional, male-dominated sexual relationship." Other stories in this collection, specifically "You," "Four Summers," "Accomplished Desires," "Demons," and "Shame," also portray a cycle of young women repeating the previous generation of women's servitude to men.

Oates has continued to thrive as a writer, despite critical charges leveled against her. The two most common criticisms, Oates believes, are based not on her writings but on the fact that she is a serious and prolific woman working in a profession dominated by men. The prevailing, and perhaps traditionally more feminine, practice in fiction is to write stories of a more personal and domestic nature. Oates, however, in the tradition of prolific Victorian novelists such as Charles Dickens, Joseph Conrad, and Anthony Trollope, is concerned with the role of men and women in the society of her own time. It has also been suggested that professional jealousy is behind the criticism (by mostly male critics) of Oates's tremendous literary output.

Oates has been compared to American writer Flannery O'Connor and, like O'Connor, has been questioned about the violence in her writing, with the suggestion that such violence is not "lady-like." She addressed this question by writing an article called "Why Is Your Writing So Violent?" for *The New York Times Book Review*. In it, she labeled the question insulting, ignorant, and sexist. Oates is a serious writer who is concerned with the moral and social conditions of her generation in a profession that has too few women role models.

Sources for Further Study

Bellamy, Joe David. "Joyce Carol Oates." In *The New Fiction Interviews with Innovative American Writers*. Urbana: University of Illinois Press, 1974. Contains comments by Oates on her writing style and several of her stories.

Bender, Eileen T. "Conclusion: Missing Views, 'Last Days.'" In *Joyce Carol Oates, Artist in Residence*. Bloomington: Indiana University Press, 1987. Examines "In a Region of Ice" and "Last Days."

Grant, Mary Kathryn. *The Tragic Vision of Joyce Carol Oates*. Durham, N.C.: Duke University Press, 1978. Discusses Oates's focus on violence and tragedy in her fiction.

Oates, Joyce Carol. *(Woman) Writer: Occasions and Opportunities*. New York: E. P. Dutton, 1988. These essays discuss writing by women, both Oates's and others'.

Phillips, Robert. "Joyce Carol Oates." *The Paris Review* 20, no. 73 (Spring, 1978): 198-226. Oates comments on her literary interests and personal experiences, and responds to criticism of her work.

Bonnie Flaig

WHERE YOU'LL FIND ME

Author: Ann Beattie (1947-   )
Type of work: Short stories
First published: 1986

Form and Content

Where You'll Find Me is a collection of fifteen short stories that depict Ann Beattie's chief concern: the alienated condition of modern women as reflected in their domestic relationships. Beattie has become famous because of her ability to describe the chronic loneliness, frustration, and hopelessness that many of her feminine readers know from personal experience. The women in these stories are often looking for love and marriage but finding that something about the modern condition makes these things hard to find and impossible to keep. Many stories deal with second or third marriages or live-in relationships doomed to self-destruction because neither party is willing to make a permanent commitment.

The men and women about whom Beattie writes are usually members of the upper middle class. They all seem depressed, anxious, confused, or self-destructive in spite of the fact that they enjoy an enviable standard of living. In fact, it often seems that their spiritual malaise is a result of their addiction to upward mobility and consumerism, along with their awareness of the failure of status and possessions to satisfy basic human needs.

The stories in *Where You'll Find Me* are all very short and are written in the style that has come to be called minimalism. An examination of these stories reveals all the characteristics that have been damned and praised by critics since minimalism appeared on the American literary scene in the 1960's.

The titles themselves are minimalistic. Many consist of a single word, such as "Snow," "Skeletons," "Lofty," "Janus," "Spiritus," "Times," and "Cards." The stories are told in simple declarative sentences. This is one of the most striking characteristics of Beattie's style. Here is an example from "Spiritus": "The man's grandson had visited. A boy seven or eight. A towhead." Beattie takes few pains to inform the reader of the factual details that journalism students are told to consider crucial to any news story: Who? What? Where? When? Why? How? She rarely gives her characters anything but first names. Her story "Coney Island" opens in a typically minimalistic fashion with the words "Drew is sitting at the kitchen table in his friend Chester's apartment in Arlington." In "Snow," she even dispenses with first names and uses "I," "me," "you," and "we."

Beattie rarely bothers to describe her characters. She often fails to provide any information about where a story is taking place. In reading a story by Beattie, the reader is forced to make all sorts of guesses and assumptions based on minimal information. The reader is made to feel like an eavesdropper and a voyeur.

Because Beattie is a "taker-out," rather than a "putter-in," as one writer has characterized minimalists, her stories are all quite short. They are short mainly because they begin *in medias res*, as if both the beginning and the ending have been snipped off with scissors. Here is a fairly characteristic example of a Beattie ending from the story "Times": "Slowly—while Peter and her mother stared—she lifted her hand, still smiling, and began to suck the chocolate off her finger."

Unlike traditional short-story writers, Beattie does not build up a climax in order to end with a surprising or thrilling conclusion. A Beattie story is not intended to inform a reader but only to communicate a mood—often a mood that has been described as a suppressed scream.

The stories in *Where You'll Find Me* do not offer answers to life's important questions or interpretations of human behavior. There are no "epiphanies," to use novelist James Joyce's term for the flashes of insight that are so common in traditional short stories, such as those in his own *Dubliners* (1914). The fact that Beattie's stories end so inconclusively leaves the reader with a feeling that human relationships are too complicated and too fragile to survive the stresses and strains of modern living.

Analysis

The reader who approaches Ann Beattie's short stories with the intention of trying to find out what they "mean" is in for frustration and disappointment. Beattie has been harshly criticized for writing pieces that are pointless, meaningless, and in fact not even stories at all but merely "vignettes." She has not defended her position but has gone on writing in the same style that has made her the most discussed, the most loved, and the most hated short-story writer in the United States. Her readers, however, find that Beattie is expressing feeling with which they are painfully familiar.

The mood induced by a typical Beattie story is similar to those produced by some of the early films of Swedish filmmaker Ingmar Bergman; T. S. Eliot's most famous poem, "The Waste Land" (1922); Samuel Beckett's absurdist play *Waiting for Godot* (1954); George Orwell's futuristic novel *1984* (1949); the conclusion to James Joyce's famous short story "The Dead" (1914); or George Meredith's collection of short poems *Modern Love* (1862).

Critics who are hostile to minimalism try to explain its popularity as a result "of the greatly shortened attention span of the generation of readers brought up on television," to quote critic John W. Aldridge. It could be argued that the popularity of minimalism is a result of the greater sophistication of a generation of readers who have been exposed from earliest childhood to a glut of media input. It is worth noting that modern readers continue to read older writers such as Jane Austen and Virginia Woolf and seem to be capable of understanding such difficult writers as deconstructionist literary critic Jacques Derrida.

In "Summer People," Beattie seems to be replying indirectly to her critics by referring to the eighteenth century novelist Henry Fielding, author of the picaresque novel *Tom Jones* (1749).

> For a second, he wanted them all to be transformed into characters in one of those novels she had read all summer. That way, the uncertainty would end. Henry Fielding

would simply step in and predict the future. The author could tell him what it would be
like, what would happen, if he had to try, another time, to love somebody.

Beattie suggests that such explanations might have been possible in Fielding's less
complicated, slower-moving world but are impossible in the hectic, fragmented,
alienated world that is rushing blindly into the twenty-first century.

In contrast to the conventional short story, which depicts a conflict proceeding to a
resolution, a Beattie story usually depicts a situation that is going nowhere. Movies
and television keep turning out an endless stream of epiphanies or points or morals.
Even animated cartoons offer happy endings with implicit messages, such as their
favorite moral that good always triumphs over evil. Beattie believes that traditional
stories create a false impression that problems can be solved, that life has meaning;
such stories provide the reader with a temporary emotional "high" or "rush" but are
not always true to life and might even be described as hypocritical.

Beattie, like all minimalists, favors nouns and verbs and is remarkably frugal with
adverbs and adjectives because they suggest an attitude, an involvement, a point of
view. She sometimes writes a story in the present tense, as in "Coney Island" and
"High School." This popular minimalistic narrative device creates the impression that
the narrator has no idea where the story is going, how it will end, or whether it has any
"point" or "meaning."

Beattie deliberately avoids abstractions and generalizations, and whenever these
appear in a story, they are usually in the form of dialogue. In other words, Beattie
seems to want to avoid attempting to say what anything means; she wants to describe
what modern life looks like, sounds like, and feels like. She does not provide answers
to any of the human problems she dramatizes because she does not believe that any
such answers are to be found.

Context

Ann Beattie has had a considerable impact on women's literature and women's
issues in general. She has inspired many women to write about their own feelings of
loneliness and alienation, and her stories have served as a model for them to follow.
She has shown women writers that it is not necessary to present solutions to contemporary women's problems if they do not believe that they possess solutions; women
writers can render a service merely by portraying the problems themselves in their
manifold aspects.

In her novel *Orlando: A Biography* (1928), Virginia Woolf proclaimed allegorically
through the sex transformation of the protagonist that fiction was becoming
feminized. This is even more true today. Fiction is read by far more women than men,
and consequently there are more and more women authors as well as women editors
and women literary agents. The field has come to be dominated by women.

The feminization of fiction has led to subtle changes in storytelling because women
tend to be more interested in such matters as personal relationships than in arriving at
pragmatic solutions to problems. Beattie is one of the leading women authors who is

reshaping both long and short fiction to reflect the tastes and interests of the vast majority of fiction readers, who happen to be women.

Feminists see a political message in Beattie's writings. They believe that her female characters are alienated, lonely, maladjusted, and confused because of the revolutionary changes taking place in women's role in society. Modern women are torn between marriage and career, between motherhood and self-fulfillment, between monogamy and sexual freedom. They are no longer willing to play subservient roles in relation to the men in their lives, but they question whether marriage as an institution can survive if they insist on complete independence.

There are no easy answers to such problems, and Beattie steadfastly refuses to try to come up with easy answers. Instead, she continues to portray the problems themselves in all their infinite variations as they affect women, men, and children in upper-middle-class, Eastern-seaboard America and will eventually come to affect women, men, and children all over the world.

Sources for Further Study

Aldridge, John W. *Talents and Technicians: Literary Chic and the New Assembly-Line Fiction.* New York: Charles Scribner's Sons, 1992. An extremely hostile discussion of minimalist writers in general by a distinguished scholar. Focuses on Beattie's stories and novels in chapter 2, "Less Is a Lot Less (Raymond Carver, Ann Beattie, Amy Hempel, Frederick Barthelme)." A good example of the strong critical reaction against writers such as Beattie, encapsulating all the arguments against minimalism.

Barth, John. "A Few Words About Minimalism." *The New York Times Book Review*, December 28, 1986, 2. A famous American fiction writer defines minimalism in art and concludes that there is a place for both minimalism and maximalism in literature. This amusing writer quotes hostile critics who have denigrated minimalism as "K-Mart realism," "hick chic," "Diet Pepsi minimalism," "post-Vietnam, and post-literary, postmodernist blue-collar neo-early Hemingwayism."

Epstein, Joseph. "Ann Beattie and the Hippoisie." *Commentary* 75 (March, 1983): 54-58. A distinguished literary critic attacks Beattie and her school of minimalists in an article that is nevertheless remarkably fair-minded and insightful. Epstein categorizes Beattie as "a generation writer" whose work chronicles the disenchantment of people who came of age during the turbulent 1960's and subsequently came to realize that the world had not been significantly changed by all their idealistic activism.

Iyer, Pico. "The World According to Beattie." *Partisan Review* 50, no. 4 (1983): 548-553. This incisive article, which dissects Beattie's plots, characters, and themes, is highly critical but still gives Beattie credit for her intelligence, style, and keen observation.

Montresor, Jaye Berman, ed. *The Critical Response to Ann Beattie.* Westport, Conn.: Greenwood Press, 1993. A collection of reviews and essays dealing with eight of Beattie's books, including *Where You'll Find Me.* The introduction contains a brief biography of Beattie as well as an overview of what has been written about her. Extensive bibliography and reference notes.

Murphy, Christina. *Ann Beattie*. Boston: Twayne, 1986. The first book-length study of Beattie. Murphy is a professor who writes in a formal but not overcomplex style. Views Beattie as an inheritor of the tradition of social realism extending from Ernest Hemingway through John Cheever to John Updike. Contains a chronology, a partially annotated bibliography, and endnotes.

Bill Delaney

THE WHITE ALBUM

Author: Joan Didion (1934-   )
Type of work: Essays
First published: 1979

Form and Content

An examination of American culture in the late 1960's, Joan Didion's second collection of essays takes as its title the popularly accepted name of the Beatles' untitled double record album, an album that many argue was the defining or capstone musical production of that decade. The metaphor of album also serves to describe the rhetorical structure of the title essay, one of Didion's most well known works. A number of the essays in this volume are structured as collages or as series of vignettes loosely strung together thematically or associatively.

The twenty essays in this volume were written between the years 1968 and 1978. Most had been previously published in magazines such as *Life, Esquire, The Saturday Evening Post, The New York Times Book Review, Travel and Leisure*, and *New West*. Many were composed and revised over a number of years, and some of those that were previously published appear in slightly different forms. The thirty-seven-page title essay occupies the first of five sections in the book. Under the heading "California Republic," the next section contains seven essays, each about significant or emblematic people and places in California. The third section, "Women," begins with one of Didion's most controversial works, "The Women's Movement." Also included in that section are essays on the British novelist Doris Lessing and the American painter Georgia O'Keeffe. The heading "Sojourns" covers seven pieces on places as varied as the Hoover Dam in Nevada and the Hawaiian Islands. The volume ends with "On the Morning After the Sixties," which gives the title to the section, and "Quiet Days in Malibu."

The White Album is very much a continuation of the sort of chronicling of American culture, particularly in California, that Didion had begun in her first collection of essays, *Slouching Towards Bethlehem* (1968). As it was in that volume, the personal voice is very much at the center of most of these essays, even when their subject is not ostensibly Didion, and thus Didion, as a woman and a writer, is often taken to be the subject of her own writing. A number of these essays have become well known by virtue of being frequently anthologized in college readers as the very best examples of the genre of personal essay.

Analysis

The title essay of *The White Album* begins with one of Didion's most well known and oft-quoted lines: "We tell ourselves stories in order to live." It is an opening that signals a central theme of both this collection and much of Didion's subsequent nonfiction. In distinguishing what she calls the "disparate images" of "actual experience" from the stories "we tell ourselves"—that is, those narratives that provide a certain coherence to experience—Didion sets out the terms for her exploration of the cultural and personal dissonance she finds in the social upheaval of the late 1960's.

As with her most important nonfiction, in "The White Album" Didion interweaves cultural analysis with threads of personal narrative, the one providing metaphors for the other. A diagnosis of multiple sclerosis represents, for example, "a precise physio-logical equivalent" for what she experienced at the time as a breakdown in the social order. A psychiatric evaluation that describes her as failing to cope adequately with the world "does not now seem," she writes, "an inappropriate response to the summer of 1968."

Didion also draws on cinematic metaphors: When she writes about "flash pictures in variable sequence, images with no 'meaning' beyond their temporary arrangement, not a movie but a cutting-room experience," it both suggests the failure of the old narratives and describes the shape of the essay itself. "The White Album" is about the breakdown of a certain kind of coherence, which Didion experiences as both cultural and personal, and her attempts to find new metaphors for that experience. The essay's form, a collage, is sometimes read as a literal analogue for this breakdown.

The essay consists of fourteen segments, each separated by white space and each numbered. Some are whole vignettes; some reproduce pieces of conversation, juxtaposed and self-consciously out of chronological sequence. A number of the segments include excerpts of other texts: trial transcripts, Didion's own psychiatric report, song lyrics from the rock group The Doors, and found texts such as a packing list from her closet door. Thematic threads are chopped, rearranged, and interwoven.

"The White Album" is Didion's most accomplished, complex use of the collage form, but a number of other essays in *The White Album* also draw on the techniques of collage and montage, often being composed as a series of vignettes. Each of the four segments of "Quiet Days in Malibu," for example, has to do with various unexpected sides of life in that Southern California beach community. In "Good Citizens," Didion arranges three separate segments in a curious and ironic juxtaposition—one on the rhetoric and cast of liberal politics in Hollywood, one on Nancy Reagan when her husband was still the governor of California, and one on the 1970 national congress of the Junior Chambers of Commerce—with only the title to connect them. Each of the segments of "In the Islands," identified by the year of each particular visit, is about a distinct feature of the geographical and psychic landscape of Hawaii.

Most of these essays are concerned with California subjects. "Many Mansions" is about the controversial and unoccupied governor's mansion that the Reagans had built; in "James Pike, American," Didion reflects on the Episcopal bishop and builder of San Francisco's Grace Cathedral whose unorthodox rise in the ecclesiastical hierarchy, she suggests, is very much a California story. "Holy Water" is about the Operations Control Center for the California State Water Project and the systems that move and keep track of water for Southern California, a subject that inspires "reverence" in her.

As with the essays in *Slouching Towards Bethlehem* and another of her nonfiction works, *Salvador*, the presence of the first person in Didion's pieces has engendered critical disagreement about whether the subject of her writing is Didion herself or the social commentary. She is praised by some for her "eye for the telling detail," and her elegant and sharp prose. Others complain about the personal elements and describe her work as neurotic or self-indulgent and her style as an affectation. As Didion herself wrote in the preface to *Slouching Towards Bethlehem*, "Since I am neither a camera eye nor much given to writing pieces which do not interest me, whatever I do write reflects, sometimes gratuitously, how I feel." Nevertheless, these rhetorical and stylistic features—her cultural analysis, her attention to detail, the quality of her voice, and the character or personality inhabited by her essays—have remained at the heart of both Didion's nonfiction and the critical response to it, despite changes in the scope and subject of her writing over the years.

Context

Didion is among the foremost American essayists, male or female, of the twentieth century. She is recognized for the elegance and distinctiveness of her style, the precision of her social critique, and the insistent presence of the first-person voice in her work. In her refusal to separate her personal voice from her cultural analysis, Didion brings her perspective as a woman into all the essays in *The White Album*. She is not, however, typically identified as a writer who is concerned with women or women's issues. Her nonfiction is rarely spoken of in terms of feminist concerns, and few reviewers or scholars have analyzed it from that critical perspective.

Response to "The Women's Movement" (first published in *The New York Times Book Review*) by feminist critics such as Catharine Stimpson and Barbara Grizzuti Harrison has taken Didion to task for displaying a superficial and inaccurate understanding of the history of the women's movement and of feminism. At the time of the publication of *The White Album*, it was Didion's only direct treatment of the issues raised by the contemporary women's or feminist movements.

In addition to her first collection of essays, *Slouching Towards Bethlehem*, Didion's nonfiction includes her third collection, *After Henry* (1992), and the book-length works *Salvador* (1983) and *Miami* (1987), both of which collect essays that had been previously published as a series. Her nonfiction in the late 1980's and early 1990's contains much less of the personal voice, as do, for example, her essays on the 1988 and 1992 U.S. presidential campaigns collected in *After Henry* and in periodicals such as *The New York Review of Books*. She has also written an introduction (1989) to *Some Women*, a selection from the work of photographer Robert Mapplethorpe.

Sources for Further Study

Anderson, Chris. *Style as Argument: Contemporary American Nonfiction*. Carbondale: Southern Illinois University Press, 1987. Anderson, a major theorist of literary nonfiction, characterizes the work of Didion, Tom Wolfe, Truman Capote, and Norman Mailer as bearing witness to disjunctions in American experience. Relying on classical and contemporary rhetorical and literary theory, he focuses on the relationship between style and theme. Rather than reading Didion's essays to explicate her fiction or explain her personality, he analyzes them as texts, attending closely to structure, tone, voice, and presence.

Duffy, Martha. "Pictures from an Expedition." *The New York Review of Books* 25 (August 16, 1979): 43-44. This review essay praises *The White Album* primarily for the quality of Didion's voice. Duffy's analysis of some of the essays, particularly "The Women's Movement," is clear and balanced, though brief.

Felton, Sharon, ed. *The Critical Response to Joan Didion*. Westport, Conn.: Greenwood Press, 1993. Felton's introduction to this collection surveys Didion's body of work up to 1993, drawing thematic connections across the genres. The volume contains reviews, selected critical response, a chronology, and an excellent bibliography.

Harrison, Barbara Grizzuti. "Joan Didion: The Courage of Her Afflictions." *The Nation*, September 29, 1979, 277-286. In an extended analysis of several of Didion's novels and essays, Harrison attempts to figure out why readers find Didion's style so appealing. A stylist herself, she finds Didion petty and whiny, entirely self-absorbed and cold. A portion of the article addresses Didion and feminism.

Henderson, Katherine Usher. *Joan Didion*. New York: Frederick Ungar, 1981. Writing for the general reader, Henderson summarizes each essay in *The White Album*, noting thematic trends and connections to *Slouching Towards Bethlehem*. Her analysis focuses on Didion's use of architecture both thematically and as a metaphor for the structuring of her essays.

Malin, Irving. "The Album of Anxiety." In *Joan Didion: Essays and Conversations*, edited by Ellen G. Friedman. Princeton, N.J.: Ontario Review Press, 1984. This very brief essay offers a close reading, section by section, of *The White Album*.

Muggli, Mark Z. "The Poetics of Joan Didion's Journalism." *American Literature* 59 (October, 1987): 402-421. Claiming that "close analysis of individual journalistic texts have been rare," Muggli reads Didion's nonfiction in *The White Album* and *Slouching Towards Bethlehem* as both journalism and literary text. He calls Didion "one of the great American prose-poets."

Schow, H. Wayne. "*Out of Africa*, *The White Album*, and the Possibility of Tragic Affirmation." *English Studies* 647 (February, 1986): 35-50. Schow compares the work of Danish writer Karen Blixen (Isak Dinesen) and Didion as women and as writers on opposites sides of what he calls the "philosophical watershed" created by two world wars. He reads the work of both as dealing with the perceived collapse of cultural meaning and social order. His analysis attends especially to form, theme, tone, and sense of place.

Towers, Robert. "The Decline and Fall of the 60's." *The New York Times Book Review*, June 17, 1979, 1. Towers begins his review by claiming that "the effectiveness" of "The White Album" as an essay is in "the use to which personal neurosis has been put." His praise for the essay, which he sees as the best in the volume, relies on a connection between Didion's psychological state and her writer's voice.

Laura Julier

WIDE SARGASSO SEA

Author: Jean Rhys (Ella Gwendolen Rees Williams, 1894-1979)
Type of work: Novel
Type of plot: Psychological realism
Time of plot: The mid-nineteenth century
Locale: Spanish Town, Jamaica; Massacre, a village on the Windward Islands; and
   Great Britain
First published: 1966

Principal characters:
   ANTOINETTE COSWAY, a girl who is rejected by her emotionally
      disturbed mother and the townspeople, who look down on
      decadent white landowners
   ANNETTE MASON, Antoinette's mother
   ROCHESTER, an Englishman who comes to Spanish Town and
      receives thirty thousand pounds for his marriage to Antoinette
   CHRISTOPHINE, the Martinique-born housekeeper who possesses
      the knowledge of voodoo
   DANIEL COSWAY, Antoinette's "coloured half-brother"
   AMELIE, the "little half-caste servant" of Antoinette

Form and Content

   In *Wide Sargasso Sea*, Jean Rhys's characters fall into mental instability as a result
of the rejection and isolation that dominate their lives. Rhys does not give a sentimental version of her characters' declines but offers a detached journalistic account from
two perspectives. The novel is divided into three sections. Section 1 is narrated by
Antoinette, who describes the rejection that penetrates her early childhood. She also
narrates section 3, which further depicts isolation as she is placed in an alien
environment in England. Section 2 is narrated by her husband, Rochester, who offers
his perspective on the peculiarities of life in the islands and of life with Antoinette.
This shift in narrators is effective because it allows readers to understand each
character's dilemma.
   To set the atmosphere of rejection, Rhys opens the novel with Antoinette describing
the attitudes of the Spanish Town residents toward her mother, Annette. Many factors
contribute to Annette's nonacceptance by the local residents, who believe that Annette
is out of place because she was born in Martinique rather than Jamaica. They believe
that she is far too young for her husband, so they question her motives for marrying
him. They also talk about Pierre, her son, who was born with a mental disability. In
addition, because the wounds of slavery have not healed, enmity exists between
former slaves and landholders. Annette had been accustomed to social status when her
husband's plantation had been prosperous, so the isolation drives her to madness.
   The impact of the rejection goes beyond Annette. Her daughter, Antoinette, is also

ostracized by the community. As the narrator of section 1, she describes the relationships of the community toward her mother and herself as well as the relationship between mother and daughter. After the loss of Coulibri, the family estate, and of Pierre, Annette completely rejects her daughter. Antoinette is sent to a convent, where she experiences a life that is totally unlike the one she knew at Coulibri. Catholicism contrasts sharply with the superstition and magic she had learned from Christophine, her family's housekeeper. Antoinette feels confusion, another factor contributing to her isolation. Section 1 ends after Antoinette attends her mother's funeral. Throughout the narration of this opening segment, Rhys depicts a childhood in which rejection and isolation are the dominant factors. The result is that Antoinette is unable to communicate; she does not know how to give of herself to others.

Antoinette seeks companionship and an end to her isolation by "buying" a husband from Britain. Rhys has this gentleman narrate the second section of *Wide Sargasso Sea*. Rochester's narration reveals his struggle to maintain his identity in this new environment, which initially entrances him but which also clashes with the values of his upbringing. Rhys establishes characters who contribute to their own undoing; blame is not assigned to others. Antoinette's inability to communicate leads her to use extreme methods in an effort to overcome her isolation. Rochester's inability to be flexible in adapting to a new way of life creates a further barrier to communication.

Section 3 is narrated by Antoinette, who describes her isolation in her husband's British estate. Instead of Rochester being the alien in her island environment, she is now the alien in his homeland. Her madness becomes complete in these final years of isolation.

In *Wide Sargasso Sea*, Jean Rhys speculates about the history that evolved the characters in Charlotte Brontë's *Jane Eyre*. Brontë's Rochester is a neurotic, embittered man who keeps his unstable wife closeted in the attic. *Wide Sargasso Sea* ends where *Jane Eyre* begins.

Analysis

Jean Rhys's *Wide Sargasso Sea* is a study of individuals who are entangled and finally consumed by their obsessions, just as divers are ensnared by the thick sargasso seaweed that surrounds the Windward Islands. Rhys's characters are similar to the grotesques described in Sherwood Anderson's "The Book of the Grotesque." He describes characters who cling to singular ideas, adapting them as personal truths. Their limited perspectives act as barriers to communication that cause the sea between individuals to widen. Isolation results as characters reside within their own psychological islands. Because the memories of slavery are so fresh in their minds, the townspeople cannot let go of their hatred of white landholders. Annette cannot release either her desire for social acceptance or her fear of the blacks. Antoinette is obsessed with the need to be loved, while Christophine cannot release her faith in obeah. Finally, Rochester cannot relinquish his civilized social decorum. All these characters have become entangled in their own truths. The tighter they hold on to their particular perspectives, the more isolated and grotesque they become. Rhys demonstrates that isolation leads to psychological demise.

Isolation is not necessarily self-inflicted. At times, historical factors influence relationships. This is seen in the rejection by the blacks in Spanish Town of Annette. The Coulibri estate had been a flourishing plantation during the days of slavery, but when slavery was abolished, workers' wages became too costly and many white "aristocrats" watched their lands decay. As property deteriorated, the respect that went along with land ownership also dwindled. The townspeople could not forget the history of slavery, and Annette could not ignore the hatred she felt directed toward her by the blacks. No communication took place, so the sea between Annette and the townspeople grew wider. After the burning of Coulibri, Annette went into complete isolation, even from her family members. Isolation drove her to madness.

Wide Sargasso Sea is also a story of cultural clashes and the isolation that results from the inability to communicate. This is best demonstrated in the character Rochester, who has been reared according to British social decorum. When he first comes into contact with the wildness of the island's vegetation and running water, he is excited. Excitement is also revealed in the early sexual play of the newlyweds. As time passes, however, the sensuality, spontaneity, and superstition of Jamaican culture appear as aggressive abandon, which conflicts with Rochester's disciplined background. Viewing his wife through the eyes of European civilization, Rochester begins to doubt her. He lets his British rationalization dominate his feelings. He chooses to maintain his cultural identity at the expense of his marriage. He returns to Britain with Antoinette, and she lives in isolation in an alien environment.

Some critics claim that *Wide Sargasso Sea* is a story of male domination. They refer to Rochester's locking his wife up in the attic of his English estate, in the environment in which he could best assert his strength. Even in the village of Massacre, however, Antoinette had isolated herself from everyone but Christophine and the bottle. Antoinette's love for Rochester was so great that she wanted to possess him. After all, she had bought him for thirty thousand pounds. Yet the free environment of the islands would not permit anyone to be owned. Antoinette's desire for Rochester led her to summon Christophine to use obeah to instill desire in her husband. Antoinette's obsession to have her husband's love drove him away from her. Rather than be possessed by his wife, Rochester took control. He gained this control in England, where he knew the rules of domination.

Antoinette does not know how to communicate. Having lived with rejection since childhood, she has never learned how to share herself with others. She believes that she can buy a husband, but this results in further loneliness. A marriage without love offers no communication, no companionship. Her obsession to possess someone, to fill the rejection she had known all of her life, is too powerful. Antoinette's obsession for love brings about her demise.

Context

Jean Rhys's works are known for depicting females as spontaneous and fragile and males as cold and destructive. In *Wide Sargasso Sea*, however, to distinguish between the oppressors and the victims is difficult. Both genders seem to be at the mercy of their environments. Annette is the victim of historical prejudices resulting from the abolition of slavery. Antoinette is the victim of growing up in a family that was filled with rejection, leaving her unable to communicate with others. Rochester is the victim of being reared in European society and then being transported to a new environment where he is surrounded by the freedom of island culture. Each character must struggle to survive in difficult or unfamiliar conditions.

Rhys avoids sentimentality for her victims and reports journalistically. In isolation, the female characters struggle to form some sense of self-identity, but they seem always to be grasping for smoke. Rhys seems to suggest that women too often base their identities on their ties with others. Women pursue dependent roles and seem to lack identity in isolation. With an absence of self, women are continually grasping and often slide into mental instability.

Some critics claim that Rhys writes of cold-hearted men who take advantage of weak, dependent women. In *Wide Sargasso Sea*, Rochester takes Antoinette's dowry and shares a passionate beginning with her before turning away from her, leaving her in a state of imbalance. Rhys, however, does not paint Rochester as a cold, heartless character. She places Rochester in an alien environment and then depicts his state of loss. He is continually investigating his new environment, continually questioning his emotions in regard to Antoinette, continually trying to explain himself in letters to his father. The struggle to maintain his European culture in the free island atmosphere is not easy for him. Rhys, however, gives him the strength to recognize the problem. He realizes that he is out of place in the island environment and returns to England. His strength is in recognizing the cause of his confusion and in having the independence to return. Women, who are dependent on others, seem to lack the ability to step out of confusion.

Antoinette lacks any sense of self, which requires years of communication with others to develop. She has never learned to communicate. She relies on money to acquire a husband, rather than relying on her own personality or character. She relies on an aphrodisiac to seduce her husband rather than believing she can accomplish the seduction herself. Each of these decisions reflects Antoinette's lack of self-esteem. Rejection has made her unknown to herself. The irony in the story is that self-identity is acquired from interaction with others, yet that same interaction often results in loss of identity. To maintain balance is difficult for everyone, regardless of gender.

In *Wide Sargasso Sea*, Rhys does not place the blame for women's passivity, lack of identity, or disorientation on men. She instead creates characters who are responsible for their own fates. In showing the negative consequences of depending on others for identity, Rhys encourages the development of a strong sense of self. She punctuates that personal goal with doubt, however, by emphasizing that people are products of their environments.

Sources for Further Study
Anderson, Sherwood. "The Book of the Grotesque." In *Winesburg, Ohio*. New York:

Penguin Books, 1992. This first chapter gives a thorough explanation of "grotesqueness," the inability to communicate with others. The rejection that results further strengthens the barriers against communication. Anderson's explanation facilitates an understanding of the characters in *Wide Sargasso Sea.*

Angier, Carole. *Jean Rhys: Life and Work.* Boston: Little, Brown, 1991. These seven hundred pages give a thorough discussion of Rhys's early life, her schooling, her clash of cultural backgrounds, her chorus line experience, her self-inflicted isolation, and her relationships. Angier connects Rhys's life with those of the characters in her books.

Hulbert, Ann. "Jean Rhys: Life and Work." *The New Republic* 206 (February 17, 1992): 38-41. This lengthy article reviews the biography of the same name by Carole Angier. Much information is given about Rhys's life and about the characters in her novels. Rhys claims, "I have only ever written about myself."

Rhys, Jean. *After Leaving Mr. Mackenzie.* New York: Harper & Row, 1931. This second novel by Rhys is the story of Julia, who marries in order to escape Britain and to go to the Continent. After the collapse of her marriage, Julia goes from man to man and takes up drinking. Julia tries to grasp the essence of herself but finds her hands empty. Other novels by Rhys include *Quartet* (1928), *Voyage in the Dark* (1934), and *Good Morning, Midnight* (1939).

Linda J. Meyers

WIFE

Author: Bharati Mukherjee (1940-   )
Type of work: Novel
Type of plot: Psychological realism
Time of plot: The 1950's to the 1970's
Locale: Calcutta, India; and Queens and Manhattan, New York
First published: 1975

>*Principal characters:*
>DIMPLE DASGUPTA, an ordinary girl from the urban Bengali
>   middle class
>AMIT BASU, Dimple's husband
>MILT GLASSER, an enormous young American who seduces
>   Dimple by treating her with sensitive casualness
>INA MULLICK, a well-educated, seemingly Americanized, and
>   "chillingly sexy" Bengali woman involved in women's
>   liberation
>JYOTI and MEENA SEN, the Bengali couple with whom Dimple
>   and Amit stay when they first arrive in New York
>MARSHA MOOKERJI, Milt Glasser's sister, a professor at Columbia

Form and Content

Wife is a tightly constructed novel that is divided into three parts. Primarily an immigrant narrative, it chronicles the cultural disorientation, alienation, and mental deterioration of a young Hindu wife who emigrates to the United States with her husband. Bharati Mukherjee uses third-person limited omniscience to tell the story from the wife's point of view and, at the same time, to develop a counterperspective on the ideological gender role models for the reader. The novel is steeped in violence.

Part 1 is set in Calcutta. In this section, the author explores, with undermining humor, the social, cultural, economic, and sexual context of the protagonist's premarital state of mind. Born into a middle-class Bengali family, in which a girl of twenty is considered past marriageable age, Dimple Dasgupta is worried about her marriage prospects because of her dark skin, "sitar-shaped body," and "rudimentary breasts." Nevertheless, haunted by erotic fantasies fed by film and beauty magazines, she entertains the vision of her marriage to a neurosurgeon as a portal to romance, freedom, love, and happiness. Her romantic vision collapses when her father arranges her match with Amit Basu, an engineer who is about to emigrate to the United States. She sadly thinks of herself as "someone going into exile."

Dimple's first night after marriage comes to her as a rude awakening when her husband ignores her wishes completely in matters of immigration and then asks her to change her name to Nandini because his mother considers the name Dimple "too frivolous and un-Bengali." Dimple resents her loss of identity, but inwardly she refuses to be diminished. Her dangerous abortion to terminate an unwanted pregnancy is not only an assertion of her choice but also an act of rebellion against patriarchal oppression. Although she rationalizes her action by thinking that the baby might have "cluttered up the preparation for going abroad," her destructive act both reinforces and prefigures the violent streak in her psyche.

Part 2 of the novel perceptively registers the culture shock experienced by Dimple as she starts her new life as an immigrant wife with her husband in Queens in the apartment of their expatriate Bengali friends, Jyoti and Meena Sen. Although she has broken from her country, she cannot erase her ancestral past and years of moral conditioning about her expected gender role. In the company of her friends, she remains the docile and dutiful wife, ready "to uphold Bengali womanhood, marriage and male pride." She obeys her husband by not drinking alcohol, by not accepting the job offered by Vinod Khanna, and by remaining in the background when it is appropriate to do so. She is elated at the social gatherings of Indians, but her confinement to the Bengali community hinders the process of her acculturation to American life. In her ignorance, and out of sheer boredom, she turns to daytime television to gain an understanding of American family life.

Part 3 dramatizes Dimple's growing sense of alienation and her paranoid obsession with violence and suicidal fantasies as she moves into an apartment in Manhattan. Haunted by fear, homesickness, and loneliness, she sinks deeper and deeper into the world of television until she becomes culturally disoriented and loses all sense of values. It is in this state of mind that she begins to fall for Milt Glasser, whom she regards as "America." She finds Milt to be manly, warm, sympathetic, and uninhibited, in contrast to her husband, who is childish, cold, prudish, and unsupportive. With her cultural values and inhibitions gone, her repressed hostility toward Amit erupts in a climactic act of violence: She stabs him to death with a kitchen knife.

Analysis

Mukherjee's central concern in her work is to fictionalize the problems of immigration, expatriation, and cross-cultural assimilation. She has taken it upon herself to illuminate the marginal and almost invisible world of immigrants to North America— most of them South Asian, and others, increasingly, from Third World countries—who pull up their traditional roots and arrive in the New World with dreams of wealth, success, and freedom. She dramatizes the conflict between their old belief systems and the New World ethos, and lends an artistic voice to their experiences of trauma and triumph.

In *Wife*, she presents the psychological portrait of a young Bengali woman who experiences problems of adjustment to an alien culture and, in the process, undergoes traumatic changes—social, cultural, and psychological. The novel focuses on her acute sense of displacement and gradually heads toward her total alienation: "She was so much worse than ever, more lonely, more cut off from Amit, from the Indians, left alone with borrowed disguises. She felt like a shadow without feelings." The novel also indicts the traditional Indian system of arranged marriage, which pushes women into oppressive roles in a dominantly patriarchal culture.

Like countless other middle-class Hindu girls in India, Dimple Dasgupta has been reared to emulate the role model of Sita, the archetype of ideal Indian womanhood in the *Ramayana*, who has been used for centuries to impose ideological hegemony of patriarchal culture. Subconsciously, in her premarital, tradition-bound dreams, she imagines herself to be Sita, who stood the test of fire at her husband's request. After marriage, however, living with her husband's extended family drives her crazy, and she feels oppressed and frustrated by playing the role that is expected of a Bengali wife. Her unrealistic expectations of love, freedom, and self-realization in marriage are not reconciled with the hard realities of her wedded life with Amit. Once again, Sita's image is evoked in a letter to the editor in an English magazine, adulating the virtues of "sacrifice, responsibility, and patience" in an ideal Hindu wife. The editor's comment, used to mock the age-old tradition of emulating Sita, seems to reflect the author's feminist stance: "What was sauce for Sita may no longer be sauce for us."

Dimple catches the hint and begins to question the values of traditional Indian culture, which sets high ideals for women but treats them as marginal persons in society. Thinking about her own husband's expectations, she reflects: ". . . all her life she had been trained to please. He expected her, like Sita, to jump into the fire if necessary." In real life, however, women who jump into fire are destroyed or maimed. Dimple, therefore, cannot realize this ideal of wifehood and remain intact. Her inability to be like Sita in a literal sense creates a schism in her personality, resulting in an inward rage beneath her docile exterior. To emancipate herself from the oppressive hold of patriarchal Hindu culture, she looks to the New World as a passport to freedom.

Although Dimple continues to behave like a dutiful wife after her arrival in New York, her docile behavior in the presence of her friends belies her internalized frustration and violence. Inwardly, she feels like an imploding star. She conceives numerous ways to commit suicide: Setting fire to her sari, slicing her jugular vein in a warm shower, and inhaling aerosol pesticides are a few of the methods she imagines. She also conjures fantasies to destroy her symbolic oppressor, her husband Amit. The terrifying freedom offered by America lures her to break loose from the constrictive marriage arranged by her father. She asserts her sexual independence by having an affair with Milt Glasser. Her transgressions in Marsha's clothes are her rebellious gestures to assert herself and to break with her cultural past. In a symbolic hallucination scene at the end of the book, she sees herself as a bird in a cage held by Amit. Milt stands outside the cage and pokes her with a stick until she is a "mangled, bleeding mess." The sexual overtones of the scene are obvious. In an ironic reversal, instead of committing suicide, she murders her husband to free herself from her marriage-cage. Her seven stabs to kill Amit are a symbolic repudiation of the seven rounds she took with him around sacrificial fire to solemnize a Hindu marriage.

Context

Wife is Mukherjee's testament for women's liberation and women's right to self-expression and self-determination. Commenting on the novel in a *Publishers Weekly* interview with Sybil Steinberg, Mukherjee states that "the wife was going through feminist and immigrant crises." By telling the story from the wife's point of view, Mukherjee provides a feminist perspective on the Indian system of arranged marriage. She offers a radical critique of patriarchal ideology by questioning the concept of the ideal woman in Hindu society. She also touches on the related issues of women's oppression and madness, and she seems to advocate a woman's right to control her sexuality and reproduction, to work outside the home, to express herself, and to seek self-fulfillment. Dimple's bitter outrage at her pregnancy—"that no one had consulted her before depositing *it* in her body"—and her subsequent attempts to successfully terminate it are both crucial issues, from the woman's viewpoint. Mukherjee's portrait of Dimple is steeped in modern feminist consciousness.

Dimple thought that the best part of marriage was "being free and expressing yourself," but she was in for a rude shock. By focusing on Dimple's inner thoughts, feelings, and behavioral patterns, Mukherjee shows how the oppressive system of arranged marriage not only deprives a woman of her identity and freedom of choice but also dehumanizes her by treating her as a marketable commodity. Through Dimple, she also questions the tyranny of social mores that require a wife to be submissive and self-effacing in order to adapt to the ways of her husband's extended family.

In a society that looks upon marriage as a sacrament for women, Mukherjee adroitly engages Dimple in reading two letters to the editor, which introduce the debate on the moral virtues of traditional wifehood versus the contemporary reality of abused wives. The editor's comments on both these letters curtly counter the dominant patriarchal ideology and advocate the feminist agenda of more political power for women to fight abuse and to assert their right to self-determination.

That Mukherjee condones Dimple's final act of liberation by murdering her husband is evident from her interviews with both *Canadian Fiction Magazine* and *Iowa Review*. She called it a "midguided act" but nonetheless a "positive" act of "self-assertion." "*Wife*," she stated, "is a novel that is very dear to me."

Sources for Further Study

Jain, Jasbir. "Foreignness of Spirit: The World of Bharati Mukherjee's Novels." *The Journal of Indian Writing in English* 13, no. 2 (July, 1985): 12-19. Considers *The Tiger's Daughter* and *Wife* primarily as "novels of and about isolation," and demonstrates how the female protagonists of the two novels remain essentially "immigrants both in place and mind."

Mukherjee, Bharati. "An Interview with Bharati Mukherjee." Interview by Geoff Hancock. *Canadian Fiction Magazine* 59 (1987): 30-44. An important interview in which Mukherjee provides useful information about her family background, formative influences, and early works, including *Wife*. She also offers illuminating comments on her fictional characters, themes, voice, and obsessions.

Nelson, Emmanuel S., ed. *Bharati Mukherjee: Critical Perspectives*. New York:

Garland, 1993. This collection of twelve essays provides a wide range of contemporary critical perspectives on Mukherjee's art, ideology, and achievement. Maya Manju Sharma's essay, "The Inner World of Bharati Mukherjee: From Expatriate to Immigrant," in particular, offers a brief feminist perspective on *Wife*. This indispensable volume includes a perceptive introduction, a selected bibliography of primary and secondary sources on Mukherjee's works, and an index.

Rustomji-Kerns, Roshni. "Expatriates, Immigrants, and Literature: Three South Asian Women Writers." *The Massachusetts Review* 29, no. 4 (1988): 655-665. An introductory comparative study of three women writers from India—Santha Rama Rau, Kamala Markandaya, and Bharati Mukherjee—who are preoccupied with recreating the lives and experiences of immigrants and expatriates in their works. Provides brief critical summaries of the major works by these three writers.

Sivaramkrishna, M. "Bharati Mukherjee." In *Indian English Novelists: An Anthology of Critical Essays*, edited by Madhusudan Prasad. New Delhi: Sterling, 1982. Sivaramkrishna offers a perceptive analysis of the theme of disintegration and displacement in Mukherjee's first two novels, *The Tiger's Daughter* and *Wife*. The author's protagonists, he argues, "are victims of life which is visionless because it is voiceless."

Chaman L. Sahni

WILD SEED

Author: Octavia E. Butler (1947-   )
Type of work: Novel
Type of plot: Fantasy
Time of plot: 1690-1840
Locale: West Africa and the United States
First published: 1980

> *Principal characters:*
> ANYANWU, an immortal shape-shifter and healer
> DORO, an immortal body-vampire
> ISAAC, Doro's favorite son
> THOMAS, an American Indian man used by Doro as a breeder
> NWEKE, daughter of Anyanwu and Thomas

Form and Content

Wild Seed follows the lives of two immortal beings, from 1690 to 1840: Doro, who can shift his "life essence" into the bodies of other people by will, causing their souls or essences to die; and Anyanwu, an Onitsha-Ibo (African) woman who possesses powerful healing skills and the ability to shape-shift, to take any human or animal shape. The story centers on Doro's struggle to create a race of immortals with extraordinary powers and Anyanwu's resistance to the cruelty of his methods.

The novel is divided into three books: "Covenant," which begins in Africa in 1690; "Lot's Children," centered in New England in 1741; and "Canaan," set in Louisiana in 1840. Each book depicts a stage in the relationship between Doro and Anyanwu. Early in book 1, Doro senses Anyanwu's presence while collecting breeding stock in West Africa. She is "wild seed," a powerful individual whose unique genes Doro has not bred into her. Anyanwu is drawn to him, for his promise of immortal children and compelling charm. She has been married numerous times during her three-hundred-year life span; Doro offers the first promise in ages of a worthy husband. Doro encourages her to leave Africa for one of his breeding settlements in America.

Aboard ship, Anyanwu learns that Doro's promises include veiled threats against her children and forced marriage to his son Isaac. Though resistant, she eventually agrees to marry Isaac. Only this woman, Isaac believes, can keep Doro from becoming completely inhuman, because she can live, potentially, as long as he. If he can feel truly connected to another person, perhaps a long-hidden caring side will emerge.

Book 2 takes place fifty years later, with Isaac an old man and father (biologically or adoptively) to Anyanwu's many new children. They live in Wheatly, a community made stable by the influence of the couple. The reader meets Nweke, the child of Anyanwu and Thomas. Although Doro intended to have the physically and emotionally ill Thomas rape Anyanwu as punishment for her resistance, Anyanwu heals him and turns the potentially violent act into one of affection. Because she comes to care for Thomas, Doro kills him. The child Nweke seems to offer incredible promise for

Doro's plans; however, she loses control of her abilities and is accidentally killed by Isaac. Deeply pained by Nweke's death and appalled by Doro's callous response, Anyanwu escapes by becoming a dolphin and living outside human contact.

Although Doro cannot sense Anyanwu when she is in animal form, she finds that she cannot live forever away from those whom she loves. In book 3, Anyanwu has returned to human form, establishing a safe community in Louisiana, insulated from the slave culture all around. Only when Doro finds her does she again begin to suffer. Doro places several difficult "breeders" in her community; including Joseph Toller, who causes the death of her son Stephen.

Despite emerging displays of affection from Doro, Anyanwu remains belligerent. Doro must kill to survive, but he also kills on whims, to emphasize his power. Anyanwu decides to end her life. This finally reaches Doro. He begs her to live; only when he begins to weep, acknowledging his vulnerability and loneliness, does she yield. The novel ends with an epilogue in which Anyanwu moves to California and changes her name to Emma. She and Doro remain separated for long periods of time, but they gain strength from being eternally bonded through their history and immortality. They have reached a compromise with which both can live.

Analysis

Wild Seed was the fourth of the five novels in Octavia Butler's "Patternist" series; chronologically, however, it takes place first. The series focuses on a race of physically linked superhumans, begun by Doro many years before *Wild Seed* takes place and continuing into the 1970's—in the novel *Mind of My Mind* (1977), in which Doro is killed by his own daughter—and on to the far future—depicted in *Patternmaster* (1976). *Survivor* (1978) and *Clay's Ark* (1984) deal with groups and events extrapolated from the future world of *Patternmaster*.

A primary theme in *Wild Seed*, and all Butler's novels, is the inevitability of power struggles between individuals and cultures. Through characters such as Doro and Anyanwu, she examines the struggles between destructive and constructive forces, as Doro seeks to build an empire and Anyanwu seeks to build places of safety and freedom. Although *Wild Seed* does not lend itself to easy moralizing, the novel encourages thought about the uses and abuses of power.

Butler writes science fiction and fantasy exclusively. These are richly metaphoric genres, meaning that ideas expressed in such fiction may offer commentary on the world outside the text from an imaginative distance. Although it is often described as predictive or extrapolative (imagining the future based on current trends or events), Butler's fiction is firmly grounded in human history and experience, and it tells about the world in which the novel was written through the critical distance of fantasy figures and situations, such as the conflict of immortal superhumans seen in *Wild Seed*. Butler relies on fantastic rather than realistic characters and situations to encourage her readers to think in new ways about human history and culture.

One way to interpret *Wild Seed* is to study Butler's characters as they relate to individuals or groups from human history. For example, one can read the way in which Doro controls and abuses Anyanwu and all of his people as being comparable to the way in which a slavemaster dominates those he has enslaved. Doro's desire to breed the people whom he collects is a motive similar to that behind the breeding of slaves. He treats his people better than slaves by placing them in comfortable communities and not using them for economic gain, yet they may not choose their own mates, live where they want, or refuse him anything.

Because the world of *Wild Seed* is clearly patriarchal, one can also read the struggle between antagonist and protagonist as commentary on the struggle between man and woman, or, more precisely, between traditionally "masculine" and "feminine" world-views. Anyanwu survives through healing and nurturance (of herself and others)—qualities traditionally associated with "femininity" in American culture; Doro, by contrast, survives through aggression and violence—traits traditionally linked with "masculinity." Anyanwu, as a matriarchal type, wishes primarily to care for and protect others; Doro, as a patriarchal type, wishes primarily to control and dominate.

To encourage a more complex understanding of history and human relations, however, Butler also challenges the opposition she invokes. This allows readers to examine their limitations. For example, although Anyanwu may fit traditional "feminine" stereotypes through her passivity and gentleness, she can also become extremely aggressive and violent. Twice in the novel, Anyanwu turns into a leopard and kills an attacker to protect herself. Similarly, Doro may well exhibit the "masculine" traits of aggression and invulnerability; however, late in the novel, one sees him expose a weaker, more fragile side: when he describes his painful childhood and when he begs Anyanwu not to commit suicide.

Butler also complicates the simplicity of the master/slave opposition. Although Doro can be viewed as a slavemaster, he is also "enslaved" by his own inability to die. One also encounters references to true slavers in the novel and can see Doro's greater respect for his people, by comparison. Doro does, eventually, come to care deeply for Anyanwu, granting her some of the respect she deserves. Anyanwu is also far more than the passive victim traditionally suggested by the term "slave." She resists her oppressor, protects those who are powerless, and must even act the role of "master" on her plantation in Louisiana.

By revealing the operation of such oppositions through fantastic characters in a realistic setting, Butler encourages her readers to consider the construction of gender, race, and human history, and to examine the ways in which battles for power damage all humanity, despite their seeming inevitability.

Context

The primary contribution of *Wild Seed* to women's literature and feminist thought is its discussion of the inseparable links between gender and racial oppression for women of color, within the specific boundaries of the fantasy genre. By setting her novel in a realistic Africa and America of the past, she shows her readers the strength, the struggles, and the survival of black women through the slave years of United States history. By granting her primary characters immortality and superhuman abilities, she makes the battles against gender and racial oppression eternal, the physical and emotional violence more devastating.

Although the novel can be termed a "dystopia," Butler seems to be less interested in such abstract labels than in showing how her doubly oppressed black female protagonists can and will survive, against all odds and despite enormous sacrifices and compromises. The world of *Wild Seed* is bleak, offering little promise of true freedom or happiness for any of her characters, but it is identifiable as a period in the world that her readers inhabit. Envisioning a more idyllic future or alternate universe will not help women of color (or the human race as a whole) to survive and evolve. Categorically overthrowing one's oppressors is a very rare option, and it is never one that Butler cares to depict. Understanding how the system works and how to win each small battle for survival is the primary goal of her always-disempowered protagonists. The enemy cannot be avoided by separatism; confrontation and continuous contact are the only options she offers her characters. This, Butler has noted in interviews, often makes her heroines unlikable, but congeniality does not help people to survive. This can only be accomplished through vigilance and eternal struggle.

For Butler, the concerns of women are part of a larger cultural whole on which she comments from a doubly oppressed position: that of a woman and an African American. One of her primary reasons for writing literature is to depict the survival of African American culture throughout history and into the future, no matter what the cost to any individual. Butler is the only African American woman writing solely in the genres of science fiction and fantasy, and her socially conscious and emotionally compelling prose has earned for her a unique place in women's literature.

Sources for Further Study

Govan, Sandra Y. "Homage to Tradition: Octavia Butler Renovates the Historical Novel." *MELUS* 13, nos. 1-2 (Spring/Summer, 1986): 79-96. Govan examines the links between Butler's novels, specifically *Kindred* and *Wild Seed*, and the tradition of African American autobiography and the slave narrative. She emphasizes Butler's reliance on these forms to create fictional worlds that are historically grounded rather than completely speculative.

Salvaggio, Ruth. "Octavia E. Butler." In *Suzy McKee Charnas, Octavia E. Butler, Joan Vinge*, edited by Marleen Barr. 1986. Reprint. San Bernardino, Calif.: Borgo Press, 1987. This collection of three texts in one volume on individual feminist science fiction and fantasy writers contains the most complete overview of Butler's early work, including a chronology of her life and works, a biocritical introduction, analysis of her fiction (novels and stories published up to 1987), and a bibliography.

_____ . "Octavia Butler and the Black Science-Fiction Heroine." *Black American Literature Forum* 18, no. 2 (Summer, 1984): 78-81. A study of Butler's methods of creating her black female protagonists, emphasizing all the heroines of the "Patternist" series.

Shinn, Thelma J. "The Wise Witches: Black Women Mentors in the Fiction of Octavia E. Butler." In *Conjuring: Black Women, Fiction, and Literary Tradition*, edited by Marjorie Pryse and Hortense E. Spillers. Bloomington: Indiana University Press, 1985. An examination of the "wise witches," or black women with extraordinary powers, who populate Butler's fiction, emphasizing what she terms "archetypal" frameworks for portraying the preservation of female knowledge within patriarchal cultures.

Weixlmann, Joe. "An Octavia E. Butler Bibliography." *Black American Literature Forum* 18, no. 2 (Summer, 1984): 88-89. A chronologically arranged list of Butler's novels, short fiction, interviews, book reviews, and criticism. Very inclusive up to 1984, but contains many references to small press publications that may be difficult to find.

Zaki, Hoda M. "Utopia, Dystopia, and Ideology in the Science Fiction of Octavia Butler." *Science-Fiction Studies* 17 (July, 1990): 239-251. A study of Butler's politicized literary strategies through the concepts of utopia and dystopia, emphasizing how Butler reflects and challenges 1970's (white) liberal feminist uses of utopia.

Elyce Rae Helford

WINTER'S TALES

Author: Isak Dinesen (Baroness Karen Blixen-Finecke, 1885-1962)
Type of work: Short stories
First published: Vinter-Eventyr, 1942 (English translation, 1942)

Form and Content

The stories in *Winter's Tales*, although they are many-faceted and highly complex, place a heavy emphasis on the role of women in human existence. Women are portrayed as insightful, resourceful, and powerful; although most of their activity takes place behind the scenes, they are in control of the truly important events of life. Other themes of the volume, such as the role of art and the place of religion, are all informed by Isak Dinesen's larger concern with the nature of the universal female force. Dinesen wrote *Winter's Tales*, which was published after Dinesen's homeland, Denmark, had been occupied by Germany during World War II, partly to encourage her countrymen in their hour of need. Her emphasis on the life-giving female power, as opposed to the destructive masculinity of war, was a way of reminding her readers that the war would not last forever; there would be better times ahead.

The eleven stories in the volume are arranged slightly differently in the American and the Danish editions. In the American version, tales 1 and 11, "The Young Man with the Carnation" and "A Consolatory Tale," are both focused on the function of art in human life. The Danish edition of the book is introduced by "The Sailor-boy's Tale," which is a forceful story about female archetypal power. The difference in organization between the two editions is probably a function of the different circumstances in Denmark and the United States at the time.

Four of the remaining eight stories offer portraits of exceptionally strong women. In "Sorrow-acre," there are actually two such figures: the young wife Sophie Magdalena, who, married to a man who is old enough to be her grandfather, has taken on the duty to provide him with a male heir; and the old woman Anne-Marie, who redeems her son from a lengthy prison sentence by reaping a large field in one day. Heloise of "The Heroine" is a woman stripper who, when she and a group of travelers are arrested by the Germans during the Franco-Prussian War, has the courage to resist an indecent demand made of her by one of the Germans, thereby saving her friends from torment of conscience. Jensine, in "The Pearls," enters into a contest of wills with her young husband, whom she endeavors to teach the meaning of fear. In the end, however, she learns to overcome her own fear of the role that nature has given her, which is to become the mother of generations yet to come. "The Invincible Slave-owners" tells about two sisters, Mizzi and Lotti, who come from a good family although their lives are cursed by poverty, but who nevertheless courageously struggle to keep up appearances.

The remaining four stories, "The Dreaming Child," "Alkmene," "The Fish," and "Peter and Rosa," all tell about moments of awakening, when an important truth of existence is understood by one or more of the characters. Truth can only be understood through struggle, however, and there are times when the struggle leads to death, as it does in "Peter and Rosa." *Winter's Tales* can fruitfully be viewed as the record of a great artist's struggle to find truth at a difficult time in the history of the world. Dinesen finds her truth in her contemplation of the essence of femaleness and its role in human life.

Analysis

Dinesen's central purpose in *Winter's Tales* is to show that women play an absolutely crucial role in life—indeed, that they are its very source and focus. The other themes of the work are linked to, and secondary to, the theme of the power of women.

From a thematic standpoint, the central story of *Winter's Tales* is "The Sailor-boy's Tale." It tells about a young sailor-boy named Simon, who during a storm climbs the mainmast of his ship in order to free a peregrine falcon that has been caught there. Two years later, in the town of Bodo in northern Norway, Simon again meets the falcon, but in a most unusual way. Having fallen in love with a girl named Nora, he is, while on his way to see her one evening, detained by a Russian sailor named Ivan. To get away, Simon stabs the Russian, who is sexually interested in him, after which he is hunted by Ivan's shipmates. While he is hiding in the crowd at a dance, an old pagan Lapp woman named Sunniva shows up, says that Simon is her son, and saves him from the Russians. She also reveals that she is a shape-shifter and that she is the falcon that Simon helped. She tells him that she admires his devotion to Nora and that the females of the earth hold together in a great matriarchal conspiracy. Referring to men as their sons, she indicates that the world is really run by the women. The story of Sunniva's pagan matriarchy is Dinesen's metaphor for the power of women in human life.

It is instructive that Sunniva is a pagan rather than a Christian, for Dinesen did not share the dualistic Christian worldview, which tends to relegate women to a secondary position. In "The Heroine," she inverts the hierarchical relationship between man and woman by casting a woman stripper in the role of savior.

Heloise, the heroine, is traveling in Germany at the outbreak of the Franco-Prussian War. Stranded at the border in the company of several other French travelers, as well as an Englishman named Frederick, she and the rest of the company are arrested for espionage. They are told by a German officer that they will be released only if Heloise will accept an indecent proposal made by him. By categorically refusing to cooperate, Heloise displays such courage that the Germans give the group their freedom anyway. Years later, however, it is understood by Frederick, the central consciousness in the story, that Heloise's real feat is not to have saved the lives of the French travelers but to have helped them avoid the guilt that they would have carried had their freedom been purchased by a scandalous act. Dinesen thus arranges the thematic material of the story so as to portray Heloise as a savior, and the imagery used in the text is such that this interpretation is confirmed. "The Heroine" is a powerfully twisted and ironic retelling of the Christian story of salvation.

In "Sorrow-acre," Dinesen takes aim at one of the most cherished notions of

Western patriarchy: the idea of biological succession from father to son in a family. The young wife of the story, Sophie Magdalena, has allowed herself to be married off to a much older man with the idea that she is to bear him a son. After the marriage, she becomes acquainted with her husband's nephew Adam, who is visiting his uncle's estate. It soon becomes clear that it is Adam, not his uncle, who will be the biological father of Sophie Magdalena's first child, who, however, will legally belong to Adam's uncle. Women, not men, have supreme power in matters of biological succession and are the guarantors of paternity.

"Sorrow-acre" also features an older woman named Anne-Marie, who spends the long day of the story's main action reaping a large rye field. Her son has been accused of a serious crime, and Adam's uncle, who essentially is the supreme ruler in the area, has promised to let the boy escape prosecution and certain conviction if his mother is able to reap the whole field between sunup and sundown. As Anne-Marie completes her task and thus redeems her son from a long sentence, she dies from exhaustion. She, like Heloise, is a female savior. In Dinesen's universe, women are the source of life and redemption, and all else is secondary to that.

Context

Dinesen became a writer out of economic necessity. Having spent many years as a coffee farmer in Africa and finally having had to sell her farm, she had nothing but her artistic talent to fall back on when she returned to Denmark in 1931. Some stories that existed in draft form in her African years found their way into her first book, *Seven Gothic Tales* (1934). She further mined her experience in Africa in the autobiographical narrative *Out of Africa* (1937), which established her as a major literary presence both in Denmark and in the English-speaking world. As a divorced, penniless woman, she wrote in order to make a living.

Winter's Tales was a great success with both the critics and the public, as were her other books. It was, as were four of her other volumes, chosen as a Book-of-the-Month Club selection. She was appointed an honorary member of the American Academy of Arts and Letters in 1957, and she was repeatedly mentioned as a candidate for the Nobel Prize in Literature.

Early on, Dinesen was not recognized specifically as a writer of women's literature; she was seen as a woman who wrote stories. Her love of the past (many of her stories are set in the 1870's) and the values of a bygone era made it easy to think of her as a cultural and political reactionary. Commentators often focused on the aristocratic values of her characters and the fantastic elements in her texts. With the renewal of the women's movement in the 1960's and 1970's, however, she began to be read differently, as it became easier to see how truly radical she is in her view of the nature of the female and its role in human life. Dinesen came to be recognized as a superb literary artist who also had some very interesting things to say about what it means to be a woman. She has attracted the attention of many gifted critics, some of whom have a feminist bent, and the criticism that has been produced has added much to her reputation. She has also been the subject of a large number of doctoral dissertations.

Sources for Further Study

Henriksen, Aage. *Isak Dinesen/Karen Blixen: The Work and the Life*. Translated by William Mishler. New York: St. Martin's Press, 1988. Written by a friend of Dinesen who is also a pioneering scholar of her works, the six articles in *Isak Dinesen/Karen Blixen* cover numerous aspects of her life and oeuvre. Commentary on the stories in *Winter's Tales* is found throughout, but especially in the essay "Karen Blixen and Marionettes."

Johannesson, Eric O. *The World of Isak Dinesen*. Seattle: University of Washington Press, 1961. From a Neo-Critical perspective, Johannesson offers close readings of Dinesen's tales, concluding that the art of storytelling is the author's central theme and the basis for her worldview. The book serves as an excellent introduction to Dinesen's work. There is a good bibliography as well as an index.

Juhl, Marianne, and Bo Hakon Jørgensen. *Diana's Revenge: Two Lines in Isak Dinesen's Authorship*. Translated by Anne Born. Odense, Denmark: Odense University Press, 1985. This volume contains two essays of considerable length. Juhl's "Sex and Consciousness" is informed by feminist theory. Jørgensen, in "The Ways of Art," discusses the relationship between Dinesen's sensuality and her art. Their book has a good bibliography and is particularly strong in its discussion of Dinesen's use of classical symbols.

Stambaugh, Sara. *The Witch and the Goddess in the Stories of Isak Dinesen: A Feminist Reading*. Ann Arbor, Mich.: UMI Research Press, 1988. Recognizing the importance of gender for a reading of Dinesen, Stambaugh offers a feminist-inspired examination of her portraits of women. Explications of the stories in *Winter's Tales* are found throughout. The book has a complete scholarly apparatus.

Thurman, Judith. *Isak Dinesen: The Life of a Storyteller*. New York: St. Martin's Press, 1982. Thurman's biography constitutes a complete overview of Dinesen's life and work. It also provides brief analyses of her works, scholarly notes, a select bibliography, and a useful index.

Whissen, Thomas R. *Isak Dinesen's Aesthetics*. Port Washington, N.Y.: Kennikat Press, 1973. Whissen discusses the role played by *logos* and *mythos* (defined as the origin of the impulse toward art as well as its manifestation in the artistic work), and the significance of these concepts to the metaphors of the bow and the blank page in Dinesen's work. Discussions of the stories in *Winter's Tales* are found throughout this tightly argued book, which is equipped with notes, bibliography, and an index.

Jan Sjåvik

WISE BLOOD

Author: Flannery O'Connor (1925-1964)
Type of work: Novel
Type of plot: Psychological realism
Time of plot: The 1940's
Locale: The American South
First published: 1952

> *Principal characters:*
> HAZEL MOTES, the grandson of a backwoods preacher
> ENOCH EMERY, a lonely young man who becomes Hazel Motes's "prophet"
> ASA HAWKS, Sabbath Lily's father, a hypocritical preacher who claims to have blinded himself as a test of faith
> SABBATH LILY HAWKS, Asa Hawks's seductive teenage daughter
> HOOVER SHOATES, an evangelist con man who uses the name Onnie Jay Holy and tries to cut in on what he supposes is Hazel's scam: sidewalk preaching
> MRS. FLOOD, Hazel's stupid, dishonest landlady

Form and Content

Wise Blood chronicles the last few months of Hazel Motes's life, beginning with his leaving the army and moving to the city and ending with his death there. His pilgrimage dramatizes his attempt to disprove the religion of his grandfather, an itinerant backwoods preacher. Two images—one of his grandfather preaching from the hood of his old car and another of a ragged Christ who stalks him from behind trees—have haunted him so thoroughly that Hazel feels compelled to test God.

From the beginning of the novel, Hazel concentrates on making a sort of antireligious testimony to anyone who will listen. He startles two women on the train to Taulkinham by suddenly announcing that he has no use for salvation. In a similar negative testimony, he spends his first few nights in the city with a prostitute, Leora Watts. Ironically, like the cab driver who took Hazel to Mrs. Watts's house, Leora Watts recognizes immediately that Hazel is driven by religion, although she supposes that he is some sort of preacher.

It is Jesus whom Hazel most wants to escape, and thus, moved partly by the sight of the false preacher Asa Hawks, Hazel creates the Church Without Christ. He believes that his church will demonstrate the truth of his belief that Jesus is only a trick. For the same reason, Hazel buys a car, an ancient, rat-colored Essex. His claim that a man with a good car has no need of salvation is a sort of parody of all the slogans of the secular world. The more he tries to escape his grandfather's vision of the purpose of life, however, the more he seems to imitate it, so that even Asa Hawks can say, in his not-quite-blindness, that a preacher has marked Hazel.

This portion of Hazel's journal culminates in his experiences with Enoch Emery.

Like the others, Enoch recognizes Hazel as a marked man almost from the moment they meet on the streets of Taulkinham. Early on, Enoch's loneliness leads him to entice Hazel into a place of mystery and power—the city museum. Together, they gaze into a glass case at the tiny mummified man that has enthralled Enoch. Thus, it is no surprise when, after elaborate and ritualistic preparations, Enoch steals the mummy and presents it to Hazel as the "new jesus."

Hazel finds the mummy in his room, cradled in the arms of Sabbath Lily, a parodic madonna and child. Rejecting the whole picture, Hazel smashes the mummy against the wall; the new jesus is worthless, filled with trash.

Soon afterward, Hazel has an even more powerful crisis. He murders the man whom Hoover Shoates hired to imitate him, Solace Layfield, the "True Prophet," by driving over him in his car. As Hazel leaves the city, intent on starting the Church Without Christ in some other place that is more receptive to it, a policeman stops him for a traffic violation and pushes his unlicensed car over a cliff.

Hazel returns to his rooming house and lives through part of the winter in an agony of self-flagellation. He binds his chest with barbed wire, puts stones in his shoes, and eventually blinds himself. At last, after staggering blindly through the winter streets, feverish with pneumonia, he dies in a ditch. After his death, his landlady, Mrs. Flood, looks at him intently, for she seems to see in his face an indication that he has followed pinpoints of light that suggest the star of Bethlehem.

Analysis

Like all Flannery O'Connor's fiction, *Wise Blood* is intended to articulate religious truths that O'Connor, writing from her faith as a Roman Catholic, took very seriously. Typically, she clothed those truths in comic, even satiric, pictures of the rural South and its inhabitants, the very world O'Connor lived in almost all of her life. O'Connor always protested the labeling of her comic characters as grotesque, claiming them to be realistic pictures of the people around her. Thus, her portrayal of Hazel Motes is both comic and serious, and Hazel's journey embodies the novel's central themes.

In a novel filled with people who make claims on religion, only Hazel Motes is truly serious about it, so serious that he feels compelled to deny religion until he is forced to face the truth. Throughout most of the novel, Hazel does everything he can to evade the truth that he finally faces. The most striking example is his "Church Without Christ," with which he intends to demonstrate the irrelevance of the Christ his grandfather preached so intently. His denial is blocked at every turn, however, as people recognize that Hazel is somehow marked by God.

Even Hazel's church is not spared; Hoover Shoates's false claims about Hazel's powers as a prophet are a mere attempt to extort money from passersby. In short, Shoates intends to corrupt Hazel's "church" in exactly the same way that he would try to corrupt any other religious movement. Like most of the novel's characters, he cannot imagine that anyone is serious about religion.

An important exception is Enoch Emery. In his desperate need for human contact, he is so willing to accept whatever Hazel says about himself or his church that he finds himself drawn into Hazel's claims, almost without conscious awareness of what is happening to him. After stealing the mummy, Enoch somehow intuits that it must be the "new jesus" of Hazel's anti-church. After he has delivered the mummy to Hazel, Enoch's role is at an end. At that point, he is symbolically reduced from man to beast when, in one of the novel's best comic scenes, he steals the gorilla suit from the actor who plays Gonga the Gorilla (Gonga has always been Enoch's hero). The reader's last view of Enoch shows him discarding his human clothing, evidently prepared to go through life as an ape.

The turning point in Hazel's attempt to escape the Jesus who haunts him comes when he kills Solace Layfield, the "True Prophet" whom Hoover Shoates hired to retaliate against Hazel for refusing to let him use the Church Without Christ for his own profit. Shoates has given Layfield a suit of clothes that is identical to Hazel's, and the message that he shouts from the curbside seems to people on the sidewalk to be identical to what Hazel says. Layfield has become Hazel's double, and Hazel somehow knows that he must kill him. He carries out the murder by running over Layfield in his Essex. As the "True Prophet" lies dying, he mutters out a confession of the major sins of his life. Hazel bends close to hear that confession and Layfield's call on Jesus for help.

Significantly, just before Layfield's death, Hazel finds Sabbath Lily and the "new jesus" in his room. Hazel cannot see clearly, because he is wearing the spectacles his mother once wore to read the Bible, but in a symbolic gesture, Hazel smashes the mummy against the wall and its worthless stuffings dribble to the floor. Once he has rid himself of the useless "new jesus," Hazel is ready to rid himself of his double, Solace Layfield. The double's death (which in some sense is Hazel's own death), however, seems to force Hazel to see the truth.

Like Oedipus, once Hazel sees the truth, he blinds himself. In fact, he spends the last months of his life in a fury of self-punishment. Here, the novel's point of view shifts to that of his venal landlady, Mrs. Flood, who cannot understand what Hazel is doing. Still, at the novel's end, even she has a sense that behind the hollows of Hazel's dead eyes lies a vision of light like the light of the star of Bethlehem, and in the novel's last lines O'Connor suggests that Mrs. Flood, like Hazel, may have begun to see that light.

Context

Flannery O'Connor's reputation has rested on her significance as a Southern writer who dealt with religious themes, a recognition she herself would probably have found more than satisfactory. As her various nonfiction writings make clear (especially the collection *Mystery and Manners: Occasional Prose*, 1969), O'Connor was very seriously interested in the craft of fiction and in using that craft to communicate her religious vision. She was emphatic in arguing that in everything she wrote there was a moment of grace in which a character somehow had a chance to recognize divine love.

To express those themes, O'Connor drew on the rural South and its people and their religion. That was the world she knew best, having lived almost her whole life in it. Indeed, after 1950, when she was diagnosed with lupus, traveling from her home in Milledgeville, Georgia, became increasingly difficult for her. As her many letters make clear, however, the inhabitants of her world were a rich source of interest and amusement to her, and she seems never to have felt any lack of richer experience. She took special delight in their language, and often represented rural white speech in her fiction and imitated it in her letters.

O'Connor lived in a world that was on the edge of great social change, particularly regarding civil rights, but she remained uninterested in social issues. In fact, sociologists (and psychologists) are frequently the objects of her satire. Although she was not unsympathetic to the plight of the disenfranchised, she argued that no white person could know enough about the black experience to write meaningfully about it. Black characters move through her fiction like shadows; her central characters are all white.

She was also not particularly interested in women's issues, although she created many female characters—some of them modeled on the rural women, both poor and middle-class, who surrounded her; some of them lumpishly intellectual and scornful of the limited world of their sisters. O'Connor satirized them both. To her, social issues were subordinate to more important themes, and her pictures of the world usually laugh at the superficiality of its allures. O'Connor was never very successful in describing romantic or sexual relationships between men and women, and she was not very interested in those themes.

O'Connor's best contribution to American fiction, however, was her combination of the comedic and the serious, a combining that was quite in keeping with her intense belief in the saving power of divine love.

Sources for Further Study

Baumgaertner, Jill P. *Flannery O'Connor: A Proper Scaring*. Wheaton, Ill.: Shaw, 1988. This study deals with O'Connor's work as religious fiction, including essays on her most frequently collected short stories and her novels. Baumgaertner treats *Wise Blood* as a semiallegory about a "Christian in spite of himself." Includes a bibliography.

Brinkmeyer, Robert H., Jr. *The Art and Vision of Flannery O'Connor*. Baton Rouge: Louisiana State University Press, 1989. Brinkmeyer's "Narrator and Narrative" chapter includes a lengthy discussion of *Wise Blood*, concentrating on the texture of the novel's world and on the relationship of point of view to theme.

Giannone, Richard. *Flannery O'Connor and the Mystery of Love*. Urbana: University of Illinois Press, 1989. Giannone devotes a thirty-five page chapter to *Wise Blood*, arguing that the novel articulates the disparity between "inept human bungling" and the power of God. Includes a bibliography.

Hendin, Josephine. *The World of Flannery O'Connor*. Bloomington: Indiana University Press, 1970. Hendin discusses *Wise Blood* as a sort of coming-of-age novel. She sees the light in Hazel's eyes at the conclusion as ambiguous.

Lawson, Lewis. "The Perfect Deformity: *Wise Blood*." In *Modern Critical Views:*

Flannery O'Connor, edited by Harold Bloom. New York: Chelsea House, 1986. Lawson examines the use of physical deformities as symbolic in the novel.

Stephens, Martha. *The Question of Flannery O'Connor*. Baton Rouge: Louisiana State University Press, 1973. Stephens devotes a fifty-two-page chapter to *Wise Blood*, concentrating particularly on the novel's structural problems.

Walters, Dorothy. *Flannery O'Connor*. New York: Twayne, 1973. Like most of the Twayne series, this is a good general introduction to O'Connor's work. The twenty-page chapter on *Wise Blood* discusses its early critical reception, summarizes the action, and analyzes its religious themes.

Ann D. Garbett

WITCHES, MIDWIVES, AND NURSES
A History of Women Healers

Authors: Barbara Ehrenreich (1941-   ) and Deirdre English (1948-   )
Type of work: Social criticism
First published: 1973

Form and Content

Considering that women have always been healers, Barbara Ehrenreich and Deirdre English set out to recover that tradition in *Witches, Midwives, and Nurses: A History of Women Healers*. Their book encourages women employed in health care, especially nurses, to work out the struggles that they face in a profession which became the bailiwick of male professionals. The authors approach their task by devoting half their book to the history of witchcraft and medicine in the Middle Ages and half to the history of women and the rise of the medical profession in the United States. In each case, they show women as both humane and empirical with respect to their attitudes toward healing. How then, they ask, were women suppressed as health workers in the development of a male-dominated profession?

In uncovering the political, religious, and economic reasons for medieval witch-hunts, Ehrenreich and English present a picture of witches as peasant women healers. With the rise of the European medical profession and the exclusion of women from universities, both by rule and by economics, independent women healers could be seen as witches. Precisely as women—seen religiously as seductive, lusty, and the reason for man's fall from grace; and not educated in university-based medical study, thereby healing by the power of evil—female healers were accused, tried, and burned at the stake.

In the early nineteenth century United States, midwives and folk healers as well as other practitioners held sway. Women's place in medicine centered on a people's medicine. They employed primarily mild herbal medications, dietary suggestions, and personal support for their patients, while the "regulars" in medicine preferred "heroic" measures, such as bloodletting and surgery. Religious arguments concerning the "nature of woman," economic considerations with regard to paying clientele, and political considerations linked to power were bolstered by arguments about biological destiny and the technical superiority of males. With the rise of medical schools, women, barred from medical study, formed their own schools. Upon graduation, they were still barred from internships and from membership in medical associations. By the early part of the twentieth century, midwives were eventually outlawed, most of the women's medical schools were closed, and the loss in the percentage of female physicians was not to be regained until the 1950's and 1960's. The nurse was the role left to women, an ancillary role for the woman healer.

The beauty of this book lies not only in its content but also in its form. Its clarity and pointedness in presenting the similarities between the witch burnings and the exclusion of women from medicine in the nineteenth and early twentieth century allow the reader to see the differences in approach and argumentation between the two eras. These differences tend to point up the double binds in which numbers of women in the healing professions still find themselves. While the work is a concise forty-seven pages, it is sweeping in approach and eminently readable; it is also interspersed with illustrations that lend to the overall feel, scope, and meaning of the text. While the book is scholarly in its conclusions, it is not so overly documented as to break the reader's attention and sense of flow. It provides a two-page bibliography indicating some of the classic works from which the authors draw their conclusions, such as *The Malleus Maleficarum* (1486) and what has been called *The Flexner Report* (1910). The gift of this book lies in its balance among scholarship, women's experience, and a call to action.

Analysis

In keeping with their sense that women's knowledge of their own history is the beginning of their opportunity to take up the struggle again, Ehrenreich and English provide two clear, readable, historic foci of women's story as health workers and uncover a history long suppressed. Written in 1973, this history not only recovered women's story as unlicensed doctors, midwives, anatomists, pharmacists, nurses, and counselors but also provided some explanation for women's contemporary experiences of facelessness and subservience in the healing professions. It pointed to women's situation as a majority of numbers with a minority of power in the health fields.

The book places this subservience within the context of a male takeover of the previously female leadership of health care, a takeover tied to larger sex and class struggles. Ehrenreich and English see the four centuries of witch-hunting as an ongoing movement by church and state to drive the "wise women" from the realm of healing. To the church, the witches' understanding of herbs, drugs, and anatomy and their use of their senses for information threatened doctrinal, misogynist, and antisexual teachings. To the state, the "wise women" may have represented organized communication networks of peasant women who were dissidents as well as healers. The medieval university-trained doctors, male and upper class, were the main beneficiaries of the witch-hunting purges that drove women out of medicine. The authors place the burning of witches in classist and sexist categories, giving fragmentary evidence that some of the women were involved in the peasant rebellions of the time.

In the nineteenth century United States, where medical practice had been traditionally open to anyone who could demonstrate healing skills, the male takeover started later but ultimately went much further. Although an early attempt by formally trained doctors to monopolize medicine by posing professionalism as an alternative to lay practice was met with indignation in the form of a popular health movement, the "regulars" eventually won the day. The popular health movement converged with the feminist movement in the 1830's and 1840's. The "irregulars," mostly lay practitioners and midwives, were seen as unscientific at a time when healing had little or no scientific foundation. By the beginning of the twentieth century, the "regulars" had European science and American ruling class power and money available to help them monopolize the medical profession. Medicine, now requiring lengthy and expensive higher education and training, became the preserve of wealthy white males. Nursing, invented by upper-class women reformers for improving hospital conditions, evolved into an elaborate set of subservient caring roles based on the Victorian notion of femininity.

In their historical approach and social critique, Ehrenreich and English uncover some of the mystique of "science" by lifting some of its disguises of power. They also lift the veil that had fallen over women's place in healing, providing an opportunity for women to reexperience pride in their contributions to curing and caring and providing an opportunity for women to learn from history.

The authors provide the seeds of a sociological analysis of the class systems that support male power and have been institutionalized in the male-dominated practice of medicine. They find that the deep-rooted nature of sexism is older than medical science itself but that it redrew its arguments in terms of biology and medicine. They point out the inconsistencies, both in terms of scientific logic and in terms of theories of "women's innate nature," in the arguments for excluding women from healing roles and relegating them to subservient ones by clarifying the shift in stereotypes used for making the same exclusionary arguments. They make a clear connection between the rise of the medical profession in the United States as part of the nineteenth century struggles around power vis-à-vis class and sex and the peak of the popular health movement coinciding with the beginnings of the feminist movement.

Drawing a clear set of distinctions between professionalism and expertise, Ehrenreich and English encourage women to challenge science rather than to be mystified by it. They encourage an open-eyed approach to the monopoly of scientific knowledge with a goal of opening medicine to all women, rather than merely opening the medical profession to women. They accomplish this by breaking down the distinctions between women as health care workers and women as health care consumers.

Context

The material in *Witches, Midwives, and Nurses* came from the authors' research and ideas for their course on women and health at State University of New York, Old Westbury. Published in 1973 by the Feminist Press, *Witches, Midwives, and Nurses* and its companion piece, *Complaints and Disorders: The Sexual Politics of Sickness* (1973), made ties between previous research and new possibilities. The authors' approach to women's history in healing opened the way for a significant amount of detailed research to come, beginning in the late 1970's. Their books provided scholarly conclusions in a style which invited a wide variety of readers to grasp, enjoy, and be moved by the recovered history and the logical and sociological critique.

Neither professional historians nor social scientists, Ehrenreich and English presented a fresh view at a time when a women's health movement in the United States was gathering and growing as a precisely feminist phenomenon. Both pieces received diverse responses from varying types of groups. The books became not only the bases for discussion in grass-roots and consciousness-raising groups but also texts on reading lists in nursing schools and women's studies programs. By 1974, when Ehrenreich and English began their book *For Her Own Good: One Hundred Fifty Years of the Experts' Advice to Women* (1979), there had been an amazing growth in women's studies programs. The women's health movement was moving toward self-help, lay midwifery, and expanded networking.

These first two pamphlets from the Feminist Press encouraged the movement for women's health and provided a mirror in which female health care workers could see themselves. They evoked a new moral force growing in consciousness-raising groups and led to women seeking increased knowledge concerning questions of their own health care (such as the pill, IUDs, hysterectomies, cesarean sections, and hormonal treatments), eventually giving rise to women's clinics and health care centers. By 1976, the Boston Health Collective's *Our Bodies, Ourselves* (2d ed., 1976) was published, as well as Adrienne Rich's *Of Woman Born: Motherhood as Experience and Institution* (1976). Feminist critiques of medical practices, as well as feminist social analysis and feminist alternatives, were on a path of growth.

Sources for Further Study
Abram, Ruth J., ed. *"Send Us a Lady Physician": Women Doctors in America, 1835-1920*. New York: W. W. Norton, 1985. A collection of essays that explore in greater detail some of the ideas presented by Ehrenreich and English. The essays present the professionalization of medicine in nineteenth century United States, women's entrance into the medical profession, and the reason for the decline in the percentage of women physicians at the end of the nineteenth century.
Achterberg, Jeanne. *Woman as Healer*. Boston: Shambala, 1990. A survey of women's healing activities from prehistory to 1990. The chapters "Fate of the Wise Women" and "Professionalization of the Healing Arts" are particularly pertinent.
Hubbard, Ruth. *The Politics of Women's Biology*. New Brunswick, N.J.: Rutgers University Press, 1990. An exploration of the relationship between science and political decision making. Hubbard finds "women's biology" to be a social construct and a political concept rather than a scientific one. She mentions pertinent nineteenth century data with regard to women's attempts at access to higher education.
Sherwin, Susan. *No Longer Patient*. Philadelphia: Temple University Press, 1992. A feminist approach to bioethics. The author shows that a feminist ethics of health care must ask its questions regarding health care practices with attention to the overall power structures of dominance and subordination. Chapter 9 considers how the construction of a medicalized view of women's experience assumes proprietorship over women's lives.
Todd, Alexandra Dundas. *Intimate Adversaries: Cultural Conflict Between Doctors and Women Patients*. Philadelphia: University of Pennsylvania Press, 1989. Based on a two-and-a-half-year study of audiotaped and observed conversations between

gynecologists and women patients. Todd examines doctor-patient relationships with a focus on the woman patient.

Frances R. Belmonte

WITH A DAUGHTER'S EYE
A Memoir of Margaret Mead and Gregory Bateson

Author: Mary Catherine Bateson (1939-   )
Type of work: Memoir
Time of work: The twentieth century
Locale: The United States and the islands of Bali and Samoa
First published: 1984

Principal personages:
    MARGARET MEAD, an anthropologist
    GREGORY BATESON, an anthropologist, ethologist, and
      philosopher of science
    MARY CATHERINE BATESON, their daughter, an anthropologist
      and linguist
    FRANZ BOAS, Mead's professor and benefactor, a principal figure
      in modern anthropology
    RUTH BENEDICT, Boas' graduate student, an anthropologist and
      Mead's intimate companion

Form and Content

Anthropologist Mary Catherine Bateson (who prefers the name Catherine) wrote *With a Daughter's Eye: A Memoir of Margaret Mead and Gregory Bateson* from her unique perspective as the couple's only child. For her sources, she deliberately ignored her parents' voluminous papers and published works, just as she studiously avoided interviewing any of their colleagues and friends, relying instead on her own memories. Much in the first four chapters, during which she describes her early childhood, is therefore impressionistic. Nevertheless, she recounts extraordinarily vivid memories of Mead and Bateson, buoyed no doubt by their photographic and film record of Catherine beginning at her birth. Mead, who spent most of her professional life exploring forms of childhood and child rearing, observed her daughter as if she were a subject for scholarly research, keeping copious notes as well as a film record. Notwithstanding, she was an affectionately attentive mother, and in *With a Daughter's Eye* Catherine Bateson provides a fond remembrance of her famous parents.

In the central section of her book, Catherine describes her parents as she recalls them during her adolescence. After their divorce in 1950, Catherine remained with her mother in New York City, while vacationing with her father in California. She ably devotes much of the last several chapters to a technical analysis of her parents' work. Her father, Gregory Bateson, the son of the renowned English geneticist William Bateson, received early training as a naturalist. In fulfillment of parental expectations, he attended the University of Cambridge, taking his first academic degree in biology in 1925. Afterward, he transferred his keen observational skills to the scrutiny of human cultures, earning a Cambridge graduate degree in anthropology in 1935.

A polymath, Bateson's accomplishments included his anthropological work on the Iatmul, chronicled in his book *Naven* (1935); his collaborative work with Mead in Bali, in which they pioneered photography and films as ethnographic research tools; and his development of the concept of schismogenesis (later known as positive feedback), in which systems, either mechanical or human, are perpetually adjusted through circular interaction. In addition, he studied dolphin communications with ethologist John Lilly, explored metalanguage or the nonverbal features of human languages, theorized on the nature of schizophrenia (which he viewed as the failure of individuals to participate effectively in the metalinguistic levels accompanying all human conversation), and treated schizophrenic patients.

For her part, Catherine's mother, Margaret Mead, provided American women with guidance and inspiration, serving as one of the few popular role models for intelligent, aspiring professional women. Mead aided women by clarifying the interaction of cultural and biological determinants in gender formation. She encouraged women to enter professions while simultaneously celebrating their maternal roles.

Analysis

Acting almost as a participant observer in the lives of her parents—an anthropological technique first used by Mead in the United States, whereby an individual assumes a role within the culture that she is studying—Catherine insightfully integrates Mead and Bateson's professional and personal lives. The contrast between her parents is striking. Mead was affectionately maternal, while Bateson was often preoccupied and emotionally distant. Puzzled as to how to entertain his daughter on her visits with him, Bateson initiated a series of excursions to national parks, continuing a tradition begun when she was an infant of encouraging her interest in the natural world. In nature, Gregory and Catherine found common ground for discussion, and through metaphor, he taught her about the world. Otherwise, he evinced little interest in Catherine's pursuits unless they meshed with his own. He seemingly expected her, even as a collaborating adult, to abandon professional or philosophical questions that did not intrigue him.

Bateson was passionate in his regard for the natural world, but he was not sanguine about humanity's future. As an upper-class British atheist, he focused on the excesses and corruptions in American society, assuming prominence among members of some California countercultures. Mead, on the other hand, valued human beings above all else and was devoted to the study of children. Animals evoked little response from Mead; she was uninterested even in pets. While Bateson was almost fatalistic, Mead was optimistic, believing in the perfectibility of humankind. She was a devout Episcopalian who celebrated tradition and provided Americans, women in particular, with affirmation for their values and lives.

Mead became a professional woman in an era when professions were virtually closed to her gender. She nevertheless viewed herself as an atypical professional because she longed for children, and after several miscarriages, became a devoted mother to Catherine, her only child. Mead rejected American child-rearing practices, which were inimical to the opinions that she had formed while observing primitive peoples. With the approval of the young and sympathetic pediatrician Dr. Benjamin Spock, Mead initiated several radical innovations in child rearing. For example, Catherine was breast-fed on a self-demand feeding schedule, shared her mother's bed as an infant, and as an older child visited Mead in her bed upon waking in the morning.

While Mead, within her family and publicly through her writing and lecturing, redefined mother-child relationships, she nevertheless valued and respected the stabilizing role of tradition and ritual. Catherine was drilled in etiquette and was admonished for using coarse language. Similarly, she was encouraged to master social conventions so that she could move freely within all levels of American society.

The requirements of fieldwork, World War II, and Mead's substantial fame resulted in extended separations for mother and daughter, a situation which Catherine apparently believes carried as much advantage as disadvantage. While she clearly missed her parents on their absences, she was left in the care of friends who functioned as extended family. For a time, Mead, Bateson, and their daughter lived with Mary and Larry Frank, the latter of whom was instrumental in the development of interdisciplinary work in the social sciences; their son Colin served as a brother to young Cathy, as she was then called.

Catherine Bateson writes affectionately and approvingly of both her parents, yet she is candid in describing her feelings of betrayal at her mother's failure to reveal to Catherine her bisexuality. While Mead had informed her daughter that it was indeed possible to love two people simultaneously if they were sufficiently different from each other, it was not until after her mother's death that Bateson realized that the relationship between Mead and fellow anthropologist Ruth Benedict was a sexual one. In *With a Daughter's Eye*, Catherine Bateson publicly revealed what Mead, fearing scandal, had chosen to keep private.

Context

With a Daughter's Eye is a personal testimony from Catherine Bateson of her mother's life as a woman who successfully combined motherhood with a thriving professional career. Furthermore, it provides an intimate portrait of a woman who provided a role model for generations of American women who had seen their own lives as narrowly proscribed by the culture in which they lived.

Mead served American women in other ways. In her early anthropological studies *Coming of Age in Samoa* (1928), *Sex and Temperament* (1935), and *Male and Female* (1949), she explored the roles of biological and cultural determinants in the formation of personality, finding that traits considered masculine in one culture (aggression, for example) could just as easily be considered feminine in another. Mead, in collaboration with Bateson, developed theories of the formation of temperament or personality types within cultures.

Mead's career was initially aided by the farsighted Franz Boas, the professor at Columbia University who was instrumental in the development of modern anthropology. Boas shrewdly recognized that some aspects of culture were more accessible to female researchers than male ones, and nearly half of the anthropology graduate students trained at Columbia during his long tenure were women. Boas sent Mead to the field with instructions for studying adolescent behavior. Mead, equipped with theoretical grounding but little practical knowledge, developed many of the techniques of modern fieldwork. She was, for example, one of the first to implement the participant observer technique in her work in Samoa. In Bali with Bateson, she exploited photographs and films as methods for researching nonverbal communications, when photography had only been used to illustrate anthropology books.

With several other anthropologists, Mead worked for the United States government during World War II in various intelligence capacities. Her contributions to the war effort included studying and lecturing about the differences between British and American culture in order to smooth over relations, analyzing the eating habits of Americans, and describing American society in *And Keep Your Powder Dry* (1942). She played a principal role with Ruth Benedict in the development of national character studies, which evolved as a means of categorizing and exploring the fundamental characteristics of complex nations about which little was known. Mead and others developed a new methodology for studying cultures in which it was not feasible to do fieldwork. They called it "culture at a distance."

Mead was also instrumental in popularizing anthropology, largely through her best-selling books of which *Coming of Age in Samoa* was the first. From 1962 until her death, she wrote a column with colleague Rhoda Metraux for *Redbook* magazine which was read by millions of American women. While she used her column as a forum for her own ideas, she also read the letters that she received as a means of remaining current regarding the concerns and opinions of her readers.

The highly respected Mead was widely mourned when she died of cancer in 1978. Her achievements in anthropological technique and theory, her broadening of the perception of gender, her government work (which included intelligence activities and congressional testimony against nuclear weapons and global pollution), and her tireless services to American women were evidence of her remarkable energy and ambition.

Sources for Further Study

Bateson, Mary Catherine. "Continuities in Insight and Innovation: Toward a Biography of Margaret Mead." *American Anthropologist* 82 (June, 1980): 270-277. Bateson describes her reasons for publishing her highly personal recollections of her mother in an attempt to record the way Mead's personal and professional lives were intertwined. Bateson views her study of her parents as anthropology, and indeed she functions as a participant observer in the culture of their lives.

Howard, Jane. *Margaret Mead: A Life*. New York: Simon & Schuster, 1984. Howard, a journalist, used as sources interviews with colleagues, friends, and acquaintances of Mead. Although the biography is informative, it is flawed by her uncritical use of her sources and the inclusion of unsubstantiated or gratuitous observations. Contains an index, bibliographies, and illustrations.

Lipset, David. *Gregory Bateson: The Legacy of a Scientist*. Englewood Cliffs, N.J.: Prentice Hall, 1980. In the first section, Lipset provides a thorough biographic treatment of Bateson, while the second section is devoted to a cogent analysis of Bateson's rich intellectual and professional pursuits. Bateson's intellectual theorizing is made readily accessible through Lipset's capable analyses. Contains an index, a bibliography, and citations.

Mead, Margaret. *Blackberry Winter: My Earlier Years*. New York: William Morrow, 1972. Mead described both her professional and her personal lives in this engaging autobiography, which is peppered with photographs of her life. Divided into three sections: Section 1 describes her early life, section 2 is a discussion of her fieldwork, and section 3 discusses her role as mother and grandmother.

Metraux, Rhoda. "Margaret Mead: A Biographical Sketch." *American Anthropologist* 82 (June, 1980): 262-269. In this opening article in an issue devoted exclusively to Mead, colleague Metraux provides a detailed yet concise biography of Mead. Includes a select bibliography.

Sahlins, Marshall. "Views of a Culture Heroine." *The New York Times Book Review*, August 26, 1984, 1, 20-21. Anthropologist Sahlins provides an overview of Bateson's biography of her parents, as well as of Mead's life and work in this extended book review.

Yans-McLaughlin, Virginia. "Margaret Mead." In *Women Anthropologists: A Biographical Dictionary*, edited by Ute Gacs et al. New York: Greenwood Press, 1988. This highly informative yet concise biography of Mead carefully chronicles her professional life. Includes a bibliography of primary and secondary sources.

Mary E. Virginia

A WIZARD OF EARTHSEA

Author: Ursula K. Le Guin (1929-   )
Type of work: Novel
Type of plot: Fantasy
Time of plot: The distant past
Locale: The world of Earthsea
First published: 1968

Principal characters:
GED, a wizard's student who is also known as Duny and
  Sparrowhawk
OGION, an aged hermit, wizard, and teacher
VETCH, a fellow wizard of limited talent who befriends Ged

Form and Content

Speaking in Sweden in 1989, Ursula K. Le Guin explained why she found it necessary to write *Tehanu: The Last Book of Earthsea* (1990). She said that she conceived of the Earthsea trilogy, of which *A Wizard of Earthsea* is the first book, as a subverted heroic tale. In the 1960's, when she was composing the stories, she thought of herself as transcending gender insofar as she was a woman successfully writing in a masculine genre for children, but she came later to see that, to a significant degree, she was writing as an "honorary or artificial man." Furthermore, she realized that by giving her lead male characters dark skins, she was doing more than simply subverting the Anglo-European conventions of heroic fantasy; she also was associating her heroes with that other, larger group from the cultural margins, women.

A Wizard of Earthsea is a heroic fantasy told as a historical legend. As a young child, Ged shows an extraordinary talent for magic and soon attracts the attention of an obscure opposing force, associated finally with the Stone of Terrenon on the island of Osskil. Characters connected with this stone tempt Ged, during various stages of his training, to gratify his vanity and pride by summoning the spirits of the dead to appear among the living, thus exerting power over death. The story of his coming to terms with the dark side of himself, his shadow, may be seen as structured by temptations and crises.

The first major temptation during his boyhood comes from a young girl, the daughter of an enchantress from Osskil. She encourages him to try a spell of transformation, but when he goes to Ogion's books in search of the spell, he is transfixed by one for summoning, and this first evokes his shadow. He receives his quest as a result of his second main temptation. In a foolish contest on Roke, he summons a departed spirit and releases his shadow into the world. This strange entity is presented as an emissary from a realm of nonbeing, the opposite and opponent of all that is. To understand the shadow thoroughly, one must turn to Le Guin's world-view as expressed in her essay collections, *The Language of the Night* (1979) and

Dancing at the Edge of the World (1989), where her discussions of Carl Jung and of Taoism help to clarify her understanding of the relations between being and nonbeing. Le Guin's epigraph to the novel and the series makes clear, however, that order in this fantasy world depends not upon the defeat of the shadow, but rather upon a kind of balance between light and shadow, between being and nonbeing: "Only in silence the word,/ only in dark the light,/ only in dying life:/ Bright the hawk's flight/ on the empty sky." Therefore, Ged sets out on a quest after releasing the shadow, to determine his proper relationship to this entity.

Ged's quest is both literal and spiritual. He must travel to certain places, overcome certain obstacles, and finally meet his shadow in the right circumstances, but he also must discover who he is, the extent of his powers, and what he is to do with his life. Should the shadow, which is blind in the world of being, find him before he knows himself, then it will possess him, transforming him into an evil wizard. On these parallel journeys, Ged coerces a dragon to give up predation upon humans, resisting the temptation to free the dragon in exchange for the name of the shadow. In the magical economy of his world, knowing the true name of a thing gives one power over it. Attempting to save the life of a dying child, Ged travels spiritually to the border between death and life, and there the shadow finds him and begins to pursue him. This pursuit drives him to Osskil and the Stone of Terrenon, where Ged almost subordinates himself to the forces of nonbeing in order to gain power over the shadow; this is his most threatening temptation. When he takes shelter with Ogion, the wizard advises him to turn on and pursue the shadow, to attempt to possess it. In the final crisis, Ged confronts his shadow and gives it his own name. So named, the shadow and Ged merge, making him a powerful adult hero.

Analysis

Although *A Wizard of Earthsea* follows the major conventions of heroic fantasy, it also subverts them. Earthsea is presented as a hierarchical world, medieval in technology, but made materially rather comfortable by the use of magic. Magic is based on a knowledge of language. Ged explains that the universe is a long word, spoken by the shining of the stars, the syllables of which are the true names of all things. The magician learns these syllables, which also make up the language of dragons, and by manipulating them can participate in and to some extent direct the form and disposition of things. This creative magic is believed to be the province of men. Only men are trained in it. Although there are female amateurs, village witches who pass on a "minor" traditional knowledge of spells associated mainly with feminine domestic life, the women who achieve special power usually are seen as connected with the dark powers opposed to creation. In this story, the few powerful women are also dangerous. As the trilogy develops, and especially as it is extended into *Tehanu*, it becomes clearer that women's association with destructive magic is more a cultural than a natural phenomenon. Kept at the margins of culture by traditional social and political structures, women seem to be forced to seek power from dark forces. Because the culture associates women with darkness and nonbeing, whatever powers they show tend also to be connected with evil.

In *A Wizard of Earthsea*, Ged's meetings with women seem to be either dangerous temptations or minor events, but in each he learns something vital to his success. The dangerous women bring him into contact with his shadow, which proves to be necessary to his maturing. The helpful women, such as Vetch's sister, Yarrow, and an aged, exiled princess, help Ged to understand the values of domestic life and the suffering that results from the current political order. Such learning becomes increasingly important in the later books, which concern themselves in part with reforming the political and social order.

Ged's quest occurs on two levels. On the level of active adventure, it appears to be more or less conventional, but when one observes Ged's internal journey, Le Guin's further subversion of the genre is more visible. The brash young hero makes a mistake and, in correcting it, discovers his identity and enters into his heroic role. This movement is shown as a series of adventures, but the adventures do not involve the traditional confrontations with villains, soldiers, and monsters that can be settled by strength, cunning, and skilled helpers. Ged confronts a dragon, but this monster speaks the language of Ged's magic, and the contest is carried on mainly by bargaining. Ged meets villainous characters but evades them rather than fighting them. He struggles with the shadow, but instead of destroying it, he absorbs it into his identity. Le Guin's narrative emphasizes travelogue and internal adventure, always subordinating external adventure and heroic action. One sign of this is that, though Ged has many helpers, he takes each of his main steps alone. The primary action is Ged's self-discovery and integration.

One cause of tension between heroic conventions and the movement of this story is that the book's worldview opposes implicit assumptions of the heroic tale as it has developed in Western civilization. The conventional Christian worldview sees evil as a temporary power introduced into a good creation and destined in the end to be utterly defeated. Le Guin's worldview derives from Taoism, and as it appears in the Earthsea books, it presents a universe that depends for its existence on a balance between being and nonbeing. All particular things emerge from nonbeing and eventually return to it, and in consequence, a dynamism of creation and destruction, renewal and decay, dominates the universe. To interfere with this balance, as does an evil wizard in search of personal immortality in *The Farthest Shore* (1972), the third book of the trilogy, leads to stopping the creative process by which the universe continuously comes into being. In Ged's metaphor from *A Wizard of Earthsea*, such a desire, carried out knowledgeably, silences the continuously spoken word of creation and ends the universe. This balance is as necessary in the self as it is in the universe, and this is why Ged must merge with rather than destroy his shadow. Here, Le Guin's interest in Taoism merges with her interest in Jungian archetypes, for Ged's shadow is his own nonbeing, the dark and unknown aspects of himself that must remain unrealized but also must be acknowledged.

In the world of life, then, people must serve being and light in the name of life and oppose nonbeing, darkness, and the service of death. To do so wisely, they must recognize that nonbeing cannot be defeated—that it is not evil, but necessary. This worldview differs markedly from the Christian worldview, so this novel differs from the traditional heroic fantasies that envision the hero's victory as an ultimate defeat of evil.

Context

Although Le Guin was not to articulate and publish her main feminist ideas until well after the appearance of the Earthsea books, the directions her thought would take are implicit in those books. The Taoist worldview of *A Wizard of Earthsea* differs from the Christian worldview that is implicit in much heroic fantasy, such as J. R. R. Tolkien's trilogy *The Lord of the Rings* (1955). One main difference is that Le Guin's worldview sees the universe as continuous, without beginning or end; therefore, human history contains no fall or last judgment. This has several implications for how women are portrayed in her work.

Although women hold inferior social and political positions, there is no ancient religious justification for this state of affairs. In *The Tombs of Atuan* (1971) and *Tehanu*, Le Guin makes it clear that the oppression of women in Earthsea results from an age of imbalance in political life, in which men have come to dominate politics and magic. It appears at the end of *Tehanu* that, as a new age begins, a woman will lead in the realm of magic, a man will lead in the realm of politics, and the two will cooperate in governing a unified Earthsea.

The worldview of the Earthsea books tends to be inclusive rather than exclusive. As the main characters, through their adventures and learning, come into line with that worldview, they are more inclined to act cooperatively, to think of community as a structure for including all who share a locale rather than as a set of concepts for including the like-minded and excluding the different. Ged's final self-integration is inclusive rather than exclusive, and his missions in the later books become communitarian rather than individualistic. He always rejects even the most needed personal gains if accepting them will harm the community.

A Wizard of Earthsea won a *Boston Globe/Horn Book* Award in 1969, the same year in which Le Guin published *The Left Hand of Darkness*, which won both of the most prestigious science-fiction awards, the Nebula and the Hugo. *The Tombs of Atuan* won a Newbery Honor Book citation, and *The Farthest Shore* (1972) won a National Book Award for children's literature. Such success, at a time when few women published science fiction or fantasy under their own names, was decisive in drawing women openly into these areas, so that within twenty-five years, dozens of women had established reputations in a field dominated by men since its beginnings, first in medieval and later in romantic fantasy and continuing into the twentieth century development of science fiction and new fantasy as highly popular genres.

Another important contribution of the Earthsea books is that they were important in changing the reputation of fantasy and science fiction as genres. Although Le Guin did expect children to read these books, they are not simple. Her admirers quickly saw that her themes were as serious socially and philosophically as her writing was beautiful and subtle. By this means, Le Guin was influential in bringing serious critical attention to these genres. She was among those writers who initiated a sort of renaissance in fantasy and science fiction, both in their production and in their recognition as important cultural products.

Sources for Further Study

Bittner, James W. *Approaches to the Fiction of Ursula K. Le Guin*. Ann Arbor, Mich.: UMI Research Press, 1984. Bittner concentrates on examining Le Guin's characteristic themes and styles.

Bucknall, Barbara J. *Ursula K. Le Guin*. New York: Frederick Ungar, 1981. This book gives special attention to relations between Le Guin's life and her fiction. Includes an extensive bibliography.

Le Guin, Ursula K. *Dancing at the Edge of the World*. New York: Grove, 1988. This important collection of Le Guin's later essays, speeches, and book reviews is very important to understanding the evolution of her feminism as it relates to her thinking about the Earthsea books and the eventual composition of *Tehanu*. See, especially, the "Bryn Mawr Commencement Address."

——————. *Earthsea Revisioned*. Cambridge, Mass.: Children's Literature of New England, 1992. This short book presents a revised version of Le Guin's 1989 lecture in Sweden on feminist ideas in the Earthsea books.

——————. *The Language of the Night*. Edited by Susan Wood. New York: Putnam, 1979. This collection of Le Guin's early essays and speeches includes several that are directly related to the Earthsea books, especially "The Child and the Shadow."

Spivack, Charlotte. *Ursula K. Le Guin*. Boston: Twayne, 1984. This book examines all Le Guin's work until the 1980's—poetry, prose, and fiction—and includes an annotated bibliography.

Terry Heller

WOMAN AND NATURE
The Roaring Inside Her

Author: Susan Griffin (1943-   )
Type of work: Social criticism
First published: 1978

Form and Content

Susan Griffin's *Woman and Nature: The Roaring Inside Her* is the result of a lecture that Griffin was asked to deliver on women and ecology, and is, in its author's words, "an unconventional book." Juxtaposing the objective, authoritative, and detached voice of patriarchy with the emotional, initially tentative, and collective voices of women, Griffin posits a dialogue between these voices that reveals the significance of cultural and gender-based points of view regarding nature. By refusing to be limited by literary conventions commonly associated with prose, Griffin manages to blend the genres of prose and poetry in a critique of the relationships between Western civilization and nature, between men and women, and between objectivity and emotion.

Woman and Nature explores the traditional Western identification of woman with Earth and, in this sense, is a cultural anthropology chronicling the attitudes surrounding this identification. Griffin's extensive research ranges from philosopher Plato to psychologist Sigmund Freud, from novelist Charlotte Perkins Gilman to poet Adrienne Rich, and the illustrations that she provides from her research result in the inclusion of many voices. The two predominating voices in the book—that of patriarchy and that of the "other," notably woman—are indicated by different typestyles both to represent the dialogue between the two voices visually and to allow the reader to see how differences in language result in profound differences in relationships with nature. Pairing these disparate viewpoints lets Griffin display and describe a completely different way of seeing the natural world that she believes is largely associated with the feminine and is, finally, incontrovertible.

Griffin begins *Woman and Nature* by tracing the history of patriarchal ideas about the nature of matter and arranges these ideas and judgments alongside patriarchal comments about the nature of woman. In "Matter," the first of four "books," Griffin discusses the land, timber, cows, and other bodies (including the female body), as well as the very nature of matter itself. The analogies drawn here between woman and nature extend throughout the other books ("Separation," "Passage," and "Her Vision") as well as in the section entitled "Matter Revisited." Griffin initially thought of the form of the book as being that of a mirror which would reflect, in reverse order, the differences in describing and seeing as ascribed to the patriarchal and to the female. Yet as Griffin notes in her preface, "'Her Vision' would not be so constricted." Written associatively rather than narratively, *Woman and Nature* utilizes insightful associations to mirror cultural attitudes about woman, history, literature, agriculture, and nature. Griffin's expansive notes and bibliography at the end of the book disclose how widely the issues that she raises range—from gynecology textbooks to office manuals—and are provocative in and of themselves.

Analysis

In *Woman and Nature*, Griffin catalogs how Western patriarchal attitudes are embodied in the language that science, commerce, and the arts generally use to describe and comprehend the natural world. This language is not neutral or value-free. The section that begins *Woman and Nature* is entitled "Matter" and immediately adopts a distanced, authoritative, and judgmental tone that is a "parody of a voice with such presumptions." One of the two voices that dominate the entire text, this voice implies that it alone is in possession of absolute truths and "recognized opinion." The voice of patriarchy is realized by Griffin's use of impersonal pronouns and declarative sentence structure ("It is said") as well as by passionless descriptions of very personal and passionate events, such as a breast operation or a clitoral excision: "The mass is exorcised. Tissue posterior to it is sectioned. Deep sutures are tied as the pins are removed." Additionally, the voice of patriarchy is represented in a standard typeface, unlike the words of woman, which are represented in italic and intervene in the spaces left by patriarchal language. As Griffin's text develops, the language of woman appears more and more frequently as well as more forcefully, eventually appropriating the text itself.

"Matter" is the longest section and sets up the dichotomies between the voices and the content of those voices that pervade the entire work. Among the analogies that Griffin offers to the reader are the comparisons of the selection of trees for timber and the perfect office worker or of women's bodies and those of horses or cows. For example, Griffin links such seemingly dissimilar "animals" as women and mules when she writes: "*And we know we are not logical. The mule balks for no apparent reason. For no rhyme or reason. We remember weeping suddenly for no good reason.*" As a result, both women and mules need to be controlled by the more objective and rational males, who apparently do not "balk" without an "apparent" or "good" reason.

After exploring the development of the patriarchal viewpoint regarding "matter," Griffin's next section, entitled "Separation," considers the implications of the many kinds of separation developing from and required by patriarchy. Like the other sections that make up *Woman and Nature*, book 2 begins with a citation from a woman, in this case Emily Dickinson's "I felt a Cleaving in my Mind—." All that follows chronicles the separations of body from mind, from distance, from time, from soul. "Separation" begins with a hysterectomy and moves on to enumerate and protest these separations from self and the world, separations that Griffin declares are required to survive in patriarchy. The dire consequences of such separation provide one of Griffin's major themes, and according to the evidence that Griffin has marshaled, these consequences have had a calamitous impact on Western culture. An example of this can be observed in the dividing up of time and space into increments that can be measured and thus controlled in an attempt to "keep watch" over chaos. Book 2 ends with a section called "Terror," which attests that what is known through patriarchy is really not certain and thus leads to terror and to the unknown.

Book 3, named "Passages," is the shortest section of *Woman and Nature*. Only seven pages in length, this book is subtitled "Her Journey Through the Labyrinth to the Cave Where She Has Her Vision." In essence, this section of the work is a leap—although a painful one—from the distanced language and isolated point of view of the patriarchy to the personalized, collective language of woman. In this section, for the first time, Griffin has the italicized language of woman supersede and replace the language of received thought, of separation, of patriarchy. This book is where the vision of nature shifts from one of control and fear to one of identification and re-vision. Instead of the labyrinth provoking fear as in the Greek myth, it invokes possibility: *"The rectangular shape of his book of knowledge, bending."* Ironically, perhaps, book 3 separates the slowly evolving feminine consciousness from the rigid, fearful patriarchal consciousness.

Book 4 is "Her" vision, and woman's vision prevails in this section; the world is no longer "his." This portion of *Woman and Nature* revises the world vision to embrace such ideas as "Mystery," "Our Dreams," and "Transformation." Subtitled "The Separate Rejoined," this book scrutinizes what Griffin calls a "New Space" and a "New Time" (as well as "Flying," "Deviling," "Dancing," and "Animals Familiar") and reunites the parts of the soul and mind that were divided by the male-dominated view of the world. She becomes "The Lion in the Den of the Prophets," and "devours them." As Griffin notes in her preface, however, "Her Vision" will not be constrained, and the response to the patriarchy spills over into another section entitled "Matter Revisited." Griffin rewrites "The Anatomy Lesson" from an earlier section of "Separation" and reveals the female body to be a witness to personal strength while tracing the history of female desire, intelligence, and possibility: *"we know what we know."*

Throughout *Woman and Nature*, Griffin resists a purely linear development of her themes of separation, isolation, patriarchal oppression, female silence, and the collective nature of woman's voice. Instead, she is recursive, layered, and complex in the ways in which she unfolds her critiques. Additionally, Griffin is very careful to let the language of the patriarchy speak for itself, and it is only when the reader reconsiders received and conventionally accepted language in the light of the more reticent language of woman as represented in *Woman and Nature* that the conflicts in perception become clear. By mixing genres—the section called "Dancing," for example, is written as a poem—and using the cumulative effects of the varying typefaces, quotations, and "official" and personal languages, Griffin manages to build a sense of discomfort with notions of things as they are—or as readers have been told that they are by Western culture. It is ultimately this discomfort that Griffin channels into an alternative viewpoint based on women's ways of seeing and knowing.

Context

Although *Woman and Nature* was hailed as "extraordinary" (*Publishers Weekly*), "stirring" (*Library Journal*), and "visionary prediction" (*Ms.*), it is not poet Susan Griffin's best-known work. Griffin—who has won such awards as the Ina Coolbrith

Award for Poetry, an Emmy Award, a National Endowment for the Arts (NEA) grant, and a Kentucky Foundation for Women grant—is perhaps best known for another work of social criticism, *Pornography and Silence: Culture's Revolt Against Nature* (1981). Griffin's scholarly interests also include the narrative techniques of Henry James and the nature of authorship. Much of Griffin's later thinking and writing, however, can be traced to many of the themes and the blendings of genre evident in *Woman and Nature.*

Like Mary Daly, whom Griffin acknowledges as an influence in her writing of *Woman and Nature*, Griffin seeks to rethink and reinvent the manner and the very words women use to name their own experiences. The resulting book is not conventional in its form or scope, but it is certainly a powerful statement and an indictment of the silencing of woman and of nature throughout Western thought. Griffin deliberately limits the scope of *Woman and Nature* to Western civilization, and she cites expansively from the traditional canons across centuries and national boundaries. By challenging literary conventions as well as received histories and interpretations, Griffin enables the reader of *Woman and Nature* to participate in a feminist revision of the Western worldview as she encourages female scholarship.

Sources for Further Study

Charney, Diane Joy. Review of *Woman and Nature: The Roaring Inside Her. Library Journal* 104 (February 1, 1979): 414. Charney gives a brief review of the book under the heading of "Social Science," summing up the main theme as being one of discoveries about the nature of matter in conjunction with man's opinions about the nature of woman.

Miner, Valerie. Review of *Woman and Nature: The Roaring Inside Her. Ms.* 7 (April, 1979): 85-86. In an extensive review of *Woman and Nature*, Miner discusses the "new words, tones and rhythm" of the book. Named an encouraging and helpful critic by Griffin in the "Acknowledgments" section of her book, Miner is a sensitive reader of the text who considers it to be a tour de force in places.

Spayde, Jon. Review of *A Chorus of Stones*, by Susan Griffin. *Utne Reader*, May/June, 1993, 120-121. Spayde reviews Griffin's *A Chorus of Stones: The Private Life of War* (1992), referring to *Woman and Nature* as "her harrowing history of Western ideas of womanhood."

Willis, Ellen. "Nature's Revenge." *The New York Times Book Review*, July 12, 1981, 9. While reviewing Griffin's *Pornography and Silence* and Andrea Dworkin's *Pornography: Men Possessing Women* (1981), Willis notes many of the techniques—the juxtaposition of conflicting viewpoints and the blending of genres—that Griffin made use of in her earlier work, *Woman and Nature.*

Virginia Dumont-Poston

WOMAN AS FORCE IN HISTORY
A Study in Traditions and Realities

Author: Mary Ritter Beard (1876-1958)
Type of work: History
Time of work: From ancient times to the twentieth century
Locale: Greece, Rome, Europe, and the United States
First published: 1946

> *Principal personages:*
> SIR WILLIAM BLACKSTONE, an eighteenth century authority on
> English common law and its effects on women
> PEARL BUCK, an author who compared the roles of Chinese and
> American women
> ELIZABETH CADY STANTON, an early advocate of suffrage and
> equal rights for women
> JOSEPH STORY, an authority on equity jurisprudence
> MARY WOLLSTONECRAFT, an advocate of women's rights in
> England

Form and Content

As a result of many years of historical research and writing with her husband, Charles A. Beard, Mary Ritter Beard cultivated a deep desire to examine the role of women in history; *Woman as Force in History: A Study in Traditions and Realities* is the fulfillment of that desire. Although the author assumed that a difference existed between the traditions and realities of women's role in history, she made no attempt to reach definite conclusions.

Throughout the book, Beard analyzes the impact of Anglo-American common law and its major exponent, Sir William Blackstone, on the position of women in a male-dominated society. The basic starting point for Beard was to see if women had been in absolute subjection to men in reality or only in tradition. She reviewed the century after the first women's rights assembly in America, the Seneca Falls Convention organized by Elizabeth Cady Stanton and Lucretia Mott in 1848. Beard's goal was to see if subjection was real, and if it was, to see if total equality based on equity jurisprudence was the answer.

Woman as Force in History traces the attitudes of both men and women concerning woman's role in history. The author reveals the sins of omission as well as the sins of commission regarding the recognition of women's impact on the history of the world. Beard looks at various types of writers, such as sociologists, anthropologists, and psychologists, as well as historians, in search of their attitudes toward women. Being a historian herself, she criticizes that group for not giving proper recognition to the accomplishments of women. As an example, Beard uses the American History series volume *The Middle Period, 1817-1858* (1897), by John W. Burgess. Beard believes that the rare references to women by Burgess do not give an accurate picture of the influence of women in that critical period of American history. Burgess refers to a law in Virginia that severely penalized white women who cohabited with African American slaves, and the only women whom he mentions are a slaveowner named Mary Brown and a fugitive slave named Ellen Crafts. Yet he makes no mention of Harriet Beecher Stowe and other women who had an impact on that period.

Beard's long experience as a historian led her back to the Greco-Roman world as the beginning of the historical analysis of her work. She refers to such documents as Rome's *Twelve Tables*, written in the fifth century B.C., and the *Corpus Juris Civilis*, under the Byzantine emperor Justinian in the sixth century A.D. Beard then proceeds to a detailed look at women's role in the economic, social, educational, and intellectual life of medieval Europe. She uses her last chapter to analyze how women have affected history, as well as how that effect has been perceived by most male writers.

Woman as Force in History offers a good balance between fact and theory. Unsupported speculation is kept to a minimum, and Beard quotes freely from many sources to substantiate her text. She gives the reader of this work the opportunity to see the totality of the force that women have exerted throughout history.

Analysis

Throughout *Woman as Force in History*, Mary Beard seems to project the idea that if women had always been the victims of a masculine plot to hold them in a slavery of subjection, they would not have exerted the force in history that she believes they have. Although she sympathizes with the intent of the Declaration of Sentiments adopted at the Seneca Falls Convention in 1848, Beard does not fully accept its unqualified assertion that the masculine goal throughout history had been to maintain absolute tyranny over women. After rejecting the idea of a forced subjection, Beard proceeds to trace how the idea developed and how it was perceived by women in the nineteenth century such as Elizabeth Cady Stanton. The author then discusses how the concept of equality was developed and advocated as a cure for the perceived subjection.

Beard begins her work by describing the relationship between men and women as one of the most visible revolutionary movements of modern times. The book is better understood and much more significant when one considers that it was written with the shadows of such men as Adolph Hitler, Benito Mussolini, and Joseph Stalin looming in the background. Beard discusses the influence of women on the momentous events of that time.

The author first covers the force exerted on Russia by Nadejda Krupskaya, the wife of Vladimir Lenin, whose marriage to Lenin created a revolutionary partnership. Krupskaya is credited with being the driving force to include women's rights as a vital part of the Bolshevik agenda in 1917. The idealistic nature of Marxist communism made it impossible for Lenin to ignore that force, which Beard credits with much of the success of the Bolshevik revolution. Beard continues by describing the same impact of women on the success of Fascism in Italy under Mussolini, in Germany under Hitler, and in Spain under Francisco Franco. Beard specifically reveals how Hitler used the concept of women's rights to persuade women to support the Nazi Party, and how that support led to his initial success. The author then reveals how Hitler used the blind support of women to produce the army of soldiers that ignited a worldwide military conflagration in 1939.

In her chapters surveying various men and women writers, Beard gives the reader a broad overview of the perceived subjection of women. She reveals certain errors that perpetuated themselves to the point that even women writers such as Dr. Elizabeth Adams accepted them. One error was that since there are few records of women's education in Ancient Greece and Rome, such education was almost nonexistent. Beard accurately points out that a lack of historical record is not proof that something did not occur. Later in the book, she cites the example of Theano, the wife of the sixth century B.C. Greek philosopher Pythagoras, who was herself a highly educated and highly respected philosopher. Beard does not adequately recognize, however, that Theano was the exception and not the rule.

Beard is critical of historians as a group for not recognizing the force that women have been in history. Even when later social historians such as Arthur Schlesinger tried to correct this problem, they were uncertain, because of a lack of precedent, of how to do so. In support of women's role in shaping early American democracy, Beard quotes the French visitor Alexis de Tocqueville. In his book *Democracy in America* (1835), Tocqueville declared that if he were asked to name the one thing most responsible for the success of American democracy, his answer would be the superiority of American women.

Woman as Force in History gives the reader an excellent evaluation of Blackstone's *Commentaries on the Laws of England* (1765), the recognized authority on common law. Beard does not accept Blackstone's belief that English common law pronounced "civil death" on women when they married; by this, he meant that all of a woman's property became the property of her husband. Beard is equally critical of Blackstone's belief that common law judges could rule statutory laws null and void if they violated common reason. Beard appreciates the good intentions of Mary Wollstonecraft and her book *A Vindication of the Rights of Woman* (1792), but she is disappointed that Wollstonecraft accepted so much of Blackstone's work. Wollstonecraft recognized the power of women to move men, but Beard believes that she described and defended that power in a way that was degrading to women as a whole.

Much of *Woman as Force in History* is devoted to the improvement of American law over its English foundation. Most American colonies and later states modified unacceptable parts of English common law, including provisions relating to women, by statutory law. Unlike Blackstone, American leaders such as Thomas Jefferson declared that statutory law must always have precedence over common law. Throughout her book, Beard traces and partially rejects the argument that the answer to women's rights is equity jurisprudence. She recognizes that this jurisprudence through chancery courts can remedy much injustice to women, but she does not see it as a solution to every problem. Instead of seeking an overall solution, Beard continually returns to her basic belief that, in spite of centuries of neglect, women have exerted a major force in the history of the world.

Context

Woman as Force in History was one of the earliest attempts, particularly by a well-known historian, to study the impact of women throughout history. By its very nature, the book immediately became a controversial topic of conversation and literary criticism. Although advocates of women's rights applauded Beard's attempt to correct historical injustice to women, many did not accept her belief that female historical subjection was only a myth. They were also critical of Beard's rejection of legal equality as a means of correcting that subjection.

Professional historians greeted *Woman as Force in History* with varying degrees of skepticism and criticism. Most of their criticism was based on Beard's style of writing rather than on the content of the book. They believed that the work was too repetitious and included too many long quotations. Some thought that Beard should have made a greater effort to reach a conclusion in her study and to offer solutions. A few historians criticized what they perceived as Beard's errors in historical research. Predictions by the more optimistic that, in the future, major historical works would include more of the impact of women failed to materialize. More than twenty years later, *A World History* (1967), by William McNeill, listed only one woman in the index.

An earlier book by Beard, *On Understanding Women* (1931), covered many of the same points as *Woman as Force in History*, but with fewer historical illustrations. The two books are much more easily understood and have a greater impact when taken together. The books coauthored by Mary Beard and her husband, Charles A. Beard, also contribute to a better understanding of their combined denial of female subjection; these books include *The Rise of American Civilization* (1927) and *The American Spirit* (1942).

Like many controversial books, *Woman as Force in History*, after several years of neglect, experienced a revival of interest. A paperbound reissue in 1962 coincided with an increase of interest in women's rights. It enjoyed significant popularity well into the 1970's, and it has had a profound impact on the liberation of women in general.

Sources for Further Study

Beard, Mary Ritter, ed. *America Through Women's Eyes*. New York: Macmillan, 1933. This volume is a collection of writings by women covering various aspects of American history. Presents viewpoints on frontier life, the Civil War, industrialization, World War I, and other significant periods not found in most sources.

_____. *On Understanding Women*. Westport, Conn.: Greenwood Press, 1931. This earlier book by Beard is more philosophical in nature than *Woman as Force in History*. Nevertheless, it does include several illustrations of how women's role in life has been misunderstood over the centuries. Includes a good bibliography of other attempts to study the subject.

_____ . *A Woman Making History: Mary Ritter Beard Through Her Letters*. Edited by Nancy F. Cott. New Haven, Conn.: Yale University Press, 1991. An anthology of some of the letters of Mary Beard. Beard did not want her letters published and therefore destroyed most before she died, but Cott secured enough to reveal much of what motivated Beard. Examines how Beard arrived at the title for *Woman as Force in History*.

Carroll, Berenice A., ed. *Liberating Women's History: Theoretical and Critical Essays*. Chicago: University of Illinois Press, 1976. An interesting source of writings evaluating historiography concerning women. Includes a critique of *Woman as Force in History* and other writings, some covering different time periods, including the medieval period. Also covers different political settings, such as Germany prior to World War I.

Christie, Jane Johnstone. *The Advance of Women: From the Earliest Times to the Present*. Philadelphia: J. B. Lippincott, 1912. This interesting study was one of the first attempts in modern times to study the role of women in history. Christie is clear and strong in her criticism of the injustice committed by men against women over the centuries, but she offers few suggestions for improving conditions in the future.

Glenn L. Swygart

WOMAN ON THE EDGE OF TIME

Author: Marge Piercy (1936-   )
Type of work: Novel
Type of plot: Science fiction
Time of plot: The late twentieth century, interspersed with visits to 2137
Locale: Several mental institutions in New York City and Mattapoisett, a village in
    Massachusetts
First published: 1976

> *Principal characters:*
> CONNIE (CONSUELO CAMACHO RAMOS), a Mexican American
>   woman unfairly institutionalized as violent
> LUCIENTE, an androgynous visitor from the future, whose lovers
>   include Jackrabbit and Bee
> DOLLY (DOLORES CAMACHO), Connie's niece, a prostitute
> GILDINA, an alternate version of either Connie or Dolly existing
>   in a dystopian future
> SIBYL, Connie's closest friend on the violent ward
> SKIP, another friend on the ward

Form and Content

Woman on the Edge of Time tells the story of Connie Ramos who, incarcerated in a mental institution, travels into a possible utopian future. Structurally, the novel alternates Connie's experiences on several mental wards with a series of visits to the future world of Mattapoisett, Massachusetts, in 2137. Moving from a false spring to a permanent winter, Connie enacts an ironic version of the hero's journey outlined by Joseph Campbell in *The Hero with a Thousand Faces* (1949). Luciente, Connie's guide, is the bright shadow of Connie's despair; Connie notes that Luciente's name in Spanish means "shining, brilliant, full of light." She provides the call to adventure, contacting Connie just before she wallops her niece's pimp, an act which takes her across the threshold of Bellevue hospital and into the "belly of the iron beast" to Rockover State.

During this time, Connie's trips to the future often mirror or compensate for aspects of her past or events on the ward. Her anguish at losing her daughter to adoption and her desire to once again live in a family are answered by her inclusion in Luciente's family and her contact with Luciente's daughter, Dawn. When an old woman on the ward dies, Connie attends the honored death of Sappho, a storyteller in the future. When her niece Dolly fails to show up for a visit, Connie attends a festival, sees one of Jackrabbit's holographs ("holis"), and has sex with Bee, a large, gentle black man who reminds her of Claud, her deceased lover.

At Rockover, Connie and her friends Sybil and Skip are selected for operations to experiment with chemical control of emotions; simultaneously, Connie learns that

Luciente and her society are at war with the remnants of a multinational powerbase whose use of "robots or cybernauts" as fighters links them to Connie's doctors, who are trying to master the technology of brain control. After seeing how the implants depersonalize another patient, Alice, Connie plans and executes an escape. Caught and returned to custody, Connie watches as the surgery finally enables Skip to commit suicide. In the parallel universe of the future, Jackrabbit is killed while serving on defense.

Once Connie herself has the operation, her contacts with Luciente's world become increasingly muddled. An attempt to reach Mattapoisett catapults her into a negative version of the future, where she meets Gildina, the debased opposite of Luciente, who like Connie's niece Dolly is a prostitute. After a visit to attend Jackrabbit's wake, Connie decides to enlist as a fighter in the war against the mechanistic future, at one point flying in what she thinks is a battle against the soldiers of the future and finally deciding to carry the war into her own time by poisoning the hospital staff with the parathion that she steals from her brother's greenhouse. The novel ends with a series of excerpts from Connie's official files, revealing that she was permanently incarcerated at Rockover. By killing her doctors, however, she may have helped Luciente's future come into existence.

Analysis

An extended, feminist revision of Ken Kesey's *One Flew over the Cuckoo's Nest* (1962), *Woman on the Edge of Time* combines a critique of authoritarian institutions with one of the most fully realized feminist utopias. Connie's visits to Luciente's world map out systematic alternatives to the abuses of power that she suffers as a patient and as a middle-aged, poor, Chicana single mother. These visits explore three interrelated categories of concern shared by all Piercy's work: a Marxist critique of economically based power hierarchies; a feminist critique of sex roles, gender inequities, and child-rearing practices; and a humanist critique of scientific ignorance of and disregard for the ecological unity of the human mind and the natural environment. As one of Luciente's family members explains, "the original division of labor" between men and women enabled "later divvies into have and have-nots, powerful and powerless, enjoyers and workers, rapists and victims. The patriarchal mind/body split turned the body to machine and the rest of the universe into booty on which the will could run rampant."

Luciente's world functions as a classless utopia whose equal distribution of labor and wealth emphasizes the importance of productive, meaningful work and indicts excessive consumption. Rejecting capitalism, they no longer buy or sell anything; they have "dumped the jobs telling people what to do, counting money and moving it about." Concentration of wealth and power in the hands of a privileged few is a central evil in every reality of the book. Luciente explains that "the force that destroyed so many races of beings, human and animal . . . was profit-oriented greed." It is the remnants of these greedy profiteers whom Luciente and her friends are battling; the misogynistic alternate reality of Gildina is run by "the richies" whom she names as "the Rockemellons, the Morganfords, the Duke-Ponts."

Luciente's future lacks not only classes but also gender hierarchies. Sex roles as Connie suffers under them are nonexistent, eliminated along with motherhood. Children are no longer born by women. Incubated in a "brooder," each child has three genetically unrelated "comothers," at least two of whom, regardless of sex, take hormone treatments that allow them to nurse. Initially repulsed by the sexual arrangements of the future, Connie hates the brooder, seeing the whole process as mechanistic reduction of children to animals. Yet despite her rage at the sight of a man breast-feeding, she finally concludes that this future fulfills her fantasy of "a better world for the children," wishing passionately that her daughter Angelina could grow up as strong, proud, and unafraid as Luciente's children.

Children in Luciente's world are allowed to explore the full range of their human potential. Nurturing mind in body, the culture educates "the senses, the imagination, the social being, the muscles, the nervous system, the intuition, the sense of beauty—as well as memory and intellect." Jackrabbit lists their priorities: They have tried to learn from "cultures that dealt well with handling conflict, promoting cooperation, coming of age, growing a sense of community, getting sick, aging, going mad, dying." Educational practices and initiation and healing rituals to deal with each of these life tasks are drawn with rich pragmatic detail during Connie's visits.

The future's holistic attitude toward the individual parallels their sense of connection to the natural world. Following the heritage of the American Indians, they "put a lot of work into feeding everybody without destroying the soil." Although they can automate whole factories, they use technology mainly for inhumanly mindless tasks. An Earth Advocate and an Animal Advocate sit on all planning councils, making sure human needs are balanced with those of the biosphere.

Life in Mattapoisett is thus a point-by-point refutation of the power structure of Connie's world where "the whole social-pigeonholing establishment" routinely reduces individuals to a category of disease, subjecting them to the absolute whim of doctors who try to manipulate the human mind while knowing almost nothing about it. Instead, Piercy crafts a culture which can accept idiosyncracy and conflict, a place where individual differences and emotions are understood and honored, where the care and nurturing of children is the central task of families supported by a unified community, and where everyone lives in a balance of useful work and creative play. Even if Connie's trips to the future are all hallucinations, the reality that she creates is saner than the world that her doctors control.

Context

Written after Piercy's two most explicitly feminist works, *Small Changes* and *To Be of Use*, both published in 1973, *Woman on the Edge of Time* details many of the same women's issues: the trauma of illegal abortion and rape, the self-abasement required by conventional gender roles, the pain and anger of mother-daughter relationships, the need to extend the nuclear family, the difficult loyalties of female friendships, and the humane recognition of alternatives to heterosexuality. Its most important contributions to feminism, however, lie in its status as a heterosexual feminist utopia, its invention of a richly nonsexist language for describing human emotions, and its imaginative embodiment of alternative motherhood.

Piercy's theoretical foundation in Marxism and practical experience in community activism makes hers one of the most rigorously conceived of all feminist utopias. Luciente's wry acknowledgement that governing by consensus means spending endless time in meetings, as well as the finely dramatized details of the "worming" process by which the community helps her resolve her conflicts with one of Jackrabbit's other lovers, are authentic renditions of the daily politics of consciousness-raising groups. Another index of the novel's realism is its genial inclusion of men. Most of the works to which the novel is usually compared—Charlotte Perkins Gilman's *Herland* (1915), Joanna Russ's *The Female Man* (1975), Suzy Charnas' *Motherlines* (1978), and Sally Gearheart's *The Wanderground* (1979)—posit separatist worlds where men have ceased to exist or appear only occasionally for necessary breeding.

Piercy's poetic ear also enriches feminist dimensions of the novel. While the invention of the gender-neutral pronoun "per" is one obvious answer to linguistic sexism, a more subtle corrective is supplied by the metaphorical richness of Luciente's language, particularly its strong, kinetic verbs such as "inknow," (to sense body-mind connections), "graze" (to contact mentally), "paint the bones" (to use euphemisms), "bottom" (to feel depressed), "grasp" (to understand), and "sling" (to criticize).

The most revolutionary of Piercy's innovations, however, is the elimination of motherhood, a literal extrapolation of Shulamith Firestone's call in *The Dialectic of Sex: The Case for Feminist Revolution* (1970) for women to socialize the technologies of biological reproduction so that they will no longer be physically or psychologically responsible for child care. Also incorporating Juliet Mitchell's emphasis in *Woman's Estate* (1971) on the need for corollary revolutions in women's work, sexual freedom, and child-rearing practices, Piercy confronts the dilemmas of mothering contemporaneously outlined in Adrienne Rich's *Of Woman Born: Motherhood as Experience and Institution* (1976) and Dorothy Dinnerstein's *The Mermaid and the Minotaur: Sexual Arrangements and Human Malaise* (1977). The solution of Luciente's world—"So we all became mothers"—anticipates Nancy Chodorow's *The Reproduction of Mothering: Psychoanalysis and the Sociology of Gender* (1978) in suggesting that women will not achieve sexual equality until men are "humanized to be loving and tender" by fully participating in child rearing.

Sources for Further Study

Adams, Karen C. "The Utopian Vision of Marge Piercy in *Woman on the Edge of Time.*" In *Ways of Knowing: Essays on Marge Piercy*, edited by Sue Walker and Eugenie Hamner. Mobile, Ala.: Negative Capability, 1991. A good general introduction, this essay summarizes the novel as a feminist utopia, comparing its central concerns with those in Charlotte Perkins Gilman's *Herland*.

Bartkowski, Frances. *Feminist Utopias*. Lincoln: University of Nebraska Press, 1989. Chapter 2, "The Kinship Web," compares Piercy's novel to Joanna Russ's *The Female Man*, discussing utopian conventions and placing the novel in the context of feminist and Marxist critiques. Good on the use of language and the role of the artist.

Gygax, Franziska. "Demur—You're Straightway Dangerous: *Woman on the Edge of Time*." In *Ways of Knowing: Essays on Marge Piercy*, edited by Sue Walker and Eugenie Hamner. Mobile, Ala.: Negative Capability, 1991. Emphasizes psychiatric critique, mentioning Piercy's involvement with the Mental Patients Liberation Front and her familiarity with the work of Phyllis Chessler. A psychological analysis of androgyny in the novel compares it to works by Adrienne Rich and Doris Lessing.

Kessler, Carol Farley. "*Woman on the Edge of Time*: A Novel 'To Be of Use.'" *Extrapolation* 28, no. 4 (Winter, 1987): 310-318. Stressing the didactic function of Piercy's novel, examines communal, ecological, and spiritual values, arguing that the violent conclusion of the novel is a call for reader involvement.

Pearson, Carol. "Coming Home: Four Feminist Utopias and Patriarchal Experience." In *Future Females*, edited by Marleen S. Barr. Bowling Green, Ohio: Bowling Green State University Popular Press, 1981. A revision of "Women's Fantasies and Feminist Utopias" in *Frontiers* 2, no. 3 (Fall, 1977): 50-61. The original article places Piercy's *Woman on the Edge of Time* in the tradition of feminist utopias such as those by Joanna Russ, Ursula Le Guin, James Tiptree, Mary Bradley Lane, Charlotte Perkins Gilman, Dorothy Bryant, and Mary Staton (only the last four are discussed in the revision), systematically discussing their similar treatments of women's work, violence against women, sex roles, and the need to revolutionize economic structures, the nuclear family, and societal attitudes toward nature.

Rosinsky, Natalie. *Feminist Futures: Contemporary Women's Speculative Fiction*. Ann Arbor, Mich.: UMI Research Press, 1984. Chapter 3, "Battle of the Sexes," contrasts Piercy and Joanna Russ's advocacy of androgyny with Sally Gearheart's separatism in *The Wanderground*. Noting the humorous, ironic elements of Piercy's novel, Rosinsky analyzes the flexibility of Piercy's feminist solutions.

Elisa Kay Sparks

THE WOMAN WARRIOR
Memoirs of a Girlhood Among Ghosts

Author: Maxine Hong Kingston (1940-   )
Type of work: Memoir
Time of work: The mythic past and the twentieth century
Locale: China, New York, and California
First published: 1976

Principal personages:
MAXINE HONG KINGSTON, the American daughter of Chinese
  immigrants who tries to make sense of her dual heritage
BRAVE ORCHID, her mother, a doctor and a ghost fighter in China
MOON ORCHID, Brave Orchid's sister and Maxine's aunt
NO NAME WOMAN, Maxine's father's sister, who kills herself and
  her illegitimate child
FA MU LAN, the legendary Chinese woman warrior
TS'AI YEN, a Chinese woman who was scholar, poet, and musician

Form and Content

In *The Woman Warrior: Memoirs of a Girlhood Among Ghosts*, Maxine Hong
Kingston presents a series of mythic and autobiographic stories that illuminate the
way in which the author must deal with the sexism and racism in her world. As a young
Chinese American girl, who is called such racist names as "gook" and who is
repeatedly told such misogynist Chinese sayings as "girls are maggots in the rice" by
her own parents, Kingston feels alienated both from the dominant American culture
and from the male-dominated Chinese culture. In her memoirs, Kingston tells of her
search for women role models, interweaving imaginative stories concerning such
characters as Fa Mu Lan, a Chinese woman warrior, with memories of her own
relationship with her strong-willed mother, Brave Orchid. Through these various
stories, the narrator searches to affirm her Chinese American female identity in the
context of her bicultural world.

The narrator begins her autobiography with her mother telling her a cautionary tale
about her Chinese aunt, whom Kingston calls the No Name Woman. Her married aunt,
who became pregnant from an illicit affair, incurs the wrath of the Chinese villagers,
who attack her family's house. Her aunt gives birth to her child and drowns both
herself and the child in the family well. Kingston calls her aunt "No Name Woman"
because her family, blaming the aunt for the shame that she brought to them,
deliberately attempts to erase her from the family's memory. Although Brave Orchid
warns Maxine not to repeat her aunt's story, Maxine uses the story as a catalyst for her
creative imagination. Maxine attempts to imagine her aunt's reason for adultery: Was
she in love? Was she raped? Most important, she tries to transform her aunt from a
mere object lesson—of misguided passion punished by communal wrath—into a

human being who should not be forgotten by the family.

Yet Brave Orchid tells Maxine stories not only of women who have been ostracized by a punitive feudal community but also of powerful women such as Fa Mu Lan, a Chinese woman warrior who saves her community. Fa Mu Lan serves as a central inspiration for Maxine who, in her imagination, becomes the woman warrior fighting battles to right the wrongs perpetrated against her people. Although she fantasizes that she is like the woman warrior who fights tyrants, Maxine acknowledges her own limitations in her everyday life; when she attempts to challenge her boss's racist comments, he simply ignores her "bad, small-person's voice."

In the latter part of her autobiography, Kingston turns her attention to the life of Brave Orchid, who acts as both an adversary and a role model for her. She depicts two ostensibly conflicting pictures of her mother. On the one hand, her mother, who married her husband right before he left for the United States, lives an independent life in China, going to medical school and becoming a doctor. On the other hand, when she goes to the United States years later to be with her husband, she reverts back to the traditional role of wife. Nevertheless, Kingston's strong-willed mother stands in stark contrast to Brave Orchid's sister, Moon Orchid, who comes to the United States after being separated from her husband for three decades. Brave Orchid commands Moon Orchid to insist that her husband, who has taken another wife, recognize her role as "first wife." Instead, Moon Orchid's husband, now a successful American doctor, rejects her with a hostile stare. Unable to endure her husband's rejection or to adapt to her new country, Moon Orchid becomes paranoid and eventually insane.

Although Brave Orchid is a powerful matriarchal figure, she ostensibly attempts to pass on patriarchal values to Maxine. Thus, in a key scene, Maxine verbally "battles" with her mother, in order to assert her own identity and autonomy. In the end, however, Maxine realizes that she and her mother—both born in the year of the dragon—have much in common; both are fighters and storytellers.

Analysis

In this work, Kingston explores the ways in which women can find their voices in patriarchal cultures that seek to silence them. Although Kingston begins her autobiography with her mother's injunction "not to tell," she breaks her silence in order to relate the story of No Name Woman and to begin a search for self-expression, finding ways to challenge sexist and racist oppression.

Kingston uses the stories of her two aunts—No Name Woman and Moon Orchid—to highlight the danger of silence, which Maxine associates with victimization and the loss of identity. Because of her illicit affair, No Name Woman's family blames her for the community's punitive actions and after her death attempts to forget her existence; they attempt to "silence" her by eradicating her very memory. When Moon Orchid confronts her unfaithful husband, he turns upon her and effectively silences her. Soon after, Moon Orchid becomes insane. Later, Maxine observes, "I thought talking and not talking made the difference between sanity and insanity. Insane people were the ones who couldn't explain themselves."

As an antidote to these "silenced" women, Maxine imagines the stories of powerful women such as Fa Mu Lan and Brave Orchid. While Fa Mu Lan is a woman warrior who fights to "right the wrongs" carved on her back by her parents, her independent mother Brave Orchid is a strong-willed matriarch, a "champion talker." There are ways, however, that both Fa Mu Lan and Brave Orchid perpetuate the values of patriarchal cultures. Fa Mu Lan is able to be a leader precisely because her followers assume that she is a man; when she finishes her fighting, she resumes the duties of the traditional Chinese wife and daughter. Although Brave Orchid lived an independent life as a doctor—a nontraditional role for a woman—in China, when she is reunited with her husband in America she resumes her traditional role as wife, bearing her husband six children and working long hours in a laundry. It is most significant, however, that she enculturates her daughter by passing on the misogynist sayings and antifemale cultural prejudices. Moreover, she cuts her daughter's frenulum, the membrane fold under the tongue—which Maxine interprets as an act of violation and repression. Although Brave Orchid later insists that she cut Maxine's frenulum precisely so that she would not be tongue-tied, Maxine, who believes that this act made her mute in school, accuses her mother of attempting to silence her.

Kingston believes that it is critical to claim her own voice, her own autonomy. In a climactic scene, the young Maxine challenges her mother in a shouting match, enacting a forbidden tirade against her mother, refusing to be a victim of silence. Yet she feels strangely dissatisfied with her verbal battle with her mother. She realizes that speech can also be used as an oppressive force—an agent of patriarchal rhetoric—to silence another. Kingston learns, in the end, not to privilege speech for its own sake. Although she sees the importance of speech as a means of self-expression, she also recognizes how speech can be used as a means of oppression.

In ending her autobiography with the story of Ts'ai Yen, Kingston is presenting a hopeful vision for the possibility of interethnic harmony and positive roles for women. Symbolically, Kingston is also relating a story of reconciliation, between her mother and herself, between the different cultures of America and China. Kingston learns of this story from her mother, but as she states, "The beginning is hers, the ending, mine." When the poet Ts'ai Yen was twenty, she was stolen by a barbarian chieftain from her people; while in captivity, she bore two children and created songs. After twelve years, she was ransomed from the barbarians, and she returned to China with her songs. Like Ts'ai Yen, Kingston learns to channel her anger against oppression into artistic acts—which, in Kingston's case, speak of the hope for racial and gender harmony. Like Ts'ai Yen's bicultural songs, Kingston's narrative crosses national boundaries; moreover, her work also crosses generic boundaries, those of autobiography, myth, history, fantasy, and folklore. Through her multiple stories, Kingston demonstrates that truth itself can be multiple; as she transcribes the Chinese oral tradition into written English, she believes that "it translates well."

Context

Although other Asian American women writers preceded her, Kingston was one of the first to garner national recognition, winning the National Book Critics Circle Award in 1976 for *The Woman Warrior*. Thus, she has been seen as a pioneer for other Asian American women writers who have succeeded her. Politically, Kingston's *The Woman Warrior* has excited interest not only because the work provides a feminist vision from a Chinese American woman's perspective but also because of the negative reaction that it has produced in such Chinese American men as Frank Chin.

On the one hand, Kingston provides a critique of a patriarchal and misogynist feudal China that can trap women in demeaning, slavelike roles, subject to such cultural practices as foot-binding. On the other hand, Kingston points out that the Chinese culture itself provides her with such powerful women role models as Fa Mu Lan and Ts'ai Yen. Out of this complex tradition, Kingston forges a bicultural self that will allow her to enact her own "woman warrior" identity in an American society with its own racist and patriarchal legacy.

Nevertheless, Chinese American playwright Frank Chin has criticized Kingston's work on the grounds that it propagates racist views of Chinese Americans. Interested in championing a Chinese heroic tradition to combat the often-emasculating vision that the dominant American culture has of Asian American men, Chin believes that Kingston's feminist views distort an authentic picture of China and Chinese Americans. Certainly, however, one can argue that Kingston's work is an autobiographic, not an ethnographic, study; Kingston is conveying her understanding of her mother's talk-stories, which reflect a living immigrant oral culture, not a series of static, "authentic" tales. Moreover, Kingston has reformulated male heroic traditions, highlighting the contributions of women to that tradition. Thus, Kingston's work broadens the concept of a Chinese mythos precisely because she embeds her hybrid American and feminist views within that tradition, claiming her own "woman warrior's" voice.

Sources for Further Study

Chan, Jeffrey Paul, Frank Chin, Lawson Fusao Inada, and Shawn Wong, eds. *The Big Aiiieeeee! An Anthology of Asian American Writers.* New York: New American Library/Meridian, 1991. Chin has accused *The Woman Warrior*, shaped by its feminist vision, of being a "fake book," providing an inauthentic picture of Chinese American history and catering to a racist American culture.

Cheung, King-Kok. *Articulate Silences: Hisaye Yamamoto, Maxine Hong Kingston, Joy Kogawa.* Ithaca, N.Y.: Cornell University Press, 1993. In her chapter on Kingston, Cheung notes the way in which historical and parental silence provokes the author to use her imagination to create possible versions of stories that her taciturn parents refuse to convey.

Johnson, Diane. *Terrorists and Novelists.* New York: Alfred A. Knopf, 1982. Comparing Kingston to Carobeth Laird and N. Scott Momaday, Johnson writes that *The Woman Warrior* is an "antiautobiography," a work which blurs the boundaries between fiction and autobiography. Johnson argues that Kingston, in challenging the "female condition," resists her culture in order to triumph over it.

Lim, Shirley Geok-lin, ed. *Approaches to Teaching Kingston's "The Woman Warrior."*

New York: Modern Language Association, 1991. This collection of essays is an excellent source for cultural background and close readings of the text. Includes a helpful bibliographic essay, a personal statement from Kingston on *The Woman Warrior*, a section providing sociohistorical information to help readers better understand references to the Chinese American culture contained in the work, and close analyses of the text. Also highlights different approaches to the text, including feminist, postmodernist, and thematic approaches.

Ling, Amy. *Between Worlds: Women Writers of Chinese Ancestry*. New York: Pergamon, 1990. Ling locates Kingston's work within a historical tradition of Chinese American writers. She highlights Kingston's need for "writing wrongs" by "writing about the wrongs."

Smith, Sidonie. *A Poetics of Women's Autobiography: Marginality and the Fictions of Self-Representation*. Bloomington: Indiana University Press, 1987. Smith notes the ways in which Kingston uses autobiography as a means of creating identity and breaking out of the silence that her culture imposes on her. She also states that *The Woman Warrior* is "an autobiography about women's autobiographical storytelling," emphasizing the relationship between genre and gender.

Sandra K. Stanley

THE WOMAN'S BIBLE

Author: Elizabeth Cady Stanton (1815-1902)
Type of work: Literary criticism
First published: 1895-1898

Form and Content

Struggling for women's rights in the nineteenth century, the early feminists were constantly told that the Bible ordains woman's sphere as helper to man and woman's status as inferior to man. Having heard this throughout her decades of labor in the women's rights movement, Elizabeth Cady Stanton determined in 1895 to investigate the Bible and what it really says about women. She attempted to obtain the assistance of a number of female scholars of Hebrew and Greek, but several turned her down, fearing that their reputations would be compromised. Other women were afraid to critique the Bible for religious reasons. Still others, Stanton notes in her introduction, did not want to bother with a book they felt was antiquated and of little importance.

She finally chose a committee of women she believed would make a valuable contribution, primarily based on her perception of their liberal ideas and ability to make sense out of what they read. This was the "Revising Committee" that shared billing with Stanton for the work. Stanton herself, however, wrote most of the commentary, and it contains her own beliefs and values.

When women struggling for their rights in the nineteenth century were referred to the Bible with the explanation that God ordained their inferior position, Stanton notes that there were a variety of responses. Some glossed over the most antiwoman aspects of the Bible and interpreted the rest liberally, thus maintaining their belief in its divine inspiration. Others noticed that biblical law, church law, and the English common law that was the basis of American jurisprudence in the nineteenth century all had a common theme and dismissed them all as human in origin. Still others simply accepted traditional interpretations and the belief that women's equality would be antireligious and dangerous to the home, the nation, and the church.

For herself, Stanton accepted that the Bible is a mixture of valuable principles of love, liberty, justice, and equality (as, she says, are the holy books of all religions) which at the same time includes passages that degrade women and make their emancipation impossible. One cannot, she says, accept or reject the Bible as a whole since, although it includes some divine, spiritual truths, it is a human book full of human error. Therefore, her goal was to analyze in detail the 10 percent of the book that she believed relevant to women.

The Woman's Bible is divided into two volumes. The first deals with the five books of the Pentateuch and the second all the other parts of the Bible upon which Stanton and her committee chose to comment. There are commentaries in the first part on Genesis, Exodus, Leviticus, Numbers, and Deuteronomy and in the second part on Joshua, Judges, Ruth, Samuel, Kings, Esther, Job, Psalms, Proverbs, Ecclesiastes, the

Song of Solomon, Isaiah, Daniel, Micah, Malachi, and even the Kabbalah, a medieval Jewish mystical writing. This section also includes commentary on the New Testament books of Matthew, Mark, Luke, John, Acts, Romans, Corinthians, Timothy, Peter, the letters of John, and Revelation. All of the book is written by women, much of it by Elizabeth Cady Stanton herself.

Analysis

Stanton's own comments on the first chapter of Genesis provide an example of her radical understanding of the Scripture. Noting that in this Creation story there is divine consultation, and therefore seemingly a plurality of divine beings, and that the man and woman were both created in the image of God, Stanton concurs with other scholars that the Trinity is represented here. Rather than three male beings, however, it is more logically made up of divine Father, Mother, and Son. She then suggests that women's lot in life would be improved if prayers were offered to the Heavenly Mother as well as to the Heavenly Father.

The next author introduces the reader to what at the time was the height of scholarly biblical criticism: the division of the Pentateuch into several original sources that were later put together by an editor. Although her understanding of biblical sources is naïve, antiquated, and overly simplistic by modern standards, Ellen Batelle Dietrick's explanation that Genesis holds two separate stories of the Creation is accepted biblical scholarship today.

Finally for this passage, Lillie Devereux Blake presents another bit of logic by pointing out that one cannot assert that woman's creation after man in the second story signifies her inferiority without at the same time admitting that man is inferior to creeping things, since he was created after them in the first story.

Later in Genesis, Stanton finds one verse (36:18) on which to comment, and one sees here not only the kinds of insights that she had and questions that she raised but also an explanation of her approach to the biblical text. The verse simply names the three sons of Esau's wife Aholibamah. Stanton's first thought is to wonder who this woman was and why one does not learn any more of her. Stanton would like to know what she thought, what she said, what she did.

Then noting that some biblical interpreters try to find deep symbolic meanings in what she reads as simple records of a people, she admits that she herself is not versed in theories of biblical interpretation. If the Bible, she says, is meant to point the way to salvation, it does not make sense for it to require great symbolic interpretations in order to understand it, any more than road signs should require complicated symbolic interpretation. She therefore gives the reader fair warning that she intends to base her comments on the Bible as she reads it in plain English.

Stanton's comments frequently do not stick to the passage under discussion. Quite often, the passage merely serves as a spark to the exposition of an idea on the author's mind. For example, in her commentary on Exodus 32, wherein the jewelry of the Israelites (which Stanton assumes belonged mostly to the women) is melted down to make a golden calf, the primary lesson she draws is one about self-sacrifice. It is a virtue highly valued in women, she notes. She would rather teach women that self-development is a higher ideal. This was one of Stanton's primary themes throughout her life, and she finds several places to repeat it in this book, including here, even though it has very little to do with the story of the golden calf.

Stanton was also not above imaginative leaps into the ludicrous. In a discussion of Elijah's ascent into Heaven in a fiery chariot in I Kings 17, in all seriousness she conjectures that he rode a balloon. The perplexed widow who witnessed the ascent, she suggests, had no idea that he did not ascend all the way to Heaven but probably landed in some farmer's cornfield.

Stanton's dictum about the virtue of self-development is repeated in her discussion of the New Testament story of the widow's mite in Mark 12. To this woman who gave all she had to the temple, Stanton would like to say that sacrificing everything to a religious organization, neglecting her own self-development, is wrong.

These are only a few of the topics addressed by Stanton and the Revising Committee. The book ends with a selection of letters from still other women, responding to the questions of whether the Bible has advanced or retarded the emancipation of women, whether it has dignified or degraded them.

Context

After the publication of the first volume, one clergyman opined that "It is the work of women, and the devil." Stanton replied: "This is a grave mistake. His Satanic Majesty was not invited to join the Revising Committee, which consists of women alone." Stanton's stand in questioning the religious authority of the Bible and the beliefs about women which were based on it led to ridicule, vitriolic attacks by the clergy, and even a move by her fellow feminists in the suffrage movement. In 1896, against the impassioned advice of Stanton's friend Susan B. Anthony, even the National American Woman Suffrage Association repudiated any connection with *The Woman's Bible*, the official reason being the nonsectarian nature of the association.

The book was controversial by its very nature, since it attacked not only the Bible's use as an authority on which to base women's subordination but also its divine inspiration. For many years, Stanton's work was all but forgotten, existing chiefly in the attics of a few remaining supporters in the early twentieth century. With the revival of feminism in the late 1960's, however, interest in the book as a historical document was revived. It was reprinted in 1972 by Arno Press and also in 1974 by the Coalition Task Force on Women and Religion.

Although full of inaccuracies and quaint interpretations, the questions that Stanton raised were still important, and the arguments from the Bible for women's subordination could still be heard. Therefore, Stanton's interest in the portrayal of women in the Bible was also revived along with the twentieth century feminist movement. *The Woman's Bible* presaged a large number of scholarly works. Because more women have had the opportunity to become learned in biblical studies, these works are highly sophisticated and professional biblical scholarship when compared with Stanton's largely amateurish work. The names of Phyllis Trible, Phyllis Bird, Elizabeth

Schussler Fiorenza, Alice Laffey, and Carol Meyers represent only a tiny sampling of the most well known of these biblical scholars. Their work stems from a similar concern about what the Bible really says about women.

Sources for Further Study

Banner, Lois W. *Elizabeth Cady Stanton: A Radical for Woman's Rights.* Boston: Little, Brown, 1980. This biography of Stanton covers the reformer's long and productive life, from her childhood through her marriage and years as a mother of seven, her organization of the first Women's Rights Convention of 1848, her association with Susan B. Anthony, and her continuing activism until her death in 1902.

Laffey, Alice L. *An Introduction to the Old Testament: A Feminist Perspective.* Philadelphia: Fortress Press, 1988. An example of modern biblical study about women. Laffey takes readers through the Old Testament/Hebrew Bible with analyses from a feminist point of view of both the texts and the cultural factors behind them. Although this work deals only with the Old Testament, it illustrates the kind of feminist biblical scholarship being done.

Oakley, Mary Ann B. *Elizabeth Cady Stanton.* Old Westbury, N.Y.: Feminist Press, 1972. Another biography of Stanton, this one is somewhat shorter than Lois Banner's (above). Written in a narrative style, including many conversational quotations. Takes the reader from Stanton's childhood in New York through her older years.

Stanton, Elizabeth Cady. *Elizabeth Cady Stanton.* Edited by Theodore Stanton and Harriet Stanton Blatch. 2 vols. New York: Arno Press, 1969. This set, compiled by two of her children, is the most complete work about Stanton's life. The first volume is a revision of her autobiography, published in 1898 under the title *Eighty Years and More.* The second volume begins with selections of her letters from 1839 to 1850 and ends with her diary from 1880 to her death in 1902.

Stanton, Elizabeth Cady, Susan B. Anthony, Matilda Jocelyn Gage, and Ida H. Harper, eds. *History of Woman Suffrage.* 6 vols. New York: Fowler and Wells, 1881-1922. Reprint. New York: Source Book Press, 1970. Originally a three-volume set which was later expanded by other editors to make a total of six. Offers a complete documentation of the struggle for women's suffrage, from the 1848 Women's Rights Convention to the final ratification of the Nineteenth Amendment granting women the vote in 1920. Speeches, reports, newspaper articles, letters, and other archival information, linked together with a running narrative by the authors.

Waggenspack, Beth Marie. *The Search for Self-Sovereignty: The Oratory of Elizabeth Cady Stanton.* New York: Greenwood Press, 1989. Part of a series on Great American Orators, this book takes readers directly into the work of Stanton as a public speaker. Although her career as an orator for women's rights was complicated both by the demands of her work in the home as a mother and by the opposition to women as public speakers, she nevertheless made many important speeches. The first part of this book discusses Stanton's life and work, and the second part reprints seven of her speeches. Complete with notes and an annotated bibliography.

Eleanor B. Amico

WOMAN'S ESTATE

Author: Juliet Mitchell (1940-   )
Type of work: Social criticism
First published: 1971

Form and Content

Woman's Estate is a compilation of several essays written by Juliet Mitchell in the late 1960's and in 1970, combined with new material that both connects the older essays and elaborates upon the implications of Mitchell's arguments. Mitchell describes the women's liberation movement (the term she uses to designate the most progressive wing of the women's movement) as the vanguard of radical political activism in the late 1960's. She likewise sees it as the key element in a new revolutionary political movement. The text itself is divided into two related sections. Part 1, entitled "The Women's Liberation Movement," gives a general description of the background and politics of the movement itself. Part 2 provides a theoretical discussion of a movement grounded in a combination of materialist and feminist theory.

Because the text is obviously a product of the intellectual and social climate of the 1960's, Mitchell appropriately begins part 1 with a chapter on the background of the 1960's. She argues that the women's liberation movement can only be understood in relation to the other major political movements of the period, those of blacks, students, and youth. Of these three movements, Mitchell finds the shift from the Civil Rights movement of the early 1960's to black radicalism in the late 1960's to be that most closely analogous to the struggle of women. Women's liberation, she theorizes, owes less to historical feminist movements, such as women's suffrage, than it does contemporaneous social struggles. Just as blacks suffer from economic and social oppression, so do women, and as many blacks shift from calls for reform to calls for revolution, so too does a sizable segment of the women's movement. Unlike the most radical elements of the black liberation movement, however, the majority of those involved in the women's liberation movement come from middle-class backgrounds. Thus the movement also shares many similarities with the various youth and college student movements.

The remainder of part 1 is devoted to a description of women's liberation politics and a cataloging of organizations as they existed in the late 1960's. Mitchell highlights the differences between various national movements and the effects of the "reformist" organizations that try to work within the existing structure. She does not include the National Organization for Women (NOW) in her discussion because she considers it to be merely a "feminist" or mainstream political group. Instead, women's liberation follows the separatist pattern set by Black Power activists. Mitchell describes the similarities between various international women's groups to be "women only" membership, collective work, and a small-group emphasis. Key concepts include consciousness-raising and the insistence upon the deleterious effects of patriarchy.

Groups that do not fit within this women's liberation paradigm are dismissed by Mitchell as being either accommodationist or sectarian.

Part 2, "The Oppression of Women," provides a theoretical explanation of the women's liberation movement. Writing from a socialist-materialist perspective, Mitchell outlines the primary structures that control women's lives: production, reproduction, sexuality, and socialization. Traditional socialist theories have been preoccupied with the predominance of production as a "base" for a "superstructure" of culture. Mitchell places reproduction on the same level as production, claiming the division of labor among the sexes as the origination of the division of labor. Likewise, she places an equivalent emphasis on sexuality and socialization. Her innovative theorizing of previously secondary levels of socialist thought serves as a precursor to Mitchell's later work on psychoanalysis and the importance of socialization in the lives of women.

Analysis

Mitchell's text serves two purposes in the women's movement: as a descriptive document of contemporaneous practices in the movement and as a prescriptive document that purports to outline the future of the movement. Mitchell's description of the 1960's political scene is primarily of historical interest: Her view is that of a British writer whose perspective on American politics is primarily informed by her fellow activists and from media accounts. Thus she incorrectly identifies the Black Power segment of the Civil Rights movement as the most important segment of the African American struggle for equality. Her writing on feminism, however, provides great insight into the movement, and her theoretical emphasis lays the groundwork for much of the current debate in feminist and cultural theory.

Mitchell is most persuasive when describing the causes and potentials of 1960's politics. Her approach is usually historically oriented, with a few notable lapses, but it is always dialectical in presentation. Materialist dialectics, as proposed by Karl Marx, can be used to explain a cultural event in relation to its material base, while also accounting for the contradictory forces of history. Mitchell focuses on the contradictions of 1960's society that caused the seemingly spontaneous growth of liberation movements, as well as the contradictions that these movements often unwittingly embraced and embodied. Her primary examples in part 1 deal with the nature of consumer culture, women's education, and the sexual revolution.

Mitchell views the expansion of capitalism into the consumer market as a contradictory phenomenon. To create and exploit any market successfully, capital must necessarily expand the individual's definition of needs, requiring a redirection of desire and a new definition of experience. Mitchell finds the 1960's philosophy of "Do your own thing" to be a perfect example of this contradiction. Society can cultivate the ideology of spontaneous expression and consumption as long as the expression assumes the form of approved activity. The ideology can lead to dangerous or subversive conduct, however, if the individual decides that her own thing is not what the advertising agencies decree. The expansion of consciousness, with its attendant dangers, is connected to another cultural institution, that of the education of women—into certain limited roles.

Women's education is necessary for the operation of an efficient consumer economy; however, Mitchell argues, education can become a threat to the system when women begin to realize for what they are being educated. Mitchell provides evidence to support her contention that women are given just enough education to make them useful secretaries or blue-collar workers but are denied educational access to advanced professions or graduate work. Here her examples from Great Britain are the most telling, because the vast majority of women in British graduate programs study for degrees in education. Mitchell argues that the system maintains itself in this way, by indoctrinating women into an ideology which they are in turn expected to spread. Mitchell conversely believes that increased educational opportunity for women will inevitably lead to a radical questioning of their role within that system.

Finally, the increased social status of women in consumer society may also be said to account for the advent of the sexual revolution. As women gain increasing control over their sexual lives, they are faced with the contradictory picture of the increased commodification of their sexuality. Mitchell provides the example of London in 1970, a city saturated with advertising, most of it using a woman's body as the primary visual element. Mitchell argues that the women's movement has yet to explain the nature of this contradiction, but she believes that the sexual revolution will eventually have a positive effect on women. Her grappling with this theoretical difficulty provides a transition and a link to the second part of her text, in which she attempts to provide a theoretical model capable of uniting the diverse groups within the women's liberation movement.

Part 2 of the text presents Mitchell's original work on the theory of women's liberation. As she notes in Part 1, women have traditionally been placed in a secondary role even in socialist and materialist theory. She proposes the placement of the issue of women's rights in the forefront of socialist theory. Two of the four areas about which Mitchell theorizes, production and reproduction, have been and are basic issues in the women's movement. The second two issues that Mitchell introduces, sexuality and the socialization of children, continue as areas of argumentation and theorization within the movement. Sexuality, traditionally explained by such male-dominated fields as psychology and psychoanalysis, is, as Mitchell finds, a field fraught with internal contradictions. Her insistence on the use of Freudian models of psychoanalytic interpretation separates her from the mass of Marxist and feminist theorists and establishes a base for her later heavily psychoanalytic work. Likewise, her insistence on the importance of the socialization of children helped to open a crucial area of feminist investigation. Mitchell's Freudian predilections lead her to emphasize the importance of infantile experience (within the early years of development), while many subsequent writers have discussed the importance of socialization throughout the adolescent years. Mitchell's assertions that an entire lifetime of decisions can be programmed through the experience of only the first year of life, however, make her one of the most determined of determinists.

Context

Along with Germaine Greer's *The Female Eunuch* (1970) and Kate Millett's *Sexual Politics* (1970), Mitchell's text represents one of the culminating products of the women's movement of the 1960's. Mitchell's theories are thoroughly grounded in the European and British traditions of radicalism and socialism. Thus her argument concentrates on class and social struggle instead of the American concentration on individual rights and spontaneous protest. She also presents a skeptical account on the important questions of a feminine essence, or an essential feminism.

Millett and Greer present a socialist and an anarchist view of women's oppression, respectively. Mitchell criticizes both for what she sees as an overgeneralizing tendency particular to American writing and ideology. While Millett presents a convincing and necessary critique of patriarchy and its prevalence in contemporary society, Mitchell criticizes her work for its antihistorical and undialectical approach. Mitchell prefers to demonstrate how patriarchy works in the individual lives of women instead of proving that it does indeed have an affect. Greer's theories are dismissed by Mitchell as being the female equivalent of the hippie and yippie movements, middle-class misbehavior that is easily reassimilated into a consumer culture increasingly based on the consumption of images (including those of entertainingly outlandish behavior).

Mitchell is even more equivocal on the issue of the essential nature of women's oppression. She asserts that all women are oppressed and that women's oppression is the oldest fact in human history, but she draws short of claiming a unique women's psyche or women's language, as many continental or American feminists have done. She eschews the term "feminist" in favor of the term "woman" in order to highlight the biological basis of women's oppression. By insisting on and accounting for both the biological and the historical nature of women's oppression, Mitchell adds a scholarly and political facet to women's studies that was previously absent or buried by abstraction.

Sources for Further Study

Beauvoir, Simone de. *The Second Sex.* Translated by H. M. Darshley. New York: Alfred A. Knopf, 1953. The early influential work on women based on the theory of historical materialism. An important source for Mitchell's work.

Engels, Friederich. *The Origin of the Family, Private Property, and the State.* 1884. Reprint. Moscow: Progress, 1977. The paradigmatic work by one of the founders of socialist theory. Based on the anthropological findings of American writer Henry Lewis Morgan, Engels argues that the family is the basis of all social structures.

Hayden, Dolores. *The Grand Domestic Revolution.* Cambridge, Mass.: MIT Press, 1982. A groundbreaking work in materialist feminism and historicism. Hayden presents convincing historical evidence indicating that the women's movement has been much less discontinuous than Mitchell asserts. Her emphasis on architectural design provides fascinating proof of the materialist interest of nineteenth century feminists.

Miller, Casey, and Kate Swift. *Words and Women: New Language in New Times*. New York: Anchor Books, 1976. A work that argues for a linguistic, instead of a materialist, approach to women's issues. The authors share Mitchell's interest in the linguistic traces of women's oppression.

Millett, Kate. *Sexual Politics*. Garden City, N.Y.: Doubleday, 1970. A influential work on women's issues contemporaneous with *Woman's Estate*. Millet shares Mitchell's materialist paradigm but pays much less attention to the question of dialectical and historical development.

Jeff Cupp

WOMEN AND MADNESS

Author: Phyllis Chesler (1940-　　)
Type of work: Social criticism
First published: 1972

Form and Content

Phyllis Chesler's *Women and Madness* is a feminist indictment of the male-dominated psycho-medical establishment. Chesler examines the gender-based power relations in psychology and psychiatry from many perspectives and uses many tools: statistical studies, transcripts of interviews, quotations from many sources, personal reminiscences, charts and graphs, illustrations, extensive (almost chatty) footnotes, tales from classical mythology, and free speculation. Throughout her investigation, she consistently finds that women have been oppressed by the power of male definitions of mental health and mental illness, of treatment and cure.

Chesler divides her book into two sections, "Madness" and "Women." In the first section, she considers the role of "madness" in the lives of four famous female mental patients: Elizabeth Packard (1816-c.1890), Ellen West (c.1890-1926), Zelda Fitzgerald (1900-1948), and Sylvia Plath (1932-1963). In trying to live authentically—faithful to her own light in terms of religion, artistic creativity, or simple physical energy and adventurousness—each of these women ran afoul of gender-based societal expectations and consequently found herself in the power of men in the psychiatric industry. Once identified as "patients," the women were then coached, coaxed, and coerced to mend their ways and return to the path of compliant wifedom. Chesler finds mental asylums, and most psychotherapy, to be bureaucratized extensions of the patriarchal family, carrying out the will of husbands of mostly female patient populations. Using epidemiological studies done by others, she demonstrates that the standard for mental health in Western society is not the same for men and women and that it is unfair to women.

In her first section, Chesler not only offers statistics and actual life stories of historical figures but also introduces Jungian tools: She recruits mythic presences into her discussion. She examines the figures of Demeter and her daughters, the Virgin Mary, and Joan of Arc for the ways in which they embody certain constellations of typical female experiences.

The second section of the book is dominated by the results of Chesler's informal interviews with sixty women. Her interview subjects were selected to represent five distinct groups: women who have sex with their therapists, who are confined to mental hospitals, who are lesbians, who are members of ethnic minority groups, and who are feminists in therapy. In each chapter concerning these issues, Chesler briefly describes the demographics of her interview group, gives transcripts from her interviews, and presents some general discussion of her results. She is careful to point out that her study population was not randomized, and she makes no claim that her interviews describe anything except the subjective experience of the group of women that she interviewed. From her eclectic, personal, and openly adversarial feminist perspective, Chesler raises many questions and advances many conclusions about the psychiatric establishment. In general, she finds that in a male-dominated society, treatment of the forms of deviance that are termed "mental illness" is necessarily patriarchal. In other words, male-dominated psychiatry and psychology stand to serve the tense and oppressive power relations that exist between men and women. Sex-role stereotypes exist for both men and women, but Chesler finds that women are allowed a much narrower margin of deviation from role than men before society labels them "mad." "Madness," according to Chesler, may consist in either going too far in acting out the devalued female role (passivity, indecisiveness, frigidity, or depression) or in rejecting one's sex-role stereotype altogether and venturing to show traits that are considered appropriate for the other gender.

Analysis

Women and Madness is organized around the central observation of the numerical gender imbalance in psychiatry: Most patients are women, but psychotherapy is in the control of men. Chesler documents both sides of this imbalance with statistics and considers why the field is so slanted in this particular direction. One possible explanation that she considers is the "help-seeking nature of the female role." Women, who are socialized to value connectedness and interdependence, may simply be more comfortable initiating relationships where they ask for and receive help and advice than are men, who are socialized to value independence, autonomy, and competitive victory. This greater comfort with "help-seeking" may manifest as a greater frequency of doctor visits.

Similarly, the parallels between psychiatric institutions and the nuclear family may make it easier for women than for men to switch from one to the other. Chesler suggests that the typical mental hospital is, dynamically speaking, a "family," with doctor-daddies, nurse-mommies, and female patients who return to the role of the "biologically owned child." In this role, the female patient is expected to be childlike in obedience and trust of her "elders." She is also expected to be childlike in another way: virginal in regard to her own needs but sexually exploitable by her therapist. The female mental patient's hospital role is congruent with her outside role (daughter and/or wife) in a way that the male patient's role is not.

Among Chesler's other plausible reasons for the preponderance of female mental patients is the objective, real-world oppression of women. Women's role as an oppressed caste may cause them to suffer greater stress, provoking greater numbers of psychiatric symptoms. Also, she notes that there has been a differentiation between the social response to extreme acting out of the male social role versus the female role. Male-style acting out—aggression and violence—is largely dealt with by the criminal justice system and not the mental health system. This leaves psychiatric hospitals full of people whose preferred mode of acting out involves extremes of the female passive, dependent role—primarily women.

Perhaps the most significant factor in the overrepresentation of women in psychopathology statistics is the possibility that, in Western society, "mentally healthy" is defined to mean "male." To support this claim, Chesler cites a 1970 study in which a group of mental health professionals of both sexes were asked to complete personality profiles describing a healthy male, a healthy female, and a healthy adult of unspecified gender. It was discovered that the personality profile of an ideal healthy male was very similar to that of a healthy adult of unspecified gender, while the ideal of the healthy female was significantly different: more submissive, less adventurous, and less independent. This suggests that there is no way for a female to be socially defined as mentally healthy: If she fits the ideal of a healthy adult, then she deviates from the ideal of a healthy woman; if she fits the ideal of a healthy woman, then she must be less than fully adult. If this study truly represents the social norm of mental health, it would seem there is no way for women to win. Therefore, women must overwhelmingly outnumber men in psychiatric treatment; womanhood is deviance, by definition.

It should be noted that Chesler's consideration of the high rates of mental illness in women focuses purely on social factors. Never does she consider physiological factors. Biochemical imbalances, genetic predispositions, hormonal disturbances, neurological lesions, allergies, toxins, enlargements of the ventricles in the brain—many of the most active areas of neuropsychiatric research in the last quarter of the twentieth century—are not discussed.

Context

In the early 1970's, when Chesler's book appeared, there was a tremendous popularization of psychotherapy. The most significant impact of *Women and Madness* was to open this territory of psychiatry and psychotherapy for feminist exploration. By 1972, a number of biographical and autobiographical works had already appeared to detail individual women's struggles with insanity and the label of "insanity," notably Nancy Milford's *Zelda* (1970) and Sylvia Plath's *The Bell Jar* (1971). What was still lacking, however, was a broader discussion that would identify common patterns in these personal stories and situate them in a general social context. It was this gap that Chesler sought to fill with *Women and Madness*.

The book's publication was greeted with extremely mixed reviews, and it was not only opponents of feminism who quarreled with its stance. Chesler's exhortation that women take power was seen by some as a call to adopt the ways of the oppressor, instead of doing away with oppression—to simply substitute male madness for female. Some claimed that she romanticized madness itself and failed to distinguish between being identified as mad by others, feeling oneself to be mad, and truly being mad in some objective sense. Others criticized the book's emphatic attack stance, which failed to address the idea of reforming the field of psychiatry. The patchwork nature of the text—with epidemiological data loosely stitched to personal narrative and mythology to polemic—seemed to some critics poorly edited. Some accused her of misinterpretations and frank errors in her statistics. In addition, as was almost obligatory with feminist writers of the period, her tone was called "strident."

In spite of such criticism, *Women and Madness* was an influential book. Turning a feminist eye on the psychiatric industry was a productive move, even if the fruit that it bore may have been more polished in later hands. Chesler's idiosyncratic and personal style in the book, while striking some readers at the time as slapdash, actually became part of a new trend of relinquishing the pretense of impersonal objectivity, the pose of standing apart and separate from the subject of study. Quite apart from its place in general historical trends is the role that this book has played in the lives of many individual women who have found it a comfort and a catalyst in their own struggles with mental health institutions in the United States.

Sources for Further Study

Bolen, Jean Shinoda. *Goddesses in Everywoman: A New Psychology of Women*. San Francisco: Harper & Row, 1984. The exploration of goddess archetypes as patterns of female personality, with which Chesler opens and closes *Women and Madness*, is more fully developed here. With this book, Bolen became one of the luminaries of the resurgent popularization of Jungian psychology in the 1980's and 1990's.

Castillejo, Irene Claremont de. *Knowing Woman: A Feminine Psychology*. 1973. Reprint. Boston: Shambhala, 1990. An attempt to map the psychic terrain of women. This work is closer to classical Jungian theory than Jean Shinoda Bolen's or Chesler's, especially in its view of the differentiation of personality into masculine and feminine.

Formanek, Ruth, and Anita Gurian, eds. *Women and Depression: A Lifespan Perspective*. New York: Springer, 1987. A collection of essays from a variety of theoretical perspectives about female depression in childhood, adolescence, adulthood, and old age. Depression is recognized by Chesler and others as being the primary psychiatric symptom of women in contemporary urban society.

Gilligan, Carol. *In a Different Voice: Psychological Theory and Women's Development*. Cambridge, Mass.: Harvard University Press, 1982. Contrasts women's imperative to nurture and protect relationships with men's imperative to achieve status and advancement.

Heilbrun, Carolyn G. *Reinventing Womanhood*. New York: W. W. Norton, 1979. Using literary, personal, psychological, historical, and mythological material, Heilbrun challenges women to create imaginatively a new, autonomous identity for themselves.

Jack, Dana Crowley. *Silencing the Self: Women and Depression*. Cambridge, Mass.: Harvard University Press, 1991. Many writers have analyzed depression in women as a response to loss. In this work, Jack, following Carol Gilligan, considers depression as a response not to an external loss but to a loss of self. Attention is given to women's sacrifice of self in primary relationships and to the impact on daughters of maternal self-sacrifice.

Milford, Nancy. *Zelda: A Biography*. New York: Harper & Row, 1970. A carefully documented biography of Zelda Fitzgerald which became a model for other women's biographies. This highly respected work was one of Chesler's sources for the much briefer account in *Women and Madness* of Fitzgerald's life as typical of the way in which women's identification as mentally ill is used to deprive them of power and freedom.

Rich, Adrienne. Review of *Women and Madness*. *The New York Times Book Review*, December 31, 1972, 1, 20-21. One of feminism's leading thinkers reviews the strengths and weaknesses of Chesler's work.

Donna Glee Williams

WOMEN IN MODERN AMERICA
A Brief History

Author: Lois W. Banner (1939-   )
Type of work: History
Time of work: The late nineteenth century to the 1970's
Locale: The United States
First published: 1974

Principal personages:
> JANE ADDAMS, a settlement house worker and social reformer
> SUSAN B. ANTHONY, a woman suffrage advocate
> CARRIE CHAPMAN CATT, a suffragist leader
> BETTY FRIEDAN, a feminist writer of the 1960's
> ALICE PAUL, an advocate of the Equal Rights Amendment
> ELEANOR ROOSEVELT, a First Lady and reformer
> ELIZABETH CADY STANTON, a woman suffrage leader

Form and Content

Designed as a supplementary text for courses in twentieth century United States history and women's history, *Women in Modern America: A Brief History* offers an analytic narrative of the actions of women from the end of the nineteenth century to the mid-1970's. Lois W. Banner's goal is to acquaint the reader with the women, both famous and obscure, who shaped the story of females in the United States and to "provide a corrective to the traditional histories from which women are absent." She wrote her book at a time when the modern interest in women's history was just getting under way, and her account became an influential contribution to the literature in the field during the 1970's.

Banner divides the time span of the book into three distinct periods: 1890 to 1920, when women pursued suffrage and other reforms; 1920 to 1960, an era of "greater complacency about women's problems"; and 1960 to 1974, when a more radical feminism emerged. Within these three broad eras, Banner considers a wide range of women, including African Americans, immigrants, the poor, and the middle class. Her goal is to portray how these groups of women responded to social changes while giving appropriate attention to the women who fought for greater rights for all females.

The years covered in the book were a time of rapid change that subjected women at all levels of society to new pressures and strains. Throughout the period, however, Banner believes that contrasting images of women as the embodiment of virtue and a source of temptation and evil have influenced society's attitude toward women and their place in the social order.

Banner also deals with the complex issue of feminism and the shifting definitions of the term during the years that her book covers. She examines the development of feminism after 1900 and tracks its varied manifestations throughout the first three-quarters of the century. Banner distinguishes among four types of followers: radical feminists, militants, social feminists, and domestic feminists. These explanatory categories help trace the occasions when divisions within feminism as a movement worked against the furtherance of the cause of women generally.

To facilitate further research, Banner provides extensive bibliographies for each chapter. There are also reference notes for the quoted materials and the sources that she used. This apparatus makes the book particularly useful as a guideline for scholarship on women and accounted in part for the impact that the book had on other scholars writing about women during the 1970's and 1980's. Banner also sought to achieve a measured and balanced tone toward the events and people she was describing, achieving a high degree of success in that regard. The book also contains an abundance of drawings and contemporary photographs that illustrate Banner's text in a very effective way.

Analysis

From the outset of her narrative, Banner stresses that progress for American women occurred when pressure from women compelled changes in male attitudes. Men sometimes yielded portions of their privileged status, but the surest course to meaningful change was for women to assert themselves in politics, in the professions, and at home. Banner's assessment of the record for women during the 1890's indicates the mixed results that came from a reliance on male willingness to move in the direction of greater gender equality.

In dealing with the turbulent years between 1900 and 1920 that brought so many important changes for women, Banner first draws a historical profile of the condition of females in the United States during these two decades. This strategy enables her to examine the diversity of women's experiences in a chapter that blends equal parts of economic and social history. The section on prostitutes is notable for its sympathetic treatment of these women and for its dispassionate analysis of the forces that led them into that profession. Banner both anticipated and stimulated the growing body of feminist scholarship that treats prostitution and society's response to it as a means of understanding more general attitudes toward women.

The suffrage movement of the Progressive Era presents Banner with an occasion when women made up a significant element in the mainstream of national reform. While discussing suffrage activities in detail, she also shows how women became involved in myriad other social justice campaigns. Organized women, especially club women, sparked efforts to beautify cities, to create better conditions in schools, and to improve the quality of municipal government. Banner devotes particular attention to the importance of settlement houses such as Hull-House, operated by Jane Addams, in this reform process.

Amid this ferment, radical feminist ideas received a hearing. Banner examines the whole spectrum of opinion among the most advanced feminist thinkers, including

Margaret Sanger, Emma Goldman, and Charlotte Perkins Gilman. In the end, woman suffrage provided a rallying point for many female reformers. Banner argues that the cause of suffrage required both the middle-class tactics of Carrie Chapman Catt of the National American Woman Suffrage Association and the more confrontational approach of Alice Paul and the Woman's Party. The text also explores how the bright promise of the suffrage campaign did not lead to the further gains for women that its more enthusiastic advocates had anticipated.

After the tumult of winning suffrage, the thirty years that followed brought setbacks and difficulties for American women. Banner traces the breakup of political unity among women after 1920 and the fragmented response of many female groups to the challenges of the new decades. The greater emphasis on home, family, and female beauty indicated to Banner a return of antifeminist attitudes to a place of dominance in society. The "flaming youth" of the 1920's expressed more interest in pleasure than social causes. For Banner, the whole decade represented a series of missed opportunities for women.

The Great Depression and World War II brought new forces that changed the situation of American women without disturbing the society's underlying assumptions about masculine superiority. The New Deal addressed some concerns about the conditions of women in the workplace during the 1930's, but not as part of any feminist agenda. Similarly, World War II produced opportunities for women to enter the labor force, but only while men were away fighting. Banner's exploration of the effects of the Depression and world conflict in this book contributed to an enhanced awareness among historians of the importance of the period between 1920 and 1945. *Women in Modern America* thus proved to be a stimulus to other historians to explore more fully this previously neglected phase of women's history in the United States.

The rise of modern feminism began during the period after the end of World War II, and this significant change in the attitudes of women in the United States forms the natural climax of Banner's narrative. The process of militancy began slowly in the late 1940's and into the 1950's because traditional values toward men had reasserted themselves after the end of the war. In the postwar decade, American society emphasized home life and domesticity; feminist issues accordingly receded for a time.

The more reformist social climate of the 1960's provided a context for a reawakening of feminist ideas. Betty Friedan's *The Feminine Mystique* (1963) alerted its readers to the discrimination that women still faced and delivered a powerful challenge to Freudian ideas about a woman's proper role. Meanwhile, the Civil Rights movement and the protests against the war in Vietnam fostered a new generation of feminist activism among women who had marched and worked in these other causes. New groups such as the Women's Political Caucus and the National Organization for Women (NOW) appeared. Banner concludes with a survey of feminism and its achievements during the 1970's. She found it encouraging that feminism had not faded away in a single generation, as it had during the Progressive Era, but she could not forecast where the struggle for female equality and opportunity would lead during the remainder of the twentieth century.

Context

Textbooks do not usually have a large effect on the direction of scholarship in their subject field. That is not the case, however, with Lois Banner's volume. Her ability to summarize the state of existing knowledge about women in the twentieth century in clear prose with relevant examples made the book a favorite with instructors in women's history courses. Banner's suggestions about further research and opportunities for new inquiries also encouraged graduate students to mine her text for potential dissertations and articles.

Decades after its publication, *Women in Modern America* also stands out for its prescience in identifying broad areas where historians would do constructive work. Banner's section on prostitution in the Progressive Era was a harbinger of numerous monographs and articles on this controversial topic. Banner also pointed the way toward the intense interest about the activities of women during the 1920's and 1930's that has characterized writing about women's history since the mid-1970's. Textbooks often become dated soon after they are published, but Banner's book remains as fresh, thoughtful, and provocative as when it first appeared. It repays reading for the beginning student of women's history and the expert alike.

After *Women in Modern America*, her first book, Banner published a biography of Elizabeth Cady Stanton in 1979, an exploration of the importance of appearance in *American Beauty* (1983), and a book on women and aging called *In Full Flower: Aging Women, Power, and Sexuality* (1992).

Sources for Further Study

Banner, Lois W. *In Full Flower: Aging Women, Power, and Sexuality*. New York: Alfred A. Knopf, 1992. Banner's more recent work offers an opportunity to see how her thinking about women and feminist issues has evolved since the publication of *Women in Modern America* in 1974.

Chafe, William. *The Paradox of Change: American Women in the Twentieth Century*. Rev. ed. New York: Oxford University Press, 1991. Chafe first published his history of American women in the twentieth century in 1972. This revised and updated volume can be used to contrast how two scholars approach what are essentially the same type of historical issues.

Evans, Sara. *Born for Liberty: A History of Women in America*. New York: Free Press, 1989. This overview of the whole history of women in the United States offers a good basis for comparison with Banner's treatment of the period between 1890 and the 1970's.

Hartmann, Susan. *From Margin to Mainstream: American Women and Politics Since 1960*. New York: Alfred A. Knopf, 1989. One of a series of brief narratives on key decades during the twentieth century, Hartmann's book offers a more detailed examination of the period covered in the last chapters of Banner's text.

Kerber, Linda K., and Jane De Hart Mathews, eds. *Women's America: Refocusing the Past*. 3d ed. New York: Oxford University Press, 1991. A collection of documents and essays about women in American history, this text provides an indication of the direction that more recent scholarship on women has taken.

Kessler-Harris, Alice. *Out to Work: A History of Wage-Earning Women in the United States*. New York: Oxford University Press, 1982. This book indicates how the study of women in the workforce evolved during the decade after Banner's book was first published.

Rosenberg, Rosalind. *Divided Lives: American Women in the Twentieth Century*. New York: Hill and Wang, 1992. Rosenberg deals with the same issues as Banner does, but her interpretations reflect the impact of feminist scholarship in the two decades since Banner's work first appeared.

Sklar, Kathryn Kish, and Thomas Dublin, eds. *Women and Power in American History: A Reader*. Vol 2. Englewood Cliffs, N.J.: Prentice Hall, 1991. This volume, which begins with 1870, is a useful collection of scholarly essays that illuminates many of the issues that Banner treated in her overview of the twentieth century American woman.

Lewis L. Gould

THE WOMEN OF BREWSTER PLACE

Author: Gloria Naylor (1950-   )
Type of work: Novel
Type of plot: Social realism
Time of plot: The 1960's, with flashbacks to the 1930's
Locale: Brewster Place, an African American inner-city neighborhood
First published: 1982

Principal characters:

MATTIE MICHAEL, a middle-aged woman from Tennessee who is like a mother to the residents of Brewster Place

ETTA MAE JOHNSON, Mattie's best friend, who has pursued worthless men

KISWANA BROWNE, an activist college dropout, the daughter of a wealthy suburban family

LUCIELIA ("CIEL") LOUISE TURNER, a sort of foster daughter to Mattie

CORA LEE, a woman who loves babies, but not children

LORRAINE and THERESA ("TEE"), a lesbian couple

BEN, the old, alcoholic janitor who drinks to forget his faithless wife and lame daughter

Form and Content

Like modernist author Sherwood Anderson's *Winesburg, Ohio* (1919), *The Women of Brewster Place* is unified by locale (an inner city in the North), and Gloria Naylor uses individual chapters to focus on the lives and affairs of one or two characters. The themes of love and loss, trust and betrayal, hope and despair all help to unify the plot and characterization in a visually appealing portrait of the hard lives and gentle strength of seven black women in the 1960's.

Each character sketch begins with the present circumstances in which the woman finds herself, and then flashbacks of a few weeks, years, or even decades reveal each character's story of love and loss. Mattie, the matriarchal figure of Brewster Place, was the darling of her old father, who wished to protect her from men but who beat her savagely with a broom handle when she refused to reveal the man who impregnated her. Like the other women in this book, Mattie's only fault is loving too much, trusting the lies of the man she loves. In almost every case, erotic love between men and women leads inevitably to illegitimate children, poverty, abuse, abandonment, and despair. Men are shown as lazy, cowardly, and brutal characters whose only joys are hard liquor or drugs, love affairs with women, and violence. The women are shown in a slightly more sympathetic light, but some of them, too, are revealed as equally culpable and willing victims of their abusive men. Even the lesbian couple, Lorraine and Tee, who have no interest in men, seek some tolerance from the other black women who themselves are victims of racism and sexism. They, too, become the victims of prejudice and brutality.

Although each woman has a different story to tell, like the people of *Winesburg, Ohio* they are all alienated from God, nature, one another, and themselves. Their only hope is the love that each woman has for the others. Ultimately, Naylor claims, it is women who are victimized by ignorance, violence, and prejudice, and even love. Together, however, women can reject the first three and hold out for appropriate objects of love. It is only when people's safe little world is shaken by the dark evil of violence that they care enough to take back what is theirs. Change can only come from within.

Yet one should not ignore the positive images that also appear in *The Women of Brewster Place*. Every woman has at least one other person whom she loves selflessly and unconditionally, and when faced with the horrors of modern life, such as the death of a child or the loss of a lover, the women come together with kindness, generosity, and the strong spirit of African American women. There is a gentle yet unshakable will that refuses to be destroyed by betrayal, loss, and violence.

Analysis

Brewster Place is a dead-end street in fact and in symbol, for the women who move there are trapped by their hopes and fears. For them, Brewster Place is both the birth and the death of their dreams. The brick wall that separates Brewster Place from the nicer neighborhoods represents the wall of prejudice and shame, racism and sexism that must be smashed by the residents. They alone can effect change in this climate of hostility and mistrust. The garbage in the alley symbolizes the character of the street toughs who run drugs, rape, and kill here. No one can stop them until the women on Brewster Place join forces and souls to fight back courageously against the human trash terrorizing their neighborhood.

Despite the violence in these women's lives, the language that Naylor uses is as potent and engaging as poetry—colorful and provocative, realistic but not bitter. Thus critics praise Naylor's style, even as some suggest that hers is not a new story. Her characters are as archetypal as the characters of Porgy and Bess in George Gershwin's 1935 black opera, as William Bradley Hooper claims, but they are also convincing and vivid, according to Anne Gottlieb.

Some suggest that Naylor's characters are too stereotypical or flat. For example, many male critics have complained about the totally negative images of black men in *The Women of Brewster Place*, the same complaint made about Alice Walker's *The Color Purple* (1982). Still others comment that Kiswana, the young activist, and the two lesbians, Lorraine and Tee, are undeveloped characters. Since early in the novel these are the only women who have not been the victims of heterosexual affairs, Naylor has been accused of failing to present black women in successful love relationships. The climactic gang rape of Lorraine reflects Naylor's theme of male violence directed at women, and the women's response—their togetherness in tearing down the wall of Brewster Place (in Mattie's dream, anyway)—underscores the difference between the sexes in terms of reactions to their environment. It is this remarkable, hope-filled ending that impresses the majority of scholars.

The book is to a certain extent a political treatise on the effects of poverty, ignorance, and violence, but it is also a love story. Yet it is not a love story in the traditional sense: There is no romance between men and women except that which ends in disappointment or tragedy, such as Ciel's love for her husband and the needless death of their only child. Maternal love is also thwarted. Mattie's sacrifice for her son, her thirty years of drudgery to give him a decent home and the opportunity that she was denied, means no more to him than a quick drink or a senseless bar fight. In Cora Lee, one sees the other end of despair, for she deserts her children emotionally, which is as devastating as Ciel's or Mattie's losses.

Yet despite poverty, fatigue, desperation, and suspicion, the women of Brewster Place hold one another in heartfelt love and care. It is not *eros* (romantic love) but the selfless *philia* (friendship love), described by fifth century B.C. Greek philosopher Plato and recommended by feminist writers Mary Wollstonecraft and Charlotte Perkins Gilman, that these women experience and in which they revel. Their friendship teaches them to survive. One cannot live without loss; it is the human condition. Naylor shows, however, that for women—and black women in particular—survival comes from the courage and support of those who share pain and anguish and yet also share the triumph of the human spirit, from families created not by genes and blood and law but by the heart and soul.

Context

As Naylor's first novel, the award-winning *The Women of Brewster Place* brought her into the realm of serious critical interest. She went on to publish *Linden Hills* (1985) and *Mama Day* (1987), which deal with black men and women struggling with the American Dream or being torn between black mysticism and the lure of the big city. Neither of these books met with as much praise as *The Women of Brewster Place*, although most critics commended Naylor's talent.

Naylor is accepted as a major contemporary writer, and scholars agree that her language is clear but gritty, like the people whom she portrays, and that her imagery is evocative and her vision consistent and believable. Some say that she is in accord with the realism of her contemporaries, black women authors Alice Walker and Toni Morrison, but that the extent of her talent has yet to be proven.

In interviews and speeches on college campuses, Naylor has repeated the story of her "traditional" schooling, of her love of reading, of coming-of-age in the revolutionary 1960's and being unaware that blacks wrote novels until she was twenty-six, when she was first introduced to literature written by and about African Americans. To those who take for granted the presence of multicultural emphases in the classroom, Naylor's story seems as unbelievable as the tales of separate drinking fountains, restrooms, and restaurants for whites and blacks that existed until the Civil Rights movement and Supreme Court decisions revolutionized race relations in the United States. It is important to recall these realities when considering the impact of *The*

Women of Brewster Place on Americans, regardless of race, gender, age, or sexual orientation.

The fact that *The Women of Brewster Place* was translated to a television film in 1989 starring Oprah Winfrey, who was also executive producer and who ensured that the film was a clear, accurate depiction of the book, suggests the popularity of the novel. More important, however, it reveals the significant impact Naylor's portrait of black urban women has had on the reading and viewing public. The favorable reception given the motion picture helped increase sales of the book to the general public, and Naylor's works have joined those of other black writers in college literature courses.

In many ways, *The Women of Brewster Place* may prove to be as significant in its way as Southern writer William Faulkner's mythic Yoknapatawpha County or Sherwood Anderson's *Winesburg, Ohio*. It provides a realistic vision of black urban women's lives and inspires readers with the courage and spirit of black women in America.

Sources for Further Study

Branzburg, Judith V. "Seven Women and a Wall." *Callaloo* 7, no. 2 (Spring/Summer, 1984): 116-119. Branzburg broaches the politically explosive topic of black women who write negatively, although truthfully, about black men and places Naylor in the company of such serious writers as Toni Morrison and Toni Cade Bambara. She praises the "rich, sensuous, rhythmic language" and "sense of reality" in *The Women of Brewster Place* and its effort to show the importance of individual responsibility to women who seek independent lives.

Gomez, Jewelle. "Naylor's Inferno." *The Women's Review of Books* 2, no. 11 (August, 1985): 7-8. An analysis of Naylor's second novel, *Linden Hills*, which concerns blacks who have achieved the financial and political success only dreamt of by the residents of Brewster Place. Linden Hills is the middle-class suburb from which Kiswana, the young activist of *The Women of Brewster Place*, came. Comparing the two novels, Gomez discusses Naylor's use of Italian Renaissance poet Dante Alighieri's *Inferno* as symbolic of the evils of greed, power, madness, and racism (even among blacks, some of whom favor lighter skin). The writer criticizes Naylor's confusion of time periods in both novels but praises her talent.

Hooper, William Bradley. Review of *The Women of Brewster Place*. *Booklist* 78, no. 19 (June 1, 1982): 1300. A review that praises Naylor's conviction, beautiful style, and characterization, which Hooper finds believable and without bitterness.

Jones, Robert. "A Place in the Suburbs." *Commonweal* 112, no. 9 (May 3, 1985): 283-285. Compares *Linden Hills* to *The Women of Brewster Place* in terms of Naylor's recognition of the symbolic foundation and effects of geography on the human heart and mind, as well as the corruption that results from loss of memory. Both works are connected in terms of the strength of spirit and belief in invincibility so common to Americans, black or white. Yet for Naylor, it is family, not land or culture, that is the psychic center for African Americans.

Wickenden, Dorothy. Review of *The Women of Brewster Place*. *The New Republic* 187, no. 10 (September 6, 1982): 37-38. Compares the novel to Alice Walker's *The Color Purple*, in terms of both books' negative images of black men. Wickenden claims that Naylor goes beyond a mere celebration of "female solidarity" to focus on the importance of redemption and maternal love.

Linda L. Labin

WOMEN, WORK, AND FAMILY

Author: Louise A. Tilly (1930-   ) and Joan W. Scott (1941-   )
Type of work: History
Time of work: 1700-1950
Locale: Great Britain and France
First published: 1978

> *Principal personages:*
> MICHAEL ANDERSON, a social historian
> ANNIE BESANT, a late nineteenth century British birth control
>   advocate
> FREDERICK LePLAY, a French sociologist
> IVY PINCHBECK, a women's historian

Form and Content

As the authors acknowledge, the effect which paid employment has on women and on the family is an old problem, but one which was still unresolved at the time they decided to write *Women, Work, and Family.* Some historians, such as Alice Clark, believed that industrial capitalism was responsible for the exclusion of women from paid employment, and thus played a crucial role in modern women's oppression. Others, including Ivy Pinchbeck, insisted that the Industrial Revolution increased women's employment opportunities and therefore was a liberating factor. Louise A. Tilly and Joan W. Scott seek to resolve this dispute by examining the impact of industrialization on female employment and on the family in Great Britain and France between 1700 and 1950.

Women, Work, and Family is divided into three parts. Part 1 examines the family economy in early modern France and Great Britain. Part 2 considers the family economy during the Industrial Revolution in those two countries. The third part traces the development of what Tilly and Scott call the family consumer economy in the period after the Industrial Revolution. Each part examines the nature of women's work, the demographic forces shaping women's lives, and the relationship between women's paid labor and women's position in the family. Twenty-four pages of notes and a nine-page bibliography enable the reader to evaluate the sources used by the authors and provide a useful guide for those who wish to do further reading on the subject.

Drawing upon the work of demographers, economists, and anthropologists, Tilly and Scott use a social-science approach to their subject rather than a traditional chronological narrative. As a result, the authors rely on aggregate statistical data to demonstrate changes in such areas as fertility rates, age at first marriage, wage rates, and the growth of women's employment in specific industries. The primary focus of the book is thus on the material structures that shaped women's lives; there is little about women's attitudes toward these developments or the cultural forces that affected their lives. By concentrating on ordinary women of the lower middle class and working class, the authors avoid the pitfall of making broad generalizations based upon the experiences of a small number of exceptional middle-class women.

Women, Work, and Family is a scholarly study which breaks new ground in directing attention to the social and economic environment within which women lived during this period. It makes use of new approaches used by social scientists, such as the concept of the life cycle, in explaining women's distinctive reaction to economic and social modernizing forces. Its strength lies in identifying the long-term economic and social trends that transformed women's lives. Indeed, one of the goals of the authors is to create a model of how work and family interact at different stages of industrialization which will apply to any society going through that process.

Analysis

Although they avoid the male-centered point of view of most previous studies by male labor historians, Tilly and Scott adopt the tone of objective social scientists rather than writing from a woman-centered or feminist perspective. *Women, Work, and Family* can perhaps most accurately be described as an attempt to apply the new social history to working women, rather than being what came to be viewed as women's history in the decade after it was published. While the extensive use of social-science concepts and language gives the work an authoritative tone, women's voices are rarely heard and it infrequently mentions individual women.

Tilly and Scott maintain that throughout the period under study most adult women married, and thus their experience with paid employment varied according to the type of family economic system that was dominant at a given point in time. In the preindustrial period, the family economy shaped women's productive and reproductive roles. Because production took place within the home, women were able to participate in productive labor. Since their contribution was essential to the family's economic survival, married women exercised greater authority within the family at this time than in later periods.

The authors suggest that the Industrial Revolution undermined this crucial economic foundation for women's status within the family by bringing about the separation of home and work. Although contemporaries believed that the factory system of production greatly increased women's employment opportunities, Tilly and Scott maintain that work, in the sense of paid employment, increasingly became a male role, while married women tended to engage in unpaid domestic duties. When married women did enter into paid employment, however, they usually did so in response to family economic needs rather than for individual advancement. Consequently, the authors refer to this stage as the family wage economy.

After World War I, a third family type emerged: the family consumer economy. It implied that families had risen above a subsistence standard of living and had surplus income to spend for consumer goods. Married women were now expected to become consumer experts able to make wise choices between competing brands of products. The authors view this as a positive development for wives in the sense that their role as the manager of family money was becoming more significant than their role as wage earner. Because they had fewer children, and thus spent fewer years preoccupied with child rearing, women's employment levels rose in this period. The authors stress, however, that when married women entered paid employment in this period, they still did so primarily to provide consumer goods or education for other family members.

Women, Work, and Family altered interpretations of women's work in several respects. In contrast to those who believed that industrialization substantially increased the level of women's employment in the nineteenth century, Tilly and Scott suggest that it resulted in reduced employment for women; it was only in the twentieth century that women's employment levels rose significantly. In addition, the authors undermine claims that women entered into employment for individual or self-centered reasons. They indicate that throughout the nineteenth and twentieth centuries, most women worked in order to provide financial support for their families. Thus, whereas others have assumed that industrialization meant radical changes in the proportion of women who worked and their motives for doing so, Tilly and Scott build a strong case for emphasizing the continuities in women's work.

In an important final chapter, the authors demonstrate that women's workforce participation after World War II was strikingly different from that in the early twentieth century. This was not simply a matter of higher levels of female employment, but a change in the composition of the female labor force involving a much higher proportion of married women working. Tilly and Scott reject the assumption that this change was attributable to World War II. Instead, they suggest demographic explanations: The supply of young single women had been reduced by the falling birth rate in the 1930's, by the increase in the postwar marriage rate, and by the reduction in the age at first marriage. The pool of young single women available for employment was also reduced by the raising of the age at which they left school.

Women, Work, and Family attracted considerable attention because it raised large questions and attempted to provide a new paradigm for the history of women workers in the modern period. Yet in some respects the authors' interpretation has drawn criticism. Their claim that industrialization brought a substantial reduction in married women's employment in the nineteenth century is based on census records that are now known to be misleading. Tilly and Scott deliberately excluded discussion of women's consciousness from their study. One result of this materialist approach is that one learns little about what women thought about the way in which they were treated. There is also surprisingly little about women's involvement in the workers' organizations that attempted to bring about change; those who rely solely upon *Women, Work, and Family* will be unaware that many women joined trade unions and political parties in an attempt to improve their conditions as workers.

Context

Women, Work, and Family is considered a classic in the field of women's history because it effectively undermined the modernization model that portrayed industrialization as leading to women's emancipation. It presents convincing evidence of the strong continuity in working-class women's participation in the labor force during the two centuries prior to 1950. Throughout this period, most married women worked to provide financial assistance to other family members, rather than for their own individual interests. The authors also show that the typical female wage earner of the nineteenth century was not the relatively highly paid factory worker but someone who worked in areas, such as domestic service, that had been considered women's work for centuries.

Sources for Further Study

Bradley, Harriet. *Men's Work, Women's Work*. Minneapolis: University of Minnesota, 1989. A sociological account which examines the theories about why work is gendered, followed by case studies of the sex segregation of jobs in several industries. Bradley suggests that the most important feature of women's paid employment is that women are invariably relegated to "women's jobs" and thus limited in what they are permitted to do.

John, Angela V., ed. *Unequal Opportunities: Women's Employment in England, 1800-1918*. Oxford, England: Basil Blackwell, 1986. A collection of essays on different aspects of women's employment between 1800 and 1918 written from the perspective of the women who worked. The authors reinforce Tilly and Scott's thesis about the continuity of women's employment roles by demonstrating in detail how this was accomplished in specific industries.

Lewis, Jane. *Women in England, 1870-1950: Sexual Divisions and Social Change*. Bloomington: Indiana University Press, 1984. An overview of the changes in women's lives from 1870 to 1950 which pays special attention to the impact of economic and demographic forces. Although sensitive to class and other differences that separated women, Lewis views women as a gender group living in a man-made world.

Roberts, Elizabeth. *A Woman's Place: An Oral History of Working-Class Women, 1890-1940*. Oxford, England: Basil Blackwell, 1984. An important study of working-class women in Lancashire which makes good use of interviews. Roberts stresses the power that women wielded within their families, and she finds that they define emancipation as being able to leave paid employment, rather than in terms of employment opportunities outside the home.

_____. *Women's Work: 1840-1940*. London: Macmillan, 1988. Perhaps the best brief summary of the contemporary state of knowledge on women's work from the mid-nineteenth century to World War II. While acknowledging the gains in women's employment opportunities, Roberts stresses the sex segregation of jobs that restricted women to lower-paid positions.

Rose, Sonya O. *Limited Livelihoods: Gender and Class in Nineteenth-Century England*. Berkeley: University of California Press, 1992. Makes extensive use of theory in constructing a sociological account of working-class women's work during the period of industrialization. Noted for its use of gender analysis in demonstrating how cultural forces shaped women's perceptions of class and gender relations.

Walby, Sylvia. *Patriarchy at Work*. Minneapolis: University of Minnesota Press, 1986. A sociological study of the way in which patriarchy shapes capitalism through a historical account of women employed in three industries: cotton textiles, engineering, and clerical work. Whereas other authors have claimed that patriarchal relations in the workplace reflected patriarchal family structures, Walby argues instead that patriarchy and capitalism are in conflict with each other.

Harold L. Smith

THE WOMEN'S ROOM

Author: Marilyn French (1929-   )
Type of work: Novel
Type of plot: Bildungsroman
Time of plot: The 1950's to the 1960's
Locale: New Jersey; Cambridge, Massachusetts; and the coast of Maine
First published: 1977

Principal characters:

MIRA, a woman disillusioned with wifehood, motherhood, and
   suburbia who searches for friendships among women
NORM, Mira's former husband, known as the Great God Norm
BEN VOLER, Mira's lover
NATALIE, one of Mira's suburban friends, married to Hamp, a
   boyish man
ADELE, one of Mira's suburban friends, unhappily married to Paul
SAMANTHA, one of Mira's suburban friends, married to the
   unemployed Simp
LILY, one of Mira's suburban friends, married to Carl, who
   abuses her
MARTHA, one of Mira's suburban friends, in an "open" marriage
VALERIE, one of Mira's Harvard friends, with a liberated sexual
   identity
AVA, one of Mira's Harvard friends, a frustrated ballet dancer
CLARISSA, one of Mira's Harvard friends, unhappily married to
   Duke
KYLA, one of Mira's Harvard friends, unhappy with Harley
ISO or ISOLDE, one of Mira's Harvard friends, a lesbian

Form and Content

   The Women's Room features a cover in which the word "Ladies'" is crossed out,
renaming the "Ladies' Room" toilet at Harvard University and, symbolically, challenging the rigid gender roles assigned to females in modern America. The title also
comically evokes the title of one of Marilyn French's feminist mentors, Virginia
Woolf, whose earlier masterpiece *A Room of One's Own* (1929) proclaimed women's
androgynous right to economic independence. Like Woolf, French creates an autobiographical voice that takes the reader on a mental journey that inquires into the theme
"what women want."
   This mid-twentieth century *Bildungsroman* is a long novel which has been called
shapeless and unplotted, but in fact its contents are carefully structured. In form, the
novel consists of six units. The opening describes thirty-eight-year-old Mira hiding in
the toilet and her new Harvard milieu, introducing the themes of gender relations,

personal freedom, and men problems. The second section flashes back to her earlier life, motherhood, and frustrating friendships with suburban women. The third unit traces the vicissitudes of Mira's marriage to Norm, ending with his request for a divorce. The fourth is a meditation on sin and civil rights that leads away from her suicide attempt and toward the "ideal" lover, Ben Voler. The fifth section follows the decline of her Harvard relationships, which are pried away from Mira. In the concluding epilogue, Mira reveals herself to be the autobiographical narrator of her life's story and identifies herself as a solitary beach walker in Maine.

Another way of viewing the novel's form is to see it as a comparison and contrast between two sociologically different American environments: the suburban enclave, whether for struggling young couples or middle-class success stories; and the academic environs of Cambridge, Massachusetts, near Harvard University. However disparate on the surface, underneath these two distinctive "cultures" turn out to be the same place, one in which men and women are incompatible. The novel's narrator and her friends passionately debate why this should be so. Why are women conditioned to be dependent upon men? How is it that women, in fact, grow away from men and become mothers whose lives revolve around their children? *The Women's Room* explores women's innocent disbelief in these problems, as well as men's possessive power. Yet the interactions between the sexes, regardless of age or marital status, turn out in the novel to be as enervating for women at Harvard as they are in America's gray suburbs.

French chose these themes and organizing devices partly from the validation that they receive from her own life experiences. French was divorced in 1957 and attended Hofstra College in the 1960's and Harvard University in the 1970's, experiences drawn upon for this novel. Its content has often been called polemical, but readers have widely accepted the contemporary validity of French's characterizations of two cultures and her criticism of men's androcentric worldview. Fiercely full of life, and refusing to compromise, Mira's story is brilliantly accurate with its dialogue, characterizations, and knowledge of changing relationships between men and women over three decades and two generations.

This novel of ideas focuses on the grinding details of a woman's daily life. Its complexity is drawn from a diverse number of characters; French's experience as a Shakespeare scholar has taught her how to pattern an elaborated narrative with character clusters that reinforce thematic patterns. The novelist works to speak candidly to the reader, avoiding a sense of the narrator's superiority over a reader but nevertheless challenging the reader to think about the philosophical issues involved in choosing selfhood rather than servitude. Thus the novel's rhetorical strategy is to address the reader as an adult friend, in effect a member of the women's gatherings—a participant in the community of women, its sufferings and celebrations.

Analysis

Marilyn French's central intention is the stretching of readers' moral sense by making them think about and examine the unpleasant aspects of men's and women's relationships. Her portrait of the enculturation of a typical American girl in the 1950's is startling in terms of its protagonist's ordinariness. Mira, the girl who thinks the world will give her a beautiful view, is presented as an Everywoman who, like her many friends, suffers from America's gender dynamics. As in such earlier protesting tales as Sylvia Plath's *The Bell Jar* (1963), French propels an anguished girl into an unhappy adulthood. French widens and deepens the theme, however, by her insistence on a broad span of time and a wide panorama that replicates the pattern of female suffering. Called mad, oversexed, undersexed, boring, or stupid, such women either refuse to submit and be destroyed by insensitive men or are driven "over the line."

Yet French's first novel is not written as an antimale polemic; the narrator repeatedly pauses in her narrative to mull over questions about men's motivation and perceptions, how life must appear to them and hence the inevitability of their viewpoint. Mira herself is a producer of male "childflesh," the mother of sons whom she cherishes and hopes to make into androgynous gentlemen. Unlike their father, who cannot "equate the act" of sex with feeling, Mira tries to teach her boys that it is possible to grow into more than their father, her friends' husbands, or Barbie's Ken, "clean-cut and polite and blank." In fact, Mira is no reverse misogynist; she "distrusts generalized hatred" and faults Val for saying that "all men are the enemy" after she has been maddened by grief over her daughter's rape, both literally and then by the patriarchal system. Mira's more reasonable view is that men need emotional education; her long narrative insists that the American Dream must not "eradicate" women in order for them to become men's possessions. It is the unquestioned political and economic gender system which must be changed so that men will cease being the thoughtlessly superior group automatically deferred to by subordinate women.

French's novel galvanized readers in 1977 when the book was published. *The Women's Room* has been called as fictionally influential as *The Feminine Mystique* (1963), Betty Friedan's study of domestic discontent. Against the background of a chaotic period in American history—the Civil Rights movement, assassinations, the Vietnam War, the peace movement, the Kent State shootings—French goes beyond other tales of women's suffering. She draws readers because of her creation of a visionary women's community, laid out against a philosophically argued background, that appeals to thoughtful analysis and humane justice. Rebutting the wide and common assumption that American women dislike one another, she presents a different reality: They need and enjoy one another's support, but they often fail to live up to its ideal. Their "jiggling moments" of intense and complete human harmony may not be sustainable, but they are real. This is French's vision of community within the novel—maintained inadequately in suburbia, sustained temporarily in the graduate school enclave, and meditated upon in the author's seaside retreat at the novel's conclusion. Nevertheless, the narrator's commitment to "the dancing moments that were a person" is cultivated within a human community. Her learned mind assures the careful reader that much about men's and women's relationships fails because of historically shaped facts that have led the two sexes in America to become two incompatible cultures.

Though she never captures the secret of two human beings sharing "togetherness and separateness," Mira's refusal to meet men's goal of "adjustment" to their role's expectations leads her to analyze the problem in terms of women's training to be fairy-tale princesses. Her *Bildungsroman* rejects the beautiful "but not true" fairyland of suburban married life and offers the Maine coastline as a better "symbol of what life is all about." Women in the novel, such as Clarissa, dream of being Sleeping Beauty, Mummy and Daddy's "little princess" for whom whatever is wanted will be whisked in by the "good fairy's" wand. This character marries a Duke and is surely kissed, but it does not save her from the consequences of disempowerment. Mira learns that she and her various friends aren't "happy children playing ring-around-the-rosy."

As a corrective, the narrator cleverly suggests a rewriting of Virginia Woolf's tale of Shakespeare's sister in *A Room of One's Own*; this revision would show the creative Renaissance woman not being destroyed but marrying, becoming a mother, and surviving through the controls available in language. This is exactly what Mira herself does. She refuses to live by her mirror like the "queen in *Snow White*" and makes a commitment to "let the voices out," to "write it all down" and make sense out of it. Thus the narrator demythicizes women's lives, rejecting men's savior role. Mira adds, "What prince is going to cut through brambles to reach me? Besides they are mostly spurious princes." Mira still believes in the potential for a "corporation of the heart." Having survived fifteen years of marriage, a soap-opera life of suburban loneliness, and even the role of being the "Old Wise Woman of Cambridge" at the end of the novel, the protagonist's adult identity is based upon a recognition that no man—indeed, no person—can create one's mental health, which must be a consequence "of lowered expectations."

Context

Marilyn French calls *The Women's Room* a "collective biography" of a large group of American citizens. Her goal was to break the mold of conventional women's novels by presenting a pattern that weaves together and emphasizes the ordinariness of her suffering women characters. Her thesis is that women must accept life as a lonely chaos in which there is no foreseeable complementarity between men and women. In fact, French believes that women are more intimately bonded to their children than to men, that romance and lust are temporary conditions, and that candor on these issues is freeing.

Called a feminist classic, *The Women's Room* draws upon French's admiration for Simone de Beauvoir's *Le Deuxième sexe* (1949; *The Second Sex*, 1953). Her first novel provides a feminine perspective that rejects the positioning of women as the "other" or object in a world determined and controlled by men. Its explosive best-seller status is probably a consequence of its verisimilitude. The phenomenal popular success of *The Women's Room* in 1977 was dependent on American women's recognition of its central theme that women inadequately oppose men's possessive power; they innately value nonjudgmental nurturance.

Many ardent feminists may have been puzzled by a polemical novel that criticizes not only men but women as well; they have not treated the book as a marching banner. Its endorsement of motherhood left it standing alone, neither a conventionally conservative nor a radical text. Later women writers, such as Alice Walker in *The Color Purple* (1982) or Margaret Atwood in *The Handmaid's Tale* (1986), borrowed French's technique of developing a microcosm of American society and using it to illustrate gender disparities in power and their damning consequences for women. Sex segregation and the oppression of women have consequently become popular themes for women writers.

Preceded by such feminist thinkers as Woolf and Beauvoir, French is an anomaly, a distinguished academic scholar whose breakthrough best-seller brilliantly engages the reader who eagerly accepts her characters' reactions to life. Brimming with energy, this novel fiercely refuses to compromise. Perhaps it straddles the ideologies of middle-American women and feminists because French's depiction of women's plight is universalized by her diverse examples and because she shows women's problems with intimacy to be universal human experiences. There is no idealized woman-to-man bond or woman-to-woman bond in *The Women's Room*; rather, French proposes that women's dominant commitment is to rearing their children, a role that is the center of their lives. This is why Valerie's abandonment of her daughter Chris is treated as a tragedy in the novel. It also illustrates how French proposes to use her fiction to clarify human values of the past such as motherhood, working within accepted moral traditions to stretch readers' moral sense by reminding them about how the past continues to shape modern lives.

Sources for Further Study

Clarke, Betsy. *The Turmoils of Gender: Marilyn French and Mary Gordon*. Rockford, Ill.: Rockford Institute, 1982. An interesting discussion by two modern feminist writers about their respective literary treatments of what some have called "the longest war."

French, Marilyn. "The Emancipation of Betty Friedan." In *Fifty Who Made the Difference*. New York: Villard Books, 1984. Praises a feminist predecessor who opened the public dialogue about middle-class housewives' discontent in America during the 1960's.

_____ . "The Masculine Mystique." *Literary Review* 36 (Fall, 1992): 17-27. Complementing Betty Friedan's analysis of women's ambivalent power base in a female mystique, French considers the background of men's power base. She addresses the question of why she does not focus her fiction upon male characters and explains why men's unselfconscious, phallocentric worldview has its dangers.

_____ . "Self-Respect: A Female Perspective." *The Humanist* 46 (November/December, 1986): 18-23. A serious philosophical consideration of gender-based class superiority. French draws upon classical thinkers such as Aristotle to provide a background for her feminist analysis of self-respect. Feminism privileges pleasure for women, not power, she argues, and balances selfhood against the external world. Adults examine options and accept the consequences, including suffering. The essay concludes that adults know virtue is its own reward.

Homans, Margaret. " 'Her Very Own Howl': The Ambiguities of Representation in Recent Women's Fiction." *Signs* 9 (Winter, 1983): 186-205. Explores French's relationship to language in the context of other contemporary women novelists.

Wagner, Linda W. "The French Definition." *Arizona Quarterly* 38 (Winter, 1982): 293-302. Discusses how French's narrative voice in *The Women's Room* and *The Bleeding Heart* (1980) defines contemporary women's ideas concerning the societally induced role of women as sufferers who exempt men from the burden of suffering.

Sandra Parker

A WORLD OF LIGHT
Portraits and Celebrations

Author: May Sarton (1912-   )
Type of work: Memoir
Time of work: The first half of the twentieth century
Locale: The United States and Europe
First published: 1976

Principal personages:

GEORGE SARTON, May Sarton's father, a historian and scholar
MABEL ELWES SARTON, May Sarton's mother, an artist
CELINE DANGOTTE LIMBOSCH, Mabel Sarton's school friend and
    a lifelong friend of the family
EDITH FORBES KENNEDY, a friend from Sarton's years in
    Cambridge, Massachusetts
GRACE ELIOT DUDLEY, a friend Sarton met on a voyage to France
ALICE and HANIEL LONG, an American poet and his wife from
    Santa Fe, New Mexico
MARC TURIAN, a Swiss winemaker
ALBERT QUIGLEY, a painter and Sarton's neighbor in Nelson,
    New Hampshire
S. S. KOTELIANSKY, a London literary figure
ELIZABETH BOWEN, a British novelist
LOUISE BOGAN, an American poet
JEAN DOMINIQUE (MARIE CLOSSET), a French poet and Sarton's
    teacher for a year

Form and Content

May Sarton notes in her preface to *A World of Light: Portraits and Celebrations* that she carried this book in her mind for twenty years. Its purpose is to fill the gap in her autobiography between *I Knew a Phoenix* (1959), which covers her life from childhood to age twenty-six, and *Plant Dreaming Deep* (1968), which begins when she was forty-five. Sarton knew all the people described in the book by the time that she was forty, but by the time that she came to write the book, all but one were dead. The book is a joyful celebration of those deep and enduring friendships that shaped Sarton as a woman and as an artist. Its importance lies as much in what it reveals about her as in what it reveals about the friends whom she "celebrates."

The twelve portraits, each introduced by a photograph, are divided into four sections, based on a loose chronology. The first section contains descriptions of Sarton's parents, whom she had already sketched in *I Knew a Phoenix*. The most significant difference between the portraits is Sarton's acceptance of and reconciliation with her father, which came only late in her life. Significant friends from her early womanhood, Celine Dangotte Limbosch and Edith Forbes Kennedy, are the subjects of the second section. The third section groups together friends from different times in Sarton's life but is unified by the sense of place that rooted all four, a sense which Sarton acquired only with her own house in Nelson, New Hampshire. For the literary critic, the last section is the most important of the book for its intimate portraits of two famous women writers, Elizabeth Bowen and Louise Bogan, as well as the iconoclastic S. S. Koteliansky and the lesser-known French woman poet Jean Dominique.

The volumes that constitute Sarton's autobiography, which also includes *Journal of a Solitude* (1973), have been called a social history of a contemporary woman writer. Sarton pays little attention, however, to her own creative process other than to maintain her position that poems must be inspired by Muses, which for her are women with whom she has had an intense relationship. She voices her distress at being ignored or dismissed as sentimental by critics. Her purpose in writing the book is to deliver the "essence" of the characters and her relationship to them. Moreover, since Sarton's life has been an exercise in solitude and rootlessness, her friendships take on for her a deeper meaning. As she notes in the preface, every day she can trace the influence of one or another of the friends whom she describes.

On the whole, Sarton's attitude toward her subjects borders on adulation, yet she carefully acknowledges that the very nature of deep friendships requires tolerance and pain. The variety of the friends she celebrates, from a struggling Swiss winemaker to famous women poets and novelists, emphasizes Sarton's own compassion, acceptance, and ability to engage herself in meaningful relationships with people from all walks of life and all levels of society. The overwhelming theme in her friendships is her independence, diligence, love of art, admiration of intelligence, and sympathy for nature. Anyone possessing these qualities was readily made part of her circle of friends.

Analysis

As with Vera Brittain's *Testament of Youth* (1933), *Testament of Friendship* (1940), and *Testament of Experience* (1957), Sarton's memoirs transcend fact to present essential truth. Indeed, the volume *Plant Dreaming Deep*, marked by its extended narrative of single experience yet unified thematically and chronologically, transforms the genre. *I Knew a Phoenix* and *A World of Light* follow the more conventional form of discrete pieces, most of which were published individually in *The New Yorker*. While critics accepted the republication of these pieces in a collection, Sarton has been criticized for lifting verbatim from the first volume the pieces on Albert Quigley, her New Hampshire friend, and S. S. Koteliansky, her Russian mentor, and at the same time claiming in the preface that she has brought to the work fresh judgments and new insights.

A similar charge might be leveled against the portraits of her mother and father, since Sarton has already written of them in *I Knew a Phoenix*. Yet Sarton's depiction of their marriage—a marriage between an obsessive, self-centered, childlike husband

and a frustrated, thwarted, artistic wife—requires much distance and compassion; it reflects the anger and courage that Sarton herself has displayed throughout her career. The "informal" portrait of her father remains a unique combination of intuitive insights and rich detail.

The portraits of the middle two sections emphasize Sarton's remarkable talent for establishing friendships. The descriptions of Sarton's two early friends, Celine Dangotte Limbosch and Edith Forbes Kennedy, acknowledge her need for stability, understanding, appreciation, and encouragement in her early years during the awakening of her sexuality and her first attempts at writing poetry. Limbosch was the closest friend of Sarton's mother; she cared for Sarton as a child during the pastoral early years in Belgium before her family was uprooted by war. Limbosch's intense love for Sarton's mother made her capable of understanding Sarton's own passionate attachments to other women. Their friendship and Limbosch's home in Belgium, which Sarton visited almost yearly, remained the only absolute continuity in Sarton's nomadic life. Edith Kennedy was a similar anchor for Sarton in Cambridge, Massachusetts, where Sarton's family finally settled. This friendship, marked by the shared love of music and conversation, made possible Sarton's early poetry.

In the middle section of four portraits, Sarton attempts to create what she calls a Renaissance portrait, in which the subject is painted with an emblematic landscape in the background. Some have criticized these sketches as being too removed by time from the intensity of Sarton's experience, yet they contain some of the best examples of Sarton's effective and accurate descriptions of nature, as the Southwestern landscape in the piece on Haniel Long and the garden at Grace Eliot Dudley's estate Le Petite Bois. Perhaps the most charming portrait in the book is of Marc Turin, the impoverished Swiss winemaker whose family tenaciously held onto their vineyards for three hundred years. His time was spent equally between the real world of his grapevines and the imaginative world of the literature that he loved.

The final section, particularly the portraits of Elizabeth Bowen and Louise Bogan, reveals Sarton at her best as a memoirist. She illuminates the character of these two well-known writers while at the same time teaching the theme of the entire volume: that love and friendship are rare and costly experiences. Sarton met Bowen in London after the failure of Sarton's theatrical career when she was just beginning as a writer. Bowen had already attained renown, and she graciously took Sarton under her wing. After a one-night love affair, they settled into a long and artistically valuable friendship that Bowen ended abruptly, much to Sarton's dismay. Sarton describes Bowen as the witty, charming host of a literary circle which included Leonard and Virginia Woolf; Bowen was also happily married to a man who either did not know or did not care to know about his wife's affairs with both men and women. Sarton recognizes that the powerful tension that Bowen creates in her work springs from the turbulent personality hidden deep within the cool, placid social persona.

In the case of Bogan, the portrait that Sarton creates is of a fragile artist, held together by sheer force of will. Sarton's compassionate understanding of Bogan's fight against depression counteracts the impression that Sarton writes as a scorned lover who gave more than she received. Unlike the cruel ending to her relationship with Bowen, Sarton and Bogan remained friends until Bogan's death. Their remarkable friendship celebrated here is also recorded in their correspondence.

Context

May Sarton has often been criticized for her sentimentality and laxity of style. *A World of Light* has not escaped such censure. She suffers, too, from her essential readability in a literary climate that prizes the difficult and obscure. Her output, nevertheless, has been prolific; she published almost a volume a year for more than fifty years. Throughout her career, she has been one of the few self-supporting women writers of her time. Indeed, one aspect of her significance to women's literature is that she has persevered in the face of almost overwhelming obstacles.

In *A World of Light*, what some have seen as self-indulgence and self-pity can also be seen as the understandable self-doubt of a serious writer who had courageously given the best of herself only to be overlooked or discounted. Taken with the other volumes of her autobiography, *A World of Light* proves the strength of Sarton as a forthright person and a skilled memoirist. It is as much a celebration of the fulfillment possible for a solitary woman as a celebration of enduring friendships. Indeed, Sarton has persistently written of women who have chosen to face and even welcome their extraordinary feelings, their independent lives, their solitude.

Although a political liberal, as seen in her journals, Sarton has refused to align herself with any particular movement. She has written courageously of her sexuality and of her choice to live a solitary life in her autobiography and in her novel *Mrs. Stevens Hears the Mermaids Singing* (1965), yet to label her a feminist or a lesbian is to deny the universality of her themes. She is at once an idealist and a humanist, proving through her memoirs the value of the struggle inherent in love and friendship. Critical acclaim has come late to Sarton; however, it has come. She has received a Guggenheim Award and the Tidewater Prize, has been nominated for a National Book Award in both fiction and poetry, and has been awarded numerous honorary degrees.

Sources for Further Study

Anderson, Dawn Holt. "May Sarton's Women." In *Images of Women in Fiction: Feminist Perspectives*. Bowling Green, Ohio.: Bowling Green University Popular Press, 1972. While this essay analyzes only three of Sarton's novels—*The Small Room* (1961), *Mrs. Stevens Hears the Mermaids Singing*, and *Joanna and Ulysses* (1963)—the entire collection offers a variety of interesting background essays on various aspects of feminist literary criticism, many of a general nature such as those in the section "Feminist Aesthetics." The lengthy annotated bibliography includes sections on women writers before the twentieth century, twentieth century women, and works about literature.

Evans, Elizabeth. *May Sarton, Revisited*. Rev. ed. Boston: Twayne, 1989. A useful study organized by the genres in which Sarton has worked, the book includes an entire chapter on the journals and memoirs. The discussion of the influential friendship of Louise Bogan is particularly interesting. Evans includes an annotated bibliography.

Heilbrun, Caroline. *Hamlet's Mother and Other Women*. New York: Columbia University Press, 1990. This fascinating study by a foremost feminist critic contains two essays on Sarton, one a study of *Mrs. Stevens Hears the Mermaids Singing* and the other of her memoirs, including *A World of Light*.

Rule, Jane. *Lesbian Images*. London: Peter Davis, 1975. In the chapter on Sarton, Rule discusses two novels, *The Small Room* and *Mrs. Stevens Hears the Mermaids Singing*. She also gives useful information about Sarton's attitude toward her sexuality as seen through her novels.

Sibley, Agnes. *May Sarton*. New York: Twayne, 1972. Published before *A World of Light*, Sibley's is the first book-length study of Sarton's work. Provides good background discussions of the novels and poetry and an annotated bibliography of reviews of her work.

Jean McConnell

A WRINKLE IN TIME

Author: Madeleine L'Engle (Madeleine Camp, 1918-   )
Type of work: Novel
Type of plot: Fantasy
Time of plot: The future
Locale: The northeastern United States and the planets of Camazotz and Uriel
First published: 1962

Principal characters:

MEG MURRY, an awkward thirteen-year-old girl

CHARLES WALLACE MURRY, her younger brother

DR. MURRY, Meg and Charles's father, a brilliant scientist sent to the planet Camazotz

MRS. MURRY, his wife and the children's mother, a biologist and bacteriologist

SANDY and DENNYS, the Murry's ten-year-old twin sons

MRS. WHATSIT, MRS. WHO, and MRS. WHICH, three supernatural beings who enable the Murry children to journey to Camazotz

CALVIN O'KEEFE, Meg's friend, who accompanies her to Camazotz

AUNT BEAST, a furry, tentacled creature

IT, a huge, disembodied brain which controls the thinking of all people on Camazotz

Form and Content

A Wrinkle in Time is Madeleine L'Engle's story of a brother and sister who seek their father, who is imprisoned on the planet Camazotz. A fantasy novel for children, the work accentuates the power of women by casting thirteen-year-old Meg Murry as the protagonist and savior.

The government of the United States has sent Meg's father to Camazotz to rectify a moral evil blighting the minds and souls of the planet's inhabitants. On Camazotz (a possible play on "comatose"), the people are placidly content because they have no conflicts. Every thought and action of their daily lives is controlled by It, a disembodied brain that functions as the communal mind; there is neither opportunity nor desire for individuality. In short, the human beings of Camazotz have become little more than robots. Pain, an inherent part of being human, is denied them; in its place is the warm bliss of mindless "happiness." Because Dr. Murry is a threat to their "perfect" society, the administrators of Camazotz have taken him captive.

The Mrs. W's—Mrs. Whatsit, Mrs. Who, and Mrs. Which, supernatural beings who combat evil—commission Meg Murry and her brother Charles Wallace to accompany them to Camazotz, so that the children might rescue their father and see the spiritual decay that he has been fighting. After arriving on the planet, the children proceed to the CENTRAL Central Intelligence Building, where they find Dr. Murry imprisoned in a transparent marble column. With the aid of magic spectacles bestowed by Mrs. Which, Meg passes through the column and frees her father. Charles Wallace, however, unconsciously surrenders himself to the power of It. The sunny and tender-hearted little boy becomes hardened and surly, mocking the sister he once loved. Meg concludes that only her love for Charles Wallace can restore the child to himself. Her conviction is correct, for when she cries, "I love you!" her brother rushes into her arms. The story swiftly comes to an end as the children "tesser" (move quickly through time and space) back to the Murrys' garden, whence they departed less than five minutes earlier. Returning with the children, Dr. Murry receives his wife's embrace. Although he has been unable to restore human spirit to Camazotz, he will presumably work to keep Earth from slipping into a similar state, in which individual thought succumbs to "group think" and feeling is nonexistent.

As Dr. Murry has come to realize the flaws of a monolithic society, Meg arrives at a truth concerning the space age: that intelligence and scientific knowledge must not be allowed to overshadow the importance of human affection. When Charles Wallace falls under the spell of It—the unadulterated mind, free from muddling emotions—it becomes clear to his sister that without genuine connection to other people, he will degenerate to the robotic level of the Camazotzians. Therefore, Meg goes to his rescue with the strongest weapon that she possesses: love.

Analysis

L'Engle's primary audience consists of children in the elementary and middle grades, those to whom appearance and "fitting in" are of utmost importance. Her themes, therefore, offer these readers a different perspective.

The novel's foremost theme is the value of nonconformity. Neither Meg nor Charles Wallace fits the stereotype of the "typical" teenager or five-year-old. Charles Wallace's linguistic precocity and Meg's mathematical skills place them far above the norm, but because few people hear Charles Wallace's speech or see Meg's mind at work, the general public regards both children as odd and slightly subnormal in intellect. Recalling the years when her father was at home, Meg remembers referring to herself as "dumb." Dr. Murry corrected his daughter's self-assessment by reminding her that everyone develops at a different pace: She will eventually "catch on" to math (with the help of the shortcuts he promised to teach her), just as Charles Wallace (then a toddler) will learn to talk.

Later, when she visits Camazotz, Meg realizes the horror of life in a community where everyone is exactly like everyone else. On Camazotz, there is a "right" way to bounce a ball, a "right" time to turn on a light, a "right" way to think. It is this extreme conformity, supposedly affording security and happiness, that Dr. Murry has attempted to conquer. It is significant that his rescue is effected not by the supposedly well-rounded twins, Sandy and Dennys, but by his "different" children, Charles Wallace and Meg. The fact that the "strange" characters perform a major and positive function attests L'Engle's belief in the worth of individuality.

In *A Wrinkle in Time*, things are not always as they seem. Meg and Charles

Wallace's "slowness" is superficial. In addition, the Murrys' fellow townspeople assume that Dr. Murry has abandoned his wife, but both Mrs. Murry and Meg suspect—correctly—that he is on a secret mission involving grave danger. Even Mrs. Murry is likely to make quick judgments based on outer appearances. When Mrs. Whatsit arrives at the door in an array of ragged, mismatching sweaters and scarves, Mrs. Murry takes her for a bag lady. Her hasty assessment of her comically clad neighbor receives a jolt, however, when the latter calmly remarks that there is actually such a thing as a "tesseract." Far from being a simple squatter, Mrs. Whatsit is a supernatural being whose understanding exceeds that of the most gifted mortals.

While the Murry children seem to accept the Mrs. W's as benevolent helpers, some religious groups have attempted to ban *A Wrinkle in Time* on the grounds that these three ladies resemble witches. If readers look only at the W's outer appearance, this objection is justifiable; if they look at the characters behind the guises, however, it is without substance. It seems possible, in fact, that L'Engle has given the Mrs. W's a witchlike description in order to advance her theme of discrepancy between appearance and reality.

The purpose of the Mrs. W's in transporting the children to outer space is twofold: They wish to help them find their father and deliver him from the evil of Camazotz; and they intend to enlighten them—Meg in particular—to the worth of individuality. Even though her physical appearance is less attractive than she desires, Meg realizes from seeing the people of Camazotz that there is nothing enviable in being a copy of someone else. Thus the mission of the "witches" is essentially good.

Mrs. Whatsit tells the children that she and the other Mrs. W's are not the first to fight against evil; leaders, such as Jesus, have striven to elucidate minds clouded by ignorance and crippled by blind obedience to dictators of collective thinking. Furthermore, she and Mrs. Who frequently quote passages from the Old and New Testaments. Therefore, the appearance of the Mrs. W's notwithstanding, *A Wrinkle in Time* can be considered a Christian, rather than a satanic, novel.

Effective children's writers educate as they entertain. L'Engle indirectly introduces her audience to mathematics, physics, foreign languages, Greek mythology, and English literature. Assisting Calvin O'Keefe with his homework, Meg makes casual reference to algebraic and physical equations; Mrs. Who quotes lines from writings in Latin, French, and German; and Mrs. Whatsit assumes the form of a flying horse on which the children ride to their first stop in outer space, the planet Uriel. The horse is reminiscent of Pegasus, while L'Engle may have named the planet for the archangel of the sun in John Milton's *Paradise Lost* (1667, 1674). Through such references, L'Engle teaches her audience within the context of a quickly moving, suspenseful fantasy.

Context

A winner of the Newbery Award for children's literature, *A Wrinkle in Time* alters the pattern of many earlier juvenile novels by casting females as the leading and more effective characters. Yet the work upholds supposedly feminine characteristics, making it clear that these very characteristics enable Meg Murry to save her father and brother. When the children and Mrs. Whatsit arrive on Camazotz, Mrs. Whatsit tells Meg that her strongest assets are her "faults": her impatience, anger, and stubbornness—traits sometimes negatively attributed to women. Although Meg does not at first understand, she soon sees that Mrs. Whatsit is correct. While Calvin advises her to proceed slowly and cautiously in rescuing her father, Meg's impatience will not let her wait; it propels her—literally—through the marble column. Similarly, her anger at the overwhelming power of It makes her stubbornly determined that the brain will not consume the mind and soul of her brother. Finally, her love for Charles Wallace, based not on his intelligence but only on the child himself, saves the little boy.

Meg's love for Charles Wallace undoubtedly derives from the love and nurture that she herself receives from other females. Mrs. Murry, for example, always has time to be a mother, her intellectual interests notwithstanding. On Uriel, Mrs. Whatsit, in the guise of a flying horse, shelters frightened Meg under her wing. Aunt Beast holds and feeds her following her passage through the Dark Thing, an embodiment of evil, until she is strong enough to return to Camazotz. Thus, it is the maternal succor of females that gives Meg the power she needs for the job that she must perform; in turn, Meg's impetuosity and fierce, unconditional love save the male characters, who are helpless in the hands of their enemies. For all of his intelligence, Dr. Murry can neither effect his own escape nor save his son. Through her characters, then, L'Engle emphasizes the importance of maintaining "womanly" qualities.

Sources for Further Study

Friedan, Betty. *The Feminine Mystique*. New York: W. W. Norton, 1963. Explains that the frustration felt by many women of the 1950's derived from their lack of personal fulfillment. With her combination of science and motherhood, Mrs. Murry represents the "new" woman Friedan is urging others to become.

Harvey, Brett. *The Fifties: A Women's Oral History*. New York: HarperCollins, 1993. Discusses the family of the 1950's, supporting theories and general observations with concrete examples from case studies. It was a decade of great conformity, which may explain why people outside the Murry family often regarded the "strange" children with hostility.

Huck, Charlotte S., Susan Helper, and Janet Hickman. *Children's Literature in the Elementary School*. 5th ed. Fort Worth, Tex.: Harcourt, Brace, Jovanovich College Publishers, 1989. Contains discussions of *A Wrinkle in Time*, including the attempts to ban the work. The authors argue that L'Engle is a Christian writer.

Lukens, Rebecca J. *A Critical Handbook of Children's Literature*. 4th ed. Glenview, Ill.: Scott, Foresman, 1992. Details the characteristics of children's fiction and the components of plot, style, and characterization. Lukens distinguishes between strict science fiction and fantasy, explaining that the former concentrates on technology while the latter emphasizes the human element in a scientific world.

Rebecca Stingley Hinton

WRITTEN ON THE BODY

Author: Jeanette Winterson (1959-   )
Type of work: Novel
Type of plot: Picaresque
Time of plot: The late twentieth century
Locale: London and Yorkshire, England
First published: 1992

> *Principal characters:*
> THE NARRATOR, a professional translator, unnamed and of
>   unspecified gender
> LOUISE, the narrator's lover, who is dying of cancer
> ELGIN, Louise's husband, a physician who specializes in the
>   treatment of cancer
> JACQUELINE, the most recent of the narrator's former lovers, an
>   animal psychologist at a zoo
> ESAU and SARAH ROSENTHAL, Elgin's parents, Jewish shop
>   owners
> INGE, a Dutch "anarcha-feminist" and a former lover of the
>   narrator
> BATHSHEBA, a married dentist and a former lover of the narrator
> CRAZY FRANK, the giant son of midgets and a former lover of the
>   narrator
> BRUNO, a mover who finds Jesus while trapped under a
>   wardrobe, also a former lover of the narrator
> GAIL, the manager of a Yorkshire wine bar in which the narrator
>   temporarily works

Form and Content

Written on the Body is a meditation on the nature of sexual love and passion as experienced by the first-person narrator, whose name and gender are never revealed. The narrative's primary focus is on the absent Louise, the most recent and apparently most passionately adored of a series of lovers, both men and women. Details of these earlier affairs are interspersed throughout the novel as points of comparison to the all-consuming passion expressed for Louise. Alternately anguished and exhilarated, cynical and romantic, the monologue immediately establishes the circumstances of lost love, although why and how this loss came about is not revealed until later. The narrator addresses his/her thoughts and ruminations at times to the absent Louise, at others to the reader.

Witty and cynical accounts of former loves punctuate this mournful, elegiac remembrance. Readers are told about Inge, the "anarcha-feminist" who is also a committed romantic and a lover of beauty. She suffers at the thought of the damage that she may do to beautiful objects or innocent lovers when, as part of her crusade against patriarchal, phallocentric monuments, she blows up buildings. Because of her qualms, she eventually limits her terrorist activities to men's toilets, abetted by the narrator. There is Bathsheba, the married dentist who insists on keeping the affair clandestine and finally ends it in favor of her husband, causing her lover some temporary pangs of deprivation and longing. Other briefly mentioned lovers include Bruno, a mover who finds Jesus while trapped for hours under a fallen wardrobe, and Crazy Frank, the six-foot, "bull-like" son of midget parents. These are caricatures, described in broad, often humorous strokes, which provide contrast to the tragic and implicitly more real and enduring passion for Louise, who is described in minute detail.

The narrator is living with Jacqueline when he/she meets Louise. Jacqueline is described as comfortable but ordinary. The narrator draws an analogy between him/herself and the traumatized animals Jacqueline works with at the zoo. Jacqueline was chosen primarily as a calm harbor in which the narrator comes to rest after a series of emotionally and physically draining affairs. When confronted with the affair with Louise, Jacqueline is devastated. In her rage at being betrayed, she destroys the shared apartment before she leaves, an action which runs contrary to her earlier characterization. Louise meanwhile has left her husband, Elgin, and moved in with the narrator.

Shortly after this, about halfway through the novel, the narrator recalls the day that Elgin came to the house and revealed that Louise is dying of lymphocytic leukemia. In anguish, the narrator decides to leave London for Yorkshire without telling Louise in order to force her to return to Elgin, who can provide the best treatment for her illness. Reluctantly, Louise does return to Elgin, and they travel to Switzerland for her treatment.

The narrative format shifts at this point to a series of short analyses, clinical descriptions of various parts of the body and the diseases that can afflict them, which reads almost like an anatomy textbook. Within each section, the general becomes specific in references to Louise's body and the cancer that is destroying it. This section acts as a break in the time sequence of the novel. The first half is a reminiscence, a recollection of the past. The narrative following the anatomical section has more immediacy and tension, and it brings events up to the present with hints of a future that the earlier part lacked. Miserable without Louise, and prompted by the lecherous but compassionate Gail, who manages the Yorkshire wine bar in which the narrator has a temporary job, the narrator returns to London to find Louise. Elgin is contacted, and it is revealed that Louise has left her treatment, and him, and disappeared. In despair, the narrator returns to Yorkshire, only to find Louise—thin and pale, but alive—waiting. The novel ends here, in the present tense, in the form of a beginning: "This is where the story starts."

Analysis

Applying and mingling different influences and genres, most notably the romantic and the picaresque, *Written on the Body* presents a reflection, at once specific and universal, on romantic and sexual love. In purposefully refusing to reveal the narrator's gender, intentionally playing with the reader's preconceptions through the narrator's reference to him/herself at various times as a Boy Scout, a Lothario, or the girl in "Rumpelstiltskin," various effects are created. As some critics have observed, Jeanette Winterson implicitly presents the experience of romantic passion as universal, transcending gender.

Through this device, however, the novel also forces the reader to acknowledge the existence of sexual stereotypes based on gender. The male/female narrator has had lovers of both sexes, though predominantly with married women who presumably are, or were, essentially heterosexual. This presents a surprising variety of sexual possibilities. The whole tone and perception can change depending on whether the narrator is believed to be male or female. For example, the impulsiveness and self-indulgence admitted to by the narrator have different conventional interpretations depending on gender. Literary portrayals of similar male characters, such as the eponymous hero of Henry Fielding's *Tom Jones* (1749), tend to present this type of behavior with some indulgence, even envy—a kind of winking acquiescence to the naughty boy. The traditional feminine corollary is the femme fatale, but this type is conventionally portrayed as distinctly uncharming: a kind of black widow who heartlessly seduces and discards men and who herself usually meets a sticky end. Perceived as female, the narrator of *Written on the Body* does not fit this mold, not only because he/she is too witty and exuberant but also because the lovers are predominantly female, which presents a very different paradigm of sexual relationship. The effect is a continually disorienting and altered perspective on sexual and gender-based stereotypes.

Further uncertainty is created as the reader, addressed as a sort of confidant by the narrator, sees glimpses of flaws and omissions of which the narrator is guilty. One of the most noticeable episodes in which this occurs is in the account of Jacqueline. It is the mousy, comfortable Jacqueline who is seen graphically to be damaged by abandonment. Her character is discomfiting because of the lack of similarity to any of her predecessors, who appear to be as robust and sexually fickle as the narrator. The disapproval tinged with disdain that marks the narrator's description of Jacqueline's ordinariness and the casual account of her desperate and embittered departure reveal a less-than-sympathetic side of the narrator.

The title of the book refers, in part, to the novel's focus on self-discovery and expression through sexuality. A recurring theme in Winterson's work is the intermingling of identities of the loved one and the self, the discovery of self in and through the lover, which is strongly evident in *Written on the Body*. In a physical sense, the narrator observes that there is more similarity than difference between him/herself and Louise, and there are many references to a merging with and possession of Louise's body: "This is the body where [my] name is written." Yet the body is analyzed in a broader sense as well. It is recurringly viewed as the vessel of both life and death in the novel. Before the revelation of Louise's illness, her body is described in adoring and lyrical (if objectified) detail, the narrator savoring every part of it in the language of a lover. What is viewed as the instrument of intense pleasure and expression of love, however, is also later seen as the enemy, the self-betrayer turning against itself through disease. The language becomes more clinical and impassive.

Winterson has stated that George Gordon, Lord Byron is one of her heroes, and there is evidence of this influence in *Written on the Body*, in the narrator's energetic pursuit of intensity of feeling (both emotional and physical) in a variety of sexual experiences. He/she admits to an obsessional search for "ecstasy without end." The language, the tragic element, and the predicament of yearning for an unattainable lover are very much in the romantic tradition. Also resonant of the romantic sensibility is the undertone of luxuriant revelling in misery, corroborated by the narrator's admission of an addiction to passion, however tormented, and scorn for contentment. "Contentment is a feeling you say? Are you sure it's not an absence of feeling?" the narrator asks the reader rhetorically.

Context

Winterson published her first novel to immediate acclaim in the mid-1980's. Although she is both a lesbian and a feminist, the themes that Winterson explores are not limited to specifically lesbian or feminist issues, nor do they display any overt political posturing. It is through form rather than content that Winterson might arguably be seen to contribute a new voice and perspective to literature by women. The richness and value of her work comes through her freely employing and mingling many different styles and literary forms in her exploration of a variety of large themes—notably sexuality, gender, time, and freedom. All of her novels experiment with narrative form, creating disorienting shifts in time and character, the latter often presented as sexually ambiguous.

Her fourth novel, *Written on the Body* is considered by some critics to be a sequel to her first novel, *Oranges Are Not the Only Fruit* (1985), whose central character, Jeanette, bears a strong resemblance to Winterson herself and her own early life and experience as a lesbian. Winterson denies that either novel is autobiographical, although both, particularly the earlier novel, contain many possible correlations to her own experience. As if in direct response to this speculation, however, *Written on the Body* seems to both set up and then undermine it in the use of a possibly similar, but clearly fickle and unreliable, first-person narrator. Winterson seems to be teasing those who presume to associate the fictional character with the author.

Winterson's work defies any pigeonholing of genre or theme. It is her diversity that is viewed by many critics as her most important contribution to literature by women. In *Into the Mainstream: How Feminism Has Changed Women's Writing* (1989), Nicci Gerrard sees Winterson as walking in the footsteps of Angela Carter, sharing with her a boldness and breadth of imagination which allows them to leave the "woman's world" and "treat the whole world as their own."

Sources for Further Study

Anna, Gabriele. Review of *Written on the Body*. *The New York Review of Books* 40, no. 5 (March 4, 1993): 22. A long and extremely thorough review which gives as much attention to previous works, particularly *Oranges Are Not the Only Fruit*, as it does to the subject text. Also contains references to and comparisons with other authors and/or literary works and interesting biographical details about Winterson.

Gerrard, Nicci. *Into the Mainstream: How Feminism Has Changed Women's Writing*. London: Pandora Press, 1989. A good survey of the social and political climate of the 1970's and 1980's and its effect on women writers and their work. Brings in the opinions of several writers, literary agents, and editors. Although only brief reference is made to Winterson, and then only to her earlier work, Gerrard's work places *Written on the Body* in an insightful and comprehensible context.

Hunt, Sally, ed. *New Lesbian Criticism: Literary and Cultural Readings*. London: Simon & Schuster, 1992. The essay on Winterson discusses *Oranges Are Not the Only Fruit* as a "crossover" text into the dominant culture, which is seen to have lost its radical lesbian content in its adaptation to a television film.

Petro, Pamela. Review of *Written on the Body*. *The Atlantic* 271, no. 2 (February, 1993): 112. A thorough and intelligent discussion of *Written on the Body* presented within the framework of Winterson's previous novels. The review clearly identifies and comments on recurring themes and formal techniques in Winterson's work.

Susan Chainey

WUTHERING HEIGHTS

Author: Emily Brontë (1818-1848)
Type of work: Novel
Type of plot: Romance
Time of plot: The late eighteenth century
Locale: The West Yorkshire moors
First published: 1847

Principal characters:

MR. LOCKWOOD, a gentleman of private means who becomes
   Heathcliff's tenant at Thrushcross Grange
NELLY DEAN, the housekeeper of Thrushcross Grange
HEATHCLIFF, a foundling brought into the Earnshaw home, a
   passionate man
CATHERINE EARNSHAW, Heathcliff's soulmate, who marries
   Edgar Linton
HINDLEY EARNSHAW, Catherine's older brother, who is brutal in
   his treatment of Heathcliff
EDGAR LINTON, a somewhat spoiled, wealthy inhabitant of
   Thrushcross Grange
ISABELLA LINTON, Edgar's sister, who marries Heathcliff
CATHERINE LINTON, the daughter of Edgar Linton and Catherine
   Earnshaw
LINTON HEATHCLIFF, the son of Heathcliff and Isabella Linton
HARETON EARNSHAW, the son of Hindley Earnshaw, who is in
   love with Catherine Linton
JOSEPH, the servant of the Earnshaws at Wuthering Heights

Form and Content

Wuthering Heights is a story of passionate love that encompasses two generations
of two families, the Earnshaws and the Lintons. It is a framed tale narrated by two
different characters, one with intimate knowledge of the families (Nelly Dean) and
one unacquainted with their history. The first narrator is the stranger, Mr. Lockwood.
A wealthy, educated man, Lockwood has chosen to rent a house in the isolated moors,
saying that he has wearied of society. Yet his actions belie his words: He pursues a
friendship with Heathcliff despite the latter's objections and seeks information about
all the citizens of the neighborhood. Lockwood is steeped in the conventions of his
class, and he consistently misjudges the people he meets at Wuthering Heights. He
assumes that Hareton Earnshaw, the rightful owner of Wuthering Heights, is a servant
and that Catherine Linton is a demure wife to Heathcliff. His statements, even about
himself, are untrustworthy, requiring the corrective of Nelly Dean's narrative.

Lockwood cultivates Nelly Dean's friendship when a long illness, brought on by his foolish attempt to visit Heathcliff during a snowstorm, keeps him bedridden for weeks. Nelly has been reared with the Earnshaws and has been a servant in both households. She has observed much of the central drama between the two families, but her statements, too, are colored by prejudice. Nelly dislikes Catherine Earnshaw, who behaved selfishly and treated the servants badly at times, and she supports Edgar Linton because he was a gentleman.

Through these two unreliable lenses are filtered the love stories of Catherine and Heathcliff, Catherine and Edgar, and in the second generation, Catherine Linton and Hareton Earnshaw. The antithesis of character—Heathcliff's past is a blank, Edgar is a gentleman's son; Heathcliff is dark and brooding, Edgar is fair and cannot conceal his feelings—is echoed with other oppositions. Wuthering Heights is an exposed, cold farmhouse; Thrushcross Grange is an orderly gentleman's home with plush furnishings, warm fires, and an enclosed park. The houses, instead of places of safety, become literal prisons for the female characters, while the wild moors (which nearly kill Lockwood) represent freedom and naturalness of behavior.

Patterns of dualism and opposition are played out between the first and second generations as well. Heathcliff, the physically strongest father, has the weakest child, Linton Heathcliff. By dying young, Linton dissolves the triangular relationship that has so plagued the older generation, undermining Heathcliff's influence. Hareton Earnshaw, abused like Heathcliff and demonstrating surprising similarities of character, nevertheless retains some sense of moral behavior and is not motivated by revenge. Catherine Earnshaw's daughter, as willful and spirited as her mother, does not have to make the same difficult choice between passionate love and socially sanctioned marriage. Instead, Catherine Linton and Hareton Earnshaw are left to help each other and inherit the positive legacies of the past, enjoying both the social amenities of Thrushcross Grange and the natural environment of Wuthering Heights.

Analysis

An essential element of *Wuthering Heights* is the exploration and extension of the meaning of romance. By contrasting the passionate, natural love of Catherine and Heathcliff with the socially constructed forms of courtship and marriage, Emily Brontë makes an argument in favor of individual choice. Catherine and Heathcliff both assert that they know the other as themselves, that they are an integral part of each other, and that one's death will diminish the other immeasurably. This communion, however, is doomed to failure while they live because of social constraints. Heathcliff's unknown parentage, his poverty, and his lack of education make him an unsuitable partner for a gentlewoman, no matter how liberated her expressions of independence. Brontë suggests the possibility of reunion after death when local residents believe they see the ghosts of Heathcliff and Catherine together, but this notion is explicitly denied by Lockwood's last assertion in the novel, that the dead slumber quietly.

The profound influence of Romantic poetry on Brontë's literary imagination is evident in her development of Heathcliff as a Byronic hero. This characterization contributes to the impossibility of any happy union of Catherine and Heathcliff while they live. Heathcliff looms larger than life, subject to violent extremes of emotion, amenable to neither education nor nurturing. Like Frankenstein's monster, he craves love and considers revenge the only fit justice when he is rejected by others. Catherine, self-involved and prone to emotional storms, has just enough sense of self-preservation to recognize Heathcliff's faults, including his amorality. Choosing to marry Edgar Linton is to choose psychic fragmentation and separation from her other self, but she sees no way to reconcile her psychological need for wholeness with the physical support and emotional stability that she requires. Unable to earn a living, dependent on a brother who is squandering the family fortune, she is impelled to accept the social privileges and luxuries that Edgar offers.

Yet conventional forms of romance provide no clear guide to successful marriage either; both Edgar and his sister, Isabella, suffer by acting on stereotypical notions of love. Edgar does not know Catherine in any true sense, and his attempts to control her force her subversive self-destruction. Isabella, fascinated by the Byronic qualities with which Heathcliff is so richly endowed, believes that she really loves him and becomes a willing victim in his scheme of revenge. What remains is a paradoxical statement about the nature and value of love and a question about whether any love can transcend social and natural barriers.

Another theme that Brontë examines is the effect of abuse and brutality on human nature. The novel contains minimal examples of nurturing, and most instruction to children is of the negative kind that Joseph provides with his lectures threatening damnation. Children demonstrably suffer from a lack of love from their parents, whose attention alternates between total neglect and physical threats. The novel is full of violence, exemplified by the dreams that Lockwood has when he stays in Wuthering Heights. After being weakened by a nosebleed which occurs when Heathcliff's dogs attack him, Lockwood spends the night in Catherine Earnshaw's old room. He dreams first of being accused of an unpardonable sin and being beaten by a congregation in church, then of a small girl, presumably Catherine, who is trying to enter the chamber's window. Terrified, he rubs her wrist back and forth on a broken window-pane until he is covered in blood. These dreams anticipate further violence: Hindley's drunken assaults on his son and animals, Catherine's bloody capture by the Lintons' bulldog, Edgar's blow to Heathcliff's neck, and Heathcliff's mad head-banging when he learns of Catherine's death. Heathcliff never recovers from the neglect and abuse that he has experienced as a child; all that motivates him in adulthood is revenge and a philosophy that the weak deserve to be crushed. Hareton presents the possibility that degraded character can be redeemed and improved through the twin forces of education and love, yet this argument seems little more than a way of acknowledging the popular cultural stereotype and lacks the conviction that Brontë reveals when she focuses on the negative effects of brutality.

A third significant theme of *Wuthering Heights* is the power of the natural setting. Emily Brontë loved the wildness of the moors and incorporated much of her affection into her novel. Catherine and Heathcliff are most at one with each other when they are outdoors. The freedom that they experience is profound; not only have they escaped Hindley's anger, but they are free from social restraints and expectations as well. When Catherine's mind wanders before her death, she insists on opening the windows to breathe the wind off the moors, and she believes herself to be under Penistone Crag with Heathcliff. Her fondest memories are of the times on the moors; the enclosed environment of Thrushcross Grange seems a petty prison. In contrast to Catherine and Heathcliff, other characters prefer the indoors and crave the protection that the houses afford. Lockwood is dependent on the comforts of home and hearth, and the Lintons are portrayed as weaklings because of their upbringing in a sheltered setting. This method of delineating character by identifying with nature is another aspect of Emily Brontë's inheritance from the Romantic poets.

Context

When it was first published, *Wuthering Heights* received almost no attention from critics, and what little there was proved to be negative. Critical opinion deemed the book immoral, and Charlotte Brontë felt moved to apologize for it after Emily's death by saying that her sister wrote during the feverish stages of tuberculosis. To publish at all, the Brontë sisters chose to submit their works using male pseudonyms because they believed that it would be impossible to market their poems and novels otherwise. They experienced many rejections and were never recompensed fairly for the value of their work. When their identity was revealed, many critics expressed surprise (that the novels could be written by inexperienced women who lived in isolated circumstances) and shock (that the violence and passion of *Wuthering Heights* could be conceived by a woman at all). There has even been a serious attempt made to prove that Emily's brother, Branwell, was the true author of *Wuthering Heights*.

This reaction suggests the reluctance of the Victorian public to accept challenges to the dominant belief that women were beneficent moral influences whose primary function was to provide a pure environment for men who, of necessity, sullied themselves in the world of work. *Wuthering Heights* provides no overt rebellion against this view, but the depiction of female characters who display anger, passion, and a desire for independence demonstrates Emily Brontë's judgment that women were suited to a wider sphere of action.

Contemporary feminist critics have seen Catherine Earnshaw as a character for whom no meaningful choices are possible. Her self-starvation and periods of madness can be read as signs of female powerlessness and rage. Even her death can be seen as the last resort of the oppressed, a kind of willed suicide which she announces is her only form of revenge against both Edgar Linton and Heathcliff for thwarting her true nature. The second half of the novel, focusing on Catherine Linton, is then an assertion of Victorian society's values countering Catherine Earnshaw's desire to be self-determining. Catherine Linton is beautiful in a conventional way, and she dutifully serves as daughter, wife, nurse, and teacher. Yet, compared to her mother's, her story has much less drama and fails to persuade the reader of its truth. In fact, it best serves to highlight the unique and deeply felt nature of her mother's subjugation.

Sources for Further Study

Craik, W. A. *The Brontë Novels*. London: Methuen, 1968. An early attempt to separate the biographical material from the artistic skill of the writers. Craik focuses on the development of character in *Wuthering Heights*.

Eagleton, Terence. *Myths of Power*. London: Macmillan, 1975. A Marxist approach to works by the Brontë sisters which places *Wuthering Heights* in a broad historical and political context.

Ewbank, Inga-Stina. *Their Proper Sphere: A Study of the Brontë Sisters as Early-Victorian Female Novelists*. Cambridge, Mass.: Harvard University Press, 1966. Addresses the contained world of *Wuthering Heights*, which despite its isolation, functions as a microcosm of the human condition.

Gérin, Winifred. *Emily Brontë*. New York: Oxford University Press, 1971. A comprehensive biography of Emily Brontë, informed by Gérin's research on other members of the Brontë family and her intimate knowledge of Haworth and the surrounding moors of West Yorkshire.

Gilbert, Sandra M., and Susan Gubar. *The Madwoman in the Attic: The Woman Writer and the Nineteenth Century Literary Imagination*. New Haven, Conn.: Yale University Press, 1979. An important feminist reading of nineteenth century women writers, including an insightful chapter on Emily Brontë.

Ratchford, Fannie. *The Brontës' Web of Childhood*. New York: Columbia University Press, 1941. The first book to examine the relationship of the childhood writings to the adult novels of the Brontë sisters. Ratchford outlines the children's collaboration on the stories about Verdopolis, and she explains how Emily and Anne created the world of Gondal.

Weissman, Judith. *Half Savage and Hardy and Free: Women and Rural Radicalism in the Nineteenth-Century Novel*. Middletown, Conn.: Weslayan University Press, 1987. Contains an examination of the Romantic influence and radical politics of *Wuthering Heights*.

Williams, Raymond. *The English Novel*. New York: Oxford University Press, 1973. Presents a Marxist reading of *Wuthering Heights* as a novel which challenges repressive structures and achieves emotional directness.

Gweneth A. Dunleavy

YEAR OF THE UNICORN

Author: Andre (Mary Beth) Norton (1912-   )
Type of work: Novel
Type of plot: Science fiction
Time of plot: After the war with Alizon
Locale: Another world
First published: 1965

> *Principal characters:*
> GILLAN, a twenty-year-old woman who elects to become the
>   bride of a Were-Rider
> KILDAS, a bride of the Were-Riders
> HERREL, called the Wronghanded, a Were-Rider who takes on
>   animal shapes, the future husband of Gillan
> HALSE, called the Strongarmed, an enemy of Herrel
> HYRON, the captain of the Were-Riders

Form and Content

Year of the Unicorn is one of a series of highly successful books that occur in a place called Witch World. All the basic characteristics of this land are established in the first novel in the series, *Witch World* (1963). Although this place is named "the Witch World" in other books in the series, it is never referred to by that name in *Year of the Unicorn*. Witch World is perhaps a distant planet, or it may exist in another dimension of Earth. Gates allow entry into Witch World from other worlds, and apparently human beings from Earth occasionally enter it. Many of the adventures confronting Gillan and Herrel are unique to this Witch World saga, while many other aspects are common to most Witch World stories. Thus, the Were-Riders are represented as a group in a number of other stories, but their history and functioning are only briefly summarized there. The land that they traverse, the Waste, is central to all the Witch World sagas.

The shape-changers, or Were-Riders, are introduced in this novel. They fought on the side of a land called High Hallack in a war against invaders called the Hounds of Alizon. The enemy used weapons from some other, unnamed world that are very similar to armaments, such as tanks and rocket launchers, found in this world. If High Hallack won the war, the Were-Riders were to receive thirteen brides, maidens between the ages of eighteen and twenty. They promised that they would then leave High Hallack and return to the unknown land called the Waste. This Great Bargain was the product of fear and desperation in High Hallack, and the novel begins when the price is demanded on the first day of the new year: the year of the unicorn.

The novel recounts adventures that occur during this year. Gillan, an orphan without a home or social status, disguises herself to become one of the chosen maids. At this time, she is unaware of the nature and depth of her own magical powers. She flees a bleak future on the chance that even a mysterious, dangerous future is an improvement. Her untrained magical powers disturb the tenuous balance of power between gods and their servants in the strange and twisted landscape called the Waste. Unlike all the other brides, she has her own vision of herself, independence, and good.

In some ways, *Year of the Unicorn* is a romance that takes place in a seemingly medieval tale of good against evil. Gillan and Herrel represent ordinary people in the sense that they have little worldly goods or social status. They are not unusually handsome or gifted with everyday graces. Gillan's unfolding discovery of her strengths as a person with magical powers, perhaps like a witch's, however, is a story of interpersonal growth. The moral of the story is that love, faith, and hope can overcome seemingly impossible odds. Thus, this is an optimistic story where good triumphs over evil and where "girl meets boy" and falls in love. It is not a simplistic story, but it echoes legends and folktales.

Year of the Unicorn has a powerful ending. The crafty evil of Halse and his thuggish followers is revealed in a battle between good and evil. Gillan dies and Herrel, who had betrayed her in a physical attack beyond his control, brings her back from the land of the dead. This is the imaginative drama one expects in a "good read," but Norton pushes beyond formulaic endings. The final battle shows the collusion of Hyron, the leader of the Were-Riders, who supports evil in order to rid himself of innocent but disliked scapegoats. Gillan and Herrel reject the entire group as one permeated with hatred not only for them but for anything good as well. This is not merely a romantic ending for a couple in love who can conquer the world alone. It is a moral decision requiring courage and hope. In the final lines of the story, Herrel reveals that Hyron is actually his father as well as the clan leader, and the betrayal of his son is even a greater crime than the reader had known.

This book examines some of the greatest themes of human storytelling: betrayal by the clan, the family, and one's mate, death, love, magic, and friendship. The heroine is an independent woman with few material or social resources. Her need for others is a continuing but problematic reality.

Analysis

Witch World offers a gripping fantasy world of mythic struggles between the gods. It emerges from the imagination of Andre Norton, a great American storyteller and author of more than ninety books. Norton draws on a rich multicultural vision culled from history, anthropology, folklore, and humans' primordial interest in adventure, fear, and courage. Witch World is paradoxically a sacred myth in secular packaging: a fantasy series in American popular culture linked to sacred dramas and universal instincts.

For example, Norton employs many of the formulas used by traditional adventure stories. Gillan is involved in a series of dirty tricks that she barely survives. Yet Norton makes these adventures more than devices to confound her readers. Her heroine continually avoids the traps set before her by learning more about herself and her enemies. She draws on physical and mental strengths. She reflects on past experiences and chooses to act with moral goodness. She ultimately chooses intimacy without surrendering her humanity.

This book and others in the Witch World series can be read by juvenile readers and appear to be wholesome yarns. This superficial reading is in itself enjoyable, but this has been a barrier to Norton's acceptance as a serious writer of cultural myths. One of the serious critiques of women's lives in this book arises from the constrictive, unexciting life that Gillan, an orphan, endures within a women's abbey. Anything, including an arranged marriage to pay a war debt, is better than her dreary future receiving charity. A rational decision to marry even a potentially inhuman, malelike being is empowering for impoverished women in a patriarchal society. After her choice of a mate, moreover, Gillan is not subject to the illusions of the other brides. They see flowers, enjoy sumptuous beds, and dine on gourmet wines and food; Gillan sees a sere wilderness, crude lodgings, and minimal rations. Gillan makes her choices without a "cloak-spell" clouding her judgment, and this infuriates the Were-Riders, who take brides without their full consent.

The men who oppose Gillan's independence, led by Halse, escalate their attacks against her. She is separated into two beings: One has her physical appearance and is controlled by the evil magic of the men, while the other exists as a shadow with dwindling physical strength but with her own mind and soul. The men in the group enjoy the mindless, soulless "fetch" while her "true spirit" endures adventure after adventure. First, the "true" Gillan is almost raped and murdered by a roving band of soldiers, the Hounds of Alizon, who lost the recent war. After using magic to kill these marauders, she encounters physical and mental barriers protecting the homeland of the Weres. Next, That Which Runs the Ridges, a foul being that is part animal and part evil spirit, attacks her during the night after she is exhausted in every meaning of the word. As Gillan explains: "Fear can kill, and I had never met such fear as this before. For this did not lurk in any dream, but in the world I had always believed to be sane and understandable."

Again, Gillan defeats a monstrous enemy, only to be confronted by further trials and magic. There is a progression in these tests—from initially physical, external battles to increasingly subjective, internal struggles. Although Norton does not dichotomize physical and mental strengths, she does portray faith and moral character as more important facets of being human than physical stamina and muscles.

Witch World draws on images similar to those of prehistoric societies such as Stonehenge, the Arthurian legends, and folktales of magical beings and woods. Norton combines these great, universal stories with popular techniques employed in the genres of adventure, romance, and juvenile literature.

Context

Although Norton has written more than ninety books, few scholars have studied her corpus. One reason for this scholarly oversight is that her books defy categorization as either highbrow or lowbrow literature. Whatever category of class and taste they fit, they are popular: 10 million copies of Witch World books had been sold worldwide by 1987. Norton's books also tap into scholarly writings and primitive images of the bestial in animal and human forms. The Were-Riders epitomize this theme and its combination in one being. Dark, light, death, life, evil, good, exhaustion, and renewal are integral components in her tales of adventure and trial.

Norton's protagonists in Witch World are often female, such as Gillan. She began writing in science fiction in the early 1950's, when it was seen as a "man's field" for both authors and readers; thus, to be accepted, she selected the male pseudonym Andre. Thus, Norton's tales balance everyday life and the sacred, and she shares this shadowy status in the world of the sacred, and she shares this shadowy status in the world of serious analysis, especially that written by feminist scholars. Despite the recent growth in feminist scholarship in science fiction, however, Norton remains caught between pulp writing, popular adventure stories, and academic acceptance.

Norton has had a tremendous impact, however, outside the groves of academe: The number of famous, "serious" science-fiction writers inspired by her is staggering. For example, Anne McCaffrey and C. J. Cherryh have each dedicated a book to Norton. Marion Zimmer Bradley, Tanith Lee, Judith Tarr, and Poul Anderson are only a few notable authors who acknowledge Norton's influence on their work and lives. Joan D. Vinge wrote an open letter to Norton in which she reflects on Norton's profound impact on her: first as a junior high school student, then as a successful adult writer. As Vinge notes, "Written in a clean, straightforward prose that never gets in the way of its images, your adventures catch the elusive 'sense of wonder' that sets apart good science fiction from all other kinds of fiction and makes a fan into an addict." Vinge, like Norton's millions of fans, concludes: "Because of you, I am." Norton's wide-ranging vision and cultural innovation may be lauded by scholars one day. Until then, her readers will continue to enjoy this great storyteller's tales of wonder and hope.

Sources for Further Study

Carter, Lin. "Andre Norton: A Profile." In *Secret of the Lost Race*, by Andre Norton. New York: Ace Books, 1959. This overview of Norton's work by a respected science-fiction author lauds and analyzes Norton's corpus as it existed in 1959. This essay appears in some of the paperback editions of the novel.

Norton, Andre. *The Book of Andre Norton.* Edited by Roger Elwood. New York: DAW Books, 1975. Primarily an anthology of Norton's short stories, with a few interesting essays on her work. The best essay is an autobiographical one in which Norton explains how she writes her fantasies.

——————, ed. *Tales of the Witch World.* 3 vols. New York: T. Doherty Associates, 1987. An anthology of short stories written by many authors following the Witch World formula established in Norton's books. Many additional details, figures, or continuing stories are found here. Norton's introductory essays give an overview of Witch World.

Shwartz, Susan, ed. *Moonsinger's Friends: An Anthology in Honor of Andre Norton.* New York: Bluejay Books, 1985. A science-fiction *Festschrift* honoring Norton. Instead of writing about Norton, the sixteen eminent authors write science-fiction stories inspired by her work. Shwartz's editorial notes and introduction discuss the authors' works and Norton's influence.

Mary Jo Deegan

THE YEARLING

Author: Marjorie Kinnan Rawlings (1896-1953)
Type of work: Novel
Type of plot: Social realism
Time of plot: 1870 and 1871
Locale: Florida
First published: 1938

Principal characters:
JODY BAXTER, a twelve-year-old boy
PENNY BAXTER, Jody's father
ORA BAXTER, Jody's mother and Penny's wife
FODDER-WING FORRESTER, a neighbor about Jody's age, one of
    his few friends
OLIVER HUTTO, Penny Baxter's close friend and neighbor
GRANDMA HUTTO, Oliver's mother
TWINK WEATHERBY, Oliver's girlfriend
FLAG, the yearling of the title, a fawn whose appetite for Penny's
    sparse crops threatens the family's precarious existence
DOC WILSON, a typical backcountry doctor

Form and Content

The Yearling is an initiatory tale in which an innocent and happy twelve-year-old boy passes into young adulthood. Some of his youthful illusions are shattered by the end of the year in his life that the book chronicles, but Jody emerges with a substantial hold on the adulthood that stretches ahead of him.

Jody Baxter lives in the scrubby inland country of central Florida not far south of the Georgia line, the area out of Gainesville in which Marjorie Kinnan Rawlings herself lived intermittently. He is the only child of Penny and Ora Baxter, two people who barely scrape by on what they can grow or catch when Penny goes hunting or fishing. Jody accompanies his father on his food-seeking adventures and also helps with the family's minimal farming. Despite the Baxter's poverty, Jody's childhood seems ideal by most standards. The boy has a particularly strong bond with his father. He is less sure of his feelings toward his mother, a large, dominating woman who rules a roost that clearly someone has to rule. Penny is easygoing and not always practical. Ora's temperament complements his. She views life realistically, forcing practicality upon her two men, even though they do not always appreciate her efforts to control them in this way.

By drawing Ora as she does, Rawlings defines important lines of conflict in her novel, which was awarded the 1938 Pulitzer Prize in fiction. Although *The Yearling* is sentimental, it had phenomenal sales in the years immediately following its publication and has regularly been a steady seller. The book, sincere and fresh, appeals to young people, among whom it is a classic. Rawlings tells her story in a straightforward, chronological way that works well for a book that is neither fraught with hidden meanings nor filled with sweeping, universal truths. Rawlings' microcosm is neatly contained and manageable.

The first portion of *The Yearling* sets up necessary relationships and establishes essential conflicts between Penny and Ora, Jody and Ora, the Baxters and the Forresters, and the Huttos and the Forresters. This business attended to, Rawlings gets to the heart of her story, which begins when Penny—out with Jody in quest of Old Slewfoot, a bear that has been devastating the area—is bitten by a rattlesnake. He faces imminent death if drastic action is not taken. In desperation, Penny shoots a doe, rips open its abdomen, and removes the warm liver, which he places on the snakebite to draw out the toxin. Doc Wilson, when he comes to treat Penny, confirms that by this action, Penny saved his life. Jody returns to where Penny was bitten and finds the fawn of the doe that his father shot. He brings it home, names it Flag, and, contrary to his mother's wishes, raises it. Flag requires food and milk, scarce commodities in the Baxter household.

As Flag reaches the yearling stage, however, the situation becomes grave. The deer roots in the Baxter's garden, destroying crops on which the Baxters are depending for their living. A crisis is inevitable, but Jody tries to forestall it by building a fence around the garden and replanting. His efforts are to no avail. Flag is able to leap over the fence and continue the damage. Finally, Ora, never a good shot, fires at the marauding Flag, wounding the animal badly. Jody has no alternative but to end Flag's suffering by firing a fatal bullet into the wounded deer. This act, more than anything else in the story, marks Jody's coming-of-age.

Analysis

Rawlings uses the first part of her novel to establish the relationship between Jody and his parents as well as to suggest the relationship between Penny and Ora, who emerges as a dominant, although not very appealing, figure. Jody, because of the physical isolation of his surroundings, has few playmates, but Rawlings establishes that he and Fodder-Wing Forrester are good friends. Fodder-Wing, however, is the atypical child in his large family. Crippled, he is kinder and more appealing than his violent, lawless brothers. Rawlings also sets up Penny and Jody's friendship with Grandma Hutto and establishes that Penny and Oliver Hutto, Grandma's son, are close friends.

When Oliver returns from sea, he is drawn into a barroom brawl with Lem Forrester over Twink Weatherby, Oliver's fiancée. When the Forrester boys join the fray, Penny and Jody try to protect Oliver. This fight is necessary to the story because it establishes the Oliver-Penny-Jody underdog status, but Rawlings also uses it to show that these simple folk, when a crisis occurs, can let bygones be bygones.

Bad blood has existed between Penny and the Forresters for some time. Penny is basically moral, but, desperate for a hunting rifle with which to hunt Old Slewfoot, the bear that has been ravaging his crops and killing livestock in the area, he traded the Forresters a worthless dog in return for a rifle that, with minor repairs, was perfectly good. Penny forewarned the Forresters that the dog was not trainable, but that made them the more eager to trade. They thought that Penny was trying to deceive them because he really wanted to keep the dog.

When Penny discovers that his hogs have disappeared, he suspects that this is the Forresters' way of repaying the disadvantageous trade that they made with him. Penny and Jody strike out to find the missing hogs, and when they wander into the swamp, a rattlesnake bites Penny. He shoots a doe, using her liver to draw the poison from his wound. Penny limps to his cabin, while Jody goes to the Forresters to beg a ride to Doc Wilson's. The Forresters, although they have just fought with Penny and Jody, hold no grudges in the face of this crisis, realizing that Penny had to come to Oliver's aid in the barroom. They not only fetch Doc Wilson, but Buck Forrester moves into the Baxter cabin to help with the chores until Penny recovers.

When Jody returns to the swamp and finds the motherless fawn, Flag, the story's main conflict begins. Obviously, the Baxters feel an obligation to the fawn, whose mother's death made Penny's survival possible. This sense of obligation, however, does not diminish the fact that Flag, in order to survive, must be fed from the Baxter's meager food supply.

Flag becomes domesticated, but, as a wild animal, it retains its animal ways. Rawlings presents the fawn so beguilingly that readers immediately identify with it, even personify it. Consequently, they develop an antipathy for Ora Baxter, who, completely rationally, realizes that the fawn's presence is threatening her family's overall welfare. She finally convinces Penny of this, and as a result, Jody begins to have violent disagreements with his father, a disaffection that mirrors his coming-of-age.

The Baxters' situation becomes desperate when Penny falls ill and a September storm ruins their crops. Old Slewfoot kills another of the Baxters' hogs, but Penny's illness prevents him from pursuing the marauding bear. By the time that wolves attack livestock in the area, Penny has recovered sufficiently to hunt them down with the Forresters, who in the course of the hunt find ten bear cubs whose mother has been shot by hunters. The Forresters take the cubs to Jacksonville and sell them, sharing the profits with Penny.

The Baxters plan to visit Grandma Hutto for Christmas, but just before they are to leave, Old Slewfoot again attacks the Baxters' livestock. Penny pursues the bear, this time killing it. When they arrive in Volusia for their Christmas celebration with Grandma Hutto, they discover that Oliver has come back to town with his bride, Twink. Lem Forrester, jealous of Twink's marriage, comes into town with his brothers and torches Grandma Hutto's house, burning it to the ground. Oliver, however, does not realize who set the fire. The next day, he and his bride, along with Grandma Hutto, leave Volusia on a riverboat to resettle in Boston.

The Baxters endure a difficult winter, and when spring arrives, Penny and Jody plant their crops, only to have them destroyed by Flag, which leads finally to the story's sad ending in which Jody must destroy Flag. The boy, now at the threshold of adulthood, feels betrayed by his parents and makes a feeble attempt to run away from home.

Context

The Yearling was perfect for its time: In 1938, Europe was arming for a war into which the United States would inevitably be drawn. The reading public badly needed a book that glorified innocence and reflected a less complicated era than the one facing a populace still suffering from the Great Depression, shocked by the Spanish Civil War and its atrocities, and apprehensive about the rise of fascism in Germany, much of Eastern Europe, and Italy.

Marjorie Kinnan Rawlings did not live in an age notable for the kind of feminism that emerged in the United States during the 1970's and 1980's, although in her early years, suffragettes were active in seeking the voting rights that women were finally accorded in 1920. In *The Yearling*, Rawlings certainly did not set out consciously to make a statement about the status of women. Nevertheless, she makes two important points about matters that are important in terms of feminist issues.

First, in her depiction of Ora Baxter, Rawlings creates a strong, almost overpowering female character who, if her actions are at times distressing, can at least be justified. The Baxters live at the edge economically. Not only does their farm produce little, but Penny's bouts of illness leave him unable to hunt for the food that the family needs and render him powerless, at times, to prevent the onslaughts that bears and wolves make on his livestock. Viewing the Baxters' situation realistically, an objective observer would have to conclude that Ora is right: The family cannot afford to keep Flag. Jody can practice small economies so that Flag's presence will seem less threatening, but when the yearling jumps the fence and eats the crops, the solution to the problem is clear: Flag must be killed. The deer cannot be released to nature because it has become a domesticated animal, but the deer's continued presence will lead to disaster for the family. Ora does the only thing that she can when she shoots Flag.

The only other female presence in the story (except for Grandma Hutto) is Twink Weatherby. She is not a major figure in *The Yearling*, but her social situation is clear. Two men are in love with her and fight over her. Twink is a pawn in a male-dominated situation. Apparently, she does not believe that she can simply tell Lem Forrester that she loves Oliver and wants to marry him. Instead, quite confounded by the barroom brawl generated by Lem's jealousy, Twink flees, leaving town on a riverboat to keep people from talking about her. Oliver continues his pursuit of her and finally wins her hand. One wonders, however, whether, had he beaten Oliver to the punch, Lem Forrester might have won Twink's hand as easily as Oliver did.

Sources for Further Study

Bellman, Samuel I. *Marjorie Kinnan Rawlings*. New York: Twayne, 1974. Offers a valuable chronological table and a solid, annotated bibliography. The first chapter, focusing on Rawlings' biography, is well researched. The following chapters provide analytical readings of her writings, including *The Yearling*.

_____ . "Marjorie Kinnan Rawlings: A Solitary Sojourner in the Florida Backwoods." *Kansas Quarterly* 2 (Spring, 1970): 78-87. Bellman writes of Rawlings' antipathy for cities and tells of how she originally went to Florida with her first husband, Charles Rawlings, also a writer. She remained at Cross Creek after her divorce and became closely identified with the area through her fiction.

Bigelow, Gordon E. *Frontier Eden: The Literary Career of Marjorie Kinnan Rawlings*. Gainesville: University of Florida Press, 1966. This comprehensive study is based upon the extensive Marjorie Kinnan Rawlings Archive housed at the University of Florida Library in Gainesville. Bigelow knows intimately the area about which Rawlings often wrote. He provides sympathetic insights into her creative process.

Rawlings, Marjorie Kinnan. *The Marjorie Kinnan Rawlings Reader*. Edited by Julia Scribner Bigham. New York: Charles Scribner's Sons, 1956. In her ten-page introduction to the well-chosen selections in this collection, Bigham provides a quick and accurate overview of Rawlings' writing. Useful for the beginning student.

Stuckey, W. J. *The Pulitzer Prize Novels: A Critical Backward Look*. Norman: University of Oklahoma Press, 1966. In his assessment of novels that have been awarded the Pulitzer Prize, Stuckey views *The Yearling* disdainfully, considering it sentimental and amateurish. He attributes some features of Rawlings' style to Ernest Hemingway's influence.

R. Baird Shuman

THE YELLOW WALLPAPER

Author: Charlotte Perkins Gilman (1860-1935)
Type of work: Novella
Type of plot: Social criticism
Time of plot: The late nineteenth century
Locale: New England
First published: 1892

> *Principal characters:*
> THE NARRATOR, an imaginative, creative woman apparently
>   suffering from postpartum depression
> JOHN, the narrator's husband, a physician
> JENNIE, John's sister, who serves as housekeeper
> WEIR MITCHELL, the real-life doctor who popularized the "rest
>   cure" prescribed to the narrator (and the author as well)

Form and Content

The structure of *The Yellow Wallpaper* creates a sense of immediacy and intimacy. The story is written in a journal-style, first-person narrative which includes nine short entries, each entry indicated by a small space between it and the last. The journal entries span three months during which John attempts to cure his wife's "nervous condition" through the rest cure of Weir Mitchell, which assumes that intellectual stimulation damages a woman physically and psychologically. In the beginning of the story, the narrator appears sane and believable, but as the story continues, the reader realizes that she is unreliable because she withholds and confuses information. By the end, the structure—short paragraphs, fragmented and disjointed thought patterns—reflects the narrator's mental disorder. Through the revelations contained in the journal, the reader is allowed an intimate view of the narrator's gradual mental breakdown.

The journal begins when John and the narrator move into a temporary home John has procured to provide the narrator the break from routine that he believes necessary for her rest and recovery. She, on the other hand, doubts the necessity of such a move and wonders if the mysterious house is haunted. John reveals his superior attitude toward his wife by laughing at her "fancies," a response which the narrator finds quite natural because, as she explains, one must expect such treatment in marriage. She even suggests that his indifference to her opinions on the house and her illness keeps her from getting well faster. Her suggestion turns out to be a fateful prediction.

Against her wishes, John decides that he and his wife will sleep in the attic room of the house, which at one point may have been a nursery. Actually, the room seems to be more of a prison than a place for children to play. The windows have bars on them, and the bed is nailed to the floor. There is even a gate at the top of the stairs. Even more disturbing to the narrator, however, is the yellow wallpaper, peeling or pulled off the walls in strips. In the beginning, the paper's pattern jolts and annoys the narrator's sensibilities, but later her attitude has a bizarre change.

The narrator's morbid fascination with the yellow wallpaper is the first clue of her degenerating sanity. She begins to attribute lifelike characteristics to the paper, saying that it knows how it affects her and that its eyes stare at her. She even begins to believe that the paper has two levels, a front pattern and a shadowy figure trapped behind its bars. The narrator betrays the progression of her illness when she begins to believe that the figure behind the wallpaper is a woman, trapped like herself.

The woman behind the wallpaper becomes an obsession. The narrator begins to crawl, like the woman behind the paper, around the edge of the room, making a groove or "smooch" on the wall. The narrator begins to catch glimpses of the woman out the windows, creeping around the garden on her hands and knees. She also starts peeling off the wallpaper in an effort to completely free the woman (or women, as she soon believes) trapped in that second layer. John and his sister, Jennie, begin to suspect that something is terribly wrong, and yet they are pleased with her apparent progress. She appears more normal to them at times because she is saving her energy for nighttime, when the woman behind the paper is most active. Her apparent normality is merely a façade.

The story's climactic scene occurs as their stay in the rented house is coming to a close. On their last night, John is once again in town attending to a patient, and the narrator asks Jennie not to disturb her. Left alone, the narrator locks herself in the nursery to allow uninterrupted time for peeling wallpaper and thus freeing the shadowy woman. As the narrator works, she identifies more closely and intensely with the trapped woman until, ultimately, she loses her sense of individual identity and merges with the woman behind the wallpaper. John breaks down the door to find his wife crawling amid the torn paper, proclaiming that she is free at last, and no one can put her back behind the wallpaper. John faints, and his wife continues her creeping over his fallen body.

Analysis

Charlotte Perkins Gilman used her personal bout with postpartum depression to create a powerful fictional narrative which has broad implications for women. When the narrator recognizes that there is more than one trapped, creeping woman, Gilman indicates that the meaning of her story extends beyond an isolated, individual situation. Gilman's main purpose in writing *The Yellow Wallpaper* is to condemn not only a specific medical treatment but also the misogynistic principles and resulting sexual politics that make such a treatment possible.

The unequal relationship between the narrator and John is a microcosm of the larger gender inequity in society. Gilman makes it clear that much of John's condescending and paternal behavior toward his wife has little to do with her illness. He dismisses her well-thought-out opinions and her "flights of fancy" with equal disdain, while he belittles her creative impulses. He speaks of her as he would a child, calling her his "little girl" and saying of her, "Bless her little heart." He overrides her judgments on the best course of treatment for herself as he would on any issue, making her live in a house she does not like, in a room she detests, and in an isolated environment which makes her unhappy and lonely. John's solicitous "care" shows that he believes the prevailing scientific theories which claim that women's innate inferiority leaves them, childlike, in a state of infantile dependence.

Gilman makes John the window through which readers can view the negative images of women in her society. In Gilman's lifetime, women's right to become full citizens and to vote became one of the primary issues debated in the home, the media, and the political arena. As women's reform movements gained the strength that would eventually win the vote in 1920, the backlash became more vicious and dangerous. Noted psychologists detailed theories that "proved" women's developmental immaturity, low cognitive skills, and emotional instability. Physicians, who actually had little knowledge of the inner workings of the female body, presented complex theories arguing that the womb created hysteria and madness, that it was the source of women's inferiority. Ministers urged women to fulfill their duty to God and their husbands with equal submission and piety. In indicting John's patronizing treatment of his wife, Gilman indicts the system as a whole, in which many women were trapped behind damaging social definitions of the female.

One can see the negative effects of John's (and society's) treatment of the narrator in her response to the rest cure. At first, she tries to fight against the growing lethargy that controls her. She even challenges John's treatment of her. Yet, while one part of her may believe John wrong, another part that has internalized the negative definitions of womanhood believes that since he is the man, the doctor, and therefore the authority, then he may be right. Because they hold unequal power positions in the relationship and in society, she lacks the courage and self-esteem to assert her will over his even though she knows that his "treatment" is harming her. Deprived of any meaningful activity, purpose, and self-definition, the narrator's mind becomes confused and, predictably, childlike in its fascination with the shadows in the wallpaper.

In the end, the narrator triumphs over John—she literally crawls over him—but escapes from him only into madness. As a leading feminist lecturer and writer, Gilman found other options than madness to end her confinement in traditional definitions of womanhood. Eventually, Gilman divorced her husband, who married her best friend, and her husband and her best friend reared her child. The public, friends, and family so sharply censured Gilman for her actions that she knew many women would stay in unhealthy situations rather than risk such condemnation. By having the story end with the narrator's descent into insanity, Gilman laments the reality that few viable options exist for creative, intellectual women to escape the damaging social definitions of womanhood represented by John. In her horrifying depiction of a housewife gone mad, Gilman attempts to warn her readership that denying women full humanity is dangerous to women, family, and society as a whole.

Context

The publication of *The Yellow Wallpaper* had both immediate and long-term effects on women's issues. Gilman writes in her essay "Why I Wrote *The Yellow Wallpaper*" that the story was meant to save women from further suffering under the rest cure, and that her plan was successful. She says that after her former physician, Weir Mitchell, read a copy of the story that she had sent to him, he altered his treatment of women with nervous disorders. Therefore, the novella served an immediate purpose in the real, everyday lives of late nineteenth and early twentieth century women.

Originally viewed as a gothic horror story in the tradition of Edgar Allan Poe, *The Yellow Wallpaper* also helped to establish Gilman as an important woman writer in this genre. While few other critics gave it much attention, William Dean Howells praised the novella for its ability to "freeze the blood" and included it in his 1920 collection of *The Great Modern American Stories*. The novella became well known among such later horror writers as H. P. Lovecraft, who included it in *Supernatural Horror in Literature* (1945).

It was not until the 1970's and the advent of feminist scholarship, however, that critics began to explore the social, political, and cultural implications of *The Yellow Wallpaper*. Since then, feminist scholars have identified the novella as an indictment of a social structure which deters women's intellectual, psychological, and creative growth in an effort to keep women childlike and submissive. The work is now often included in American literature anthologies and feminist resources as a fine early example of fiction that criticizes social restrictions placed on women.

Feminist scholars have also found that the destructive impact of social definitions of womanhood on women of the late nineteenth and early twentieth centuries illustrated in this novella appear in other women's fiction of the time. For example, the central protagonist of Kate Chopin's *The Awakening* (1899) faces similar damaging social definitions of womanhood and, not finding a place for herself among them, commits suicide (not madness, but a similar escape). In another example, Mary E. Wilkins Freeman writes of a woman, "Old Woman Magoun," who allows her beloved granddaughter to die rather than be traded in a card deal; she then goes mad. Gilman was not alone in showing how misogynistic attitudes destroy women.

Sources for Further Study

Gilbert, Sandra M., and Susan Gubar. *The Madwoman in the Attic: The Woman Writer and the Nineteenth-Century Literary Imagination.* New Haven, Conn.: Yale University Press, 1979. One of the premier critical works on nineteenth century women writers. Includes a discussion of *The Yellow Wallpaper* linking the pattern in the wallpaper to patriarchal text patterns that women writers had to escape.

Gilman, Charlotte Perkins. "Why I Wrote *The Yellow Wallpaper*." *Forerunner* 4 (1913): 271. A one-page article in which Gilman explains that her main reason for writing *The Yellow Wallpaper* was to save other women from fates similar to her own under the rest cure.

Golden, Catherine. *The Captive Imagination: A Casebook on "The Yellow Wallpaper."* New York: Feminist Press, 1992. This indispensable compilation includes the text of *The Yellow Wallpaper* with the original illustrations, useful biographical and background information, well-selected critical essays, and a solid introduction.

Kolodny, Annette. "A Map for Rereading: Or, Gender and the Interpretation of Literary Texts." *New Literary History* 11, no. 3 (1980): 451-467. In this article, Kolodny argues that Gilman's contemporaries did not understand the implications of *The Yellow Wallpaper* because they did not have the context to understand her point.

Meyering, Sheryl L., ed. *Charlotte Perkins Gilman: The Woman and Her Work*. Ann Arbor, Mich.: UMI Research Press, 1989. An important collection of critical essays on Gilman and her works, including one by Linda Wagner-Martin focusing on *The Yellow Wallpaper*.

Amy E. Hudock

YONNONDIO
From the Thirties

Author: Tillie Olsen (1913-   )
Type of work: Novel
Type of plot: Social realism
Time of plot: The early 1920's
Locale: Wyoming, South Dakota, and Nebraska
First published: 1974

> *Principal characters:*
> ANNA HOLBROOK, a woman of the working class
> JIM HOLBROOK, her husband, who loses much of his humanity
>   through hardship
> MAZIE HOLBROOK, their child, who must face adversity
> WILL, BEN, JIM, and BESS HOLBROOK, Mazie's siblings
> ANNA MAE, GERTRUDE ("JINELLA") SKOLNICK, ERINA, ELLIE,
>   KATIE, and CHAR, Mazie's friends and playmates
> ELIAS ("OLD MAN") CALDWELL, a dying man who takes an
>   interest in Mazie's life
> SHEEN MCEVOY, Jim's coworker in the mine

Form and Content

Through the Holbrook family, *Yonnondio: From the Thirties* tells the stories of working people in three states and at least as many forms of employment. In particular, the novel shows Mazie Holbrook approaching her teen years and simultaneously developing a consciousness of the injustices and perplexities of the world, ranging from violence to avarice. Mazie stands on the developmental threshold between childhood and young adulthood, the emotional threshold between hope and despair, and the artistic threshold between creating beauty and yielding to the forces that would preempt or corrupt such beauty.

Yonnondio, Tillie Olsen's first novel, was published for the first time in 1974, but its writing was begun as early as 1932. At that time, Olsen hoped to unite her commitments as an artist and an activist by generating this socially conscious text. The novel's opening chapter, "The Iron Throat," originally appeared in *Partisan Review* in 1934. It is the only portion of the novel published when first written. Olsen completed the rest of the text in two stages spanning the intervening years. Therefore, the novel that she published in 1974 represents a painstaking reconstruction of text.

During the 1970's, Olsen received a grant from the MacDowell Colony, an artists' community, to attempt completion of her as yet unpublished novel. She resolved to assemble the novel entirely from extant manuscript pages, adding no new writing to the published text. Olsen spent five months there, weaving together remaining fragments of the earlier manuscript. Of the novel she first envisioned, Olsen laments in her epilogue to the 1974 book, "These pages you have read are all that is deemed publishable of it. Only fragments, rough drafts, outlines, scraps remain—to tell what might have been, and never will be now." This reclaiming of a Depression era story helps explain the work's subtitle, *From the Thirties*. The slender volume has an eight-chapter structure.

The novel's allusion in both title and epigram to poet Walt Whitman's "Yonnondio" underscores this issue of lost or vanishing speech. Indeed, narrative strategies employed throughout the novel recall the struggle to be heard. *Yonnondio* is a multivocal text, switching perspectives and forms of address frequently. At times, the narration reflects the awareness of young Mazie Holbrook. At other points, the narrative foregrounds the concerns of Mazie's mother, Anna Holbrook. Still other passages address the reader directly with commentary concerning matters of social, economic, and political injustice. Elements of dialogue provide acoustic detail through the speech patterns of individual characters. The shifting narrative voices of *Yonnondio* bring texture and dimension to the unfolding of its events and relationships. In keeping with this chorus of narrative voices, settings used within the novel—from mines to slaughterhouses—have one feature in common: a dense screen of industrial, agricultural, and human sound, over which characters must strain to make themselves heard. Contemplation and reflection, whether in overcrowded homes or mechanized work sites, seem nothing short of impossible within this environment.

Analysis

Olsen began *Yonnondio* as a novel of protest, which may explain why many literary critics have tended to discuss the novel chiefly in terms of the genre of 1930's proletarian fiction. This characterization of Olsen's text seems fitting from a thematic standpoint, because the story concerns a working-class family grappling with unemployment, workplace hazards, industrial strikes, illness, and poverty. It chronicles the plight of the working poor whose circumstances constantly threaten survival. In service of this objective, the novel documents even the smallest details of life for the Holbrooks, both inside and outside the home. Olsen suggests the spirit of ordinary citizens by demonstrating the full extent of the hardships that they endure. Therefore, without idealizing characters, Olsen furnishes the reader with ways to understand their actions and responses, even their acts of cruelty and desperation.

Yonnondio is not easily classified as exclusively a proletarian novel, however, because it has other important textual dimensions. Even if viewed as a work of proletarian fiction, Olsen's novel remains somewhat atypical of that genre of writing in the United States. Although *Yonnondio* registers Olsen's rejection of the prevailing orders of industrial capitalism and agribusiness, the novel declines to offer hope (to characters or to readers) in the form of a revolution or radical transformation of those orders. Apart from the implicit suggestions that existing gender roles constrain familial relations and that unorganized and nonunion workers become subject to endless indignities, relocations, and risks, Olsen's principled dissent stops short of establishing a specific position of political advocacy. Furthermore, although Olsen was once a member of the Young Communist League, her characters undergo no conversions to revolutionary consciousness.

Because Olsen writes *Yonnondio* from the perspective of a working woman and about the perspective of working women, she also helps address a rather large gap in the body of 1930's proletarian fiction, which concentrated chiefly on the plight of male workers. As a woman-centered text attentive to the working class, *Yonnondio* proves unusual among political fiction of the day, with the exception of the rediscovered texts of a few of Olsen's contemporaries, such as Fielding Burke, Agnes Smedley, Meridel Le Sueur, Tess Slesinger, and Josephine Herbst.

Olsen has asserted that her writings forgo the familiar preoccupation in fiction with heroic quests for identity. Forsaking such literary conventions as too much of a luxury for the people who populate *Yonnondio*, she calls attention to the more basic issue of human survival—social, economic, physical, and spiritual. Identity and self-determination, the ultimate attainments of heroic quest in literature, are far from sufficient to address the inequalities of conditions at work in this class-stratified world. Consequently, Olsen does not develop her characters as fully as is traditional within fiction. Instead, she sketches figures who are representative of a larger group or situation. Anna, for example, stands as the embattled familiar center. In efforts to sustain her family, Anna maintains some hope for her children, although she no longer hopes much for herself. Anna's dreams seem to have receded with her youth. Therefore, although a significant portion of the novel chronicles the experiences and perspective of Anna, she is not engaged in a heroic voyage of discovery. If anything, she has discovered more than she cares to of what this world has to offer her.

As published, *Yonnondio* concludes with a scene of the Holbrook family feverish in the heat of a summer night, a situation offset in some measure (and underlined in another) by the contrasting exuberance of young Bess at play. Anna's is the last voice heard in the text, uttering a modest hope for the day to come. Of that coming day, nothing is said and little more implied. Based upon the writer's early outlines for *Yonnondio*, however, Olsen anticipated a labor strike, Jim's abandonment of the family, and Anna's recurrent fate of pregnancy, this time faced alone. Left to support a large family on her own, Anna subsequently tries to secure an abortion. As the 1934 outline continues, Anna and Ben Holbrook both meet untimely deaths. The Holbrook children are then distributed to friends, other family members, and—in the case of Bess—an orphanage. In time, a homeless Mazie and Will venture to California, where Will becomes a political organizer for the American Communist Party.

Context

Through her poems, essays, and fictions, Tillie Olsen has devised and demonstrated a theory of women's writing as it is variously silenced in an androcentric culture. This novel, published belatedly and rescued from textual fragments written decades earlier, represents a case study in women's literary silence. It is the novel readers nearly did not see; it is a reconstituted work through which Olsen attempted "to tell what might have been, and never will be now." Even the women who appear in *Yonnondio*, most notably Mazie and Anna, find themselves restrained from artistic expression or fulfillment by the oppressive contexts in which they must operate. Therefore, Olsen calls attention not only to those silences that customarily punctuate cycles of writing activity but also to "unnatural" silences that, through circumstance, thwart otherwise productive writers or condemn them to obscurity.

With her concern for reconstructing narratives of the literary and cultural past, and her examples of how that objective might be approached (through both fiction and nonfiction), Olsen inspires readers and writers alike to take note of such silencing forces as gender roles limiting women's authority to engage writing with "totality of self" and notions of excellence that tend to render women's perspectives minor, marginal, or invisible. Among other factors, Olsen notes that the demands of marriage and motherhood compete with women's time and energy for written expression. Drawing from the lives of many of the most famous figures of women's literature written in English, Olsen observes that many such women never married: Louisa May Alcott, Jane Austen, Emily Brontë, Willa Cather, Emily Dickinson, Ellen Glasgow, Sarah Orne Jewett, Marianne Moore, Christina Rossetti, Gertrude Stein, and Eudora Welty. Other women writers did not marry until their thirties: Charlotte Brontë, Elizabeth Barrett Browning, George Eliot, and Olive Schreiner. Many writers, though married, were childless: Lillian Hellman, Katherine Mansfield, Dorothy Parker, Katherine Anne Porter, Dorothy Richardson, Edith Wharton, and Virginia Woolf.

Through her vivid reenvisioning of literary history, of voices both heard and unheard, Tillie Olsen has helped to initiate a praxis of feminist criticism, scholarship, and fiction directing itself toward a collective consciousness of women's journey into speech and struggle toward empowerment. Olsen's influence on both feminists and writers of the New Left can be discerned in the work of such women writers as Adrienne Rich and Susan Griffin.

Sources for Further Study
Duncan, Erika. *Unless Soul Clap Its Hands: Portraits and Passages*. New York: Schocken, 1984. Duncan's chapter on Tillie Olsen's life and work, based in part on her own interviews with Olsen, makes frequent reference to *Yonnondio*. Of particular interest is a rather detailed description of the original outline for elements not incorporated in the published text.
Olsen, Tillie. *Silences*. New York: Delacorte Press/Sarah Lawrence, 1978. Within this volume, Olsen has collected a number of her writings directly relating to women's struggle for a literary voice. Especially notable among these are two critical pieces, "Silences in Literature" and "One Out of Twelve: Writers Who Are Women in Our Century," in which Olsen renders the loss to literary history because of prohibitive economic and social restraints to women's writing.
Orr, Elaine Nell. *Tillie Olsen and a Feminist Spiritual Vision*. Jackson: University Press of Mississippi, 1987. In her treatment of *Yonnondio*, Orr maintains that while Olsen's novel incorporates motifs associated with working-class literature, its

writing is more aptly considered as an act of women's political and spiritual consciousness.

Pearlman, Mickey, and Abby H. P. Werlock. *Tille Olsen*. Boston: Twayne, 1991. This volume devotes a fifteen-page chapter to *Yonnondio*. Pearlman and Werlock characterize the novel in terms of its portrayal of themes such as disillusionment and loss, offset by Olsen's representations of moments marked by a transcendent human will.

Rosenfelt, Deborah. "From the Thirties: Tillie Olsen and the Radical Tradition." *Feminist Studies* 7, no. 3 (Fall, 1981): 389-394. This rich source of historical information situates Olsen in the context of radical literature associated with the 1930's Old Left. In this way, Olsen's work becomes linked to that of Edna St. Vincent Millay, Katherine Anne Porter, Mary McCarthy, and Dorothy Parker.

Stimpson, Catharine. *Where the Meanings Are*. New York: Methuen, 1988. In her sixth chapter, "Tillie Olsen: Witness as Servant (1977)," Stimpson explores the responsibilities of the writer as citizen as well as artist. She sees Olsen's novel as bearing witness to the lives of those often belittled or denied by previous literature, and she praises Olsen's ability to represent the interlocking oppressions of gender and class.

Yalom, Marilyn, Ed. *Women Writers of the West Coast: Speaking of Their Lives and Careers*. Santa Barbara, Calif.: Capra Press, 1983. The essay on Olsen included here has its origins in a dialogue between Olsen and Yalom. These conversations yielded a discussion of the experience of marginality. Also discusses the effect that Olsen achieves when she reads her works aloud.

Linda S. Watts

MASTERPLOTS II

WOMEN'S
LITERATURE
SERIES

TITLE INDEX

MASTERPLOTS II

TITLE INDEX

AUTHOR INDEX

AUTHOR INDEX

AUTHOR INDEX

TYPE OF WORK INDEX

TYPE OF WORK INDEX

GEOGRAPHICAL INDEX

GEOGRAPHICAL INDEX

GEOGRAPHICAL INDEX